Developments in International Accounting – General Issues and Classification

The New Library of International Accounting

Series Editor: Christopher W. Nobes

> *PricewaterhouseCoopers Professor of Accounting, University of Reading, UK*

1. Developments in International Accounting – General Issues and Classification
    Christopher W. Nobes

Future titles will include:

Developments in Country Studies in International Accounting – Europe
Sally Aisbitt and Lisa Evans

Developments in Country Studies in International Accounting – Americas and the Far East
Gary K. Meek

Developments in the International Harmonization of Accounting
Christopher W. Nobes

Developments in Financial Reporting by Multinationals
Clare B. Roberts

For a list of all Edward Elgar published titles visit our site on the World Wide Web at
www.e-elgar.com

Developments in International Accounting – General Issues and Classification

Edited by

Christopher W. Nobes

PricewaterhouseCoopers Professor of Accounting
University of Reading, UK

THE NEW LIBRARY OF INTERNATIONAL ACCOUNTING

An Elgar Reference Collection
Cheltenham, UK • Northampton, MA, USA

Published by
Edward Elgar Publishing Limited
Glensanda House
Montpellier Parade
Cheltenham
Glos GL50 1UA
UK

Edward Elgar Publishing, Inc.
136 West Street
Suite 202
Northampton
Massachusetts 01060
USA

225 96399

A catalogue record for this book is available from the British Library.

ISBN   1 84376 098 3

Printed and bound in Great Britain by MPG Books Ltd, Bodmin, Cornwall

Contents

Acknowledgements

The editor and publishers wish to thank the authors and the following publishers who have kindly given permission for the use of copyright material.

Accounting and Business Research for articles: T.E. Cooke (1993), 'The Impact of Accounting Principles on Profits: The US versus Japan', *Accounting and Business Research*, **23** (92), Autumn, 460–76; Margaret Lamb, Christopher Nobes and Alan Roberts (1998), 'International Variations in the Connections Between Tax and Financial Reporting', *Accounting and Business Research*, **28** (3), Summer, 173–88.

American Accounting Association for article: Marilyn Taylor Zarzeski (1996), 'Spontaneous Harmonization Effects of Culture and Market Forces on Accounting Disclosure Practices', *Accounting Horizons*, **10** (1), March, 18–37.

Blackwell Publishing Ltd for articles: Nabil Baydoun and Roger Willett (1995), 'Cultural Relevance of Western Accounting Systems to Developing Countries', *Abacus*, **31** (1), March, 67–92; Julie Norton (1995), 'The Impact of Financial Accounting Practices on the Measurement of Profit and Equity: Australia Versus the United States', *Abacus*, **31** (2), September, 178–200; Rafael La Porta, Florencio Lopez-de-Silanes, Andrei Shleifer and Robert W. Vishny (1997), 'Legal Determinants of External Finance', *Journal of Finance*, **LII** (3), July, 1131–50; Samantha Miles and Christopher Nobes (1998), 'The Use of Foreign Accounting Data in UK Financial Institutions', *Journal of Business Finance and Accounting*, **25** (3 and 4), April/May, 309–28; Christopher Nobes (1998), 'Towards a General Model of the Reasons for International Differences in Financial Reporting', *Abacus*, **34** (2), September, 162–87; Peter F. Pope and Martin Walker (1999), 'International Differences in the Timeliness, Conservatism, and Classification of Earnings', *Journal of Accounting Research*, **37**, Supplement, 53–87; Christopher Nobes (2002), 'An Analysis of the International Development of the Equity Method', *Abacus*, **38** (1), February, 16–45.

Elsevier Science for articles: Timothy S. Doupnik and Stephen B. Salter (1995), 'External Environment, Culture, and Accounting Practice: A Preliminary Test of A General Model of International Accounting Development', *International Journal of Accounting*, **30** (3), 189–207; Alan Roberts (1995), 'The Very Idea of Classification in International Accounting', *Accounting, Organizations and Society*, **20** (7/8), 639–64; Christopher Nobes and Julie Norton (1996), 'International Variations in the Accounting and Tax Treatments of Goodwill and the Implications for Research', *Journal of International Accounting, Auditing and Taxation*, **5** (2), 179–96; Ray Ball, S.P. Kothari and Ashok Robin (2000), 'The Effect of International Institutional Factors on Properties of Accounting Earnings', *Journal of Accounting and Economics*, **29**, 1–51; Donna L. Street, Nancy B. Nichols and Sidney J. Gray (2000), 'Assessing the Acceptability of International Accounting Standards in the US: An Empirical Study of the Materiality of US GAAP Reconciliations by Non-US Companies Complying with IASC Standards', *International Journal of Accounting*, **35** (1), 27–63; John Craner, Danuta Krzywda, Jiri Novotny and Marek Schroeder (2000), 'The Determination of a Group for Accounting Purposes in the UK, Poland, and the Czech Republic in a Supranational Context', *International Journal of Accounting*, **35** (3), 355–97.

Journal of Accounting Literature for articles: Shahrokh M. Saudagaran and Gary K. Meek (1997), 'A Review of Research on the Relationship Between International Capital Markets and Financial Reporting by Multinational Firms', *Journal of Accounting Literature*, **16**, 127–59; Shalin Chanchani and Alan MacGregor (1999), 'A Synthesis of Cultural Studies in Accounting', *Journal of Accounting Literature*, **18**, 1–30.

Taylor and Francis Ltd (http://www.tandf.co.uk/journals) for articles: Niclas Hellman (1993), 'A Comparative Analysis of the Impact of Accounting Differences on Profits and Return on Equity: Differences between Swedish Practice and US GAAP', *European Accounting Review*, **2** (3), December, 495–530; Carol A. Adams, Pauline Weetman, Edward A.E. Jones and Sidney J. Gray (1999), 'Reducing the Burden of US GAAP Reconciliations by Foreign Companies Listed in the United States: The Key Question of Materiality', *European Accounting Review*, **8** (1), 1–22; R.H. Parker (2001), 'European Languages of Account', *European Accounting Review*, **10** (1), 133–47.

University of Chicago Press for article: Rafael La Porta, Florencio Lopez-de-Silanes, Andrei Shleifer and Robert W. Vishny (1998), 'Law and Finance', *Journal of Political Economy*, **106** (6), December, 1113–55.

Every effort has been made to trace all the copyright holders but if any have been inadvertently overlooked the publishers will be pleased to make the necessary arrangement at the first opportunity.

In addition the publishers wish to thank the Marshall Library of Economics, Cambridge University, the Library of the University of Warwick and the Library of Indiana University at Bloomington, USA for their assistance in obtaining these articles.

Introduction

Christopher W. Nobes

This book is the second edition of the first volume of a five-volume series of readings on international accounting. The new series comprises the second editions of the five volumes; the first editions having been published in 1996. As before, the coverage of the volumes is as follows:

Volume 1. Developments in International Accounting – General Issues and Classification
Volume 2. Developments in Country Studies in International Accounting – Europe
Volume 3. Developments in Country Studies in International Accounting – Americas and the Far East
Volume 4. Developments in International Harmonization of Accounting
Volume 5. Developments in Financial Reporting by Multinationals

A brief discussion of the scope of international accounting was included in the first edition of Volume 1, pp. ix–x.

The editorship of most of the volumes remains the same for the second editions, although Volume 2 has new editors (who were doctoral students at the time of the first edition, but are now well-established researchers). Volume 5 has been edited by one of the two editors of its first edition.

Whereas the second editions of many books are a re-working of the original material, the second editions of these volumes contain entirely different material from the first editions. They take the story further, starting around 1993–94 where the first editions left off.

As before, we have restricted our choice of works to those published in English. This is a major restriction. However, we suspect that most of our readers would find difficulty if any one particular language were added, and that the difficulties would rise as the number of languages was increased. Also, although some of the editors are familiar with literature in a few languages other than English, none of us could achieve a balanced coverage of all non-English works.

Naturally, the scope of the volumes overlaps. For example, a paper on the harmonization of certain features of French and German accounting could be put in Volume 2 or Volume 4. However, the authors have liaised to avoid repeats of papers. In these editions, the papers on currency translation and segment reporting are in Volume 5, rather than in Volume 3 as they were in the first editions.

Introduction to this Volume

Part I of this volume looks at introductory issues, including some papers on classification of accounting systems. Readers should note that a number of the papers on harmonization in Volume 4 also refer to classification or have implications for it.

Doupnik and Salter (Chapter 1) construct a general model to explain how financial reporting has developed differently in different countries. They use the ideas of Gray (1988; see first edition of this volume) concerning cultural influences, coupled with some non-cultural influences. They use measures of eleven such influences as independent variables, and measures of 100 accounting practices as dependent variables. They find some explanatory power for their model. Elsewhere, Salter and Niswander attempt a test of Gray's cultural hypothesis for 29 countries. However, they had difficulty in measuring Gray's 'accounting values', retreating to indirect measures. For example, the degree of uniformity was partly measured by whether a country had common law or code law, but this is not really a test of differences in accounting practices but of a possible influence on them. The research supported some of Gray's hypothesized relationships, but not most of them.

Baydoun and Willett (Chapter 2) examine the assertions of some previous writers that the type of accounting used in developed countries may lack relevance for the needs of developing countries. They suggest that this may be true for disclosure requirements in particular. They develop Gray's (1988) framework for this purpose.

In the third Chapter, the paper by Zarzeski continues the cultural theme. By examining companies in seven countries, it is found that market forces can persuade companies to override a culture of secrecy. A useful summary by Chanchani and MacGregor of the cultural literature is found in Chapter 4.

Attention now turns to more direct influences on accounting: law, finance and tax. In two papers (Chapters 5 and 6), La Porta *et al.* examine the relationship between a country's legal system and its financing system. They find correlation between the existence of a common law system and stronger investor protection. This is also associated with less concentration of ownership of shares.

Saudagaran and Meek (Chapter 7) provide a helpful review of the literature on the relationship between financing systems and financial reporting systems. Some aspects of this, including greater timeliness of reporting in common law countries, are then further investigated by Ball *et al.* (Chapter 8). Elsewhere, Jaggi and Low (2000) find that companies in common law countries tend to make greater disclosures.

The connections between tax and financial reporting are investigated by Lamb *et al.* (Chapter 9), with a concentration on four countries. They suggest that international tax differences should not be seen as a major cause of accounting differences between major classes of accounting systems. Rather, accounting in some countries is disconnected from tax in various ways because of differences in the purposes of financial reporting, which themselves are connected to financing systems.

Nobes (in Chapter 10) draws several of these strands together to propose a general theory of the reasons for international differences in financial reporting. The suggestion is that, unless there is an overwhelming foreign influence, a country's financing system can be used to predict its financial reporting. If the former changes, the latter is likely to follow. This paper includes some implications for classification, taking account of the suggestions by Roberts (in Chapter 11), including that the objects to be classified should be accounting systems not countries. Roberts provides a critical appraisal of the purposes and procedures for accounting classification. He suggests that classifications should not be seen as good or bad, except in the context of their usefulness for a desired purpose.

The next three papers examine some further issues that are typical of the field of international accounting: language issues, the concept of the group, and the international transfer of accounting techniques. In Chapter 12, Parker examines for Europe the languages in which accounting records are kept and in which financial reporting is carried out. He charts and explains the widespread use of English (particularly US English) for some purposes, but observes that most companies in countries in which English is not an official language do not produce statements in English. In Chapter 13, Craner *et al.* examine the concept of the 'group' for financial reporting purposes in the UK, Poland and the Czech Republic. The international differences and changes over time result partly from inaccurate or incomplete implementations of international rules. In Chapter 14, Nobes traces the development of the equity method across time and space. Its original uses were as an early form of consolidation and then as a substitute for consolidation for certain subsidiaries. The current use (for associates and joint ventures) developed later, with no good reason for the commonly found threshold of a 20% interest. Objections to the spread of the method in some countries were swept aside in the march towards international standardization.

Part II of the volume contains papers on the measurement of, and the effects of, international accounting diversity. The first three papers in this part apply the conservatism index of Gray (1980; see first edition of this volume) to various countries. In Chapter 15, Cooke finds some greater conservatism in Japan than in the USA. However, the paper's real value is in its investigation of some of the problems of this type of research. In Chapter 16, Hellman looks at Sweden, which had also been included in the study by Weetman and Gray (1991; see first edition of this volume). Hellman studies reconciliations to US GAAP for 1981 to 1990 and is unable to support previous suggestions of Swedish conservatism. In Chapter 17, Norton applies the approach to Australia. She can find support for the hypothesis that US GAAP reporting of equity is more conservative than Australian reporting, but no support for a similar hypothesis related to earnings. A paper by Weetman *et al.* (1998) also uses the Gray index for the UK, but as a measure of harmonization between two dates. Therefore, that paper is included in Volume 4.

In Chapter 18 of this volume, Pope and Walker compare two measures of differential UK/US conservatism for the period 1976 to 1996. They show that the results depended on the measure of earnings chosen; it changed in the UK during the period. Chapters 19 and 20 examine some other aspects of reconciliations to US GAAP. Adams *et al.* suggest ways of reducing the burden of the reconciliations, particularly for UK companies, given that very few adjustments are larger than 10%. Street *et al.* continue this theme in the context of potential SEC acceptance of financial statements prepared in compliance with International Accounting Standards (IAS). They studied reconciliations from IAS to US GAAP, and suggest that SEC acceptance of IAS without condition might be suitable.

The subject now changes to how users of financial statements cope with the international differences. Miles and Nobes (in Chapter 21) look at the use of foreign accounting data by analysts and fund managers in the City of London. They find a low level of knowledge about the differences, and very little adjustment to a common benchmark. Whittington (2000; see Volume 5) examines the previous research that used conservatism indices and notes that it may not be helpful when trying to interpret the statements of individual companies. A case study approach is adopted for two major European steel companies.

In the last chapter, Nobes and Norton present an extended comment paper on a number of previous papers that concerned the effects of international differences in the accounting and tax treatments of goodwill. One of these previous papers (Lee and Choi, 1992) was included in the first edition of this volume. Nobes and Norton suggest that previous research findings on the effects of international tax differences cannot be right because they focus on the tax rules for the amortisation of non-consolidation goodwill rather than on the fact that goodwill on consolidation is generally not relevant for tax.

References

Gray, S.J. (1980), 'The impact of international accounting differences from a security-analysis perspective: some European evidence', *Journal of Accounting Research*, **18** (1), Spring, 64–76.

Gray, S.J. (1988), 'Towards a theory of cultural influence on the development of accounting systems internationally', *Abacus*, **24** (1), March, 1–15.

Jaggi, B. and P.Y. Low (2000), 'Impact of culture, market forces, and legal systems on financial disclosures', *International Journal of Accounting*, **35** (4).

Lee, C. and F.D.S. Choi (1992), 'Effects of alternative goodwill treatments on merger premia: further empirical evidence', *Journal of International Financial Management & Accounting*, **4** (3), Autumn, 220–36.

Salter, S.B. and F. Niswander (1995), 'Cultural influence on the development of accounting systems internationally: a test of Gray's [1988] theory', *Journal of International Business Studies*, **26** (2), 379–97.

Weetman, P. and S.J. Gray (1991), 'A comparative international analysis of the impact of accounting principles on profits: the USA versus the UK, Sweden and the Netherlands', *Accounting and Business Research*, **21** (84), Autumn, 363–79.

Weetman, P., E.A.E. Jones, C.A. Adams and S.J. Gray (1998), 'Profit measurement and UK accounting standards: a case of increasing disharmony in relation to US GAAP and IASs', *Accounting and Business Research*, Summer.

Whittington, M. (2000), 'Problems in comparing financial performance across international boundaries: a case study approach', *International Journal of Accounting*, **35** (3), 399–413.

Part I
Introductory Issues, Including Classification

[1]

Int J Acctg (1995) 30:189–207
© 1995 The University of Illinois

**The International
Journal of
Accounting**

External Environment, Culture, and Accounting Practice: A Preliminary Test of A General Model of International Accounting Development

Timothy S. Doupnik[a] and Stephen B. Salter[b]

[a]*University of South Carolina, Columbia, SC, USA*
[b]*Texas A&M University, College Station, TX, USA*

Key words: Classification; Environmental factors; Culture; International accounting

Abstract: Previous theoretical frameworks of accounting development and change are synthesized in a general model of accounting system development. The general model is then subjected to a preliminary empirical test of its explanatory power by examining the relationship between countries' accounting practices and a set of environmental factors and cultural dimensions hypothesized as relevant elements of the model. The results lend support for the general model and provide insight into the importance of various factors in explaining existing accounting diversity worldwide.

A considerable amount of literature has been written with regard to classification and explanation of the diversity of accounting practice across countries. This literature has emphasized the description of similarities and differences in accounting systems around the world. Despite the volume of literature, it is disappointing that, at the end of an extensive review, Wallace and Gernon[1] conclude that international accounting scholars lack theories and their research efforts lack rigor. This paper reports the results of a study which attempts to address these concerns.

The objectives of this study are twofold. First, the various attempts in the literature to develop a theoretical model of accounting development are synthesized to form a general model of international accounting development. The model describes a country's accounting development as a complex interaction among external environment, institutional structure, and culture. The second objective is to test whether relationships exist between accounting practice and elements of the model across a broad range of countries. This study introduces the use of hierarchical

Accepted for publication: November 1, 1994

cluster analysis and canonical correlation analysis as tools for examining those relationships.

An understanding of how external environment, institutional structure, and cultural factors affect cross-national accounting diversity can be useful in efforts to reduce that diversity and enhance the comparability of accounting information worldwide. Empirical evidence on the relative importance of the different elements of the model can provide information as to where comparability efforts need to be intensified and also can provide insight as to the feasibility of reducing cross-national differences. If differences in accounting practice are significantly affected by national differences in institutional structure or culture, for example, then, to the extent that these model elements do not change (or change very slowly) over time, achieving comparability of accounting across countries might be extremely difficult.

This study represents a first step in examining empirically the interrelationship between environment, institutional structure, culture, and accounting. The results suggest that all three elements contribute to accounting diversity, but that on a global level institutional structure is of greatest importance.

Prior Research

The major questions that have been examined in international comparative financial accounting research are:

(1) What differences and similarities exist across national accounting systems (classification studies)?
(2) What factors explain these differences and similarities (environmental factors studies)?

Concerning both questions there has been a limited attempt to develop theories to explain how various factors affect national accounting systems.

Classification Studies

A number of studies have attempted to classify countries by accounting practices either inductively[2] or deductively.[3] The inductive studies primarily rely on factor analysis of survey data on financial reporting practices collected by Price Waterhouse.[4] The primary result of these studies has been to establish on an ongoing basis the continued diversity of financial reporting practices across countries.

The deductive studies have used deductive reasoning and personal knowledge of countries' accounting to develop classifications of accounting systems. These studies do not attempt to develop a formal theory but rather to arrive at an accurate description of what the world appears to be.

Environmental Factors Studies

The earliest attempts to explain cross-national differences in accounting consist of lists of environmental factors explaining often undefined differences in financial reporting practices.[5] An extension of this approach is contained in a comprehensive framework which attempts to incorporate the Farmer and Richman model of business environments into an accounting context.[6] This model does not specify the weight of the factors influencing the accounting system or the level at which the influence is applied.

Classification/Environmental Factors Studies

A number of inductive classification studies[7] have attempted to use subsets of environmental variables to predict clusters of countries with similar accounting practices. These research efforts are useful in that they empirically establish some connection between the environment and accounting practices. These studies do not provide or test a theoretical framework which explains how environmental factors affect cross-national accounting diversity.

Theoretical Frameworks of Account Development

Schweikart[8] attempted to develop a theory of international accounting within the general framework of contingency theory. In his financial accounting model, the environment (education, economic, political, social, etc.) is seen as an external contingency on institutional structure (e.g., corporations, stock exchanges, and regulatory agencies) and decision makers (e.g., investors and lenders). The environment provides the types of institutions and these institutions, within a nation's cultural framework (availability filter), provide information to the public for decision-making purposes. Changes in the external environment may change the decision environment which causes decision-makers to put pressure on the institutional structure to provide more relevant information.

Harrison and McKinnon[9] developed a framework which attempts to explain the process of change in a society's accounting system. Change is analyzed in terms of four major elements: intrusive events, intra-systems activity, trans-systems activity, and cultural environment.

Within the model, accounting system change is the product of both the intrusion of events and the continuous interactions among the accounting system and its neighboring systems. Change occurs as a specific system identifies an intrusion, chooses to deal with that intrusion, and produces a series of response events based on its perception of suitable reactions. The response events occur after the subject systems and neighbouring system have made clear to each other what needs to be done and have determined a culturally appropriate way of achieving these objectives.

Robson[10] hypothesizes and demonstrates that the process of accounting change involves translating accounting needs into a form that permits discourse with other systems. This process, by moving accounting issues into the wider social, political, and economic realm, allows accounting to assess its role, select options for change, and, in turn, influence societal decisions. The ability to translate accounting to wider issues appears to be a cultural one.

Gray[11] extended Hofstede's[12] model of societal culture patterns to develop a model of culture, societal values, and the accounting subculture. In Hofstede's model, societal values (culture) are determined by environmental factors (geographic, economic, demographic, etc.) modified by external influences (forces of nature, trade, conquest, etc.). Societal values, in turn, have institutional consequences in the form of legal system, political system, nature of capital markets, and so on. Gray extends this model to propose that the value systems or attitudes of accountants (accounting values) are related to and derived from societal values, and these accounting values, along with the institutional structure, affect the accounting system.

A General Model of Accounting Development

A synthesis of the various frameworks discussed above leads to a general model of accounting system development as presented in Exhibit 1. There are three elements which appear to determine a nation's accounting development: (1) the *external environment*, which affects both a society's culture and its institutional structure and provides external stimuli (intrusive events) that initiate change; (2) *cultural values,* which affect the institutional structure, and which govern the interactions between components of the institutional structure in evaluating suitable responses to external stimuli; and (3) the *institutional structure* within which responses are made. The importance of these three elements is echoed by Hopwood who notes that

rather than being isolated and thereby a more influenceable technical phenomenon, accounting is now recognized as being something shaped by cultures, institutional configurations and socio-historical circumstances of the specific societies in which it emerged.[13]

In an international context, these elements vary across national borders and therefore can be expected to lead to differences in accounting systems across countries.

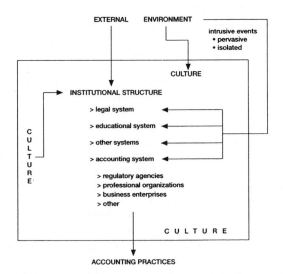

Exhibit 1. A general model of accounting development.

Although culture appears to be depicted in the model as being wholly extraneous to the institutional structure, this is not the case. Culture permeates the various systems that constitute the institutional structure, impacting on accounting practice through norms and values held by members of the accounting system and norms and values held by members of other systems with which the accounting system interacts. Among other things these norms and values influence the importance (weighting) attached to intrusive events as they disrupt individual systems. This model is based on the following propositions:

(1) There exists in every country an institutional structure comprised of various systems (accounting, legal, educational, etc.).

(2) The accounting system, in turn, is comprised of various subsystems (regulatory agencies, professional organizations, corporations, etc.). The accounting practices followed within a country derive from the accounting system.

(3) A society's institutional structure, including the accounting system, is determined by the external environment and cultural norms and values.

(4) A society's cultural norms and values, in turn, are influenced by the external environment.

(5) The external environment creates intrusive events which act as stimuli for action by the institutional structure. Each intrusion is evaluated by a member or members of the set of systems within society. Cultural norms and values affect the importance attached to a particular intrusive event.

(6) If an intrusive event relevant to accounting is not initially sourced within the accounting system it will be transmitted to the accounting system by a neighbouring system.

(7) The accounting subsystems interact to develop a response to the intrusive event. Cultural norms and values affect the interaction among the various subsystems.

(8) The accounting system does not act in a vacuum but interacts with other systems in developing culturally appropriate responses to intrusive events. Culture affects the interaction among the various systems.

(9) Intrusive events are conceptualized in two categories: (i) pervasive intrusions, such as colonization, EC Directives, inflation, and change from a planned to a market economy, which require extensive changes in the financial reporting system; and (ii) isolated intrusions, such as foreign currency fluctuations, banking scandals, and rising health care costs, which require changes in individual reporting practices only.

These propositions lead to a number of interesting avenues of research, including examination of such questions as:

(1) How does the external environment affect the institutional structure, especially the accounting component?

(2) How does culture affect the institutional structure, especially the accounting component?

(3) With which neighboring systems does the accounting system interact, in what manner, and how does culture affect this interaction?

(4) How does culture affect the interaction among the subsystems within the accounting system?

(5) How does culture affect the weight attached to a specific intrusive event?

(6) What are the past intrusive events (either pervasive or isolated) that are embodied in current accounting practice?

Case studies of individual countries would appear to be a fruitful method to address these questions.

Before embarking on research to address such questions, however, it is necessary to test whether the model is generally valid in a cross-national context. This implies testing whether there exists a relationship between the external environment and accounting practice, between the institutional structure and accounting practice, and between cultural values and accounting practice across a broad range of countries. A logical hypothesis to be developed from the model is that if the external environment, institutional structure, and/or cultural norms and values differ across countries, then it is likely that existing accounting practices will differ across countries as well. The corollary is that countries with similar environments and cultures should have similar accounting practices. The remainder of this paper reports on a study designed to address this general research question.

A Preliminary Test of the General Model

To test the general model, it is necessary to identify elements of the external environment likely to affect accounting either through their impact on the institutional structure or through intrusive events and identify the cultural values that shape the institutional structure and guide the interaction of the elements within the structure.

External Environment

In terms of the model, the external environment encompasses everything in society other than the institutional structure that society has devised to regulate itself and the cultural norms and values shared by members of society. Thus, the external environment encompasses diverse influences, such as economic conditions, geography, colonization, climate, technology, disease, relationships with other societies, and past history.

The external environment is seen as influencing a nation's accounting system in two ways: indirectly through its impact on the institutional structure and directly through the emanation of intrusive events which disrupt the accounting or neighboring systems. Some aspects of the external environment do not affect accounting or do so in such an indirect manner that the link is no longer discernible. This would appear to be true for such factors as geography and climate.

Some environmental factors may influence accounting only indirectly through their impact on those systems within the institutional structure with which the accounting system interacts. It may be no longer possible to identify these factors. For example, the type of legal system used within a country might be the result of historical factors, relations with other countries, colonization, and so on. To test the proposition that the external environment affects accounting indirectly, it becomes necessary to examine whether the form of the institutional system (which is a result of indeterminable external influences) affects accounting practice.

Other environmental factors may influence accounting both directly and indirectly. For example, a country's level of economic development is likely to have an impact on the institutional structure within that country and at the same time be the source of ongoing intrusive events which elicit response from the accounting system.

Finally, there are environmental factors that might influence accounting directly (intrusive events) without affecting the institutional structure. Examples might be inflation or the collapse of the system of fixed exchange rates.

Numerous environmental factors that influence accounting practice have been hypothesized in the literature.[14] In a review of this literature, Meek and Saudagaran[15] indicate that there is general agreement (without empirical support) that the following environmental factors influence accounting:

(1) legal system;
(2) nature of the relationship between business enterprises and providers of capital;
(3) tax laws;
(4) inflation levels; and
(5) political and economic ties.

The current study examines six factors; the first four enumerated above plus:

(5) level of education; and
(6) level of economic development.

These last two factors were originally suggested by Mueller[16] in an accounting context.

The number of factors examined in this study was limited to six to ensure a reasonable ratio of observations to independent variables in subsequent statistical testing. The factor "political and economic ties" was not examined because of difficulty in developing an objective, meaningful scale usable in testing.

Legal System

The legal system is a part of the institutional framework with which the accounting system is very likely to interact. Legal system (code vs. common law) influences the way in which accounting rules are promulgated (legislated vs. non-legislated), which in turn could influence the nature of the rules themselves.[17] To test the relationship between legal system (LEGAL) and accounting, countries are coded on a binary scale according to a classification provided by David and Brierley.[18]

Relationship Between Business and Providers of Capital

Meek and Saudagaran[19] indicate that this factor relates to sources of financing, whether the group of capital providers is large and the level of development and sophistication of capital markets. These factors can be viewed as elements of the institutional structure with which the accounting system interacts, as well as intrusive events to which the accounting system must react.

A strong equity market with a diverse group of shareholders has generally been viewed as conducive to the production of sophisticated information. When banks dominate as a source of financing, accounting assumes a creditor protection orientation and disclosure levels are lower.

To test the relationship between this variable and accounting, market capitalization as a percentage of GNP (MC) and trading volume as a percentage of market capitalization (TVOMC) were determined for each country. Data on mean level of market capitalization and trading volume were gathered from the International Finance Corporation's *Emerging Stock Markets Factbook*. GNP data were obtained from the World Bank's *World Development Report* and the International Monetary Fund's *International Financial Statistics*.

Tax Laws

In many countries, tax laws effectively determine accounting practice by requiring companies to book revenues and expenses in order to claim them for tax purposes.[20] In other countries, tax accounting and financial accounting are separate. In countries in which a strong link between taxation and accounting exists, companies are likely to adopt very conservative accounting practices so as to minimize their tax liabilities. This is likely to be especially true in countries with relatively high rates of taxation. Taxation, in general, can be seen as an intrusion on the accounting system with a potentially significant impact on accounting practice.

To test whether taxation is an intrusive event that has significantly impacted international accounting, this study examines the relationship between marginal tax rates (MTAX) and accounting practice. Data on corporate tax rates were obtained from Price Waterhouse's *Corporate Taxes: A Worldwide Summary*.

Inflation

Inflation has been one of the most intrusive economic challenges since the Great Depression. Inflation (INF) was included in the study by determining the mean annual rate of inflation over the period 1980–1987 from data provided in *World Development Report* and *International Financial Statistics*.

Level of Education

It is often suggested that the level of education in a country or in its accounting profession affects accounting practice.[21] Level of education can be seen as an intrusion on the accounting system as accounting practices are developed within the constraints of the educational environment. The hypothesis is that a simple educational environment prevents development of sophisticated accounting practices. With regard to managerial accounting information, Schweikart[22] found that a stronger educational environment was associated with less relevance for formal reports and more relevance for informal reports. In this study, the percentage of the population with tertiary education as reported in the United Nations' *UNESCO Statistical Yearbook* or the International Labor Organization's *Yearbook of ILO Statistics* was used to measure a country's level of education (EDUC).

Level of Economic Development

Mueller[23] suggested that stage of economic development, type of economy, and growth pattern of an economy can exert an impact on a country's accounting practices. The stage of development affects the type of business transactions conducted in a country and the type of economy determines which transactions are more prevalent, each of which is an intrusion on the accounting system. Cooke and Wallace[24] have found that a simple dichotomous variable based on level of economic development (developed/underdeveloped) absorbs the explanatory power of several economic variables considered jointly in explaining differences in countries' accounting systems. For this study, a country's level of development (LDEV) was scored on a binary scale (developed/underdeveloped) based upon classifications provided in *World Development Report*.

Culture

Culture can been defined as "the collective programming of the mind which distinguishes the members of one group or category of people from another."[25] While it affects many levels of society, it is assumed to exist primarily at a regional or national level.

Based upon an extensive cross-national survey, Hofstede[26] identified four underlying dimensions of societal value along which countries can be positioned: individualism, power distance, uncertainty avoidance, and masculinity.

Gray[27] suggests that these cultural dimensions may be useful in explaining international differences in accounting practices and develops two hypotheses which posit a directional relationship between financial reporting practices and culture. These are:

The higher a country ranks in terms of uncertainty avoidance and the lower it ranks in terms of individualism and masculinity then the more likely it is to rank highly in terms of conservatism.

The higher a country ranks in terms of uncertainty avoidance and power distance and the lower it ranks in terms of individualism and masculinity then the more likely it is to rank highly in terms of secrecy.[28]

Conservatism is defined as a cautious approach to income measurement and secrecy as a preference for the disclosure of business information only to those closely involved with the business.

To test the relationship between culture and accounting practice proposed in the general model, culture is operationalized along Hofstede's four dimensions: individualism (INDIV), power distance (POWER), uncertainty avoidance (UNCERT), and masculinity (MASC). Scores for these variables were obtained from Hofstede.[29] Regional scores for West Africa, East Africa, and the Arab world were applied to those countries included in the study from those geographic areas.

Accounting Practices

To examine the relationship between accounting and the independent variables identified above, a practitioner survey was conducted to obtain data on accounting practices in a broad range of countries. A survey approach was used, because it allows data to be gathered on a broader range of both disclosure and measurement practices than is possible using annual reports or international accounting summaries.

Based upon reviews by an expert panel of accounting practitioners, academicians, and financial analysts, 100 accounting issues (55 disclosure and 45 measurement items) were selected for inclusion in the survey. To facilitate input into statistical analysis, respondents were asked to indicate the percentage of companies in their country following a particular practice. To avoid the criticism of subjectivity, multiple respondents within the public accounting profession were contacted in each country with interjudge consistency used as the criterion for inclusion of respondents and countries in the database. Only those countries for which at least two responses that were not significantly different were obtained were included in the study. The resultant database contains information from 174 respondents in 50 countries on the utilization of 100 accounting practices as at January 1, 1990.

To develop a measure of national accounting practice that can be used as a dependent variable in a statistical analysis, the raw data on 100 accounting practices were input into cluster analysis. A country's membership in a particular cluster was used as the dependent variable in a test of the relationship between the independent variables and accounting practice. Because Nobes[30] suggests a multi-level structure to accounting diversity, hierarchical cluster analysis was used as the tool for developing the dependent variable. Algorithm selection, heuristics for determining optimal solutions, and validation techniques as detailed in Punj and Stewart[11] were employed.

Results

Cluster Analysis

Significant solutions were determined by examining pseudo F statistics for peaks and pseudo t^2 statistics for breaks or rapid drops in value. The strongest solution occurs at two clusters with weaker solutions at six and nine clusters. The hierarchy and cluster membership is presented in Exhibit 2. The clusters emerged as broadly consistent with previous inductive literature, especially Nobes.[32] For example, at the nine cluster level, only three countries are classified differently from Nobes' classification of 14 developed countries.[33]

The two cluster solution shown in Exhibit 2 is broadly consistent with the two "classes" of accounting system hypothesized in Nobes. Accordingly, cluster A1 is labeled "micro-based" and cluster A2 is labeled "macro-uniform" per Nobes (1983). Significant differences (at the 0.05 level) in mean score between clusters A1 and A2 exist for 65 out of 100 financial reporting issues.

The hierarchical nature of the cluster solutions suggests that there might be environmental factors and cultural dimensions of universal importance which cause national accounting systems to fall into one of two major classes. There then appear to be factors of secondary and tertiary importance which cause the two major classes of accounting to subdivide creating the six and nine cluster solutions.

For descriptive purposes only, financial reporting practices were categorized as measurement or disclosure and mean scores were computed for each cluster. High

| | Number of Clusters | | |
Country	Two	Six	Nine
Japan		B6	C9
Germany		B5	C8
Finland / Sweden		B4	C7
Egypt / Saudi Arabia / Belgium / UAE / Liberia / Thailand / Panama	A2 Macro uniform	B3	C6
Portugal / Spain / Colombia / Italy / Korea / Denmark / Norway / France			C5
Argentina / Mexico / Brazil / Chile		B2	C4
Costa Rica			C3
Malaysia / S. Africa / Zimbabwe / Hong Kong / Singapore / Namibia / Ireland / United Kingdom / Zambia / Australia / Papua N. Guinea / New Zealand / Trinidad / Nigeria / Sri Lanka / Botswana / Jamaica / Philippines / Taiwan / Netherlands / Neth. Antilles / Luxembourg	A1 Micro based	B1	C2
Bermuda / Israel / Canada / United States			C1

Exhibit 2. Results of hierarchical cluster analysis.

scores indicate relatively complex, less-conservative measurement practices and relatively high disclosure. Exhibit 3, which presents a plot of the scores at the two and nine cluster levels, suggests a strong inverse relationship between level of disclosure and conservatism.

Canonical Correlation Analysis

Countries coded on a 0,1 scale as being non-member/member of a particular cluster served as dependent variables. The independent variables consisted of country scores on the six environmental factors and the four cultural variables described earlier. Because the dependent and several independent variables in this study were non-metric, canonical correlation analysis (Cancorr) was used to examine the relationships among them. In Cancorr, linear combinations (canonical variates) are derived for each of a set of independent and dependent variables so that the correlation between the two variates is maximized. A number of pairs of variates (canonical functions) are extracted. Each canonical function provides insight into which independent variables are associated with the various stages in the development of the hierarchy of accounting systems.

Three criteria were used in deciding which canonical functions to interpret: (1) statistical significance of the squared canonical correlation, (2) magnitude of the

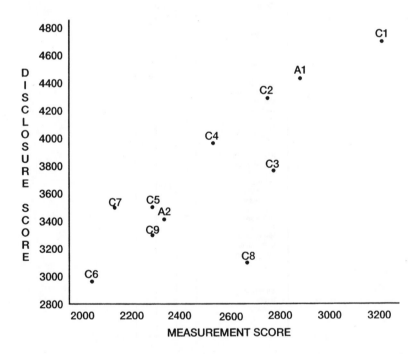

Exhibit 3. Plot of disclosure and measurement scores by cluster.

canonical correlation, and (3) a redundancy index analogous to R^2.[34] Cross loadings were used to interpret the canonical variates. Cross loadings directly correlate the original dependent variables with the independent canonical variate and, when squared, indicate the total percentage of variation in group membership explained by each independent variate. The relative power of each independent variable within the independent variate is contained in the canonical loadings on that variate. Loadings of 0.40 or greater were used in interpreting the canonical variate of the independent variables. Separate Cancorr solutions were developed for the two, six, and nine cluster solutions.

Two Cluster Solution

Using the two cluster solution to define the dependent variable, one canonical function was significant at $\alpha = 0.05$. The canonical correlation coefficient was 0.9163. The redundancy index was 0.8388, which indicates that the independent variate explained 83.88 percent of the variance in the country clusters.

Panel A in Table 1 shows that the cross loadings for the dependent variables A1 (micro-based cluster) and A2 (macro-uniform cluster) were 0.9158 and –0.9158, respectively, indicating that the independent variate explains approximately 83 percent of the variance for both clusters of countries. The independent variate FUNC1 was, dominated by LEGAL (–0.9271), with significant loadings on UNCERT (–0.6664), and MC (0.5316). Given the signs of the cross loadings and the coding scheme used for the independent variables, cluster A1 countries can be characterized as being

Table 1. Canonical structure at the two cluster level
A. Cross loadings on variates of significant functions
    Correlations between the clusters of countries and
    the canonical variates of the independent variables

	Cluster	FUNC1
Macro-based	A1	0.9158
Macro-uniform	A2	–0.9158

B. Canonical loadings on variates on significant functions
   Correlations between the independent variables and their
   canonical variates

	FUNC1
LEGAL	–0.9271
EDUC	0.0100
INF	–0.2227
LDEV	0.0765
MTAX	–0.0410
MC	0.5316
TVOMC	0.1914
UNCERT	–0.6664
POWER	–0.1610
INDIV	0.2110
MASC	0.2664

predominantly common law countries with a lower score on the uncertainty avoidance dimension of culture and higher market capitalization.

Referring to Exhibit 3 it can be seen that cluster A1 has a higher level of disclosure which is consistent with a lower level of uncertainty avoidance and greater reliance on equity investors as providers of capital. Cluster A1 also has a higher measurement score, consistent with Gray's hypothesis that low uncertainty avoidance groups tend to be less conservative.

Six Cluster Solution

The Cancorr solution at the six cluster level explains the breakup of the macro-uniform group, with the separation of Sweden/Finland (B4), Germany (B5), Japan (B6), and a Latin American (B2) cluster from a Core Macro group (B3). Three canonical functions are significant at $\alpha = 05$. The canonical correlations of these three functions are 0.9216, 0.8028, and 0.6982, respectively. The redundancy indices are 0.2229, 0.1242, and 0.0878. The independent variates cumulatively explain 43.5 percent of the variance in the country clusters.

Panel A in Table 2 shows the cross loadings for the dependent variable. The first function (FUNC1) discriminates between the micro-based group of countries (B1) and the various macro-uniform groups (B2–B6). As in the two cluster solution, the significant independent variables on FUNC1 are LEGAL, UNCERT, and MC.

Table 2. Canonical structure at the six cluster level

A. Cross loadings on variates on significant functions
   Correlations between the clusters of countries and the canonical variates
   of the independent variables

	Cluster	FUNC1	FUNC2	FUNC3
Micro-based	B1	0.9049	0.1214	0.0053
Latin American	B2	-0.3901	0.6358	0.2363
Core Macro	B3	-0.5947	-0.2855	-0.2348
Sweden/Finland	B4	-0.0897	-0.1571	-0.3137
Germany	B5	-0.0138	-0.3012	0.0981
Japan	B6	-0.0663	-0.3562	0.5550

B. Canonical loadings on significant variates
   Correlations between the independent variables and their
   canonical variates

	FUNC1	FUNC2	FUNC3
LEGAL	-0.9033	-0.1506	0.0220
EDUC	0.0187	0.0642	0.0047
INF	-0.3074	0.6935	0.3097
LDEV	0.1664	-0.5064	-0.0748
MTAX	0.0272	-0.3437	0.1792
MC	0.5689	-0.2238	0.4290
TVOMC	0.2380	-0.1262	0.3216
UNCERT	-0.6929	0.0400	0.3718
POWER	-0.2092	0.0905	0.0486
INDIV	0.2666	-0.2470	-0.1582
MASC	0.2767	-0.1680	0.7514

The second function (FUNC2) appears to discriminate the Latin American group (B2) from the other macro-uniform clusters. The independent variables with significant loadings on FUNC2 are, INF (0. 6935) and LDEV (−0.5064). This indicates that the Latin American group of countries generally has higher inflation and a lower level of economic development than the other macro-uniform groups.

The third significant canonical function (FUNC3) primarily appears to discriminate Japan (B6) from the other macro-uniform groups especially B4 (Sweden/Finland). The independent variate was dominated by MASC (0.7514) and MC (0.4290), indicating that Japan has a higher level of masculinity and higher level of market capitalization than the other macro groups. This result is somewhat unexpected as Gray associates higher masculinity with higher disclosure and less conservatism. Yet, Exhibit 3 shows that Japan (C9) has a lower measurement and lower disclosure score than most of the other macro-uniform clusters (C3–C8).

Nine Cluster Solution

Four canonical functions are significant at the nine cluster level. The canonical correlation coefficients were 0.9311, 0.8671, 0.7695, and 0.7086, respectively. The redundancy index was 0.1206 for Function 1, 0.0961 for Function 2, 0.0713 for Function 3, and 0.0643 for Function 4, indicating that the independent variates cumulatively explained 34.2 percent of the variance in the country clusters.

The cross loadings in Table 3 (Panel A) show that FUNC 1 discriminates between the micro-based clusters, Cl and C2, and the macro-uniform clusters. The loadings on the independent variate were once again dominated by the variables LEGAL, UNCERT, and MC.

The second function appears to separate Latin America (C4) from the other macro-uniform clusters much as occurred in the six cluster solution. The significant independent variables in this second function are again INF and LDEV.

The third function discriminates Japan (C9) from the other macro-uniform groups as was the case in the six cluster solution. Once again, the significant independent variables on FUNC3 are MASC and MC.

The fourth function primarily distinguishes cluster C6 from the Latin American group (C4). The significant independent variables on FUNC4 are EDUC, INF, and Power. Thus, cluster C6 has a lower level of tertiary education, lower inflation and highest power distance than the Latin America group. Exhibit 3 shows that clusters C6 and C4 represent opposite poles within the macro-uniform class of accounting systems.

While not significant at normal levels ($\alpha = 0.14$), FUNC5 explains a further 5 percent of the overall variance in country clusters and helps explain the separation of the Sweden/Finland (C7) group from the other macro-uniform groups. The significant independent variables on FUNC5 are cultural (UNCERT and MASC). Sweden and Finland are low masculinity, low uncertainty avoidance countries. Exhibit 3 shows that group C7 (Sweden/Finland) has the second lowest measurement score but has a relatively high level of disclosure which is consistent with low uncertainty avoidance. The key issues of disclosure are social with Sweden/Finland exhibiting a propensity to provide pension and shareholder disclosures. Disclosure of this type of information would appear to be consistent with a low-masculinity society.

Table 3. Canonical structure at the nine cluster level

A. Cross loadings on variates of significant function correlations between the cluster of countries and the canonical variates of the independent variables

	Cluster	FUNC1	FUNC2	FUNC3	FUNC4	FUNC5
USA/Canada	C1	0.4875	−0.1116	−0.3258	0.3258	0.2671
British	C2	0.6414	0.3181	0.2308	−0.2565	−0.1878
Costa Rica	C3	−0.1713	0.0837	−0.3266	0.0270	0.0960
Latin American	C4	−0.3839	0.4951	0.2157	0.4480	−0.0468
European	C5	−0.3290	−0.4583	−0.0874	0.0366	−0.0771
Arab/Hybrid	C6	−0.3754	0.1487	−0.2158	−0.3822	0.2391
Sweden/Finland	C7	−0.0637	−0.2940	−0.1114	0.0402	−0.4467
Germany	C8	0.0367	−0.3147	0.1787	0.2200	0.0995
Japan	C9	−0.0717	−0.2854	0.4802	−0.0879	0.2595

B. Canonical loadings on significant variates
Correlations between the independent variables and their canonical variates

	FUNC1	FUNC2	FUNC3	FUNC4	FUNC5
LEGAL	−0.8689	−0.2950	0.0092	0.1632	−0.0299
EDUC	0.1507	−0.1999	−0.2797	0.6010	0.1740
INF	−0.3410	0.5073	0.2419	0.6738	−0.1224
LDEV	0.2774	−0.6613	0.0071	0.2075	−0.0935
MTAX	0.0776	−0.4641	0.2650	0.1885	−0.1751
MC	0.5084	−0.8865	0.5367	−0.2350	−0.0840
TVOMC	0.2673	−0.1389	0.3480	0.3774	0.1287
UNCERT	−0.6315	−0.0917	−0.0229	0.2876	0.5325
POWER	−0.3054	0.3977	0.1675	−0.4610	0.1857
MASC	0.2487	0.1020	0.6115	−0.0458	0.6526
INDIV	0.3471	−0.3341	−0.0352	0.2423	−0.1278

The overall explanatory power at the nine cluster level can be seen by examining the squared multiple correlations provided in Table 4. For example, Panel A shows that the first five canonical functions explain 66.7 percent of the variance in cluster C2 (British). These five functions explain more than 30 percent of the variance in seven of the nine clusters. Panel B shows that the independent variables with the greatest explanatory power after five functions are: legal system (LEGAL), level of inflation (INF), uncertainty avoidance (UNCERT), masculinity (MASC), market capitalization (MC), and level of economic development (LDEV).

Summary and Conclusions

This study presented and tested a model of accounting development in which accounting practice is hypothesized as being the result of the complex interaction among a society's external environment, cultural norms and values, and institutional structures. Variables related to each of the three elements of the model were found to have significant explanatory power in discriminating across countries. Thus, the results lend support for the general model.

The analysis was not helpful in explaining some of the emergent clusters, most notably Germany. Assuming the model's general validity, there are obviously other

Environment, Culture, and Accounting Practice   205

Table 4. Squared cross loadings on significant variates nine cluster level
A. Squared multiple correlation between the clusters of countries ad the first five canonical variates of the independent variables

	Cluster	1	2	3	4	5
USA/Canada	C1	0.2376	0.2501	0.3562	0.4624	0.5337
British	C2	0.4114	0.5126	0.5658	0.6316	0.6669
Costa Rica	C3	0.0293	0.0363	0.1430	0.1437	0.1529
Latin American	C4	0.1474	0.3925	0.4391	0.6398	0.6420
European	C5	0.1083	0.3183	0.3260	0.3273	0.3332
Arab/Hybrid	C6	0.1409	0.1630	0.2096	0.3557	0.4129
Sweden/Finland	C7	0.0041	0.0905	0.1029	0.1045	0.3041
Germany	C8	0.0013	0.1004	0.1323	0.1807	0.1906
Japan	C9	0.0051	0.0866	0.3172	0.3249	0.3922

B. Squared multiple correlations between the independent variables and the first five canonical variates of the clusters of countries

	1	2	3	4	5
LEGAL	0.6546	0.7200	0.7200	0.7334	0.7338
EDUC	0.0197	0.0497	0.0960	0.2774	0.2900
INF	0.1008	0.2943	0.3290	0.5569	0.5632
LDEV	0.0667	0.3955	0.3956	0.4172	0.4208
MTAX	0.0052	0.1672	0.2087	0.2266	0.2394
MC	0.2241	0.2297	0.4003	0.4291	0.4310
TVOMC	0.0620	0.0765	0.1482	0.2197	0.2266
UNCERT	0.3458	0.3521	0.3524	0.3939	0.5124
POWER	0.0809	0.1998	0.2161	0.3228	0.3372
MASC	0.0536	0.615	0.2829	0.2804	0.4618
INDIV	0.1045	0.1884	0.1891	0.2186	0.2254

environmental factors and cultural dimensions that explain the complete range of international accounting diversity.

Perhaps the most important finding of this study is the emergence of two major classes of accounting systems whose country members differ significantly on the basis of type of legal system. If differences between these two classes of accounting are rooted in differences in institutional structure, the power that intrusive events might have to cause change in accounting practice is likely to be mitigated and comparability of accounting across classes might be extremely difficult to achieve.

In attempting to reduce differences between these two classes of accounting system, the immediate relevant task might be to understand better how a country's legal system and accounting system relate to one another. The answer to this and other questions exploring the interrelationship between institutional structure, culture, external environment, and accounting might prove fruitful in understanding and ultimately reducing accounting diversity worldwide.

References

1. Wallace, R.S.O. and H. Gernon, "Frameworks for International Comparative Financial Accounting." *Journal of Accounting Literature* (1991), 209–264.

2. DaCosta, R.C., J.C. Bourgeois, and W.M. Lawson, "A Classification of International Financial Accounting Practices." *International Journal of Accounting Education and Research* (Spring 1978), 73–85; Frank, W., "An Empirical Analysis of International Accounting Principles." *Journal of Accounting Research* (Autumn) 1979), 593–605; Nair, R. and W. Frank, "The Impact of Disclosure and Measurement Practices on International Accounting Classifications." *Accounting Review* (July 1980), 426–450; Doupnik, T.S., "Evidence of International Harmonization of Financial Reporting." *International Journal of Accounting Education and Research* (Fall 1987), 47–67; Goodrich, P.S., "Cross-national Financial Accounting Linkages: An Empirical Political Analysis." *British Accounting Review* (1986), 42–60.

3. Mueller, G.G. 'Accounting Principles Generally Accepted in the United States Versus Those Generally Accepted Elsewhere." *International Journal of Accounting Education and Research* (Spring 1968), 91–103; Seidler, L.J., International Accounting: The Ultimate Theory Course." *Accounting Review* (October 1967), 775–781; American Accounting Association, "Report of the 1975-76 Committee on International Accounting Operations and Education." *Accounting Review* (Suppl. 1977), 65–132; Al Najjar, F. "Standarization in accounting practices: A Comparative International Study." *International Journal of Accounting Education and Research* (Spring 1986), 161–176; Nobes, C.W., "A Judgemental International Classification of Financial Reporting Practices." *Journal of Business Finance and Accounting* (Spring 1983), 1–19.

4. Price Waterhouse International, *Accounting Principles and Reporting practices: A survey in 38 countries* (London: Price Waterhouse International, 1973); *Accounting Principles and Reporting Practices: A survey in 46 countries* (London: Price Waterhouse International, 1975); *International Survey of Accounting Principles and Reporting Practices* (London: Price Waterhouse International, 1979).

5. Mueller, G.G. (1968); AAA, 1977.

6. Radebaugh, L.H., "Environmental Factors Influencing the Development of Accounting Objectives, Standards and Practices in Peru." *International Journal of Accounting Education and Research* (Fall 1975), 39–56.

7. DaCosta et al., 1978; Frank, 1979; Nair and Frank, 1980; Goodrich, 1986.

8. Schweikart, J.A., "Contingency Theory as a Framework for Research in *International Accounting*." *International Journal of Accounting Education and Research* (Fall 1985, 89–98.

9. Harrison, G.L. and J.L. McKinnon, "Culture and Accounting Change: A New Perspective on Corporate Reporting Regulation and Accounting Policy Formulation." *Accounting, Organizations and Society* (No. 3, 1986), 233–256.

10. Robson, K. "On the Arenas of Accounting Change: The Process of Translation." *Accouting Organizations and Society* (No. 5/6, 1991), 547–570.

11. Gray, S.J., "Towards a Theory of Cultural Influence on the Development of Accounting Systems Internationally." Abacus (March 1988), 1–15.

12. Hofstede, G., *Culture's Consequences: International Differences in Work Related Values.* (Beverly Hill: Sage Publications, 1980).

13. Hopwood, A., "The Future of Accounting Harmonization in the Community." *European Accounting* (1991), 12–21.

14. See, for example, Mueller, 1968; AAA, 1977; Radebaugh, 1975.

15. Meek, G. and S. Saudagaran, "A Survey of Research on Financial Reporting in a Transnational Context." *Journal of Accounting Literature* (1990), 145–182.

16. Mueller (1968).

17. Meek and Saudagaran (1990), 9.

18. David, R. and J. Brierley, *Major Legal Systems in the World Today.* (London: Stevens, 1985).

19. Meek and Saudagaran (1990), 9–10.

20. Ibid., p. 10.

21. Mueller (1968); Radebaugh (1975); and AAA (1977).

22. Schweikart, J.A., "The Relevance of Managerial Accounting Information: A Multinational Analysis." *Accounting, Organizations and Society* (No. 6, 1986), 541–554.

23. Mueller (1968).

24. Cooke, T.E. and R.S.O. Wallace, "Financial Disclosure Regulation and its Environment: Review and Further Analysis." *Journal of Accounting and Public Policy* (Summer 1990), 79–110.

25. Hofstede, G., *Cultures and Organizations: Software of the Mind.* (London: McGraw-Hill, 1991), 5.

26. Hofstede (1980).

27. Gray (1988).

28. Ibid., 10–11.

30. Nobes (1983).

31. Punj, G. and D.W. Stewart, "Cluster Analysis in Marketing Research: Review and Suggestions for Application." *Journal of Marketing Research* (May 1983), 134–148.

Environment, Culture, and Accounting Practice   207

32. Nobes (1983).
33. The misclassified countries are Belgium, Japan and the Netherlands.
34. See Hair, J.F., R.E. Anderson, and R.L. Tatham, *Multivariate Data Analysis with Readings* (New York: McMillan, 1987), 194, 199–200, 249 for heuristics used to interpret results of canonical correlation analysis.

Correspondence and offprint requests to: Professor Timothy S. Doupnik, College of Business Administration, University of South, Carolina, Columbia, SC 29208, USA.

[2]

ABACUS, Vol. 31, No. 1, 1995

NABIL BAYDOUN AND ROGER WILLETT

Cultural Relevance of Western Accounting Systems to Developing Countries

It has been suggested recently that the accounting systems used in developing countries may be irrelevant to their needs because they originate in Western countries with different cultural values. The accounting literature on this point, however, is vague in its assessment of exactly what aspects of Western accounting systems fail to meet the test of relevance. Furthermore, it is not clear whether the differences between the needs of users in various countries are differences in kind or only differences in degree. This article analyses these issues by introducing technical considerations in addition to the behavioural ones usually discussed and by separating out problems of accounting *measurement* from problems of accounting *disclosure*. This distinction is used to argue that it is the specific disclosure rules of particular calculations inherent in Western accounting systems rather than the transaction cost database that are most likely to fail to satisfy the needs of users in developing countries. The effect of the importation of the French Unified Accounting System to Lebanon is examined and an amended version of the Hofstede–Gray cultural accounting framework is used to clarify the concept of cultural relevance.

Key words: Accounting theory; Culture; Disclosure; Measurement.

In recent years increasing attention has been paid to the cultural dimension of accounting (Gray, 1988; Tay and Parker, 1990; Hamid et al., 1993). AlHashim and Arpan (1992) argued that the needs of users are influenced by environmental factors specific to the locality in which their decisions are made. Similarly, according to Perera (1989a), accounting practices evolve to suit the circumstances of a particular society at a particular time. However, many developing countries have adopted accounting systems from Europe and North America (Briston, 1978). Consequently it is difficult to judge the validity of these arguments directly. A number of studies have been carried out to assess the impact of Western accounting systems on individual developing countries (e.g., Briston and Liang, 1990; Briston and Wallace, 1990; Parry and Grove, 1990) and others have undertaken comparative analysis of two or more developing countries (e.g., AICPA, 1964, 1975; Briston, 1990). Consensus is lacking as

NABIL BAYDOUN is Lecturer in Accounting, City Polytechnic of Hong Kong, and ROGER WILLETT is Professor in Accounting, University of Otago.

The authors gratefully acknowledge the helpful comments of Alan MacGregor, Rob Gray, Hector Perera, Ng Su-May, Jill McKinnon and members of staff in the Department of Accountancy at Otago University.

to the accounting system that would best suit each country, but there does seem to be general agreement that Western accounting systems are deficient to some extent in meeting the requirements of users in developing countries.

The existing literature is rather vague in its assessment of what aspects of Western accounting systems fail to meet the test of relevance to developing nations' needs. For example, is it the case that the recording and analysis of costs through the double entry bookkeeping system is at fault or is there some less fundamental defect in the system, such as the need for a change in some of the regulations regarding the specific items to be disclosed in annual financial statements? One of the main theoretical paradigms which has been used to address the question of the relevance of Western accounting systems to developing nations is due to Hofstede (1980) and Gray (1988). This article discusses the application of Hofstede–Gray theory in these circumstances. The theory is illustrated by examining the use of the French Unified Accounting System (UAS) in Lebanon. It is argued that although Gray's 'dimensions' may possibly help us to understand how social factors affect the technology of accounting, certain purely technical aspects of accounting which are also pertinent to the question of cultural relevance should be considered more formally. The analysis depends upon appreciating that the measurement–disclosure distinction recognized by Gray and others in the literature on harmonization and the cultural impact of accounting (e.g., Fechner and Kilgore, 1994) brings with it a certain amount of information about what is most likely to be influenced by cultural context. This extension of the Hofstede–Gray theory is used to argue that the specific disclosure rules of particular calculations inherent in Western accounting systems rather than the transaction cost database are most likely to fail to satisfy the needs of users in developing countries. Due to the limited nature of the evidence currently available, the generality of the analysis is limited. In return, however, it allows relationships between some aspects of culture and items of financial information to be discussed more specifically.

Developing Countries and Hofstede–Gray Theory
The description 'developing country' refers to a country falling within the rather vague definition used by Wallace (1990): a country in the midstream of economic development.[1] Developing countries possess a monetary economy, some parts of the social and economic infrastructure of developed countries (Makdisi, 1977; Perera, 1989b) and, in particular, accounting systems. Since one of the functions of accounting systems, presumably, is to serve some purpose (FASB, 1978) it is natural to ask whether the accounting systems adopted by developing countries are most suitable for those countries.

---

[1] As Wallace (p. 3) states, developing countries are typically African, Asian, South American, Middle Eastern and South Pacific which were decolonized by the European powers in the 1950s and in which there is often a sizeable section of the population who would be considered poor by Western standards. This definition ties in reasonably well to those used in the statistical analysis of economic development (e.g., World Bank, 1991). Osmańczyk (1985) is a useful reference for the United Nations definitions of developing and developed countries.

ACCOUNTING AND CULTURE IN DCS

An answer to this question either requires a piecemeal, case-by-case judgment on what elements constitute an appropriate accounting system for a specific developing country, region or cultural group, or it requires a theory of what is relevant to the needs of users in developing countries. The theory which has so far found the most favour in this regard is due to Hofstede (1980) and Gray (1988). Hofstede's is a theory from the literature of cross-cultural psychology and is not concerned with accounting per se. Gray's is an extension of Hofstede's theory which attempts to understand some of the mechanisms through which cultural variables might impact on the correct design of accounting technology. The remainder of this section describes this composite theory in detail.

Hofstede (1987) defined 'culture' as a collective programming process by a society which distinguishes the belief systems of its members from other societies. Four characteristics of culture were specified: symbols, heroes, rituals and values. The last (which is relevant here) is the most difficult to change, according to Hofstede, and he suggested that differences in institutional behaviour can be explained by differences in four dimensions of value. These are: large versus small Power Distance; strong versus weak Uncertainty Avoidance; Individualism versus Collectivism; and Masculinity versus Femininity. All of these dimensions are assumed to be ordinally measurable. Power Distance depends upon the extent to which members of society accept the unequal distribution of power within institutions and society generally. Uncertainty Avoidance is reflected in the extent to which ambiguous situations are tolerated and the extent to which institutions insist on conformity. Individualism refers to the relationship of members of society to their families vis-à-vis other societal units. Cultures are more individualistic to the extent that the self and immediate family claim priority over the interests of broader social groupings such as the firm and the state. Masculinity implies strongly differentiated sex roles and stresses material success in competitive societies.[2]

It seems plausible to suggest the existence of an effect by culture on accounting practices (e.g., Burchell et al., 1980, p. 19; Meyer, 1986) but the mechanisms by which such an effect might be transmitted are not immediately obvious. Hofstede's framework is shown in Figure 1. Societies are influenced by different underlying technological and environmental factors and consequently develop different societal

---

[2] These dimensions seem to be independent of one another according to Hofstede (1980) and were the outcome of a factor analysis of the questionnaire responses of a large sample of IBM employees in over forty countries. Hofstede claimed that his values relate to three cultural dimensions identified in anthropological research and sociological theory. These are relationship to authority, the concept of the self and gender role differentiation (Parsons and Shils, 1951; Inkeles and Levinson, 1969). It is important to understand that Hofstede's cultural values are to be interpreted as social attributes of collections of people, not as psychological attributes of individuals (Hofstede, 1991, Chapter 1). Hofstede (1991) discusses a possible fifth dimension extracted from a study of Chinese cultural values which appears to be independent of the four dimensions discussed in this paper and relates to the degree to which people take a short-term view or a long-term view of life. This has some possibly interesting implications for certain accounting issues such as cash flow versus accrual accounting. However, due to the fact that it is not yet clear how Gray's framework would accommodate this additional value, and also to the absence of data with respect to Lebanon on this issue at the present time, the 'Confucian' dimension is not incorporated into the analysis.

FIGURE I

HOFSTEDE'S FRAMEWORK

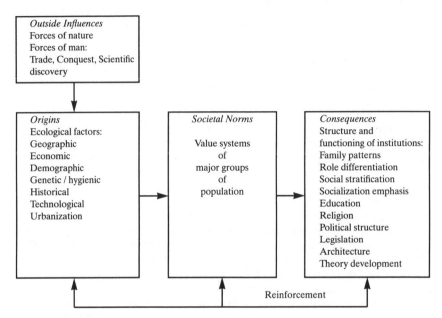

Source: Hofstede (1980).

values. These in turn effect institutional processes including, presumably, information needs about those processes. This appears to be the basic argument supporting the contention that each culture should develop its own accounting system to serve its own distinct requirements.

Gray attempted to use Hofstede's theoretical framework to explain more specifically the effect of cultural values on accounting practices. Gray related four accounting variables to Hofstede's dimensions: Professionalism, Uniformity, Conservatism and Secrecy. Basically to use Gray's framework one must be able to determine, by some means, whether an accounting system scores high or low on each of the dimensions. Then, Gray hypothesized, the relationship between his accounting values and Hofstede's cultural values is as shown in Table 1. The specific areas of practice which these variables are supposed to affect is shown in Figure 2, reproduced from Radebaugh and Gray (1993), and described originally by Gray as those of authority, measurement and disclosure. Gray would expect a high value for Individualism in a society to be associated with the willing exercise of individual judgment and thus, the reasoning goes, relatively influential professional accounting bodies. High Individualism similarly implies a suspicion of Uniform or Secretive

70

ACCOUNTING AND CULTURE IN DCS

TABLE 1

RELATIONSHIPS BETWEEN GRAY'S ACCOUNTING DIMENSIONS
AND HOFSTEDE'S CULTURAL DIMENSIONS

Cultural Values (Hofstede)	Accounting values (Gray)			
	Professionalism	Uniformity	Conservatism	Secrecy
Power Distance	–	+	?	+
Uncertainty Avoidance	–	+	+	+
Individualism	+	–	–	–
Masculinity	?	?	–	–

Note: '+' indicates a direct relationship between the relevant variables; '–' indicates an inverse relationship. Question marks indicate that the nature of the relationship is indeterminate.

FIGURE 2

GRAY'S ACCOUNTING DIMENSIONS AND MEASUREMENT AND DISCLOSURE

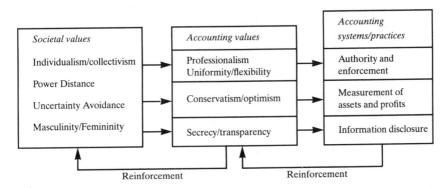

Source: Radebaugh and Gray (1993).

disclosure practices and a Conservative calculation rule like the lower of cost and market value might be expected to be less popular on the basis that undue pessimism is associated with Conservatism. The interpretation of Gray's variables will be discussed in more detail throughout this paper.

A number of studies have been carried out at the theoretical level utilizing the Hofstede–Gray framework. For example, Perera (1989a) applied the approach to developing countries generally and Gerhardy (1990) to the specific case of West

A B A C U S

Germany.[3] To our knowledge, however, the theory has yet to be empirically tested. Indeed such is the nature of the concepts involved and the state of the available evidence that it is questionable whether Gray's adaptation of Hofstede's theory can in fact be empirically validated in the usual scientific sense.

The problem of substantiating the Hofstede–Gray theory is particularly acute in the context of understanding the relevance of accounting practices to the needs of developing countries. Widely differing accounting practices have evolved in the EEC and other Western countries, as has been highlighted by recent attempts at harmonization. These differences can be explained in terms of local, cultural conditions (Pratt and Behr, 1987; Schreuder, 1987) and a number of environmental factors (Nair and Frank, 1980; Goodrich, 1982; Nobes, 1983). If such clear differences have evolved among relatively similar developed economic systems it is quite possible that had accounting systems evolved independently in developing countries they would have had a rather different form from any we now witness in present day Europe. However, most accounting systems used in developing countries have been directly imported from the West through a variety of channels: by colonialism in the past (Engleman, 1962; Heatly, 1979); and through Western multinational companies (Seidler, 1969), the influence of local professional associations (usually founded originally by Western counterpart organizations) and aid and loan agencies from the industrialized nations in the present (Heatly, 1979). The consequence of this transmission of technology is that it *may* have once been relevant to the information needs of the colonisers and *may* today be relevant to the information needs of the managers of multinational companies, Western governments and the International Monetary Fund.[4] However the process of importation makes it extremely difficult to determine in a straightforward, positive fashion, by simple correspondence of the theory with the facts, whether Western technology is relevant to the current needs of developing societies. Due to the interference in what would otherwise have been the natural evolution of financial information requirements there are no uncontaminated examples of modern accounting practices in developing countries. Consequently great care has to be taken in using data from developing countries to draw inferences about relevance on the basis of the Hofstede–Gray framework. Probably the best that can be achieved presently is to adopt the Hofstede–Gray framework as an implied definition of cultural relevance and apply it to specific cases to see if the results of such an enterprise are consistent with the available evidence. This method is applied to the case of Lebanon in the next section.

---

[3] At the theoretical level with respect to developing countries in general, Perera traced the societal values inherent in Power Distance, Uncertainty Avoidance, Individuality and Masculinity together with institutional characteristics such as the legal system, capital markets, education and professional associations back to underlying ecological, economic, historic and technological factors.

[4] It may not, of course. Some would argue that the present form of Western financial statements fails even to satisfy the needs of Western users (e.g., see Briston, 1978). As Hopwood states: 'It is just not true that current or past practice necessarily reflect desirable practice' (1974, p. 166).

ACCOUNTING AND CULTURE IN DCS

THE CASE OF LEBANON AND THE FRENCH UAS

The French UAS

In order to apply the Hofstede–Gray schema to analyse the relevance of the UAS in both France and Lebanon it is necessary to examine the latter's attributes with respect to the accounting value dimensions. There is a difficulty of interpretation with this exercise in that Gray's values are defined in terms of social dispositions rather than the attributes of financial reports. The theoretical significance of this matter will be taken up later. In the meantime Gray's dimensions will be informally analysed as if they were attributes of the UAS itself.

Descriptions of the French accounting system lead one to conclude that Professionalism, under Gray's definitions, is low and that Uniformity is high (e.g., AlHashim and Arpan, 1992).[5] The reasons for the present pattern of French accounting practices appear to be largely historical (Nobes and Parker, 1991). Since then there has been a long tradition of accounting legislation in France. The *Code Napoleon*, for example, was a forerunner of much Continental accounting regulation and the present UAS is a modern version of the 1947 *Plan Comptable Général.*[6] The basic form of these accounts developed out of the belief on the part of successive French governments that a national uniform system would both help to promote a more equitable distribution of wealth through a more effective taxation policy (Scott, 1970) and would also benefit the national economy through a more informed planning strategy (Holzer, 1984). The necessary involvement of the French government in the creation of this grand design, together with a strong legislative influence on company disclosure practices, has resulted in a system of accounting in which the exercise of Professional judgment is substantially reduced in order to achieve higher Uniformity of practice.

Gray's definition of conservatism (1988, p. 8) is similar to Chambers' (1966) interpretation of it as a deliberate downward bias or 'pessimism' in accounting estimates. This emphasises a statistical aspect of accounting measurement which is likely to be context specific and the effects of which will be seen mainly in the choice of valuation method and income determination. It is usually accepted from the earlier work of Gray (1980) and others (e.g., Nobes and Parker, 1991) that the UAS, like German accounting, is inherently more conservative than Anglo-American

---

[5] Professionalism, in this context, refers to the extent to which individual accountants have the discretion to depart from detailed rules and guidelines in measurement and disclosure issues (Gray, 1988; Perera, 1989a). It is not always clear in the literature that 'professionalism' is an attribute of an accounting system rather than an attribute of the cultural environment. For example, it is unclear how 'self-regulation' as a defining characteristic of professionalism is a quality that one might expect to find in an accounting system instead of a quality that is exhibited by professional organizations within a particular society. In fact, solely in the context of accounting systems, 'uniformity' often appears to simply be the inverse attribute of 'professionalism'.

[6] The basis of the *Plan Comptable* actually seems to have been laid down by the occupying German authorities in World War II. More details of the French UAS may be found in Baydoun and Gray (1990).

systems in this respect. For example, depreciation policies are determined strictly in accordance with taxation law and rather large portions of annual profit (5 per cent) have to be set aside to a statutory reserve until the latter reaches a level of 10 per cent of the issued share capital. Again, the reason behind this practice appears to be historical and culturally specific: the dominant position of banking institutions and government in the ownership structure of French companies (Nobes, 1989).

Gray's fourth accounting dimension of Secrecy relates to an issue of disclosure: the extent to which accounting information about the firm finds its way into the hands of third parties. The evidence strongly supports the belief that the UAS provides less information to third parties and hence is considerably more Secretive than the accounting disclosures required of their British and American counterparts (Barrett, 1980). The position of investors seems to be particularly affected in this regard (Scott, 1970). The reason for the appearance of this trait in the UAS is presumably similar to the causes of Conservatism, that is, the close control of companies by government and large financial institutions which have powers of access to the information they require.

The UAS was developed by the French and therefore it is to be expected that correlations would be observed between Hofstede's cultural dimensions and Gray's accounting dimensions in the directions described in Table 1 if Gray's theory of relevance is valid. If either Perera's or Hofstede's data on cultural values is used (Perera, 1989a, p. 53; Hofstede, 1980, pp. 92–152), this is the case for the first three cultural dimensions, namely Power Distance, Uncertainty Avoidance and Masculinity. Power Distance and Uncertainty Avoidance in France are both relatively high compared to most other democratic European and Anglo-Saxon countries.[7] Masculinity is on the low side of the international average for France, particularly when the organizational role aspect of the concept is applied to perceived differences between the sexes at the expert strata of management, that is, the level at which accounting information might be thought to be especially relevant (Hofstede, 1980, p. 281). However, the pattern of Individualism in French society appears to run in the opposite direction to the way predicted by Gray. The comparison of French cultural values with Gray's accounting values may thus indicate that, in this regard, the UAS fails to meet the needs of French accounts users. Alternatively it may be that this cultural dimension is not appropriate to the question being asked, or that Gray's theory is invalid.

For the reasons given in the preceding section, one possible use of Gray's theory as applied to developing countries is as a definition of relevance. In this context it is instructive to apply the definition to the case of Lebanon, to see if the result leads to conclusions which appear to be sensible in the light of what we know about Lebanese history, environment and culture.

---

[7] This has been attributed to the preference of the French for highly centralized bureaucratic structures, a trait which seems to be a stable and accepted characteristic of French society over a long period of time and to be exhibited in political and economic hierarchies at all levels (Most, 1984).

ACCOUNTING AND CULTURE IN DCS

Historical, Environmental and Cultural Background of Lebanon
Lebanon is a relatively small country with limited natural resources. It is densely populated with about three and a half million people occupying only 10,452 square kilometres of the Levant. The country's strategic position on the Eastern Mediterranean seaboard has assured the region and its surrounding area of the role of an important trading centre since ancient times.[8] Following World War I in 1920, the Allied Supreme Council granted France a mandatory authority over Lebanon. The components of this new state consisted of Arabic-speaking people, both Muslim and Christian, and had been part of the Ottoman Empire since 1518. Despite the long period of Turkish rule there is little evidence of Turkish influence in the everyday life of the Lebanon today.[9] Lebanon was a French colony until 1943 and French troops remained in the country until 1946. During the period of French occupation the Lebanese Pound was tied to the French Franc, which had the effect of exporting the economic problems of France during the years of the Great Depression (Badrud-Din, 1984). In the first thirty years following World War II Lebanon experienced a period of relative economic prosperity with an annual average GDP growth rate of approximately 6 per cent.

Since 1975 Lebanon has been subjected to a crippling civil war. The main economic effect of this and the more general conflict in the Middle East in recent years has been significant levels of inflation and destabilization of the economy (Baydoun and Gray, 1990). The civil war has reduced the level of commerce and virtually eliminated a once-healthy tourist industry (Saidi, 1986). Lebanon's limited manufacturing industry, which has also been badly affected by the war, is light, modern (e.g., food processing) and depends heavily upon imported raw materials (Badrud-Din, 1984). The country exports mainly food and tobacco products to the Arab market. The industrial sector now consists mainly of small firms owned and operated chiefly by private interests with little government involvement. A trend towards greater privatization has continued despite the present conflict (Labaki, 1991).

The influence of the French style of life is clearly visible in Lebanon today, especially among the Maronite community. The French period led to the establishment of schools, hospitals and other institutions which acted as vehicles for the transmission and assimilation of French culture (Bucheiry, 1991). Strong trading relations between France and Lebanon still exist, French law is deeply embedded in Lebanon's constitution and French is the official second language (Gordon, 1983). Most importantly, the French government sponsored the transfer of the French UAS to Lebanon in 1983 and it has since been adopted by all Lebanese firms.[10]

---

[8] This is the land in which the Phoenicians once dwelt and is part of what was once referred to as 'Asia Minor', an area colonized in turn by Persians, Greeks, Romans, Arabs and Turks among others.

[9] Apart from some elements in the Lebanese vocabulary, the typical Lebanese menu, dress and some family relationships.

[10] A grant of 500,000 French Francs was given by the French government to finance the transfer (personal interview in 1990 with A. Mattar, Chairman of the Technical Affairs Committee, Lebanese Association of Certified and Public Accountants).

Nevertheless, despite the strong French influence in Lebanon there exist significant environmental and cultural differences between the two countries today, some of which may affect the relevance of the UAS to Lebanese user needs.

Unlike the case of France, no direct assessments of Lebanon's four cultural dimensions are publicly available. However, Hofstede (1991) provides data on a group of Arab countries including Lebanon and this can be used as the starting point for the analysis. Hofstede's values for the Arab countries compared to France are shown in Table 2. As can be observed, as a group the Arab countries exhibit higher Power Distance and Masculinity and lower Individualism and Uncertainty Avoidance than France.

There are a number of reasons, however, why these scores are unlikely to reflect Lebanese cultural values. The group of countries Hofstede described as 'Arab' consists of Egypt, Iraq, Kuwait, Libya, Saudi Arabia and the United Arab Emirates as well as Lebanon. Included in this sample are countries belonging to the Gulf region, North Africa and the Mediterranean, areas of great cultural diversity with representatives from among the richest (e.g., Kuwait) and poorest of nations (e.g., Egypt) on a per capita GNP basis. Furthermore the effects of colonization on individuals within this group are likely to have been diverse since Saudi Arabia was never colonized directly; Egypt, Iraq and Kuwait were colonized or influenced less

TABLE 2

HOFSTEDE'S ARAB COUNTRIES CULTURAL
VALUES SCORES COMPARED TO THOSE OF FRANCE

	Arab countries	France
Power Distance		
Score rank	7	15/16
Score	80	68
Reference page (Hofstede, 1991)	26	26
Individualism		
Score rank	26/27	10/11
Score	38	71
Reference page	53	53
Masculinity		
Score Rank	23	35/36
Score	53	43
Reference page	84	84
Uncertainty Avoidance		
Score rank	27	10/15
Score	68	86
Reference page	113	113

Source: Hofstede (1991).

ACCOUNTING AND CULTURE IN DCS

directly by the British; Libya by the Italians; and Lebanon by the French. Given these factors we might expect considerable variability on some of the dimension scores by the countries within the group.

Since the Arab countries score is an aggregate it acts as a measure of location for the scaled values for each individual country in the group. This enables us to estimate very roughly how Lebanon's cultural values stand in relation to these 'average' measures and thus to the values of the cultural dimensions of France. In the assessment of Lebanon's cultural values which follows, the analysis relies upon a triangulation of Hofstede's data with impressionistic emic data and with observations of some of the institutional processes, which, according to Hofstede's theory, are consequences of cultural values.[11] It also serves to raise the question of the extent to which it is sensible to ask questions about *the* culture of Lebanon, since there may be several cultures seeking to coexist within the same Lebanese geographical boundary. This point is returned to in the concluding discussions.

Power Distance. The Arab countries as a group ranked seventh out of fifty national groupings with a score of 80 compared to a ranking of fifteenth and a score of 68 for France (see Table 2). Consideration of Lebanese institutional arrangements and general norms suggest that, comparatively with the other Arab countries in Hofstede's group, Lebanon's Power Distance score would be below the aggregate score of 80.

Lebanon possesses a written constitution originally based upon the French model which was introduced in 1926 and which established a parliamentary democracy (Gordon, 1983; Salem, 1991). The constitution has been amended several times since then, the last time being in 1990. It guarantees certain fundamental rights of the individual, including 'respect for public liberties, especially the freedom of opinion and belief' (Salem, 1991). The political intention behind the clauses in the preamble to the latest amendment of the constitution and in particular the *mithaq al-aysh al-mushtarak*[12] may be interpreted as an attempt to lower the level of Power Distance in Lebanese society.

Most of the effects of the recent civil war have tended to further reduce Power Distance. Indeed, the war may be interpreted as evidence of the rejection of inequalities in the power structure implicit in the pre-1975 political system. The powers of the Maronite president, for example, have been substantially curtailed in the amended constitution. The former executive powers of the president have now been ceded to a Council of Ministers, thus establishing a more non-French, collegial political decision making apparatus. The Lebanese presidential office, as modified by

---

11 Hofstede's values have certain consequences for the institutional arrangements societies develop. Hofstede's theory therefore justifies our making inferences about cultural values on the basis of observed patterns of institutional behaviour. From a mechanistic point of view, group decision making processes which manifest themselves in institutional actions are presumably determined with some degree of probability by the common norms held by individuals who collectively constitute the relevant organization.

12 Literally, 'communal coexistence'. This principle reaffirms the interconfessional amity between Muslims and Christians which in principle has existed since the inception of the Lebanese state.

the recent constitutional changes, now has a ceremonial role more reminiscent of Ireland, Germany and Israel (all of which score low on the Power Distance scale) than of France.[13]

At the level of individual organizations as well as at the lower, non-ministerial levels of political institutions, the proposed aboliton of the 'six to five' employment policy which requires the appointment of six Christians for every five Muslims (including Druze) seeks to redress a perceived imbalance between the different religious groups (Article 95, Salem, 1991; Soffer, 1986; Faour, 1991). These movements toward more equal power distribution in Lebanese society are typical of changes in the political and social structure which have occurred since the 1970s and reflect a current system of values which strongly rejects the distribution of power imposed by the French (Fawaz, 1991).

On Hofstede's scale, a high reading of Power Distance depends upon two basic characteristics both being present: one is that significant inequalities in the distribution of power exist; the other is that members of society accept the inequalities. Given the present difficult circumstances in Lebanon, the extent of the first characteristic is difficult to gauge although, by comparison with the Arab grouping, the basis of Lebanese power-sharing structures appears to be in a state of transition towards a more egalitarian template. The absence of the second characteristic, however, is clear: as evidenced by the current conflicts and recent changes in the constitution the *acceptance* of inequality between at least some of the important groupings in Lebanese society is low.

These institutional characteristics of Lebanese society suggest that, if the Lebanese power distance value is greater than the moderate position of France it is probably much closer to the French value than the average 'Arab countries' score of 80 would indicate. A more moderate score on the Power Distance scale is also suggested by consideration of the family, school and workplace norms described by Hofstede (1991, p. 37). The norms which characterize Lebanese communities are fairly evenly distributed between those associated with small and large Power Distances. For example, while parents teach children obedience and children are expected to treat parents with respect, there is also a belief that inequalities among people should be minimized and that subordinates should be consulted. Furthermore, decentralization is one of the main characteristics of Lebanese history in stark contrast to, say, the position in Egypt (e.g., Khalaf, 1987). This reasoning suggests that the Lebanese value for Power Distance probably falls into the middle range.

Uncertainty Avoidance. Hofstede's Uncertainty Avoidance score for the Arab countries of 68, with a ranking of twenty-seventh, is low in comparison with France, which scored 86 and was ranked tenth equal in the study. The traits exhibited by Lebanon suggest a relatively low level of Uncertainty Avoidance compared to the other countries in the Arab group, which implies that this value is relatively weak in Lebanese society compared to France's quite high score.

---

[13] See Article 17 of the 1990 Lebanese Constitution (translated in Salem, 1991).

ACCOUNTING AND CULTURE IN DCS

This trait is particularly well illustrated in Lebanon by a strongly free-enterprise economy. The Lebanese region has old commercial and trading traditions and economic growth, past and present, has been mainly due to the investment of private capital (Labaki, 1991). Government economic policies have, in fact, long been based upon the implicit objective of allowing the private sector to lead economic expansion, sometimes with the encouragement of large investment and tax incentives for both home and foreign investors (Gordon, 1983). This is unlike most other Arab countries and is representative of a more free-market philosophy than that which would be found in many European countries, particularly France. Uncertainty is a normal feature of life. There is no unemployment benefit in Lebanon and health is mostly privately funded (Kuvian, 1982). Although the state makes free education available at both elementary and higher levels, 70 per cent of Lebanese nevertheless chose private education (McDowall, 1986).

The general norms of Lebanon are mostly on the weak Uncertainty side: the Lebanese are, for instance, comfortable in ambiguous situations with unfamiliar risks and are motivated by achievement (Hofstede, 1991, p. 125). While some norms are indicative of stronger Uncertainty Avoidance (e.g., the display of aggression at appropriate times is socially acceptable) they are relatively few compared to those reflecting weak Uncertainty Avoidance. The key differences in politics and ideas between Lebanon and the typical Arab country in Hofstede's data also point in the same direction. Citizen protest is more acceptable and Lebanon is more regional and international, with stronger human rights traditions (Hofstede, 1991, p. 134). The institutional facts of life in Lebanon, therefore, as well as some strong cultural characteristics, impose a greater tolerance of Uncertainty on Lebanese society than in the other Arab countries in Hofstede's sample, and thus its Uncertainty index must be low relative to that of France.

Individualism: The Arab countries score low on Individualism (scoring 38 and ranked equal twenty-sixth) compared to France (scoring 71 and ranked equal tenth). However, many traits on the continuum of Individualism run parallel to those of Uncertainty Avoidance and suggest that Individualism in Lebanese society is considerably higher than in other Arab countries.

Interference in private life by the organs of state is relatively low, for example. There are low levels of taxation (Torbey, 1986) and there are absolutely no controls over foreign exchange (Badrud-Din, 1984). The Lebanese family is the strongest social unit, dominating economic and political life at the expense of affection for non-family and state organizations and cutting across the boundaries of wealth and education (McDowall, 1986), something which Hofstede describes as 'fragmented collectivism'. Individualism and private property rights are, in fact, basic principles which are now enshrined in the written constitution (pp. 122–6, Salem, 1991), which itself embodies a long-running, free-market oriented philosophy.[14]

---

[14] It should be noted that, in respect of Individualism, Lebanese society is considerably less clannish than other countries in the Middle East (Khalaf, 1987).

The written constitution guarantees individual liberties in specific ways. For example, Article 9 of the amended 1990 constitution pledges absolute freedom of conscience (Salem, 1991). The toleration of individualism has led over a number of years to Lebanon being seen as a refuge for asylum seekers (Gordon, 1983, p. 41) and it is a country traditionally renowned for its free press (Salem, 1991, p. 166). There is not a single government-owned newspaper and, since 1980, no state involvement in the television services (Kuvian, 1982). A further manifestation of the Lebanese tolerance for free thinking can be found in the content of the typical syllabi of political and economic studies in the higher education system. For example, commercial subjects studied at the Lebanese University include both Western capitalist economic theory as well as the theories of Communism and Third World developing economies (Centre for Lebanese Studies, 1991). Foreign languages such as English and French are also more important than usual among Middle Eastern countries (Badrud-Din, 1984). Private educational institutions enjoy almost complete autonomy (*Middle East and North Africa Yearbook,* 1992, p. 675). This liberal style of education is considered so fundamental that it was singled out for special mention in the 1990 amendment to the constitution (Salem, 1991). Lebanon thus possesses many of the characteristics of freedom taken for granted in Western societies and also, perhaps, places greater emphasis on individual self-reliance than would usually be expected in modern welfare-state capitalist societies.

The norms of Lebanese society are predominantly Individualistic (Hofstede, 1991, p. 67): people focus on the nuclear family, identity is based on the individual and employee–employer relationships are based upon mutual advantage; and the politics and ideas of Lebanon are overwhelmingly individualistic in contrast to the typical Arab country; people have a right to privacy, a personal opinion, equality under the law and so on. Lebanon's value for Individualism would lie well above the score for the composite of the Arab countries and probably lies along with France in the high individualism category.

Masculinity: Hofstede's data on Masculinity placed the Arab country group in the middle range of the index with a score of 53 and ranked twenty-third. France lies toward the more Feminine end of the scale with a score of 43 and ranked equal thirty-fifth with Iran. As is typical of the Arab group as a whole, the role of the sexes is typically more clearly differentiated than it is in the West. This may be due to family size, which is larger than it is in Europe.[15] Male children are more highly valued than female children (Khalaf, 1987) and, given the biological imperative, the number of women available to enter the workforce is severely curtailed. Historically, the number of women actually in the workforce is relatively low, particularly in higher management positions.[16] Within the Arab group, Lebanon is probably among

---

[15] Official demographic statistics about Lebanon appear to be virtually impossible to obtain (Faour, 1991). Our information in this respect is based upon personal estimates of family sizes in Lebanon.

[16] The participation rate of Lebanese males in the workforce in 1975 was 42.1 per cent and that of Lebanese females was 9.6 per cent. This compares to male and female rates of 55.6 per cent and 29.3 per cent respecively in France for the same year (International Labour Office, 1978). No official statistics are available after 1975 for Lebanon on this matter.

ACCOUNTING AND CULTURE IN DCS

the most strongly masculine societies. The war has tended to emphasize gender differences. Women do not serve in the Lebanese Army, for example. War by its very nature emphasises toughness and male assertiveness. Moreover, the armed forces as organizations usually have what Hofstede (1980, p. 261) refers to as Masculine goals.

The typical modern role model reinforced by literature such as that of Barakat (1974), Pound (1986) and Mahfouz (1989) and by the free-market economic environment is of a self-reliant, competitive male with strong family loyalties and a woman whose main duty is still that of a housewife and mother. The general norms of Lebanese society (Hofstede, 1991, p. 96) are overwhelmingly masculine, the dominant values in society being material success and progress with men being assertive and women tender. These characteristics and those relating to politics and ideas (such as the importance of economic growth, Hofstede, 1991, p. 103) place Lebanon toward the higher end of the Masculinity scale, on the other side of the Arab countries away from France.

Information Mismatch in the Lebanese UAS

This analysis of Lebanese society in terms of Hofstede's cultural values has, of necessity, been brief and selective. Lebanese society has undergone substantial changes in recent years in the characteristics described and will presumably continue to do so in the future. Aspects such as Power Distance have noticeably changed in the last two decades and not all influences point in the expected direction. It might be expected, for example, that war may increase Power Distance in certain ways (Hofstede, 1980, Chapter 8). Again, religion is a key factor in the Middle East but it is often difficult to gauge its effect on cultural values. One might argue that the Muslim faith professed by a substantial number of the Lebanese population is a force towards egalitarianism and against Power Distance. The *zakat* (taxation) and the *mirath* (inheritance) laws, for instance, are based upon a principle of equal distribution of wealth (Gambling and Abdel-Karim, 1991). On the other hand, the strong hierarchical structure of some of the religious sects in Lebanon might be argued to lead in the opposite direction.

These considerations make it necessary to handle the available evidence with a great deal of care and only to infer that which is relatively obvious. In this case the evidence is sufficiently clear for a reasonably strong conclusion to be drawn about the relative positions of Lebanon and France on the Power Distance and Individualism scales. There appears to be sufficient cause, however, for concluding that Uncertainty Avoidance is low compared to France's high score and that Lebanon's Masculinity value is high compared to France. On this basis, using the definition of cultural relevance implied by Table 1, it would appear that Lebanon's requirements are for less Uniformity, Conservatism and Secrecy in financial reporting practices. This conclusion may possibly strike the reader as a reasonable result based upon the general impression one receives of the Lebanese environment. However, this is some way from determining what specific information would be more relevant to Lebanese users. To achieve more definite recommendations it is necessary to extend the Hofstede Gray Theory further by explicitly considering the nature of the basic technical accounting dimensions of measurement and disclosure.

MEASUREMENT AND DISCLOSURE

The charge that Western accounting systems fail to serve users in developing countries is often stated in a vague manner and a part of the function of a theory like Gray's is to make this sort of claim more precise. As shown in the previous section, it probably does go some way to achieving this objective, but does it go far enough? To claim that more or less Uniformity, Conservatism and Secrecy are desirable or to be expected in a Lebanese accounting system does not reveal the detailed structural relationships through which cultural predispositions are translated into definite policy recommendations on the detailed physical appearance of accounting reports.

As was shown in Figure 2, Gray's theory attempts to link his accounting values to specific attributes of accounting practice in the form of authority, enforcement, measurement and disclosure. The first two of this latter group are seen as being distinct from the last two in that the former are influenced by the values of Professionalism and Uniformity and represent characeristics of the social and political framework in which the activity of accounting takes place, while the latter are influenced by Conservatism and Secrecy and represent what and how financial information is reported to users. Both of these issues are clearly of important theoretical and practical interest, but the first is of an entirely different character from the second. The linkages between cultural values and the authority and enforcement characteristics found in the arrangements developed by society to organize its accounting activities are a direct application of Hofstede's theory that cultural values will impact on the forms institutions take and the processes they use. On the other hand, the linkages between cultural values and the physical attributes of financial reports (i.e., what they look like, what they contain and how much information they contain, etc.) is an entirely different type of question because it demands assessing the impact of the social dimension of accounting on the technical.

One of the problems with using Gray's theory to address either issue is that it is not entirely clear whether, to the extent that they are meant to be cultural attributes of social groups rather than physical attributes of the technology of accounting, his accounting values serve any useful purpose as intervening explanatory variables between Hofstede's basic cultural dimensions and the characteristics one might expect to find in accounting practice. All of Gray's accounting values are defined in terms of preferences for particular courses of action rather than in terms of apparent attributes of financial statements, such as the qualitative characteristics described in the FASB's Conceptual Framework project (FASB, 1980). Professionalism, for example, appears from Gray's description to refer to the disposition either of individual accountants to use judgments rather than mechanically follow pre-imposed rules, or possibly of professional bodies to prefer self-regulation as opposed to regulation by the State. Uniformity as defined by Gray (1988, p. 8) really appears to be little more than an inverse quality to Professionalism although there is clearly another sense (which may have been what Gray implicitly intended it to take) in

ACCOUNTING AND CULTURE IN DCS

which Uniformity could also be interpreted as the physical attribute of an accounting system (e.g., the extent to which the financial reports of one accounting entity are physically similar to those of other accounting entities).

The treatment of Professionalism and Uniformity by Gray is consistent with the framework described in Figure 2. These values are argued to influence authority and enforcement aspects of accounting systems, which are part of the social and political structure of accounting rather than the technical processes of accounting. Nevertheless, the need for such supposed relationships is far from obvious. For example, Uncertainty Avoidance supposedly has the relationship to Professionalism and Uniformity shown in Table 1 and the latter also supposedly relate to Authority in the way shown in Figure 2. However, given the very close connections between Uncertainty Avoidance and 'concepts of authority' in Hofstede's original theory (1991, pp. 120–3), these linkages appear to be superfluous.

Gray's discussion of the other two accounting value concepts, Conservatism and Secrecy, in relation to the issues of measurement and disclosure suggest that they would be expected to be more influential in determining the technical nature of accounting. This raises the question of whether such an interpretation is tenable. In the first place, it is not self-evident that the social characteristic of Secrecy is any more important in the determination of financial statement attributes than is the social attribute of Uniformity. A trait of high Secrecy in a culture, for instance, may mean that financial reports are less likely to contain certain types of information than in other, less secretive societies. However a high Uniformity score might be expected to directly influence the uniformity with which financial statements of differing entities are prepared, something about which Secrecy apparently would have little to say. Consequently the justification for choosing the particular linkages suggested in Figure 2 is unclear. In the second place, there are obvious questions of interest in understanding the possible forms which financial reports might take which do not seem, at least at a superficial level, to be formally addressed at all in Gray's theory. For instance, under what circumstances might a Statement of Value Added be more culturally relevant than a Profit and Loss Account? Consequently, Gray's theory seems, on the one hand, to overlook some important accounting effects of culture, and on the other hand, to say less than it could about some important aspects of the form and content of financial statements.

It is probably unrealistic to expect to be able to obtain complete agreement on a full and comprehensive theory of the form and exact content of corporate reports. Nevertheless, at least some part of the difficulty in applying Gray's theory and variants of it such as Mathews and Perera (1993) to providing answers to more specific questions about the form and content of financial statements lies in the need to consider certain basic characteristics of accounting technology itself. It seems a lot of thought has been given to the behavioural aspects of accounting but an insufficient amount has been given to the effect of limitations on the influence of cultural factors imposed by the tehnical dimension of accounting. Culture does exert an influence on the technology of accounting but it does so differentially, affecting some parts strongly, other parts less so and certain parts hardly at all. Consideration of why this

ABACUS

is so, therefore, is an essential exercise in any attempt to determine the type of financial statements (as opposed to the forms of social and political organization) which are culturally relevant to a society.

The conventional wisdom in the literature holds that the relevance of accounting numbers depends upon some perceived purpose such as decision usefulness or accountability (Gray et al., 1988). Cultural differences may lead to many specific differences in the requirements of users for accounting information but it is likely that users in developing and developed societies also have many information requirements in common. Therefore, are those who argue that Western accounting systems are irrelevant to the needs of developing countries (Briston, 1978; Perera, 1989b; Samuels and Oliga, 1982; Wallace 1990) suggesting that transaction costs should not be recorded and analysed into economic activities? Or are they simply arguing that the detail and type of information about calculations which are disclosed in Western financial statements should be amended in some way to accommodate differing cultural perspectives?

The first suggestion is extremely radical. Without careful recording of the effects of transactions on activities it is difficult to see how it would be possible for developing countries to enjoy the benefits obtainable from economic analysis. Where independent evolution has taken place, developing countries seem to attach the same significance as do developed countries to the analysis of economic activities through the recording of transactions by systems of bookkeeping (Hayashi, 1989);[17] although developing societies differ in the level of complexity of the events that take place, the transactions these events generate and the variety of decision needs accounting information has to serve.

The second, weaker suggestion, that patterns of disclosure should be adjusted but that basic measurement processes should be left intact, seems more plausible and in fact has a certain theoretical significance in the context of the distinction made between measurement and disclosure issues in accounting noted by a number of writers (Solomons, 1983; Sterling, 1987; Willett, 1987).[18] The main features of this distinction are illustrated in the hierarchy shown in Figure 3.

Measurement issues split into two main types: *fundamental* measurements which involve the direct assignment of a number to an object or event by a relatively objective procedure; and indirect or *derived* measurements which usually involve a calculation based upon fundamental measurements. In accounting, the assignment of debt values to transactions is an example of a fundamental measurement while the profit figure (which includes calculations like the depreciation adjustment) is an

---

[17] Both Japan ('Daifuku-cho') and the Islamic word, *before Paciolo,* independently developed bookkeeping systems of this sort according to Hayashi (1989, p. 8).

[18] In particular, in the conceptual framework literature the distinction between representational faithfulness and relevance (Sterling, 1987) is similar to that between measurement and disclosure, as is the distinction between the political and technical dimensions of accounting, in the standard setting literature (Solomons, 1983). There also appears to be a growing awareness of the significance of this distinction in the recent literature on cultural values (e.g., Fechner and Kilgore, 1993) and on harmonization (e.g., van der Tas, 1988).

ACCOUNTING AND CULTURE IN DCS

example of a derived measurement. The common characteristic of both types of measurement is that they represent observed properties of something in the real world.[19] Disclosure issues are, in contrast, not issues of representational faithfulness at all but of whether anybody wants the information concerned — even if it is properly measured. Relevance does not determine whether an accounting measurement is valid but it does determine, with some degree of probability, whether it is or ought to be disclosed in a set of financial statements. Consequently, the major significance of the concepts of cultural values and cultural relevance is likely to be in terms of their effect on practices which have more to do with disclosure than measurement.

The distinction between measurement and disclosure is, however, not entirely black and white in this context. The framework outlined in Figure 3 identifies the levels at which accounting information is more likely to be open to the charge of cultural irrelevance. The lowest, most fundamental level activity cost measurements (e.g., the cost of inventories and fixed assets) rely much more on purely technological

FIGURE 3

LEVELS OF MEASUREMENT AND DISCLOSURE IN ACCOUNTING

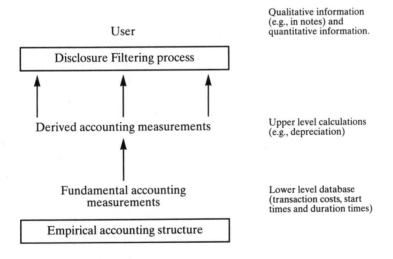

---

[19] See Hines (1988) for an unusual discussion of the doctrine of realism as applied to accountancy. Details of the argument that issues of measurement must logically be considered prior to issues of disclosure can be found in Willett (1987, 1991).

relationships than do the higher levels, and consequently are less affected by social and cultural differences. Higher level, derived measurements such as depreciation calculations and market values, in contrast, are decision-specific statistics and more likely to become irrelevant to user needs if arbitrarily transferred across cultural boundaries. Finally, at the interface between measurements and user, the disclosure filtering mechanisms are by definition culturally determined and it is at this level particularly, the *disclosure* level, that Western accounting practices are most likely to be irrelevant to user needs in developing countries.

This analysis suggests that the subject matter which forms the basis of *any* disclosed financial information is relatively fixed. Essentially, this basis consists of an activity analysis of a defined subset of the population of invoice costs, the subset chosen depending upon whether the accounting is actual cost or current value. Asset analysis requires at least the three main financial reports of position statement, income statement and funds statement to fully account for the data base in aggregate (Hodgson et al, 1993). However, precisely how much of the information contained in the chosen basis is disclosed to users is very much determined by factors such as the cultural forces discussed here. This is what makes it theoretically useful to try to more formally relate the *qualitative characteristics* of financial statements to Hofstede's cultural values via the intervening social attributes suggested by Gray. By extending Gray's framework in this way, it may be possible to explain more formally some of the important, overt characteristics of financial reports. In fact, by grouping the commonly cited qualitative characteristics of financial statements (Mathews and Perera, 1993) in the way decribed in Table 3, it appears that a suitable, technical, reinterpretation of Gray's values of Uniformity, Conservatism and Secrecy can satisfactorily accommodate many of those characteristics in so far as they are pertinent to matters of disclosure. Furthermore, since the reinterpreted concepts can be expected to have the same relationships with Hofstede's cultural values as the original concepts, the amendment allows the Hofstede–Gray framework to be extended to more specific policy prescriptions in a straightforward manner.

Table 3 suggests some relationships between the technical, disclosure characteristics of financial reports, Gray's three concepts of Uniformity, Conservatism and Secrecy and some examples of the manner in which the qualitative characteristics are manifested in the form and content of published accounts. Uniformity as a technical characteristic of financial statements is interpreted as encompassing the two qualities of consistency and comparability, each in different ways relevant to the question of apparent uniformity of accounting policies over time and uniformity of presentation of accounting information between accounting entities. Conservatism and Secrecy overlap in their effects on the remaining qualitative characteristics. Conservatism is pertinent to the *quality* of disclosed information and is thus associated with such physical characteristics as objectivity, verifiability, reliability, neutrality and substance over form. They determine such specific issues of the form and content of financial reports as the communication of historic cost versus current value accounting and the use of rules such as 'lower of cost and market'. These characteristics may, if scaled in the appropriate manner, be

ACCOUNTING AND CULTURE IN DCS

TABLE 3

RELATIONSHIPS BETWEEN GRAY'S REINTERPRETED DIMENSIONS, QUALITIVE
CHARACTERISTICS AND THE FORM AND CONTENT OF CORPORATE REPORTS

Accounting dimensions — technical aspects	Qualitative characteristics relating to disclosure	Examples of issues relating to the form and content of corporate reports
Uniformity	Uniform content and presentation:	
	Consistency	Standardized accounts
	Comparability	Accounting policies
	Quality of Information:	
Conservatism	Timeliness	Normal publication date
	Materiality	Cost versus market values
	Objectivity	Cash flow accounting
	Verifiablity	Lower of cost and market
Secrecy	Reliability	
	Neutrality	
	Substance over form	
	Amount of information:	Extent of disaggregated data:
	Accountability	Number of items disclosed
	Decision usefulness	Group accounts
		Supplementary statements

expected to be correlated in the same way with underlying cultural values, as is Gray's original concept of Conservatism. Gray's original Secrecy concept can be similarly related in a consistent manner both to the quality characteristics and to the *amount* of information in financial reports, the latter being manifested in such traits as the number of items disclosed and the extent to which aggregated data is disclosed in contrast to disaggregated data. This allows the possibility of bringing into the analysis the attributes of accountability and decision usefulness. These notions are concerned with patterns of disclosure such as user focus and the nature of the accounting entity,[20] matters which are not clearly addressed in Gray's original analysis.

In the case of Lebanon the relationships shown in Table 3 suggest a number of policy prescriptions which are more specific than those determined at the close of the discussion in the previous section. Assuming that cultural relevance is or should be a factor in determining the form of financial statements, we would expect Lebanese financial statements to be less uniform across time and between entities, to contain more market value information and provide more items of disaggregated

---

[20] In the sense that the greater the extent of the accounting entity (e.g., a group entity) and the wider the focus of the accounts in terms of users, the greater is the potential amount of information disclosed.

information. Normal publication dates should be relatively flexible and there should be less call for conservative valuation rules such as lower of cost and market.

It would appear that these and other similar prescriptions implied by Table 3 cannot be tested directly at present. Since 1983 all Lebanese firms have been required to follow the UAS and this system has not yet been modified to accommodate any cultural differences between France and Lebanon. If the Hofstede–Gray theory is to amount to anything more than a statement of what some theorists believe to be the cultural relevance of accounting information, however, our analysis suggests that modifications along the lines described above either will or should take place in Lebanese accounting in the future.

CONCLUSION

This article has discussed the issue of the relevance of Western accounting to developing societies. The difficulty with much of the existing literature in this area is that it is not clear exactly what aspects of Western accounting systems are irrelevant to the needs of users in developing countries and it is not always obvious what the term 'relevance' means. The analysis was based on Hofstede's (1980, 1991) characterization of cultural values and Gray's (1988) accounting-value hypotheses were used to define the notion of 'relevance of an accounting system'. These were used to analyse the relevance of the French UAS to the Lebanon. It was argued that although the Hofstede–Gray framework does appear to provide a structure within which to examine issues of the cultural relevance of accounting systems, insufficient notice has been taken of important technical aspects of accounting technology. In particular it was suggested that the charge of irrelevance aimed at an accounting system applied to a developing society was most likely to be substantiated against disclosure rules rather than against the underlying fundamental recording systems upon which most accounting information is based. This led to an extension of the Hofstede–Gray theory which redefined the concepts of Uniformity, Conservatism and Secrecy in terms of the physical characteristics of financial statements.

As in many areas in accounting research, great care has to be taken in pursuing analysis of this kind. Interesting insights into fundamental accounting issues can be revealed but there are also significant qualifications, two of which deserve special mention. One qualification is the delicate juxtaposition of the positive and the normative in analysis of this kind. It was stated earlier that in order to descriptively test a theory of cultural relevance like Gray's it is necessary, from a strictly logical point of view, to already have in one's possession a definition of cultural relevance. Unfortunately, in the context of cultural analysis we do not have such a definition. The usual 'decision usefulness' definitions in the literature will not do, for example, because they focus on the level of the individual and this does not necessarily translate in a simple manner to the macro-social, cultural level. Therefore, in the absence of an independent definition there is a danger that testing hypotheses relating cultural values to accounting characteristics will degenerate into circular

ACCOUNTING AND CULTURE IN DCS

reasoning. The analysis in this paper attempted to avoid this mistake by taking Gray's hypotheses as a tentative implied definition of cultural relevance and to then use it to see if the results produce reasonable conclusions in the light of the available evidence. This is clearly not a strong scientific methodology but it is internally consistent and non-trivial in the sense that, should the evidence for instance turn out to never or only infrequently synchronize with Gray's concept of cultural relevance, then it would surely eventually be discarded in favour of something else. Given the paucity of culturally uncontaminated evidence in the case of studying the accounting practices of developing countries, this means that the possibility of convincingly accepting or rejecting the Hofstede–Gray theory in this context is likely to be a long and arduous process based upon carefully examining those elements of practice which have evolved distinctly within such societies.

A second qualification relating to the Hofstede–Gray framework lies in the scope of its application. Hofstede places great importance on the fact that his cultural values relate to the characteristics of nations and that it is meaningful to reason at this level, despite the many differences which exist within subcultures at the many levels of society. To apply this thesis to the question of the relevance of accounting information is a significant departure from the normal way in which this concept is normally discussed in the modern literature. Virtually all analysis of this matter takes as its reference point the needs of a relatively homogeneous group of users (e.g., shareholders, creditors, investors, trade unionists, etc.). The focus in the cultural relevance literature is different from this mainstream approach to the issue of usefulness. It is uncertain whether it will eventually lead to similar conclusions, or even whether it will ultimately be possible to reconcile the two approaches. In the context of Lebanon, this is especially obvious. It contains a number of important religious groups which have significantly distinct subcultural characteristics, some of which may run counter to the apparent national cultural values. In Lebanon the question of the Islamic community is a case in point. Under Islam the social order is closer to collectivism and the rights of private ownership are ultimately subordinate to Allah. Consequently, the forms of presentation and disclosure which are most applicable to a moderately individualistic society may not be so relevant to the kind of accountability required by the Islamic *Shari'a*. The issue of the extent to which Hofstede's concepts are applicable to the analysis of more specific social groups is an open question at the present time.

It would be interesting to apply the kind of analysis used in this paper to other developing societies. Perhaps further research will reveal patterns of relevance common to developing nations. One of the main problems for research in this area is access to data. Most of the data we have used is in the public domain. Pertinent data of this type, which has the advantage of helping to build a general picture, is often less easy to acquire in the case of developing countries than in the case of developed countries. Direct data from questionnaires is also less easy to acquire in developing countries. Nevertheless, given that the position of the Lebanon makes it more difficult to obtain usable data than in most countries, this should not be an insurmountable problem.

A B A C U S

REFERENCES

AlHashim, D., and J. Arpan, *International Dimension of Accounting*, 3rd edn, PWS-Kent Publishing Co., 1992.

American Institute of Certified Public Accountants, *Professional Accounting in Twenty-Five Countries*, AICPA, 1964.

_____ , *Professional Accounting in Thirty Countries*, AICPA, 1975.

Badrud-Din, A. A., *The Bank of Lebanon: Central Banking in a Financial Centre and Entrepot*, Frances Pinter, 1984.

Barakat, H., *Days of Dust*, The Mediana University Press International, 1974.

Barrett, M. E., 'Financial Reporting Practices: Disclosure and Comprehensiveness in an International Setting', *Journal of Accounting Research*, Spring 1980.

Baydoun, N., and R. Gray, 'Financial Accounting and Reporting in The Lebanon: An Exploratory Study of Accounting in Hyperinflationary Conditions', *Research in Third World Accounting*, Vol. 1, 1990.

Briston, R. J., 'The Evolution of Accounting in Developing Countries', *International Journal of Accounting Education and Research*, Fall 1978.

_____ , 'Accounting in Developing Countries: Indonesia and the Solomon Islands as Case Studies for Regional Cooperation', *Research in Third World Accounting*, Vol. 1, 1990.

Briston, R. J., and F. S. Liang, 'The Evolution of Corporate Reporting in Singapore', *Research in Third World Accounting*, Vol. 1, 1990.

Briston, R. J., and R. S. O. Wallace, 'Accounting Education and Corporate Disclosure Regulations in Tanzania', *Research in Third World Accounting*, Vol. 1, 1990.

Bucheiry, M., *Beirut's Role in the Political Economy of the French Mandate: 1919–39*, Centre for Lebanese Studies, Oxford, 1991.

Burchell, S., C. Clubb, A. Hopwood, J. Hughes and J. Nahapiet, 'The Roles of Accounting in Organizations and Society', *Accounting, Organization and Society*, Vol. 5, No. 1, 1980.

Chambers, R. J., *Accounting, Evaluation and Economic Behavior*, Prentice-Hall, 1966.

Engleman, K., 'Accounting Problems in Developing Countries', *Journal of Accountancy*, January 1962. *Europa World Yearbook*, Vol. 1, Europa Publication, 1992.

Faour, M., 'The Demography of Lebanon: A Reappraisal', *Middle Eastern Studies*, October 1991.

Fawaz, T. L., *Merchants and Migrants in Nineteenth-Century Beirut*, Harvard University Press, 1983.

_____ , *State and Society in Lebanon*, The Centre for Lebanese Studies and Tufts University, 1991.

Fechner, H. E., and A. Kilgore, 'The Influence of Cultural Factors on Accounting Practice', *The International Journal of Accounting Education and Research*, Vol, 29, No. 3, 1994.

Financial Accounting Standards Board, SFAC 1, *Objectives of Financial Reporting by Business Enterprises*, FASB, 1978.

_____ , Statement of Financial Accounting Concepts No. 3, *Qualitative Characteristics of Accounting Information*, FASB, 1980.

Gambling, T., and R. A. A. Abdel-Karim, *Business and Accounting Ethics in Islam*, Mansell, 1991.

Gerhardy, P. G., *An Evaluation of the Role of Culture in the Development of Accounting Principles in West Germany*, Accounting and Finance Research Paper 90/2, The Flinders University of South Australia, 1990.

Goodrich, P. S., 'A Typology of International Accounting Principles and Policies', *British Accounting Review*, Spring 1982.

Gordon, C. D., *The Republic of Lebanon: Nation in Jeopardy*, Westview Press, 1983.

Gray, R., D. Owen and K. Maunders, 'Corporate Social Reporting: Emerging Trends in Accountability and the Social Contract', *Accounting Auditing and Accountability*, Vol. 1, No. 1, 1988.

Gray, S. J., 'The Impact of International Accounting Differences from a Security Analysis Perspective: Some European Evidence', *Journal of Accounting Research*, Spring 1980.

_____ , 'Towards a Theory of Cultural Influence on the Development of Accounting Systems Internationally', *Abacus*, March 1988.

ACCOUNTING AND CULTURE IN DCS

Hamid, S. R., R. Craig and F. L. Clarke, 'Religion: A Confounding Cultural Element in the International Harmonization of Accounting?', *Abacus*, September 1993.

Hayashi, T., *On Islamic Accounting: Its Future Impact on Western Accounting,* The Institute of Middle Eastern Studies, The International University of Japan, Working papers series, No. 18, 1989.

Heatly, R., *Poverty and Power,* Zed Press, 1979.

Hines, D. R., 'Financial Accounting: In Communicating Reality, We Construct Reality', *Accounting, Organization and Society,* No. 3, 1988.

Hodgson, A., J. Okunev and R. J. Willett, 'Accounting for Intangibles: A Theoretical Perspective', *Accounting and Business Research,* Spring 1993.

Hofstede, G., *Culture's Consequences: International Differences in Work-Related Values,* Sage Publications, 1980.

_____ , 'The Cultural Context of Accounting', in B. E. Cushing (ed.), *Accounting and Culture,* American Accounting Association, 1987.

_____ , *Cultures and Organisations: Software of the Mind,* McGraw-Hill, 1991.

Holzer, H. P. (ed), *International Accounting,* Harper and Row, 1984.

Hopwood, A., 'Accounting and Human Behavior', *Accountancy Age Books,* Haymarket Publishing Limited, 1974.

Inkeles, A., and D. J. Levinson, 'National Character: The Study of Modal Personality and Sociocultural Systems', in G. Lindsey and E. Aronson (eds), *Handbook of Social Psychology*, 2nd edn, Vol. 4, Addison-Wesley, 1969.

International Labour Office, *Yearbook of labour statistics,* ILO, 1978.

Khalaf, S., *Lebanon's Predicament,* Columbia University Press, 1987.

Kuvian, G. T., *Encyclopedia of the Third World,* Vol. 2, Mansell, 1982.

Labaki, B., 'The Challenge of Socioeconomic Reconstruction', in Fawaz, L. (ed.), *State and Society in Lebanon,* The Centre for Lebanese Studies and Tufts University, 1991.

Mahfouz, N., *Palace Walk,* W. M. Hutchins and O. E. Kenny (trans.), Doubleday, 1989.

Makdisi, S., *Financial Policy and Economic Growth: The Lebanese Experience*, Columbia University Press, 1977.

Mathews, M. R. and M. H. B. Perera, *Accounting Theory and Development,* 2nd edn, Nelson, 1993.

McDowall, D., *Lebanon: A Conflict of Minorities*, The Minority Rights Group, London, Report No. 61, 1986.

Meyer, J. W., 'Social Environments and Organizational Accounting', *Accounting, Organizations and Society,* Vol. 11, No. 4/5, 1986.

Middle East and North Africa Yearbook, Europa Publication, 1992.

Most, K. S., 'Accounting in France', in H. P. Holzer (ed.), *International Accounting,* Harper and Row, 1984.

Nair R. D., and W. G. Frank, 'The Impact of Disclosure Measurement Practices on International Accounting Classifications', *Accounting Review,* July 1980.

Nobes, C., 'A Judgemental International Classification of Financial Reporting Practices', *Journal of Business, Finance and Accounting,* Spring 1983.

_____ , *Interpreting European Financial Statements: Towards 1992,* Butterworth, 1989.

Nobes, C., and R. Parker, *Comparative International Accounting,* Prentice-Hall, 1991.

Osmanczyk, E. J., *The Encyclopedia of the United Nations and International Agreements*, Taylor and Francis, 1985.

Parry, M., and R. Grove, 'Does Training More Accountants Raise the Standards of Accounting in Third World Countries? A study of Bangladesh', *Research in Third World Accounting,* Vol. 1, 1990.

Parsons, T., and E. A. Shils, *Toward a General Theory of Action,* Harvard University Press, 1951.

Perera, H., 'Towards a Framework to Analyze the Impact of Culture on Accounting', *International Journal of Accounting,* Vol. 24, 1989a.

91

ABACUS

_____ , 'Accounting in Developing Countries: A Case for Localised Uniformity', *British Accounting Review*, June 1989b.

Pound, S. O., *Arabic and Persian Poems*, The National Poetry Foundation, University of Maine at Orono, 1986.

Pratt, J., and G. Behr, 'Environmental Factors, Transaction Costs, and External Reporting: A Cross-National Comparison', *International Journal of Accounting Education and Research*, Spring 1987.

Radebaugh, L. H., and S. J. Gray, *International Accounting and Multinational Enterprises*, Wiley, 1993.

Saidi, N., *Economic Consequences of the War in Lebanon*, Centre for Lebanese Studies, Oxford, 1986.

Salem, P., 'The New Constitution of Lebanon and the Taif Agreement', *The Beirut Review*, Spring 1991.

Samuels, J. M., and J. C. Oliga, 'Accounting Standards in Developing Countries', *International Journal of Accounting Education and Research*, Fall 1982.

Schreuder, H., 'Accounting Research, Practice and Culture: A European Perspective', in B. E. Cushing (ed.), *Accounting and Culture*, American Accounting Association, 1987.

Scott, G. M., *Accounting and Developing Nations*, University of Washington Graduate School of Business Administration, 1970.

Seidler, L. J., 'Nationalism and the International Transfer of Accounting Skills', *International Journal of Accounting Education and Research*, Fall 1969.

Soffer, A., 'Lebanon — Where Demography is the Core of Politics and Life', *Middle Eastern Studies*, April 1986.

Solomons, D., 'The Political Implication of Accounting and Accounting Standard Setting', *Accounting and Business Research*, Spring 1983.

Sterling, R. R., *An Essay on Recognition*, Accounting and Finance Foundation within the University of Sydney, 1987.

Tay, J. S. W., and R. H. Parker, 'Measuring International Harmonization and Standardisation', *Abacus*, March 1990.

Torbey, J., *Income Taxation in Lebanon* (in Arabic), Dar-Annahar, 1986.

Van der Tas, L. G., 'Measuring Harmonization of Financial Reporting Practice', *Accounting and Business Research* Vol. 18, No. 70, 1988.

Wallace, R. S. O., 'Accounting in Developing Countries', *Research in Third World Accounting*, Vol. 1, 1990.

Willett, R. J., 'An Axiomatic Theory of Accounting Measurement', *Accounting and Business Research*, Spring 1987.

_____ , 'The Measurement Theoretic and Statistical Foundations of the Transactions Theory of Accounting Numbers', *Proceedings of AAANZ*, 1991.

World Bank, *World Development Report*, International Bank for Reconstruction and Development, 1991.

[3]

© 1996 American Accounting Association
Accounting Horizons
Vol. 10 No. 1
March 1996
pp. 18–37

Spontaneous Harmonization Effects of Culture and Market Forces on Accounting Disclosure Practices

Marilyn Taylor Zarzeski

Marilyn Taylor Zarzeski is Assistant Professor of Accounting at the University of Central Florida.

SYNOPSIS: With several institutions striving to harmonize international accounting rules across various sectors of the world, this study asks whether accounting is so culturally driven that harmonization is unattainable. The study also asks what, if anything, can change culture in relation to information disclosure behavior. Two hundred fifty-six corporate annual reports from France, Germany, Hong Kong, Japan, Norway, the United Kingdom and the United States were examined in order to determine whether cultural and market forces correlate with the level of investor-oriented disclosure. Tests also examined whether the culture-disclosure relationship is different for local versus international enterprises.

The primary findings show that the secretiveness of a *culture* does underlie disclosure practices of its business enterprises. There is evidence that *market* forces also affect disclosure behavior: (1) higher levels of relative foreign sales relate to higher levels of disclosure, (2) lower debt ratios relate to higher disclosure, and (3) larger firms tend to disclose more information. Secondary findings show that local enterprises, but not international enterprises, disclose financial information commensurate with the secretiveness of their local culture. Enterprises operating in the global culture, on the other hand, appear to be disclosing higher levels of information than dictated by their local culture, perhaps in order to obtain resources at reasonable costs.

These findings may be useful to the International Organization of Securities Commissions in their effort to harmonize the financial reporting of companies listing on foreign stock exchanges. Although local culture permeates accounting disclosure, there is evidence that *firms operating in the international marketplace* may be willing to adhere to a mandated set of minimal accounting disclosures in order to compete for international resources. Firms already do disclose differently when operating in the global culture, thereby providing evidence of spontaneous "harmonization" effects of culture and market forces upon accounting disclosure behavior.

Data Availability: Data for this study were taken from company annual reports. A list of sample firms is available from the author upon request.

Motivation for this research originates from ongoing international accounting harmonization efforts. Such efforts attempt to alleviate alleged investors' decision-making problems via mandated international accounting standards. *Proponents* of harmonization contend that a mandatory setting of standards across countries is a reasonable approach for improving comparability among international financial statements. Such comparability, it is assumed, would increase protection of "for-eign"[1] investors and would thereby foster the expansion of international financial markets.

[1] "Foreign" is relative to the disclosing company.

This paper received the Association of Charted Accountants in the United States 1995 Education Award for accounting manuscripts.

The author would like to thank her dissertation committee (Chairman Bipin Ajinkya, Anwer Ahmed, Roy Crum and Ron Ward) for their invaluable guidance, two anonymous reviewers, Jeannie Johnson, Robert Larson, and Cindy Parks for their very helpful comments.

Submitted July 1995
Accepted December 1995

Opponents of accounting harmonization argue that enterprises competing in international markets will spontaneously disclose financial information in order to be competitive. Regulated disclosures, therefore, are unnecessary. Additionally, regulated international harmonization may not be possible in a business world of cultural, legal, political and economic differences. Financial reporting systems have evolved over time, and each country's reporting system serves the needs of a distinct group of constituents such as public investors, private creditors or governments.

Several international organizations responsible for the establishment of accounting guidelines are attempting to harmonize accounting standards across different segments of the world. Progress of the International Accounting Standards Committee (IASC) is evident by their 32 International Accounting Standards (IASs). Although there is no requirement for countries to adhere to the IASs, there are growing numbers of companies reporting in compliance with them. Progress with the European Union (EU) standards has occurred over several years, but important measurement and disclosure issues were resolved by permitting two alternative methods rather than only one. These options reduce the comparability across EU financial statements.

The International Organization of Securities Commissions (IOSCO) is attempting to find an acceptable financial reporting system for enterprises that list securities on a foreign exchange. There is a possibility that IOSCO will recommend the IASC standards for companies listing on foreign exchanges. Securities regulators across the world are seeking relevant *and* comparable disclosures that may improve economic resource allocations. For financial information to be comparable, there are actually three aspects that must be addressed: (1) is the *same amount* of information presented (i.e., disclosure issues); (2) is the *same information* presented (i.e., recognition and measurement issues); and 3) is the information equally *reliable*? (i.e., audit issues).

This research addresses the first question by examining disclosure levels. It examines whether enterprises dependent upon international markets for major resources are spontaneously providing levels of financial disclosure sought by investors. This research also proposes that local enterprises, but not international enterprises, disclose financial information commensurate with their home culture. If such evidence exists, then the legitimacy of forced accounting harmonization for *all firms across countries* is questionable. However, *firms operating in the international marketplace* may be willing to adhere to a mandated set of minimal accounting disclosures in order to compete for international resources. This paper attempts to answer Salter and Niswander's (1995, 394) question: "What, if anything, can change culture?"

The remainder of this paper is organized as follows. The next three sections set the background: the evolution of accounting, the culture-market influences upon information disclosure, and an overview of prior accounting disclosure studies. The hypotheses and model development are then described, followed by the research results. The last section of the paper summarizes the findings and their implications.

EVOLUTION OF ACCOUNTING

Before there is agreement on articulated rules, the implied rules of conduct over time are followed (Hayek 1967). Accounting *practices* (implied rules) often become accounting *standards* (articulated rules). Accounting practices evolve differently across countries because business relationships evolve differently. Business relationships differ because of environmental stimuli, e.g., politics, law, economics and culture. If standards come from practices (voluntary) and practices come from culture (through business relationships, government, capital markets, financial intermediaries and the accounting profession), then accounting standards appear to be *culture-driven through market forces*.

A culture grows and develops in response to environmental stimuli, similar to the growth of firms' accounting disclosure behaviors and countries' accounting disclosure standards. There are several classification studies that show evidence of environmental patterns associated with national systems of accounting (e.g., Mueller 1967; Radebaugh 1975; Belkaoui 1983; Salter and Niswander 1995). Gray (1985) explains that enterprises in economically developed countries are probably more candid so that business performance can be evaluated by society. More secretive countries,[2] though, may have developed business and financing relationships that encourage direct, private interactions. Such countries may have developed financial reporting systems *not* intended mainly for outside investors. Salter and Niswander (1995) find evidence that cultural secrecy relates negatively to the development of financial markets.

To understand the development of *international* financial markets and the feasibility of international accounting standards, we now view the culture-market-standards paradigm in the global environment. Perhaps the harmonization issue can be more readily untangled by thinking of the cultural differences as *culture-driven through market forces*. The global market is just a different "culture" than the one the firm faces at home. When a firm does business in the global market, it is operating in a different "culture" and therefore may need to have different "practices." Higher levels of financial disclosures may be necessary for international survival because disclosure of quality operations should result in lower resource costs. When enterprises from more secretive countries perceive economic gain from increasing their financial disclosures, cultural borrowing may occur. The culture being borrowed will be a "global market culture," rather than a specific country culture.

Hayek (1988) believes that individuals adapt their activities to events that occur in a market system. He advances Menger's (1883) spontaneous ordering of the market in which practices and institutions arise from activities of numerous individuals using economic information in pursuit of their own interests. In other words, disclosure practices in the international marketplace arise spontaneously. The question remains whether institutional-ized disclosure standards are possible in a global culture. Is a competitive international marketplace a strong enough inducement for countries (or international firms) to borrow the global culture and agree upon international accounting standards?

Bloom and Naciri (1989) note that the nine countries in their study show evidence that local standard setting lags behind environmental and cultural changes. Perhaps international standard setting also lags behind environmental and cultural changes. If the current study finds evidence of global cultural borrowing,[3] then *international* accounting standard setting may be feasible at least for firms operating in the global market.

INFORMATION DISCLOSURE: CULTURE-DRIVEN THROUGH MARKET FORCES

Although it is difficult to separate the impact of cultural forces and market forces on accounting disclosure practices, this section examines prior research related to these forces. First is a discussion of Gray's (1988) theory of cultural influence on accounting. Second, there is an overview of multinationals and competitive strategy, nationally and internationally. Third, resource dependence theory helps to explain the behavior of firms in a competitive environment.

Gray's Theory of Cultural Influence on Accounting

As discussed earlier, culture underlies the business activities of a nation. Utilizing accounting as a subculture, Gray (1988) proposes several hypotheses that relate Hofstede's (1980) four cultural dimensions (individualism-collectivism, uncertainty avoidance, masculinity-femininity and power distance) to accounting systems. Gray (1988) develops a framework for analyzing the de-

---

[2] Information disclosure, denoting openness of a society, relates to the degree of secretiveness of a culture.
[3] Such evidence includes: (a) firms in the international marketplace providing higher levels of disclosure practices than their domestic counterparts and (b) international firms disclosing similarly across firms.

velopment of accounting systems by using accountants' value systems, purported to be derived from societal values. The accounting
values used by Gray (1988) include professionalism versus statutory control, uniformity versus flexibility, conservatism versus optimism,
and secrecy versus transparency. The last
value grouping forms the foundation for the
current study because information disclosure
may depend upon the level of secrecy in each
culture.

Perera (1989) uses Gray's theory (1988) in
a descriptive analysis of different cultural environments and their accounting systems.
Perera concludes that the Anglo-American accounting model espoused by the IASC is likely
to encounter relevance problems in Continental Europe and other countries with different
culture-driven markets from the United
States and the United Kingdom. Gray and
Vint (1994) also test Gray's theory (1988) by
using the database of disclosure practices from
a 1984 project conducted by the University of
Glasgow and Deloitte Haskins and Sells. With
27 countries in a *univariate* regression analysis, the researchers find significant correlations between each cultural dimension and the
average accounting disclosure score of each
country's enterprises.[4] A *multivariate* regression analysis with all four cultural variables
shows individualism positively related to accounting disclosure and uncertainty avoidance, negatively related to accounting disclosure. Gray's (1988) culture-accounting theory
also has been shown to explain financial reporting practices, with disclosures derived by
the Center for International Financial Analysis and Research (Salter and Niswander 1995).

The current study uses Gray's (1988)
theory of cultural influence upon accounting
disclosures. Gray's theory explains how culture affects the development of businesses and
their institutions, including accounting systems. The current study examines the culture-
accounting relationship in a resource dependence context, specifically in a competitive
global market context. This study questions
whether innovation in disclosure occurs in the
financial reporting behavior of enterprises

dependent on foreign resources. In particular,
do enterprises in the international marketplace disclose contrary to the secretiveness of
their home culture? If so, then what causes
such "contrary" behavior?

Multinationals and Competitive Strategy

There are increasing pressures for higher
levels of accountability from multinational
enterprises (Gray et al. 1981). Such pressures
result not only from multinational firms' significant power over resources, but also from
the risk-reducing incentive of firms to display
themselves as quality firms. Competition involves the revelation and exchange of knowledge or information about quality (Alchian
and Demsetz 1972).

In an analytical *capital market* scenario,
Verrecchia (1983) shows that traders are unable to interpret withheld information of a
firm as good or bad, in comparison to the firm's
competitors. The traders are likely to discount
the value of the firm, thereby encouraging
thorough disclosure practices by the firm. In
a *product market* scenario, Darrough and
Stoughton (1990) use game theory to show
that competition in the product market en-
courages voluntary disclosure because disclosure helps the financial market to value the
entrenched firm more accurately.[5]

To compete successfully with firms that possess knowledge of local business conditions and
traditions, the multinational firm must hold
some form of competitive advantage. Porter
(1986) points out that competitive advantage of
a firm can only be understood by analyzing discrete activities and not the firm as a whole. His
examples of discrete activities include *accounting activities*, e.g., disclosures, that are physically distinct and readily observed.

---

[4] As hypothesized, individualism and masculinity are
positively related to accounting disclosure, while uncertainty avoidance and power distance are negatively
related to accounting disclosure.
[5] The cited study is applicable to the sample of entrenched international firms in the current study because the sample firms are *not* new to the international marketplace.

Firms adopting a *national* competitive strategy may either maintain stable local sources of capital, materials, labor and customers, or obtain resources via changes in their organization structure, e.g., vertical or horizontal integration. Williamson (1975) explains how firms form hierarchies of suppliers and wholesalers in order to lower transaction costs. Such hierarchies encourage private sharing of financial information, thereby decreasing information demands from outsiders.

Firms adopting an *international* competitive strategy are operating in a global culture that depends upon global resources. To obtain foreign customers and enhance public image, firms may choose to disclose at least as much as their competitors, which may or may not be "more" than they are already disclosing in their home country[6] (Lundblad 1991). To obtain foreign capital at lower costs, firms may likewise provide disclosures similar to their competitors in order to demonstrate the quality of earnings and assets (Choi 1973; Diamond and Verrecchia 1991). For further explanation of the resource-disclosure relationship, next is an explanation of resource dependence theory.

Resource Dependence

Resource dependence theory is an explanation of how firms manage uncertainty surrounding business transactions (Pfeffer and Salancik 1978). Firms develop and modify practices to solve problems that arise as they attempt to realize value from business transactions. International activity involves added risks and uncertainties for business firms and the parties that do business with them. In order to obtain resources at reasonable costs, firms competing for customers, labor, materials and capital in a global market are likely to exhibit higher levels of investor-oriented disclosures than exhibited domestically. Firms anticipate that increased disclosure will lower uncertainty about their operations. The current study examines the degree to which dependence on local versus international resource providers affects accounting disclosure behavior of resource seekers, i.e., business firms.

ACCOUNTING DISCLOSURE STUDIES

There has been research interest in accounting disclosure behavior in annual reports since, at least, the 1960s. Disclosure research pertinent to the current study can be divided into two categories. The first category includes accounting disclosure questionnaires sent to various parties within the financial reporting process. Using the relevance ranking of disclosure items, researchers developed accounting disclosure indices or performed statistical tests of disclosure rankings (Cerf 1961; Singhvi and Desai 1971; Buzby 1974; Chandra 1974; Baker et al. 1977; Firth 1978; McKinnon 1984). These studies show that user groups assess the value of financial disclosures differently. Therefore, it is important for the current study about investor-oriented disclosures to include those items that investors deem important.

The second category of relevant disclosure studies involves the use of a disclosure index to measure required, voluntary or total accounting disclosure in annual reports. With disclosure as the dependent variable, correlations are investigated not only for U.S. firms but also for foreign firms (Singhvi 1968; Choi 1973; Barrett 1976; Firth 1979; McNally et al. 1982; Cooke 1991). Regression studies of India, Japan, Mexico, New Zealand and the U.K. show that firm size is related positively to the level of accounting disclosure. Other variables related to disclosure are stock market listing and industry sector (manufacturing). Choi (1973) found evidence of increased disclosure when firms enter the Eurobond market. Barrett (1976) found that the annual report disclosures of U.S. and U.K. companies differed from those in France, Germany, Japan, Netherlands and Sweden. Salter and Niswander (1995) used Bavishi's (1991) tabulated disclosure scores for the world's leading 1,000 companies and found that cultural se-

---

[6] Even though the U.S. and U.K. firms face high disclosure standards domestically, they can increase their total disclosure by providing more *nonfinancial* information such as employee data, production and backlog information.

crecy is negatively related and market capitalization is positively related to level of annual report disclosure.

Also important here is an empirical study of accounting disclosure *requirements*[7] across 34 stock exchanges (Adhikari and Tondkar 1992). From their English-language disclosure-preference survey of financial executives across 41 countries, the researchers develop a disclosure scoring method and use it to measure each country's dependent variable (required disclosure for listing on stock exchange). Because this scoring method is recent, is based upon investors' opinions across countries, and encompasses several items not included in other scoring methods, I combine it with prior methods for the measure of the dependent variable in the current study. Further explanation is provided below in the discussion of the dependent variable.

MODEL DEVELOPMENT

In order to link culture and market forces to investor-oriented disclosure practices of enterprises across countries, I develop the International Disclosure Model. The market forces are relative foreign sales, debt ratio and total assets,[8] while the cultural forces are uncertainty avoidance, individualism-collectivism, masculinity-femininity and power distance (Hofstede 1980). The rationale for each independent variable and its relationship to accounting disclosure follows the pictorial display of the model in figure 1. Later, the International Dependence Model, a variation of the International Disclosure Model, examines whether the culture-accounting relationship is different when businesses operate in the international marketplace.

Development of Research Hypotheses

This section presents the International Disclosure Model and the International Dependence Model.

International Disclosure Model

Dependent Variable. *Investor-oriented disclosure practices,* the dependent variable, includes both required and voluntary disclosure items in English-version annual reports

from seven countries. Other international comparative studies have followed the approach that I have followed (see, for example, Barrett 1976, Choi 1973). To develop a comprehensive scoring method, I use all disclosure items in the following accounting disclosure studies: Adhikari and Tondkar (1992), Barrett (1976), Choi (1973) and Singhvi and Desai (1971). Table 1 provides the disclosure items and their one-to-four weightings, with a *four* indicating highest importance to analysts.[9] It is important to use investor-oriented disclosures for the dependent variable because investors are typically the main users of annual reports. Annual reports appear to be the intended outlet of most accounting harmonization efforts.

Each company's weighted dependent variable is calculated as follows. If the disclosure item appears in the annual report, then the weighting is added to the total disclosure score. After scoring the entire annual report, the total disclosure score is divided by the total possible score; this percentage becomes the dependent variable. The unweighted score is calculated similarly, except that each disclosure item receives one point rather than a weighted number.

Independent Variables. Three market forces and four cultural forces comprise the independent variables of the International Disclosure Model. The plus or minus in the parentheses indicates the hypothesized relationship between disclosure and each independent variable. Figure 2 provides the Model in equation format and summarizes the measurement of each variable. Each hypothesis below is stated in the alternate form, rather

---

[7] An examination of *country* disclosure requirements provides a view different from the *enterprise* disclosure studies discussed above.

[8] Total assets acts more as a control variable than a market variable.

[9] First, the Adhikari and Tondkar (1992) one-to-five rankings are converted to one-to-four rankings in order to be comparable to the other three studies. If available in the Adhikari and Tondkar (1992) study, I use their ranking because it is most recent and global. Then, for the remaining disclosure items, I use the average of the other researchers' scores or just the score itself if only one researcher used the disclosure item.

FIGURE 1
Development of International Disclosure Model

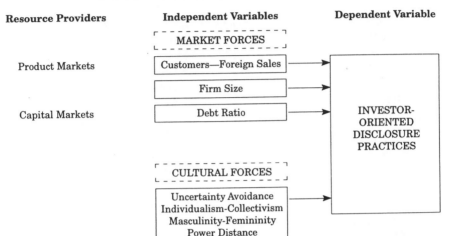

than the null form that the study hopes to reject. The measures for the market variables are in the corporate annual reports, and the measures for the cultural variables are in Hofstede's study (1980).

FSALES%(+), foreign sales divided by total sales, is a relative value. Foreign sales is an international market force that is expected to influence accounting disclosure behavior of business enterprises. If companies have more foreign sales, they are likely to have more foreign operations, labor and capital. To obtain such resources at reasonable costs, it is important that companies share information about the quality of their operations. Saudagaran (1988) found a significant positive relationship between the percentage of a firm's foreign sales to total sales and the listing of its shares in foreign markets.

Hypothesis 1: Companies with higher levels of *foreign sales to total sales* are likely to provide higher levels of investor-oriented disclosures.

DEBTRATIO(–), total debt divided by total assets, is both a local and international

market force because debt structures vary within countries and across countries (Sekely and Collins 1988). If companies have higher debt ratios, it is likely that they share more private information with their creditors. Companies with higher debt ratios, on the average, probably exist in countries with high uncertainty avoidance and likely have developed banking relationships and interlocking corporate ownerships as alternate capital sources to public ownership. Conversely, companies with lower debt have a higher percentage of stock ownership, which could encourage investor demand for information.

Hypothesis 2: Companies with lower *debt ratios* are expected to have higher levels of investor-oriented disclosures.

FIRMSIZE(+), the total assets of a company, is expected to relate positively to disclosure because larger companies, on the average, are likely to have higher public demands for information. Larger companies are often more internationally dependent on foreign resources. As mentioned earlier, numerous studies show firm size to be positively related

TABLE 1
Disclosure Weights for Comprehensive Scoring Method

DISCLOSURE ITEMS	Weight	DISCLOSURE ITEMS	Weight
GENERAL INFORMATION		**FINANCIAL INFORMATION**	
Company objectives	2.95	Segment earnings—products and cust.	3.05
PP&E function, location, size	2.6	Segment earnings—geographic	3.05
Products, including new	2.95	Segment revenue—products and cust.	2.47
R&D information/progress	3	Segment revenue—geographic	3.47
R&D info/progress, incl. expense	3.5	Discussion of company results	3.1
Employee information	3.3	Discussion of signif. accounting policies	3
Capital expenditures—current	3.15	Allowance for doubtful accounts	3.3~
Capital expenditures—planned	3.15	Inventory breakdown	1.67
Dependent on major customers	3	Order backlog information	1
Industry trends/position	3.2	Tangible asset breakdown—PP&E	3
		Orig.cost, accum.deprn, depr exp.	2
INFORMATION ABOUT MANAGEMENT		Current market value of market. sec.	2.5
Company director information	2.7	Plant capacity used/output	3
Management information	2.7	Changing price levels information	3
		Deferred taxes—expensed vs. paid	1.75
COMPANY'S CAPITAL		Income statement—single	3
Stock details	3.2	Income statement—comparative	4
Number and types of shareholders	2.5	Income statement—relevant subclasses	1
Large shareholders—name&size	2.95	Distribution of Income	1
Substantial interest shareholders	3.3	Balance sheet—single	3
Options,warrants, conversion rights	3.1	Balance sheet—comparative	4
Historical price range & trading volume	2.7	Balance sheet—relevant subclasses	1
Co. & subs—loan capital detail/prin.&int.	3.65	Earned surplus—reconciliation	3.17
		Sales or gross margin only	1.5
FINANCIAL INFORMATION		Both sales and gross margin	3
Hist. of operating & fin. data—5 years	2.1	Past pension fund liability	2.1~
Hist. of operating & fin. data—9 years	2.9	Advertising expense	1
Audited financial statements	3.75	Contingent liabilities	1
Statement of cash flows—comparative	3.3		
Statement of cash flows—single	3	**RECENT DEVELOPMENT/PROSPECTS**	
Dividend record and future policy	3.3	Major factors to influence next year	3.4
Consol. & uncon. subs, incl. consol.stmts	3.35	Profit Forecast	3.4
Investments not subs—information	2.85	Cash projections for 1 to 5 years	3.3~
		TOTAL NUMBER OF DISCLOSURES	52 *

~ = Disclosure item deemed important by creditors (Chow and Wong-Boren 1987).
* = Although there are 58 rows of disclosure items, only 52 are unique to a firm.

to accounting disclosure within a country; therefore, firm size[10] is considered more as a control variable than a market variable. This study examines whether larger companies across several countries are more likely to

[10] The natural log transformation of total assets is deemed appropriate for this study because the data shows a positive skewness, indicating nonlinearity. Note that the nontransformed raw data for firm size has no heteroscedasticity problem; the coefficients are significant but in hundred thousandths.

FIGURE 2
International Disclosure Model
Directional Relationships and Measurement of Variables

Panel A: Directional Relationships

$$DISC_i = b_0 + b_1FSALES\%_i - b_2DEBTRATIO_i + b_3FIRMSIZE_i \\ - b_4UNCER_c + b_5INDIV_c + b_6MASCU_c - b_7POWER_c + \varepsilon$$

Panel B: Measurement of Variables

Dependent Variable

DISC	=	Total enterprise disclosure/total possible disclosure points

Market Forces

FSALES%	=	Foreign sales/total sales
DEBTRATIO	=	Total debt/total assets
FIRMSIZE	=	Natural log of total assets ($U.S. millions)

Cultural Forces

UNCER[1]	=	Uncertainty avoidance
INDIV	=	Individualism versus Collectivism
MASCU	=	Masculinity versus Femininity
POWER	=	Power distance

Subscripts: i = Enterprise-specific   c = Country-specific

[1] For each of the four cultural dimensions of the Hofstede (1980) study, the country values range from 6 to 112. A higher value indicates more of that particular cultural trait.

---

have higher levels of investor-oriented disclosures.

Hypothesis 3: *Larger* companies are more likely to have higher levels of investor-oriented disclosures.

The following *four cultural forces* are measured as continuous variables, ranging from 6 to 112. These measures were developed by Hofstede (1980)[11] in a multidimensional scaling of work-related surveys from over 160,000 IBM employees across 64 countries. This study uses Gray's (1988) secrecy/transparency hypotheses that relate each cultural dimension to information disclosure. Companies of more secretive countries (with more private means of obtaining resources) are more likely to disclose less public information. As hypothesized, Salter and Niswander (1995) found a negative relationship between secrecy and disclosure practices, with uncertainty avoidance and individualism being significantly related to disclosure.[12]

UNCER(–), uncertainty avoidance, one of Hofstede's (1980) four cultural dimensions, signifies the degree to which a society can accept ambiguity. Companies in strong uncertainty avoidance countries are more likely to disclose less information publicly because more certain[13] relationships exist, e.g., bank financing and closely-held company owner-

[11] Although this study is dated 1980, it is applicable to today's environment because country culture changes slowly. Although Hofstede's work has enhanced our awareness of global cultural characteristics, it is important to remember that environment changes within and outside a company are continually changing corporate culture at a pace more rapid than country culture changes.

[12] Salter and Niswander (1995) use *secrecy* rather than *disclosure* for their dependent variable. The disclosure scores are multiplied by minus one in order to hypothesize, for example, that higher individualism relates to lower secrecy. Therefore, their expected directional relationships are opposite of the current study's hypotheses.

[13] "Certain" refers to direct relationships that are more private and predictable.

ship. On the contrary, societies exhibiting weak uncertainty avoidance are more likely to have developed business relationships and institutions that do not necessarily reduce uncertainties. Such societies are more likely to have companies with widely-held ownership and capital markets exhibiting substantial new financing and ongoing trading activity. Companies in such weak uncertainty avoidance countries are more likely to disclose higher levels of public investor-oriented information in order to compete in open market settings.

Hypothesis 4: Companies from weak *uncertainty avoidance* countries are more likely to disclose more investor-oriented information than those of strong uncertainty avoidance countries.

INDIV(+), individualism versus collectivism, represents the degree of separateness within a society. Collectivist societies, with less individuality, are expected to disclose lower levels of public information because their families and in-groups, for example, foster secrecy. Individualistic societies are *less* likely to have developed large closely-held companies and are likely to be *less* dependent on banking relationships for capital. Because there are relatively less secretive business relationships in an individualistic society, its companies are more likely to exhibit higher levels of public investor-oriented information.

Hypothesis 5: Companies from *individualistic* countries are more likely to disclose more investor-oriented information than those of collectivist countries.

MASCU(+), masculinity, is a cultural tendency toward assertiveness and achievement. More masculine countries are likely to be growth-oriented, economically and otherwise. Such countries are more likely to advocate business relationships and institutions that foster growth activities. To compete cost effectively in the business world, businesses in masculine societies are more likely to disclose higher levels of information.

Hypothesis 6: Companies from *masculine* countries are more likely to disclose more

investor-oriented information than those of feminine countries.

POWER(–), power distance, denotes the dispersion of authority in a society. In a society with high power distance, there is less dispersion of and less questioning of authority figures. High power distance societies are likely to have developed businesses and related institutions that discourage extensive sharing of information. Contrarily, enterprises in low power distance countries are likely to face the demands of their constituents by disclosing higher levels of information.

Hypothesis 7: Companies from low *power distance* countries are more likely to disclose more investor-oriented information than those of high power distance countries.

International Dependence Model

A second model, the International Dependence Model, includes the variables of the International Disclosure Model. However, subsamples of the total sample of companies, are used to examine whether enterprises doing business mainly in their home country are more likely to disclose information commensurate with their home culture, while enterprises doing business internationally are likely to disclose information commensurate with the global culture. If an enterprise competes in the international marketplace, it faces additional risks and uncertainties with the procurement of competitive resources. To reduce the costs of risks and uncertainties, an enterprise from a more secretive country may be willing to disclose more information to the public.

The international dependence proxy is the level of *total foreign sales of an enterprise within its own country*.[14] It is deemed necessary to perform the split within each country

---

[14] Note that *total foreign sales* is not the same as *foreign sales percentage*. Pearson correlation tests show a .05 relationship between the two foreign sales figures. This allows me to keep the foreign sales percentage variable as an independent variable in the International Dependence Model.

because countries exhibit varying dependence on world markets. As in the International Disclosure Model, the dependent variable of the International Dependence Model is total disclosure.

Each country's enterprises are split in half to obtain two subsamples: high international firms and low international firms. For example, of the 31 firms in the French sample, the 16 firms with foreign sales of less than 6 billion French francs are in the first subset representing low international dependence. The 15 firms with foreign sales of more than 6 billion French francs are in the second subset representing high international dependence. All countries' low international dependence firms are then combined, as are the high international dependence firms. The two resulting subsets are used to measure whether low versus high international dependence makes a difference in the culture-disclosure relationship.

Hypothesis 8: Firms exhibiting low *dependence on international resources* are likely to exhibit a significant relationship between disclosure and the secretive nature of their home culture, but the firms exhibiting high dependence on international resources are likely to show little or less culture-accounting relationship.[15]

Research Design

The random sample of enterprises is selected from Compustat *Global Vantage* (1990) or the *International Brokers' Estimate System* (1986–1992) in order to ensure that there is investor appeal. The sample is a composite of small, medium and large business firms, by size of revenue; this size variation allows for examination of disclosure behavior of local versus international firms because (in the sample selection stage) larger firms are assumed to have higher levels of foreign sales. The variation in firm size in this study differs from the Salter and Niswander (1995) study that included companies from the largest 1,000 in the world.

Because disclosures across *industries* vary somewhat, this research primarily includes six manufacturing industries: building construction, chemicals, electronic equipment, fabricated products, machinery and transportation equipment. These industries represent several of the major imports and exports of the countries in this study. Saudagaran and Biddle (1995) found that industry exports to specific countries positively relate to the choice of foreign listing locations. In other words, companies in certain industries appear to list on certain foreign stock exchanges because the firms have more exports to those countries.

Seven industrialized countries are examined: France, Germany, Hong Kong, Japan, Norway, the U.K. and the U.S. The cultural diversity of these countries makes possible an analysis of the culture-disclosure relationship.

From 795 requests for English version annual reports, I received a 33 percent response rate. Of the 266 annual reports received, 256 provided the information needed for this study.[16] A test for non-response bias indicated no bias present. The intent of this study, to obtain companies with varying levels of international resource dependence, appears to have been achieved with the receipt of small, medium and large companies' annual reports.

I use descriptive analysis to examine averages and ranges of the company data and cross-sectional analysis to investigate the research hypotheses. Ordinary least squares regression analysis statistically examines the International Disclosure Model to determine whether culture and market forces correlate with investor-oriented disclosures. A Wald test statistically examines the International Dependence Model to determine whether there

---

[15]"Less relationship" implies that the statistical significance of any relationship between culture and accounting in the high international firms will not be as strong as its significance in the low international firms. In other words, the high international firms will act more like the global competitive culture then possibly their local culture.

[16] The 256 annual reports are disbursed as follows: 1991 (1), 1992 (108), and 1993 (147). My requests for "the most recent" annual reports were sent between January and April of 1994.

are differences in the culture-disclosure relationships when firms have low versus high international dependence.[17]

RESEARCH RESULTS
Descriptive Analysis

Table 2 presents descriptive statistics for the total sample of companies and for country samples. First, the statistics for the *total* and *country* samples show that the intended research design has been attained. The total company sample ranges in size from U.S.$24 million to U.S.$192 billion assets. With the wide ranges of each cultural variable in the total sample, it is clear that cultural diversity has been achieved with this sample of business enterprises. The ranges of the dependent variable and the other independent variables also show wide variation across enterprises, thereby providing for the possibility of statistical relationships. Note that the debt ratio of a few enterprises is higher than 100 because the stockholders' equity is negative.[18]

Second, the statistics for the *country* samples in table 2 show that the U.S. enterprises have the highest average disclosure (73%) in their annual reports, with the U.K. being a close second with 68.7%. These high disclosure scores are as expected because prior studies have shown high disclosure in Anglo-American countries. While Japan and the U.S. exhibit the lowest average foreign sales to total sales (about 27%), Norway and France show the largest (in the 54–59% range). These results may indicate that Japanese and U.S. companies have large local populations to which they sell their products, while Norwegian and French companies seek more foreign customers. Norway has the highest average debt ratio (72.8%), with Germany at 71.6% and Japan at 68.7%. Several studies have noted that Germany and Japan rely heavily upon bank debt. In this sample, the largest firms, on the average, are located in Japan, the U.S. and Germany, in descending order. This result is consistent with these countries being noted for their high level of industrial growth. Of the seven countries, the U.K. exhibits, on average, the smallest firms.

Third, because the Pearson correlation coefficients show very little multicollinearity present across the independent variables, a table is not presented. Individualism and power distance show moderate collinearity at $-.67$, which is expected because each of these cultural variables defines a person's relationship in society. Individualism defines a person's relationship with other people in a society, while power distance defines a person's relationship with powerful institutions in a society. Variance inflation factors are examined and no severe multicollinearity is found. Total foreign sales, the international proxy, is highly related to total assets, but barely related to the natural log of total assets (Pearson correlation coefficients of .94 and .32, respectively).

Finally, although not displayed in table 2, the six industry samples show some interesting statistics. The highest average disclosure (72.1%) is found in the chemical companies, with the lowest disclosure (59.6%) found in building construction firms. The building construction firms also display the lowest average foreign sales at 14%. The building construction findings are consistent with its regional and local nature. The highest foreign sales are made by firms in the chemical industry (45.6%) and in the transportation equipment industry (45.5%). The highest average debt ratio (68.2%) occurs in the transportation equipment enterprises, probably because almost half of those enterprises are German or Japanese. In this study, the largest firms exist in the transportation equipment and electrical equipment industries,

---

[17] The Wald test is performed on *each* cultural variable in the two reduced models (low and high). The F-test compares the low versus high international dependence samples to determine whether there is a different effect of each cultural variable on disclosure. For this study, the Wald test is more appropriate than the Chow test because it can examine structural differences between individual parameters and groups of parameters, while using only one covariance matrix. The Chow test examines overall structural differences only.

[18] Tests that exclude these four firms show similar results to the tests that include these firms.

Accounting Horizons / March 1996

TABLE 2
International Disclosure Model Descriptive Statistics
Total Sample

All Enterprises (n=256)	Mean	Std. Dev.	Minimum	Maximum
DISC (%)	61.8	13.5	12	89
FSALES%	38.9	27.3	0	100
DEBTRATIO (%)	59.7	20.3	2	171
FIRMSIZE ($U.S. mil.)	6,853	22,006	24	192,876
UNCER	56.3	22.5	29	92
INDIV	69.7	22.3	25	91
MASCU	61.9	20.0	8	95
POWER	46.6	13.5	31	68

Country Models

France (n=31)	Mean	Std.Dev.	Minimum	Maximum
DISC (%)	62.8	12.2	29	87
FSALES%	54.8	20.5	12	91
DEBTRATIO (%)	65.5	15.6	36	93
FIRMSIZE ($U.S. mil.)	5,222	8,466	83	44,311

Germany (n=29)				
DISC (%)	57.3	10.6	26	80
FSALES%	49.4	17.0	7	75
DEBTRATIO (%)	71.6	13.2	43	93
FIRMSIZE ($U.S. mil.)	8,443	14,834	55	53,284

Hong Kong (n=29)				
DISC (%)	56.8	6.3	47	69
FSALES%	38.3	37.7	0	98
DEBTRATIO (%)	34.3	16.8	2	66
FIRMSIZE ($U.S. mil.)	1,972	3,034	38	10,461

Japan (n=39)				
DISC (%)	59.7	11.6	27	80
FSALES%	26.1	21.0	0	74
DEBTRATIO (%)	68.7	15.5	36	95
FIRMSIZE ($U.S. mil.)	12,071	18,245	455	80,465

Norway (n=16)				
DISC (%)	59.3	17.6	32	81
FSALES%	59.0	34.3	0	78
DEBTRATIO (%)	72.8	28.2	47	171
FIRMSIZE ($U.S. mil.)	1,365	2,839	24	11,705

United Kingdom (n=47)				
DISC (%)	68.7	8.7	52	86
FSALES%	41.4	30.2	0	85
DEBTRATIO (%)	55.9	17.0	19	107
FIRMSIZE ($U.S. mil.)	675	1,061	53	5,629

United States (n=65)				
DISC (%)	73.0	8.2	48	87
FSALES%	27.8	18.2	0	70
DEBTRATIO (%)	57.1	17.7	15	103
FIRMSIZE ($U.S. mil.)	11,787	38,796	32	192,876

Note: The country samples do not include culture because Hofstede's (1980) cultural variables do not allow for cultural variation *within* a country. No such study exists.

with average assets of U.S. $23 billion and U.S.$9 billion, respectively.

International Disclosure Model
Total Sample

Results of the ordinary least squares (OLS) regression of the total sample in table 3 show strong support (p < .0001) for the hypotheses of the International Disclosure Model. All variables except power distance are highly significant and are related to disclosure in the hypothesized directions. Together, the independent variables explain 48% of the variation in investor-oriented disclosures of business enterprises.

The estimated coefficient for foreign sales (FSALES%) is positively related to disclosure, thereby indicating that firms dependent on foreign customers are more willing to disclose higher levels of investor-oriented information in their annual reports. The DEBTRATIO is negatively related to disclosure, an indication that firms with more debt are likely to disclose less public information. The FIRMSIZE coefficient exhibits a positive relationship, thereby suggesting that larger firms disclose more annual report information.

Three of the four culture-accounting relationships are highly significant. As predicted, individualism (INDIV) and masculinity (MASCU) are positively related to disclosure, while uncertainty avoidance (UNCER) is negatively related. Because power distance (POWER) is moderately correlated with INDIV, a multivariate analysis, such as this model, can result in confounding effects with variables that are correlated. The culture-accounting results are evidence that the secretiveness of a country is associated with the investor-oriented disclosure levels of its business enterprises and are support for Gray's (1988) hypotheses.

Alternate Tests (not presented in tabular form)

In addition to the weighted disclosure scores, I examined *unweighted* scores for the dependent variable. In other words, for each item disclosed by a company, one point is assigned, rather than a number between one and

four. Cross-sectional analysis of the unweighted disclosure scores in a regression model show results that are extremely similar to those with the weighted scores. In the unweighted model, the explanatory power is one percentage point lower and the estimated coefficients of the variables are somewhat lower, when compared with the weighted model. The only significance level that is slightly lower relates debt ratio to disclosure; the significance drops from a .05 to a .10 level.

The total sample for the International Disclosure Model is also tested with weighted scores using the disclosure scoring methods of Adhikari and Tondkar (1992), Barrett (1976), Choi (1973) and Singhvi and Desai (1971). Results are very similar to those of the comprehensive scoring method of this study. The explanatory power of the four additional models ranges from 45 percent to 50 percent, with all variables except power distance significantly related to disclosure, in the directions predicted.

Country Models

Also in table 3 are OLS results of each country's enterprise disclosures regressed on foreign sales, debt ratio and firm size. All three independent variables significantly help to explain 28 percent of the disclosure variation in French annual reports and 49 percent of the disclosure variation in Japanese annual reports.[19] In each country model, firm size is positively associated with disclosure at a significance level of p < .05 or better. The coefficient of debt ratio is negatively related to disclosure in three countries, France, Germany and Japan, evidence of their strong banking and government relationships. Foreign sales

---

[19] Only English version annual reports are used in this study because the point of view is that of an English-reading investor. The prior accounting disclosure studies cited in this paper are based upon U.S. investors, except for: (1) Firth's (1978) study about U.K. users and (2) the Baker et al. (1977) study about U.S. and Australian users. The 1992 stock exchange disclosure survey of Adhikari and Tondkar (1992) was sent to 41 countries, but all the surveys were written in English. English is considered to be the global language of business. It is the language to which companies most often translate their annual report.

32   *Accounting Horizons / March 1996*

TABLE 3
International Disclosure Model Regression Results

$$DISC_i = b_0 + b_1 FSALES\%_i - b_2 DEBTRATIO_i + b_3 FIRMSIZE_i$$
$$- b_4 UNCER_c + b_5 INDIV_c + b_6 MASCU_c - b_7 POWER_c + \varepsilon$$

Total Sample (n=256)

Variable	Expected Relationship	Estimated Coefficient	t-Statistic	One-Tail p-Value
Intercept	NA	17.020	2.965	0.0016
FSALES%	+	0.105	4.972	0.0001
DEBTRATIO	−	−5.799	−1.772	0.0388
FIRMSIZE	+	3.120	9.297	0.0001
UNCER	−	−0.184	−5.700	0.0001
INDIV	+	0.307	9.046	0.0001
MASCU	+	0.099	3.157	0.0009
POWER	−	0.159	2.610	0.0048 nps

F-value: 34.37 (Prob. > F = .0001)   Adjusted R-Square: 0.48

Country Models

Variable	Expected Relationship	Estimated Coefficient	t-Statistic	One-Tail p-Value
France (n=31)				
Intercept	NA	44.719	3.057	.0025
FSALES%	+	0.118	1.261	.1091
DEBTRATIO	−	−30.937	−2.468	.0101
FIRMSIZE	+	4.110	2.853	.0041

F-value: 5.01 (Prob. > F = 0.0068)   Adjusted R-Square: 0.28

Variable	Expected Relationship	Estimated Coefficient	t-Statistic	One-Tail p-Value
Germany (n=29)				
Intercept	NA	45.288	4.067	.0002
FSALES%	+	0.046	0.407	.3438
DEBTRATIO	−	−19.631	−1.319	.0995
FIRMSIZE	+	3.141	2.741	.0056

F-value: 3.25 (Prob. > F = 0.0386)   Adjusted R-Square: 0.19

Variable	Expected Relationship	Estimated Coefficient	t-Statistic	One-Tail p-Value
Hong Kong (n=29)				
Intercept	NA	46.017	9.000	.0001
FSALES%	+	0.055	1.454	.0792
DEBTRATIO	−	1.567	0.200	.4217
FIRMSIZE	+	1.323	1.762	.0451

F-value: 1.65 (Prob. > F = 0.2027)   Adjusted R-Square: 0.06

Variable	Expected Relationship	Estimated Coefficient	t-Statistic	One-Tail p-Value
Japan (n=39)				
Intercept	NA	22.797	2.423	.0103
FSALES%	+	0.141	1.991	.0271
DEBTRATIO	−	−13.171	−1.447	.0783
FIRMSIZE	+	4.997	4.583	.0001

F-value: 13.32 (Prob. > F = 0.0001)   Adjusted R-Square: 0.49

(Continued on next page)

TABLE 3 (Continued)

Variable	Expected Relationship	Estimated Coefficient	t-Statistic	One-Tail p-Value
Norway (n=16)				
Intercept	NA	−12.129	−0.876	.1991
FSALES%	+	−0.041	−0.464	.3253
DEBTRATIO	−	22.857	2.131	.0272 nps
FIRMSIZE	+	9.438	5.193	.0001

F-value: 9.94 (Prob. > F = 0.0014)   Adjusted R-Square: 0.64

United Kingdom (n=47)				
Intercept	NA	44.585	8.217	.0001
FSALES%	+	0.138	4.169	.0001
DEBTRATIO	-	3.707	0.666	.2545
FIRMSIZE	+	2.823	3.213	.0012

F-value: 14.64 (Prob. > F = 0.0001) Adjusted R-Square: 0.47

United States (n=65)				
Intercept	NA	55.412	18.199	.0001
FSALES%	+	0.203	4.489	.0001
DEBTRATIO	−	1.286	0.270	.3939
FIRMSIZE	+	1.525	3.221	.0010

F-value: 21.58 (Prob. > F = 0.0001) Adjusted R-Square: 0.49

---

nps = not predicted sign

---

is most positively related to disclosure in the U.K., the U.S. and Japan. These three country models have high explanatory power (adjusted R-squares of at least .47), which means that the independent variables help to explain 47 percent of the variation in annual report disclosures.

Norway, with the smallest sample size, has explanatory power of 64%, with larger firms disclosing more information, but *higher* debt ratios influencing higher disclosure levels, opposite of the prediction. In the sample, Norway has moderate uncertainty avoidance, but high debt ratios. Norwegian companies have been shown to have high debt structures (Sekely and Collins 1988). With a population of four million people, Norway may not have significant equity ownership of companies.

Except for Hong Kong, the overall significance of the F-value for each country model is .05 or better, which is the conventional levels.

Hong Kong's country model explains the least amount of disclosure variation that occurs in their corporate annual reports. Per the standard deviation of disclosure in table 2, these reports also have the least variation to be explained.

International Dependence Model

In general, the Wald test of the International Dependence Model shows strong evidence to support H8. There is evidence that companies more dependent on *local* resources (low international dependence) disclose information consistent with their local culture, while companies more dependent on *international* resources (high international dependence) disclose either *less like* their home culture or *unlike* their home culture. In particular, table 4 presents the results of the various Wald tests for the International Dependence Model.

Total Foreign Sales as International Dependence Proxy

First, in the upper portion of table 4 is a summary of the structural changes tested by the Wald tests. Between low versus high international firms, there is a significant change in the relationship of disclosure and the independent variables in total (whole model). The significance level is a p-value of .05 or better. That overall model measure, however, does not tell us specifics about the focus of this test—the culture-accounting relationship.

Next, the *cultural grouping (i.e., all four cultural forces)*[20] is tested for structural change, with evidence that international firms disclose differently than local firms because of cultural secretiveness. All four cultural variables are examined here as a group in relation to accounting disclosure. The group mea-

[20] The *market grouping*, not part of the hypothesis, also shows changes in disclosure from the low to the high internationally dependent firms. Firm size drives the results, with less of a positive relationship occurring between firm size and disclosure as the companies get larger.

TABLE 4
International Dependence Model
Test of Structural Change in the Culture-Disclosure Relationship

International Proxy: Total Foreign Sales Within a Country
Dependent Variable: Total Disclosure

Wald Test Summary Results	Low Versus High International Dependence	Structural Change (Prob > F)
	Whole Model	.05
	Market Grouping	.05
	Culture Grouping	.01
	UNCER	.01
	INDIV	ns
	MASCU	.05
	POWER	ns

Wald Test Detail Results (Culture Only)	Low International Dependence	High International Dependence
	Coefficients and t-Statistics	
UNCER (–)	–0.35 (–6.59) ****	–0.11 (–2.39) ***
INDIV (+)	0.35 (6.99) ****	0.35 (7.47) ****
MASCU (+)	0.12 (2.45) ***	0.02 (0.63) ns
POWER (–)	0.29 (3.13) nps	0.15 (1.81) **

Sample Size n = 256   Adj. R-Square 0.52

Note 1: A one-tail t-test is used.
Note 2: White's Test shows no heteroscedasticity present.

**** = $p < .001$;   *** = $p < .01$;   ** = $p < .05$;   * = $p < .10$
npd = not predicted directional change
nps = not predicted sign
ns = not significant

sure tells us there is a change (at the $p < .01$ significance level) in the culture-accounting relationship, but it does not tell us what particular cultural variables are influential or in which direction the change occurs.

Finally, the *separate* cultural variables are tested via a third Wald test. Results in the lower portion of table 4 provide relatively strong evidence that uncertainty avoidance and masculinity are cultural traits that relate differently with accounting disclosure, depending upon the degree of internationalism of a firm. For example, at a significance level of .01 or better, table 4 provides evidence that the relationship of uncertainty avoidance and accounting disclosure is stronger for the low international firms. As predicted, *local* firms disclose more like their culture than do *international* firms (the absolute value of the UNCER coefficient of local firms is stronger at –0.35 than is the –0.11 coefficient). Masculinity is significantly related to disclosure for local firms, but not significantly related for international firms, as predicted. Individualism has no structural change. Power distance, probably because it is negatively correlated with individualism and therefore has confounding effects, is not significant or of the proper sign.

SUMMARY AND IMPLICATIONS

This study examines the relationship between enterprise accounting disclosure and both market and cultural forces across seven countries. It attempts to ascertain whether culture underlies corporate disclosure behavior and whether international resource dependence causes firms to disclose higher levels of information. The study also investigates whether *local* firms disclose information commensurate with the secretiveness of their home culture, while *international* firms disclose information commensurate with the global culture that is differently market-driven. I argue that international firms from secretive countries are likely to be motivated to disclose higher levels of public information than they would at home, in order to show the quality of their operations.

The results of the International Disclosure Model are consistent with resource dependence theory. There is evidence that companies with higher foreign sales (customers) are more likely to disclose higher levels of investor-oriented information. Companies with greater dependence on debt financing, i.e., usually a more local resource, are found to disclose less public information. Being more likely to compete internationally for resources, larger companies disclose higher levels of investor-oriented information. The International Disclosure Model also provides evidence of Gray's (1988) theory of cultural influence upon accounting, that the secretive nature of a culture relates to the level of accounting disclosure practices. Companies domiciled in cultures possessing more individualism, more masculinity and less uncertainty avoidance are more likely to disclose higher levels of information.

The theory of cultural borrowing is manifest in the results of the International Dependence Model. When firms are more internationally dependent, their disclosure behavior is different from their home culture. In other words, international firms from more secretive countries *borrow* the global culture of their competitors, as evidenced by less secretive disclosure practices of international firms. This study not only provides additional support for the relationship between levels of financial disclosure and cultural secrecy, but also goes further by answering Salter and Niswander's (1995) question about what can change culture: dependence on international resources. Total foreign sales has been shown to be a viable proxy for international dependence, with potential usefulness in future international research studies.

The results of this empirical study are important because they suggest that *total* accounting harmonization may be difficult since accounting disclosure practices appear to be culture-driven through market forces. The quest to harmonize accounting standards across all companies in all countries is a debatable position.

The results imply, though, that firms operating in the international marketplace are spontaneously disclosing high levels of public information. These firms show evidence of harmonization effects of global culture and market forces on their accounting disclosure behavior. The global market may exert sufficient force as to make regulated harmonization for multinational corporations unnecessary. On the other hand, the findings suggest that it may be possible for the IASC and IOSCO to harmonize accounting disclosures for firms listing on foreign stock exchanges.

REFERENCES

Adhikari, A., and R. H. Tondkar. 1992. Environmental factors influencing accounting disclosure requirements of global stock exchanges. *Journal of International Financial Management and Accounting* 4: 75–105.

Alchian A., and H. Demsetz. 1972. Production, information costs, and economic organization. *The American Economic Review* 62: 777–795.

Baker, H. K., R. Chenhall, J. Haslem, and R. Juchau. 1977. Disclosure of material information: A cross-national comparison. *The International Journal of Accounting* 13 (1): 1–18.

Barrett, M. E. 1976. Financial reporting practices: Disclosure and comprehensiveness in an international setting. *Journal of Accounting Research* 14 (1): 10–26.

Bavishi, V. 1991 *International Accounting and Auditing Trends,* 2nd edition. Princeton, NJ: Center for International Financial Analysis and Research.

Belkaoui, G. F. 1983. Economic, political and civil indicators and reporting and disclosure adequacy: Empirical investigation. *Journal of Accounting and Public Policy* 2: 207–219.

Bloom, R. and M. A. Naciri. 1989. Accounting standard setting and culture: A comparative analysis of the United States, Canada, England, West Germany, Australia, New Zealand, Sweden, Japan, and Switzerland. *The International Journal of Accounting* 24: 70–97.

Buzby, S. L. 1974. Selected items of information and their disclosure in annual reports. *The Accounting Review* 49: 423–436.

Cerf, A. R. 1961. *Corporate Reporting and Investment Decisions.* Berkeley, California: Public Accounting Research Program.

Chandra, G. 1974. A study of the consensus on disclosure among public accountants and security analysts. *The Accounting Review* 49: 733–742.

Choi, F. 1973. Financial disclosure and entry to the European capital market. *Journal of Accounting Research* 11: 159–175.

Chow, C., and A. Wong-Boen. 1987. Voluntary financial disclosure by Mexican corporations. *The Accounting Review* 62: 533–541.

Cooke, T. E. 1991. An assessment of voluntary disclosure in the annual reports of Japanese corporations. *The International Journal of Accounting* 26: 174–189.

Darrough, M. N., and N. M. Stoughton. 1990. Financial disclosure policy in an entry game. *Journal of Accounting and Economics* 12: 219–43.

Diamond, D., and R. Verrecchia. 1991. Disclosure, liquidity, and the cost of capital. *The Journal of Finance* 46: 1325–1359.

Firth, M. 1978. A study of the consensus of the perceived importance of disclosure of individual items in corporate annual reports. *The International Journal of Accounting* 14 (1): 57–70.

———. 1979. The impact of size, stock market listing, and auditors on voluntary disclosure in corporate annual reports. *Accounting and Business Research* 9: 273–280.

Global Vantage. 1990. New York: Standard & Poor's Compustat Services.

Gray, S. 1985. Cultural influences and the international classification of accounting systems. *EIASM Workshop on "Accounting and Culture."* Amsterdam.

———. 1988. Towards a theory of cultural influence on the development of accounting systems internationally. *ABACUS* 24: 1–15.

———, J. Shaw, and L. McSweeney. 1981. Accounting standards and multinational   corporations. *Journal of International Business Studies* 12: 121-136.

———, and H. M. Vint. 1994. The impact of culture on accounting disclosures: some international evidence. Working paper: University of Warwick, England.

Hayek, F. A. 1967. *Studies in Philosophy, Politics, and Economics.* Chicago, Illinois: The University of Chicago Press.
——. 1988. *The Fatal Conceit: The Errors of Socialism.* Chicago, Illinois: The University of Chicago Press.
Hofstede, G. 1980. *Culture's Consequences: International Differences in Work-Related Values.* Beverly Hills: SAGE Publications.
International Brokers Estimate System (IBES). 1986–1992. Summary Data Tapes. New York: I/B/E/S, Inc.
Lundblad, H. 1991. Factors underlying voluntary disclosure: An application of multi-attribute utility theory to financial disclosure. Working paper, California State University, Northridge, California.
McKinnon, J. L. 1984. Application of Anglo-American principles of consolidation to corporate financial disclosure in Japan. *ABACUS* 20: 16–33.
McNally, G., L. Eng, and C. Hasseldine. 1982. Corporate financial reporting in New Zealand: An analysis of user preferences, corporate characteristics and disclosure practices for discretionary information. *Accounting and Business Research* 13: 11–20.
Menger, C. 1883. *Investigations into the methods of the Social Sciences with Special Reference to Economics.* New York: New York University Press.
Mueller, G. 1967. *International Accounting.* New York: Macmillan.
Perera, M. 1989. Towards a framework to analyze the impact of culture on accounting. *The International Journal of Accounting* 24: 42–56.
Pfeffer, J., and G. Salancik. 1978. *The External Control of Organizations: A Resource Dependence Perspective.* New York: Harper & Row, Publishers.
Porter, M. E. 1986. Changing patterns of international competition. *California Management Review* 28 (2): 9–41.
Radebaugh, L. H. 1975. Environmental factors influencing the development of accounting objectives, standards and practices in Peru. *International Journal of Accounting Education and Research* 11 (1): 39–56.
Salter, S. B., and F. Niswander. 1995. Cultural influence on the development of accounting systems internationally: A test of Gray's [1988] theory. *Journal of International Business Studies* 26 (2): 379–397.
Saudagaran, S. M. 1988. An empirical study of selected factors influencing the decision to list on foreign stock exchanges. *Journal of International Business Studies* 19 (1): 101–127.
——, and G. C. Biddle. 1995. Foreign listing location: A study of MNCs and stock exchanges in eight countries. *Journal of International Business Studies* 26 (2): 319–341.
Sekely, W. S., and J. M. Collins. 1988. Cultural influences on international Capital Structure. *Journal of International Business Studies* : 87–100.
Singhvi, S. 1968. Characteristics and implications of inadequate disclosure: A case study of India. *The International Journal of Accounting* 3 (2): 29–43.
——, and H. Desai. 1971. An empirical analysis of the quality of corporate financial disclosure. *The Accounting Review* 46: 129–138.
Verrecchia, R. E. 1983. Discretionary disclosure. *Journal of Accounting and Economics* 5: 179–194.
Williamson, O. 1975. *Markets and Hierarchies: Analysis and Antitrust Implications.* New York: Free Press.

[4]

Journal of Accounting Literature
Vol. 18, 1999, pp. 1 - 30

A SYNTHESIS OF CULTURAL
STUDIES IN ACCOUNTING

Shalin Chanchani*
Victoria University of Wellington

Alan MacGregor
University of Otago

1.0 INTRODUCTION

If contributions to the accounting literature are any gauge, the impact of culture on various facets of accounting has become of increasing interest to accounting researchers. Despite this increase in interest there is a lack of studies summarising and critically examining such contributions. This paper seeks to fill this gap and in so doing assess the current state of empirical and theoretical literature, synthesize and review findings, redirect the literature where necessary and increase our understanding of a growing field of inquiry.

The relevance of culture and its effect on accounting practices has been the subject of much debate [Burchell *et al*, 1980; Meyer, 1986; and Fechner and Kilgore 1994]. For example, previous researchers have identified the relationship of accounting with (i) the needs of developing countries [Makdisi, 1977; Perera 1989; Wallace, 1990]; (ii) the role of religion [Mansor, 1984; Hamid *et al*, 1993]; (iii) development of control systems [Harrison 1992, 1993; O'Connor, 1995]; and (iv) the need for harmonization [Rivera, 1989; Barthes, 1989; Goeltz, 1991]. Choi and Mueller [1984] summarize this argument succinctly by suggesting that if accounting is a service function, and the accounting environments differ among countries, then accounting must differ amongst these countries. One central variable that helps us understand values within a country is culture. The link between culture and accounting values has been elaborated by Gray [1988].

This paper is organized around the chronological development of contributions to the cultural relevance literature. Section two reviews the pre-Gray literature as it arose prior to 1988. Gray's attempt to provide a theory of cultural relevance [1988] is discussed in section 3. The literature from 1989 [post Gray] to the present time is reviewed in section 4. In section 5, the conclusion, we attempt to identify the gaps in the literature which highlight possible directions for future research.

2.0 PRE-GRAY LITERATURE

To gain a richer understanding of the leading thoughts of this period the pre-Gray literature is classified into two groups of studies. The first group is identified as stud-

* This paper is based partly upon the first author's doctoral dissertation submitted to the University of Otago, Dunedin, New Zealand. The authors would like to thank Professor Roger Willett of Queensland University of Technology, Dr Paul Theivananthampillai of the University of Otago, and an anonymous referee for their comments.

2   *Journal of Accounting Literature*   Volume 18

ies adopting an anthropological approach to accounting while the second group of studies classifies accounting practices globally by means of a judgmental or statistical analysis. The latter includes deductive studies [Mueller [1967], Choi and Mueller [1984], Nobes [1983]] and inductive approaches [Nair and Frank [1980]].

2.1 Anthropological Approaches to Accounting

This segment of the literature may broadly be described as a cluster of studies attempting among other things to: view accounting as a social function; describe accounting as an uncertainly absorbing process; and explain the behavior of accountants in business.

Violet [1983] appears to be the earliest author to explicitly consider international accounting from a systems view of culture. He visualized accounting systems from the position of a cultural relativist examining accounting as a social function, i.e., accounting as a product of its culture. Basing his analysis on Levi-Strauss' structuralism[1], Violet claimed that the rudiments of accounting for resources exist in even the most basic societies [p 4]. Citing the literature that studies accounting as a language, he analyzed the cultural relativism of the International Accounting Standards and suggested that the success of the International Accounting Standards Committee is limited by cultural variables. Violet attempted to delineate cultural determinants that influence the promulgation and acceptance of international accounting theories and standards. More specifically Violet discusses the influence and importance of customs as they relate to social institutions[2].

March and Olson [1976] described accounting as an uncertainty absorbing process that may absorb uncertainty to such an extent that it absorbs all useable information as well. In an amusing comparison between business and primitive society, Cleverly [1973] labelled accountants as the priests of business. Gambling [1977] drew a parallel between accounting and magic and gave many examples which showed that accounting information is often an after the fact justification of decisions that are taken for non-logical reasons. He claimed that the main function of accounting information is to maintain morale in the face of uncertainty[3]. Among the other studies in this area: Burcheel *et al.* [1980] examine how accounting is implicated in both organizational and social practice; Meyer [1986] develops and presents hypotheses about the factors

---

[1]   Structuralism was an interdisciplinary movement of thought originating on the European Continent in the fifties. Hoebel, [1972] in *Anthropology: The Study of Man* provides an excellent explanation of this concept. The term refers to the study of the ways in which groups and individuals are organised and related to one another in the functioning entity that is a society [p 308]. Boon [1972] also provides a detailed description of Structuralism in 'From Symbolism to Structuralism'.
       For a complete discussion of structuralism and the relationship of classification as a universality, see Levi-Strauss [1963] which expanded Maslow's classification of social needs to include a need for order.
[2]   He also discusses the importance of language as the most pervasive of cultural variables and contends that language and accounting, as a symbolic written system, are determinants of behavior, personality and thought process.
[3]   'In short, the accountant is the person who enables a distinctly demoralised modern industrial society to live with itself, by reassuring it that its models and data can pass for truth' [1977, p 18-19].

affecting work in organizations; Pratt and Behr [1987] explain external reporting systems in terms of the cost of transactions in capital markets and Schreuder [1987] identifies the accounting research cultures in Europe and compares these to the ones in the United States[4].

This literature seems to be rather disjoint and *ad hoc* in its approach, but certainly provides some insights by way of either a structuralist interpretation of accounting or some anecdotal insights about the role of accounting and accountants in business.

2.2 Classifying Accounting Practices

Comparative international accounting research has contributed to a growing realization that fundamentally different accounting patterns exist, which are argued to result from environmental differences, and that international classification differences may have significant implications for harmonization and economic integration[5]. Such efforts have been divided by Gray [1988] into deductive [e.g., Mueller, 1967, 1968; Nobes, 1983, 1984] and inductive [e.g., Frank, 1979; Nair and Frank, 1980] approaches. While the deductive approach identifies environmental factors and links them to national accounting practices to propose international classifications, the inductive approach identifies development patterns, analyses practices and proposes explanations by referring to various factors.

The deductive approach: Mueller [1967, 1968] broke new ground by suggesting classifications of accounting systems and business environments. His classification of accounting systems into four patterns of development[6] was simple but he failed to explain the methods employed to obtain the groupings. Mueller, however, considered the four categories sufficient to embrace accounting as it is known and practiced in various parts of the world [1968, p 2]. Nobes [1983, 1984] extended Mueller's analysis and based his classification on an evolutionary approach. He adopted a structural approach to the identification of accounting practices and assessed major features including the importance of tax rules, the use of conservative valuation procedures, the strictness of application of historical costs, the making of replacement cost adjustments, the use of consolidation techniques, the generous use of provisions, and uniformity between companies in the application of rules[7]. The results do not go beyond providing a support for the classification of countries as either micro or macro based. No

---

4   Mounting a cultural relativist argument Schreuder [1987] concludes that it is no coincidence that behavioral accounting in the United States mainly denotes the relation between accounting and individual behavior, while in Europe the association is with accounting and organisational behavior. Similarly behavioral accounting in the United States is motivated by psychology; while in Europe this is motivated by Sociology.

5   See for instance Mueller, 1967; Zeff, 1971; Radebaugh, 1975; Choi and Mueller, 1984; Arpan and Radebaugh, 1985; Nobes and Parker, 1985.

6   These four distinct approaches to accounting development in Western nations with market oriented economic systems identified by Mueller are: *the macroeconomic pattern* where business accounting interrelates closely with national economic policies; *the microeconomic pattern* where accounting is viewed as a branch of business economics; *the independent discipline approach* where accounting is viewed as a service function; and *the uniform accounting approach* where accounting is viewed as an efficient means of administration and control.

7   In a later work, Nobes [1992] identified six factors which may be important causes of international differences between financial reporting systems: legal systems, business ownership, stock exchanges, tax systems, profession and other factors.

explicit mention is made of culture as an explanatory variable[8]. The classification scheme, although apparently plausible, remains hypothetical and needs further empirical analysis to be convincing. This group is included despite the fact that culture has not been used, to date, in this approach. As culture could potentially inform classification, it is useful to examine an approach which has not yet used it but could.

The inductive approach: Frank [1979] and Nair and Frank [1980] made the most significant contribution related to this approach by conducting a statistical analysis of accounting practices in forty four countries using the Price Waterhouse data[9]. They made a distinction between measurement and disclosure practices, identifying five groups in terms of measurement practices and seven with regard to disclosure practices. These groupings followed Seidler's [1967] *spheres of influence* classification[10]. Subsequent to the identification of groupings, Nair and Frank [1980] attempted to assess the relationships of these groups with a number of explanatory variables. However, the hypotheses that (a) cultural and economic variables might be more closely associated with disclosure practices, and (b) trading variables might be more closely associated with measurement practices are not supported. Nair and Frank [1980] used language as a proxy for culture, which was perceived to capture similarities in legal systems. They provided no explanation for these suppositions.

These studies are interesting and may provide useful classifications for empirical research. However, there are some problems with these approaches. The deductive approach is very broad but does not even allude to culture as an explanatory variable for the diversity of observed reporting practices. The inductive approach has been criticized for weaknesses in its data[11]. Gray suggested that cultural influences had been subsumed in economic factors and that the influence of culture on accounting appeared to have been neglected in the various classifications. Only a very broad country groupings and accounting patterns had been identified. There is neither a general consensus about the nature of these groupings or patterns among the authors nor has any specific relationship been established between environmental factors and accounting patterns. Moreover, there appears to be very little, if any, causality implied in terms of what underlying factors may actually be responsible for causing the observed differences among the different categories of the accounting system[12]. Lastly, the literature seems to have been developed on an *ad hoc* empirical basis lacking an underlying theoretical structure to support the statistical analysis of the data.

---

8   In this instance, it should be clarified that Nobes [1983,1984] did not mention culture as a possible variable in explaining differences across countries. Given the development in international accounting literature pertaining to the importance of cultural relevance in accounting, it appears that a variable which may have significant explanatory power may have been overlooked by Nobes. This however, does not in any way reflect upon the inductive-deductive classification of accounting practice forwarded by Nobes. We wish to thank the referee for pointing this out and for assisting us in clarifying this.

9   Two other studies were based on the same Price Waterhouse data: a study by Da Costa *et al.*, [1978] on which Frank's study is based and one by Goodrich [1982].

10   Seidler [1967] identified the following *spheres of influence:* The British Commonwealth, Latin American / South European, Northern and Central European and US models. In AAA [1977] fives *zones of influence:* British, Franco-Spanish-Protugese, Germanic-Dutch, US and Communistic were listed.

11   Among other the Price Waterhouse data was criticised for its suitability of purpose, misleading cases and errors. Nobes stated that 'the results from this data must be used with caution and such caution has not always been present [1992, p 60].

12   In this case, culture as a variable is probably the cause, while the effect is manifested by the observation in the variation of accounting systems and practices.

3.0 GRAY'S THEORY OF CULTURAL RELEVANCE

Gray [1988] was a pioneering paper in the development of the idea that culture might influence accounting practices. It attempted to bring together constructs from culture and accounting, relate them in meaningful way and proposed quite specific hypotheses of the form of these relationships. Nothing similar had been attempted prior to Gray's [1988] work in the international accounting literature and therefore warrants a more detailed review. This section discusses Gray's [1988] theory which identified accounting sub-cultural values[13] and related them to Hofstede's societal values producing a series of relationships which were translated into four hypotheses. Gray's claim of a cultural influence on accounting rests on the framework he proposed, which is reproduced below in Figure 1.

Figure 1

Culture, societal values and the accounting subculture

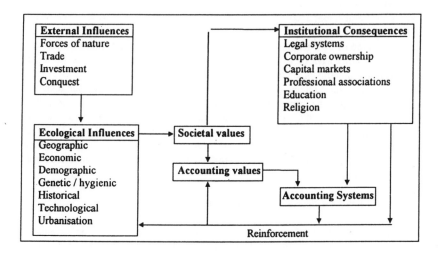

[Source: Gray, 1988, p7]

The origins of cultural values are found in a variety of factors effecting the ecological or physical environment. These societal values lead to the development and maintenance of institutions within a society including education, social and political systems and legal, financial and corporate structures. Once in place these systems tend

---

[13] Although Gray does not specifically attribute these dimensions to any particular study, Arpan and Radebaugh [1985] identified values directly associated with the accounting profession as Conservatism, Secrecy, attitudes towards the accounting profession and attitudes towards business.

6   *Journal of Accounting Literature*   Volume 18

to reflect and reinforce the societal values as depicted in the reinforcement loop in Figure 1. This structure tends to remain stable and changes at the national level are mainly due to major external acts of nature or of man. International trade, investment, multi-national companies and colonisation are examples of the latter. The external forces, as depicted in Figure 1, effect these societal values primarily via the environmental influences. The societal values in turn influence the institutional settings like the legal or educational system within a country.

Culture or societal values at the national level permeate through to occupational subcultures with varying degrees of integration. Gray incorporated accounting in this framework with accounting systems and practices shown as being influenced by, and in turn reinforcing, societal values. He suggested that, in this way, one may gain novel insights into the process of identifying and explaining the differences between accounting practices internationally. The model in Figure 1 presents societal values at the level of accounting subculture. Accordingly, the value systems of accountants are seen to be derived from the societal values with specific reference to work-related values. Consequently, these accounting values in turn influence accounting systems including the reporting and disclosure of information. Thus, depending on the varying degrees of external and ecological forces shaping societal values in different societies, different accounting systems are deemed to develop, reflect and reinforce these values.

External influences and different ecological factors thus, through varying societal values, create different accounting values and systems in different parts of the world. This appears to be the basic argument supporting the contention that each culture should develop its own accounting systems to serve its own distinct requirements [e.g., Jaggi 1975]. Gray went on to suggest that there should be a close match between culture areas and patterns of accounting systems. This is the basis upon which Gray rests his theory of cultural relevance to accounting and, although Gray does not acknowledge it in his paper, the framework as depicted in Figure 1 above is based substantially upon Hofstede's [1980, ch 1] framework. Having laid the foundations for cultural relevance to accounting, Gray links Hofstede's dimensions of *Power Distance, Uncertainty Avoidance, Individualism and Masculinity*[14] to accounting sub-cultural values[15]. Gray's accounting values are described and discussed individually in the following four subsections.

3.1 Professionalism Versus Statutory Control

Gray proposed *Professionalism* as a significant accounting value dimension because accountants adopt independent attitudes and exercise their individual professional judgement to varying degrees. A major controversy in many Western countries surrounds the issue of the extent to which the accounting profession should be subject

---

[14] Power distance is the degree of inequality among people which the population of a country considers normal: from relatively equal to extremely unequal. Uncertainty avoidance is the degree to which people in a country prefer structured over unstructured situations: from relatively flexible to extremely rigid. Individualism is the degree to which people in a country learn to act as individuals rather than as members of a cohesive group: from collectivist to individualist. Masculinity is the degree to which 'masculine' values like assertiveness, performance, success and competition prevail over 'feminism' values like quality of life, care of the weak, warm personal relationships: from tender to rough.

[15] Hofstede [1980, 1991] derived these dimensions on the basis of theoretical reasoning and empirical analysis of data collected via 116,000 questionnaires from IBM employees in over fifty countries.

to public regulation and statutory control or be permitted to retain control over accounting standards as a matter for private self-regulation [Taylor and Turley, 1986]. Professional associations, for instance, are firmly established in countries such as the US and UK, less so in Continental Europe and to an even lesser extent in the less developed countries, if at all [Holzer, 1984; Nobes and Parker, 1995]. In the UK, *a true and fair* view of a company's financial position relies heavily on the accountant's professional judgement which is entirely different from the situation in France and Germany where the professional accountant's role is reduced to implement rather prescriptive and detailed legal requirements [Gray and Coenenberg, 1984]. There is little disagreement about Professionalism being considered a significant construct in the accounting literature.

Gray argues that Professionalism is most closely related to the societal values of Individualism and Uncertainty Avoidance. A preference for independent professional judgement is consistent with a preference for a loosely knit social framework where there is more emphasis on individual decisions and respect for individual endeavor. This is consistent with weak Uncertainty Avoidance. Practice is all important, there is a belief in fair play and in as few rules as possible and a variety of professional judgements tend to be tolerated. Gray also saw a link between Professionalism and Power Distance in that Professionalism is more likely to be accepted in a small Power Distance society where there is more concern for equal rights, where people at various power levels feel less threatened and more prepared to trust people, and where there is a belief in the need to justify the imposition of laws and codes. Gray, however, did not observe any significant link of Masculinity with Professionalism. Summarizing his perception of the link between Professionalism and Hofstede's dimensions of culture he formulated the following hypothesis:

H_1: The higher a country ranks in terms of Individualism and the lower it ranks in terms of Uncertainty Avoidance and Power Distance then the more likely it is to rank highly in terms of Professionalism.

3.2 Uniformity Versus Flexibility

Gray identified Uniformity versus Flexibility as a significant accounting sub-cultural value dimension because attitudes about Uniformity, Consistency or Comparability are incorporated as a fundamental feature of accounting principles globally [Choi and Mueller, 1984; Arpan and Radebaugh, 1985; Nobes and Parker, 1995]. This accounting sub-cultural value is open to interpretations ranging from a relatively strict inter-company and inter-temporal Uniformity, to consistency within companies over time and, for some, to the flexibility of accounting practices to suit the circumstances of individual companies. In countries like France, a uniform accounting plan has long been in operation, together with the imposition of tax rules for measurement purposes, where there is a concern to facilitate national planning. In the US, on the other hand, there is more concern with inter-temporal consistency with a certain degree of inter-company comparability subject to a perceived need for flexibility [Choi and Mueller, 1984; Holzer, 1984; Arpan and Radebaugh, 1985].

Gray argued that Uniformity is linked most closely with the Uncertainty Avoidance and Individualism dimensions. A preference for Uniformity is consistent with a preference for strong Uncertainty Avoidance leading to a concern for law and

8   *Journal of Accounting Literature*   Volume 18

order and rigid codes of behavior, a need for written rules and regulations, a respect for conformity and the search for ultimate, absolute truths and values. This value dimension is also consistent with a preference for Collectivism, as opposed to Individualism, with its tightly knit social framework, a belief in organization and order, and respect for group norms. Gray also argued for a link between Uniformity and Power Distance in that Uniformity is more easily facilitated in a large power-distance society where the imposition of laws and codes of a uniform character are more likely to be accepted. For Gray, however, Masculinity did not appear to have any significant link with Uniformity. He thus expressed the relationship of Uniformity with Hofstede's cultural dimension of Uncertainty Avoidance, Power Distance and Individualism as follows:

H_2: The higher a country ranks in terms of Uncertainty Avoidance and Power Distance and the lower it ranks in terms of Individualism then the more likely it is to rank highly in terms of Uniformity.

3.3 Conservatism Versus Optimism

Gray identified Conservatism as a significant accounting value dimension because it is arguably 'the most ancient and probably the most pervasive principle of accounting valuation' [Sterling, 1967, p 10]. Conservatism or prudence in asset measurement and the reporting of profits is perceived as a fundamental attitude of accountants the world over. Moreover, Conservatism varies according to country, ranging from a strongly conservative approach in Continental Europe to much less conservative attitudes of accountants in the US and UK [Beeny, 1975, 1976; Nobes, 1984; Choi and Mueller, 1984; Arpan and Radebaugh, 1985]. The differential impact of Conservatism on accounting measurement practices internationally has also been demonstrated empirically [Gray, 1980; Choi and Mueller, 1984]. Gray suggested that such differences seem to be reinforced by the relative development of capital markets, the differing pressures of users interests, and the influence of tax laws on accountants in the countries concerned.

Gray argued that Conservatism can be linked most closely with Hofstede's dimensions of Uncertainty Avoidance since a preference for more conservative measure of profits is consistent with strong Uncertainty Avoidance following from a concern with security and a perceived need to adopt a cautious approach to cope with the uncertainty of future events. He also saw a link, though less strong, between high levels of Individualism and Masculinity on one hand, and weak Uncertainty Avoidance on the other. An emphasis on individual achievement and performance is likely to foster a less conservative approach to measurement. As regards the Power Distance dimension Gray did not theorize any significant link with Conservatism. This reasoning led to the following hypothesis:

H_3: The higher a country ranks in terms of Uncertainty Avoidance and the lower it ranks in terms of Individualism and Masculinity, the more likely it is to rank highly in terms of Conservatism.

3.4 Secrecy Versus Transparency

Gray suggested that Secrecy versus Transparency is a significant dimension which stems from the influence of management on the quantity of information disclosed to outsiders. Moreover, Secrecy in business relationships is a fundamental accounting attitude [Arpan and Radebaugh, 1985]. Secrecy also seems to be closely related to Conservatism in that both values imply a cautious approach to corporate financial reporting in general. However, Gray argued that Secrecy relates to the disclosure dimension and Conservatism relates to the measurement dimension. Although, the extent of Secrecy would seem to vary across countries with lower levels of disclosure, including instances of secret reserves, evident in Continental Europe compared to the US and UK [Barrett, 1976; Choi and Mueller, 1984; Arpan and Radebaugh, 1985]. These differences would also seem to be reinforced by the differential development of capital markets and the nature of share ownership which may provide incentives for the involuntary disclosure of information [Watts, 1977].

Gray argued that Secrecy can be linked most closely with Uncertainty Avoidance, Power Distance and Individualism. A preference for Secrecy is consistent with strong Uncertainty Avoidance following from a need to restrict information disclosures to avoid conflict and competition and to preserve security. A close relationship with Power Distance also seems likely in that high Power Distance societies are likely to be characterized by the restriction of information to preserve power inequalities. Secrecy is also consistent with a preference for Collectivism (as opposed to Individualism) and Masculinity, to the extent that more caring societies (where more emphasis is given to the quality of life, people and the environment) will tend to be more open, especially as regards socially related information. Gray thus proposed that:

H_4: The higher a country ranks in terms of Uncertainty Avoidance and Power Distance and the lower it ranks in terms of Individualism and Masculinity then the more likely it is to rank highly in terms of Secrecy.

Although Gray provided this seminal effort by proposing to relate accounting sub-cultural values to societal values on a conceptual basis, he appeared to have paid lesser attention to a number of factors which may significantly question his hypotheses formulation. The first problem in testing the hypotheses is a conceptual one, for the hypotheses are rather rigid in their wording. In the case of hypothesis one, for example, it is not clear what the state of Professionalism should be in the context of both high Individualism and high Uncertainty Avoidance[16]. Gray's hypotheses are in fact compound hypotheses, and as such are restricted in terms of the situations that are permitted to be tested[17]. Furthermore, the links between accounting values and practices are not specified. It is not evident as to how accounting practices will differ between cultures of differing accounting values[18]. Even if the cultural values and accounting were related in a certain way, how should this effect the qualitative characteristics of financial statements? Questions such as how would users and preparers benefit from such apparent linkages were also left unanswered.

Arguably, one of Gray's hypotheses [H4, p 11, Gray 1988] may be shown to be inconsistent with argument leading up to it[19]. In constructing an argument leading up

---

16   As opposed to high individualism a low uncertainty avoidance, as posited by Gray.

17   For example, only in situations of high Power Distance, low Individualism, low Maculinity, high Uncertainty Avoidance will high Conservatism exist.

18   For example, it is not clear how much less disclosure (and of what form) one may expect between highly secretive and less secretive countries? It is this level of specificity that will lend itself better to empirical testing and insights relating to accounting practice.

19   We are grateful to Joanna Yeoh for this observation.

10   *Journal of Accounting Literature*   Volume 18

to the hypothesis on secrecy Gray states that "more caring ... will tend to be more open especially as regards socially related information" [p 11]. This argument states that low masculinity will cause low secrecy, an intuitive and acceptable proposition. H_4, however, states that "... the lower it (a society) ranks in terms masculinity then the more likely it is to rank *highly* in terms of secrecy". This hypothesis states that (among other relationships), lower masculinity causes high secrecy, which is inconsistent with the argument leading up to the hypothesis.[20]

The relationships identified by Gray regarding the cultural influence of accounting were summarized by Baydoun and Willett [1995] in a testable form within the following table:

Table 1

The Hofstede - Gray Framework

	Power Distance	Individualism	Masculinity	Uncertainty Avoidance	Long term orientation
Conservatism	+	–	–	+	+
Uniformity	+	-	?	+	+
Professionalism	–	+	?	–	–
Secrecy	+	–	–	+	+

'+' indicates a direct relationship between the variables, '-' indicates an

inverse relationship and '?' indicates that the relationship is indeterminate.

[Source: Adapted from Baydoun & Willett, 1995]

4.0 POST GRAY LITERATURE

The literature saw a sharp increase in studies relating culture and accounting subsequent to Gray's proposed framework. There was also an increase in studies applying Hofstede's value dimensions to various aspects of accounting. This section reviews the

---

[20] This inconsistency has been carried through the literature including the works of Baydoun & Willett [1995] as well as Salter and Niswander [1995].

related literature incorporating studies from 1988 through to the present and can be classified into three parts. The first part includes the literature that develops and critically evaluates the Hofstede-Gray framework on a theoretical basis. The second part attempts to apply Hofstede's constructs to other areas of accounting like auditing and management control. The third part of post Gray literature discusses studies not classified in above two parts.

4.1 Theoretical Development of the Hofstede-Gray Framework

This section traces the evolution of the Hofstede-Gray framework. The studies by Perera [1989], Fechner and Kilgore [1994] and Baydoun and Willett [1995] are reviewed below. Each study has built on the previous one and strengthened Gray's proposed theory of cultural relevance to accounting.

4.1.1   Perera [1989]

Perera [1989] and Perera and Matthews [1990] built on Gray's theory to propose a number of hypotheses relating societal values to accounting sub-cultural values. In particular, Perera provided a useful explanation of cultural factors in the context of developing countries' accounting systems. Perera's main contribution seems to lie in his suggestion that a combination of accounting sub-cultural dimensions have considerable influence on accounting practices. He related accounting values to certain aspects of accounting practice: authority of accounting systems, force of application, measurement practices used and the extent of information disclosed as follows:

Table 2

Societal values and accounting practices

Societal values ———▶	Accounting values ———▶	Accounting practice
Individualism	Professionalism	Authority
Uncert. Avoidance	Uniformity	Application
Power Distance	Conservatism	Measurement
Masculinity	Secrecy	Disclosure

[Source: Adapted from Perera, 1989]

Having identified how accounting values may be influenced by societal values Perera postulated how one or more accounting value may influence or determine accounting practice. These relationships, as depicted in the Table above appear to follow a logic which suggests that societies with, say, high Individualism will tend to have higher levels of Professionalism and consequently practice lower levels of authority in accounting practice, and so forth. He, however, remained silent on the nature, magnitude and direction of the relationship between accounting values and practice. Another contribution was that the hypotheses Perera formulated which appeared to lend themselves to testing to a greater extent than those originally proposed by Gray. However, although the links in the above relationships appear to be meaningful and attempt to simplify Gray's constructs, it is not entirely clear that the constructs of Authority and Application for instance, are any less abstract than Gray's labels of Professionalism or Uniformity. Nevertheless Perera's work must be credited as an attempt to develop ideas of cultural relevance which were then in a stage of infancy.

Perera further suggested that societal values are affected by a broad set of environmental factors including economic variables and analyzed the Anglo-American and Continental European systems of accounting (the latter typified by France and Germany). He concluded that the requirements imposed through the General Accounting Plan have greatly influenced the development of accounting practices in France. He pointed to similar developments in Germany suggesting that France and Germany have developed accounting systems which are based on enforceable legal prescriptions. He supported this analysis by linking these practices to Hofstede's cultural dimensions for these countries, claiming that they had a very similar ranking. Perera extended this discussion to developing countries and suggested that transferring accounting skills from Anglo-America countries to developing countries is unlikely to be appropriate as these countries typically have inadequate professional subcultures to develop suitable standard accounting skills.

Perera and Perera and Matthews' conclusion, was consistent with Gray's, that is Uncertainty Avoidance and Individualism appear to most influence accounting. Table 3, adapted from Fechner and Kilgore [1994], compares the hypotheses proposed by Gray [G] and Perera and Matthews [P&M]. The shaded region shows the dimensions along which Gray and Perera and Matthews differed in their analysis.

4.1.2   Fechner and Kilgore [1994]

Fechner and Kilgore [1994] challenged Perera's classification of France and Germany. Drawing upon Hofstede's work, the accounting literature[21] and a detailed analysis of accounting practices in these countries, they claimed that France and Germany are not similar enough to represent a Continental European group, which is contrary to Perera's suggestion. They also asserted that Australia and New Zealand display similarities in measurement, but not disclosure, practices, a finding contrary to the dichotomy proposed by Gray [1988] who classified Australia and New Zealand into one group for measurement and disclosure practices. Since the literature prior to 1994 failed to explain the differences in accounting practices within and across countries in

---

[21] In particular the classifications of Nair and Frank [1980], and Nobes [1983].

Table 3

Proposed hypotheses based on frameworks suggested by Gray and Perera

	Professionalism		Uniformity		Conservatism		Secrecy	
	G	P, P&M	G	P, P&M	G	P, P&M	G	P, P&M
Individualism	High	High	Low	High	Low	Low	Low	Low
Uncert. avoidance	Low	Low	High	Low	High	High	High	High
Power Distance	Low		High				High	
Masculinity					Low		Low	
Predicted outcome	High	High	High	Low	High	High	High	High

[Source: Fechner and Kilgore, 1994, p 269]

either the Anglo-American, Continental European or other cluster groupings identified by Gray, Fechner and Kilgore [1994] proposed a modified theoretical framework to explain the cultural influence of accounting as follows:

Figure 2

Modified theoretical framework

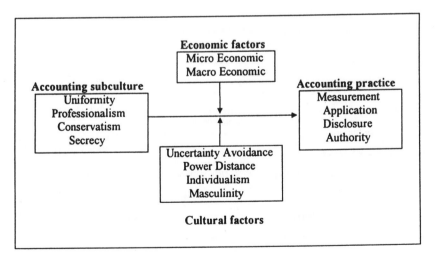

[Source: Fechner and Kilgore, 1994]

In justifying this framework Fechner and Kilgore suggested that while both economic and cultural factors influence accounting and accounting practice, the economic factor variable has a moderating influence on the association between accounting sub-cultural values and accounting practices. Their analysis of the divergence in disclosure practices supported an association between accounting subculture values and the accounting practice dimensions of authority and disclosure. Fechner and Kilgore's modified framework, presented cultural factors as variables which may, perhaps, moderate the relationship between accounting subculture and practice. In Perera and Gray's framework, in contrast, cultural factors are a part of the societal values which cause changes in accounting subculture [see Figure 1 and Perera, 1989, p 48]. In addition, Fechner and Kilgore failed to comment on how aspects of the measurement, form or content of a set of financial accounts may be expected to differ from one country or region to another. Furthermore, they provided no indication of how hypotheses may be constructed, how the numerous variables in the framework may be operationalized, the degree to which they may interact, and how statistical tests might be conducted to investigate the apparent interactions between the variables of interest.

4.1.3   Baydoun and Willett [1995]; Willett et al., [1997]

Baydoun and Willett [1995] and Willett *et al.*, [1997] critically evaluated Gray's theory and suggested that although Gray's dimensions may possibly help us understand how social factors affect the technology of accounting, certain purely technical aspects of accounting which are also pertinent to the question of cultural relevance should also be considered more formally. The contribution of this theory lies in its critical evaluation of the relationships between Gray's accounting sub-cultural values, Hofstede's societal values and accounting practice as depicted by Gray and reproduced below in Figure 3.

Figure 3

Gray's accounting dimensions and measurement and disclosure

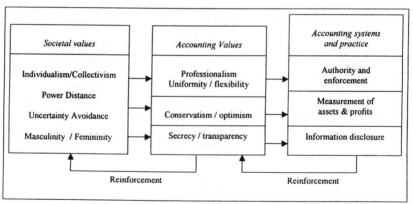

[Source: Radebaugh and Gray, 1993]

Gray defined his accounting values in terms of preferences for particular course of action rather than in terms of qualitative characteristics of financial statements. Professionalism as depicted by Gray was either an accountant's preference to use judgement or the preference of a professional body to self-regulate. Uniformity as defined by Gray, Baydoun and Willett suggested, appeared little more than an inverse quality to Professionalism (although they pointed out that there is another sense in which Uniformity could also be interpreted as the physical attribute of an accounting system). They reasoned that Gray's theory was clear neither about the role of accounting values as cultural attributes of social groups or physical attributes of technology of accounting. They, therefore, cast doubt on whether his accounting values served any useful purpose as intervening variables between Hofstede's dimensions of culture and the characteristics of accounting practice as indicated in Figure 3.

Another point related to the above referred to the fact that little justification was provided by Gray to support the linkages shown in Figure 3. For instance, a trait of high Secrecy in a culture may mean that financial reports are less likely to contain certain types of information than in other, less secretive societies. However, a high Uniformity score might be expected to directly influence the Uniformity with which financial statements of differing entities are prepared, something about which Secrecy apparently has little to say. Consequently, Baydoun and Willett argued that the justification Gray provided for choosing the particular relationships shown in Figure 3 was unclear.

While such criticism of Gray's theory by Baydoun and Willett may be instructive it does little to elucidate the cultural relevance of accounting. In order to establish cultural relevance, they proposed that a distinction be made between aspects of *measurement* and *disclosure* in financial statements. Baydoun and Willett noted that although behavioral aspects of accounting have been studied in some detail, insufficient attention has been given to the effect of the technical dimensions of accounting in limiting the influence of cultural factors. They pointed out that culture influences the technology of accounting differentially: affecting some parts strongly, other parts less so and certain parts hardly at all. An understanding of why this may be the case is critical in determining the form and content of financial statements which are culturally relevant to a society and is the focus of Baydoun and Willett's theory of cultural relevance, which is summarized below in Figure 4.

The smaller box in Figure 4 contains the technology of accounting, that is the process developed by a society for recognizing events for accounting measurements, making calculations based upon those measurements and disclosing those calculations to users. The larger box, with darker border, contains the elements of the accounting environment, users, preparers and their decision models. The most physically determined aspects of accounting technology and the accounting environment are shown towards the bottom of the figure while the most socially determined aspects, such as the rules for proper disclosure, appear towards the top. The implication of the triangle on the right hand side of the figure is that culture has a differential effect on different parts of the accounting technology. By definition culture will affect those parts of the accounting environment mostly determined by social factors to a greater degree than it will affect those parts mostly determined by physical factors. For instance, the measurement of physical input-output relationships in the production of commodities is little, if at all, affected by culture. More susceptible are the management structures of firms which correspond with the base of the inverted triangle. This analysis suggested

16   *Journal of Accounting Literature*   Volume 18

Figure 4

The accounting environment

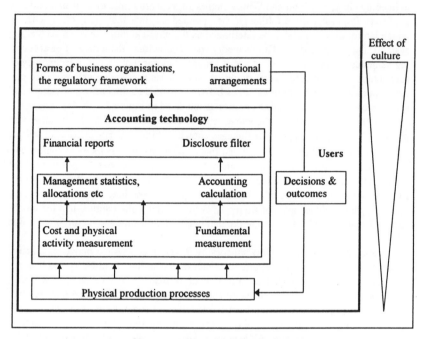

[Source: Willett *et al.*, 1997, ch 19]

that the measurement subject matter that forms the basis of any disclosed financial information is relatively fixed. However, how much of the information contained in the chosen basis is disclosed to users is very much determined by factors such as the cultural forces discussed here.

By extending Gray's framework in this way Baydoun and Willett [1995], suggested that it may be possible to explain more precisely some of the important characteristics of financial reports. The linkages between cultural values and the physical attributes of financial reports (i.e., what they look like, what and how much information they contain, etc.) requires assessing the impact of the social dimensions of accounting on the technical. By grouping the commonly cited qualitative characteristics of financial statements in the way described in Table 4, Baydoun and Willett argued that a suitable, technical reinterpretation of Gray's values of Uniformity, Conservatism and Secrecy could satisfactorily accommodate many of those characteristic regarding matters of disclosure. Furthermore, since the reinterpreted concepts could be expected to have the same relationships with Hofstede's cultural values as the original concepts, the amendment allowed the Hofstede-Gray framework to be extended to more specific policy prescriptions in a straightforward manner. These relationships between Gray's reinterpreted dimensions and qualitative characteristics and the form and content of corporate reports are presented in Table 4 below.

Table 4 suggests some relationships between the technical, disclosure characteristics of financial reports, Gray's three concepts of Uniformity, Conservatism and Secrecy and some examples of the manner in which the qualitative characteristics are manifested in the form and content of published accounts. Uniformity, as a technical characteristic of financial statements, is interpreted as encompassing the two qualities of consistency and comparability. Each of these, in different ways, is relevant to the question of apparent Uniformity of accounting policies over time and Uniformity of presentation of accounting information between accounting entities.

Table 4 developed Gray's Figure 3 to understand if it might be possible to test how aspects of accounting values are manifested in the financial statements. For instance, if one had *a priori* expectations about a particular accounting value being high or low in, say, Secrecy, one could sample a set of financial statements and measure the items in the third column to compare these against those from another country's financial statements. However, like the other literature discussed in this sub-section, Baydoun and Willett's theories lack substantive evidence, empirical or otherwise, to test the

Table 4

Gray's reinterpreted dimensions and qualitative characteristics

Accounting dimensions – technical aspects		Qualitative characteristics relating to disclosure	Examples of issues relating form & content of corporate reports
Uniformity		*Uniform content & presentation* Consistency Comparability	Standardised accounts Accounting policies
Secrecy	Conservatism	*Quality of information:* Timeliness Materiality Objectivity Verifiability Reliability Neutrality Substance over form	Normal publication date Cost versus market values Cash flow accounting Lower of cost and market
		Amount of information: Accountability Decision usefulness	*Extent of disaggregated data:* Number of items disclosed Group accounts Supplementary statements

[Source: Baydoun and Willett, 1995]

18   *Journal of Accounting Literature*   Volume 18

validity of their theory. In a recent work, Roberts [1995] discusses issues and problems associated with attempts to classify national systems of accounting. His analysis demonstrates the incoherence of taxonomies that rely upon appeals to objectivity and presents a case for the development of classifications that explicitly focus on the concept of an accounting system. Roberts argues that if we are to proceed with the classification of the attributes of accounting in different countries, we should be aware that there is a danger of enthnocentrism in doing so. He concludes that any classification, by definition, imposes its own world view and sets up patterns of thinking, characterization and influence which may mislead and veil the nature of accounting in different countries.

4.2 Accounting Applications of Hofstede's Theory

This section reviews some of the studies that have attempted to apply Hofstede's theory and his proposed dimensions of culture to aspects of accounting. The reviewed literature in this area appears to fall into two distinct sets. The first set applies the Hofstede-Gray framework to a particular country or a set of countries to test the validity of the underlying theory. These studies are reviewed in the following sub-section. The second set employs Hofstede's dimensions in the context of studying management control systems within firms. These studies are reviewed in the second sub-section.

4.2. Hofstede-Gray Framework Applied

Gehrardy [1990] is an example of an attempt to test the Hofstede-Gray framework by applying it to accounting systems found in West Germany. While Gerardy does not entirely refute Gray's theory, he concludes that 'in the case of West Germany, Gray's theory is unable to explain the relationship between accounting and cultural value dimensions in an entirely satisfactory manner' [p 28][22]. A major failing of studies such as this, however, is that they are *ad hoc*, based upon selected information and are somewhat subjective in their analysis of culture and accounting systems and practices of the respective countries. It is quite possible that by using a slightly different set of information a contrary conclusion might have been reached.

Eddie's [1991] study of the thirteen countries of the Asia Pacific region, which looked for association between societal values and accounting sub-cultural values, found support for Gray's theory, confirming all the predicted signs of association between societal and accounting values [p 29]. Eddie used Hofstede's [1980] index scores for dimensions of culture and created a subjective index for Gray's values based on information available in 1991. Although Eddie's study appeared to be empirical in nature, it suffered from the possibility of bias since the factors comprising each of the accounting sub-cultural value indices and the weights assigned to the factors comprising the index were determined subjectively by the author. Consequently, it is perfectly possible that the judgemental scoring of each of the factors on a four point scale would produce significantly different results should a different researcher be responsible for assigning the weights. In addition to this problem, no justification was provided either

---

[22] In a recent study, MacGregor *et al.*, [1997], drew a similar conclusion with respect to the application of Gray's theory to the case of Malaysia and Singapore [p 118].

for selecting the factors, assigning the weights and there was lack of rigour in the method resulting from an absence of triangulation in terms of measurement. Not only did Eddie use two different sets of data based on information sets twenty years apart, but the data was secondary in nature. Although this study carries the merit of being one of the first attempts to test Gray's theory empirically, the results should be viewed with caution.

Chow *et al* [1995] applied the Hofstede-Gray model to the case of China. In doing so they describe the accounting system and processes in China and suggest that given the current state of the accounting profession, and accounting measurement and disclosure in China, the development of the accounting systems will be constrained by the influence of China's culture and its accounting sub-culture. They further suggest that while financial reporting will be governed by accounting standards, their development and enforcement will remain a governmental and legalistic function.

Salter and Niswander [1995] make a more useful contribution. Their study tests the Hofstede-Gray framework based upon data from countries drawn from Gray [1988]. The study concludes that Gray's model is best at explaining actual financial reporting practices and is relatively weak in explaining extant professional and regulatory structures from a cultural base. The study further suggests that both the development of financial markets and levels of taxation enhance the explanations offered by Gray.

4.2.2   Culture and Management Control

The cross-cultural generalizability of research results and the associated transferability of management control systems (MCS) is gaining importance as the movement towards the globalization of business and economies continues. This section reviews some of the ideas in the literature pertaining to MCS and culture. However, this brief overview is a sampling of such studies and not comprehensive.

The general direction of the research in this area tests the hypotheses that MCSs across nations do not necessarily operate in an identical manner. This general claim has been extended to testing the role of MCS with respect to organizational culture settings. Daley *et al.*, [1985] found empirical evidence of both similar and different attitudes towards specific aspects of control systems design between US and Japanese managers and controllers. These findings supported the reasonable assumption that it is unlikely that all MCS characteristics are generalizable and transferable across cultures, but equally unlikely that none is. Chow *et al.*, [1989] used a controlled experiment consisting of American and Singaporean students representing high and low Individualism, respectively, and find partial support for one of their cultural hypotheses in that when pay was (in)dependent, (high) low Individualism subjects had a significantly higher mean normalized job performance. While this study's findings only partially supported an association between Individualism, MCS and job performance, both Hwang [1989] and Harrison [1993] reported significant results of a similar association.

Birnberg and Snodgrass' [1988] appears to be the earliest attempt to conduct field research on the implications of different cultural settings on the perception of a firm's MCS. They compared the perceptions of MCS's which are held by US and Japanese

20   *Journal of Accounting Literature*   Volume 18

workers. They hypothesized that Japanese workers are as aware of the presence of controls as are their US counterparts. Subject to the limitations inherent in exploratory research, Birnberg and Snodgrass stated that 'the findings are encouraging to those who argue that culture affects control' [p 447].

Hwang [1989] used Hofstede's Power Distance concept to study the effect of national culture on the relationship between budgetary participation and motivation. He concluded that motivation of middle-level management cannot be improved in high Power Distance countries through the use of participative management. Frucot and Shearon [1991] similarly tested the cross-cultural generalizability of the interaction of the locus of control and budgetary participation in influencing job satisfaction and performance using respondents from multinational and local firms in Mexico. Mexico is distinguished from the US in terms of lower Individualism and higher Power Distance and Uncertainty Avoiding culture. These differences were employed to formulate a theory which implicated a non-generalizable result for Brownell's [1982] hypotheses[23]. It was found that the Brownell result generalized for first level managers with regard to managerial performance, but no generalizable result was found for lower level manager performance, nor with regard to job satisfaction for both levels of management. Brownell's results were confirmed only for the less than 100% foreign-owned firms, and it was stated that 'within the Mexican culture, different conclusions are obtained depending on whether the firm is controlled by local or foreign interests' [p 81].

Harrison's [1992] study used Hofsede's cultural dimensions of Power Distance and Individualism to examine the cross-cultural generalizability of a participation effect on the relation between budget emphasis on superior evaluative style and subordinates' job related attitudes. It was hypothesized that the effect of participation would be the same in low Power Distance / high Individualism and high Power Distance / low Individualism cultures. Samples from Australia and Singapore were used as proxy cultures. The results lent support to the hypothesis and carried implications for the cross-cultural transferability of the designs of MCSs.

O'Connor [1995] pointed out that while the results of some of the above studies provided support for the influence of national culture, little guidance has been provided for multinationals as to what is needed to adapt to the local environment in adopting a particular control system. To assess the role of organizational control in this context, a field study was conducted to investigate whether organizational cultural differences between local and foreign manufacturing firms affect the previously identified role of budgetary participation in a high Power Distance nation, Singapore. The results from interview and survey data analysis provided support for the hypothesis that Power Distance moderates the usefulness of participation in budget setting and performance evaluation at the organizational culture level in terms of decreased role ambiguity and enhanced superior-subordinate relationship.

In a more recent study, Chow *et al* [1999] investigate the effects of national culture on firms' design of and employees' preference for management controls. The data for the study was obtained from Taiwanese managers working in Japanese, Taiwanese and US owned firms. The results were consistent with national culture affecting the firms's design and employees' preference for seven management controls. Among

---

[23] Studying the relationship between budgetary participation and performance, Brownell [1982] identified antecedents and consequences effecting such a relationship. Antecedents included managers' locus of control and the influence of national culture and consequences included factors like job satisfaction.

other things, this study noted that 'Hofstede's definition of each cultural dimension is insufficiently precise to guide consistent applications across studies' [p 456].

Bhimani [1999] reviews and critically examines the methodologies deployed in cross-national management control research and considers other modes of analysis. He discusses the societal effects approach, new institutionalism and new historical analyses, and provides a comprehensive and useful classification and positions the alternative perspectives in comparative management control research.

Harrison and McKinnon [1999] provide a comprehensive review of cross-cultural research in MCS over the past 15 years. This review analyzes the theoretical and methodological strengths and weaknesses within the literature and identifies four major weaknesses of this literature as a whole. These are: a failure to consider the totality of the cultural domain in theoretical exposition; a tendency to not consider explicitly the differential intensity of cultural norms and values across nations; a tendency to treat culture simplistically; and, an excessive reliance on the conceptualization of culture in terms of value dimensions.

Although such studies provide insight into the relationship between national and organizational cultures on one hand and aspects of MCSs on the other, caution is warranted in interpreting the results especially with regard to culture or organization specific factors. There is a need to replicate these study in countries which have a similar ranking in terms of their culture patterns. Another common limitation of the cross-sectional analysis typically used is that it does not provide unambiguous evidence to test predictions of causal relationships. In addition, a lack of cross-validation of the Power Distance difference between the local and foreign companies is apparent; other factors may significantly differ between the two groups. Yet another criticism of these studies is that none employ all the dimensions of culture proposed by Hofstede and are therefore lacking in comprehensiveness. The samples employed in these studies were quite often restricted to a particular organization. These studies are therefore open to the criticism that organization culture scores are likely to be confounded with national culture scores.

4.3 Other Approaches

This sub-section provides a brief overview of three other approaches to study the cultural relevance of accounting of which, two having been proposed by Belkaoui. The first approach is the linguistic study of accounting i.e., studying accounting as a language of business [Belkaoui, 1995]. The second approach is based upon a model of cultural relativism [Belkaoui, 1990]. Belkaoui's framework of cultural relativism appears to potentially offer an alternative framework to Gray's model of cultural relevance. The third approach clusters other studies that don't fit in the above framework.

Language is an essential part of culture. Belkaoui postulates that accounting may be perceived as a language and identifies three theses: the linguistic relativity thesis, the socio-linguistic thesis, and the bilingual thesis. It is the linguistic characteristic of accounting that dictates the judgement / decision process in accounting. The concept of linguistic relativity is due to Sapir who refers to the linguistic symbolism of culture and perceives language as an instrument and communication of thought, predisposing its users to a distinct belief system. All these premises lead to the formulation of the principle of linguistic relativity: language is an active determinant of thought. The linguistic relativity hypothesis is preceded by a linguistic determinism hypothesis which

22   *Journal of Accounting Literature*   Volume 18

implies that the structure of language determines the structure of thought [Belkaoui, 1990, p 70]. Regarding the linguistic relativity hypothesis, Belkaoui claimed that users' behavior is based on their relative understanding of certain lexical distinctions and grammatical rules in accounting and this may imply that a research attempt should be made in both practice and accounting academia to identify for each type of user the lexical and grammatical accounting distinctions most conducive to efficient behavior [1995, p 73].

Sociolinguistics recognizes the existence of different linguistic repertoires in a single language associated with different social strata, ethnic status and gender which results in different linguistic behavior. Belkaoui demonstrated its applicability to accounting by identifying specific accounting linguistic codes associated with different speech communities: professional and academic groups in accounting. The existence of different linguistic codes in accounting is responsible for (1) the existence of a schism in accounting; (2) the recourse to rhetoric in the selling of accounting research to targeted audiences; (3) different perceptions of accounting concepts by members of different accounting professional groups; and (4) the different human information processing, cognitive, and task performances of novices versus experts [1995, p 115].

The bilingual thesis studies the impact of the bilingual requirements of business practices in the world of accounting. Proficiency in more than one language is shown to lead to greater mental flexibility and cognitive flexibility, increased metalinguistics ability, some advantages in concept formation abilities, a predisposition to divergent thinking and advanced skills in cognitive style [24]. All these advantages can be assumed to be present in all the situations where accountants who are bilingual are functioning in contexts requiring the use of more than one language. Belkaoui concluded with a call for the rethinking of some of the requirements for accounting expertise to include the learning of foreign languages [1995, p 147].

In addition to the above hypothesis, Belkaoui [1990] proposed a model of cultural relativism in accounting. This model, as illustrated in Figure 5 below, postulates that culture dictates the organizational structures adopted, the micro-organizational behavior, and the cognitive functioning of individuals. In turn, these affect the judgement-decision process when individuals are faced with an accounting or auditing phenomenon.

According to Belkaoui this model avoids the two main problems that has beset the earlier operationalization and use of culture as a construct in accounting studies. The first problem is the equating of culture with nations and the second problem is the *ad hoc* use of culture as a residual factor in explaining variations that had not been explained by other factors. In explaining this model Belkaoui follows Hofstede's definition of culture and perceives culture as a collective programming of the mind, an ideological system forming the backdrop for human activity and providing people with a theory of reality. This backdrop is composed of distinct elements and includes definite dimensions. Each of these cultural elements — language, religion, values and attitudes, law, education, politics, technology, material culture and social organization - is assumed in the cultural relativism model to have the potential of dictating the organizational structures adopted, the cognitive functioning of individuals and micro-organizational behavior all of which may shape the judgement-decision process in accounting.

---

[24] See Belkaoui [1995, Ch 2] for an excellent review of such studies.

Figure 5

Cultural relativism in accounting

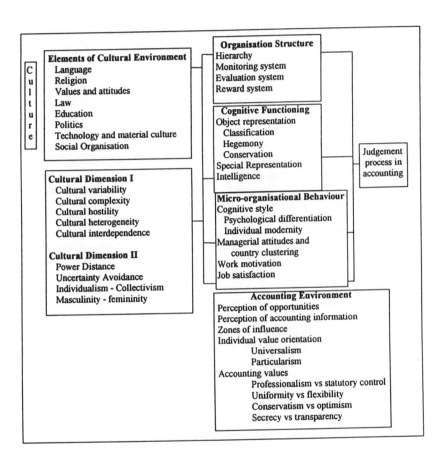

[Source: Belkaoui, 1990, p 41]

Cultures vary along five dimensions: cultural variability, cultural complexity, cultural hostility, cultural heterogeneity, and cultural interdependence. The first three refer to conditions within cultures while the latter two refer to conditions among cultures. The cultural relativism model as set out in Figure 5 assumes that differences in these five dimensions generate different cultural environments. In addition to this, Belkaoui's model allows for cultures to vary along Hofstede's dimensions that reflect the cultural orientations of a country. The cultural relativism model assumes that differences among Hofstede's postulated dimensions of culture create different cultural arenas. The essential argument underlying Belkaoui's model is that cultural processes guide the decision processes in accounting and that culture, through its various levels of manifestations, determines the organization structure, micro-organization behavior, the accounting environment, and the cognitive functioning of individuals facing accounting phenomena.

Although Belkaoui's cultural relativism model is insightful and includes some of the more subtle elements of organizational and cultural environment it provides no guidance as to how it could be useful in practical circumstances or how it might be tested. As a test of a sub-section of this theory Belkoui and Picur [1991] tested the perception of a set of accounting concepts to evaluate the intercultural perceptual differences. The cultural relativism thesis provided the research hypothesis on the relationship between cultural and perception. Their findings supported the contention that accountants from different cultures differ in their perceptions of accounting concepts and called for further research on the nature and consequences of cultural determinism in accounting.

In addition to the above there is a group of studies in the literature which, while not clearly related to the main area we cover, relate accounting to culture. Thus this coverage is only indicative. For instance, Auyeung and Sands [1996] studied how individualism-collectivism is reflected in the learning styles of accounting students in Australia, Hong Kong and Taiwan. This is typical of studies in this area. Soeters and Schreuder [1988] study the interaction between national and organizational cultures at the firm level. They found pronounced effects of the US national culture upon the organizational cultures of the firms under study. Lamb *et al* [1998] constructed a method for assessing the degree of connection between tax rules and practices and financial reporting rules and practices in a country. Among other things, they suggest that it may be more fruitful to compare systems of financial accounting according to the reciprocal patterns of influence and interrelations between tax and accounting, rather than to label systems according to national stereotypes.

5.0 CONCLUSION AND FUTURE RESEARCH

This paper has reviewed the influence of culture on accounting at two levels: the theoretical level and the empirical level. On the theoretical side, the literature has developed in several ways: through anthropological approaches, Gray's theory and methods proposed by Belkaoui. Gray's theory has received the most attention and has consequently been developed more than the other approaches evidenced within the literature. Whether this is desirable is questionable for it is far from established that Gray's proposed theory provides a superior or more insightful view of the influence of culture on accounting than do the other approaches. Because of the parsimony of the Hofstede-Gray framework, Gray's theory lends itself more readily than other theories to hypotheses formulation and consequently to the operationalization of its variables. However, the gains made by simplifying the complex concepts of cultural dimensions and accounting sub-cultural values into a four by four matrix may be offset by loss of the richness of the constructs of culture.

Whereas at the theoretical level there appears to be a certain amount of agreement among authors about the potential for culture to influence accounting, it is the extent and nature of this influence that is in debate. Violet [1983] claimed that 'accounting is in fact determined by culture' whereas Hofstede [1985] concluded that 'the lack of consensus across different countries as to what represents proper accounting methods is because their purpose is cultural, not technical'. While in general both authors agree, they nonetheless have slightly varying emphasis on the extent of culture's influence on accounting.

The attempts to study the influence of culture on accounting have come a long way from Jaggi's [1975] attempt to examine the influence of Parsons and Shils' pattern variable Universalism vs Particularism on the reliability of disclosed information in financial statements to Gray's 'first step in the development of a theory of cultural influence on the development of accounting systems' [1988, p 1]. Willett *et al.*,'s [1997] theory of cultural relevance along with the distinction between *measurement* and *disclosure* probably represents the most contemporary thought in this area of literature. Nobes [1998] contribution is also worthy of note. He proposed a general model for international differences in accounting practices. For Nobes' accounting systems mean the financial reporting practice used by an enterprise. He contends that a country may use several such systems in any one year or over time. Nobes' theory identified two explanatory factors for the first split of accounting systems into classes. This classification includes the effects of a number of factors including colonial inheritance, tax, level of education, economic development, legal system, inflation and culture. This provides a rich ground and a completely novel area of inquiry in this area of literature.

The empirical strand of the literature seems to have evolved in that Hofstede's dimensions and theories have been applied quite meaningfully to the management accounting literature with particular reference to culture and its role in MCS. The success of this application is at best variable[25]. The studies which have attempted to empirically test the Hofstede-Gray framework seem to lack in both method and data[26]. This literature review failed to locate any study that used primary data to test the Hofstede-Gray framework. Future research may benefit from exploring factors other than those forwarded by Gray for it is likely that he (like Hofstede readily admits to) may have left out dimensions of accounting sub-cultural values which may be critical to his proposed model.

Our review of the literature identifies a number of areas where further investigations could be conducted[27]. The first gap with this literature is the universal reliance and acceptance of Hofstede's definition of culture and cultural classifications. This potential deficiency is supported by Harrison and McKinnon [1999], who suggest that an excessive reliance on the value dimension conceptualization of culture has produced

---

[25] See Harrison and McKinnon [1999].

[26] These include Gerhardy [1990] to West Germany, Baydoun and Willett [1995] to Lebanon, Eddie [1991] to thirteen Asian Pacific nations and Niswander and Salter [1995].

[27] Some of the areas we identify overlap with 21 research topics proposed by Gray [1989] which remain nascent.

a highly restricted conception and focus. Researchers will be well advised to investigate alternative definitions and classifications of culture in the social sciences literature and apply the new classification to cross-cultural accounting issues. A particularly useful framework for investigation is forwarded by Belkaoui [1990, 1991, 1995] in the form of cultural relativism, cognitive relativism, linguistic relativism, organizational culture relativism and contractual relativism hypothesis.

The second area of gap identified is the universal acceptance of Gray's dimensions of accounting sub-cultural values. A worthwhile question to investigate here is whether the four dimensions forwarded by Gray are the only dimensions of accounting value? Are there other dimensions, and if so, what are these? Also, would it be possible to identify a more dominant accounting sub-cultural value operating within a society? And if so, how would the linkages in the Hofstede-Gray framework change to incorporate this?

The third area in the literature that is likely to be a fertile ground for research is to extend the study of influence of culture on accounting practices in a generic way to more specific instances by applying this analysis to different countries and cultures. In this regard while some insightful work has been conducted, a lot remains to be done[28]. Related areas worthy of inquiry would be the study of culture as it is a function of ethics in accounting practice. Culture's effect on judgement is also an area that is worthy of further investigation[29].

The fourth area of literature that warrants investigation is the measurement-disclosure distinction drawn by Baydoun and Willett [1995]. While this cultural relevance distinction on disclosure aspects of accounting rather than measurement appears to be fundamental, there is value in rigorously testing this assertion. For if this is indeed the case then future research will be well directed towards identifying and studying disclosure.

A consideration of the development in this literature leads us to also suggest that the theoretical / qualitative development of the literature is not complete. Empirical tests of the Hofstede-Gray framework may therefore be premature. This assertion will be particularly true should further research locate incompleteness in the dimensions forwarded by either Hofstede and/or Gray. Thus the fifth area for further research may be a renewed emphasis on theoretical development and robustness.

The sixth and final area of research we wish to propose is the possible change in the causal variables in the cultural relativism argument. While traditionally literature has presented cultural influences causing variations in accounting practice, moderated by economics, we suggest an investigation of accounting practices as a function of economics moderated by cultural factors. An important paper in this vein is Zarzeski [1996] who tests whether disclosure levels can be explained by company size, foreign sales, debt ratios and Hofstede's cultural dimensions. Zarzeski finds all of the variables bar power distance are significant in a regression which explains 48% of the variance in disclosure levels.

A related but separate avenue for research is proposed by Nobes [1998], who suggests an alternative model of examining variations in accounting systems. His model

---

[28] Harrison and McKinnon [1999], reviewed earlier, provide an excellent insight in this area.

[29] While Belkaoui's *Judgement in International Accounting* [1990] is a leading work into judgement as it relates to cognition, cultures, language and contracts, investigation into each of the specific aspects of judgement would be worthwhile.

of reasons for international accounting differences essentially consists of a class of accounting being effected by the strength of equity-outsider system [p 177]. This in turn is influenced by culture, which is a function of the broad external environment. One key idea Nobes [1998] proposes is that accounting practices should be classified based upon systems and not countries. This is a novel idea and provides a new avenue for inquiry.

In summary, this paper reviewed literature studying the cultural relevance of accounting and critically examined different strands within this literature. Research on culture and its influence on accounting values will continue to be of substantial interest to academic research and practice. While the accounting literature has only begun to examine cultural influences in accounting since Gray [1988], there has been a surge in such studies in this growing area of research. Discussions of the directions for future research as identified in this study pose exciting research opportunities in a paradigm which is beginning to receive the attention it deserves.

28   *Journal of Accounting Literature*   Volume 18

REFERENCES

Arpan, J.S. and L.H. Radebaugh. 1985. International Accounting and Multinational Enterprises. Wiley.

Auyeung, P. and J. Sands. 1996. A cross cultural study of the learning styles of accounting students. *Accounting and Finance*. Vol. 36, 261-174.

Barrett, M.E. 1976. Financial reporting practices: Disclosure and comprehensiveness in an international setting. *Journal of Accounting Research*. (Spring):10-26.

Barthes, G. 1989. IASC News. Meeting the expectations of global capital markets. 1-2.

Baydoun, N. and R.J.W. Willett. 1995. Cultural relevance of western accounting systems to developing countries. *Abacus*. (March):67-91.

Beeny, J.H. 1975. European Financial Reporting: West Germany. Institute of Chartered Accountants of England and Wales.

Benny, J.H. 1976. European Financial Reporting: France. Institute of Chartered Accountants of England and Wales.

Belkaoui. A. 1979. Is there a Consensus on Disclosure? The Reality Challenges Common Belief. *Chartered Accountant Magazine*. (May):44-46.

Belkaoui, A.R. 1990. Judgement in International Accounting. Quorum books.

Belkaoui, A.R. 1994. International and Multinational Accounting. London: Dryden Press.

Belkaoui, A.R. 1995. The Linguistic Shaping of Accounting. Quorum Books.

Belkaoui, A.R. and R.D. Picur. 1991. Cultural determinism and the perception of accounting concepts. *International Journal of Accounting*. Vol. 26, 118-130.

Bhimani, A. 1999. Mapping methodological frontiers in cross-national management control research. *Accounting Organisation and Society*. Vol. 24, 413-440.

Birnberg, J.G. and C. Snodgrass. 1988. Culture and control: A field study. *Accounting Organisations and Society*. 447-464.

Brownell, P. 1982 The role of accounting data in performance evaluation, budgetary participation and organizational effectiveness. *Journal of Accounting Research*. (Spring):12-27.

Burchell, S., C. Clubb, A. Hopwood, J. Huges and J. Nahapiet. 1980. The roles of accounting in organizations and society. *Accounting Organization and Society*, Vol. 5, No. 1.

Choi, F.S. 1973 Financial disclosure and entry to the European capital market. *Journal of Accounting Research*. (Autumn):159-175.

Choi, F. and G. Mueller, G. 1984. International Accounting. Prentice Hall.

Choi, F. and G. Mueller. 1992. International Accounting. Prentice Hall.

Chow, L.M., G.K. Chau and S.J. Gray. 1995. Accounting reforms in China: cultural constrains on implementation and development. *Accounting and Business Research*. Vol. 26, No. 1, 29-49.

Chow, W.C., M.D. Shields and A. Wu. 1999. The importance of national culture in the design of and prefer ence for management controls for multi-national operations. *Accounting Organizations and Society*. Vol. 24, 441-461.

Chow, C.W., M.D. Shields and Y.K. Chan. 1989. The effects of management controls and national Culture on manufacturing performance: An experimental investigation. Working paper presented at the 12th Annual Congress of the European Accounting Association, Stuttgart.

Cleverley, G. 1973. Managers and Magic. London: Longman.

Committee on Concepts and Standards for External Financial Reports. 1977. Statement on Accounting Theory and Theory Acceptance. American Accounting Association: Sarasota.

Da Costa, R.C., R.C. Bourgeois and W.M.A. Lawson 1978. Classification of International Financial Accounting Practices. *International Journal of Accounting Education and Research*. Vol. 11, 95-106.

Daley, L., J. Jiambalvo, G.L. Sundem and Y. Kondo, Y. 1985. Attitudes towards financial control systems in the United States and Japan. *Journal of International Business Studies*. (Fall):91-110.

Eddie, I.A. 1991. Asia pacific cultural values and accounting systems. *Asia Pacific International Management Forum*. Vol. 16, No. 3, 22-30.

Farag, S.M. 1991. Accounting in the 1990s: An international perspective. *The International Journal of Accounting*. Vol. 26, 243-251.

Fechner, H.E. and A. Kilgore. 1994. The influence of cultural factors on accounting practice. *International Journal of Accounting*. Vol. 29, 265-277.

Frank, W.G. 1979. An empirical analysis of international accounting principles. *Journal of Accounting Research*. (Autumn):593-605.

Frucot, V. and W.T. Sheraton. 1991. Budgetary participation, locus of control, and Mexican managerial performance and job satisfaction. *Accounting Review*. (January): Vol. 66, 80-99.

Gambling, T. 1977. Magic, accounting and morale. *Accounting Organizations and Society*. Vol. 2, 141-151.

Gerhardy, P. 1990. An evaluation of the role of culture in the development of accounting principles in West Germany. *Accounting and Finance Research Paper*. 90/2, Flinders University, South Australia.

Goodrich, P.S. 1982. Accounting and political systems, University of Leeds school of economic studies. Discussion Paper No. 109.

Goletz, R.K. 1991. International accounting harmonization: the impossible (and unnecessary?) dream. *Accounting Horizons*. (March):85-88.

Gray, S.J. 1980. The impact of international accounting differences from a security analysis perspective: Some European evidence. *Journal of Accounting Research*. (Spring).

Gray, S.J. 1988. Towards a theory of cultural influence on the development of accounting systems internationally. *Abacus*. (March):1-15.

Gray, S.J. and A.G. Coencberg (eds). 1984. EEC Accounting Harmonisation: Implementation and Impact of the Fourth Directive. North Holland.

Gray, S.J. 1989. International accounting research: The global challenge. *The International Journal of Accounting*. Vol. 24, 291-307.

Hamid, S., R. Craig and F. Clarke. 1993. Religion: a counfounding cultural element in the international harmonization of accounting? *Abacus*. Vol. 29, No. 2, 131-148.

Harrison, G.L. 1992. The cross-cultural generalizationability of the relation between participation, budget emphasis and job related attitudes. *Accounting Organisation and Society*. (January), Vol. 17, 319-339.

Harrison, G.L. 1993. Reliance on accounting performance measures in superior evaluative style - the influence of national culture and personality. *Accounting Organizations and Society*. 319-339.

Harrison, G.L and J.L. McKinnon. 1999. Cross-Cultural research in management control systems: a review of the current state. *Accounting Organizations and Society*. Vol. 24, 483-506.

Hoebel, E.A. 1972. Anthropology: The Study of Man. 4th Ed, New York, McGraw-Hill.

Hofstede, G. 1980. Cultures Consequences. McGraw-Hill.

Hofstede, G. 1985. The ritual nature of accounting systems. Paper presented at EIASM Workshop on Accounting and Culture. (June):5-7.

Hofstede, G. 1991. Cultures and Organisations: Software of the Mind. McGraw-Hill.

Holzer, H.P. (eds). 1984. International Accounting. Harper and Row.

Hwang, S.C. 1989. The effect of culture on the relationship between participation and motivation. (Unpublished Ph.D dissertation, Macquarie University, Sydney, Australia).

Jaggi, B.L. 1975. The impact of the cultural environment on financial disclosures. *International Journal of Accounting*. (Spring).

Lamb, M., C. Nobes and A. Roberts. 1998. International variations in the connections between tax and financial reporting. *Accounting and Business Research*. (Summer): Vol. 28, No. 3, 173-188.

Levi-Strauss, C. 1961. The Elementary Structures of Kinship. (Rev ed; J.H.Bell, J.R. von Sturmer, & R. Needham, Trans) Boston: Beacon Press.

Levi-Strauss, C. 1963. Structural Anthropology. New York, Basic Books.

MacGregor, A., M. Hossain and K. Yap. 1997. Accounting in Malaysia and Singapore: Culture's lack of consequences? Accounting in the Asia-Pacific region, Baydoun, N., Nishimura, A. and Willett, R.J.W. (eds), 99-127.

Makdisi, S. 1977. Financial Policy and Economic Growth: The Lebanese Experience. Columbia University Press.

Mansor, M. 1984. Undang-Undang Perdagongan Dalom Islam. Penerbitan Alharamain (M) And. Bhd., Kuala Lumpur.

March, J.G. and J.P. Olsen. 1976. Ambiguity and Choice in Organisations. Bergen, Norway: Universitetsforlaget.

Meyer, J.W. 1986. Social environments and organizational accounting. *Accounting Organizations and Society*. Vol. 11, No. 4/5.

Mueller, G.G. 1967. International Accounting. New York: Macmillan.

Mueller, G.G. 1968. Accounting principles generally accepted in the United States versus those generally accepted elsewhere. *The International Journal of Accounting*. (Spring):91-103.

Nair, R.D. and W.G. Frank. 1980. The impact of disclosure and measurement practices on international accounting classifications. *The Accounting Review*. (July):426-450.

Nobes, C. 1998. Towards a general model of the reasons for international differences in financial reporting. *Abacus*. Vol. 34, No. 2, 162-187.

Nobes, C. and R.H. Parker. 1995. Comparative International Accounting. Prentice Hall.

Nobes, C. 1992. International Classification of Financial Reporting. Second edition, Routledge.

Nobes, C. A 1983. Judgmental classification of financial reporting practices. *Journal of Business Finance and Accounting*. (Spring):1-18.

Nobes, C. 1984. International Classification of Financial Reporting. Croom Helm.

O'Connor, N. 1995. The influence of national culture on the use of performance evaluation systems in Singapore and South Korea. PhD thesis, Faculty of Business and Hotel Management, Griffith University, Australia.

Perera, H. 1989. Towards a framework to analyse the impact of culture on accounting. *International Journal of Accounting*. Vol. 24, 42-56.

Perera, M.H.B. and M.R. Mathews. 1990. The cultural relativity of accounting and international patterns of social accounting. *Advances in International Accounting*. Vol. 3, 215-251.

Pratt, J. and G. Behr. 1987. Environmental factors, transaction costs and external reporting: A cross-national comparison. *International Journal of Accounting Education and Research*. (Spring).

Radebaugh, L.H. 1975. Environmental factors influencing the development of accounting objectives, standards and practices in Peru. *International Journal of Accounting Education and Research*. (Fall).

Radebaugh, L. and S.G. Gray. 1993. International Accounting and Multinational Enterprises. Wiley.

Rivera, J.M. 1989. International Journal of Accounting. The internationalization of accounting standards: Past problems and current prospects. 320-341.

Roberts, A. 1995. The very idea of classification is international accounting. *Accounting Organizations and Society*. Vol. 20, No. 7/8, 639-664.

Salter, S.B. and F. Niswander. 1995. Journal of International Business Studies. Second Quarter, 379-397.

Schreuder, H. 1987. Accounting research, practice and culture: A European perspective, in B. E. Cushing (ed). *Accounting and Culture*. American Accounting Association.

Soeters, J. and H. Schreuder. 1988. The interaction between national and organizational cultures in accounting firms. *Accounting Organization and Society*. Vol. 13, No. 1, 75-85.

Sterling, R.R. 1967. Conservatism: The fundamental principle of valuation in traditional accounting. *Abacus*. (December).

Sterling, R.R. 1972. Decision oriented financial accounting. *Accounting and Business Research*. (Summer):198-208.

Taylor, P. and S. Turley. 1986. The Regulation of Accounting. Blackwell.

Violet, W.J. 1983. The development of international accounting standards: An anthropological perspective. *International Journal of Accounting Education and Research*. (Spring):1-12.

Walace, R.S.O. 1990. Accounting in developing countries. *Research in Third World Accounting*. Vol. 1.

Watts, R.L. 1977. Corporate financial statements: A product of the market and political processes. *Australian Journal of Management*. (April).

Willett, R.J.W., A. Nishimura and N. Baydoun. 1997. Reflections on the relationship between culture and accounting in the Asia-Pacific region, in Accounting in the Asian Pacific Region, Baydoun, N., A. Nishimura and R.J.W. Willett (eds). 400 426.

Zarzeshi, M.T. 1996. Spontaneous harmonization effects of culture and market forces on accounting disclosure practices. *Accounting Horizons*. Vol. 10, No. 1, (March):18-37.

Zeff, S.A. 1971. Forging Accounting Principles in Five Countries:A History and an Analysis of Trends. Stipes.

[5]

THE JOURNAL OF FINANCE • VOL. LII, NO. 3 • JULY 1997

Legal Determinants of External Finance

RAFAEL LA PORTA, FLORENCIO LOPEZ-DE-SILANES, ANDREI SHLEIFER,
and ROBERT W. VISHNY*

ABSTRACT

Using a sample of 49 countries, we show that countries with poorer investor protections, measured by both the character of legal rules and the quality of law enforcement, have smaller and narrower capital markets. These findings apply to both equity and debt markets. In particular, French civil law countries have both the weakest investor protections and the least developed capital markets, especially as compared to common law countries.

WHY DO SOME COUNTRIES have so much bigger capital markets than others? Why, for example, do the United States and the United Kingdom have enormous equity markets, while Germany and France have much smaller ones? Why do hundreds of companies go public in the United States every year, while only a few dozen went public in Italy over a decade (Pagano, Panetta, and Zingales (1995))? Why do Germany and Japan have such extensive banking systems, even relative to other wealthy economies? If we look at a broader range of countries, why in fact do we see huge differences in the size, breadth, and valuation of capital markets? Why, to take an extreme example, do Russian companies have virtually no access to external finance and sell at about one hundred times less than Western companies with comparable assets (Boycko, Shleifer, and Vishny (1993))?

In our earlier article (La Porta, Lopez-de-Silanes, Shleifer, and Vishny (1996), henceforth LLSV (1996)), we have conjectured that the differences in the nature and effectiveness of financial systems around the world can be traced in part to the differences in investor protections against expropriation by insiders, as reflected by legal rules and the quality of their enforcement. We presented evidence indicating that legal rules protecting investors and the quality of their enforcement differ greatly and systematically across countries. In particular, these rules vary systematically by legal origin, which is either English, French, German, or Scandinavian. English law is common law, made by judges and subsequently incorporated into legislature. French, German, and Scandinavian laws, in contrast, are part of the scholar and legislator-made civil law tradition, which dates back to Roman law (David and Brierley (1985)). Most countries have adopted their legal systems through occupation or colo-

* La Porta, Lopez-de-Silanes, and Shleifer are from Harvard University, and Vishny is from the University of Chicago. We are grateful to Alex Chang, Mark Chen, and Magdalena Lopez-Morton for research assistance, to Ed Glaeser, Stewart Myers, and Luigi Zingales for helpful comments, and to the HIID and the National Science Foundation for support of this research.

nization by one of the European powers to which they owe the origin of their laws. Some other countries, such as those in Latin America, have adopted their legal systems after attaining independence, but have still typically chosen the laws of their former colonizers.

By comparing legal rules across 49 countries, we showed that legal rules from the different traditions differ in content as well as in the history of their adoption. In the area of protection against expropriation by insiders, common law countries protect both shareholders and creditors the most, French civil law countries the least, and German civil law and Scandinavian civil law countries somewhere in the middle. We also showed that richer countries enforce laws better than poorer countries, but, controlling for per capita income, French Civil law countries have the lowest quality of law enforcement as well. In our earlier article, we did not pursue the consequences of differences in legal environments at great length, except to show that countries with poor investor protections have more highly concentrated ownership of shares. The broader question, of course, is whether they also have inferior opportunities for external finance and thus smaller capital markets.

Accordingly, in this article we try to assess the ability of firms in different legal environments to raise external finance through either debt or equity. Presumably, the willingness of an entrepreneur to sell his equity, or to assume debt, depends to a large extent on the terms at which he can obtain external finance. For equity, these terms are reflected by valuation relative to the underlying cashflows; for debt, they are reflected by the cost of funds. If the terms are good, an entrepreneur would sell more of his shares or raise more debt. Countries whose financial systems offer entrepreneurs better terms of external finance would then have both higher valuations of securities and broader capital markets in the sense that more firms would access them. To the extent that better legal protections enable the financiers to offer entrepreneurs money at better terms, we predict that the countries with better legal protections should have more external finance in the form of both higher valued and broader capital markets.

Measuring the size of financial markets—whether debt or equity—is a bit tricky. The values of these markets are dominated by the largest firms. To address this problem, we supplement an aggregate stock market valuation measure with the number of domestic listed firms as well as the number of Initial Public Offerings (IPOs). We also focus on a debt measure that includes all private debt and bond market borrowing. Finally, we examine a sample of all firms from the WorldScope database, a subset consisting of the largest listed firms.

We compare external finance across 49 countries as a function of the origin of their laws, the quality of legal investor protections, and the quality of law enforcement. We find strong evidence that the legal environment has large effects on the size and breadth of capital markets across countries.

Our article is related to several recent strands of research. Shleifer and Vishny (1997) and LLSV (1996) focus on the legal solutions to agency problems between entrepreneurs and investors, and in particular emphasize the cross-country differences in these solutions. Modigliani and Perotti (1996) also focus on contract enforcement as a determinant of external finance, and in particular stress the choice between bank loan and equity finance. Rajan and Zingales (1995) look at G-7 evidence on the determinants of capital structure, or debt and equity choice, although they do not emphasize investor protection. It is possible that the relative legal treatment of shareholders and creditors affects capital structure as well as the availability of either kind of finance, but we do not focus on this issue here. Finally, a growing literature surveyed by Levine (1996), and including recent contributions by King and Levine (1993) and Rajan and Zingales (1996), examines the consequences of developed financial markets for investment and growth. Our article, in contrast, focuses on the determinants of financial development, but does not follow through on its "real" consequences. Unlike the rest of the literature, then, our article aims to empirically establish the link between the legal environment and financial markets.

Section I describes our data. Section II presents the results, and Section III concludes.

I. Data

We are interested in the ability of companies in different countries to raise external funds in the form of either equity or debt. Since we do not have direct measures of external financing for smaller companies, we use primarily aggregate data, which partly capture the breadth of various markets. Table I summarizes the data we use and the sources they come from.

We use three measures of equity finance. Our first variable looks at the ratio of stock market capitalization to GNP in 1994, scaled by a rough measure of the fraction of the stock market held by outside investors. Conceptually, it is not appropriate to look at just the ratio of stock market valuation to GNP. For example, if 90 percent of a firm's equity is held by the insiders and 10 percent is held by the outsiders, then looking at the market capitalization of the whole firm gives a tenfold overestimate of how much has actually been raised externally. For each country, we roughly estimate the average fraction of equity held by the insiders by looking at the country's 10 largest publicly traded nonstate firms, finding the combined ownership stake of the three largest shareholders in each of these firms, and averaging that stake over the 10 firms (see LLSV (1996)). Since we made this calculation for only the largest firms, and since we do not take account of cross-holdings, this procedure probably overestimates the share of equity held by the true outsiders. With all the roughness, this procedure is still conceptually preferred to looking at the uncorrected ratio of market capitalization to GNP. We also note that the results presented below hold for that uncorrected ratio as well, although with lower explanatory power.

We look at two further measures of the extent of equity finance that focus more specifically on market breadth. The first is the number of listed domestic firms in each country relative to its population. The second is the number of

1134   *The Journal of Finance*

Table I

Description of the Variables

Origin	Identifies the legal origin of the Company Law or Commercial Code of each country. Source: Reynolds and Flores (1989) and La Porta *et al.* (1996).
External cap/ GNP	The ratio of the stock market capitalization held by minorities to gross national product for 1994. The stock market capitalization held by minorities is computed as the product of the aggregate stock market capitalization and the average percentage of common shares not owned by the top three shareholders in the ten largest non-financial, privately-owned domestic firms in a given country. A firm is considered privately owned if the State is not a known shareholder in it. Source: *Moodys International, CIFAR, EXTEL, WorldScope, 20-Fs, Price-Waterhouse*, and various country sources.
Domestic firms/ Pop	Ratio of the number of domestic firms listed in a given country to its population (in millions) in 1994. Source: *Emerging Market Factbook* and *World Development Report 1996*.
IPOs/Pop	Ratio of the number of initial public offerings of equity in a given country to its population (in millions) for the period 1995:7–1996:6. Source: *Securities Data Corporation, AsiaMoney, LatinFinance, GT Guide to World Equity Markets*, and *World Development Report 1996*.
Debt/GNP	Ratio of the sum of bank debt of the private sector and outstanding non-financial bonds to GNP in 1994, or last available. Source: *International Financial Statistics, World Bondmarket Factbook*.
GDP growth	Average annual percent growth of per capita gross domestic product for the period 1970–1993. Source: *World Development Report 1995*.
Log GNP	Logarithm of the Gross National Product in 1994. Source: *World Development Report 1996*.
Rule of law	Assessment of the law and order tradition in the country. Average of the months of April and October of the monthly index between 1982 and 1995. Scale from 0 to 10, with lower scores for less tradition for law and order. Source: *International Country Risk Guide*.
Antidirector rights	An index aggregating shareholder rights. The index is formed by adding 1 when: (1) the country allows shareholders to mail their proxy vote; (2) shareholders are not required to deposit their shares prior to the General Shareholders' Meeting; (3) cumulative voting is allowed; (4) an oppressed minorities mechanism is in place; or (5) when the minimum percentage of share capital that entitles a shareholder to call for an Extraordinary Shareholders' Meeting is less than or equal to 10% (the sample median). The index ranges from 0 to 5. Source: Company Law or Commercial Code and La Porta *et al.* (1996).
One-share = one-vote	Equals one if the Company Law or Commercial Code of the country requires that ordinary shares carry one vote per share, and 0 otherwise. Equivalently, this variable equals one when the law prohibits the existence of both multiple-voting and non-voting ordinary shares and does not allow firms to set a maximum number of votes per shareholder irrespective of the number of shares she owns, and 0 otherwise. Source: Company Law or Commercial Code and La Porta *et al.* (1996).

Legal Determinants of External Finance   1135

Table I—Continued

Creditor rights	An index aggregating creditor rights. The index is formed by adding 1 when: (1) the country imposes restrictions, such as creditors' consent or minimum dividends, to file for reorganization; (2) secured creditors are able to gain possession of their security once the reorganization petition has been approved (no automatic stay); (3) the debtor does not retain the administration of its property pending the resolution of the reorganization; (4) secured creditors are ranked first in the distribution of the proceeds that result from the disposition of the assets of a bankrupt firm. The index ranges from 0 to 4. Source: Company Law or Bankruptcy Laws and La Porta *et al.* (1996).
Market cap/ sales	The median ratio of the stock market capitalization held by minorities to sales in 1994 for all nonfinancial firms in a given country on the *WorldScope* database. Firm's *j* stock market capitalization held by minorities is computed as the product of the stock market capitalization of firm *j* and the average percentage of common shares not owned by the top three shareholders in the ten largest nonfinancial, privately-owned domestic firms in a given country. A firm is considered privately owned if the State is not a known shareholder in it. Source: *WorldScope*.
Market cap/ cash-flow	The median ratio of the stock market capitalization held by minorities to cash flow in 1994 for all nonfinancial firms in a given country on the *WorldScope* database. Firm's *j* stock market capitalization held by minorities is computed as the product of the stock market capitalization of firm *j* and the average percentage of common shares not owned by the top three shareholders in the ten largest nonfinancial, privately-owned domestic firms in a given country. A firm is considered privately owned if the State is not a known shareholder in it. Source: *WorldScope*.
Debt/sales	Median of the total-debt-to-sales ratio in 1994 for all firms in a given country on the *WorldScope* database. Source: *WorldScope*.
Debt/cash flow	Median of the total-debt-to-cash-flow ratio for all firms in a given country on the *WorldScope* database. Source: *WorldScope*.

initial public offerings of shares in each country between mid-1995 and mid-1996 (the period for which we have been able to obtain the data), also relative to the population. These two variables obviously reflect the stock and the flow of new companies obtaining equity finance. It may make sense to look at both of them because the development of financial markets has accelerated greatly in the last decade, and hence the IPO evidence provides a more recent glance at external equity financing.

Finding data on debt finance that do not just focus on the largest companies is more difficult, since bank financing information is not readily available. However, we do have data on the total bank debt of the private sector in each country, as well as on the total face value of corporate bonds in each country. The aggregate of these two variables relative to the GNP is a plausible measure of the overall ability of the private sector to access debt finance. The fact that we are looking at the whole private sector rather than just corporations may actually be an advantage, since in many countries entrepreneurs raise money on their personal accounts to finance their firms (for example, by mortgaging their properties).

Although the principal focus of our analysis is on the aggregate data, we devote some attention to the microdata on the largest firms, obtained from the WorldScope Database for 1996. For this sample, we also develop measures of equity and debt finance in different countries. For each country, we use four measures of access of their WorldScope companies to capital markets. The first equity variable is the median ratio of market capitalization to sales of the companies in the WorldScope sample for that country, corrected as in the aggregate data by the estimated share of equity of large companies held by outsiders. (We use the exact same correction here as for the aggregate data rather than assembling outside ownership data for all companies.) The second variable for each country is the median ratio of market capitalization to cash flow, again corrected for outside ownership. The first of these two variables is roughly the analog of the aggregate equity valuation variable, and the second is just a different—but perhaps more easily interpretable—normalization.

For debt, we also define two variables for each country. The first is the median ratio of total debt to sales of all the firms in the WorldScope database in that country. The second is the median ratio of total debt to cash flow. The first variable in particular is roughly parallel to our aggregate debt measure.

Our measures of investor protection draw on our earlier work, which has developed measures of shareholder and creditor protections in different legal regimes (LLSV (1996)). Theoretically, we are interested in the legal rights that shareholders and creditors have that enable them to extract a return on their investment from the insiders. For equity, these rights are most importantly the voting rights in the election of directors and other important corporate matters, as well as the rights to make specific claims against the corporation. For debt, these rights cover the liquidation and reorganization procedures when the borrower defaults. In LLSV (1996), we quantified many of these rights for a sample of 49 countries from around the world.

In this article, we use some of the summary variables from the earlier article. First, we know for each country the legal origin of its laws. Second, we have a survey-based estimate of the quality of law enforcement, called "rule of law," which is an assessment by investors in different countries of the law and order environment they operate in. Third, we have measures of how well legal rules themselves protect investors in different countries. For shareholders, we have constructed an antidirector rights index described in detail in Table I. The index aggregates such elements of minority shareholder rights as the ability to vote by mail, the ability to retain control of shares during the shareholders' meeting, the possibility of cumulative voting for directors, the ease of calling an extraordinary shareholder meeting, and perhaps most importantly, the availability of mechanisms of allowing oppressed minority shareholders to make legal claims against the directors (e.g., the possibility of class action suits). We also use another shareholder rights variable, namely the requirement that each ordinary share carry only one vote in the country's commercial law.

For creditors, we use a creditor rights index that aggregates the various rights that secured creditors might have in liquidation and reorganization. Restrictions on the managers' ability to seek unilateral protection from creditors, mandatory dismissal of management in reorganization, lack of automatic stay on assets, and absolute priority for secured creditors all contribute to this index. Again, the precise definition of the index is presented in Table I.

II. Results

A. Presentation of the Data

Table II presents the aggregate data used in this study, with countries organized by origin of their legal system. It also presents comparisons across legal origins. Several interesting results jump out. First, on all measures, common law countries provide companies with better access to equity finance than civil law countries, and particularly French civil law countries. Common law countries have the average ratio of outsider held stock market to GNP of 60 percent, compared to 21 percent for the French civil law countries, 46 percent for the German civil law countries, and 30 percent for the Scandinavian countries. The United States, incidentally, is below the common law average in this sample, which is not entirely surprising given that it is growing much slower than Hong Kong, Malaysia, or Singapore. Common law countries have 35 listed firms per one million people (on average), compared to 10 for the French civil law countries, 17 for the German civil law countries, and 27 for the Scandinavian countries. It is actually quite striking to see that France has 8 listed firms per million people, Italy has 4, and Germany has 5, compared to 36 in the United Kingdom, 30 in the United States, and 128 in Israel. Finally, during the year we look at, common law countries averaged 2.2 IPOs per million people, compared to 0.2 of an IPO for the French origin, 0.12 of an IPO for German origin, and 2.1 IPOs for the Scandinavian origin. During that year, Germany had 7 IPOs, France had 10, while the United States had 803 and India had 1114. On all the equity measures, the differences in means between the English and the French origin are statistically significant.

As Table II indicates, our antidirector rights measure is by far the highest in common law countries, intermediate in Scandinavian and German civil law countries, and the lowest in the French civil law countries. In contrast, there is not much difference in the incidence of one-share-one-vote rules. These results give a preliminary indication that low shareholder protection may be the reason why some legal origins have smaller equity markets as well as lower access of firms to equity finance.

Aggregate debt as a share of GNP is 68 percent for common law countries, 45 percent for the French civil law countries, 97 percent for the German civil law countries, and 57 percent for the Scandinavian countries. Again, debt finance is more accessible in the English than in the French origin. However, indebtedness is even higher in the German civil law countries—also sometimes described as countries with bank-focused financial systems. The creditor rights

Table II

External Capital Markets

This table classifies countries by legal origin. Definitions for each of the variables can be found in Table I. Panel B reports tests of means for the different legal origins.

Country	External Cap/GNP	Domestic Firms/Pop	IPOs/Pop	Debt/GNP	GDP growth	Log GNP	Rule of Law	Antidirector Rights	One-Share = One-Vote	Creditor Rights
					Panel A: Means					
Australia	0.49	63.55	—	0.76	3.06	12.64	10.00	4	0	1
Canada	0.39	40.86	4.93	0.72	3.36	13.26	10.00	4	0	1
Hong Kong	1.18	88.16	5.16	—	7.57	11.56	8.22	4	1	4
India	0.31	7.79	1.24	0.29	4.34	12.50	4.17	2	0	4
Ireland	0.27	20.00	0.75	0.38	4.25	10.73	7.80	3	0	1
Israel	0.25	127.60	1.80	0.66	4.39	11.19	4.82	3	0	4
Kenya	—	2.24	—	—	4.79	8.83	5.42	3	0	4
Malaysia	1.48	25.15	2.89	0.84	6.90	11.00	6.78	3	1	4
New Zealand	0.28	69.00	0.66	0.90	1.67	10.69	10.00	4	0	3
Nigeria	0.27	1.68	—	—	3.43	10.36	2.73	3	0	4
Pakistan	0.18	5.88	—	0.27	5.50	10.88	3.03	4	1	4
Singapore	1.18	80.00	5.67	0.60	1.68	11.68	8.57	3	1	3
South Africa	1.45	16.00	0.05	0.93	7.48	10.92	4.42	4	0	4
Sri Lanka	0.11	11.94	0.11	0.25	4.04	9.28	1.90	2	0	3
Thailand	0.56	6.70	0.56	0.93	7.70	11.72	6.25	3	0	3
UK	1.00	35.68	2.01	1.13	2.27	13.86	8.57	4	0	4
US	0.58	30.11	3.11	0.81	2.74	15.67	10.00	5	0	1
Zimbabwe	0.18	5.81	—	—	2.17	8.63	3.68	3	0	4
English origin avg	**0.60**	**35.45**	**2.23**	**0.68**	**4.30**	**11.41**	**6.46**	**3.39**	**0.22**	**3.11**
Argentina	0.07	4.58	0.20	0.19	1.40	12.40	5.35	4	0	1
Belgium	0.17	15.50	0.30	0.38	2.46	12.29	10.00	0	0	2
Brazil	0.18	3.48	0.00	0.39	3.95	13.03	6.32	3	1	1
Chile	0.80	19.92	0.35	0.63	3.35	10.69	7.02	3	1	2
Colombia	0.14	3.13	0.05	0.19	4.38	10.82	2.08	1	0	0
Ecuador	—	13.18	0.09	—	4.55	9.49	6.67	2	0	4
Egypt	0.08	3.48	—	—	6.13	10.53	4.17	2	0	4
France	0.23	8.05	0.17	0.96	2.54	14.07	8.98	2	0	0
Greece	0.07	21.60	0.30	0.23	2.46	11.25	6.18	1	1	1
Indonesia	0.15	1.15	0.10	0.42	6.38	11.84	3.98	2	0	4
Italy	0.08	3.91	0.31	0.55	2.82	13.94	8.33	0	0	2
Jordan	—	23.75	—	0.70	1.20	8.49	4.35	1	0	—
Mexico	0.22	2.28	0.03	0.47	3.07	12.69	5.35	0	0	0
Netherlands	0.52	21.13	0.66	1.08	2.55	12.68	10.00	2	0	2
Peru	0.40	9.47	0.13	0.27	2.82	10.92	2.50	2	1	0
Philippines	0.10	2.90	0.27	0.10	0.30	10.44	2.73	4	0	0
Portugal	0.08	19.50	0.50	0.64	3.52	11.41	8.68	2	0	1
Spain	0.17	9.71	0.07	0.75	3.27	13.19	7.80	2	0	2
Turkey	0.18	2.93	0.05	0.15	5.05	12.08	5.18	2	0	2
Uruguay	—	7.00	0.00	0.26	1.96	9.40	5.00	1	1	2
Venezuela	0.08	4.28	0.00	0.10	2.65	10.99	6.37	1	0	—
French origin avg	**0.21**	**10.00**	**0.19**	**0.45**	**3.18**	**11.55**	**6.05**	**1.76**	**0.24**	**1.58**
Austria	0.06	13.87	0.25	0.79	2.74	12.13	10.00	2	0	3
Germany	0.13	5.14	0.08	1.12	2.60	14.46	9.23	1	0	3
Japan	0.62	17.78	0.26	1.22	4.13	15.18	8.98	3	1	2
South Korea	0.44	15.88	0.02	0.74	9.52	12.73	5.35	2	1	3
Switzerland	0.62	33.85	—	—	1.18	12.44	10.00	1	0	1
Taiwan	0.88	14.22	0.00	—	11.56	12.34	8.52	3	0	2
German origin avg	**0.46**	**16.79**	**0.12**	**0.97**	**5.29**	**13.21**	**8.68**	**2.00**	**0.33**	**2.33**
Denmark	0.21	50.40	1.80	0.34	2.09	11.84	10.00	3	0	3
Finland	0.25	13.00	0.60	0.75	2.40	11.49	10.00	2	0	1
Norway	0.22	33.00	4.50	0.64	3.43	11.62	10.00	3	0	2
Sweden	0.51	12.66	1.66	0.55	1.79	12.28	10.00	2	0	2
Scandinavian origin avg	**0.30**	**27.26**	**2.14**	**0.57**	**2.42**	**11.80**	**10.00**	**2.50**	**0.00**	**2.00**
Sample average	**0.40**	**21.59**	**1.02**	**0.59**	**3.79**	**11.72**	**6.85**	**2.44**	**0.22**	**2.30**

Legal Determinants of External Finance   1139

Table II—Continued

Country	External Cap/GNP	Domestic Firms/Pop	IPOs/Pop	Debt/GNP	GDP growth	Log GNP	Rule of Law	Antidirector Rights	One-Share = One-Vote	Creditor Rights
				Panel B: Tests of Means (*t*-statistics)						
Common vs civil law	3.12	3.16	3.97	1.33	1.23	−1.06	−0.77	5.24	−0.03	3.61
English vs French origin	3.29	3.16	4.50	2.29	1.97	−0.28	0.51	5.13	−0.11	3.61
English vs German origin	0.68	1.24	2.34	−1.88	−0.78	−2.31	−1.82	3.66	−0.52	1.43
English vs Scand. origin	1.25	0.44	0.08	0.71	1.81	−0.44	−15.57	2.14	2.20	1.71
French vs German origin	−2.38	−1.85	0.78	−3.39	−1.96	−2.48	−2.55	−0.47	−0.45	−1.29
French vs Scand. origin	−0.91	−3.31	−5.45	0.82	0.97	−0.33	−20.80	−1.25	2.50	−0.60
German vs Scand. origin	0.94	−1.21	−2.76	2.71	1.32	2.11	−11.29	−0.98	1.58	0.63

index is the highest in common law countries, intermediate in German and Scandinavian civil law countries, and the lowest in the French civil law countries. Again, low rights line up with small markets when we compare French and English origin, but German civil law countries are somewhat of a mystery. A possible explanation of this mystery is suggested by Rajan and Zingales (1995), who find that German companies have high overall liabilities, though not necessarily high debt per se. Overall, the results on debt, like those on equity, suggest that legal rules influence external finance.

Table III abstracts away from origin and examines in more detail the determinants of external financing. It suggests that stronger antidirector rights (and perhaps also one-share-one-vote rules) are associated with larger and broader equity markets. The association between creditor rights and indebtedness is more tenuous. Better law enforcement, as measured by rule of law, is associated with more domestic firms and IPOs per capita, as well as a greater ratio of private sector debt to GNP. There is also some weak evidence that larger countries have higher debt. Table III confirms our preliminary impressions from Table II, points to the importance of law enforcement as well as of the legal rules, and indicates the need for more systematic testing in a regression framework.

B. Regression Analysis

Tables IV–VII present a series of regressions of capital market size measures on various controls as well as estimates of the quality of investor protection. We include several control variables in all the regressions. First, we control for historical GDP growth because growth is likely to affect both valuations and market breadth. Second, we control for the (logarithm of) real GNP on the theory that setting up capital markets might be an increasing returns to scale activity, and therefore larger economies might have larger capital markets. Third, because all the regressions include our rule of law measure, and the correlation between rule of law and GDP per capita is 0.87, we do *not* include GDP per capita as a control. Including it does not have much of an effect on the coefficients on legal rights variables, but does eliminate the significance of rule of law. In a sense, rule of law is a theoretically more appropriate variable.

Table III

Investor Rights and External Finance

This table classifies countries according to their ranking in: (a) Antidirector Rights; (b) One-Share = One-Vote; (c) Creditor Rights; (4) Rule of Law; (5) GDP Growth; and (5) Log GNP. For each panel, the table shows the average value of different external finance measures for the bottom quartile, the middle two quartiles, and the top quartile. The last row of each panel shows the *t*-statistic for a test of means between the bottom and the top quartiles.

	External Cap/ GNP	Domestic Firms/Pop	IPOs/Pop	Debt/GNP
Means by antidirector rights				
Bottom 25%	0.19	12.05	0.14	0.44
Mid 50%	0.39	20.03	0.97	0.63
Top 25%	0.58	35.68	2.05	0.63
Test of means (*t*-statistic)				
Bottom 25% vs. Top 25%	−2.50	−2.35	−2.55	−1.22
Means by one-share = one-vote				
Not One Vote	0.32	20.10	0.87	0.59
One Vote	0.65	26.76	1.48	0.56
Test of means (*t*-statistic)				
One Vote vs Not One Vote	−2.61	−0.76	−1.08	0.29
Means by creditor rights				
Bottom 25%	0.27	18.43	0.85	0.49
Mid 50%	0.40	18.25	0.62	0.66
Top 25%	0.59	31.30	2.37	0.65
Test of means (*t*-statistic)				
Bottom 25% vs. Top 25%	−2.09	−1.11	−1.95	−1.15
Means by rule of law				
Bottom 25%	0.28	8.51	0.28	0.34
Mid 50%	0.47	22.36	0.89	0.63
Top 25%	0.36	33.08	1.85	0.70
Test of means (*t*-statistic)				
Bottom 25% vs. Top 25%	−0.73	−4.11	−2.30	−3.84
Means by GDP growth				
Bottom 25%	0.42	22.83	0.74	0.54
Mid 50%	0.28	15.90	0.86	0.60
Top 25%	0.62	30.43	1.64	0.62
Test of means (*t*-statistic)				
Bottom 25% vs. Top 25%	−1.05	−0.61	−1.20	−0.56
Means by log GNP				
Bottom 25%	0.25	15.36	0.27	0.43
Mid 50%	0.46	26.12	1.33	0.50
Top 25%	0.39	19.82	0.98	0.82
Test of means (*t*-statistic)				
Bottom 25% vs. Top 25%	−1.31	−0.63	−1.24	−3.26

Table IV looks at the ratio of our estimate of externally held market capitalization to GNP. Not surprisingly, the results show that faster growing economies have higher capitalization stock markets: a 1 percent faster growth rate between 1970 and 1993 raises the ratio by about 4 to 6 percentage points (where the worldwide mean is 40 and the standard deviation is 37 percentage

Table IV

External Market Capitalization of Equity/GNP Regressions

Ordinary least squares regressions of the cross-section of 49 countries around the world. The dependent variable is "External Cap." The independent variables are (1) GDP Growth; (2) Log GNP; (3) Rule of law; (4) French origin; (5) German origin; (6) Scandinavian origin; (7) Antidirector Rights; (8) One-share = One-Vote. Standard errors are shown in parentheses.

Independent Variables	Dependent Variable: External Cap/GNP				
GDP growth	0.0617[b]	0.0544[b]	0.0584[b]	0.0562[b]	0.0441[b]
	(0.0232)	(0.0201)	(0.0238)	(0.0242)	(0.0209)
Log GNP	−0.0129	−0.0168	0.0038	−0.0053	0.0091
	(0.0333)	(0.0334)	(0.0386)	(0.0382)	(0.0324)
Rule of law	0.0378[c]	0.0455[b]	0.0417	0.0424[b]	0.0437[c]
	(0.0206)	(0.0203)	(0.0250)	(0.0243)	(0.0231)
French origin			−0.3225[a]	−0.2142[c]	−0.3341[a]
			(0.1131)	(0.1194)	(0.1084)
German origin			−0.2962[c]	−0.1849	−0.3230[b]
			(0.1497)	(0.1599)	(0.1438)
Scandinavian origin			−0.3391[b]	−0.2816[c]	−0.3056[b]
			(0.1373)	(0.1479)	(0.1218)
Antidirector rights	0.1171[a]			0.0675[c]	
	(0.0353)			(0.0354)	
One-share = one-vote		0.2745[b]			0.2890[b]
		(0.1235)			(0.1111)
Intercept	−0.2437	0.0100[b]	0.0336	−0.0860	−0.0475
	(0.2880)	(0.3063)	(0.3677)	(0.3629)	(0.3066)
Observations	45	45	45	45	45
Adjusted R²	0.2936	0.2347	0.2867	0.3016	0.3801

[a] Significant at 1%; [b] Significant at 5%; [c] Significant at 10%.

points). Country size does not matter. The coefficient on the rule of law is around 4 in all specifications: raising rule of law from the sample average of 6.85 to a perfect 10 increases outsider held market capitalization by about 13 percent of the GNP.

The five specifications in Table IV look at the different combinations of origin dummies and shareholder rights variables. We find that individually, both the antidirector rights score and the one-share-one-vote dummy have a relatively large effect on the market capitalization ratio. Raising the antidirector rights score from its French origin average of 1.76 to its common law average of 3.39 raises the market capitalization to GNP ratio by 19 percentage points—half of the difference between the French and the English means. Countries with mandatory one-share-one-vote rules have a 27 percentage points higher ratio. Each of the three civil law families has an about 30 percentage points lower outsider held market capitalization relative to GNP than the common law family does. The reason that these results looked less pronounced in the raw data in Table II is that German and Scandinavian origin countries have extremely high rule of law scores, which contribute to larger stock markets. Once these scores are controlled for, all civil law families have much smaller stock markets than those in common law countries, presumably because of inferior investor protections.

The last two columns of Table IV include both the origin dummies and the two shareholder rights variables, included one at a time. The coefficients on all variables fall relative to their values when included in isolation. Taken on face value, the estimates suggest that our shareholder rights variables account for some of the difference between relative market capitalizations of different legal families, but that the family effects are also significant.

The results on the number of listed domestic firms per (million) capita are presented in Table V. Here, higher GDP growth is not associated with a statistically significantly higher number of listed firms, suggesting that the result of Table IV is explained by a higher valuation of listed firms in faster growing economies rather than by a higher number of listed firms. The results also show that countries with bigger economies have fewer listed firms per capita, other things equal. Rule of law again comes in very significantly: a move from the world mean of 6.85 to a perfect score of 10 is associated with 15 more domestic listed firms per million people (the world mean is 22). When included alone, our antidirector rights score is highly significant: a move from the French to the English mean in that score raises the number of listed domestic firms per million people by 12. The one-share-one-vote dummy is no longer significant, although it has a relatively large estimated effect of the predicted sign.

The dummies for civil law origins again point to much narrower stock markets for countries in the French, German, and Scandinavian legal families than in common law countries. The parameter estimates of about -20 indicate that civil law countries have about 20 fewer listed firms per million people. This is 0.8 of a standard deviation, and is a pretty impressive estimate given that the sample-wide mean of the dependent variable is 21. When the antidirector rights score is included together with origin dummies, the coefficient estimates on the dummies fall only slightly, while the coefficient on the antidirector score falls sharply. As far as market breadth is concerned, there is more to the difference between legal families than is captured by our antidirector rights score.

Our last, and relatively direct, measure of firms' access to capital markets is the number of IPOs between mid-1995 and mid-1996, again per million people. In Table VI, the GDP growth rate has a statistically significant effect on the number of IPOs in specifications that control for legal origin; the coefficient

Legal Determinants of External Finance   1143

Table V

Domestic Firms/Population Regressions

Ordinary least squares regressions of the cross-section of 49 countries around the world. The dependent variable is "Domestic Firms/Pop." The independent variables are (1) GDP growth; (2) Log GNP; (3) Rule of law; (4) French origin; (5) German origin; (6) Scandinavian origin; (7) Antidirector rights; (8) One-share = one-vote. Standard errors are shown in parentheses.

Independent Variables	Dependent Variable: Domestic Firms/Pop				
GDP growth	1.0767 (1.4000)	1.3461 (1.3318)	1.0111 (1.2661)	0.8950 (1.2733)	0.5763 (0.9884)
Log GNP	−4.3181[b] (1.6588)	−4.0659[b] (1.7697)	−2.9126 (1.7698)	−3.3073[b] (1.8165)	−2.7979 (1.6816)
Rule of law	4.5093[a] (1.2579)	4.8584[a] (1.4023)	4.8422[a] (1.3616)	4.8577[a] (1.3377)	4.9582[a] (1.3356)
French origin			−21.9069[a] (7.4014)	−17.5313[b] (8.9183)	−22.5204[a] (7.2884)
German origin			−25.1485[a] (8.4882)	−20.5611[b] (9.7216)	−26.3007[a] (7.8639)
Scandinavian origin			−22.2680[b] (10.1744)	−19.9575[c] (10.0144)	−21.3009[b] (10.0541)
Antidirector rights	7.3034[a] (1.8052)			2.7304 (1.6591)	
One-share = one-vote		8.1382 (7.5228)			10.0675 (6.3165)
Intercept	19.3863 (15.4445)	29.0780[c] (17.0108)	33.0485 (20.6317)	28.6987 (21.4015)	30.6212 (20.2510)
Number of observations	49	49	49	49	49
Adjusted R²	0.2198	0.1153	0.2197	0.2495	0.2681

[a] Significant at 1%; [b] Significant at 5%; [c] Significant at 10%.

estimates indicate that a one percentage point higher historical growth rate raises the number of IPOs by about 0.2, or less than one-tenth of a standard deviation. The size of the economy is again insignificant. Rule of law has a large positive effect on the number of IPOs: the move from the world mean to a perfect 10 in the rule of law raises the number of IPOs by 0.8, where the world mean is 1 per million people per year. The antidirector rights score is highly significant (just as in Table V): moving from the French to the English origin mean raises the number of IPOs by 0.8. In contrast, one-share-one-vote is not significant when included alone, just like what we found in Table V.

The results on the effects of the legal origin are a bit different than before. The French and German civil law countries average 2 fewer IPOs (per million

1144   *The Journal of Finance*

Table VI

Initial Public Offerings/Population Regressions

Ordinary least squares regressions of the cross-section of 49 countries around the world. The dependent variable is "IPOs/Pop." The independent variables are (1) GDP growth; (2) Log GNP; (3) Rule of law; (4) French origin; (5) German origin; (6) Scandinavian origin; (7) Antidirector rights; (8) One-share = one-vote. Standard errors are shown in parentheses.

Independent Variables	Dependent Variable: IPOs/Pop				
GDP growth	0.1222	0.1320	0.1937[b]	0.1916[c]	0.1633[b]
	(0.1281)	(0.1193)	(0.1012)	(0.1037)	(0.0744)
Log GNP	−0.1672	−0.1225	0.0662	0.0452	0.1255
	(0.1453)	(0.1692)	(0.1086)	(0.1129)	(0.1002)
Rule of law	0.2549[a]	0.2943[a]	0.2122[b]	0.2108[b]	0.2127[a]
	(0.0889)	(0.0926)	(0.0842)	(0.0830)	(0.0731)
French origin			−1.5982[a]	−1.2949[a]	−1.6677[a]
			(0.3552)	(0.3696)	(0.3132)
German origin			−2.8118[a]	−2.5450[a]	−3.027[a]
			(0.5698)	(0.5909)	(0.5543)
Scandinavian origin			−0.3123	−0.1421	−0.1367
			(0.8666)	(0.8486)	(0.8414)
Antidirector rights	0.5352[a]			0.1937[c]	
	(0.1364)			(0.0989)	
One-share = one-vote		0.6359			1.0287[a]
		(0.5422)			(0.3450)
Intercept	−0.5546	−0.2720	−0.9201	−1.3071	−1.7268
	(1.3472)	(1.7534)	(1.3233)	(1.3204)	(1.2088)
Number of observations	41	41	41	41	41
Adjusted R^2	0.3082	0.1571	0.4907	0.4927	0.5643

[a] Significant at 1%; [b] Significant at 5%; [c] Significant at 10%.

people) than the common law countries—more than a standard deviation of the IPO variable. Scandinavian countries, however, do not appear to have fewer IPOs in any of the specifications. The adverse effects of the French and German origin on IPOs remain once we include the antidirector rights score and the one-share-one-vote dummy. Both of our rights measures are significant after controlling for origin. Overall, the results in this table, like those of the previous one, show that our shareholder rights measures explain some of the variation in equity finance across countries, but that there is more to the origin effect than is captured by these measures. The regressions also confirm all our earlier results that civil law—particularly of the French or German

Legal Determinants of External Finance   1145

Table VII
Debt/GNP Regressions

Ordinary least squares regressions of the cross-section of 49 countries around the world. The dependent variable is "Debt/GNP." The independent variables are (1) GDP growth; (2) Log GNP; (3) Rule of law; (4) French origin; (5) German origin; (6) Scandinavian origin; (7) Creditor rights. Standard errors are shown in parentheses.

Independent Variables	Dependent Variable: Debt/GNP		
GDP growth	0.0310[c]	0.0251[c]	0.0197
	(0.0171)	(0.0134)	(0.0152)
Log GNP	0.0667[b]	0.0370	0.0404
	(0.0252)	(0.0255)	(0.0250)
Rule of law	0.0615[a]	0.0698[a]	0.0694[a]
	(0.0132)	(0.0147)	(0.0148)
French origin		−0.1516[b]	−0.1163
		(0.0740)	(0.0825)
German origin		0.1080	0.1082
		(0.1010)	(0.0982)
Scandinavian origin		−0.2764[b]	−0.2618[b]
		(0.1037)	(0.1075)
Creditor rights	0.0518[c]		0.0270
	(0.0267)		(0.0298)
Intercept	−0.8621[a]	−0.3496	−0.4414
	(0.2579)	(0.2524)	(1.341)
Number of observations	39	39	39
Adjusted R^2	0.5522	0.5191	0.5984

[a] Significant at 1%; [b] Significant at 5%; [c] Significant at 10%.

variety—reduces the breadth of the stock markets. In Scandinavian countries, the IPOs picture is brighter than that for the number of listed issues.

Table VII presents the results for our aggregated indebtedness measure. Note a somewhat smaller sample owing to the lack of data. In the specification that does not include origin dummies, both the level of the nation's GNP and the historical growth of GDP are associated with higher total debt relative to GNP; however, the statistical significance of these results does not carry over once origin is controlled for. In the specification without origin dummies, the coefficient on the creditor rights index is also statistically significant, but this result loses significance, and the coefficient falls sharply once origin is controlled for. The effect of rule of law is more robust, as before. Rule of law yet again has a large and statistically significant effect on the size of the capital market: the move from world mean to a perfect 10 is associated with a 20 percentage point increase in debt to GNP ratio, or 0.7 of a standard deviation.

The origin effects are interesting. Relative to common law countries, French legal origin countries have a lower ratio of debt to GNP (which becomes insignificant when creditor rights are also included, perhaps because of a high negative correlation between creditor rights and the French dummy). French origin countries have a 12 to 15 percentage point lower ratio of debt to GNP, where the overall sample mean is 59 percent. German origin countries again have a higher ratio of debt to GNP, but the effect is not statistically significant. Finally, Scandinavian origin countries have a hugely (almost one standard deviation) lower ratio of debt to GNP, a difference not much diminished by the inclusion of the creditor rights index. In sum, French and Scandinavian civil law countries do have more narrow debt markets than common law countries, a difference not adequately captured by our creditor rights index.

The overall results of Tables IV to VII are straightforward to summarize. We find that good law enforcement has a large effect on the valuation and breadth of both debt and equity markets. We also find large systematic differences between countries from different legal origins in the size and breadth of their capital markets. Whether measured by capitalization of equity held by outsiders, by the number of listed firms, or by IPOs, common law countries have larger equity markets than civil law, and particularly French civil law, countries, and at least part of the differences is captured by the differences in shareholder protections *that we measure*. Common law countries also have larger aggregate liabilities than do the French civil law and Scandinavian, though not German, countries. Our measure of creditor rights is less effective in capturing the difference between origins than our measure of shareholder rights. The results add up to a rather consistent case that the quality of the legal environment has a significant effect on the ability of firms in different countries to raise external finance.

C. Who gets External Finance?

Our analysis has focused on aggregate measures of the valuation and breadth of markets. An alternative approach is to look at microdata. The key issue about these data is that they cover primarily large firms that may have exposure to international capital markets, access to government finance, and captive banks. In this section, we attempt a very preliminary investigation of whether large firms are different, and in what ways.

To this end, we examine the WorldScope Database for 1996, which provides data for 38 of our 49 countries. The exclusion of smaller firms is pronounced both in that only a fraction of listed firms is included from each country, and in that relatively fewer firms are included from the emerging markets. For rich countries, WorldScope appears to cover 30–50 percent of the listed firms, whereas for developing countries, the share may be just a couple of percentage points (see the last column of Table VIII). For example, we have 2161 firms for the United States compared to nearly 7,770 listed firms, 93 firms for Italy compared to 223 listed firms, and 54 firms for India compared to 7,000 listed firms.

Legal Determinants of External Finance   1147

Table VIII

External Funding at the Firm Level

The sample of thirty-eight countries includes all the firms on the Worldscope database for 1996. The table shows median values for all the firms in each country. Panel A show the medians based on a classification by legal origin. The definition for each of the variables can be found in Table I. Panel B gives the tests of means for the different legal origins. Panel C shows mean of medians and *t*-tests for countries sorted by levels of "External Cap/GNP." Panel D shows mean of medians and *t*-tests for countries sorted by "Debt/GNP."

Country	Market Cap/Sales	Market Cap/Cash-Flow	Debt/Sales	Debt/Cash-Flow	WorldScope Firms/Domestic Firms
Panel A: Median Values by Legal Origin					
Australia	0.75	6.15	0.19	1.42	0.12
Canada	0.76	4.66	0.30	2.07	0.26
Hong Kong	0.66	4.01	0.31	2.50	0.12
India	0.73	8.75	0.47	4.26	0.01
Ireland	0.75	3.51	0.16	0.74	0.29
Israel	0.34	3.79	0.17	1.41	0.03
Malaysia	1.46	6.82	0.24	1.45	0.23
New Zealand	0.38	4.26	0.23	2.74	0.11
Pakistan	0.50	4.18	0.33	2.34	0.05
Singapore	0.83	5.68	0.07	0.83	0.19
South Africa	0.40	3.23	0.29	2.06	0.22
Thailand	0.71	4.65	0.54	3.45	0.32
UK	0.64	5.77	0.11	1.06	0.51
US	0.67	6.70	0.18	1.86	0.28
Average English origin	**0.69**	**5.16**	**0.26**	**2.01**	**0.20**
Argentina	0.63	4.18	0.28	1.78	0.10
Belgium	0.16	2.28	0.25	2.52	0.39
Brazil	0.24	1.97	0.18	1.52	0.11
Chile	1.68	8.15	0.29	1.59	0.13
France	0.29	4.28	0.19	2.36	0.67
Greece	0.25	5.99	0.21	2.55	0.04
Indonesia	0.48	3.03	0.37	3.25	0.23
Italy	0.17	2.21	0.32	3.04	0.44
Mexico	0.47	4.06	0.66	1.54	0.29
Netherlands	0.27	3.93	0.11	1.33	0.42
Philippines	1.61	5.17	0.29	0.86	0.14
Portugal	0.19	2.48	0.33	3.73	0.17
Spain	0.27	3.28	0.25	2.33	0.15
Turkey	0.46	2.87	0.11	0.50	0.12
Average French origin	**0.51**	**3.85**	**0.27**	**2.06**	**0.24**
Austria	0.21	2.29	0.24	2.38	0.17
Germany	0.21	3.29	0.10	1.24	0.55
Japan	0.63	13.80	0.34	6.99	0.50
South Korea	0.29	—	0.58	—	0.09
Switzerland	0.26	3.06	0.30	3.14	0.36
Taiwan	2.21	14.94	0.26	2.16	0.20
Average German origin	**0.63**	**7.48**	**0.30**	**3.18**	**0.31**
Denmark	0.30	3.30	0.22	1.88	0.38
Finland	0.30	2.90	0.31	2.58	0.80
Norway	0.49	3.70	0.36	3.62	0.46
Sweden	0.40	3.10	0.21	1.59	0.82
Average Scandinavian origin	**0.37**	**3.25**	**0.28**	**2.42**	**0.61**
Sample average	**0.58**	**4.77**	**0.27**	**2.24**	**0.28**

Table VIII—Continued

Country	Market Cap/Sales	Market Cap/Cash-Flow	Debt/Sales	Debt/Cash-Flow	WorldScope Firms/Domestic Firms
Panel B: Tests of Means (t-statistics)					
Common vs. civil law	1.04	0.64	−0.60	−0.87	
England vs. France	1.10	2.11	−0.36	−0.14	
England vs. Germany	0.20	−1.33	−0.71	−1.61	
England vs. Scandinavia	2.17	2.38	−0.32	−0.73	
France vs. Germany	−0.42	−2.04	−0.43	−1.59	
France vs. Scandinavia	0.54	0.69	−0.06	−0.68	
Germany vs. Scandinavia	0.64	1.32	0.30	0.64	

	Panel C: Sorted by External Cap/GNP		Panel D: Sorted by Debt/GNP	
Means				
Bottom 25%	0.29	3.23	0.26	1.94
Mid 50%	0.53	4.31	0.29	2.17
Top 25%	0.97	7.28	0.24	2.52
Test of means				
Bottom 25% vs. Top 25%	−3.03	−2.68	0.33	−0.80

Table VIII presents the results for the two debt and two equity variables developed for each country, and described in Section I and in Table I. To begin, Panel A presents the data on country medians, and Panel B shows the *t*-tests of comparison between families. For the outsider held market capitalization to sales ratio (which is closest to the variable in Table IV), we get the same pattern of results as before: common law countries have a higher outsider-held capitalization of the largest companies than does any other group, with the difference being most pronounced for the Scandinavian and the French origin. However, the statistical significance of the results is considerably lower. When we normalize by cash flow rather than sales, we actually get that the German legal origin countries have the highest capitalization, in part because of extremely high market valuations in Japan and Taiwan. Basically, the picture on equity for the largest firms is similar to the aggregate picture, but less pronounced. These results, incidentally, continue to hold if we consider, for each country, the median market capitalization to sales and to cash flow ratios, without correcting for the share of equity held by insiders.

For both measures of debt, the differences between the English law, the French, and the Scandinavian origins essentially disappear, although debt of large companies in German origin countries remains the highest, especially relative to cash flow. Still, the similarity of these debt numbers across origins is remarkable, and suggests to us—albeit somewhat indirectly—a potentially important conclusion: large publicly traded firms get external debt finance in almost all countries, regardless of legal rules. A possible reason for this is debt financing *of the largest publicly traded firms* comes from the government and its banks. The countries whose large companies have unusually high debt levels compared to these countries aggregate ratio of liabilities to GNP are Mexico, India, and South Korea—all with heavy state intervention in banking. We cannot be sure given the available data that this is the right interpretation.

Legal Determinants of External Finance   1149

Still, the focus on large, publicly-traded firms in assessing the ability of firms in different countries to raise external funds may be misleading.

Panels C and D focus even more directly on the comparison of the results for large firms with our earlier results. In Panel C, we sort countries into bottom 25 percent, middle 50 percent, and top 25 percent by their aggregate ratio of external market capitalization to GNP (the variable in Table IV). For each of these three groups, we compute the average of the market capitalization to sales ratio and the average market capitalization to cash flow ratio for the countries in that group, from Panel A. The results in Panel C confirm the consistency of the aggregate and large firm data for equity: countries with high aggregate outsider held market capitalization are also the countries with the relatively high relative valuation of the largest firms. In Panel D, we make the same calculation for the two debt variables used in Panel A. The striking result is that our debt measure for large firms does not vary nearly as much as the aggregate measure: large publicly traded firms in countries with low aggregate debt do not have unusually low debt levels. The largest firms appear to get external finance even in countries where smaller listed firms do not.

III. Conclusion

The results of this article confirm that the legal environment—as described by both legal rules and their enforcement—matters for the size and extent of a country's capital markets. Because a good legal environment protects the potential financiers against expropriation by entrepreneurs, it raises their willingness to surrender funds in exchange for securities, and hence expands the scope of capital markets.

Our results show that civil law, and particularly French civil law, countries, have both the weakest investor protections and the least developed capital markets, especially as compared to common law countries. Our measures of investor protection capture some, though not all, of the difference between legal environments across origins. It is interesting to note in this regard that our earlier article (LLSV (1996)) has been criticized for choosing measures of investor protection that paint a selectively bleak picture of investor protection in the French civil law family. If anything, the results of this article show the reverse: our measures of investor protection do not fully account for outside investors' predicament in these countries.

While this article has further developed the theme that legal environments differ across countries, and that these differences matter for financial markets, we have again refrained from answering the deeper question: what is it about the civil law family, and particularly about the French civil law subfamily, that accounts for the relative unfriendliness of laws to investors? Is it just by coincidence that these countries have investor-unfriendly laws? Or, have the laws been designed to keep investors relatively weak, and to assure family firms and the state a larger role in economic development? Alternatively, are poor laws just a proxy for an environment that is hostile to institutional development, including that of capital markets? In this connection, we have found some evidence (La Porta, Lopez-de-Silanes, Shleifer, and Vishny (1997)) that public and private institutions are less effective in countries exhibiting low levels of trust among citizens. It is possible that some broad underlying factor, related to trust, influences the development of all institutions in a country, including laws and capital markets. We cannot resolve these issues now, but hope to address them in future work.

REFERENCES

Boycko, Maxim, Andrei Shleifer, and Robert W. Vishny, 1993, Privatizing Russia, *Brookings Papers on Economic Activity* 2, 139–192.

David, Rene, and John Brierley, 1985, *Major Legal Systems in the World Today*, (Stevens and Sons, London, U.K.).

King, Robert and Ross Levine, 1993, Finance and growth: Schumpeter might be right, *Quarterly Journal of Economics* 108, 717–738.

La Porta, Rafael, Florencio Lopez-de-Silanes, Andrei Shleifer, and Robert W. Vishny, 1996, Law and Finance, NBER Working paper 5661.

La Porta, Rafael, Florencio Lopez-de-Silanes, Andrei Shleifer, and Robert W. Vishny, 1997, Trust in large organizations, *American Economic Review Paper and Proceedings* 87, 333–338.

Levine, Ross, 1996, Financial development and economic growth, *Journal of Economic Literature*, forthcoming.

Modigliani, Franco, and Enrico Perotti, 1996, Protection of minority interest and development of security markets, Mimeo, MIT.

Pagano, Marco, F. Panetta, and Luigi Zingales, 1995, Why do companies go public?: An empirical analysis, NBER Working paper 5367.

Rajan, Raghuram, and Luigi Zingales, 1995, What do we know from capital structure: Some evidence from the international data, *Journal of Finance* 50, 1421–1460.

Rajan, Raghuram, and Luigi Zingales, 1996, Financial dependence and growth, NBER Working paper 5758.

Reynolds, Thomas, and Arturo Flores, 1989, *Foreign Law: Current Sources of Basic Legislation in Jurisdictions of the World*, (Rothman and Co., Littleton, CO).

Shleifer, Andrei, and Robert W. Vishny, 1997, A survey of corporate governance, *Journal of Finance*, 52, 737–783.

[6]

Law and Finance

Rafael La Porta, Florencio Lopez-de-Silanes,
and Andrei Shleifer

Harvard University

Robert W. Vishny

University of Chicago

This paper examines legal rules covering protection of corporate shareholders and creditors, the origin of these rules, and the quality of their enforcement in 49 countries. The results show that common-law countries generally have the strongest, and French-civil-law countries the weakest, legal protections of investors, with German- and Scandinavian-civil-law countries located in the middle. We also find that concentration of ownership of shares in the largest public companies is negatively related to investor protections, consistent with the hypothesis that small, diversified shareholders are unlikely to be important in countries that fail to protect their rights.

I. Overview of the Issues

In the traditional finance of Modigliani and Miller (1958), securities are recognized by their cash flows. For example, debt has a fixed promised stream of interest payments, whereas equity entitles its

We are grateful to Mark Chen, Steven Friedman, Magdalena Lopez-Morton, and Katya Zhuravskaya for excellent research assistance; to Robert Barro, Eric Berglof, Bernard Black, Bertyl G. Bylund, Francesco DeNozza, Yoshikata Fukui, Edward Glaeser, Zvi Griliches, Oliver Hart, Martin Hellwig, James Hines, Louis Kaplow, Raghu Rajan, Roberta Romano, Rolf Skog, Eddy Wymeersch, Luigi Zingales, and three anonymous referees for comments; and to the National Science Foundation for financial support of this research. Documentation of the data on legal rules presented in this paper is available from the authors on request.

owner to receive dividends. Recent financial research has shown that this is far from the whole story and that the defining feature of various securities is the rights that they bring to their owners (Hart 1995). Thus shares typically give their owners the right to vote for directors of companies, whereas debt entitles creditors to the power, for example, to repossess collateral when the company fails to make promised payments.

The rights attached to securities become critical when managers of companies act in their own interest. These rights give investors the power to extract from managers the returns on their investment. Shareholders receive dividends *because* they can vote out the directors who do not pay them, and creditors are paid *because* they have the power to repossess collateral. Without these rights, investors would not be able to get paid, and therefore firms would find it harder to raise external finance.

But the view that securities are inherently characterized by some intrinsic rights is incomplete as well. It ignores the fact that these rights depend on the legal rules of the jurisdictions in which securities are issued. Does being a shareholder in France give an investor the same privileges as being a shareholder in the United States, India, or Mexico? Would a secured creditor in Germany fare as well when the borrower defaults as one in Sri Lanka or Italy, with the value of the collateral assumed the same in all cases? Law and the quality of its enforcement are potentially important determinants of what rights security holders have and how well these rights are protected. Since the protection investors receive determines their readiness to finance firms, corporate finance may critically turn on these legal rules and their enforcement.

The differences in legal protections of investors might help explain why firms are financed and owned so differently in different countries. Why do Italian companies rarely go public (Pagano, Panetta, and Zingales 1998)? Why does Germany have such a small stock market but also maintain very large and powerful banks (Edwards and Fischer 1994)? Why is the voting premium—the price of shares with high voting rights relative to that of shares with low voting rights—small in Sweden and the United States, and much larger in Italy and Israel (Levy 1983; Rydqvist 1987; Zingales 1994, 1995)? Indeed, why were Russian stocks nearly worthless immediately after privatization—by some estimates 100 times cheaper than Western stocks backed by comparable assets—and why did Russian companies have virtually no access to external finance (Boycko, Shleifer, and Vishny 1993)? Why is ownership of large American and British companies so widely dispersed (Berle and Means 1932)? The content of legal rules in different countries may shed light on these corporate governance puzzles.

In recent years, economists and legal scholars have begun to examine theoretically the costs and benefits of alternative legal rules regarding investor rights (e.g., Grossman and Hart 1988; Harris and Raviv 1988; Gromb 1993; Bebchuk 1994). The trouble is, there have been no systematic data available on what the legal rules pertaining to corporate governance are around the world, how well these rules are enforced in different countries, and what effect these rules have. There is no systematic knowledge, for example, of whether different countries actually do have substantially different rules that might explain differences in their financing patterns. Comparative *statistical* analysis of the legal underpinnings of corporate finance—and commerce more generally—remains uncharted territory.

In this paper, we attempt to explore this territory. We examine empirically how laws protecting investors differ across 49 countries, how the quality of enforcement of these laws varies, and whether these variations matter for corporate ownership patterns around the world.

Our starting point is the recognition that laws in different countries are typically not written from scratch, but rather transplanted—voluntarily or otherwise—from a few legal families or traditions (Watson 1974). In general, *commercial* laws come from two broad traditions: common law, which is English in origin, and civil law, which derives from Roman law. Within the civil tradition, there are only three major families that modern commercial laws originate from: French, German, and Scandinavian. The French and the German civil traditions, as well as the common-law tradition, have spread around the world through a combination of conquest, imperialism, outright borrowing, and more subtle imitation. The resulting laws reflect both the influence of their families and the revisions specific to individual countries. As a result of this spread of legal families and the subsequent evolution of the laws, we can compare both the individual legal rules and whole legal families across a large number of countries.

To this end, we have assembled a data set covering legal rules pertaining to the rights of investors, and to the quality of enforcement of these rules, in 49 countries that have publicly traded companies. For shareholders, some of the rules we examine cover voting powers, ease of participation in corporate voting, and legal protections against expropriation by management. For creditors, some of these rules cover the respect for security of the loan, the ability to grab assets in case of a loan default, and the inability of management to seek protection from creditors unilaterally. In effect, these rules measure the ease with which investors can exercise their powers against management. We also consider measures of the quality of enforcement of legal rules in different countries and of the quality of their accounting systems.

We show that laws vary a lot across countries, in part because of differences in legal origin. Civil laws give investors weaker legal rights than common laws do, independent of the level of per capita income. Common-law countries give both shareholders and creditors—relatively speaking—the strongest, and French-civil-law countries the weakest, protection. German-civil-law and Scandinavian countries generally fall between the other two. The quality of law enforcement is the highest in Scandinavian and German-civil-law countries, next highest in common-law countries, and again the lowest in French-civil-law countries.

Having shown that law and its enforcement vary across countries and legal families, we ask how the countries with poor laws or enforcement cope with this problem. Do these countries have other, *substitute,* mechanisms of corporate governance? These adaptive mechanisms may in fact be incorporated into the law, or they may lie outside the law. One potential adaptation to fewer laws is strong enforcement of laws, but as we pointed out above, this does not appear to be the case empirically. Another adaptation, sometimes referred to as "bright-line" rules, is to legally introduce mandatory standards of retention and distribution of capital to investors, which limit the opportunities for managerial expropriation. We find that only French-civil-law countries have mandatory dividends, and German-civil-law countries are the most likely to have legal reserve requirements of all the legal families.

A further response to the lack of legal protections that we examine is a high ownership concentration. Some concentration of ownership of a firm's shares is typically efficient to provide managers with incentives to work and large investors with incentives to monitor the managers (Jensen and Meckling 1976; Shleifer and Vishny 1986). However, some dispersion of ownership is also desirable to diversify risk. As argued by Shleifer and Vishny (1997) and explained further in Section VI, a very high ownership concentration may be a reflection of poor investor protection. We examine ownership concentration in the largest publicly traded companies in our sample countries and find a strong negative correlation between concentration of ownership, as measured by the combined stake of the three largest shareholders, and the quality of legal protection of investors. Poor investor protection in French-civil-law countries is associated with extremely concentrated ownership. The data on ownership concentration thus support the idea that legal systems matter for corporate governance and that firms have to adapt to the limitations of the legal systems that they operate in.

Section II of the paper describes the countries and their laws. Sections III and IV then compare shareholder and creditor rights, respectively, in different countries and different legal traditions. Section V compares the quality of law enforcement and accounting standards in different countries and legal traditions. Section VI focuses on ownership. Section VII presents concluding remarks.

II. Countries, Legal Families, and Legal Rules

Countries

Most studies of corporate governance focus on one or a few wealthy economies (see, e.g., Berglof and Perotti 1994; Kaplan and Minton 1994; Rajan and Zingales 1995; Gorton and Schmidt 1996). However, corporate governance in all of the three economies that scholars typically focus on—the United States, Germany, and Japan—is quite effective. To understand better the role of legal protection of investors, we need to examine a larger sample of countries. To this end, we have assembled as comprehensive a sample as possible of countries that have some nonfinancial firms traded on their stock exchanges. The sample covers 49 countries from Europe, North and South America, Africa, Asia, and Australia. There are no socialist or "transition" economies in the sample. A country is selected for inclusion if, on the basis of the WorldScope sample of 15,900 firms from 33 countries and the Moody's International sample of 15,100 non-U.S. firms from 92 countries, that country had at least five domestic nonfinancial publicly traded firms with no government ownership in 1993. We restrict attention to countries that have publicly traded firms since our primary focus is on protecting investor rights, and without public shareholders a discussion of investor rights would be limited. Having at least five nonfinancial private firms is also essential for construction of ownership data.

Legal Families

Comparative legal scholars agree that, even though no two nations' laws are exactly alike, some national legal systems are sufficiently similar in certain critical respects to permit classification of national legal systems into major families of law. Although there is no unanimity among legal scholars on how to define legal families,

> among the criteria often used for this purpose are the fol-
> lowing: (1) historical background and development of the
> legal system, (2) theories and hierarchies of sources of law,
> (3) the working methodology of jurists within the legal sys-
> tems, (4) the characteristics of legal concepts employed by
> the system, (5) the legal institutions of the system, and (6)
> the divisions of law employed within a system. [Glendon,
> Gordon, and Osakwe 1994, pp. 4–5]

On the basis of this approach, scholars identify two broad legal traditions that pertain to matters discussed in this paper: civil law and
common law.[1]

The civil, or Romano-Germanic, legal tradition is the oldest, the
most influential, and the most widely distributed around the world.
It originates in Roman law, uses statutes and comprehensive codes
as a primary means of ordering legal material, and relies heavily on
legal scholars to ascertain and formulate its rules (Merryman 1969).
Legal scholars typically identify three currently common families of
laws within the civil-law tradition: French, German, and Scandinavian. The French Commercial Code was written under Napoleon in
1807 and brought by his armies to Belgium, the Netherlands, part
of Poland, Italy, and western regions of Germany. In the colonial
era, France extended its legal influence to the Near East and Northern and sub-Saharan Africa, Indochina, Oceania, and French Carib-
bean islands. French legal influence has been significant as well in
Luxembourg, Portugal, Spain, some of the Swiss cantons, and Italy
(Glendon et al. 1994). When the Spanish and Portuguese empires
in Latin America dissolved in the nineteenth century, it was mainly
the French civil law that the lawmakers of the new nations looked
to for inspiration. Our sample contains 21 countries with laws in the
French civil tradition.

The German Commercial Code was written in 1897 after Bis-
marck's unification of Germany, and perhaps because it was produced several decades later, was not as widely adopted as the French
code. It had an important influence on the legal theory and doctrine
in Austria, Czechoslovakia, Greece, Hungary, Italy, Switzerland, Yu-
goslavia, Japan, and Korea. Taiwan's laws came from China, which

---

[1] The religious traditions, such as Jewish law, Canon law, Hindu law, and Muslim
law, appear to be less relevant in matters of investor protection. "Thus the Arabian
countries unquestionably belong to Islamic law as far as family and inheritance law
is concerned, just as India belongs to Hindu law, but economic law of these countries
(including commercial law and the law of contract and tort) is heavily impressed
by the legal thinking of the colonial and mandatory powers—the Common Law in
the case of India, French law in the case of most of the Arab States" (Zweigert and
Kotz 1987, p. 66). We focus on the principal secular legal traditions in this study.

borrowed heavily from the German code during its modernization. We have six countries from this family in our sample.

The Scandinavian family is usually viewed as part of the civil-law tradition, although its law is less derivative of Roman law than the French and German families (Zweigert and Kotz 1987). Although Nordic countries had civil codes as far back as the eighteenth century, these codes are not used anymore. Most writers describe the Scandinavian laws as similar to each other but "distinct" from others, so we keep the four Nordic countries in our sample as a separate family.

The common-law family includes the law of England and those laws modeled on English law. The common law is formed by judges who have to resolve specific disputes. Precedents from judicial decisions, as opposed to contributions by scholars, shape common law. Common law has spread to the British colonies, including the United States, Canada, Australia, India, and many other countries. There are 18 common-law countries in our sample.

To classify countries into legal families, we rely principally on Reynolds and Flores (1989). In most cases, such classification is uncontroversial. In a few cases, while the basic origin of laws is clear, laws have been amended over time to incorporate influences from other families. For example, Ecuador, a French-civil-law country, revised its company law in 1977 to incorporate some common-law rules; Thailand's first laws were based on common law but since received enormous French influence; and Italy is a French-civil-law country with some German influence. Most important for our study, after World War II, the American occupying army "Americanized" some Japanese laws, particularly in the company law area, although their basic German-civil-law structure remained. In these and several other cases, we classify a country on the basis of the origin of the initial laws it adopted rather than on the revisions.[2] In the United States, states have their own laws. We generally rely on Delaware law because a significant fraction of large U.S. companies are incorporated in Delaware. In Canada, our data come from Ontario laws, even though Quebec has a system based on French civil law.

---

[2] The European Community is currently attempting to harmonize West European laws, including those pertaining to corporate governance, by issuing directives (Andenas and Kenyon-Slade 1993; Werlauff 1993). Several countries have changed parts of their laws to adhere to E.C. directives. However, in most instances, the directives are not mandatory, and the countries are given some time to change their laws. Moreover, the E.C. directives accommodate a great deal of diversity among countries. As of 1993–94—the point in time for which we examine the legal rules of the countries in our sample—E.C. harmonization has not generally affected the legal rules that we focus on. The one area in which the E.C. impact has been large, namely mergers and acquisitions, is not an area that we examine in this paper (see below).

Legal Rules

We look only at laws pertaining to investor protection, and specifically only at company and bankruptcy/reorganization laws. Company laws exist in all countries and are concerned with (1) the legal relations between corporate insiders (members of the corporation, i.e., shareholders and directors) and the corporation itself and (2) the legal relations between the corporation and certain outsiders, particularly creditors. Bankruptcy/reorganization laws apply more generally than just to companies but deal specifically with procedures that unfold in the case of failure to pay back debt. All these laws are part of the commercial codes in civil-law countries and exist as separate laws, mainly in the form of acts, in common-law countries.

There are several conspicuous omissions from the data set. First, this paper says little about merger and takeover rules, except indirectly by looking at voting mechanisms. These rules are spread between company laws, antitrust laws, security laws, stock exchange regulations, and sometimes banking regulations as well. Moreover, these rules have changed significantly in Europe as part of E.C. legal harmonization. Until recently, takeovers have been an important governance tool in only a few common-law countries, although the situation may change.[3]

Second, this paper also says little about disclosure rules, which again come from many sources—including company laws, security laws, and stock exchange regulations—and are also intended for harmonization across the European Community. We do, however, look at the quality of accounting standards, which to a large extent is a consequence of disclosure rules.

Third, in this paper we do not use any information from regulations imposed by security exchanges. One instance in which this is relevant is exchange-imposed restrictions on the voting rights for the shares that companies can issue if these shares are to be traded on the exchange.

Finally, a potentially important set of rules that we do not deal with here is banking and financial institution regulations, which might take the form of restricting bank ownership, for example. Much has been made of these regulations in the United States by Roe (1994).

---

[3] Several readers have pointed to the U.S. state antitakeover laws as evidence of an anti–minority shareholder position in the U.S. legal system that our data do not capture. Even with all these antitakeover laws, the United States and the United Kingdom still have by far the most takeovers of any country in the world, so their laws are evidently not nearly as antitakeover as those elsewhere.

An inspection of company and bankruptcy laws suggests numerous potentially measurable differences among countries. Here we focus only on some of the most basic rules that observers of corporate governance around the world (e.g., American Bar Association 1989, 1993; White 1993; Institutional Shareholder Services 1994; Investor Responsibility Research Center 1994, 1995; Vishny 1994) believe to be critical to the quality of shareholder and creditor legal rights. Moreover, we focus on variables that prima facie are interpretable as either pro-investor or pro-management since this is the dimension along which we are trying to assess countries and legal families. There are obvious differences in rules between countries, such as, for example, tier structures of boards of directors, that we do not examine because we cannot ascertain which of these rules are more sympathetic to shareholders. Investor rights, as well as the other variables we use in this paper, are summarized in table 1. We discuss individual variables in more detail in the sections in which they are analyzed and present all the data on individual rights that we use in the paper in the relevant tables.

Some Conceptual Issues

Our goal is to establish whether laws pertaining to investor protection differ across countries and whether these differences have consequences for corporate finance. This research design immediately poses some conceptual problems. To begin, some scholars, such as Easterbrook and Fischel (1991), are skeptical that legal rules are binding in most instances, since often firms can opt out of these rules in their corporate charters, which effectively serve as contracts between entrepreneurs and investors. Indeed, in many countries, firms can opt out of some of the rules we examine. As a practical matter, however, it may be costly for firms to opt out of standard legal rules since investors might have difficulty accepting nonstandard contracts and, more important, judges might fail to understand or enforce them. The question of whether legal rules matter is fundamentally empirical: if opting out were cheap and simple, we would not find that legal rules matter for patterns of corporate ownership and finance.

A closely related question is whether more restrictive rules, which reduce the choices available to company founders, are necessarily more protective of shareholders than the alternative of greater flexibility. In an environment of perfect judicial enforcement, the benefits of flexibility probably outweigh the risks when entrepreneurs use nonstandard corporate charters to take advantage of investors, since investors can appeal to a court when they are expropriated in an

TABLE 1

VARIABLES

Variable	Description	Sources
Origin	Identifies the legal origin of the company law or commercial code of each country. Equals one if the origin is English common law, two if the origin is the French commercial code, three if the origin is the German commercial code, and four if the origin is Scandinavian civil law	Reynolds and Flores (1989)
One share–one vote	Equals one if the company law or commercial code of the country requires that ordinary shares carry one vote per share, and zero otherwise. Equivalently, this variable equals one when the law prohibits the existence of both multiple-voting and nonvoting ordinary shares and does not allow firms to set a maximum number of votes per shareholder irrespective of the number of shares owned, and zero otherwise	Company law or commercial code
Proxy by mail allowed	Equals one if the company law or commercial code allows shareholders to mail their proxy vote to the firm, and zero otherwise	Company law or commercial code
Shares not blocked before meeting	Equals one if the company law or commercial code does not allow firms to require that shareholders deposit their shares prior to a general shareholders meeting, thus preventing them from selling those shares for a number of days, and zero otherwise	Company law or commercial code
Cumulative voting or proportional representation	Equals one if the company law or commercial code allows shareholders to cast all their votes for one candidate standing for election to the board of directors (cumulative voting) or if the company law or commercial code allows a mechanism of proportional representation in the board by which minority interests may name a proportional number of directors to the board, and zero otherwise	Company law or commercial code
Oppressed minorities mechanism	Equals one if the company law or commercial code grants minority shareholders either a judicial venue to challenge the decisions of management or of the assembly or the right to step out of the company by requiring the company to purchase their shares when they object to certain fundamental changes, such as mergers, asset dispositions, and changes in the articles of incorporation. The variable equals zero otherwise. Minority shareholders are defined as those shareholders who own 10 percent of share capital or less	Company law or commercial code

Preemptive rights	Equals one when the company law or commercial code grants shareholders the first opportunity to buy new issues of stock, and this right can be waived only by a shareholders' vote; equals zero otherwise	Company law or commercial code
Percentage of share capital to call an extraordinary shareholders' meeting	The minimum percentage of ownership of share capital that entitles a shareholder to call for an extraordinary shareholders' meeting; it ranges from 1 to 33 percent	Company law or commercial code
Antidirector rights	An index aggregating the shareholder rights we labeled as "antidirector rights." The index is formed by adding 1 when (1) the country allows shareholders to mail their proxy vote to the firm, (2) shareholders are not required to deposit their shares prior to the general shareholders' meeting, (3) cumulative voting or proportional representation of minorities in the board of directors is allowed, (4) an oppressed minorities mechanism is in place, (5) the minimum percentage of share capital that entitles a shareholder to call for an extraordinary shareholders' meeting is less than or equal to 10 percent (the sample median), or (6) shareholders have preemptive rights that can be waived only by a shareholders' vote. The index ranges from zero to six	Company law or commercial code
Mandatory dividend	Equals the percentage of net income that the company law or commercial code requires firms to distribute as dividends among ordinary stockholders. It takes a value of zero for countries without such a restriction	
Restrictions for going into reorganization	Equals one if the reorganization procedure imposes restrictions, such as creditors' consent, to file for reorganization; equals zero if there are no such restrictions	Bankruptcy and reorganization laws
No automatic stay on secured assets	Equals one if the reorganization procedure does not impose an automatic stay on the assets of the firm on filing the reorganization petition. Automatic stay prevents secured creditors from gaining possession of their security. It equals zero if such a restriction does exist in the law	Bankruptcy and reorganization laws
Secured creditors first	Equals one if secured creditors are ranked first in the distribution of the proceeds that result from the disposition of the assets of a bankrupt firm. Equals zero if nonsecured creditors, such as the government and workers, are given absolute priority	Bankruptcy and reorganization laws
Management does not stay	Equals one when an official appointed by the court, or by the creditors, is responsible for the operation of the business during reorganization. Equivalently, this variable equals one if the debtor does not keep the administration of its property pending the resolution of the reorganization process. Equals zero otherwise	Bankruptcy and reorganization laws

continued overleaf

1123

TABLE 1 (*Continued*)

Variable	Description	Sources
Creditor rights	An index aggregating different creditor rights. The index is formed by adding 1 when (1) the country imposes restrictions, such as creditors' consent or minimum dividends to file for reorganization; (2) secured creditors are able to gain possession of their security once the reorganization petition has been approved (no automatic stay); (3) secured creditors are ranked first in the distribution of the proceeds that result from the disposition of the assets of a bankrupt firm; and (4) the debtor does not retain the administration of its property pending the resolution of the reorganization. The index ranges from zero to four	Bankruptcy and reorganization laws
Legal reserve	The minimum percentage of total share capital mandated by corporate law to avoid the dissolution of an existing firm. It takes a value of zero for countries without such a restriction	Company law or commercial code
Efficiency of judicial system	Assessment of the "efficiency and integrity of the legal environment as it affects business, particularly foreign firms" produced by the country risk rating agency Business International Corp. It "may be taken to represent investors' assessments of conditions in the country in question." Average between 1980 and 1983. Scale from zero to 10; with lower scores, lower efficiency levels	Business International Corp.
Rule of law	Assessment of the law and order tradition in the country produced by the country risk rating agency International Country Risk (ICR). Average of the months of April and October of the monthly index between 1982 and 1995. Scale from zero to 10, with lower scores for less tradition for law and order (we changed the scale from its original range going from zero to six)	International Country Risk guide
Corruption	ICR's assessment of the corruption in government. Lower scores indicate that "high government officials are likely to demand special payments" and "illegal payments are generally expected throughout lower levels of government," in the form of "bribes connected with import and export licenses, exchange controls, tax assessment, policy protection, or loans." Average of the months of April and October of the monthly index between 1982 and 1995. Scale from zero to 10, with lower scores for higher levels of corruption (we changed the scale from its original range going from zero to six)	International Country Risk guide

Risk of expropriation	ICR's assessment of the risk of "outright confiscation" or "forced nationalization." Average of the months of April and October of the monthly index between 1982 and 1995. Scale from zero to 10, with lower scores for higher risks	International Country Risk guide
Repudiation of contracts by government	ICR's assessment of the "risk of a modification in a contract taking the form of a repudiation, postponement, or scaling down" due to "budget cutbacks, indigenization pressure, a change in government, or a change in government economic and social priorities." Average of the months of April and October of the monthly index between 1982 and 1995. Scale from zero to 10, with lower scores for higher risks	International Country Risk guide
Accounting standards	Index created by examining and rating companies' 1990 annual reports on their inclusion or omission of 90 items. These items fall into seven categories (general information, income statements, balance sheets, funds flow statement, accounting standards, stock data, and special items). A minimum of three companies in each country were studied. The companies represent a cross section of various industry groups; industrial companies represented 70 percent, and financial companies represented the remaining 30 percent	International accounting and auditing trends, Center for International Financial Analysis and Research
Ownership, 10 largest private firms	The average percentage of common shares owned by the three largest shareholders in the 10 largest nonfinancial, privately owned domestic firms in a given country. A firm is considered privately owned if the state is not a known shareholder in it	Moodys International, CIFAR, EXTEL, WorldScope, 20-Fs, Price-Waterhouse, and various country sources
GNP and GNP per capita	Gross national product and gross national product per capita in constant dollars of 1994	World Bank and International Monetary Fund
Gini coefficient	Gini coefficient for income inequality in each country. When the 1990 coefficient is not available, we use the most recent available	Deininger and Squire (1996); World Bank (1993a, 1993b)

unanticipated way. However, with imperfect enforcement, simple, restrictive, bright-line rules, which require only a minimal effort from the judicial system to enforce, may be superior (Hay, Shleifer, and Vishny 1996). Again, the question does not have a clear theoretical answer, and the issue of how legal rules affect corporate finance is ultimately empirical.

Even if we were to find that legal rules matter, it would be possible to argue that these rules endogenously adjust to economic reality, and hence the differences in rules and outcomes simply reflect the differences in some other, exogenous, conditions across countries. Perhaps some countries chose to have only bank finance of firms for political reasons and then adjusted their laws accordingly to protect banks and discourage shareholders. Some individual rules are probably endogenous. However, this is where our focus on the legal origin becomes crucial. Countries typically adopted their legal systems involuntarily (through conquest or colonization). Even when they chose a legal system freely, as in the case of former Spanish colonies, the crucial consideration was language and the broad political stance of the law rather than the treatment of investor protections. The legal family can therefore be treated as exogenous to a country's structure of corporate ownership and finance. If we find that legal rules differ substantially across legal families and that financing and ownership patterns do as well, we have a strong case that legal families, as expressed in the legal rules, actually cause outcomes.

III.   Shareholder Rights

We begin by considering shareholder rights from company laws. The rights measures in this section are refined versions of those presented in our working paper (La Porta et al. 1996).[4]

Because shareholders exercise their power by voting for directors and on major corporate issues, experts focus on voting procedures in evaluating shareholder rights. They include voting rights attached to shares, rights that support the voting mechanism against interference by the insiders, and what we call remedial rights. To begin, investors may be better protected when dividend rights are tightly linked to voting rights, that is, when companies in a country are subject to one-share–one-vote rules (Grossman and Hart 1988; Har-

---

[4] We made two significant changes: we redefined the cumulative voting variable to also cover the right of minority shareholders for proportional representation, and we added a variable on preemptive rights of minority shareholders to buy new issues of stock (see below). In this and the following sections, all dummies have been defined so that 1 means more protective.

ris and Raviv 1988).[5] When votes are tied to dividends, insiders cannot have substantial control of the company without having substantial ownership of its cash flows, which moderates their taste for (costly) diversion of cash flows relative to payment of dividends. There are many ways out of the one-share–one-vote principle that laws in different countries accommodate. Companies can issue nonvoting shares, low- and high-voting shares, founders' shares with extremely high voting rights, or shares whose votes increase when they are held longer, as in France. Companies can also restrict the total number of votes that any given shareholder can exercise at a shareholders' meeting, regardless of how many votes he or she controls. We say that a country has one share–one vote if none of these practices is allowed by law. In our sample, only 11 countries impose genuine one-share–one-vote rules.

The next six rights, which we refer to as antidirector rights, measure how strongly the legal system favors minority shareholders against managers or dominant shareholders in the corporate decision-making process, including the voting process. First, in some countries, shareholders must show up in person or send an authorized representative to a shareholders' meeting to be able to vote. In other countries, in contrast, they can mail their proxy vote directly to the firm, which both enables them to see the relevant proxy information and makes it easier to cast their votes. In Japan, for example, annual shareholder meetings are concentrated overwhelmingly on a single day in late June, and voting by mail is not allowed for some shareholders, which makes it difficult for shareholders to exercise their votes.

Second, in some countries, law requires that shareholders deposit their shares with the company or a financial intermediary several days prior to a shareholder meeting. The shares are then kept in custody until a few days after the meeting. This practice prevents shareholders from selling their shares for several days around the time of the meeting and keeps from voting shareholders who do not bother to go through this exercise.

Third, a few countries allow cumulative voting for directors, and a few have mechanisms of proportional representation on the board, by which minority interests may name a proportional number of directors. The effect of either rule, in principle, is to give more power for minority shareholders to put their representatives on boards of directors.

[5] One of the E.C. directives recommends the adoption of one-share–one-vote rules throughout the Community. It does not appear that this directive is being incorporated into national laws too rapidly.

Fourth, some countries give minority shareholders legal mechanisms against perceived oppression by directors (in addition to outright fraud, which is illegal everywhere). These mechanisms may include the right to challenge the directors' decisions in court (as in the American derivative suit) or the right to force the company to repurchase shares of the minority shareholders who object to certain fundamental decisions of the management or of the assembly of shareholders, such as mergers or asset sales.

Fifth, some countries grant shareholders a preemptive right to buy new issues of stock, which can be waived only by a shareholder vote. This right is intended to protect shareholders from dilution, whereby shares are issued to favored investors at below-market prices.

Sixth, we look at the percentage of share capital needed to call an extraordinary shareholders' meeting.[6] Presumably, the higher this percentage is, the harder it is for minority shareholders to organize a meeting to challenge or oust the management. This percentage varies around the world from 3 percent in Japan to 33 percent of share capital in Mexico.

For each of the first five antidirector rights measures, a country gets a score of 1 if it protects minority shareholders according to this measure and a score of 0 otherwise. We also give each country a 1 if the percentage of share capital needed to call an extraordinary shareholder meeting is at or below the world median of 10 percent. Finally, we add up these six antidirector rights scores into an aggregate score, which ranges from 0 for Belgium to 5 for Canada and the United States, for example.

The last shareholder rights measure, which we treat differently from others, is the right to a mandatory dividend. In some countries, companies are mandated by law to pay out a certain fraction of their declared earnings as dividends. Because earnings can be misrepresented within the limits allowed by the accounting system, this measure is not as restrictive as it looks. The mandatory dividend right may be a legal substitute for the weakness of other protections of minority shareholders.

Table 2 presents the data on shareholder rights. The values of all variables are listed by country, and countries are organized by legal origin. Columns in table 2 correspond to particular legal provisions concerning shareholder rights, and the values in the tables are dum-

---

[6] For the United States, our reliance on Delaware presents a problem since the state leaves up to corporations the percentage of shares needed to call an extraordinary shareholder meeting. We use 10 percent for the United States because the majority of U.S. states (27) use this number.

mies equal to one if the country has shareholder protections in that particular area. Table 2 also presents equality of means tests for all the variables by origin.

An examination of world means of the variables in table 2 suggests that relatively few countries have legal rules favoring outside shareholders. Only 22 percent of the countries have one share–one vote, only 27 percent allow cumulative voting or give minorities a right of proportional board representation, only 18 percent allow voting by mail, only 53 percent have some oppressed minorities mechanism, and only 53 percent give minority shareholders a preemptive right to buy new shares.

The other clear result in table 2 is that, for many variables, the origin of laws matters. The means of shareholder rights variables are statistically significantly different between legal families. The two variables in which most legal families are similar are one share–one vote, which is an uncommon restriction everywhere (and never happens in Scandinavia, which is therefore different), and cumulative voting/proportional representation, which is also uncommon everywhere (and again never happens in Scandinavia). For the other variables, the differences in shareholder rights between legal origins are more substantial.

Specifically, two major findings emerge from table 2. First, along a variety of dimensions, common-law countries afford the best legal protections to shareholders. They most frequently (39 percent) allow shareholders to vote by mail, they never block shares for shareholder meetings, they have the highest (94 percent) incidence of laws protecting oppressed minorities, and they generally require relatively little share capital (9 percent) to call an extraordinary shareholder meeting. The only dimension on which common-law countries are not especially protective is the preemptive right to new share issues (44 percent). Still, the common-law countries have the highest average antidirector rights score (4.00) of all legal families. Many of the differences between common-law and civil-law countries are statistically significant. In short, relative to the rest of the world, common-law countries have a package of laws most protective of shareholders.

Second, along a broad range of dimensions, French-civil-law countries afford the worst legal protections to shareholders. Although they look average on one share–one vote (29 percent) and cumulative voting (19 percent) and better than average on preemptive rights (62 percent), they have the lowest (5 percent) incidence of allowing voting by mail, a low (57 percent, though not as low as German-civil-law countries) incidence of not blocking shares for shareholder meetings, a low (29 percent, though not as low as Nor-

TABLE 2
SHAREHOLDER RIGHTS AROUND THE WORLD

A. Shareholder Rights (1 = Investor Protection Is in the Law)

Country	One Share–One Vote	Proxy by Mail Allowed	Shares Not Blocked before Meeting	Cumulative Voting/ Proportional Representation	Oppressed Minority	Preemptive Right to New Issues	Percentage of Share Capital to Call an Extraordinary Shareholder Meeting	Antidirector Rights	Mandatory Dividend
Australia	0	1	1	0	1	0	.05[a]	4	.00
Canada	0	1	1	1	1	0	.05	5	.00
Hong Kong	0	1	1	0	1	1	.10	5	.00
India	0	0	1	1	1	1	.10	5	.00
Ireland	0	0	1	0	1	1	.10	4	.00
Israel	0	0	1	0	1	0	.10	3	.00
Kenya	0	0	1	0	1	0	.10	3	.00
Malaysia	1	0	1	0	1	1	.10	4	.00
New Zealand	0	1	1	0	1	0	.05	4	.00
Nigeria	0	0	1	0	1	0	.10	3	.00
Pakistan	1	0	1	1	1	1	.10	5	.00
Singapore	1	0	1	0	1	1	.10	4	.00
South Africa	0	1	1	0	1	1	.05	5	.00
Sri Lanka	0	0	1	0	1	0	.10	3	.00
Thailand	0	0	1	1	0	0	.20[b]	2	.00
United Kingdom	0	1	1	1	1	1	.10	5	.00
United States	0	1	1	1	1	0	.10	5	.00
Zimbabwe	0	0	1	0	1	1	.05	3	.00
English-origin average	**.17**	**.39**	**1.00**	**.28**	**.94**	**.44**	**.09**	**4.00**	**.00**
Argentina	0	0	0	1	1	1	.05	4	.00
Belgium	0	0	0	0	0	0	.20	0	.00
Brazil	1	0	1	0	1	0	.05	3	.50
Chile	1	0	1	1	0	1	.10	5	.30
Colombia	0	0	1	0	0	1	.25	3	.50
Ecuador	0	0	1	0	0	0	.25	2	.50
Egypt	0	0	0	0	0	0	.10	2	.00
France	0	1	0	0	0	1	.10	3	.00
Greece	1	0	0	0	0	1	.05	2	.35

Indonesia	0	0	1	0	0	.10	2	.00
Italy	1	0	0	1	1	.20	1	.00
Jordan	0	0	1	0	0	.25	1	.00
Mexico	0	0	0	0	1	.33	1	.00
Netherlands	1	0	0	1	1	.10	2	.00
Peru	0	0	1	0	0	.20	3	.00
Philippines	0	0	1	1	1	open	3	.00
Portugal	0	0	0	0	0	.05	4	.00
Spain	0	0	1	0	1	.05	2	.00
Turkey	1	1	0	1	1	.10	2	.00
Uruguay	0	0	0	0	0	.20	1	.00
Venezuela	0	0	1	1	0	.20		
French-origin average	**.29**	**.05**	**.57**	**.29**	**.29**	**.62**	**.15**	**2.33**	**.11**
Austria	0	0	0	0	0	1	.05	2	.00
Germany	0	0	0	0	0	0	.05	1	.00
Japan	1	0	1	1	1	0	.03	4	.00
South Korea	1	0	1	0	1	0	.05	2	.00
Switzerland	0	0	0	0	0	1	.10	2	.00
Taiwan	0	0	0	1	1		.03	3	.00
German-origin average	**.33**	**.00**	**.17**	**.33**	**.50**	**.33**	**.05**	**2.33**	**.00**
Denmark	0	0	1	0	0	0	.10	2	.00
Finland	0	0	1	0	0	1	.10	3	.00
Norway	0	1	1	0	0	1	.10	4	.00
Sweden	0	0	1	0	0	1	.10[b]	3	.00
Scandinavian-origin average	**.00**	**.25**	**1.00**	**.00**	**.00**	**.75**	**.10**	**3.00**	**.00**
Sample average	**.22**	**.18**	**.71**	**.27**	**.53**	**.53**	**.11**	**3.00**	**.05**

B. Tests of Means (t-Statistics)

Common vs. civil law	−.72	3.03*	4.97*	.15	5.59*	−.91	1.48	5.00*	−2.55**
English vs. French origin	−.87	2.82*	3.87*	−.05	5.45*	−1.08	−2.53**	4.73**	−2.67**
English vs. German origin	−.85	3.29*	5.00*	.00	2.83*	.46	−2.54**	3.59*	.00
English vs. Scandinavian origin	1.84***	.50	.00	2.55**	17.00*	−1.09	−1.00	1.91***	.00
French vs. German origin	−.22	1.00	−1.78***	−.22	−.96	1.23	2.64**	.00	2.67**
French vs. Scandinavian origin	2.83**	−1.37	−3.87*	2.82**	2.83	−.48	2.43**	−1.06	2.67**
German vs. Scandinavian origin	1.58	−1.00	−5.00*	1.58	2.23***	−1.27	−4.62*	−1.08	.00

NOTE.—Variables are defined in table 1.
a As a percentage of votes.
b As a percentage of the number of shares.
* Significant at the 1 percent level.
** Significant at the 5 percent level.
*** Significant at the 10 percent level.

1131

dic countries) incidence of laws protecting oppressed minorities, and the highest (15 percent) percentage of share capital needed to call an extraordinary shareholders' meeting. The aggregate antidirector rights score is the lowest (2.33) for the French-civil-law countries. The difference in this score between French civil law and common law is large and statistically significant. It is interesting to note that France itself, except for allowing proxy voting by mail and having a preemptive right to new share issues, does not have strong legal protections of shareholders. These results suggest that shareholders in the two most widely spread legal regimes—common law and French civil law—operate in very different legal environments.

The German-civil-law countries are not particularly protective of shareholders either. They have a relatively high frequency of one-share–one-vote rules (because of East Asia), require few votes to call an extraordinary meeting, and offer preemptive rights in a third of the cases. But they usually block shares before shareholder meetings, never allow voting by mail, and have oppressed minority mechanisms in only half of the countries. The average antidirector score for this family is 2.33, exactly the same as that for the French family. In Scandinavia, no country has oppressed minority protections, a one-share–one-vote restriction, or a cumulative voting/proportional representation mechanism, and only Norway allows voting by mail. At the same time, no country blocks shares before a shareholder meeting, and three out of four give shareholders preemptive rights. The average Scandinavian antidirector rights score is 3.

The one remedial measure in table 2, namely mandatory dividend, shows that mandatory dividends are used *only* in French-civil-law countries. This result is broadly consistent with the rest of our evidence and suggests that mandatory dividends are indeed a remedial legal protection for shareholders who have relatively few other legal rights.

The results in panel B of table 2 suggest that the differences in the various measures of shareholder rights between different legal families are often significant and almost always significant when common- and civil-law families are compared. One further question is whether the difference in scores by legal origin just reflects differences in per capita income levels. To address this question, table 3 divides all countries into the bottom 25 percent, middle 50 percent, and top 25 percent by gross national product per capita. The results show, in particular, that antidirector rights scores are independent of per capita income, rejecting the notion that legal rules that are more protective of investors are a reflection of higher per capita income.

In sum, common-law countries have the relatively strongest, and

TABLE 3

DEVELOPMENT AND INVESTOR RIGHTS

Countries Sorted by GNP per Capita	GNP per Capita	One Share–One Vote	Antidirector Rights	Mandatory Dividend	Creditor Rights	Legal Reserve as a Percentage of Capital
A. Means						
Bottom 25%	705	.17	2.92	.08	3.18	.15
Mid 50%	9,465	.32	3.16	.05	2.13	.16
Highest 25%	25,130	.08	2.75	.00	1.83	.15
Total average	11,156	.22	3.00	.05	2.30	.15
B. Tests of Means (*t*-Statistics)						
Bottom 25% vs. mid 50%	-4.59*	-.97	-.56	.54	2.08**	-.20
Bottom 25% vs. top 25%	-18.63*	.60	.30	1.48	2.49**	-.05
Mid 50% vs. top 25%	-7.44*	1.58	.85	2.02***	.69	.16

* Significant at the 1 percent level.
** Significant at the 5 percent level.
*** Significant at the 10 percent level.

the French-civil-law countries the weakest, protections of shareholders, independent of per capita income. Minority shareholders in Australia can vote by mail, can trade their shares during a shareholders' meeting, are protected from certain expropriations by directors, and need to organize only 5 percent of the votes to call an extraordinary meeting. Minority shareholders in Belgium, in contrast, cannot vote by mail, have their shares blocked during the shareholder meeting, are not protected from expropriation by directors, and need 20 percent of share capital to call for an extraordinary meeting. The differences between legal families come out clearly from this analysis of shareholder rights.

IV. Creditor Rights

Conceptually, creditor rights are more complex than shareholder rights, for two reasons. First, there may be different kinds of creditors, with different interests, so protecting rights of some creditors has the effect of reducing the rights of others. For example, in the case of a default, senior secured creditors may have a simple interest in getting possession of collateral no matter what happens to the firm, whereas junior unsecured creditors may wish to preserve the firm as a going concern so that they can hope to get some of their money back if the firm turns a profit. In assessing creditor rights, we take the perspective of senior secured creditors, in part for concreteness and in part because much of the debt in the world has that character.

Second, there are two general creditor strategies of dealing with a defaulting firm: liquidation and reorganization, which require different rights to be effective. The most basic right of a senior collateralized creditor is the right to repossess—and then liquidate or keep—collateral when a loan is in default (see Hart 1995). In some countries, law makes it difficult for such creditors to repossess collateral, in part because such repossession leads to liquidation of firms, which is viewed as socially undesirable. In these countries, creditors may still have powers against borrowers, namely their votes in the decisions for how to reorganize the company. The debate between the wisdom of reorganization and liquidation from the social viewpoint has been extensive (Aghion, Hart, and Moore 1992; White 1993; Baird 1995) and has raised the question of whether both procedures or just one is needed to protect creditors. Thus a country with a perfect liquidation procedure but totally ineffective reorganization might be extremely protective of creditors simply because reorganization never needs to be used. We score creditor rights in

LAW AND FINANCE   1135

both reorganization and liquidation and add up the scores to create a creditor rights index, in part because almost all countries rely to some extent on both procedures.

We use five creditor rights variables in this analysis. First, in some countries, the reorganization procedure imposes an automatic stay on the assets, thereby preventing secured creditors from getting possession of loan collateral. This rule obviously protects managers and unsecured creditors against secured creditors and prevents automatic liquidation. In Greece, for example, secured creditors have the right to foreclose on their property when their claim matures and not when the borrower defaults (Houghton and Atkinson 1993, p. 112). In other countries, in contrast, secured creditors can pull collateral from firms being reorganized without waiting for completion of reorganization, a right that is obviously of value to them.

Second, some countries do not assure the secured creditors the right to collateral in reorganization. In these, admittedly rare, countries, secured creditors are in line behind the government and workers, who have absolute priority over them. In Mexico, for example, various social constituencies need to be repaid before the secured creditors, often leaving the latter with no assets to back up their claims.

Third, management in some countries can seek protection from creditors unilaterally by filing for reorganization, without creditor consent. Such protection is called Chapter 11 in the United States and gives management a great deal of power, since at best creditors can get their money or collateral only with a delay. In other countries, in contrast, creditor consent is needed to file for reorganization, and hence managers cannot so easily escape creditor demands.

Finally, in some countries, management stays pending the resolution of the reorganization procedure, whereas in other countries, such as Malaysia, management is replaced by a party appointed by the court or the creditors. This threat of dismissal may enhance creditors' power.

As with shareholder rights, we use one remedial creditor rights measure, namely the existence of a legal reserve requirement. This requirement forces firms to maintain a certain level of capital to avoid automatic liquidation. It protects creditors who have few other powers by forcing an automatic liquidation before all the capital is stolen or wasted by the insiders.

The results on creditor rights are presented in table 4. In general, the protections of creditor rights analyzed here occur more frequently than the protections of shareholder rights. Nearly half of the countries do not have an automatic stay on assets, 81 percent

TABLE 4
CREDITOR RIGHTS AROUND THE WORLD

Country	No Automatic Stay on Assets	Secured Creditors First Paid	Restrictions for Going into Reorganization	Management Does Not Stay in Reorganization	Creditor Rights	Legal Reserve Required as a Percentage of Capital
	A. Creditor Rights (1 = Creditor Protection Is the Law)					
Australia	0	1	0	0	1	.00
Canada	0	1	0	0	1	.00
Hong Kong	1	1	1	1	4	.00
India	0	1	1	1	4	.00
Ireland	1	1	0	0	1	.00
Israel	1	1	1	1	4	.00
Kenya	1	1	1	1	4	.00
Malaysia	1	1	1	1	4	.00
New Zealand	1	0	1	1	3	.00
Nigeria	1	1	1	1	4	.00
Pakistan	1	1	1	1	4	.00
Singapore	1	1	1	1	4	.00
South Africa	0	1	1	1	3	.00
Sri Lanka	1	1	0	1	3	.00
Thailand	1	1	0	1	3	.10
United Kingdom	1	1	1	1	4	.00
United States	0	1	0	0	1	.00
Zimbabwe	1	1	1	1	4	.00
English-origin average	**.72**	**.89**	**.72**	**.78**	**3.11**	**.01**
Argentina	0	1	0	0	1	.20
Belgium	1	1	0	0	2	.10
Brazil	0	0	1	0	1	.20
Chile	0	1	0	0	2	.20
Colombia	0	0	0	0	0	.50
Ecuador	1	1	1	1	4	.50
Egypt	1	1	1	1	4	.50
France	0	0	0	0	0	.10
Greece	0	0	0	0	1	.33
Indonesia	1	1	0	1	4	.00

Italy	0	1	1	0	2	.20
Jordan	na	na	na	na	na	.25
Mexico	0	0	0	0	0	.20
Netherlands	0	0	1	0	2	.00
Peru	0	0	0	0	0	.20
Philippines	0	1	0	0	1	.00
Portugal	0	1	0	0	2	.20
Spain	1	1	1	0	2	.20
Turkey	0	1	1	0	2	.20
Uruguay	0	1	0	1	2	.20
Venezuela	na	1	na	na	na	.10
French-origin average	**.26**	**.65**	**.42**	**.26**	**1.58**	**.21**
Austria	1	1	1	0	3	.10
Germany	1	1	1	0	3	.10
Japan	0	1	0	1	2	.25
South Korea	1	1	0	1	3	.50
Switzerland	0	1	0	0	1	.50
Taiwan	1	1	0	0	2	1.00
German-origin average	**.67**	**1.00**	**.33**	**.33**	**2.33**	**.41**
Denmark	1	1	1	0	3	.25
Finland	0	1	0	0	1	.00
Norway	0	1	1	0	2	.20
Sweden	0	1	1	0	2	.20
Scandinavian-origin average	**.25**	**1.00**	**.75**	**.00**	**2.00**	**.16**
Sample average	**.49**	**.81**	**.55**	**.45**	**2.30**	**.15**

B. Tests of Means (t-Statistics)

Common vs. civil law	2.65*	1.04	1.86***	4.13*	3.61*	−4.82*
English vs. French origin	3.06*	1.75**	1.89***	3.55*	3.61*	−5.75*
English vs. German origin	.25	−1.46	1.74***	2.10**	1.43	−5.21*
English vs. Scandinavian origin	1.83***	−1.46	−.11	7.71*	1.71***	−5.90*
French vs. German origin	−1.85***	−3.20*	.37	−.32	−1.29	−2.14**
French vs. Scandinavian origin	.05	−3.20*	−1.18	2.54***	−.60	.59
German vs. Scandinavian origin	1.27	.00	−1.26	1.58	.63	1.37

* Significant at the 1 percent level.
** Significant at the 5 percent level.
*** Significant at the 10 percent level.

pay secured creditors first, over half restrict the managers' right to seek protection from creditors unilaterally, and 45 percent remove management in reorganization proceedings.

As in table 2, we see that, for many creditor rights, the legal origin matters. Common-law countries offer creditors stronger legal protections against managers. They have the highest (72 percent) incidence of no automatic stay on assets; with two exceptions, they guarantee that secured creditors are paid first (the German-civil-law and Scandinavian families have no exceptions); they frequently (72 percent, behind only Scandinavia) preclude managers from unilaterally seeking court protection from creditors; and they have far and away the highest (78 percent) incidence of removing managers in reorganization proceedings. The United States is actually one of the most anticreditor common-law countries: it permits automatic stay on assets, allows unimpeded petition for reorganization, and lets managers keep their jobs in reorganization. The average aggregate creditor rights score for common-law countries is 3.11—by far the highest among the four families—but this score is only 1 for the United States.

The French-civil-law countries offer creditors the weakest protections. Few of them (26 percent, tied with Scandinavia) have no automatic stay on assets; relatively few (65 percent) assure that secured creditors are paid first; few (42 percent—still more than German-civil-law countries) place restrictions on managers seeking court protection from creditors; and relatively few (26 percent) remove managers in reorganization proceedings. The average aggregate creditor rights score for the French-civil-law countries is 1.58, or roughly half of that for the common-law family.

On some measures, countries in the German-civil-law family are strongly pro-creditor. For instance, 67 percent of them have no automatic stay, and secured creditors in all of them are paid first. On the other hand, relatively few of these countries (33 percent) prevent managers from getting protection from creditors unilaterally, and most (67 percent) allow managers to stay in reorganization. One view of this evidence is that the German-civil-law countries are very responsive to secured creditors by not allowing automatic stay and by letting them pull collateral. As a consequence of making liquidation easy, these countries rely less on reorganization of defaulting firms, and hence being soft on such firms by letting managers stay may not be a big problem. The overall average creditor rights score of 2.33 for the German family may therefore understate the extent to which secured creditors are protected.

Finally, Scandinavia has an overall average score of 2.00, which is a bit lower than that of the German family but higher than that of the French.

The evidence on the one remedial pro-creditor legal rule in the sample, the legal reserve requirement, shows that it is almost never used in common-law countries, where other investor protections presumably suffice, but is more common in all civil-law families. Since this requirement is likely to protect unsecured creditors in particular, it is not surprising that it is relatively common in the German-civil-law countries, which tend to be as unprotective as the French-civil-law countries of unsecured creditors. The evidence suggests that, for creditors as well, remedial rights are used as a substitute for the weakness of other investor protections.

From table 4, we see that the ranking of legal families is roughly the same for creditor and shareholder protections. It is not the case that some legal families protect shareholders and others protect creditors. This result can be confirmed formally by looking at the (unreported) correlations of creditor and shareholder rights scores across countries, which are generally positive. The one possible exception is that German-civil-law countries are protective of secured creditors, though generally not of shareholders. A final interesting result, presented in table 3, is that creditor rights are, if anything, stronger in poorer than in richer countries, perhaps because poor countries adapt their laws to facilitate secured lending for lack of other financing opportunities.

In summary so far, laws differ a great deal across countries, and in particular they differ because they come from different legal families. Relatively speaking, common-law countries protect investors the most, and French-civil-law countries protect them the least. German-civil-law countries are in the middle, though closer to the civil-law group. The one exception is the strong protections that German-civil-law countries afford secured creditors. Scandinavian countries are in the middle as well. The evidence also indicates that these results are not a consequence of richer countries' having stronger investor rights; if anything, the results for creditors are the reverse.[7]

If poor investor protections are actually costly to companies in terms of their ability to raise funds, then do countries compensate for these shortcomings in other ways? We have already shown that French-civil-law countries have a higher incidence of remedial legal protections, such as mandatory dividends and legal reserves. But

---

[7] We have also examined whether investor rights are a consequence of geography by dividing the world into Australia, Europe, Africa, Asia, and America. They do not appear to be.

1140   JOURNAL OF POLITICAL ECONOMY

there may be other strategies to compensate, at least in part, for investor-unfriendly laws. One of them—examined in Section V—is strict and effective enforcement of the laws that do exist. The other—examined in Section VI—is concentrated ownership.

V. Enforcement

In principle, a strong system of legal enforcement could substitute for weak rules since active and well-functioning courts can step in and rescue investors abused by the management. To address these issues, we examine proxies for the quality of enforcement of these rights, namely estimates of "law and order" in different countries compiled by private credit risk agencies for the use of foreign investors interested in doing business in the respective countries. We use five of these measures: efficiency of the judicial system, rule of law, corruption, risk of expropriation—meaning outright confiscation or forced nationalization—by the government, and likelihood of contract repudiation by the government. The first two of these measures obviously pertain to law enforcement proper; the last three deal more generally with the government's stance toward business. Some of these measures have been previously shown to affect national growth rates (Knack and Keefer 1995).

In addition, we use an estimate of the quality of a country's accounting standards. Accounting plays a potentially crucial role in corporate governance. For investors to know anything about the companies they invest in, basic accounting standards are needed to render company disclosures interpretable. Even more important, contracts between managers and investors typically rely on the verifiability in court of some measures of firms' income or assets. If a bond covenant stipulates immediate repayment when income falls below a certain level, this level of income must be verifiable for the bond contract to be enforceable in court even in principle. Accounting standards might then be necessary for financial contracting, especially if investor rights are weak (Hay et al. 1996). The measure of accounting standards we use, like the rule of law measures, is a privately constructed index based on examination of company reports from different countries. Unfortunately, it is available for only 44 countries, 41 of which are in our sample.[8]

[8] The measure of accounting standards we use was published in 1991. At around the same time, European countries began to harmonize their accounting standards under pressure from the European Community. Over time, accounting standards may converge in Europe. However, for the purposes of our analysis of country differences and of determinants of ownership, historical differences in the quality of standards are obviously more important than the future convergence.

Table 5 presents country scores for the various rule of law measures, as well as for their accounting standards. It arranges countries by legal origin and presents tests of equality of means between families. The table suggests that quality of law enforcement differs across legal families. In law enforcement, Scandinavian countries are clearly on top, with German-civil-law countries close behind. These families have the highest scores of any group on the efficiency of the judicial system, the rule of law, corruption, risk of expropriation, and risk of contract repudiation by the government. On all the measures of rule of law, common-law countries are behind the leaders but ahead of the French-civil-law countries. The statistical significance of these results varies from variable to variable.

With quality of accounting, Scandinavia still comes out on top, though common-law countries are second, statistically significantly ahead of the German-civil-law countries. The French family has the weakest quality of accounting.

These results do not support the conclusion that the quality of law enforcement substitutes or compensates for the quality of laws. An investor in a French-civil-law country is poorly protected by both the laws and the system that enforces them. The converse is true for an investor in a common-law country, on average.

An inspection of table 5 suggests that, for the enforcement measures, the level of per capita income may have a more important confounding effect than it did for the laws themselves. In table 6, we investigate whether quality of enforcement is different in different legal families through regression analysis across countries, controlling for each country's level of per capita income. The omitted dummy in the regressions is the one for common-law countries.[9]

By every single measure, richer countries have higher quality of law enforcement. Nonetheless, even when one controls for per capita income, the legal family matters for the quality of enforcement and the accounting standards. A great deal of the cross-sectional variance in these rule of law scores is explained by per capita income and the legal origin. In some cases, these variables together explain around 80 percent of the cross-sectional variation in rule of law scores, with the lion's share of the explanatory power coming from per capita income.

Once income is controlled for, French-civil-law countries still score lower on every single measure, and statistically significantly

---

[9] We have also estimated these equations using Tobits, with very similar results. One difference is that the Tobit procedure does not produce a standard error on the Scandinavian dummy because all Scandinavian countries have the same values for some of the variables.

TABLE 5

RULE OF LAW

COUNTRY	ENFORCEMENT VARIABLES					ACCOUNTING: Rating on Accounting Standards	GNP PER CAPITA (U.S. $)
	Efficiency of Judicial System	Rule of Law	Corruption	Risk of Expropriation	Risk of Contract Repudiation		
	A. Country Scores						
Australia	10.00	10.00	8.52	9.27	8.71	75	17,500
Canada	9.25	10.00	10.00	9.67	8.96	74	19,970
Hong Kong	10.00	8.22	8.52	8.29	8.82	69	18,060
India	8.00	4.17	4.58	7.75	6.11	57	300
Ireland	8.75	7.80	8.52	9.67	8.96	na	13,000
Israel	10.00	4.82	8.33	8.25	7.54	64	13,920
Kenya	5.75	5.42	4.82	5.98	5.66	na	270
Malaysia	9.00	6.78	7.38	7.95	7.43	76	3,140
New Zealand	10.00	10.00	10.00	9.69	9.29	70	12,600
Nigeria	7.25	2.73	3.03	5.33	4.36	59	300
Pakistan	5.00	3.03	2.98	5.62	4.87	na	430
Singapore	10.00	8.57	8.22	9.30	8.86	78	19,850
South Africa	6.00	4.42	8.92	6.88	7.27	70	2,980
Sri Lanka	7.00	1.90	5.00	6.05	5.25	na	600
Thailand	3.25	6.25	5.18	7.42	7.57	64	2,110
United Kingdom	10.00	8.57	9.10	9.71	9.63	78	18,060
United States	10.00	10.00	8.63	9.98	9.00	71	24,740
Zimbabwe	7.50	3.68	5.42	5.61	5.04	na	520
English-origin average	**8.15**	**6.46**	**7.06**	**7.91**	**7.41**	**69.62**	**9,353**
Argentina	6.00	5.35	6.02	5.91	4.91	45	7,220
Belgium	9.50	10.00	8.82	9.63	9.48	61	21,650
Brazil	5.75	6.32	6.32	7.62	6.30	54	2,930
Chile	7.25	7.02	5.30	7.50	6.80	52	3,170
Colombia	7.25	2.08	5.00	6.95	7.02	50	1,400
Ecuador	6.25	6.67	5.18	6.57	5.18	na	1,200
Egypt	6.50	4.17	3.87	6.30	6.05	24	660
France	8.00	8.98	9.05	9.65	9.19	69	22,490
Greece	7.00	6.18	7.27	7.12	6.62	55	7,390

Indonesia	2.50	3.98	2.15	7.16	6.09	na	740
Italy	6.75	8.33	6.13	9.35	9.17	62	19,840
Jordan	8.66	4.35	5.48	6.07	4.86	na	1,190
Mexico	6.00	5.35	4.77	7.29	6.55	60	3,610
Netherlands	10.00	10.00	10.00	9.98	9.35	64	20,950
Peru	6.75	2.50	4.70	5.54	4.68	38	1,490
Philippines	4.75	2.73	2.92	5.22	4.80	65	850
Portugal	5.50	8.68	7.38	8.90	8.57	36	9,130
Spain	6.25	7.80	7.38	9.52	8.40	64	13,590
Turkey	4.00	5.18	5.18	7.00	5.95	51	2,970
Uruguay	6.50	5.00	5.00	6.58	7.29	31	3,830
Venezuela	6.50	6.37	4.70	6.89	6.30	40	2,840
French-origin average	**6.56**	**6.05**	**5.84**	**7.46**	**6.84**	**51.17**	**7,102**
Austria	9.50	10.00	8.57	9.69	9.60	54	23,510
Germany	9.00	9.23	8.93	9.90	9.77	62	23,560
Japan	10.00	8.98	8.52	9.67	9.69	65	31,490
South Korea	6.00	5.35	5.30	8.31	8.59	62	7,660
Switzerland	10.00	10.00	10.00	9.98	9.98	68	35,760
Taiwan	6.75	8.52	6.85	9.12	9.16	65	10,425
German-origin average	**8.54**	**8.68**	**8.03**	**9.45**	**9.47**	**62.67**	**22,067**
Denmark	10.00	10.00	10.00	9.67	9.31	62	26,730
Finland	10.00	10.00	10.00	9.67	9.15	77	19,300
Norway	10.00	10.00	10.00	9.88	9.71	74	25,970
Sweden	10.00	10.00	10.00	9.40	9.58	83	24,740
Scandinavian-origin average	**10.00**	**10.00**	**10.00**	**9.66**	**9.44**	**74.00**	**24,185**
Sample average	**7.67**	**6.85**	**6.90**	**8.05**	**7.58**	**60.93**	**11,156**

B. Tests of Means between Origins (*t*-Statistics)

Common vs. civil law	1.27	-.77	.39	-.46	-.51	3.12*	-.94
English vs. French origin	2.65*	.51	1.79***	.90	1.06	4.66*	.85
English vs. German origin	-.41	-1.82***	-.93	-2.19**	-2.79*	2.22**	-2.86*
English vs. Scandinavian origin	-3.78*	-15.57*	-5.38***	-2.06**	-2.26**	-1.05	-3.24*
French vs. German origin	-2.53*	-2.55*	-2.49*	-3.20*	-3.90*	-2.10**	-3.79*
French vs. Scandinavian origin	-9.34*	-20.80*	-9.77*	-2.94*	-3.17*	-3.32*	-4.28*
German vs. Scandinavian origin	-2.06***	-11.29*	-2.88*	-.63	.10	-2.66**	-.36

* Significant at the 1 percent level.
** Significant at the 5 percent level.
*** Significant at the 10 percent level.

TABLE 6

ORDINARY LEAST SQUARES REGRESSIONS: CROSS SECTION OF 49 COUNTRIES

DEPENDENT VARIABLE

INDEPENDENT VARIABLE	Efficiency of Judiciary System (N = 49)		Rule of Law (N = 49)		Corruption (N = 49)		Risk of Expropriation (N = 49)		Repudiation of Contracts by Government (N = 49)		Accounting Standards (N = 41)	
	(1)	(2)	(1)	(2)	(1)	(2)	(1)	(2)	(1)	(2)	(1)	(2)
Log of GNP per capita	.8421* (.1450)	.9763* (.1355)	1.4761* (.1584)	1.5541* (.1379)	1.3088* (.1138)	1.4020* (.0993)	.9099* (.0932)	.9679* (.0772)	.9951* (.0832)	1.0976* (.0734)	4.3348* (1.2453)	5.7747* (1.2908)
Civil-law dummy[a]	...	-1.3774* (.4235)	...	-.3642 (.4290)	...	-1.1388* (.3024)	...	-.3855*** (.2132)	...	-.4111*** (.2228)	...	-14.331* (2.7407)
French origin	-1.6609* (.4796)	...	-.5250 (.4563)	...	-1.3236* (.3190)	...	-.5164** (.2518)	...	-.6459** (.2520)	...	-17.366* (2.9445)	...
German origin	-1.0305*** (.6033)	...	-.2715 (.6312)	...	-1.2422* (.4749)	...	-.0009 (.2097)	...	.3803*** (.1946)	...	-11.890* (2.9104)	...
Scandinavian origin	.2392 (.3550)	...	.7174 (.4681)	...	.4369 (.3152)	...	.0054 (.2242)	...	.1300 (.2095)	...	-1.5272 (4.7556)	...
Intercept	1.2677 (1.3598)	.1702 (1.2862)	-5.6050* (1.3600)	-6.2421* (1.2087)	-3.6367* (.9881)	-4.3986* (.8711)	.4732 (.8431)	-.0018 (.7181)	-.7290 (.7250)	-1.5671* (.6493)	31.807* (10.844)	19.249 (11.442)
Adjusted R^2	.5719	.5185	.7744	.7605	.8442	.8056	.8120	.7998	.8465	.8146	.6125	.5131

NOTE.—Robust standard errors are in parentheses.
[a] The dummy variable civil law takes a value equal to one when the country belongs to the civil-law tradition (i.e., all French, German, and Scandinavian codes) and zero when the country belongs to the common-law tradition (i.e., English common law).
* Significant at the 1 percent level.
** Significant at the 5 percent level.
*** Significant at the 10 percent level.

lower for almost all measures, than the common-law countries do. However, German-civil-law countries now tend to score lower than the common-law countries on all measures other than repudiation of contracts by government, although the effect is significant only for the efficiency of the judiciary and the accounting standards. Scandinavian countries are similar to common-law countries in rule of law measures. The regression results continue to show that legal families with investor-friendlier laws are also the ones with stronger enforcement of laws. Poor enforcement and accounting standards aggravate, rather than cure, the difficulties faced by investors in the French-civil-law countries.

VI. Ownership

In this section, we explore the hypothesis that companies in countries with poor investor protection have more concentrated ownership of their shares. There are at least two reasons why ownership in such countries would be more concentrated. First, large, or even dominant, shareholders who monitor the managers might need to own more capital, ceteris paribus, to exercise their control rights and thus to avoid being expropriated by the managers. This would be especially true when there are some legal or economic reasons for large shareholders to own significant cash flow rights as well as votes. Second, when they are poorly protected, small investors might be willing to buy corporate shares only at such low prices that make it unattractive for corporations to issue new shares to the public. Such low demand for corporate shares by minority investors would indirectly stimulate ownership concentration. Of course, it is often efficient to have some ownership concentration in companies since large shareholders might monitor managers and thus increase the value of the firm (Shleifer and Vishny 1986). But with poor investor protection, ownership concentration becomes a substitute for legal protection, because only large shareholders can hope to receive a return on their investment.

To evaluate this hypothesis, we have assembled a database of up to the 10 largest (by market capitalization) nonfinancial (i.e., no banks or insurance companies), domestic (i.e., no foreign multinationals), totally private (i.e., no government ownership), publicly traded (i.e., not 100 percent privately held) companies in each country in our sample. For some countries, including Egypt, India, Nigeria, Philippines, and Zimbabwe, we could not find 10 such companies and settled for at least five.

For each company, we collected data on its three largest shareholders and computed the combined (cash flow) ownership stake of these three shareholders. We did not correct for the possibility that some of the large shareholders are affiliated with each other or that the company itself owns the shares of its shareholders. Both of these corrections would raise effective concentration of cash flow ownership. On the other hand, we also did not examine the complete ownership structure of firms, taking account of pyramidal structures and the fact that corporate shareholders themselves have owners. Doing this is likely to reduce our measure of ownership concentration. Finally, we could not distinguish empirically between large shareholders who are the management, are affiliated with the management, or are separate from the management. It is not clear that a conceptual line between management and, say, a 40 percent shareholder can be drawn.

Subject to these caveats, it is possible to construct measures of ownership concentration for 45 of our 49 countries. For each country, we took the average and the median ownership stake of the three largest shareholders among its 10 largest publicly traded companies. This measure resembles measures of ownership concentration used for American companies by Demsetz and Lehn (1985) and Mørck, Shleifer, and Vishny (1988).

Table 7 presents, by legal origin, this concentration variable for each country. In the world as a whole, the average ownership of the three largest shareholders is 46 percent, and the median is 45 percent. Dispersed ownership in large public companies is simply a myth. Even in the United States, the average for the 10 most valuable companies is 20 percent (which is partly explained by the fact that Microsoft, Walmart, Coca-Cola, and Intel are on the list and all have significant ownership concentration), and the median is 12 percent. The average concentration measure we use is under 30 percent only for the United States, Australia, United Kingdom, Taiwan, Japan, Korea, and Sweden. Presumably, if we looked at smaller companies, the numbers we would get for ownership concentration would be even larger. The finance textbook model of management faced by multitudes of dispersed shareholders is an exception and not the rule.

Table 7 also shows that ownership concentration varies by legal origin. By far the highest concentration of ownership is found in the French-civil-law countries, with the average ownership by the three largest shareholders a whopping 54 percent for the 10 largest non-government firms. The lowest concentration, in the German-civil-law countries, is 34 percent. This puzzlingly low concentration comes from East Asia, where as we already mentioned company law has been significantly influenced by the United States, rather than from Germany, Austria, or Switzerland. Scandinavian countries are also

TABLE 7

OWNERSHIP OF 10 LARGEST NONFINANCIAL DOMESTIC FIRMS BY LARGE
SHAREHOLDERS: CROSS SECTION OF 49 COUNTRIES

COUNTRY	OWNERSHIP BY THREE LARGEST SHAREHOLDERS		AVERAGE MARKET CAPITALIZATION OF FIRMS (Millions of U.S. $)
	Mean	Median	
	A. Ownership		
Australia	.28	.28	5,943
Canada	.40	.24	3,015
Hong Kong	.54	.54	4,282
India	.40	.43	1,721
Ireland	.39	.36	944
Israel	.51	.55	428
Kenya	na	na	27
Malaysia	.54	.52	2,013
New Zealand	.48	.51	1,019
Nigeria	.40	.45	39
Pakistan	.37	.41	49
Singapore	.49	.53	1,637
South Africa	.52	.52	6,238
Sri Lanka	.60	.61	4
Thailand	.47	.48	996
United Kingdom	.19	.15	18,511
United States	.20	.12	71,650
Zimbabwe	.55	.51	28
English-origin average	**.43**	**.42**	**6,586**
Argentina	.53	.55	2,185
Belgium	.54	.62	3,467
Brazil	.57	.63	1,237
Chile	.45	.38	2,330
Colombia	.63	.68	457
Ecuador	na	na	na
Egypt	.62	.62	104
France	.34	.24	8,914
Greece	.67	.68	163
Indonesia	.58	.62	882
Italy	.58	.60	3,140
Jordan	na	na	63
Mexico	.64	.67	2,984
Netherlands	.39	.31	6,400
Peru	.56	.57	154
Philippines	.57	.51	156
Portugal	.52	.59	259
Spain	.51	.50	1,256
Turkey	.59	.58	477
Uruguay	na	na	na
Venezuela	.51	.49	423
French-origin average	**.54**	**.55**	**1,844**
Austria	.58	.51	325
Germany	.48	.50	8,540
Japan	.18	.13	26,677
South Korea	.23	.20	1,034

TABLE 7 (*Continued*)

COUNTRY	OWNERSHIP BY THREE LARGEST SHAREHOLDERS		AVERAGE MARKET CAPITALIZATION OF FIRMS (Millions of U.S. $)
	Mean	Median	
	A. Ownership		
Switzerland	.41	.48	9,578
Taiwan	.18	.14	2,186
German-origin average	**.34**	**.33**	**8,057**
Denmark	.45	.40	1,273
Finland	.37	.34	1,980
Norway	.36	.31	1,106
Sweden	.28	.28	6,216
Scandinavian-origin average	**.37**	**.33**	**2,644**
Sample average	**.46**	**.45**	**4,521**
	B. Tests of Means (*t*-Statistics)		
Common vs. civil law	−1.10	−.91	1.00
English vs. French origin	−3.24*	−2.68*	1.22
English vs. German origin	1.38	1.31	−.20
English vs. Scandinavian origin	1.05	1.22	.46
French vs. German origin	3.87*	3.29*	−2.61**
French vs. Scandinavian origin	3.93*	3.32*	−.61
German vs. Scandinavian origin	−.24	−.06	1.05

NOTE.—A firm is considered privately owned if the state is not a known shareholder in it.
* Significant at the 1 percent level.
** Significant at the 5 percent level.
*** Significant at the 10 percent level.

relatively low, with a 37 percent concentration. Finally, common-law countries are in the middle, with a 43 percent average ownership concentration. The differences between the French and other legal families are statistically significant, although other differences are not. In sum, these data indicate that the French-civil-law countries have unusually high ownership concentration. These results are at least suggestive that concentration of ownership is an adaptation to poor legal protection.

In table 8, we examine empirically the determinants of ownership concentration, in two steps. First, we regress ownership concentration on legal origin dummies and several control variables to see whether origin matters. The controls we use are (the logarithm of) GNP per capita on the theory that richer countries may have different ownership patterns; (the logarithm of) total GNP on the theory that larger economies have larger firms, which might therefore have a lower ownership concentration; and the Gini coefficient for a country's income on the theory that more unequal societies have a

LAW AND FINANCE   1149

TABLE 8

ORDINARY LEAST SQUARES REGRESSIONS: CROSS SECTION OF 49 COUNTRIES

Dependent Variable: Mean Ownership

Independent Variable	Basic Regression	Shareholder and Creditor Rights
Log of GNP per capita	.0077	.0397
	(.0097)	(.0242)
Log of GNP	−.0442*	−.0428*
	(.0119)	(.0118)
Gini coefficient	.0024***	.0027
	(.0014)	(.0023)
Rule of law		−.0143
		(.0115)
Accounting		−.0029***
		(.0016)
French origin	.1296*	.0733
	(.0261)	(.0802)
German origin	−.0113	−.0025
	(.0666)	(.0728)
Scandinavian origin	−.0496	−.0430
	(.0371)	(.0473)
Antidirector rights		−.0315**
		(.0150)
One share–one vote		−.0497
		(.0406)
Mandatory dividend		.2197***
		(.1113)
Creditor rights		−.0128
		(.0171)
Legal reserve required		−.2237**
		(.0766)
Intercept	.7785*	.8686*
	(.1505)	(.2952)
Number of observations	45	39
Adjusted R^2	.5582	.7348

NOTE.—Variables are defined in table 1. Robust standard errors are in parentheses.
* Significant at the 1 percent level.
** Significant at the 5 percent level.
*** Significant at the 10 percent level.

higher ownership concentration. Second, we add to the first regression several measures of legal protections, including accounting standards, enforcement quality, shareholder rights, creditor rights, and remedial rights. Given the large number of variables collected for this paper, we cannot estimate all the possible regressions, and we need to make some choices. We pick "rule of law" as our measure of quality of enforcement and use aggregate antidirector and creditor rights scores from tables 2 and 4. The results we present are representative of other specifications.

The first regression in table 8, with all 45 observations, has an adjusted R^2 of 56 percent. It shows that larger economies have a lower ownership concentration and more unequal countries have a higher ownership concentration, consistent with the conjectured effects of these controls. In addition, this regression confirms the sharply higher concentration of ownership in the French-civil-law countries. The second regression in table 8 adds investor rights, rule of law, and accounting standards. It has only 39 observations because the data on accounting standards are incomplete. Still, the adjusted R^2 rises to 73 percent. The coefficient on the logarithm of GNP remains significant, but not that on the Gini coefficient. The coefficient on the French-origin dummy turns insignificant, which suggests that our measures of investor protections actually capture the limitations of the French-civil-law system. Indeed, countries with better accounting standards have a (marginally) statistically significantly lower concentration of ownership, though rule of law is insignificant. A 20-point increase in the accounting score (roughly the distance between the common-law and French-civil-law averages) reduces average ownership concentration by six percentage points. Countries with better antidirector rights, as measured by our aggregate variable, also have a statistically significantly lower concentration of ownership. A 1.6-point increase in the antidirector rights score (roughly the distance between common-law and French-civil-law averages) reduces ownership concentration by five percentage points. In contrast, one share–one vote is not significant.

The creditor rights score is insignificant. One could argue that when creditor rights are good, bank borrowing becomes more common, and small shareholders can free-ride on the monitoring by banks, making dispersed ownership possible. One could alternatively argue that easier bank borrowing enables firms to finance their investment through debt rather than equity, leading to a higher ownership concentration in equilibrium.

Finally, the regression shows a large positive effect of the mandatory dividend rule and a large negative effect of the legal reserve requirement on ownership concentration. The former variable is correlated with the French origin and the latter with the German origin.

Some of our independent variables, but particularly accounting standards, might be endogenous. Countries that for some reason have heavily concentrated ownership and small stock markets might have little use for good accounting standards, and so fail to develop them. The causality in this case would go from ownership concentration to accounting standards rather than the other way around. Since we have no instruments that we believe determine accounting but not ownership concentration, we cannot reject this hypothesis.

More generally, the only truly exogenous variable in these regressions is the legal origin, and hence the result that is most plausibly interpreted as causal is the positive effect of French origin on ownership concentration.

In sum, the message of this section is that the quality of legal protection of shareholders helps determine ownership concentration, accounting for the higher concentration of ownership in the French-civil-law countries. The results support the idea that heavily concentrated ownership results from, and perhaps substitutes for, weak protection of investors in a corporate governance system. The evidence indicates that weak laws actually make a difference and may have costs. One of these costs of heavily concentrated ownership in large firms is that their core investors are not diversified. The other cost is that these firms probably face difficulty raising equity finance, since minority investors fear expropriation by managers and concentrated owners.

VII. Conclusion

In this paper, we have examined laws governing investor protection, the quality of enforcement of these laws, and ownership concentration in 49 countries around the world. The analysis suggests three broad conclusions.

First, laws differ markedly around the world, though in most places they tend to give investors a rather limited bundle of rights. In particular, countries whose legal rules originate in the common-law tradition tend to protect investors considerably more than the countries whose laws originate in the civil-law, and especially the French-civil-law, tradition. The German-civil-law and the Scandinavian countries take an intermediate stance toward investor protections. There is no clear evidence that different countries favor different types of investors; the evidence rather points to a relatively stronger stance favoring all investors in common-law countries. This evidence confirms our basic hypothesis that being a shareholder, or a creditor, in different legal jurisdictions entitles an investor to very different bundles of rights. These rights are determined by laws; they are not inherent in securities themselves.

Second, law enforcement differs a great deal around the world. German-civil-law and Scandinavian countries have the best quality of law enforcement. Law enforcement is strong in common-law countries as well, whereas it is the weakest in the French-civil-law countries. These rankings also hold for one critical input into law enforcement in the area of investor protections: the accounting standards. The quality of law enforcement, unlike the legal rights themselves, improves sharply with the level of income.

Third, the data support the hypothesis that countries develop substitute mechanisms for poor investor protection. Some of these mechanisms are statutory, as in the case of remedial rules such as mandatory dividends or legal reserve requirements. We document the higher incidence of such adaptive legal mechanisms in civil-law countries. Another adaptive response to poor investor protection is ownership concentration. We find that ownership concentration is extremely high around the world, consistent with our evidence that laws, on average, are only weakly protective of shareholders. In an average country, close to half the equity in a publicly traded company is owned by the three largest shareholders. Furthermore, good accounting standards and shareholder protection measures are associated with a lower concentration of ownership, indicating that concentration is indeed a response to poor investor protection.

The ultimate question, of course, is whether countries with poor investor protections—either laws or their enforcement—actually do suffer. Recent research has begun to provide partial answers to this question. King and Levine (1993) and Levine and Zervos (1998) find that developed debt and equity markets contribute to economic growth. In a similar vein, Rajan and Zingales (1998) find that countries with better developed financial systems show superior growth in capital-intensive sectors that rely particularly heavily on external finance. Levine (1998) confirms the King-Levine findings that financial development promotes economic growth using our legal origin variable as an instrument for his measures of financial development. And finally, La Porta et al. (1997) show that countries with poor investor protections indeed have significantly smaller debt and equity markets.[10] Taken together, this evidence describes a link from the legal system to economic development. It is important to remember, however, that while the shortcomings of investor protection described in this paper appear to have adverse consequences for financial development and growth, they are unlikely to be an insurmountable bottleneck. France and Belgium, after all, are both very rich countries.

References

Aghion, Philippe; Hart, Oliver; and Moore, John. "The Economics of Bankruptcy Reform." *J. Law, Econ., and Organization* 8 (October 1992): 523–46.

---

[10] La Porta et al. (1997) use the original La Porta et al. (1996) data. We have reconfirmed their results using the refined measures presented in this paper.

LAW AND FINANCE   1153

American Bar Association. *Multinational Commercial Insolvency.* Chicago: American Bar Assoc., 1989, 1993.

Andenas, Mads, and Kenyon-Slade, Stephen, eds. *E.C. Financial Market Regulation and Company Law.* London: Sweet and Maxwell, 1993.

Baird, Douglas. "The Hidden Values of Chapter 11: An Overview of the Law and Economics of Financially Distressed Firms." Manuscript. Chicago: Univ. Chicago, Law School, 1995.

Bebchuk, Lucian A. "Efficient and Inefficient Sales of Corporate Control." *Q.J.E.* 109 (November 1994): 957–93.

Berglof, Erik, and Perotti, Enrico. "The Governance Structure of the Japanese Financial Keiretsu." *J. Financial Econ.* 36 (October 1994): 259–84.

Berle, Adolf A., and Means, Gardiner C. *The Modern Corporation and Private Property.* New York: Harcourt, Brace and World, 1932.

Boycko, Maxim; Shleifer, Andrei; and Vishny, Robert W. "Privatizing Russia." *Brookings Papers Econ. Activity,* no. 2 (1993), pp. 139–81.

Deininger, Klaus, and Squire, Lyn. "Measuring Income Inequality: A New Data-Base." Manuscript. Washington: World Bank, 1996.

Demsetz, Harold, and Lehn, Kenneth. "The Structure of Corporate Ownership: Causes and Consequences." *J.P.E.* 93 (December 1985): 1155–77.

Easterbrook, Frank H., and Fischel, Daniel R. *The Economic Structure of Corporate Law.* Cambridge, Mass.: Harvard Univ. Press, 1991.

Edwards, Jeremy, and Fischer, Klaus. *Banks, Finance and Investment in West Germany since 1970.* Cambridge: Cambridge Univ. Press, 1994.

Glendon, Mary Ann; Gordon, Michael W.; and Osakwe, Christopher. *Comparative Legal Traditions: Text, Materials and Cases on the Civil and Common Law Traditions, with Special References to French, German and English.* St. Paul, Minn.: West, 1994.

Gorton, Gary, and Schmidt, Frank. "Universal Banking and the Performance of German Firms." Working Paper no. 5453. Cambridge, Mass.: NBER, February 1996.

Gromb, Denis. "Is One-Share–One-Vote Optimal?" Manuscript. London: London School Econ., 1993.

Grossman, Sanford J., and Hart, Oliver. "One Share–One Vote and the Market for Corporate Control." *J. Financial Econ.* 20 (January/March 1988): 175–202.

Harris, Milton, and Raviv, Artur. "Corporate Governance: Voting Rights and Majority Rules." *J. Financial Econ.* 20 (January/March 1988): 203–35.

Hart, Oliver. *Firms, Contracts, and Financial Structure.* London: Oxford Univ. Press, 1995.

Hay, Jonathan R.; Shleifer, Andrei; and Vishny, Robert W. "Toward a Theory of Legal Reform." *European Econ. Rev.* 40 (April 1996): 559–67.

Houghton, Anthony R., and Atkinson, Nigel G. *Guide to Insolvency in Europe.* Chicago: Commerce Clearing House (for Deloitte Touche Tohmatsu Internat.), 1993.

Institutional Shareholder Services. *Proxy Voting Guidelines.* Washington: ISS Global Proxy Services, 1994.

Investor Responsibility Research Center. *Proxy Voting Guide.* Washington: Investor Responsibility Res. Center, 1994, 1995.

Jensen, Michael C., and Meckling, William H. "Theory of the Firm: Managerial Behavior, Agency Costs and Ownership Structure." *J. Financial Econ.* 3 (October 1976): 305–60.

Kaplan, Steven N., and Minton, Bernadette A. "Appointments of Outsiders

1154   JOURNAL OF POLITICAL ECONOMY

to Japanese Boards: Determinants and Implications for Managers." *J. Financial Econ.* 36 (October 1994): 225–57.

King, Robert G., and Levine, Ross. "Finance and Growth: Schumpeter Might Be Right." *Q.J.E.* 108 (August 1993): 717–37.

Knack, Stephen, and Keefer, Philip. "Institutions and Economic Performance: Cross-Country Tests Using Alternative Institutional Measures." *Econ. and Politics* 7 (November 1995): 207–27.

La Porta, Rafael; Lopez-de-Silanes, Florencio; Shleifer, Andrei; and Vishny, Robert W. "Law and Finance." Working Paper no. 5661. Cambridge, Mass.: NBER, July 1996.

———. "Legal Determinants of External Finance." *J. Finance* 52 (July 1997): 1131–50.

Levine, Ross. "The Legal Environment, Banks, and Long-Run Economic Growth." *J. Money, Credit and Banking* 30, no. 3, pt. 2 (August 1998).

Levine, Ross, and Zervos, Sara. "Stock Markets, Banks, and Economic Growth." *A.E.R.* 88 (June 1998): 537–58.

Levy, Haim. "Economic Evaluation of Voting Power of Common Stock." *J. Finance* 38 (March 1983): 79–93.

Merryman, John H. *The Civil Law Tradition: An Introduction to the Legal Systems of Western Europe and Latin America.* Stanford, Calif.: Stanford Univ. Press, 1969.

Modigliani, Franco, and Miller, Merton H. "The Cost of Capital, Corporation Finance and the Theory of Investment." *A.E.R.* 48 (June 1958): 261–97.

Mørck, Randall; Shleifer, Andrei; and Vishny, Robert W. "Management Ownership and Market Valuation: An Empirical Analysis." *J. Financial Econ.* 20 (January/March 1988): 293–315.

Pagano, Marco; Panetta, F.; and Zingales, Luigi. "Why Do Companies Go Public: An Empirical Analysis." *J. Finance* 53 (February 1998): 27–64.

Rajan, Raghuram G., and Zingales, Luigi. "What Do We Know about Capital Structure? Some Evidence from International Data." *J. Finance* 50 (December 1995): 1421–60.

———. "Financial Dependence and Growth." *A.E.R.* 88 (June 1998): 559–86.

Reynolds, Thomas H., and Flores, Arturo A. *Foreign Law: Current Sources of Codes and Basic Legislation in Jurisdictions of the World.* Littleton, Colo.: Rothman, 1989.

Roe, Mark J. *Strong Managers, Weak Owners: The Political Roots of American Corporate Finance.* Princeton, N.J.: Princeton Univ. Press, 1994.

Rydquist, Kristian. "Empirical Investigation of the Voting Premium." Working Paper no. 35. Evanston, Ill.: Northwestern Univ., 1987.

Shleifer, Andrei, and Vishny, Robert W. "Large Shareholders and Corporate Control." *J.P.E.* 94, no. 3, pt. 1 (June 1986): 461–88.

———. "A Survey of Corporate Governance." *J. Finance* 52 (June 1997): 737–83.

Vishny, Paul. *Guide to International Commerce Law.* New York: McGraw-Hill, 1994.

Watson, Alan. *Legal Transplants: An Approach to Comparative Law.* Charlottesville: Univ. Virginia Press, 1974.

Werlauff, Erik. *EC Company Law: The Common Denominator for Business Undertakings in 12 States.* Copenhagen: Jurist- og Okonomforbundets Forlag, 1993.

LAW AND FINANCE   1155

White, Michelle. "The Costs of Corporate Bankruptcy: The U.S.-European Comparison." Manuscript. Ann Arbor: Univ. Michigan, Dept. Econ., 1993.

World Bank. *Social Indicators of Development, 1991–1992.* Baltimore: Johns Hopkins Univ. Press, 1993. (*a*)

———. *World Development Report.* Washington: Oxford Univ. Press, 1993. (*b*)

Zingales, Luigi. "The Value of the Voting Right: A Study of the Milan Stock Exchange Experience." *Rev. Financial Studies* 7 (Spring 1994): 125–48.

———. "What Determines the Value of Corporate Votes?" *Q.J.E.* 110 (November 1995): 1047–73.

Zweigert, Konrad, and Kotz, Hein. *An Introduction to Comparative Law.* 2d rev. ed. Oxford: Clarendon, 1987.

[7]

Journal of Accounting Literature
Vol. 16, 1997, pp. 127 - 159

A REVIEW OF RESEARCH ON THE RELATIONSHIP BETWEEN INTERNATIONAL CAPITAL MARKETS AND FINANCIAL REPORTING BY MULTINATIONAL FIRMS

Shahrokh M. Saudagaran
Santa Clara University

Gary K. Meek
Oklahoma State University

1.0 INTRODUCTION

In this paper we extend an earlier survey (Meek and Saudagaran [1990]) on research in transnational financial reporting.[1] An impressive amount of research has been published in the area since that paper appeared. [2] The trend toward global capital, including international share listings, has accelerated in the 1990s.[3] As a result, issues surrounding transnational financial reporting figure more prominently on the agendas of accounting policy making bodies around the world, and they concern an increasing number of investors and companies.

Our purpose is to review and synthesize this recent research literature.[4] Since the earlier survey, the literature has taken several new directions. As such, our goal is to

We appreciate the comments of Mike Chatham, Carol Frost, Don Hermann, Carol Houston, Wayne Thomas, Olusegun Wallace, Peter Walton, the reviewer, and participants at research colloquia at the University of Washington, Oklahoma State University, and the University of Arkansas, as well as participants at the 1997 Annual Congress of the European Accounting Association and the 1997 Annual Meeting of the AAA International Accounting Section.

The first author acknowledges the financial support provided by Santa Clara University's Accounting Development Fund.

[1] The term "transnational financial reporting" refers to financial reporting across national boundaries or, more specifically, to reporting financial results to user groups located in countries other than the one where the company is headquartered. Section 4.1 of Meek and Saudagaran [1990, pp. 160-162] discusses the various approaches that companies take to accommodate foreign readers of their financial reports.

[2] Prather and Rueschhoff [1996] document that, insofar as U.S. academic journals are concerned, financial reporting is the most prevalent topic in international accounting, occupying almost 45 percent of the total since 1980. They also note that the number of financial reporting articles in the 1990s increased over earlier periods. Zeff [1996] notes that five new accounting journals with a specific international focus have been launched or announced since 1987, in response the the growth in international and comparative research.

[3] Truly "global" capital is the seamless flow of capital around the world, unincumbered by restrictions or other market frictions. In reality, capital markets are national, but increasingly linked via information technology, as barriers to seamless capital flows fall. The term "international capital markets" refers to this latter phenomenon.

[4] We limit our survey to research published in English, but we canvassed U.S. and non-U.S. journals that were available through July 1997.

128   *Journal of Accounting Literature*   Volume 16

identify the major themes and to discuss selected papers that, in our view, have advanced or best exemplify those themes. Besides describing and evaluating what we have learned from the research, we also suggest further research that may be essential. We provide a framework which we hope is useful to researchers in tying this literature together.

Our paper shares some of the subject matter discussed in other recent review articles, notably Prather and Rueschhoff [1996], Wallace and Gernon [1991], and Gernon and Wallace [1995]. However, the thrust and overall framework of our paper is different from these. Prather and Rueschhoff [1996] provide descriptive information on the trends since 1980 in topics and research methods used in the entire spectrum of international accounting research, but they do not attempt to synthesize it, nor do they comment on individual pieces of research. Wallace and Gernon [1991] are concerned with how to compare international accounting research; their emphasis is on the methodology of comparative international accounting research. Gernon and Wallace [1995] elucidate the underlying theories that support current international accounting research and they evaluate contending methodologies that have or can be used. While there is some overlap in the literature we both include, their motivation for discussing it differs from ours, and so our respective comments reflect different points of view.

This paper is organized as follows: Section 2 deals with diversity versus harmonization. Diversity prevails internationally in both generally accepted accounting principles (GAAP) and actual financial reporting practices, notwithstanding significant attempts to harmonize them. We look at the recent literature on the causes, effects, and measures of diversity, along with the extent to which harmonization has been achieved. Section 3 is about disclosures by internationally-listed companies. These are the companies most affected by the issues surrounding diversity and harmonization. Section 4 is concerned with multiple GAAP reporting, an increasing trend in transnational financial reporting. Section 5 provides concluding observations. Generally speaking, we do not repeat papers discussed in Meek and Saudagaran [1990] unless they bear on recent work.

The foregoing embrace the principal streams of recent research on transnational financial reporting. However, there are several areas that we omit. First is the literature on accounting in emerging economies. The shift towards open market economies in countries that until recently had communist or socialist centrally-planned economic systems is having a dramatic effect on their financial reporting. To attract capital from abroad, these countries are being forced to revamp their financial reporting so that foreign investors have meaningful and relevant information. This phenomenon is currently in a state of flux with different countries at different stages of drafting and adopting new standards and practices. Much of the accounting literature is descriptive and reflects the authors' opinions as to what is likely to happen in these countries. In our opinion, it will take a few more years before a clear picture emerges of their financial reporting models. Second is an emerging literature on disclosures of a social nature, particularly as they relate to corporate environmental performance (e.g., Fekrat, Inclan, and Petroni [1996] and Gamble, Hsu, Jackson, and Tollerson [1996]). We omit this literature because, in our view, the influence of international capital markets on these disclosures is not apparent: whether international capital markets are developing a social conscience and an environmental awareness is not yet clear. Finally, we have not updated the survey on geographic segment reporting (Meek and Saudagaran [1990],

Section 4.2) because this literature was recently reviewed by Herrmann and Thomas [1997].

2.0 DIVERSITY VERSUS HARMONIZATION

2.1 Causes of Diversity

A nation's accounting standards and practices are the result of a complex interaction of cultural, historical, economic, and institutional factors. It is unlikely that the mix is alike in any two countries, and diversity is to be expected. The factors that influence accounting development at the national level also help explain accounting diversity across nations. Meek and Saudagaran [1990] note that there is general agreement that the following five factors influence accounting development: (1) legal system, (2) nature of the relationship between business enterprises and providers of capital, (3) tax laws, (4) inflation levels, and (5) political and economic ties.[5] Other factors that have also been mentioned in the literature are (6) level of economic development and (7) education levels.

Cultural variables underlie nations' institutional arrangements (such as systems of law), and Meek and Saudagaran [1990] discuss a framework proposed by Gray [1988] for analyzing the relationship between culture and accounting. Gray's framework is developed from the pioneering work of Hofstede [1980] who enunciated four national cultural dimensions: (1) power distance, (2) uncertainty avoidance, (3) individualism, and (4) masculinity. The influence of culture on accounting is an area that has received attention since Meek and Saudagaran [1990]. The Hofstede/Gray framework is the basis for most of this work. Figure 1 summarizes Gray's proposed relationships between four "accounting values" and Hofstede's four cultural dimensions.[6]

---

[5] Related to this last factor is history and historical accidents. For example, Walton [1995, p. 6] notes that many continental European countries adopted the Napoleonic Commercial Code in the nineteenth century and only introduced income tax later. Thus, they had established accounting rules before they had an income tax, which gave the tax authorities something to rely on. By contrast, income tax came at the end of the eighteenth century in the U.K., well before there were any established accounting rules. This seems to have left British accounting disconnected from taxation. Therefore, why tax laws and legal systems are important in Europe is their timing in history.

[6] The societal values (cultural dimensions) enunciated by Hofstede [1980] are: (1) *power distance* - the extent to which hierarchy and an unequal distribution of power in institutions and organizations are accepted, (2) *uncertainty avoidance* - the degree to which society feels uncomfortable with ambiguity and an uncertain future, (3) *individualism (versus collectivism)* - "I" versus "we," a preference for a loosely knit social fabric or and independent, tightly knit fabric, and (4) *masculinity (versus femininity)* - the extent to which gender roles are differentiated and performance and visible achievement (traditional masculine values) are emphasized over relationships and caring (traditional feminine values).

The accounting values proposed by Gray [1988] are: (1) *professionalism (versus statutory control)* - a preference for the exercise of individual professional judgement and maintaining professional self-regulation as opposed to compliance with prescriptive legal requirements and statutory control, (2) *uniformity (versus flexiblity)* - a preference for uniformity and consistency over flexibility in accordance with perceived circumstances, (3) *conservatism (versus optimism)* - a preference for a cautious approach to measurement so as to cope with the uncertainty of future events as opposed to a more optimistic, laissez-faire, risk taking approach, and (4) *secrecy (versus transparency)* - a preference for confidentiality and the restriction of information about business only to those who are closely involved with its management and financing, in contrast to a more transparent, open and publicly accountable approach.

130   *Journal of Accounting Literature*   Volume 16

Salter and Niswander [1995] test Gray [1988] and find only mild support overall. Their results indicate that uncertainty avoidance is most strongly associated with Gray's accounting values. Individualism, which Gray thought would be relatively important overall, is only related to secrecy.[7] Power distance has no relationship to Gray's four accounting values, and masculinity is more strongly associated than Gray hypothesized. Fechner and Kilgore [1994] report Hofstede's admission that uncertainty avoidance significantly correlates with his other three cultural dimensions and it is the only one that does so. Thus, one explanation for the finding that uncertainty avoidance dominates the other three cultural dimensions is that it is a "summary index" for the other three cultural dimensions.

Gray's [1988] hypotheses have been refined by several authors. For example, he only proposes directional ("sign") relationships between cultural and accounting

Figure 1

RELATIONSHIPS BETWEEN GRAY'S ACCOUNTING VALUES
AND HOFSTEDE'S CULTURAL DIMENSIONS

Cultural Dimension (Hofstede)	Accounting values (Gray)			
	Professionalism	Uniformity	Conservatism	Secrecy
Individualism	+	–	–	–
Power Distance	–	+	?	+
Uncertainty Avoidance	–	+	+	+
Masculinity	?	?	–	–

Note: "+" indicates a direct relationship between the variables; "–" indicates an inverse relationship. Question marks indicate that the nature of the relationship is indeterminate. Gray hypothesizes that individualism and uncertainty avoidance will influence accounting the most, followed by power distance, then masculinity.

Adapted from: Baydoun and Willett [1995, p. 71].

It should be noted that later work by Hofstede (Hofstede and Bond [1988] and Hofstede [1991]) documents a fifth cultural dimension, called "Confucian dynamism" (or, "long-term orientation"). This later work contends that only three of the original four cultural dimensions are universal: power distance, individualism, and masculinity. Uncertain avoidance is a unique characteristic of Western societies, whereas Confucian dynamism applies to Eastern societies but not to Western ones. However, Yeh and Lawrence [1995] note a data problem in this work. According to them, once the outlier is removed, Confucian dynamism no longer emerges as an independent construct; it reflects the same cultural dimension as individualism.

[7] Gray and Vint [1995], focusing exclusively on the secrecy dimension, find that it is significantly related to uncertainty avoidance and individualism. These results are consistent with Salter and Niswander [1995].

dimensions. This has been extended to the relative influence of cultural dimensions on various accounting dimensions ("sign" and "size"). Thus, Baydoun and Willett [1995] argue that culture has a more important bearing on disclosure (i.e., the secrecy dimension) than on measurement (the conservatism dimension). Along the same lines, Fechner and Kilgore [1994] argue that cultural factors directly influence disclosure, while economic factors influence measurement. These proposals have yet to be tested empirically.

Integrating prior research, Doupnik and Salter [1995] model accounting development as a function of three interacting elements: the external environment, cultural values, and institutional structures. They also conduct a test of the ability of their model to explain measurement and disclosure practices in 50 countries using proxies for the seven factors enumerated above and from Hofstede's cultural variables. In addition, they provide some insights into the relative importance of environmental and cultural factors in explaining accounting development. Their results indicate that the type of legal system (code versus common law) is the dominant explanatory variable, and the basic point of departure in classifying accounting practices internationally. This is consistent with another study by the same authors (Salter and Doupnik [1992]) as well as earlier works, such as Nobes [1983]. The significance of equity as a source of finance and the cultural dimension of uncertainty avoidance are two other dominant factors. Next in importance are inflation, level of economic development, and masculinity, which are followed by level of education and power distance. Despite using recent data on accounting practices, the findings with respect to economic and institutional variables indicate that the same causes of diversity identified in earlier research[8] continue to explain diversity today. One must also be careful in interpreting the results of this study. For one, environmental and cultural factors are clearly correlated. For example, in looking at the three dominant ones identified by the study (legal system, source of finance, and uncertainty avoidance), code law countries tend to be uncertainty avoidant and rely less on stock markets as a source of finance, whereas common law countries tend to be less uncertainty avoidant and they have strong stock markets. Also, it is not clear whether cultural variables ought to "compete" head-to-head with, especially, institutional variables as explanations of accounting diversity. Since cultural variables underlie institutional arrangements, their impact on accounting is second-order. Third, the authors combine measurement and disclosure practices in constructing their dependent variable. While they present evidence that measurement and disclosure are correlated in their database (less conservative measurement practices associate with higher disclosure and vice versa), it is not clear why the two should be influenced in the same way by the same factors.

Overall, it is not clear to us that recent research on the causes of diversity has yielded much that is new and/or definitive. "Culture" remains a rather imprecise generic concept, one that is difficult to operationalize. Gernon and Wallace [1995, p. 91] worry that culture has often become "a residue for everything that cannot be explained by other factors" and question whether culture is really a homogeneous phenomenon within countries. While Hofstede may be the "best" framework that we have, it is incomplete. For example, religion—which extends beyond national boundaries—

---

[8] Nor apparently have classifications changed very much. The authors also cluster countries according to accounting practices and get basically the same groupings as earlier research. See Sections 2.3 and 3.0 in Meek and Saudagaran [1990].

underlies business practices, institutional arrangements, and therefore accounting practices.[9] Language is another cultural input. Perera [1994] paraphrases comments made by Gerhard G. Mueller that accounting seems to flourish in English-speaking countries and to languish in most others, particularly Romance language countries.[10] Most of the related accounting literature has taken Hofstede [1980] as a given and accepted it uncritically, but Perera [1994] and Gernon and Wallace [1995] point out some reasons to have reservations. For example, Hofstede developed his framework based on data from one large MNC (IBM), and so may not be generalizable. Also, his data are old and there may have been some cultural shifts since the time of collection. Thus, there is substantial scope for refining the measures and other operationalizations of culture as a concept. Moreover, other cultural frameworks besides Hofstede's may yield different insights.

An area that has received relatively little attention is the comparative analysis of accounting standard setting. How accounting standards are set and the influences on the process in different countries help explain why standards vary around the world. Different standards are another cause of diverse practices. (However, the relationship between practice and standards is not one-way: in some cases practice derives from standards, but in others, standards confirm or legitimize practice.) Examples of this literature are Gorelik [1994], who looks at standard setting in Canada, the U. K., and the U. S., and McKinnon [1993], who compares Australia and Japan.

The extent to which the causes of diversity at the national level extend to the transnational level is an open question. Section 3.0 presents evidence on disclosures by companies competing for capital in international capital markets. Such companies are increasingly tailoring their financial reporting for a worldwide audience, notwithstanding the need to prepare financial statements in the first instance according to the rules of the country of their domicile. For this group of companies, international capital market pressures seem to be a counterforce to the causes of diversity at the national level. We conjecture that international capital market pressures are likely to be a primary cause for moderating accounting diversity in the future.

2.2 Effects of Diversity

A number of studies have looked at the diversity in financial reporting practices and their effect on firms. Issues examined include the effects of differences in disclosure levels on listing decisions (Biddle and Saudagaran [1991], Saudagaran and Biddle [1992, 1995], Cheung and Lee [1995]), effects of regulatory differences on user groups (Choi and Levich [1991] and Bhushan and Lessard [1992]), and the effects of differences in goodwill treatments on mergers and acquisitions (Choi and Lee [1991], Lee and Choi [1992], Dunne and Rollins [1992], Dunne and Ndubizu [1995]).

One stream of research in this area has examined how accounting and regulatory factors that result in differing levels of financial disclosure affect where companies list their stocks. For some time now there has been a fairly heated debate as to the level of disclosure that should be required by regulators and stock exchanges from foreign

---

[9] Hamid, Craig, and Clarke [1993] examine these relationships in the case of Islam.

[10] Of course, it may be that language is not a causal factor *per se*, rather correlated with other factors.

firms listing within their jurisdictions.[11] From the regulators' perspective, the goal of protecting domestic investors from potentially misleading financial disclosures by foreign firms must be weighed against demands for increased access to investment opportunities (in foreign firms). The competitiveness of domestic stock exchanges and securities industries often hangs in the balance. In the United States, the Securities and Exchange Commission (SEC) and the New York Stock Exchange (NYSE) have been on opposite sides of the issue. The SEC insists that foreign firms' financial statements must be reconciled to U.S. GAAP for the protection of U.S. investors. The NYSE and others have argued that the reconciliation requirement imposes an unnecessary burden on foreign issuers which is keeping them from listing their securities on the NYSE and other U.S. stock exchanges. They complain that this has a number of adverse effects for the U.S. economy. It deprives U.S. investors of the opportunity to invest in many global "blue chip" companies. It reduces the competitiveness of domestic stock exchanges and securities industries relative to countries where the net regulatory burden is less than in the United States (Freund [1993], Cochrane [1994]).

Biddle and Saudagaran [1991] address three main issues related to the interaction between accounting diversity and the increasing globalization of the world's capital markets. They discuss 1) the benefits and costs of listing on a foreign stock exchange, 2) the effects of accounting disclosure levels on foreign listing decisions, and 3) accounting policy issues posed by foreign stock exchange listings and how authorities have responded.

From the accounting and financial reporting perspective, a key question in the debate outlined above is whether firms' choices regarding alternative foreign stock exchange listings are influenced by financial disclosure levels. Saudagaran and Biddle [1992] examine the listings of 302 internationally traded firms with at least one foreign listing, on one of the nine major exchanges, as of year-end 1987. Given the SEC's introduction of streamlined reporting requirements for foreign issuers via the Integrated Disclosure System (IDS) in 1982 and similar measures by Japan's Ministry of Finance in 1984, they also examine the changes in listings between 1981 to 1987. Financial disclosure levels for the eight countries in the study were obtained from a survey of 142 experts actively involved in the foreign listing process. Their results are consistent with the hypothesis that exchange choices are influenced by financial disclosure levels. Tests based on changes in listings between 1981 and 1987 provide evidence that financial disclosure levels remained a significant factor even after the relaxations in disclosure requirements by the SEC and the Ministry of Finance in Japan during 1982 and 1984, respectively.

Saudagaran and Biddle [1995] revisit the question of whether disclosure levels affect listing choices by looking at a significantly expanded sample of firms—450 firms from eight countries—that are listed on at least one of the major stock exchanges at year-end 1992. This allows them to study a ten year period (1982-1992) versus a five year period (1982-1987) since the 1982 implementation of the IDS rules in the U.S. to determine whether IDS has indeed facilitated foreign firms listing in the U.S. The results of this study are consistent with the findings in their earlier work that financial disclosure levels were still a significant factor in the choice of foreign stock

---

[11] See, for example, Torres [1990, 1991], LaBaton [1991], Freund [1993], Breeden [1994], and Cochrane [1994].

exchanges. Overall, the evidence lends credence to the concerns expressed about the effects of stringent disclosure levels on capital market participants. Accounting academics have traditionally refrained from making policy recommendations based on their research. However, developments in the capital markets combined with the mounting evidence on the costs and benefits of certain reporting requirements suggest that academics might need to be more forceful in the conclusions they draw and the conviction with which they discuss the implications of their findings. The following quote from Edwards [1993, p. 36] succinctly sums up the criticism of the SEC's stance on reporting requirements for foreign private issuers:

> First, to the extent that foreign countries currently impose less burdensome reporting standards on firms, U.S. firms now operate at a competitive disadvantage. U.S. investors are already trading the securities of unregistered foreign firms in volume in foreign markets. Second, the SEC's argument implicitly assumes that its present disclosure requirements are now optimal; that is, it implicitly assumes that investors are unwilling to pay for the additional information U.S. firms are required to disclose. Stated another way, if a foreign firm reports less information and investors recognize this as a deficiency, the firm's cost of capital will be higher than for a similar American firm. Alternatively, if by providing the information required by the SEC, an American firm's cost of capital is lower, there will be no incentive for U.S. firms to abandon the current disclosure policy. Third, to the extent that neither the U.S. firms nor U.S. investors value the additional information required by the SEC, but seek to relax disclosure standards to make them more compatible with those of foreign countries, current SEC requirements can be said to be sub-optimal—or too burdensome.

Cheung and Lee [1995] treat the level of disclosure required on exchanges as a signaling mechanism in a study that attempts to theoretically model the foreign listing behavior of companies. They consider a listing by a company on an exchange with stricter disclosure requirements as a credible signal of the company's future prospects. This means that such listings will result in better pricing for the shares of the firm. The benefits of this signaling come with the higher costs that are associated with listings on stock exchanges with more comprehensive disclosure requirements. Thus, according to Cheung and Lee [1995] for each firm the choice of a foreign stock exchange involves weighing the benefits of better pricing with the greater listing costs. The model in this paper is limited to one of many other potential benefits from listing (Saudagaran [1988]) that are likely to affect the choice of specific foreign stock exchanges by firms.

In related research, Choi and Levich [1991] and Bhushan and Lessard [1992] discuss the behavioral effects of accounting diversity on major categories of capital market participants. Both studies use surveys to gather their data. Choi and Levich [1991] ask 52 institutions consisting of investors, issuers, underwriters, regulators, standards boards, and credit rating agencies, located in Frankfurt, Zurich, London, New York, and Tokyo, 1) whether they perceive accounting diversity to be a problem, 2) whether and how these institutions attempt to cope with the diversity, and 3) whether problems associated with accounting diversity lead to capital market effects. They find that accounting differences are important and affect the capital market decisions (i.e., the geographic spread of investments, the types of securities selected, assessment of security returns or valuation, and information processing costs) of a significant number of the surveyed capital market participants regardless of nationality, size, experience, scope of international activity and organizational structure.

Bhushan and Lessard [1992] survey international investment managers from the U.S. and U.K. to determine whether and how they are affected by accounting diversity and by the presence or absence of quantitative reconciliation. The SEC has steadfastly held the opinion that reconciliation to U.S. GAAP is critical for investor protection. However, Bhushan and Lessard [1992] find that professional investors, while they regard reconciliation (along with all forms of additional information) to be useful, do not regard it as essential. The reason for this includes the fact that primary financial statements and local valuation are still most important. This paper has important policy implications because it both attempts to distinguish between the financial information that investors need as opposed to what they would like (particularly if they do not bear the costs of producing it), and it focuses on the cost of reconciliation. Since reconciliation is not costless it requires a serious cost-benefit analysis. Bhushan and Lessard [1992] conclude that the SEC's emphasis on reconciliation is not well-founded.

Another stream of research studies the effects of differing rules of goodwill on merger activity. Choi and Lee [1991] and Lee and Choi [1992] examine whether national differences in the accounting treatment of purchased goodwill are associated with differences in merger premia offered by non-U.S. acquirers when bidding for U.S. target companies. Choi and Lee [1991] focuses on acquirers from the U.K. while Lee and Choi [1992] looks at acquirers from Germany and Japan. They assess 1) whether U.K., German and Japanese acquirers consistently pay higher premia for U.S. targets than U.S. acquirers, 2) whether these premia are associated with accounting measures of goodwill, and 3) whether observed premium differentials are attributable to differences in goodwill accounting treatments. They find merger premia offered by foreign acquirers based in countries with more favorable accounting and tax treatments for goodwill than the U.S. to be higher than those offered by U.S. acquirers. Their analysis shows that goodwill accounting treatment does explain merger premia, and that the premia paid by British firms are substantially more than that paid by German and Japanese firms.

In a case study that uses identical acquisition scenarios for acquirer firms from the U.S., U.K., and Japan, Dunne and Rollins [1992] discuss the effects of differences in accounting for goodwill for financial reporting and tax purposes. Based on hypothetical scenarios they conclude that since Japan alone, of the three countries studied, allows the amortization of goodwill to be deducted for tax purposes Japanese firms have a cash flow, and thereby a competitive, advantage over firms from the U.S. and U.K. They also demonstrate that the U.K. acquirer experiences the highest reported income and rates of return because it is able to write off goodwill immediately against stockholders equity. The U.S. acquirer enjoys neither enjoys neither a cash flow nor a reported earnings advantage relative to firms from Japan and the U.K.

Dunne and Ndubizu [1995] study the effect of diversity in accounting and tax treatments for goodwill on target shareholders' wealth. *Ceteris paribus*, the odds of a successful acquisition increase as more wealth is transferred to target shareholders. They find that non-U.S. companies that write off goodwill against a reserve account transfer more wealth to the target shareholders than those that amortize goodwill against income. Foreign acquirers that deduct goodwill for tax purposes transfer more wealth to the target stockholders at the acquisition announcement than other acquirers. They conclude that this puts U.S. bidders at a disadvantage in their competition with foreign bidders to acquire U.S. firms.

Nobes and Norton [1996] and Nobes [1996] question the evidence and conclusions reached by the studies discussed above on the effects of differing rules of goodwill on merger activity on the grounds that these studies fail to distinguish between consolidation goodwill and non-consolidation goodwill (i.e., other purchased goodwill). While this may not be a problem for financial reporting in English-speaking countries because the accounting rules are generally similar for the two types of goodwill, they assert that the lack of distinction can cause problems when dealing with other countries or with tax reporting. Nobes and Norton [1996] argue that since the context of the goodwill studies is consolidated financial statements and the purchase of shares these studies are in error when they refer to the tax deductibility of goodwill because deductibility relates to goodwill arising on the acquisition of the assets of a business rather than the shares in it. In their response to Nobes [1996], Dunne and Ndubizu [1996] point out that Dunne and Ndubizu [1995] attempt to examine the differences in accounting and tax treatments for goodwill across countries and their possible effects on returns to U.S. target companies and that differences in goodwill were simply not a focus of their paper.

Overall, these findings indicate that diversity in accounting and/or tax treatments affects international merger activity. This conclusion makes sense to the extent that tax treatments are involved, since taxes have direct cash flow consequences. However, in environments where there is a dichotomy between financial reporting and tax reporting, such as in the U.K., it is puzzling why financial reporting diversity alone should have any effect on the terms of international mergers. Perhaps accounting treatments correlate with other variables such as market share and cost of capital that are the real causes.

The evidence presented in this section indicates that the effects of international accounting diversity are real. Various capital market participants and the terms of international transactions seem to be affected by it. As such, diversity imposes costs on the resource allocation system worldwide. Harmonization of this diversity may provide one solution and is discussed next.

2.3 Harmonization

With the dramatic growth in global trade and the accelerated internationalization of capital markets, financial statements produced in one country are used in other countries more and more frequently. This has brought accounting harmonization to the forefront as an international business issue. While accounting academics and others have offered several definitions of harmonization, some of which will be discussed below, very simply stated it is the process by which differences in financial reporting practices among countries are reduced with a view to making financial statements more comparable and decision-useful across countries. In this section, we address the following three questions in the area of accounting harmonization: 1) Is there a need for harmonization? 2) What factors help and hinder harmonization? and 3) What are appropriate measures of harmonization? We also discuss the evidence in extant research on the level of harmonization that has been achieved to date.

2.3.1 Need for Harmonization

As noted in Meek and Saudagaran [1990], the debate over the need for and desirability of accounting harmonization began in the academic accounting literature in the 1960s and has continued unabated since.[12]   The primary economic rationale in favor of harmonization is that major differences in accounting practices act as a barrier to capital flowing to the most efficient uses. Investors are more likely to direct their capital to the most efficient and productive companies globally if they are able to understand their accounting numbers (and so, presumably, their economic reality). However, if the accounting practices between countries are different to the point of imposing unreasonable burdens on capital providers then they may direct their capital to less efficient and productive companies simply because they can understand the latter's financial statements and thus consider them less risky investments. According to the law of comparative advantage this is a less than optimal solution which makes us economically worse off globally than we could otherwise be. A related rationale for harmonization is that it will enhance comparability of financial statements thus making them easier to use among countries. Wyatt [1989] and Beresford [1990] both point to the need for harmonization in view of the rapid growth in international capital markets and increased cross-border financing. According to them, harmonization is necessary to produce comparable and credible data for use across borders. Beresford, ex-chairman of the U.S. Financial Accounting Standards Board (FASB), rebuts suggestions that the FASB has been "uninterested" and "uncooperative" regarding the international harmonization of accounting standards. He provides his views on how the FASB will participate in the evolution of international standards. The focus is on the positive aspects of internationalization and the FASB's commitment to improving international standards.[13]

Among those that oppose harmonization there are some who consider it to be unnecessary (Goeltz [1991]), and others who are even more critical and view it as being harmful (Fantl [1971]; Samuels and Oliga [1982]; Hoarau [1995]). Goeltz [1991] argues that full harmonization of international accounting standards is probably not practical, nor truly valuable. He opines that global GAAP will not likely be achieved given the institutional impediments in the standard setting process. Also, a well-developed global capital market already exists, so there is no real need to increase the already robust international capital markets. Investors and issuers can make investment decisions without the convenience of international accounting standards. Goeltz's final argument against the need for harmonization is that investors are rational enough to spend the necessary time and money to correctly analyze investment opportunities and focus on real economic results.

Opponents generally cite differences in the economic, political, legal and cultural environment in countries as a justification for financial reporting differences. They typically express concerns that the accounting regimes in developed Western countries

---

[12] Walton [1995] and Forrester [1996] point out that harmonization has been a preoccupation of European accountants since the nineteenth century when most continental European countries adopted the Napoleonic Commercial Code.

[13] See Beresford [1990] and [1997] for his views on the FASB's role and participation in the internationalization of accounting standards.

are likely to dominate global harmonization efforts. Imposing Western accounting practices on developing non-Western countries, they argue, is likely to do more harm than good. Hoarau [1995] is critical about the international accounting harmonization movement based on France's experience with implementing international standards. He contends that in France the influence of international harmonization is limited to consolidated financial statements and that because harmonization disregards the economic, social and cultural context of French accounting it has broken down the homogeneity of the French accounting model, ruptured its unity and reduced the social functions of accounting in France. Hoarau considers the current harmonization process to be synonymous with harmonization to the Anglo-Saxon, and particularly the American, accounting model and its focus on the stockholder as the primary stakeholder. According to him, there remain unanswered questions about the nature and means of achieving harmonization, about its consequences at a national level and about the obstacles and political difficulties to be overcome. Nobes [1995] disagrees with Hoarau's views and refutes a number of points made by Hoarau including the scope of harmonization, alternatives in preparing consolidated financial statements, information needs of creditors and employees, and American 'imperialism' in the harmonization effort. Nobes argues that countries, including France, have adopted certain accounting rules not because of any pressure from the IASC or the U.S. but because they were best suited to those countries' needs in the increasingly international capital markets. In a similar vein, van der Tas [1995] points out that France made certain choices on accounting standards when implementing the Seventh Directive. However, he agrees with Hoarau's view that national standard-setters should be allowed greater involvement in the development of international accounting standards.

We believe that France, unlike a number of the developing countries, has the political will and clout to act in its perceived national interest including in the arena of accounting harmonization. We are concerned, however, that a number of industrializing and economically developing countries that lack the resources to develop their own standards might succumb to the wholesale adoption of IASs in an effort to gain global respectability for their financial reporting. It is our view that such countries should endeavor to make their voices heard in IASC discussions to ensure that their concerns and requirements are considered in any international standards that emerge. Their growing economic prowess gives them the collective ability to do so.

2.3.2 Pressure for and Obstacles to Harmonization

In recent years the pressure for global harmonization has come from a variety of quarters including users, preparers, and regulators of financial statements. Users such as investors and financial analysts are concerned about the reliability and comparability of financial statements prepared in countries other than their own. If they cannot understand the financial statements of foreign companies they may be unwilling to invest in them. As companies increasingly tap foreign sources of capital, this is also a reason for preparers of financial statements to support the harmonization effort. Multinational companies can also expect additional benefits from harmonization such as the reduced cost of preparing consolidated financial statements, ease in monitoring subsidiaries, more relevant managerial accounting reports and comparable performance evaluation methods with harmonization than without it.

Regulators face higher costs with the growth in cross-border listings by companies since they now need to monitor compliance not just by domestic firms but also by foreign firms that are listed in their jurisdiction. While one way of coping with this might be to simply require foreign firms to provide financial statements that conform to the host country's requirements there is considerable debate as to the wisdom of this approach. Critics such as Baumol and Malkiel [1993], Edwards [1993], and Freund [1993] argue that the high costs of financial reporting and other regulatory compliance thereby imposed on foreign firms causes them to stay away. (Empirical evidence supporting this claim has been discussed in section 2.2 above.) This hurts the very investors that the regulator is mandated to protect by depriving them of attractive investment opportunities. If one accepts this proposition then regulators would also be expected to benefit from harmonization in that it would reduce their monitoring costs and yet allow domestic individual investors the option of investing in foreign companies without incurring unduly high transactions costs.

One of the reasons that global accounting harmony is still an objective rather than a reality is that there remain a number of obstacles to harmonization. Some of these are economic while others are political. On the economic front, harmonization is often opposed due to its economic impact on countries or segments of society within countries. Grinyer and Russell [1992] discuss the lobbying effort in the U.K. in the case of accounting for goodwill and provide evidence that managers and auditors lobbied against the IASC proposal to further their own vested interests. Thus to the extent that economic consequences of accounting practices vary by country and to the extent that they are considered in the standard-setting process this acts as an important obstacle to global harmonization.

Nationalism represents a political obstacle to harmonization. As in many other arenas, countries are wary of ceding control of their accounting regulation to outsiders particularly if it is perceived as replacing their own accounting regulations with those of other countries. It helps if the external standards originate from a multi-country organization such as the IASC since it is more politically palatable for countries to adopt "international standards" rather than the standards of another country. Wallace [1990] discusses the emergence of the IASC as a legitimate organization due to its acceptance by its constituents. According to him, the IASC continues to survive because of (a) the increasing internationalization of business and finance which make global harmonization of accounting and disclosure practices desirable, (b) the composite nature of its standards and its preoccupation with topics of a general nature, (c) its evolutionary strategy, and (d) the absence of a rival organization with keen and prolonged interest in the development and marketing of global accounting standards. However, critics of the IASC have argued that until it undertook its Comparability Project, its standards were so flexible as to be irrelevant and that the IASC was a "Trojan Horse which conceals the Anglo-Saxon accounting enemy inside a more respectable international facade" (Nobes and Parker [1995, p. 127]).

Another political obstacle to harmonization is the absence of strong professional accounting bodies in a number of countries (Nobes and Parker [1995]). This means that an organization such as the IASC, which seeks to operate through national accounting bodies, will not be effective in a number of countries. This obstacle may be overcome, at least as it relates to listed companies, if the International Organization of Securities Commissions (IOSCO) endorses the IASC's standards and provides enforcement in its member countries. There are indications that IOSCO may accept this role in the near future [IASC 1997a].

2.3.3 Measures of Harmonization

Harmonization, in the accounting context, may be defined as the process aimed at enhancing the comparability of financial statements produced in different countries' accounting regulations. van der Tas [1988] and Tay and Parker [1990] draw a distinction between material (de facto) and formal (de jure) harmonization. The former refers to the harmony of actual accounting practices while the latter refers to the harmony of financial accounting regulations. van der Tas [1988] draws a second distinction dealing with measurement and disclosure issues. He suggests that the harmonization of both accounting practices and accounting regulations can focus either on measurement issues such as methods of recognition, valuation, and estimation or on disclosure issues such as the level of transparency provided by entities via their financial reporting. Harmonization measurement studies purport to explore the similarity or lack thereof of accounting practices and requirements.

Tay and Parker [1990] analyze six such studies to demonstrate problems involved in measuring the concepts of 'harmonization' and 'standardization' in the context of international accounting. They discuss methodological issues and problems related to the definition and operationalization of terms, data sources, and statistical methods. They draw distinctions between the terms *harmonization and standardization* (i.e., a movement away from total diversity versus a movement towards uniformity), *regula - tion and practice* (i.e., de jure versus de facto), and *strict* and *less strict* regulation (viz., (i) apply to all companies versus apply to some companies, (ii) the law versus a professional accounting standard, and (iii) defined precisely versus defined loosely to allow discretion). These distinctions were also noted in Meek and Saudagaran [1990]. Finally, they also distinguish between *harmony and uniformity* which are states and *harmonization and standardization* which are processes. They point out that there are numerous differences between how the six studies in their analysis approach their stated task of measuring harmonization and consequently it should not be surprising that they come up with different conclusions.

Tay and Parker [1990] suggest an alternative methodology for measuring harmonization. They make four specific recommendations on how to conduct such research. First, in the interest of comparability the focus ought to be on *de facto* (practice) rather than *de jure* (regulation) harmonization. Second, in the interest of measuring reporting practices they recommend that data be obtained from annual reports or surveys of annual reports rather than surveys of legal and accounting regulation. Third, data on proportions of companies using different accounting practices should be obtained. Then an operational definition of harmonization could be a significance test for differences between the observed distribution of companies using different methods and either a random distribution or some expected distribution. Fourth, the level of harmony could be quantified using a concentration index describing the entire distribution. This would allow comparison over different time periods and provide evidence of harmonization or the lack thereof.[14]

---

[14] See Gernon and Wallace [1995] for a critique of this area of research.

2.3.4 Evidence of Current Harmonization

Since the European Union (EU, formerly the European Community — EC) is the only multi-country organization engaged in harmonization that also has the ability to enforce its accounting directives, a number of studies have attempted to measure the level of harmonization attained within the EU. Some of these studies address accounting practice by looking at the extant reporting in corporate annual reports from selected EU member countries while others look at the state of regulation on specific accounting items in selected countries. Hermann and Thomas [1995] look at the level of harmonization in accounting measurement practices among eight member countries in the European Union. Adapting van der Tas' [1988] *I* index to measure harmonization, they find that accounting for foreign currency translation of assets and liabilities, treatment of translation differences, and inventory valuation are harmonized while accounting for fixed asset valuation, depreciation, goodwill, research and development costs, inventory costing, and foreign currency translation of revenues and expenses are not harmonized. They also find some evidence that there is greater harmonization among fairness-oriented countries than among legalistic countries. van der Tas [1992] tests for harmonization of accounting for deferred taxes in the EC and finds mixed evidence for the years 1978-88. Emenyonu and Gray [1992] also use van der Tas's *I* index to measure harmonization of accounting practices between France, Germany and the U.K. They also find little evidence of harmonization across the three countries. Using groups of British and French accountants in a laboratory study, Walton [1992] finds that there is not only a lack of harmonization in the application of the EU Fourth Directive between the two jurisdictions but also a general absence of consensus even within each country group. Garrod and Sieringhaus [1995] compare the regulations for accounting for leased assets in Germany and the U.K. and conclude that the regulations are ambiguous and result in dissimilar accounting treatment in the two countries. Adhikari and Tondkar [1995] study the success of the EU in harmonizing stock exchange disclosure requirements for 11 EU stock exchanges. They find that EU requirements do not eliminate the differences in the disclosure requirements between stock exchanges. Rather they establish a lower bound below which the disclosure requirements may not fall. These studies indicate that the EU has achieved minimal harmony in its accounting practices and regulations (Bindon and Gernon [1995]).

There is a small but emerging literature that addresses accounting harmonization in economic blocks other than the EU. Saudagaran and Diga [1997] study accounting regulation in five countries (i.e., Indonesia, Malaysia, Philippines, Singapore, Thailand) belonging to the Association of South East Asian Nations (ASEAN) in the context of the global and regional paradigms of harmonization. They use a comparative framework to highlight the similarities and differences in the regulatory environment of the five countries. The study examines forces driving global harmonization in ASEAN and discusses the economic and political conditions for regional harmonization that, unlike the EU, do not yet exist in ASEAN. Saudagaran and Diga [1997] conclude that this has led to the dominance of the global paradigm of harmonization in ASEAN. Agami and Monsen [1995] examine accounting standards and practices within Scandinavian countries and find that a fair level of harmonization has been achieved among these countries driven in no small measure by the fact that three (i.e., Denmark, Finland, Sweden) of the four countries (Norway being the exception) are members of the European Union. Other studies dealing with the subject of regional harmonization have proposed rather than measured the level of harmony attained among geographically proximate countries. Two such studies are Rahman, Perera, and Tower [1994] and Rivera and Salva [1995]. Rahman, Perera, and Tower [1994] consider the current arrangements relating to accounting standard-setting structures in Australia and New Zealand. They conclude that a merger of the two countries' standard-setting structures would be the most appropriate means of achieving accounting harmony between Australia and New Zealand and offer some ideas to bring about such a merger. Rivera and Salva [1995] propose the European Union model of accounting standard-setting to achieve accounting harmony within Latin America. Among the interesting issues in regional harmonization are 1) whether its effect is to further global harmonization or detract from it, and 2) what factors influence whether countries belonging to economic blocks choose the regional or the global paradigm of harmonization.

Until this point in time there has been very little empirical research measuring the success of harmonization at the global level. Meek and Saudagaran [1990] noted that the research on the extent of harmonization with the IASC's standards, prior to the start of its Comparability Project in 1989, showed that the IASC had little impact on reporting practices even among MNCs. They expressed the view that it was necessary to undertake a systematic analysis of the reasons for the apparent reluctance to adopt IASC standards before setting up enforcement mechanisms for these standards. The need for such research still remains. The less than enthusiastic initial response may be largely due to the fact that the original series of accounting standards promulgated by IASC were very broad and did little to enhance the comparability of financial statements. That particular concern ought to be alleviated to a considerable extent with the tightening of IASC standards through its Comparability and Improvements Project begun in 1989. This project was initiated with a view to enhancing comparability in part to gain the approval and thereby enforcement of its standards by the International Organization of Securities Commissions (IOSCO). Research looking into whether the level of global harmony has increased as a result of the tightening of standards would only be meaningful after the passage of a reasonable period of time since the promulgation of the revised IASC standards.

3.0 DISCLOSURES BY INTERNATIONALLY-LISTED COMPANIES

Meek and Saudagaran [1990] point out that a distinction should be made between the financial reporting practices of domestic and multinational companies. International operations create new stakeholders with new, and possibly different, demands for information. A further distinction can be made for companies raising capital in international capital markets. Additional disclosures, especially of a voluntary[15] nature, can be expected by these companies in response to international capital market

---

[15] Distinguishing a voluntary disclosure from one that is required is more difficult in an international context that it is in a strictly domestic one. For example, something required in one jurisdiction may be voluntary in another. If an internationally listed company must meet both jurisdiction's requirements, is the item required or voluntary? In addition, disclosures that are required in statutory filings may encourage similar disclosures in, say, company annual reports where, strictly speaking, they are voluntary. Should this disclosure in the annual report be considered voluntary or required?

pressures associated with the competition for investment funds. Meek and Saudagaran [1990] state that internationally-listed companies are the ones for whom international harmonization efforts are most relevant.[16]   However, if voluntary disclosures are already sufficiently harmonized, then the rationale for extensive regulation of transnational financial reporting is less clear. For example, Choi and Levich [1990] report that voluntary disclosures are one way that MNCs cope with international diversity in accounting principles.

Zarzeski [1996] specifically looks at the influence of multinationality on annual report disclosures in relation to so-called "market forces" (leverage and size) and national cultural characteristics. She finds that while cultural attributes underlie disclosure behavior, culture is overridden to some extent by market forces. Specifically, the study finds that a high cultural tendency toward secrecy exerts a general dampening influence on disclosure levels, but that disclosure levels increase as companies grow larger and increasingly multinational, and as they increase their sourcing of finance from stockholders (that is, as leverage decreases).[17] The findings are consistent with observations by Meek and Saudagaran [1990] from research in the early 1980s that reporting by MNCs is anchored in national requirements. Zarzeski [1996] demonstrates that financial statements of MNCs continue to reflect the primary orientation of accounting in their home countries. However, her study is also consistent with the point made above that reporting practices of domestic and MNCs are different. Zarzeski [1996] examines "overall" disclosure levels (i.e., without distinguishing between voluntary and mandatory disclosures) and a refinement would be separating disclosures into voluntary and mandatory items. As noted above, the effects of market forces are likely to be more obvious on voluntary disclosures. In addition, her arguments for why multinationality and leverage should increase disclosure relate more to voluntary than to mandatory disclosures. Finally, note that the study considers the effects of "market forces" generally, not specifically international capital market forces.

Several national studies of corporate reporting behavior have documented an international capital market effect on the extent of voluntary disclosure. Countries include Japan (Cooke [1991]), Malaysia (Hossain, Tan, and Adams [1994]), New Zealand (Hossain, Perera, and Rahman [1995]), and Sweden (Cooke [1989b]).[18] In addition,

---

[16] This is in contrast to the official view of the International Accounting Standards Committee, which is that international standards should apply to al companies. Nevertheless, the IASC acknowledges (IASC [1997b]) that its "top priority is to complete the package of 'core' standards required by IOSCO for cross-border listings" (p. 1) Further, the argument about focusing harmonization (and international standards) on certain types of companies is not new. For example, Gray, Shaw, and McSweeney [1981] reason that international standards should be aimed at multinational corporations, while Nobes and Parker [1985, pp. 341-342] argue that harmonization should be aimed at listed companies. Our view that international harmonization is most relevant for internationally-listed companies is based on the assumption that the information needs of capital market participants is the same worldwide. The relevance of internationally harmonized accounting standards for companies that only raise capital in their home country market is less clear (at least to us).

[17] Note that this is opposite of agency arguments that disclosure increases as leverage increases.

[18] Cooke [1991] and Cooke [1992] on Japanese companies are essentially the same analysis, except that the former is concerned with voluntary disclosures, while the latter is concerned with total disclosures (voluntary and mandatory). Both studies examine the same exploratory variables and reach the same conclusions. Similarly, Cooke [1989b] is the same as Cooke [1989a], except that the former is about voluntary Swedish disclosures and the latter is about total disclosures. Again, the same factors are examined in both studies and the same results are found.

these studies have assessed other factors that explain voluntary annual report disclosures by companies from the countries represented, though they differ in terms of specific explanatory factors examined and some of the results are inconsistent.[19]   The only other factor besides international listing status consistently observed across all four studies to explain voluntary disclosures is company size.

Gray, Meek, and Roberts [1995] and Meek, Roberts, and Gray [1995] examine the effect of international capital market pressures on voluntary disclosures by MNCs. Gray, Meek, and Roberts [1995] look at whether internationally-listed U.S. and U.K. MNCs voluntarily disclose more, as well as more harmonized, information in their annual reports than U.S. and U.K. MNCs listed only on their respective domestic stock markets. One innovation in this study is that voluntary disclosure items are grouped by type of information, since there may be differences in disclosure behavior depending on the nature of the information concerned. They form three categories of information: strategic, financial, nonfinancial. Overall, they find that participation in international capital markets is significantly associated with additional voluntary disclosures. However, the effect varies across information type. International capital market pressures are important in explaining strategic information disclosures, but not nonfinancial. For the latter, country effects are observed. Financial information disclosures seem to be weakly influenced by both capital market and country effects, with neither factor dominating. The authors conclude that international capital market pressures exert only a mild harmonization effect on voluntary disclosures.

In Meek, Roberts, and Gray [1995], the authors extend their analysis by including Continental European companies and by examining additional factors beyond listing status and national influences. Additional explanatory factors considered in this study are company size, industry, leverage, extent of multinational operations, and profitability. The study finds that company size, country (or region), international listing status, and, to a lesser extent, industry are the most important factors explaining voluntary annual report disclosures overall. However, as with their other study, the importance of the factors varies by information type.[20]   The results point to the importance of distinguishing between types of information in examining voluntary disclosures.[21]

All of the studies discussed in this section so far have focused on disclosures in annual reports. Of course, this is not the only vehicle by which companies reveal information to investors and other interested parties. For example, there are also press releases (including interim and annual earnings announcements), special-purpose

---

[19] For example, Cooke [1991] and Cooke [1989b] document a mild industry effect for Japanese and Swedish companies, respectively. The other two studies do not include an industry variable. Hossain, Tan, and Adams [1994] find that ownership concentration is statistically significant for Malaysian companies, but the other studies do not include this variable. Leverage is statistically significant in Hossain, Perera, and Rahman [1995] on New Zealand companies, but it is not in Hossain, Tan, Adams [1994] on Malaysian companies. Neither Cooke paper [1991 and 1989a] considers leverage.

[20] In other words, different types of information are voluntarily disclosed for different reasons. As the authors suggest, this has implications for future research on voluntary disclosures. The existing empirical and theoretical literature has tended to treat voluntary disclosures somewhat generically. This may be one reason why, for example, the single nation studies referred to earlier in this section have some inconsistent results.

[21] One limitation of both papers is that the authors only look at one year's worth of data (1989). Whether their results generalize to other years is not known.

reports, and formal and informal meetings with financial analysts. Frost and Pownall [1994a] examine a number of types of accounting disclosures made public to U.S. and U.K. securities markets by firms cross-listed in both markets. The disclosures include annual reports, statutory filings (such as with the SEC), and news releases of forecasts and other announcements. They consider both voluntary and mandatory disclosures. Their purposes are to see whether the frequency and timing of such disclosures differ between the two markets, and to relate firms' disclosure practices to factors such as the enforcement of disclosure rules. Generally speaking, disclosures by the sample firms should be comparable in the two markets. However, they find that more, and more timely, disclosures are made in the U.S. than in the U.K., consistent with more stringent enforcement in the United States. The finding is also consistent with higher investor demand for information in the U.S. Frequency and timing is related to firm size and, in the case of the U.S. market, whether firms are on the New York and American Stock Exchanges or on NASDAQ. Finally, they document substantial non-compliance with disclosure requirements in both jurisdictions. Research such as Frost and Pownall [1994a] provide important evidence about transnational information flows that support the functioning of capital markets around the world, and there is scope for additional work such as this. That the U.S. market has a richer information set than the U.K. market means that U.K. investors are, relatively speaking, informationally disadvantaged. Whether this type of market friction affects securities prices is another question. However, a companion study (Frost and Pownall [1994b]) suggests that it may. It documents that the stock price response to earnings disclosures by cross-listed firms is significantly greater in the United States than the United Kingdom, consistent with greater liquidity and more frequent trading in the U.S. The two papers together raise interesting cause-and-effect questions about how enforcement, disclosures, trading, and price reactions interact.

In summary, the research reported in this section suggests that while reporting practices continue to be anchored in national requirements, they should be distinguished for domestic versus multinational versus internationally-listed companies. International capital market pressures result in additional voluntary disclosures, but the effects vary by type of information. At the same time, disclosure requirements are not always met, and companies do not release the same information everywhere, even when they are required to do so. Thus, the pressures for disclosures by internationally-listed companies are quite complex. Finally, international capital market pressures have only a mild harmonization effect.

The role of accounting information in international capital markets and the impact of international capital markets on the corporate release of accounting information are barely understood. Most of the research so far has focused on the most visible forms, namely, the annual report and earnings announcements (the latter are also discussed in Section 4). Yet other forms of communication may be just as or more important. Therefore, there is scope for extending this research into, for example, press releases (other than earnings announcements) and meetings with financial analysts. Moreover, the extent to which disclosures by multinationals and internationally-listed companies is driven by regulation versus user demand (i.e., is voluntary) is an open question. Why, for example, do companies voluntarily disclose some types of information, while at the same time, refuse to disclose certain mandatory items? Both the incentives for and the effects of different types of voluntary information disclosure are also ripe for

146   *Journal of Accounting Literature*   Volume 16

research. For example, proprietary costs have been modeled analytically, but empirical research on their effects on disclosure in an international context is notably absent. Thus questions such as the following await future research: What drives disclosure policy? What channels of communication are used? How do firms coordinate their disclosures across different types of communication? How are disclosures timed and for what reason? These are not easily answered in an international context and securing data is likely to be a significant issue. However, Frost and Pownall [1994a] represents an innovative approach to overcoming the data problem. Case studies and interviews are another approach that can be taken. Then there are questions about the effects of disclosures by internationally-listed companies. For example, how does disclosure policy affect analyst behavior? How do disclosures affect cost of capital? (See Lang and Lundholm [1996] and Botosan [1997], respectively, for recent answers to these two questions for U.S. companies.) Finally, international capital market pressures on disclosure can be expected to grow if the trends toward the use of the increasingly-global capital market continues. In time, we may see them exerting more and more of a harmonization effect on disclosure.

4.0 MULTIPLE GAAP REPORTING

This section deals broadly with multiple GAAP reporting. The subject is divided into three categories, though there is some overlap between the groups. Two developments have spawned this literature. The first is the "discovery" of restatement information in Form 20-F SEC filings by non-U.S. companies. The SEC requires non-U.S. companies with U.S. share listings to include a restatement of income and stockholders' equity to U.S. GAAP in their Form 20-F filings whenever domestic GAAP is used in the primary financial statements.[22]   Many companies required to provide restatement information in their 20-Fs also include this information voluntarily in their annual reports. Thus, restatement information can be found in both 20-F filings and annual reports.[23]

The second development is the availability of *Global Vantage*, an international version of the *Compustat* database containing financial statement, market, and other information for companies from over 30 countries. In addition, *Datastream* has price and returns data from the world's major stock exchanges. The use of these two databases has extended traditional capital markets research with a national focus to the international arena. At the time of writing, Meek and Saudagaran [1990] observed that there was almost no research on the impacts of transnational financial reporting on users or on its general usefulness. This is now changed. Sections 4.2 and 4.3 explore the directions the research has taken.

[22] SEC requirements are summarized in such papers as Amir, Harris, and Venuti [1993] and Frost and Lang [1996], and more extensively in works such as Hanks, Farmey, and Walmsley [1992].

[23] Since these companies have already borne the costs of developing restatement information (due to SEC rules), the marginal cost of including it in the annual report is negligible. However, restatements can also be found in annual reports of companies not subject to SEC rules. Some of these (voluntary) restatements are based on International Accounting Standards, not U.S. GAAP. Perhaps these companies provide restatement information in response to capital market pressures or because of a "follow the leader" effect.

4.1 Descriptions of Alternative GAAP

SEC Form 20-F restatements have been used to analyze GAAP differences between a number of countries and the United States, and they provide a backdrop to the research discussed in Section 4.3. Studies include Weetman and Gray [1990], Weetman and Gray [1991], Hellman [1993], and Norton [1995].[24] These studies use the "conservatism index" developed by Gray [1980] as the focus of their comparisons.[25] Weetman and Gray [1990] examine U.S. GAAP earnings restatements by British companies, and they extend their analysis to Dutch and Swedish companies in Weetman and Gray [1991]. Hellman [1993] examines restatements to U.S. GAAP by Swedish companies, while Norton [1995] compares Australian and U.S. GAAP. Weetman and Gray [1990] and [1991] both find that U.S. GAAP is systematically more conservative than U.K. GAAP. Further, the dominant effects on differences in reported earnings are the result of differing GAAP for goodwill and deferred taxation. Weetman and Gray [1991] find that Dutch GAAP earnings is less conservative, but this is due to the flexibility for income smoothing allowed under Dutch GAAP, rather than any systematic differences between Dutch and U.S. GAAP. For Swedish companies, they report that Swedish GAAP earnings tends to be more conservative than U.S. GAAP earnings, but there is no systematic pattern; the main difference is related to taxation accounting. In contrast, Hellman [1993] finds no support for the notion that Swedish accounting practice is more conservative than U.S. GAAP. Indeed, there is some support that Swedish accounting is less conservative. However, the author noted much variation in differences across companies and over time. Norton [1995] finds little support that U.S. GAAP earnings is more conservative than Australian GAAP earnings. The most important differences involve asset remeasurement, the equity method for investments, and accounting for intangibles. She does find that U.S. GAAP stockholders' equity is more conservative than the amount under Australian GAAP. Overall, the impacts of GAAP differences vary across Australian companies.

Studies such as these are potentially useful for pinpointing differences between U.S. GAAP and that of other countries. Such information might be useful, for example, to investors in assessing differences that exist for other companies from the represented countries not providing a restatement. If the differences are systematic, then it should be possible to develop restatement algorithms. Moreover, the SEC could potentially target the most significant areas of difference for disclosure and forget about the

---

[24] Cooke [1992] compares Japanese and U.S. GAAP based on a case analysis of five Japanese companies, using a combination of SEC filings and private information provided by the companies. Since Japanese companies use U.S. GAAP in their SEC filings, rather than provide a restatement, this study does not examine restatements per se. He finds some evidence that Japanese GAAP is more prudent than U.S. GAAP. Another study, by Adams, Weetman, and Gray [1993], compares earnings and stockholders' equity under Finnish GAAP to International Accounting Standards. They find that Finnish GAAP is more conservative than IAS overall, but that there are no systematic patterns across companies. They also conclude that there is not enough disclosure to enable a user to restate on his/her own, or even understand the restatements that Finnish firms disclose.

[25] The conservatism index expresses which GAAP's income amount is more (or less) conservative than the other, i.e., which one is lower or higher. With U.S. GAAP as the benchmark, an index value less than 1.0 means that non-U.S. GAAP income is more conservative, while an index greater than 1.0 means that U.S. GAAP is more conservative.

rest in order to alleviate some of the burden that complete restatement allegedly imposes on companies. Similarly, if the GAAP of some countries are essentially in harmony with U.S. GAAP, then mutual recognition is possible.[26] Unfortunately, the overall findings provide little hope for such uses. There seem to be no systematic patterns; variations are reported across companies within countries and over time. Therefore, restatement algorithms based on past time series (alone) seem likely to be unsuccessful as a tool for predicting future restatements.[27] Moreover, generalizations are probably limited anyway. Firms disclosing restatements (either in compliance with SEC requirements or voluntarily) self-select and are probably not representative of other companies from their home countries. Companies providing restatements conceivably choose domestic GAAP practices that minimize differences with U.S. GAAP.[28] For these reasons, the potential for additional research in this area to yield useful findings seems limited.

4.2 Comparisons of National GAAP

Accounting information plays an important role in the valuation of equity securities traded in stock markets around the world. Yet the purpose of GAAP and financial accounting information varies from one nation to the next. Comparisons of the relationships between securities prices/returns and the accounting information produced by various national GAAP may yield insights to securities markets regulators as to whether to accept accounting information based on another country's GAAP. It should not be surprising if different relationships are observed from one country to the next. Pownall [1993] points out that national stock markets will not necessarily react the same way to similar disclosures. For example, the opportunities for income smoothing vary greatly from one country to the next. Therefore, if earnings are managed differently in different countries, then returns/earnings associations will be different. Furthermore, feeding information to stock markets is not the primary purpose of accounting information in many countries. Returns/earnings relationships are further complicated when one considers that in some countries national GAAP apply at the legal entity level and need not be followed in preparing consolidated financial statements. (As discussed in Mueller, Gernon, and Meek [1997, pp. 64-66], secondary reporting is most often based on IASs or U.S. GAAP.)

Alford, Jones, Leftwich, and Zmijewski [1993] compare the information content of accounting earnings in 17 countries, using the United States as a benchmark. They find differences across the 17 countries, and compared to the United States, both in the

---

[26] This idea was behind the proposed reciprocity agreement between the United States and Canada, which was stopped after the SEC learned that, contrary to conventional wisdom, substantial differences exist between U.S. and Canadian GAAP (Bandyopadhyay, Hanna, and Richardson [1994]).

[27] van Offeren [1994] describes a method to restate financial statement amounts for European companies to a common basis. However, it is not designed to restate amounts to the GAAP of any particular country, and some of the adjustments are arbitrary. The method involves analyzing specific financial statement information provided by individual companies for individual years. Thus, it is not a general purpose restatement algorithm. While the author shows that the restatement technique results in significantly different ratios, the usefulness of the restated information is not tested.

[28] One company explained that it does so because U.S. GAAP is "the most accepted benchmark of accounting worldwide" (Warbrick [1994, p. S 113]).

overall information content of accounting earnings and in how quickly it is impounded in prices (which the authors call "timeliness"). They also find that accounting earnings based on the domestic GAAP of four countries - Australia, France, the Netherlands, and the United Kingdom - is either more informative or more timely than U.S. GAAP earnings in the United States. Considering the size and liquidity of the U.S. capital market, the extensive U.S. requirements for timely disclosures, and the effectiveness with which the SEC enforces disclosure requirements, this result would puzzle many U.S. observers (at least), and is not explained by the authors. Pownall [1993] points out that data questions, such as whether earnings is defined consistently across sample countries, also obscure interpretations of the results. Cautious interpretations are in order.

Harris, Lang, and Möller [1994] compare the associations of earnings and stockholders' equity to prices/returns for German and U.S. companies on their respective stock exchanges. They find that the overall explanatory power of earnings on returns is similar for German and U.S. companies, though German earnings are valued at a higher multiple than U.S. earnings, reflecting the more conservative nature of German GAAP. However, they also find that the explanatory power of stockholders' equity on price is significantly less for German companies. Arguably, the most surprising aspect of these results is that German GAAP earnings are just as value relevant as U.S. GAAP earnings. Differences between the two countries in the importance of capital markets as a source of finance, the fundamental purpose of accounting, and particularly German income smoothing practices would lead one to expect lower explanatory power for German companies. The authors claim that this "suggests that German earnings are not as garbled as is often perceived" [p. 207].

Hall, Hamao, and Harris [1994], among other issues, compare returns/earnings associations between Japan and the United States. They find little evidence of an association in Japan, concluding that Japanese investors seem to rely less on earnings and other accounting information when pricing securities than U.S. investors do. Though these results are perhaps not surprising, just what Japanese investor use instead of accounting information is unanswered.

There is scope for extending comparative analyses such as these to other countries, and for further investigation of puzzling results discussed above. How accounting information is associated with securities prices/returns in any country depends critically on that nation's institutional framework, involving the purpose and practice of accounting and the capital market microstructure. Controlling for these differences across countries is difficult, if not impossible. Thus, it behooves the researcher to understand the institutional frameworks and the accounting regulations involved, and to describe them, so others can assess their work. Studies such as these arguably raise more questions than they answer.

4.3 Value Relevance of Restatements

Meek [1991] and Frost and Pownall [1994b] demonstrate that the U.S. stock market reacts similarly to earnings announcements based on U.S. and non-U.S. GAAP.[29]

---

[29] The reaction is related to the timeliness and frequency of disclosure and to market liquidity. Frost and Pownell [1994b] also find that the same thing cannot be said for the U.K. market. Reactions to U.K. firms' earnings announcements in the U.K. are significant, while reactions to foreign firms' announcements are not.

Implicit in any restatement disclosure (either in compliance with the SEC requirement or voluntarily) is the presumption that the restatement has relevance to investors over and above accounting information based on the firm's domestic GAAP. Results of a survey by Choi and Levich [1990] indicate that restatement to U.S. GAAP is one approach that institutional investors use to deal with worldwide GAAP differences. The authors also report that the restatement algorithms used by investors are ineffective in dealing with the differences, primarily because corporate disclosures are insufficient for complete restatement. This suggests that it may be difficult for investors to form expectations about U.S. GAAP-based amounts, and given the findings from the descriptive studies discussed above, this would not be surprising. If so, the revelation of U.S. GAAP amounts by non-U.S. firms (in the 20-F or annual report) should provide new (unexpected) information, or have value relevance. Nevertheless, Bhushan and Lessard [1992], based on a survey of investors, conclude that restatements are desirable but not necessary to make informed decisions. The efficacy of restatements is a controversial practical issue. Moreover, there is the long-standing argument of the "single domicile" notion of reporting discussed in Meek and Saudagaran [1990] which attacks restatements on a theoretical basis.[30] The evidence to date has not been overwhelming in supporting the value relevance of restatements. Published papers include Pope and Rees [1992], who look at U.K. companies; Amir, Harris, and Venuti (AHV) [1993], whose sample is a cross-section of companies from 20 countries, excluding Canada (with 40 percent of the sample from the U.K. and roughly 10 percent each from Australia, the Netherlands, and Sweden); Bandyopadhyay, Hanna, and Richardson (BHR) [1994], focusing on Canadian companies; Rees [1995] whose sample is drawn from 17 countries (with roughly one-third of it from the U.K. and one-fourth from Canada); Barth and Clinch [1996], who look at Australian, Canadian, and U.K. firms, Chan and Seow [1996], with a cross-section of companies from 13 countries (and nearly half the sample from the U.K.); and Rees and Elgers [1997], three-fourths of whose sample is from Australia, Canada, and the U.K. (the total number of countries is not reported). Figure 2 presents a summary comparison of the aforementioned studies.

AHV [1993], BHR [1994], and Rees [1995] conduct short window returns tests [31] examining price reactions to the release of restatement information (in the 20-F or annual report). AHV [1993] and BHR [1994] find no price reaction, while Rees [1995] does, both for his overall sample and a separate subsample of Canadian companies. AHV and BHR caution that their (non)results may be due to errors in specifying when the restatement information is actually released. Additionally, short window returns

---

[30] Foster [1986, pp. 134-136, 153] contrasts the *interactive* and *filter* perspectives of accounting method choice. Briefly, the interactive perspective holds that choices of accounting methods (and other financial reporting decisions) interact with a company's operating decisions, financing decisions, and mix of business decisions. In other words, accounting method choices are not independent of other managerial decisions. In contrast, the filter perspective holds that choices of accounting methods transform ("filter") the results of fixed operating, financing, and mix-of-business decisions into reported financial statement numbers, such as income and assets. In other words, accounting method choices are independent of other managerial decisions. Research supports the interactive perspective, yet restatements rely on the filter perspective of accounting method choice. Frost and Kinney [1996] present evidence that non-U.S. companies enter U.S. capital markets with an overall financial and disclosure strategy.

[31] Daley and Runkle [1996] discuss a number of econometrics and other issues associated with capital markets research which are relevant to the studies discussed here.

Figure 2

The Value Relevance of 20-F Restatements

	Pope & Rees [1992]	AHV [1993]	BHR [1994]	Rees [1995]	Barth & Clinch [1996]	Chan & Seow [1996]	Rees & Elgers [1997]
Countries in Sample	U.K.	20 countries, not Canada	Canada	17 countries, including Canada	Australia, Canada, U.K.	13 countries, including Canada	More than 8, including Canada
Type of Tests: Price reaction to filing (short return window)	No	Yes	Yes	Yes	No	No	No
Returns/earnings association (long window)	Yes	Yes	Yes	No	Yes	Yes	Yes
Market-to-book value/stockholders' equity association	No	Yes	No	No	Yes	No	Yes
Relative or incremental information content	Relative	Incremental	Incremental	Incremental	Incremental	Relative	Incremental
Conclusions	Both (U.S. and U.K.) GAAP have value relevance, but neither dominates the other	Mixed	No value relevance	Value relevance	Mixed	Foreign GAAP dominates U.S. GAAP	Restatement information is anticipated

tests are indicative of the "surprise" value of the restatement. If investors have accurate expectations about the contents of the restatement, then little reaction to its announcement would be expected. However, as noted above, restatement algorithms based on time series alone are unlikely to be successful. Nevertheless, domestic financial statements, interim earnings announcements, and other types of information are available prior to the restatement release which should improve investor predictions. While the evidence on short return window reactions to restatement is therefore conflicting, it should also be noted that the Rees [1995] results are sensitive to the event window specified. When Day t_{-2} is included, the statistical significance goes away. Overall, these studies seem to provide little evidence of an investor reaction to restatement releases.

Long returns windows tests involving returns-earnings associations have also been conducted. Pope [1993] notes that a distinction should be made between the incremental information content and the relative information content of alternative GAAP. The former focuses on the value relevance of the restatement, given domestic GAAP information, while the latter is concerned with which GAAP's information is more value relevant than the other.

AHV [1993] provide mixed evidence of the incremental value relevance of earnings restatements. While the restatement amount is found to be statistically significant in their tests overall, the results seem to be driven by one particular year and by the systems of accounting represented by the countries in the sample (Pope [1993]). The results from the tests by BHR [1994] suggest that the earnings restatement is irrelevant for valuing Canadian companies. Barth and Clinch [1996] find that earnings restatements are incrementally value relevant for Australian and U.K. firms, but generally not for Canadian companies. The Pope and Rees [1992] results indicate that both U.S. and U.K. GAAP have information content alone, each has incremental information content over the other, but that neither one clearly dominates the other. Finally, Chan and Seow [1996], using an approach advocated by Biddle, Seow, and Siegel [1995],[32] compare the relative information content of non-U.S. companies' domestic and U.S. GAAP earnings. They find that foreign GAAP earnings have greater information content than U.S. GAAP earnings.

Besides the earnings restatement, the SEC also requires a stockholders' equity restatement. This restatement has received less research attention, but is where AHV [1993] find their strongest evidence of the (incremental) value relevance of restatement information. Barth and Clinch [1996] also find that the stockholders' equity restatement has value relevance, but, as with the earnings restatement, for Australian and U.K. firms and generally not for Canadian firms.

Summarizing, the empirical evidence suggests the following: (1) non-U.S. GAAP accounting information has value relevance; (2) restatement information seems to have some (though not overwhelming) value relevance, but evidence on the general direction of relevance is mixed; (3) such value relevance as exists seems to vary by country of domicile, or perhaps system of accounting. In other words, the restatement may be more important for some countries that it is for others.

---

[32] The procedure involves a pair of three-stage returns/earnings regressions wherein U.S. and foreign GAAP earnings amounts are introduced into the regression sequence in alternating order. One pair "begins" with U.S. GAAP, while the other pair "begins" with foreign GAAP. Relative information content is assessed by comparing third-stage regression coefficients from the pair of regressions.

As noted above, one reason for the mixed evidence so far on the value relevance of restatements is that investors may be able to anticipate (some or all of) the restatement information through alternative information sources, such as domestic financial statements and interim earnings announcements. This is the premise behind Rees and Elgers [1997]. First-time filers provide shareholders' equity and net income reconciliations for the previous two and three years, respectively. These retrospective reconciliations to U.S. GAAP provide an opportunity to test for the existence of alternative information sources: finding an association between price and retrospective restatements in the periods prior to their disclosure suggests that the 20-F filing is not the exclusive source of this information. This is what Rees and Elgers [1997] find, though they do not identify what the alternative sources of information are.

Overall, the mixed evidence on the value relevance of restatements does not resolve the debate on the efficacy of the SEC's requirement for them. The evidence to date also raises other questions, such as whether restatements are more relevant for companies from certain countries than they are for others. Alternatively, restatements may be relevant for some, but not all companies, regardless of domicile. For example, they may be more informative for small companies or those from certain industries. Thus, there is scope for research aimed at clearing up the mixed results, of which Rees and Elgers [1997] is an example. Further, the relevance of restatements can be assessed using other data besides prices and returns, such as volume and transactions data. There is also a question of whether, and if so how, restatement disclosures affect the way companies are managed. For example, there is anecdotal evidence that Daimler-Benz changed management practices in response to reporting to U.S. GAAP earnings, following its 1993 New York Stock Exchange listing (*Economist* [1994], [1996a], [1996b]). Lowenstein [1996] argues that "you manage what you measure" (p. 1335). So far, research has been framed on the basis of restatements from various non-U.S. to U.S. GAAP. An alternative is to produce secondary financial statements based on International Accounting Standards. These may be even more value relevant than restatements to U.S. GAAP. IAS financial statements seem to be gathering momentum, especially because of anticipated endorsement of IASs by IOSCO (as discussed in Section 2.3). Research on this issue awaits future developments (and data). Also, relevance is but one characteristic of useful accounting information: reliability is another. The integrity of the information (are the standards followed enforced?; is there compliance with the rules?) may matter more than the type of GAAP. Gernon and Wallace [1995] point out that research is needed on whether capital markets even need harmonized accounting information. The theoretical objection to restatements based on the single domicile notion of financial reporting is also unanswered.

5.0 CONCLUSION

During the past decade there have been a number of significant developments in transnational financial reporting including a concerted move to harmonize financial reporting and the change in users' information needs based on the globalization of capital markets. Stakeholders, including stockholders, have become more interested (and invested) in foreign companies, and so reporting issues have gained greater relevance to their evaluation and projection of company performance. In this paper we have extended Meek and Saudagaran [1990] on research in transnational financial reporting by providing a review and synthesis of the relevant literature that addresses the major changes in the financial reporting arena.

In the context of developments in the harmonization area, we have examined the causes of diversity in financial reporting, the effects of this diversity and the extant debate over the need for and the optimal model of harmonization. We have also discussed research on regional harmonization particularly in the EU. There are some important questions as to whether harmonization must exclusively occur within the global paradigm which treats regional harmonization as an intermediate step or whether countries perceive regional harmonization as a legitimate alternative to global harmonization based on their particular needs. If the latter view were to gain support, it would have serious implications on current global harmonization efforts centered on the IASC.

As suggested in Meek and Saudagaran [1990], the globalization of capital markets has emerged as a very significant influence in transnational financial reporting. As more and more companies list on foreign stock exchanges there is growing evidence that financial reporting both affects and is affected by the resultant globalization of capital markets. There is growing evidence in the literature that the listing status of companies (i.e., whether and where they have foreign listings) is an important determinant of their financial reporting practices. Financial reporting represents one of the major costs involved in a foreign listing and thus the level of disclosure called for by regulators in different countries is a significant factor in determining the number and type of companies listing in each country. Since this affects the stock exchanges and securities industries in countries, both stock exchanges and securities industries are actively involved in lobbying for that level of disclosure they deem appropriate. Recent studies in this area have examined both mandatory and voluntary disclosure in this context. Related research has also looked at how differing rules on financial reporting items such as goodwill have affected capital market activities in various countries.

The concept of usefulness has begun, and will continue, to play a significant role in transnational financial reporting. The usefulness of alternative as well as multiple GAAP reporting has been a particular focus of recent research. Unfortunately, no clear picture has yet emerged to settle accounting policy debates that encircle the related issues.

As evidenced by the work reviewed in this paper, the international accounting area is dynamic and offers many interesting research opportunities. Global harmonization and the usefulness of financial disclosure will continue to pose important research questions for accounting academics and professionals seeking a better understanding of the interaction between international capital markets and financial reporting by multinational firms.

REFERENCES

Adams, A. C., P. Weetman, and S. J. Gray. 1993. Reconciling national with international accounting standards. Lessons from a study of Finnish corporate reports. *European Accounting Review* 3 (December): 471-494.

Adhikari, A. and R. H. Tondkar. 1995. An examination of the success of the EC directives to harmonize stock exchange disclosure requirements. *Journal of International Accounting Auditing & Taxation* (Vol. 4 No. 2): 127-146.

Agami, A. and N. Monsen. 1995. An appraisal of efforts by the Nordic countries toward accounting standards harmonization. *Journal of International Accounting Auditing & Taxation* (Vol. 4 No. 2): 185-203.

Alford, A., J. Jones, R. Leftwich, and M. Zmijewski. 1993. The relative informativeness of accounting disclosures in different countries. *Journal of Accounting Research* 31 (Supplement): 183-223.

Amir, E., T. S. Harris, and E. K. Venuti. 1993. A comparison of the value-relevance of U.S. versus non-U.S. GAAP accounting measures using Form 20-F reconciliations. *Journal of Accounting Research* 31 (Supplement): 230-264.

Bandyopadhyay, S. P., J. D. Hanna, and G. Richardson. 1994. Capital market effects of U.S.-Canada GAAP differences. *Journal of Accounting Research* 32 (2) (Autumn): 262-277.

Barth, M. and G. Clinch. 1996. International accounting differences and their relation to share prices: Evidence of U.K., Australian, and Canadian firms. *Contemporary Accounting Research* (Spring): 135-170.

Baumol, W. and B. Malkiel. 1993. Redundant regulation of foreign security trading and U.S. competitiveness. *Journal of Applied Corporate Finance* (Winter): 19-27.

Baydoun, N. and R. Willett. 1995. Cultural relevance of western accounting systems to developing countries. *Abacus* 31 (1) (March): 67-92.

Beresford, Dennis. 1990. Internationalization of accounting standards. *Accounting Horizons* (March): 99-107.

Beresford, Dennis. 1997. How to succeed as a standard-setter by trying really hard: A comment. *Accounting Horizons* (September): 81-92.

Bhushan, R. and D. R. Lessard. 1992. Coping with international accounting diversity: Fund managers' views on disclosure, reconciliation and harmonization. *Journal of International Financial Management & Accounting* (Summer): 149-164.

Biddle, G. C. and S. M. Saudagaran. 1991. Foreign stock listings: Benefits, costs, and the accounting policy dilemma. *Accounting Horizons* (September): 69-80.

Biddle, G. C., G. S. Seow, and A. F. Siegel. 1995. Relative versus incremental information content. Contemporary Accounting Research (Fall): 1-23.

Bindon, K. R. and H. Gernon. 1995. The European Union: Regulation moves financial reporting toward comparability. In *Research in Accounting Regulation* 9, edited by G. Previts. Greenwich, CT: JAI Press.

Botosan, C.A. 1997. Disclosure level and the cost of equity capital. *The Accounting Review* (July): 323-349.

Breeden, R.C. 1994. Foreign companies and U.S. securities markets in a time of economic transformation. *Fordham International Law Journal* (Vol. 17): S77-S96.

Chan, K. C. and G. S. Seow. 1996. The association between stock returns and foreign GAAP earnings versus earnings adjusted to U.S. GAAP. *Journal of Accounting & Economics* (Vol. 21): 139-158.

Cheung, C. S. and J. Lee. 1995. Disclosure environment and listing on foreign stock exchanges. *Journal of Banking and Finance* (Vol. 19): 347-362.

Choi, F. D. S. and C. Lee. 1991. Merger premia and national accounting differences in accounting for goodwill. *Journal of International Financial Management and Accounting* (Autumn): 219-240.

Choi, F. D. S. and R. M. Levich. 1990. *The capital market effects of international accounting diversity.* Homewood: Dow Jones-Irwin.

Choi, F. D. S. and R. M. Levich. 1991. Behavioral effects of international accounting diversity. *Accounting Horizons* (June): 1-13.

Cochrane, J. L. 1994. Are U.S. regulatory requirements for foreign firms appropriate? *Fordham International Law Journal* (Vol. 17): S58-S67.

Cooke, T. E. 1989a. Disclosure in the corporate annual reports of Swedish companies. *Accounting and Business Research* 19 (74) (Spring): 113-124.

Cooke, T. E. 1989b. Voluntary corporate disclosure by Swedish companies. *Journal of International Financial Management and Accounting:* 171-195.

Cooke, T. E. 1991. An assessment of voluntary disclosure in the annual reports of Japanese corporations. *International Journal of Accounting* 26 (3): 174-189.

Cooke, T. E. 1992. The impact of size, stock market listing and industry type on disclosure in the annual reports of Japanese listed corporations. *Accounting and Business Research* 22(87): 229-237.

Daley, L. A., and D. E. Runkle. 1996. Emerging methods in capital markets research. In A. J. Richardson (ed.), *Research issues in accounting: Issues and debates.* Vancouver: CGA-Canada Research Foundation, 117-131.

Doupnik, T. S. and S. B. Salter. 1995. External environment, culture, and accounting practice: A preliminary test of a general model of international accounting development. *International Journal of Accounting* (Vol. 30, No. 3): 189-207.

Dunne, K. M. and G. Ndubizu. 1995. International acquisition accounting method and corporate multinationalism: Evidence from foreign acquisitions. *Journal of International Business Studies* (Second Quarter): 361-378.

Dunne, K. M. and G. Ndubizu. 1996. The effects of international differences in the tax treatment of goodwill: A reply. *Journal of International Business Studies* (Vol. 27 No.3): 593-596.

Dunne, K. M. and T. P. Rollins. 1992. Accounting for goodwill: A case analysis of the U.S., U.K. and Japan. *Journal of International Accounting Auditing and Taxation* (Vol.1 No. 2): 191-207.

Edwards, F. 1993. Listing of foreign securities on U.S. exchanges. *Journal of Applied Corporate Finance* (Winter): 28-36.

Economist. 1994. A capital suggestion (April 9): 69.

Economist. 1996a. Hotels and planes (January 27): 17.

Economist. 1996b. Unhappy families (February 10): 23-25.

Emenyonu, E. N. and S. J. Gray. 1992. European Community accounting harmonization: An empirical study of measurement practices in France, Germany and the United Kingdom. *Accounting and Business Research* (Winter): 49-58.

Fantl, I. L. 1971. The case against international uniformity. *Management Accounting* (May): 13-16.

Fechner, H. H. E. and A. Kilgore. 1994. The influence of cultural factors on accounting practice. *International Journal of Accounting* 29 (3): 265-277.

Fekrat, M. A., C. Inclan, and D. Petroni. 1996. Corporate environmental disclosures: Competitive disclosure hypothesis using 1991 annual report data. *International Journal of Accounting* (Vol. 31, No. 2): 175-195.

Forrester, D. A. R. 1996. European congresses of accounting: A review of their history. *European Accounting Review* 5 (1): 91-104.

Foster, G. 1986. *Financial Statement Analysis,* Second edition. Englewood Cliffs: Prentice-Hall.

Freund, W. C. 1993. That trade obstacle, the SEC. *Wall Street Journal* (August 27): A12.

Frost, C.A. and W.R. Kinney, Jr. 1996. Disclosure choices of foreign registrants in the United States. *Journal of Accounting Research* (Spring): 67-84.

Frost, C. A. and M. H. Lang. 1996. Foreign companies and U.S. securities markets: Financial reporting policy issues and suggestions for research. *Accounting Horizons* 10 (1) (March): 95-109.

Frost, C. A. and G. Pownall. 1994(a). Accounting disclosure practices in the United States and the United Kingdom. *Journal of Accounting Research* 32 (1) (Spring): 75-102.

Frost, C. A. and G. Pownall. 1994(b). A comparison of the stock price response to earnings disclosures in the United States and the United Kingdom. *Contemporary Accounting Research* 11 (1-I) (Summer): 59-83.

Gamble, G. O., K. Hsu, C. Jackson, and C. D. Tollerson. 1996. Environmental disclosures in annual reports: An international perspective. *International Journal of Accounting* (Vol. 31, No. 3): 293-331.

Garrod, N. and I. Sieringhaus. 1995. European Union accounting harmonization: The case of leased assets in the United Kingdom and Germany. *European Accounting Review* (Vol. 4 No. 1): 155-164.

Gernon, H. and R. S. O. Wallace. 1995. International accounting research: A review of its ecology, contending theories and methodologies. *Journal of Accounting Literature* (Vol 14): 54-106.

Goeltz, R. K. 1991. International accounting harmonization: The impossible (and unnecessary) dream. *Accounting Horizons* (March): 85-88.

Gorelik, G. 1994. The setting of accounting standards: Canada, the United Kingdom, and the United States. *International Journal of Accounting* (Volume 29, No. 2): 95-122.

Gray, S. J. 1980. The impact of international accounting differences from a security-analysis perspective: Some European evidence. *Journal of Accounting Research* (Spring): 64-76.

Gray, S. J. 1988. Towards a theory of cultural influence on the development of accounting systems internationally. *Abacus* (March): 1-15.

Gray, S. J., G. K. Meek, and C. B. Roberts. 1995. International capital market pressures and voluntary annual report disclosures by U.S. and U.K. multinationals. *Journal of International Financial Management and Accounting* 6 (1): 45-68.

Gray, S. J., J. C. Shaw, and L. B. McSweeney. 1981. Accounting standards and multinational corporations. *Journal of International Business Studies* (Spring-Summer): 121-136.

Gray, S. J., and H. M. Vint. 1995. The impact of culture on accounting disclosures: Some international evidence. *Asia-Pacific Journal of Accounting* (December): 33-43.

Grinyer, J. R. and A. Russell. 1992. National impediments to international harmonization: Evidence of lobbying in the U.K. *Journal of International Accounting Auditing & Taxation* (Vol. 1 No. 1): 13-31.

Hall, C., Y. Hamao, and T. S. Harris. 1994. A comparison of relations between security market prices, returns and accounting measures in Japan and the United States. *Journal of International Financial Management and Accounting* 5 (1): 47-73.

Hamid, S., R. Craig, and F. Clarke. 1993. Religion: A confounding cultural element in the international harmonization of accounting? *Abacus* 29 (2) (September): 131-148.

Hanks, S., P. Farmey, and K. Walmsley (eds.). 1992. *United States securities and investment handbook.* London: Graham and Troutman.

Harris, T. S., M. Lang, and H. P. Möller. 1994. The value relevance of German accounting measures: An empirical analysis. *Journal of Accounting Research* 32 (2) (Autumn): 187-209.

Hellman, N. 1993. A comparative analysis of the impact of accounting differences on profits and return on equity. *European Accounting Review* 3 (December): 495-530.

Herrmann, D. and W. Thomas. 1995. Harmonization of accounting measurement practices in the European Community. *Accounting and Business Research* (Autumn): 253-265.

Herrmann, D. and W. Thomas. 1997. Geographic segment disclosures: Theories, findings, and implications. *International Journal of Accounting* (Forthcoming).

Hoarau, C. 1995. International accounting harmonization: American hegemony or mutual recognition with benchmarks. *European Accounting Review* (Vol. 4, No. 2): 217-233.

Hofstede, G. 1980. *Culture's consequences: International differences in work-related values.* Beverly Hills, CA: Sage Publications.

Hofstede, G. 1991. *Cultures and Organizations: Software of the Mind.* London: McGraw-Hill.

Hofstede, G. and H. H. Bond. 1988. The Confucian connection: From cultural roots to economic growth. *Organizational Dynamics* (Vol. 16, No. 4): 4-21.

Hossain, M., M. H. B. Perera, and A. R. Rahman. 1995. Voluntary disclosure in the annual reports of New Zealand companies. *Journal of International Financial Management and Accounting* 6 (1): 69-87.

Hossain, M., L. M. Tan, and M. Adams. 1994. Voluntary disclosure in an emerging capital market: Some empirical evidence from companies listed on the Kuala Lumpur stock exchange. *International Journal of Accounting* 29 (4): 334-351.

International Accounting Standards Committee. 1997a. IOSCO update. *IASC Insight* (June): 3.

International Accounting Standards Committee. 1997b. One size fits all? *IASC Insight* (June): 1, 4.

LaBaton, S. 1991. U.S. may ease rules affecting foreign stocks. *New York Times* (June 5): 17.

Lang, M. H., and R. J. Lundholm. 1996. Corporate disclosure policy and analyst behavior. *The Accounting Review* (October): 467-492.

Lee, C. and F. D. S. Choi. 1992. Effects of alternative goodwill treatments on merger premia: Further empirical evidence. *Journal of International Financial Management and Accounting* (Autumn): 220-236.

Lowenstein, L. 1996. Financial transparency and corporate governance: You manage what you measure. *Columbia Law Review* (June): 1335-1362.

McKinnon, J. 1993. Corporate disclosure regulation in Australia. *Journal of International Accounting Auditing & Taxation* (Vol. 2, No. 1): 1-21.

Meek, G. K. 1991. Capital market reactions to accounting earnings announcements in an international context. *Journal of International Financial Management and Accounting* (Summer): 93-109.

Meek, G. K., C. B. Roberts, and S. J. Gray. 1995. Factors influencing voluntary annual report disclosures by U.S., U.K., and continental European multinational corporations. *Journal of International Business Studies* (Third Quarter): 555-572.

Meek, G. K. and S. M. Saudagaran. 1990. A survey of research on financial reporting in a transnational context. *Journal of Accounting Literature* (Vol. 9): 145-82.

Mueller, G. G., H. Gernon, and G. Meek. 1997. *Accounting: An International Perspective*. Burr Ridge: Irwin.

Nobes, C. 1995. International accounting harmonization: A commentary. *European Accounting Review* (Vol. 4 No. 2): 249-254.

Nobes, C. W. 1983. A judgmental international classification of financial reporting practices. *Journal of Business Finance & Accounting* (Spring): 1-19.

Nobes, C. W. 1996. The effects of international differences in the tax treatment of goodwill: A comment. *Journal of International Business Studies* (Vol. 23 No. 3): 589-592.

Nobes, C. and J. Norton. 1996. International variations in the accounting and tax treatments of goodwill and the implications for research. *Journal of International Accounting, Auditing & Taxation* (Vol. 5 No. 2): 179-196.

Nobes, C. W., and R. W. Parker. 1985. *Comparative International Accounting*, 2/E. Oxford: Philip Allan.

Nobes, C. and R. Parker. 1995. *Comparative International Accounting*, 4/E. London: Prentice Hall.

Norton, J. 1995. The impact of financial accounting practices on the measurement of profit and equity: Australia versus the United States. *Abacus* 31 (2): 178-200.

Perera, H. 1994. Culture and international accounting: Some thoughts on research issues and prospects. *Advances in International Accounting* 7: 267-285.

Pope, P. F. 1993. Discussion of 'A comparison of the value-relevance of U.S. versus non-U.S. GAAP accounting measures using Form 20-F reconciliations.' (Volume 31 Supplement): 265-275.

Pope, P. F. and W. P. Rees. 1992. International differences in GAAP and the pricing of earnings. *Journal of International Financial Management and Accounting* (Autumn): 190-219.

Pownall, G. 1993. Discussion of 'The relative informativeness of accounting disclosures in different countries'. *Journal of Accounting Research* 31 (Supplement): 224-9.

Prather, J. and N. Rueschhoff. 1996. An analysis of international accounting research in U.S. academic accounting journals, 1980 through 1993. *Accounting Horizons* (March): 1-17.

Rahman, A R., M. H. B. Perera, and G. D. Tower. 1994. Accounting harmonization between Australia and New Zealand: Towards a regulatory union. *International Journal of Accounting* (Vol. 29): 316-333.

Rees, L. L. 1995. The information contained in reconciliations to earnings based on U.S. accounting principles by non-U.S. companies. *Accounting and Business Research* (Vol. 25, No. 100): 301-310.

Rees, L., and P. Elgers. 1997. The market's valuation of nonreported accounting measures: Retrospective reconciliations of non-U.S. and U.S. GAAP. *Journal of Accounting Research* (Spring): 115-127.

Rivera, J. M. and A. S. Salva. 1995. On the regional approach to accounting principles harmonization: A time for Latin American integration. *Journal of International Accounting Auditing & Taxation* (Vol. 4 No. 1): 87-100.

Salter, S. B. and T. S. Doupnik. 1992. The relationship between legal systems and accounting practices: A classification exercise. *Advances in International Accounting* (Vol. 5): 3-22.

Salter, S. B. and F. Niswander. 1995. Cultural influence on the development of accounting systems internationally: A test of Gray's [1988] theory. *Journal of International Business Studies* 26 (2)(Q2): 379-397.

Samuels, J. M. and J. C. Oliga. 1982. Accounting standards in developing countries. *International Journal of Accounting* (Fall): 69-88.

Saudagaran, S. M. 1988. An empirical study of selected factors influencing the decision to list on foreign stock exchanges. *Journal of International Business Studies* (Spring): 101-127.

Saudagaran, S. M. and G. C. Biddle. 1992. Financial disclosure levels and foreign stock exchange listing decisions. *Journal of International Financial Management and Accounting* (Summer): 106-148.

Saudagaran, S. M. and G. C. Biddle. 1995. Foreign listing location: A study of MNC's and stock exchanges in eight countries. *Journal of International Business Studies* (Vol. 26 No. 2): 319-341.

Saudagaran, S. M. and J. G. Diga. 1997. Accounting regulation in ASEAN: A choice between the global and regional paradigms of harmonization. *Journal of International Financial Management and Accounting* (Vol. 8 No. 1): 1-32.

Tay, J. S. W. and R. H. Parker. 1990. Measuring international harmonization and standardization. *Abacus* (Vol. 26 No. 1): 71-88.

Torres, C. 1990. NYSE's new chief seeks to make Big Board more international. *Wall Street Journal* (December 21): C1.

Torres, C. 1991. Big Board facing serious erosion as market for stocks, chief warns. *Wall Street Journal* (March 13): C1.

van der Tas, L. G. 1988. Measuring harmonization of financial reporting practice. *Accounting and Business Research* (Spring): 157-169.

van der Tas, L. G. 1992. Evidence of European Community financial reporting practice harmonization: The case of deferred taxation. *European Accounting Review* (May): 59-104.

van der Tas, L. G. 1995. International accounting harmonization: A commentary. *European Accounting Review* (Vol. 4 No. 2): 255-260.

van Offeren, D. 1994. Financial statement restatement of the 105 largest European companies. *Advances in International Accounting* 7: 183-201.

Wallace, R. S. O. 1990. Survival strategies of a global organization: The case of the International Accounting Standards Committee. *Accounting Horizons* (June): 1-22.

Wallace, R. S. O. and H. Gernon. 1991. Frameworks for international comparative financial accounting. *Journal of Accounting Literature* (Vol. 10): 209-264.

Walton, P. 1992. Harmonization of accounting in France and Britain: Some evidence. *Abacus* (Vol. 28 No. 2): 186-199.

Walton, P. 1995. *European financial reporting: A history*. London: Academic Press.

Warbrick, M. S. 1994. Practical company experience in entering U.S. markets: Significant issues and hurdles from the issuer's perspective. *Fordham International Law Journal* (Vol. 17): S112-S119.

Weetman, P. and S. J. Gray. 1990. International financial analysis and comparative corporate performance: The impact of UK versus US accounting principles on earnings. *Journal of International Financial Management and Accounting* 2 (2&3): 111-130.

Weetman, P. and S. J. Gray. 1991. A comparative international analysis of the impact of accounting principles on profits: The USA versus the UK, Sweden and The Netherlands. *Accounting and Business Research* 21 (84): 363-379.

Wyatt, A. 1989. International Accounting Standards: A New Perspective. *Accounting Horizons* (September): 105-108.

Yea, R. and J. J. Lawrence. 1995. Individualism and Confucian dynamism: A note on Hofstede's cultural root to economic growth. *Journal of International Business Studies* (Third Quarter): 655-669.

Zarzeski, M. T. 1996. Spontaneous harmonization effects of culture and market forces on accounting disclosure practices. *Accounting Horizons* 10 (1) (March): 18-37.

Zeff, S. A. 1996. A study of academic research journals in accounting. *Accounting Horizons* (September): 158-177.

[8]

ELSEVIER   Journal of Accounting and Economics 29 (2000) 1–51

JOURNAL OF
Accounting
& Economics

www.elsevier.com/locate/econbase

The effect of international institutional factors on properties of accounting earnings[☆]

Ray Ball[a], S.P. Kothari[b,*], Ashok Robin[c]

[a]*Graduate School of Business, University of Chicago, Chicago, IL 60637, USA*
[b]*Sloan School of Management, Massachusetts Institute of Technology, Cambridge, MA 02142, USA*
[c]*College of Business, Rochester Institute of Technology, Rochester, NY 14623, USA*

Received 3 August 1998; received in revised form 9 June 2000

Abstract

International differences in the demand for accounting income predictably affect the way it incorporates economic income (change in market value) over time. We characterize the 'shareholder' and 'stakeholder' corporate governance models of common and code law countries respectively as resolving information asymmetry by public disclosure and private communication. Also, code law directly links accounting income to current

☆We gratefully acknowledge the helpful comments of David Alexander, Eli Bartov, Sudipta Basu, Gary Biddle, Sir Bryan Carsberg, Dan Collins, Peter Easton, Bob Holthausen (the editor), Scott Keating, Christian Leuz, Gerhard Mueller, Christopher Nobes, the late Dieter Ordelheide, Peter Pope, Abbie Smith, Peter Taylor, Ross Watts, Greg Waymire, Steve Zeff, Jerry Zimmerman, the referee, and seminar participants at: Carnegie Mellon University, University of California at Berkeley, University of California at Los Angeles, CUNY Baruch College, EIASM Workshop in European Accounting in Krakow, 1999 Financial Accounting and Auditing Conference of the Institute of Chartered Accountants in England & Wales, Universität Frankfurt am Main, Hong Kong University of Science and Technology 1998 Summer Symposium, IAAER/CIERA 1998 Conference, Inquire Europe Autumn 1998 Seminar, University of Iowa, Harvard Business School, KPMG-AAA International 1999 Accounting Conference, London Business School, London School of Economics, Massachusetts Institute of Technology, Melbourne Business School, New York University, Ohio State University, University of New South Wales, University of Technology in Sydney, and Washington University in St Louis. The paper has received a Vernon K. Zimmerman Award and an Inquire Europe Prize. Ball and Kothari received financial assistance from the John M. Olin Foundation and the Bradley Policy Research Center, and Kothari acknowledges financial assistance from the New Economy Value Research Lab at the MIT Sloan School of Management.

* Corresponding author. Tel.: + (617) 253-0994; fax: + (617) 253-0603.
E-mail address: Kothari@mit.edu (S.P. Kothari).

2   *R. Ball et al. / Journal of Accounting and Economics 29 (2000) 1–51*

payouts (to employees, managers, shareholders and governments). Consequently, code law accounting income is less timely, particularly in incorporating economic losses. Regulation, taxation and litigation cause variation among common law countries. The results have implications for security analysts, standard-setters, regulators, and corporate governance. © 2000 Elsevier Science B.V. All rights reserved.

JEL classification: F00; F30; G15; M41

Keywords: International accounting; Standard setting; Regulation; Conservatism

---

1. Introduction

We show that differences in the demand for accounting income in different institutional contexts cause its properties to vary internationally. The properties of accounting income we study are timeliness and conservatism. Timeliness is defined as the extent to which current-period accounting income incorporates current-period economic income, our proxy for which is change in market value of stockholders' equity. Conservatism is defined in the Basu (1997) sense as the extent to which current-period accounting income asymmetrically incorporates economic losses, relative to economic gains.

A central result is that accounting income in common-law countries is significantly more timely than in code-law countries, due entirely to quicker incorporation of economic losses (income conservatism). Conversely, information asymmetry more likely is resolved in code-law countries by institutional features other than timely and conservative public financial statements, notably by closer relations with major stakeholders. In contrast with Roe (1994), we conclude that enhanced common-law disclosure standards reduce the agency costs of monitoring managers, thus countering the advantage of closer shareholder–manager contact in code-law countries.

We believe that timeliness and conservatism together capture much of the commonly used concept of financial statement 'transparency.' In comparison with a system that allows economic losses to be reflected in accounting income gradually over time, timely incorporation of economic losses in accounting income incents managers to stem the losses more quickly. Because accounting income flows into balance sheet accounts, conservatism as we define it also makes leverage and dividend restrictions binding more quickly. It makes optimistic non-accounting information released by managers less credible to uninformed users. Conservative accounting thus facilitates monitoring of managers and of debt and other contracts, and is an important feature of corporate governance.

The principal institutional variable we study is the extent of political influence on accounting. Our simplest proxy for political influence is a dichotomous classification of countries into code law systems with high political influence versus common law systems in which accounting practices are determined primarily in the private sector. We hypothesize that politicization of accounting standard setting and enforcement weakens the demand for timely and conservative accounting income, and conversely increases the demand for an income variable with low volatility. In our sample, Australia, Canada, UK and USA are classified as common-law countries (they comprise a group known as G4 + 1, exclusive of New Zealand) and France, Germany and Japan are classified as code-law.

In code-law countries, the comparatively strong political influence on accounting occurs at national and firm levels. Governments establish and enforce national accounting standards, typically with representation from major political groups such as labor unions, banks and business associations. At the firm level, politicization typically leads to a 'stakeholder' governance model, involving agents for major groups contracting with the firm. Current-period accounting income then tends to be viewed as the pie to be divided among groups, as dividends to shareholders, taxes to governments, and bonuses to managers and perhaps also employees. Compared to common-law countries, the demand for accounting income under code law is influenced more by the payout preferences of agents for labor, capital and government, and less by the demand for public disclosure. Conversely, because these groups' agents are represented in corporate governance, insider communication solves the information asymmetry between managers and stakeholders. We hypothesize that their preferences penalize volatility in payouts and thus in income. Thus, code-law accounting standards give greater discretion to managers in deciding when economic gains and losses are incorporated in accounting income. Managers reduce income volatility by varying the application of accounting standards or by influencing operating, financing and investment decisions (for example, by deferring discretionary expenditures such as R&D in bad earnings years).

Under the 'shareholder' governance model that is typical of common-law countries, shareholders alone elect members of the governing board, payouts are less closely linked to current-period accounting income, and public disclosure is a more likely solution for the information asymmetry problem. In comparison with the more political process in code-law countries, the desirable properties of accounting income in common law countries are determined primarily in the disclosure market. We hypothesize those properties include timeliness in incorporating negative economic income (i.e., asymmetric conservatism).

We caution that the code/common classes are by no means homogeneous, with financial reporting in no country being determined in a purely market or planning system. Notable historical examples of overlapping include the codification imposed on a predominantly common-law reporting system by the Companies Acts in the UK and by the Securities and Exchange Acts in the US, and the enactment of French and German legislation to permit consolidated financial statements prepared under common-law accounting standards. Despite these limitations, our results indicate the code/common classification is a valid proxy for the extent of political relative to market determination of financial reporting. Nevertheless, we develop finer hypotheses based on tax and regulatory differences across individual countries.

We also caution that institutional determinants of financial reporting vary over time. As a coarse test, we divide the sample into two sub-periods, and observe an increase in asymmetric conservatism of accounting income in most countries. One interpretation is that timely incorporation of economic losses in accounting income is an efficient corporate governance mechanism, providing better incentives to attend to losses and hence maximize value, which increased international product market competition has created incentives for even code-law corporations to adopt.

The sample studied is more than 40,000 firm-year accounting incomes reported during 1985–95, under the accounting rules of seven countries. Code-law income in this sample is substantially less timely and less conservative on average than common-law income. It does not even exhibit more timeliness than dividends. Within the common-law group, there is less asymmetric conservatism in accounting income in the United Kingdom, a country we characterize in terms of lower political involvement in accounting, lower litigation costs and less issuance of public debt. In addition to a detailed analysis of seven countries, we also study properties of accounting income in a sample of eighteen other countries. The results are consistent with our general thesis, that important properties of accounting income (conservatism in particular) around the world are a function of the varying demands that accounting income satisfies under different institutional arrangements.

Our research design addresses the incorporation of economic income in accounting income over time, under different international institutions. This has several advantages over simply studying international variation in accounting standards. First, much accounting practice is not determined by accounting standards, for reasons that include: practice is more detailed than standards; standards lag innovations in practice; and companies do not invariably implement standards.[1] Second, the extent to which accounting practice is determined by formal standards varies internationally, and the incentive to follow accounting standards depends on penalties under different enforcement institutions, so studying accounting standards per se is incomplete and potentially

---

[1] Asset impairment standards such as SFAS 121 in the US are an important example of accounting standards linking accounting and economic incomes. Information asymmetry implies that implementation of impairment standards depends on the incentive of financial statement preparers (managers and auditors) to disclose information about economic losses, which varies internationally (compare US and Japan).

R. Ball et al. / Journal of Accounting and Economics 29 (2000) 1–51   5

misleading in an international context. Third, reported income is influenced by managers' operating, financing and investment decisions, as well as by accounting standards. For example, managers can reduce volatility in accounting income by deferring discretionary expenditures (such as R&D) in bad years. Because the use of accounting income in corporate governance varies internationally, we expect managers' operating, financing and investment decisions to affect accounting income differentially across countries, and report evidence consistent with that expectation. For both these reasons, we study international variation in properties *of the actually reported income numbers*, inferred from the way they incorporate economic income over time.

Our research design's validity depends on two measures. First, we study the flow of *market-valued* economic income into *book-valued* accounting income, using the fiscal-year change in market value of equity (adjusted for dividends and capital transactions) as a proxy for economic income. A major concern is that the accuracy of this proxy is correlated with the institutional independent variables in the study, and in particular that code-law countries have endogenously lower market liquidity and public disclosure standards. Second, the research design requires us to infer independent variables, such as the degree of political versus market determination of reported income, from our characterization of salient institutional facts. While our characterization is based on surveying a wide range of sources, it undoubtedly is subject to error. In the concluding section, we argue that both types of measurement error create a bias *against* our hypotheses.

We contribute to a growing literature on the effects of international accounting differences, including Jacobsen and Aaker (1993), Alford et al. (1993), Amir et al. (1993), Bandyopadhyay et al. (1994), Harris et al. (1994), Joos and Lang (1994), Barth and Clinch (1996), and Pope and Walker (1999). We also contribute to the literature on international corporate governance, including Baums et al. (1994) and La Porta et al. (1997).

The following section outlines the model used to test the timeliness and conservatism of accounting income. The third section describes the data. Section four surveys the salient institutional facts used to develop and then test hypotheses on properties of income internationally. Section five extends these tests to a comparison of income with dividends and cash flows. The sixth section reports specification tests and the concluding section discusses the research design and the implications of the results.

2. A model of incorporation of economic income in accounting income

The research design infers timeliness and conservatism from the way firms' accounting incomes incorporate their economic incomes over time. We therefore specify accounting income as the dependent variable. We measure firms' economic incomes as fiscal-year changes in market values of equity, adjusted for dividends and capital contributions (Hicks, 1946).

'Clean surplus' accounting (Ohlson, 1988) implies two relevant identities for all firms. First, accounting income equals fiscal-year change in book value of equity, adjusted for dividends and capital contributions. Second, a firm's accounting and economic incomes summed over its lifetime are identical.[2] We investigate the temporal process of the incorporation of economic income in accounting income, i.e., the accounting model of income determination, and how it is affected by international institutional factors. Our research design allows for three fundamental features of the accounting model of income determination: accounting 'recognition' principles that generally reduce the timeliness of accounting income by smoothing its incorporation of economic income over time; the effectiveness of accounting accruals in ameliorating serial correlation in operating cash flows; and accounting income-statement conservatism.

The most fundamental feature of accounting determining the incorporation of economic income in accounting income over time is the accounting 'recognition' principles (FASB, 1985, Paras 78–89), including the Revenue Realization and Expense Matching principles. Whereas economic income immediately incorporates changes in expectations of the present values of future cash flows, the recognition principles incorporate such changes in accounting income gradually over time, generally at points close to when the actual cash flow realizations occur. Hence, accounting income systematically lags economic income (Ball and Brown, 1968) and the lag extends over multiple periods (Beaver et al., 1980; Easton et al., 1992; Kothari and Sloan, 1992). The recognition principles therefore cause economic income to be incorporated in accounting income in a lagged and 'smoothed' fashion over time.

This feature of accounting income arises because there is demand for an income variable with properties additional to timeliness. While timeliness per se is desirable, information asymmetry between managers and users creates a demand for an income variable that is observable independently of managers. Accounting income thus incorporates only the subset of available value-relevant information that is independently observable, whereas economic income incorporates information that is not independent of managers, such as plans and forecasts (our proxy for economic income incorporates the sharemarket reaction to managers' forward-looking statements). In other words, accounting income does not attempt to anticipate future cash flows to the same extent as economic

---

[2] We use clean surplus accounting as a concept to motivate the research design. We assume the degree of violation of clean surplus accounting is not systematically related to the international institutional factors we investigate. Research on the return-earnings relation typically exacerbates clean-surplus violation by excluding extraordinary items.

R. Ball et al. / Journal of Accounting and Economics 29 (2000) 1–51　　7

income. The first-order effect of the recognition principles thus is to make accounting income a complex moving average of past economic incomes.

The second fundamental feature of the accounting income-determination model is that accounting accruals imperfectly ameliorate serial correlation in operating cash flows. The accounting model provides for some anticipation of future cash flows through accrual accounting. For example, if managers pay an account for inventory early, then there is a decrease in current-period operating cash flow and, ceteris paribus, an offsetting increase in subsequent periods. Accrual accounting rules attempt to insulate income from the effect of the early payment, by expensing an amount in both periods that is based on inventory usage, not payments. In general, short term variation in firms' operational financing and investment decisions (such as changes in inventories, accounts payable and accounts receivable) causes negative serial correlation in operating cash flows, which accrual accounting attempts to remove from accounting income (Dechow et al., 1998). Hence, operating cash flow can be viewed as a noisier and less timely version of accounting income. However, accrual accounting is imperfect, because it is costly, so anticipation of future cash flows via accruals does not completely remove the noise in the cash flow time series.

The first two features of the accounting model of income determination together imply:

$$Y_{it} = f_j(\Delta V_{it}, \Delta V_{it-1}, \Delta V_{it-2}, \Delta V_{it-3}, \ldots, V_{it}) \tag{1}$$

where Y and ΔV, respectively, denote accounting and economic income, and V denotes noise due to imperfect accounting accruals. Economic income, ΔV, is fiscal-year change in the market capitalization of equity plus dividends and minus capital contributions during the year (Hicks, 1946). We hypothesize that the accounting model is applied differently across countries, and assume the model's parameters hold for all firms i that report under the accounting systems of country j. Assuming that ΔV is independent over time, this simplifies to

$$Y_{it} = g_j(\Delta V_{it}, \eta_{it}) \tag{2}$$

The disturbance η_{it} incorporates lagged changes in market values (ΔV_{it-1}, $\Delta V_{it-2}, \Delta V_{it-3}, \ldots$) as well as noise due to the residual serial correlation in cash flows not removed by accounting accruals (V_{it}). Both components of the disturbance term affect the R^2 of regression (2), which is used as a proxy for the timeliness property of accounting income. After scaling by opening market value, V_{it-1}, the dependent and independent variables are annual rate of return ($R_{it} \equiv \Delta V_{it}/V_{it-1}$) and earnings yield ($NI_{it} \equiv Y_{it}/V_{it-1}$), and a linear specification gives

$$NI_{it} = \alpha_{0j} + \alpha_{1j} R_{it} + \xi_{it} \tag{3}$$

The third fundamental feature of the accounting income model we study is conservatism. A longstanding example of income conservatism is the 'lower of cost or market' inventory rule, which incorporates inventory losses more quick-ly in income than gains. A topical example is new information about future cash flows from long-term assets. The recognition principles normally incorporate this information in accounting income at or near the point when the actual cash flow realizations occur. However, a variety of accounting rules and practices cause immediate write-offs against income when expected future cash flows *decrease*, without waiting for the cash flow decreases to be realized. In the US, SFAS 121 recently formalized longstanding write-off practices for long-lived assets in the form of asset impairment rules.[3] Upward revaluation is compara-tively rare in the US: it has not been practiced since the Securities and Exchange Commission (SEC) was established in 1934, though it is practiced in some countries. Consequently, unrealized increases in asset values generally do not flow into income until approximately when the underlying cash flow increases occur, but unrealized decreases are more likely to be incorporated quickly.[4]

Following Basu (1997), we incorporate conservative asymmetry in accounting income timeliness by modifying (3) for asymmetric incorporation of negative economic income:

$$NI_{it} = \beta_{0j} + \beta_{1j} RD_{it} + \beta_{2j} R_{it} + \beta_{3j} R_{it} RD_{it} + \varepsilon_{it} \tag{4}$$

The dummy variable RD_t assumes its value based on the sign of stock return, not earnings: one if return R_t is negative, and zero otherwise. β_{2j} and $(\beta_{2j} + \beta_{3j})$ capture the incorporation in current-year accounting income of positive and negative economic income respectively, in country j.

This specification has several attractive features. One advantage of specifying accounting income as the dependent variable is avoiding the need for a noisy earnings expectations model. Here, the independent variable (annual stock return) is relatively free of short-term microstructure, liquidity or mispricing effects. An additional advantage of the specification is that it incorporates the fundamental tenets of accounting income recognition. In particular, it incorpor-ates lags that arise from the demand for an independent income measure, and piecewise linearity allows us to study international differences in asymmetric timeliness, or conservatism.

Initially, we estimate separate individual-country relations for each country j, pooling all firms i reporting under the country's accounting standards and all years t. International differences in income timeliness, for positive and negative

---

[3] This 1995 accounting standard formalized what already had become common practice. Elliott and Hanna (1996) report an increase in negative 'one time' charges against income for US firms around 1970, rising to 20% of firms annually by the early 1990s. Collins et al. (1997) report a similar increase, and that by the early 1980s 25–30% of US firms reported negative incomes *before* one-time charges. These data are consistent with our view that formalized common-law accounting standards primarily arise endogenously from common practice in the market for accounting.

[4] Asset revaluations occur for acquisitions accounted under the purchase method, but do not flow through income.

economic income combined, are reflected in the R^2's of individual-country regressions (4).

3. Data

Accounting income, cash flow, and dividends over 1985–95 are from the Global Vantage Industrial/Commercial (IC) file. Accounting income NI_t is net income before extraordinary items (IC data 32).[5] Dividends *(DIV)* is dividends paid (IC data 36). Operating cashflow *(OCF)* is net income before extraordinary items (IC data 32) plus depreciation (IC data 11), minus the change in non-cash current assets (IC data 75 minus data 60), plus the change in current liabilities other than the current portion of long-term debt (IC data 104 minus data 94). All variables are scaled by market value of equity, calculated from the Global Vantage Issue file as price times number of outstanding shares, adjusted for stock splits and dividends using the Global Vantage adjustment factor. Change in accounting income ΔNI_t is $NI_t - NI_{t-1}$. Stock return R is the holding-period return, including dividends, over the firm's fiscal accounting year. Each firm/year observation is assigned to a country based on Periodic Descriptor Array 13 on the IC file, indicating the accounting standards used in preparing its financial statements that year (normally the country of the firm's home exchange).[6]

We exclude the two extreme percentiles of each variable (NI, ΔNI, DIV, OCF and R).[7] Next, we exclude each firm/year with a missing value for any variable, giving the same observation set for the various variables and models estimated. Finally, we exclude countries with less than 1000 firm/year observations over the thirteen years. This leaves us with a final sample of 40,359 firm/year observations in eleven years from seven countries: Australia, Canada, UK and USA (common law countries) and France, Germany and Japan (code law countries). We also summarize results for a secondary sample of 18 countries with at least 100 firm-year observations.

Table 1 contains sample descriptive statistics. Individual-country samples are pooled firm-years, ranging in size from 1054 (France) to 21,225 (US). In Panel A,

---

[5] German companies do not deduct minority interest from consolidated net income, but Global Vantage alters their numbers to comply with US practice. We therefore define German Y as IC data 32 + data 27, which reconciles to the numbers actually reported. The adjustment has only a trivial effect on the results.

[6] In correspondence, Christian Leuz and the late Dieter Ordelheide note that some French and German firms recently have issued consolidated financial statements prepared under International Accounting Standards. This practice largely post-dates our sample. If Global Vantage classifies these observations as 'German,' the errors create a potential bias against our hypotheses.

[7] The rationale is to eliminate observations potentially with errors or with extreme values due to scaling. The disadvantage is that potentially informative observations are deleted and there is the danger of an incorrect inference.

Table 1
Sample characteristics[a]

Panel A: descriptive statistics

	N	R			NI			DIV			OCF		
		μ	Med	σ	μ	Med	σ	μ	Med	σ	μ	Med	σ
Australia	1,321	17.3	9.9	52.6	2.6	6.7	19.0	3.5	3.6	3.3	11.6	10.9	33.3
Canada	2,901	12.1	6.0	46.8	3.2	5.3	15.4	2.0	1.4	2.4	15.1	12.2	28.9
US	21,225	12.7	8.1	42.8	3.1	6.2	14.4	1.9	1.0	2.4	11.7	10.3	21.4
UK	5,758	13.5	9.8	38.0	6.6	7.2	8.8	3.4	3.3	2.0	12.7	10.4	18.8
France	1,054	14.9	6.6	43.0	6.1	6.6	10.8	2.3	2.1	1.9	22.1	15.7	36.2
Germany	1,245	8.9	4.2	31.5	3.7	4.2	9.0	2.0	2.0	1.7	18.4	14.3	26.8
Japan	6,855	3.7	− 2.8	33.4	1.7	1.8	2.1	0.7	0.7	0.4	4.7	4.2	7.8

Panel B: Observations by fiscal year end (month)

	1	2	3	4	5	6	7	8	9	10	11	12	Total
Australia	5	0	32	4	30	964	32	2	45	0	6	201	1,321
Canada	113	26	131	51	21	105	47	144	155	72	31	2,005	2,901
US	964	405	872	401	446	2,094	562	506	1,666	700	425	12,184	21,225
UK	297	119	1,222	333	119	344	121	143	590	164	66	2,240	5,758
France	0	2	23	0	0	3	0	12	24	5	0	985	1,054
Germany	0	19	4	0	0	75	9	0	183	7	3	945	1,245
Japan	94	19	5,341	39	68	29	9	14	150	67	144	537	6,855
Total	1,473	934	7,625	828	684	3,614	780	821	2,813	1,015	675	19,097	40,359

Panel C: Observations by year

	85	86	87	88	89	90	91	92	93	94	95	Total
Australia	11	29	88	91	116	165	160	164	181	178	138	1,321
Canada	189	221	277	276	306	325	306	311	317	325	48	2,901
US	1,586	1,661	2,234	2,240	2,159	2,098	2,006	2,111	2,153	2,189	788	21,225
UK	98	314	438	508	621	703	722	751	756	733	114	5,758
France	9	66	74	72	98	147	155	151	131	146	5	1,054
Germany	20	74	83	76	90	145	180	189	170	192	26	1,245
Japan	3	328	668	739	841	881	850	857	874	814	0	6,855
Total	1,916	2,693	3,862	4,002	4,231	4,464	4,379	4,534	4,582	4,577	1,119	40,359

[a]*Sample* consists of 40,359 firm-year observations selected from the Global Vantage Industrial/Commercial and Issue files over 1985–95, using the following procedure. First, for each variable (see below) we eliminate the two extreme percentiles of firm-year observations. Second, we eliminate all firm-year observations with missing values for one or more variables, to facilitate comparability with results in previous tables. Third, we eliminate all firm-year observations from countries with less than 1,000 observations, leaving seven countries represented. Australia, Canada, United States, and the United Kingdom are the common-law countries, the rest are code-law countries.

R = buy-and-hold security return inclusive of dividends over the fiscal year;

NI = annual earnings per share before extraordinary items deflated by beginning of period price;

DIV = annual dividends per share deflated by beginning of period price;

OCF = annual operating cash flow per share deflated by beginning of period price;

N = the number of firm/year observations.

mean fiscal-year returns range from 3.7% (Japan) to 17.3% (Australia). Mean *NI* ranges from 1.7% (Japan) to 6.6% (UK). All countries' mean and median *OCF* (from which capital investments are not deducted) exceed *NI* (from which depreciation, a weighted average of past capital investments, is deducted).

Consistent with asymmetric conservatism, accounting income is negatively skewed (all medians exceed means), which contrasts with the positive skew of stock returns (all means exceed medians). That is, conservative accounting tends to incorporate economic losses as larger but transitory, capitalized amounts, and to incorporate economic gains as smaller but persistent flows over time, thus generating the negative skew of accounting income. The differential skew of earnings relative to returns calls into question the traditional linear earnings-returns specification, and supports the Basu (1997) piecewise linear version.

Also consistent with our model, in all seven countries the rank order of volatilities across variables is (highest first): *R*, *OCF*, *NI* and *DIV*. Our interpretation is: (i) accounting income is a lagged function of present and past years' returns (a type of moving average), and hence has lower volatility than individual-year stock returns; (ii) cash flow from operations is noisier than income, and hence is more volatile; and (iii) dividends is a further lagged function of accounting income, and hence is the least volatile variable. We comment on the relative magnitudes of the *R* and *NI* volatilities below.

Panel B reports the distribution of ending months for companies' fiscal years. December is the norm in Canada, France, Germany and US. March is the norm in Japan and June is the norm in Australia. Code law countries exhibit more conformity with their norm, presumably due to the greater influence of regulation and tax accounting in those countries, discussed below. UK, which we categorize below as the least regulated country in the sample, exhibits the greatest dispersion in fiscal year-ends. Panel C reports the sample distribution by calendar year.

4. Hypotheses and tests: international timeliness and conservatism of accounting income

We develop hypotheses concerning the influence of institutional variables on the two properties of accounting income captured by our model: timeliness and conservatism (or asymmetric timeliness). There have been numerous attempts to classify nations' accounting systems, based on a variety of institutional variables, but little empirical research has been directed at determining

R. Ball et al. / Journal of Accounting and Economics 29 (2000) 1–51   13

which variables explain differences in important properties of accounting income.[8]

4.1. Demand for timely accounting income in code and common law governance

Perhaps the most fundamental institutional variable causing accounting income to differ internationally is the extent of political influence on both standard setting and enforcement. An admittedly imperfect proxy for political influence – but a proxy our results legitimate – is whether standard setting and enforcement occur under codified law (a governmental process) or common law (a market process).[9] We hypothesize that the demand for timely incorporation of economic income in accounting income is lower under the code-law 'stake-holder' model of corporate governance than under the common-law 'share-holder' model. Below we describe the origins of and salient features of code- and common-law institutional environments. The discussion highlights the differences between the two systems and their differential implications for properties of accounting income. However, there is overlap between the code- and common-law institutions and accounting standard setting, which likely weakens empirical support for the hypotheses we develop.

Common law arises from individual action in the private sector. It emphasizes following legal procedure over rules (David and Brierley, 1985, p. 24; Posner, 1996). Common laws – including accounting standards – evolve by becoming commonly accepted in practice. While it might be efficient for private-sector bodies to codify generally accepted accounting rules and make them binding on their members, such standards arise in an accounting market, not in government. Common law enforcement is a private matter, involving civil litigation. Common law originated in England and it is now found in UK and many former British colonies. The common-law countries in our sample are Australia, Canada, UK and US.

Common law historically has evolved to meet the demands of contracting in markets. The 'shareholder' model of corporate governance, in which

---

[8] American Accounting Association (1977) classifies accounting systems using eight variables: political system (traditional oligarchy, totalitarian oligarchy, modernizing oligarchy, tutelary democracy, political democracy), economic system, stage of political development, financial reporting objectives, source of accounting standards, education and licensing of accountants, mechanism to enforce standards, and accounting client (public or private). Nobes (1992) and Nobes and Parker (1995, Chapter 4) survey classification schemes. How these variables affect important properties of accounting information internationally is largely untested. International accounting texts typically list variables to justify classifications, without correlating them with the national accounting standards listed in subsequent chapters, let alone with properties of the financial statements actually prepared under those standards.

[9] David and Brierley (1985) provide a survey.

14   *R. Ball et al. / Journal of Accounting and Economics 29 (2000) 1–51*

shareholders alone elect the governing board, predominates in common-law countries. Alchian and Demsetz (1972) argue this is efficient due to the additional incentive of residual claimants to effectively monitor managers. Compared to code-law governance, board members are less likely to hold large blocks, there is more monitoring of managers by external debt and equity markets (including analysts), and lenders and employees seldom have board representation. We hypothesize that, because parties contracting with the firm operate at greater 'arm's length' from managers, information asymmetry in common-law countries is more likely to be resolved by timely public disclosure.

Code-law originates from collective planning in the public sector. Governments or quasi-governmental bodies, such as France's *Conseil National de la Comptabilité* or Japan's Business Accounting Deliberation Council (which advises the Ministry of Finance) establish code-law accounting standards.[10] The code prescribes regulations ranging from abstract principles (e.g. 'prudence') to detailed procedures (e.g. the format of financial statements). Code-law enforcement is a governmental function, involving administrative bodies undertaking criminal prosecution for code violation. Code-law countries in our sample are France, Germany and Japan.

The code- and common-law common classes overlap in practice, in that financial reporting in no country is determined in a purely market or planning system. The UK Companies Acts imposed codification on a predominantly common-law system during the 19th century. In the US, the Securities and Exchange Acts played a similar role in the 1930s, among other things creating the SEC as a US government agency with responsibility for regulation of accounting standards. We acknowledge that the code- and common-law separation is not watertight and that there is some overlap in the nature of standard setting in the two categories of countries. Nevertheless, we believe the distinction is informative because, after reviewing the institutional details, we conclude it captures differences in the extent of political influence on accounting standard-setting (versus private contracting in the markets).

An important difference between common-law and code-law countries is the manner of resolving information asymmetry between managers and potential users of accounting income, including debt and equity investors, employees, suppliers and customers. Code-law corporate governance tends to be conducted by elected or appointed agents for these parties.[11] These agents tend to be

---

[10] Romans implanted code-law (also referred to as civil law, La Porta et al., 1997) in many continental European countries. The most detailed accounting code is the French *Plan comptable général*, adapted under occupation from Germany's 1937 standardization of accounting for war planning (Standish, 1997, p. 60). Japan has a code-law system, derived from the German legal and French accounting systems during the Meiji Era (1868–1910). Scandinavian law is another code-law category with origins in Roman law (David and Brierley, 1985 and La Porta et al., 1997).

[11] See Nobes and Parker (1995, Chapter 12), Roe (1994) and Miwa (1996).

informed by private 'inside' access to information. Thus, employees and stock-holders each elect 50% of the supervisory board of German *Aktiengesellschaft* (stock corporations). Banks typically dominate stock voting due to their large-block holdings and due to the German practice of banks voting individuals' stocks as agents (Köndgen, 1994). The supervisory board appoints and monitors the managerial board, and approves the financial statements. For the system to be tractable, the number of contracting parties must be small, so managers have close relations with intermediaries: notably, banks, other financial institutions, labor unions, governments, major customers and suppliers. There is no presumption that parties operate at a distance. Consequently, the demand for timely public disclosure in code-law countries is not as great as in common-law countries.[12] We propose that this reduces the demand for timely incorporation of economic income in code-law accounting income.

Conversely, we propose that code-law accounting income meets other demands. The stakeholder model views accounting income as a common 'pie' divided among stakeholders, as dividends to shareholders, taxes to governments, and bonuses to managers and perhaps employees. The portfolio weights of managers and employees typically are skewed toward their employer firms, so their incentive is to reduce volatility in payouts. Regulation of bank leverage ratios penalizes volatility in bank income and thus in the accounting income and/or dividends on their equity investments. Code-law banking systems typically are hierarchical, so bank representatives are well aware of governments' incentives to reduce volatility of tax receipts. Employee representatives typically are re-elected annually. While incentives to reduce volatility in accounting income exist in common-law countries (Healy, 1985), we hypothesize that code-law governance amplifies them.

Volatility can be reduced, at the expense of timeliness, through accounting methods that 'smooth' accounting income over time, incorporating economic income gradually over several periods. The Recognition Rules inherently smooth accounting income in all countries (though we also argue they frequently are overridden in the case of negative economic income). Nevertheless, code-law accounting gives managers considerably more latitude in timing income recognition. In good years, income can be reduced by asset write-downs (e.g. excessive allowances for bad debts), by provisions (e.g. excessive provisions for future losses or future expenses) and by transfers to reserves. In bad years, accounting income can be increased by reversing these adjustments.[13] We

---

[12] La Porta et al. (1997) predict that, in addition to differences in legal systems, differences in the extent of law enforcement affects the development of capital markets across countries. It is possible that variation in law enforcement has predictive power with respect to the demand and supply of accounting information that we ignore.

[13] Daimler-Benz reported 1993 German-rule income of DM615 million, but subsequent US GAAP disclosure revealed that a loss of DM1839 million had been hidden by various accounting adjustments (Ball, 1998).

predict that code-law accounting income incorporates a lower proportion of current-period economic income, 'smoothing' its incorporation to a greater extent over time.

H_1: *Code-law countries' accounting incomes are more 'smoothed' and less timely in incorporating current-period changes in market value than common-law countries'.*

The summary statistics reported in panel A of Table 1 are broadly consistent with this hypothesis, in that code-law countries exhibit a lower ratio of *NI* volatility to *R* volatility.[14] We formally test the hypothesis using a variety of Basu regressions (4): individual-country regressions with observations pooled across time; annual Fama/MacBeth cross-sectional regressions for individual countries; a secondary sample of eighteen other countries; and (in Section 4.3) a pooled-countries regression that allows formal tests of differences among countries.

4.1.1. Evidence from country regressions with observations pooled across time
    Initially, we test Hypothesis 1 by comparing the adjusted R^2's of the individual country, each estimated from pooled time series and cross-section data. While we make a distinction between common- and code-law countries, the categories are by no means homogeneous. For example, in Section 4.4 we argue that the UK is different from the remaining three common-law countries due to differences in the extent of accounting regulation, litigation environment, and the existence of public versus private debt. The empirical analysis therefore reports results separately for the common-law countries excluding the UK, for the UK, and for the code-law countries.
    The left-hand side of panel A of Table 2 reports the results and Fig. 1 graphs them. With the possible exception of France, there is a clear difference between individual code-law country R^2s (ranging from 4.2% to 12.6%) and common-law country R^2's (from 9.1% to 17.0%), consistent with the hypothesis. When countries are grouped, the R^2 for the pooled code-law sample is 5.2%, approximately one-third the common-law equivalent of 14.4% (excluding UK). The international differences in the degree of income-return association we document are similar to those in Alford et al. (1993), despite slightly different time periods and models.
    To assess whether the differences in R^2's are statistically significant, we estimate the standard deviation of estimated R^2's, which Cramer (1987) shows is a function of sample size, the number of independent variables and the true R^2. For four independent variables including intercepts, a true R^2 of 5%, and sample size 1,000 (5,000, 20,000), the standard deviation of the estimate is 1.3%

---

[14] The code-law ratio range is 0.06–0.29; common-law is 0.33–0.36 (excluding 0.23 for UK, discussed below).

R. Ball et al. / Journal of Accounting and Economics 29 (2000) 1–51   17

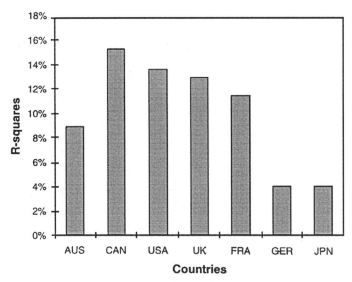

Fig. 1. International differences in earnings timeliness R-squares from individual country regressions of earnings on (a) annual return and (b) annual return times negative return dummy.

(0.6%, 0.3%). For a true R^2 of 15%, it is 2.0% (0.8%, 0.5%). Assuming independence across countries, differences in the order of 5% between our sample countries are significant, and the pooled common-law sample R^2 of 14.4% significantly exceeds the code-law R^2 of 5.2%. Since independence likely is violated, we report alternative tests below.

4.1.2. Annual cross-sectional regressions

An alternative test, due to Fama and MacBeth (1973), estimates separate annual cross-sectional Basu regressions (4), using observations for each country as well as for each of three pooled country groups (code-law, common-law and UK). We exclude the 6 of 77 country-years with fewer than 20 firm observations. For each country and each country-group, the right-hand side of panel A of Table 2 reports the time-series average of the estimated annual slope coefficients and the average of the annual regression R^2's and their t-statistics. The t-statistic is the ratio of the sample mean to the standard deviation of the time-series distribution of the estimated coefficients or R^2's, divided by the square root of the number of annual cross-sections (= 11 or 10 depending on the availability of 20 or more observations). From this test, the mean R^2 for the common-law group is 16.7% (t-statistic = 12.85) compared to 7.0% (t-statistic = 6.07) for the code-law group and 16.8% (t-statistic = 8.81) for the UK. The common-law countries' average R^2 is significantly greater than that for the code-law countries at the 0.01 level.

Table 2

Contemporaneous association between earnings and returns. Statistics based on pooled cross-section and time-series regressions and annual cross-sectional regressions using firm-year observations for each country. Intercepts are not reported[a]

Panel A: $NI = \beta_0 + \beta_1 RD + \beta_2 R + \beta_3 R^*RD + \varepsilon$

	Pooled regressions						Annual cross-sectional regressions					
	β_2	$t(\beta_2)$	β_3	$t(\beta_3)$	Adj. R² (%)	N	Avg. β_2	$t(\beta_2)$	Avg. β_3	$t(\beta_3)$	Adj. R² (%)	$t(R^2)$
Australia	−0.01	−0.53	0.37	8.63	9.1	1,321	0.02	0.99	0.33	6.12	11.15	3.68
Canada	0.00	0.12	0.40	17.21	17.0	2,901	0.01	0.51	0.39	6.82	18.19	5.59
USA	0.03	8.57	0.29	34.02	14.7	21,225	0.03	3.43	0.33	14.34	17.15	13.82
UK	0.04	10.14	0.15	13.32	13.8	5,758	0.05	4.23	0.14	5.41	16.76	8.81
France	0.08	7.30	0.07	2.30	12.6	1,054	0.06	2.95	0.14	2.71	17.59	4.52
Germany	0.05	4.28	0.10	3.27	5.4	1,245	0.04	2.01	−0.01	−0.06	7.47	4.85
Japan	0.01	5.95	0.01	2.58	4.2	6,855	0.00	0.55	0.02	3.26	6.88	4.07
Common	0.02	7.07	0.31	39.10	14.4	25,447	0.02	2.36	0.34	15.31	16.74	12.85
UK	0.04	10.14	0.15	13.32	13.8	5,758	0.05	4.23	0.14	5.41	16.76	8.81
Code	0.04	13.27	0.01	2.19	5.2	9,154	0.04	4.55	0.04	1.91	7.00	6.07

Table 2 (continued)

Panel B:	$R = \beta_0 + \beta_1 NI + \varepsilon$			$R = \beta_0 + \beta_1 NI + \beta_2 \Delta NI + \varepsilon$					
	β_1	$t(\beta_1)$	Adj. R^2(%)	β_1	$t(\beta_1)$	β_2	$t(\beta_2)$	Adj. R^2(%)	N
Australia	0.47	6.30	2.9	0.44	5.75	0.12	2.84	3.4	1,321
Canada	0.79	14.49	6.7	0.72	13.06	0.26	6.44	8.0	2,901
USA	0.90	46.08	9.1	0.76	36.52	0.37	18.58	10.5	21,225
UK	1.44	26.67	11.0	1.21	20.40	0.46	9.07	12.2	5,758
France	1.40	12.22	12.3	1.28	10.86	0.46	4.23	13.7	1,054
Germany	0.76	7.84	4.6	0.71	6.78	0.13	1.30	4.7	1,245
Japan	3.16	16.82	4.0	2.23	11.04	2.85	11.83	5.9	6,855
Common	0.85	47.52	8.2	0.74	39.71	0.30	18.92	9.4	25,447
UK	1.44	26.67	11.0	1.21	20.40	0.46	9.07	12.2	5,758
Code	1.44	22.44	5.2	1.29	19.10	0.47	7.04	5.7	9,154

[a]*Sample* consists of 40,359 firm-year observations selected from the Global Vantage industrial/Commercial and Issue files over 1985–95, using the following procedure. First, for each variable (see below) we eliminate the two extreme percentiles of firm-year observations. Second, we eliminate all firm-year observations with missing values for one or more variables, to facilitate comparability with results in previous tables. Third, we eliminate all firm-year observations from countries with less than 1,000 observations, leaving seven countries represented. Australia, Canada, United States, and the United Kingdom are the common-law countries, the rest are code-law countries.

R = buy-and-hold security return inclusive of dividends over the fiscal year;

RD = equals one if return R is negative and zero otherwise.

NI = annual earning per share before extraordinary item deflected by beginning of period price;

ΔNI = change in NI per share, adjusted for stock splits and stock dividends, deflated by beginning of period price;

N = the number of firm/year observations.

In panel A, the reported t-statistics for the average of the slope coefficients from annual cross-sectional regressions for each country are the ratios of the mean estimated coefficients to the standard deviation of the distribution of 11 annual estimated slope coefficients, divided by the square root of 11 (see Fama and MacBeth, 1973).

4.1.3. Secondary sample of eighteen countries

A secondary sample of eighteen countries with between 100 and 1000 firm-year observations provides similar results. We use the Mueller et al. (1997, pp. 11–12, Exhibits 1–4) classifications of countries as following a British–American or a Continental accounting model to proxy for our private-sector common-law and public-sector code law categories. We thereby classify eight additional countries as common-law (Hong Kong, India, Ireland, Malaysia, Netherlands, New Zealand, Singapore, and South Africa), nine as code-law (Austria, Belgium, Denmark, Finland, Italy, Norway, Spain, Sweden, and Switzerland), and add Thailand as a code-law country based on our own assessment. While the Mueller et al. classifications agree with ours for each of the seven countries in our primary sample, we are less confident of the eighteen additional country classifications. Specifically, we suspect that many countries following British–American accounting rules nevertheless lack common-law litigation enforcement and exhibit reduced demand for timely accounting income. Classification errors are expected to reduce the significance of the secondary sample results.

For each of the eight common-law and ten code-law countries, we estimate a pooled Basu regression (4). Annual cross-sectional regressions for each country are not feasible due to insufficient observations. In the interest of parsimony, we summarize the main results. Detailed results in tabulated form are available to interested readers upon request. The average R^2 for the code-law countries is 6.5%, the median is 7.0%, the minimum is 1%, and the maximum is 14.6%. In comparison, the average R^2 for the common-law countries is 15.3%, the median is 12.4%, the minimum is 9.8%, and the maximum is 22.5%. The difference in mean R^2's of the common and code-law countries is statistically significant. The results are consistent with those reported for the seven countries in Table 2 and provide an independent confirmation of H_1.

4.2. Universal demand for conservative accounting income

In this section we argue that conservatism, defined as asymmetric timeliness in incorporating economic gains and losses (Basu, 1997), is a general property of accounting income.[15] This section serves as a lead-in to Section 4.3, which

---

[15] We describe asymmetric timeliness in incorporating economic losses as 'income conservatism.' The concept is related to, but different from, balance sheet conservatism (reporting low book value of equity by under-stating assets and/or over-stating liabilities). Income conservatism implies balance sheet conservatism, but not vice versa: while code-law companies typically report conservative book values, they also are more likely to boost income in bad years. This *reduces* the asymmetric timeliness of accounting income and is difficult to describe as 'conservative' in its effect *on income*. Asymmetric timeliness is different from, but related to, Gray's (1980) concept of conservatism.

focuses on the effect of code- and common-law institutional differences on the degree of accounting conservatism.

Accountants contract to supply users with asymmetrically conservative income (i.e., to incorporate economic losses in a more timely fashion than gains) due to three properties of the accounting information market. First, managers possess specific information (Alchian, 1984) that is costly for external users to produce themselves (is not independently verifiable). Because managers have asymmetric incentives to disclose positive and negative specific information, information of negative innovations in expected future cash flows (economic losses) is more credible than positive innovations, and accountants are more likely to incorporate it in income. Second, lenders are important users of accounting information, including income and book value (a function of income), and they are asymmetrically affected by economic gains and losses (Watts and Zimmerman, 1986). Third, we propose that timely disclosure of economic losses is an important corporate governance mechanism. We assume that reversing bad investment decisions and strategies is personally more costly to managers than continuing good ones, and that informed monitoring by boards, analysts, investors and lenders is a mechanism to force them to undertake the cost. For these reasons, accountants supply income and book values that incorporate economic losses in a more timely fashion than economic gains.

The above properties of the market for accounting information are universal (though we argue below that they vary in degree internationally). We therefore expect accounting income to be asymmetrically conservative in all countries. Empirically, accounting income should exhibit higher R^2's for bad news (i.e. negative fiscal-year return) observations than for positive. Table 3 reports that negative-return R^2's exceed their positive-return counterparts in all common-law countries and in Germany.[16] The exceptions are the code-law countries France and Japan, discussed below.

Table 3 and Fig. 2 show that in all seven countries the coefficient on negative returns exceeds its counterpart on positive returns. Accounting income in the US is approximately ten times as sensitive to negative as to positive returns (estimated slopes of 0.32 and 0.03). The median country in terms of relative sensitivity to negative versus positive returns is the UK, with a ratio of approximately five (0.19 : 0.04). A formal test of the asymmetry is provided in Table 2, panel A. The incremental slope β_3 on negative fiscal-year returns (i.e. return interacted with the return dummy variable, $R*RD$) is significantly positive for all seven countries. A Fama–MacBeth test, with the β_3 coefficients estimated from

---

[16] For the separate positive and negative return regressions, we examined plots of the residuals against returns, and found no evidence of non-linearity (which was a concern for the negative-return sample in particular).

Table 3
Contemporaneous association between earnings and returns separately in good and bad news years
    Statistics from pooled cross-section and time-series regressions using firm-year observations for
each country. Intercepts are not reported[a]

	Good news: $NI = \beta_0 + \beta_1 R + \varepsilon(R \geq 0)$			Bad news: $NI = \beta_0 + \beta_1 R + \varepsilon(R < 0)$		
	β_1	Adj. R^2 (%)	N	β_1	Adj. R^2 (%)	N
Australia	−0.01	−0.1	813	0.36	10.1	508
Canada	0.00	−0.1	1,688	0.40	17.9	1,213
USA	0.03	0.8	12,721	0.32	11.7	8,504
UK	0.04	3.2	3,612	0.19	11.6	2,146
France	0.08	9.0	611	0.16	4.7	443
Germany	0.05	2.4	712	0.16	4.9	533
Japan	0.01	1.1	3,141	0.02	0.8	3,714
Common	0.02	0.4	15,222	0.33	12.2	10,225
UK	0.04	3.2	3,612	0.19	11.6	2,146
Code	0.04	3.3	4,464	0.05	1.7	4,690

[a]*Sample* consists of 40,359 firm-year observations selected from the Global Vantage indus-
trial/Commercial and Issue files over 1985–95, using the following procedure. First, for each variable
(see below) we eliminate the two extreme percentiles of firm-year observations. Second, we eliminate
all firm-year observations with missing values for one or more variables, to facilitate comparability
with results in previous tables. Third, we eliminate all firm-year observations from countries with
less than 1,000 observations, leaving seven countries represented. Australia, Canada, United States,
and the United Kingdom are the common-law countries, the rest are code-law countries.
    R = buy-and-hold security return inclusive of dividends over the fiscal year;
    NI = annual earnings per share before extraordinary items deflated by beginning of period price;
    N = the number of firm/year observations.

separate annual cross-sectional country regressions, also is reported in Table 2,
panel A. The average incremental slope is significant for all countries except
Germany.

    Unreported results for the secondary sample of 10 code-law and 8 common-
law countries also are consistent with asymmetric timeliness being a universal
property of accounting income. The incremental slope on negative returns is
positive in 12 of the 18 countries.

4.3. Demand for greater income conservatism under common-law governance

    We propose that common-law accounting income is more asymmetrically
conservative than code-law, due to greater demand for timely disclosure of
economic losses. Each of the three properties of the market for accounting
information described above is qualitatively weaker in code-law governance.
First, the closer code-law relation between managers and agents for contracting

R. Ball et al. / Journal of Accounting and Economics 29 (2000) 1–51   23

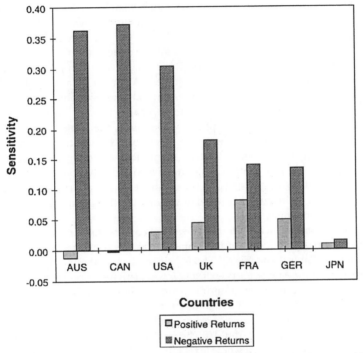

Fig. 2. International differences in asymmetry in earnings response to good and bad news; sensitivity to positive and negative returns from pooled regression of earnings on (a) annual return and (b) annual return times negative return dummy.

groups (banks, labor unions) reduces information asymmetry. Second, banks and other financial institutions tend to supply both debt and equity capital, making their loss function more symmetric. Third, there is less reliance on external monitoring of managers. Consistent with lower demand for timely incorporation of economic losses, the expected litigation cost of untimely incorporation is lower. Conversely, in code-law countries there is a demand for a low-volatility income variable, due to the more direct relation between current-year accounting income and short-term payouts such as dividends and bonuses. Reluctance to cut dividends (Lintner, 1956) leads to a preference for gradually incorporating an economic loss in income over time, for example by waiting for the reduced underlying cash flow realizations to occur, as distinct from recognizing it as a large, capitalized, transitory amount.

H_2: *Common-law accounting income is more asymmetrically conservative than code-law.*

The separate positive and negative return samples in Table 3 reveal that the greater *overall* timeliness of common-law accounting income reported above is due entirely to years with economic losses. For the common-law group, the 12.2% negative-return year R^2 significantly exceeds the 0.4% in positive-return years. In all common-law countries, R^2's in negative-return years exceed those in positive-return years. Accounting income in Australia, Canada and the US over the sample period essentially ignores current-year economic gains. Common-law accounting income seems directed primarily toward incorporation of economic losses. With the exception of Germany, the same cannot be said of code-law accounting. For the code-law sample, the negative-return year R^2 of 1.7% actually is lower than 3.3% for the positive-return years. These results are consistent with the hypothesis that, relative to code-law countries, the common-law demand for accounting income originates more in arm's length corporate governance, debt contracts, and investor litigation, and less in determining short-term payouts.

As another test of a differential degree of conservatism in code- and common-law countries, we focus on the slope coefficients from the Basu regression (4) results in Table 2 and Fig. 2. The β_{2j} slopes 2 show that accounting income in every common-law country exhibits *less* sensitivity to positive returns than in France and Germany (accounting income in Japan exhibits the least timeliness for both return samples). In contrast, the incremental negative-return slopes β_{3j} for common-law countries range from 0.15 to 0.40, considerably larger than the code-law range of 0.01–0.10. The pooled incremental slopes are 0.31 for the common-law group as a whole (excluding UK) and 0.01 for the code-law group. The difference is statistically significant at the 0.01 level.[17]

The incremental β_{3j} slope of 0.01 for Japan is the lowest in the sample (due to relative sample sizes it dominates the code-law group slope). Low income conservatism is consistent with the stylized institutional facts for Japan, in which one-time accounting write-offs are rare, economic losses reputedly are dribbled slowly into reported income over time (the banking sector being a notorious case), there is no provision for under-funded pension liabilities or other post-retirement liabilities, and the 'lower of cost or market' rule is not even used for inventories.[18]

---

[17] Unreported incremental negative return slopes in the additional 18-country sample are inconsistent with our hypothesis. While the R^2's are consistent with greater conservatism in common-law countries and the slopes are consistent with universal conservatism, the slopes do not suggest greater conservatism in common-law countries. However, due to small sample sizes many of the positive code-law country incremental slopes are not significant.

[18] Nobes and Parker (1995, pp. 298–300).

4.3.1. Pooled sample

To formally test for international differences in the degree of conservatism, we estimate (4) using data pooled across countries:

$$NI = \beta_0 + \sum_j \beta_{0j}\, CD_j + \beta_1\, RD + \sum_j \beta_{1j}\, RD\, CD_j + \beta_2 R$$

$$+ \sum_j \beta_{2j} R\, CD_j + \beta_3 R\, RD + \sum_j \beta_{3j} R\, RD\, CD_j. \tag{5}$$

Six dummy variables identify the country of the accounting standards used for each firm/year, with $CD_j = 1$ for firm/years under country j and $= 0$ otherwise. US is the 'base country,' with zero values for all country dummy variables. The coefficient β_2 on return measures the incorporation of current economic income into US firms' accounting incomes. The coefficient β_{2j} on the product of return and the country j dummy variable measures the country's *incremental* incorporation, relative to the US. The coefficients β_3 and β_{3j} measure the asymmetric conservatism of accounting income under US standards and the incremental conservatism under other countries' standards. Thus, $\beta_2 + \beta_{2j} + \beta_3 + \beta_{3j}$ measures the incorporation of negative economic income in country j. Table 4 reports results of the pooled country-dummy regression Eq. (5). Accounting income in all sample code-law countries (France, Germany and Japan) exhibits significantly less incremental sensitivity to negative economic income than under US standards.

4.4. Regulation, litigation and debt differences among common-law countries

The distinction between common-law and code-law countries provides useful insights, but as we observe above the categories are by no means homogeneous. We consider two important institutional differences within the class of common-law countries: the method and extent of their regulation of accounting; and the extent to which their securities litigation rules favor plaintiffs.

4.4.1. Regulation

We propose that, among common-law countries, income conservatism increases with regulation of accounting standard setting and enforcement. Building on Peltzman (1976), Watts and Zimmerman (1986, pp. 229–231) argue that the political process and the SEC as its agent have an incentive to avoid perceived responsibility for investor losses. We argue that responsibility is attributed more to managers, and less to the political process, if losses are disclosed in financial statements in a more timely fashion. Consequently, regulation adds criminal penalties to the common-law civil remedy of damages for untimely disclosure of material bad news. Accounting is regulated to varying degrees in all common-law countries. For reasons summarized below, we

Table 4
Comparative asymmetry in the contemporaneous returns-earnings relation: pooled regressions with individual-country effects[a]

Reported statistics are for the following model using the pooled cross-section and time-series of firm/year observations for all countries:

$$NI = \beta_0 + \sum_j \beta_{0j}\, CD_j + \beta_1\, RD + \sum_j \beta_{1j}\, RD\, CD_j + \beta_2 R + \sum_j \beta_{2j} R\, CD_j + \beta_3 R\, RD$$

$$+ \sum_j \beta_{3j} R\, RD\, CD_j + \varepsilon$$

Results are not reported for the intercept, the negative-return intercept, and their respective country dummies. The country category models use the common law countries of Australia, Canada and the US as the base category; dummies are used for (1) the UK and (2) the code law countries of France, Germany and Japan.

	Coeff.	t-Stat.
Panel A: country dummies model		
Earnings 'good news' sensitivity		
β_2 *(Return)*	0.03	*9.88*
β_{2j} *(Return∗Country Dummies):*		
Australia	− 0.03	*− 3.95*
Canada	− 0.03	*− 3.80*
UK	0.02	*2.40*
France	0.05	*4.16*
Germany	0.03	*1.57*
Japan	− 0.02	*− 2.64*
F-stat. for country return dummies		*11.35*
		p < 0.01
Incremental 'bad news' sensitivity		
β_3 *(Return Dummy∗Return)*	0.29	*39.21*
β_{3j} *(Return Dummy∗Return∗Country Dummies)*		
Australia	0.07	*2.64*
Canada	0.11	*5.28*
UK	− 0.14	*− 8.26*
France	− 0.22	*− 5.81*
Germany	− 0.19	*− 4.41*
Japan	− 0.29	*− 15.74*
F-stat.: Country Negative Ret Dummies		*67.44*
		p < 0.01
Regression		
N		*40,359*
Adj. R²		*15.4%*
F		*272.98*

R. Ball et al. / Journal of Accounting and Economics 29 (2000) 1–51   27

Table 4 (continued)
Panel B: country category dummies model

Earnings 'good news' sensitivity	Coeff.	*t*-stat.
β_2 *(Return)*	0.02	8.36
β_{2j} *(Return*Country Category Dummy):*		
UK	0.02	3.52
Code	0.01	2.37
F-stat. for country category return dummies		7.94
		$p < 0.01$

Incremental 'bad news' sensitivity		
β_3 *(Return Dummy*Return)*	0.31	46.23
β_{3j} *(Return Dummy*Return*Country Category Dummy):*		
UK	−0.16	−9.50
Code	−0.30	−19.00
F-stat.: Country Category Negative Return		200.92
Dummy		$p < 0.01$

Regression		
N		40,359
Adj. R^2		14.9%
F		642.07

[a]*Sample* consists of 40,359 firm-year observations selected from the Global Vantage industrial/Commericial and Issue files over 1985–95, using the following procedure. First, for each variable (see below) we eliminate the two extreme percentiles of firm-year observations. Second, we eliminate all firm-year observations with missing values for one or more variables, to facilitate comparability with results in previous tables. Third, we eliminate all firm-year observations from countries with less than 1,000 observations, leaving seven countries represented. Australia, Canada, United States, and the United Kingdom are the common-law countries, the rest are code-law countries.

R = buy-and-hold security return inclusive of dividends over the fiscal year;

NI = annual earnings per share before extraordinary items deflated by beginning of period price;

RD = the proxy for bad news = 1 if $R < 0$ and = 0 otherwise;

CD_j = country identifier = 1 for firm/years in country j and = 0 otherwise. USA is the 'base country' with $CD_j = 0$ $\forall j$.

characterize UK as the least regulated accounting market among our sample common-law countries.

The Securities Exchange Act of 1934 created the SEC as a US Government agency authorized to mandate and administer accounting standards. The SEC by-and-large has accepted the standards of the accounting profession, but

28   *R. Ball et al. / Journal of Accounting and Economics 29 (2000) 1–51*

nevertheless has retained a close supervisory role. It has intervened in standard setting on several occasions, as has Congress on occasions (e.g., in the debate on mark-to-market accounting, and by examining some firms' in-process R&D write-offs). We conclude that the US operates a closely regulated common-law system.

The effect is to compound the civil and criminal penalties for non-disclosure of material bad news. It has become a violation of both the common-law obligation to disclose (the civil law penalty for which is remedial damages awarded in private litigation) and a similar and sometimes stronger statutory obligation (the criminal law penalty for which is a fine, incarceration and/or prohibition from practice). We conjecture that this dual system of penalties creates additional incentives to recognize economic losses in regulated common-law countries.

Australia and Canada are widely viewed as having evolved from the loosely regulated UK model (described below) to the US regulatory model. Both commenced with a largely self-regulating profession, initially adopted provincial (rather than federal) regulation, and then moved to a system in which governmental or semi-governmental bodies set national accounting standards. Australia created a regulatory body (now constituted as the Australian Securities Commission) 'obviously modeled on the SEC' (Nobes and Parker, 1995, p. 106). It also removed standard setting from the private sector, assigning it in 1984 to a government-appointed authority (now the Australian Accounting Standards Board), whose accounting standards can be overturned only by the Australian Parliament. These changes predate our sample period, so we characterize Australian accounting as highly regulated (see Choi and Mueller, 1992, p. 86).

Canada has evolved to a regulated federal model in a similar fashion. Accounting was increasingly regulated with the establishment of the provincial securities commissions, and the enactment of provincial and federal securities laws. Various revisions of the Ontario Companies Act have been particularly influential. In 1975, federal regulations required financial statements to comply with the accounting standards promulgated in the Canadian Institute of Chartered Accountants' *CICA Handbook*, thereby giving them statutory status. The SEC has indirectly influenced Canadian accounting, due to large Canadian corporations listing in New York.

Among the common-law countries in our sample, we classify the UK as having the least regulated accounting market over our sample period. There is no UK regulatory body comparable to the SEC in the US. UK financial markets (the City of London) have historically been viewed as primarily 'self-regulating,' and the UK parliament has seldom intervened in accounting matters (Choi and Mueller, 1992, Chapter 3; Nobes and Parker, 1995, Chapter 6; Radebaugh and Gray, 1997, Chapter 5). In 1990, UK established the Accounting Standards Board (ASB), modeled on the US FASB and accountable to a newly created Financial Reporting Council. The ASB was authorized to issue Financial Reporting Standards (FRSs) that are backed by law (Radebaugh and

R. Ball et al. / Journal of Accounting and Economics 29 (2000) 1–51   29

Gray, 1997, pp. 91–92; Choi and Mueller, 1992, pp. 116–118). Nevertheless, the law allows a company to deviate from FRSs if it discloses the effect on its accounts. Even these changes did not take place until near the end of our sample period, 1985–95. We therefore treat UK accounting as less regulated than other sample common-law countries (Australia, Canada and US).

4.4.2. Litigation

Among common-law countries, we also propose that income conservatism increases in the expected costs to accounting firms and their clients from securities litigation. Expected litigation costs affect managers' and auditors' disclosure decisions (Kothari et al., 1988). The expected costs are a function of lawsuit probability, award size and legal fees. Securities lawsuits induce a demand for conservatism because the payoff function is asymmetric: they almost invariably allege investor losses arising from insufficiently conservative disclosures. We expect countries with higher expected litigation cost of nondisclosure are more likely to demand accounting income that incorporates economic losses in a timely fashion.

Our assumption is that expected litigation costs are lower in the UK than in Australia, Canada and US. Relevant UK institutional facts include: punitive damages are more difficult to obtain; juries are seldom used in civil litigation; absence of class action suits; and the so-called 'English rule,' under which losing plaintiffs pay part of defendants' costs.[19] In code-law countries, civil litigation is comparatively rare and the size of awards is comparatively small.

4.4.3. Private debt

UK corporate debt is predominantly private. We conjecture there is less information asymmetry between managers and private lenders than in the case of public debt, thus reducing the demand for timely incorporation of economic losses in UK accounting income.

4.4.4. Regulation, litigation and private debt considered jointly

Overall, we classify UK as having lower regulatory and litigation costs and predominantly private debt, so we predict less conservatism in UK accounting income than in other common-law countries. Nevertheless, relative to code-law countries, UK is expected to be more income conservative.

---

[19] The English rule is applied in UK, Australia, and most of Western Europe (Posner, 1986, p. 537), though not uniformly. It affects expected litigation costs via the frequency of litigation and the legal costs of the defendant, but not the size of awards, with unclear net effect. Katz (1987) argues: 'While it is conceivable that the English rule would lower the total number of cases brought to trial, it would likely increase the average expenditure per case. ... Even if the number of cases were to fall by as much as 30 percent, total expenditure could rise by more than 50 percent under the English rule.' Katz' analysis does not take account of one institutional detail, however: English courts award only *reasonable* costs of successful defendants, thus reducing the incentive to spend. See also Shavell (1982), Posner (1986, pp. 534–540), Hughes and Snyder (1995), Posner (1996) and Miceli (1997).

H₃: *U.K. accounting income is less conservative than in other common-law coun-tries and more conservative than in code-law countries.*

The data weakly support this hypothesis. The UK negative-return R^2 of 11.6% in Table 3 falls between that of the common-law group (12.2%) and the code-law group (1.7%). The incremental negative-return slope β_3 of 0.15 in panel A of Table 2 is significantly smaller than those for the other common-law countries (β_3 from 0.29 to 0.40), and it is marginally significantly greater than those for the code-law countries (β_3 from 0.01 to 0.10).[20]

4.5. Advantage of the Basu (1997) piecewise linear model

The misspecification in linear models for the common-law countries is seen from their generally lower R^2's in panel B of Table 2, compared with the Basu piecewise linear regressions in panel A, which is graphically depicted in Fig. 3. Code-law countries exhibit considerably less asymmetry, and hence their R^2's differ little between the specifications. In contrast, the asymmetry is sufficiently strong in Australia, Canada and US to cause R^2's from the Basu model to be approximately 1.6 to 3.2 times their linear model equivalents. Thus, linear earnings-returns models are potentially misleading in a common-law context and in international comparisons, due to substantial international differences in timing of economic loss incorporation.

5. Hypotheses and tests: accounting income versus dividends and cash flows

In this section, we compare accounting income with dividends and cash flows internationally. We argue that code-law institutional links between current-year income and dividends imply they incorporate similar information. Consistent with this hypothesis, we report that accounting income is timelier than divi-dends in common-law countries but not in code-law countries. Income is *less* timely than dividends in Germany and Japan. In contrast, accounting income is timelier than cash flows from operations in all countries.

5.1. Laws and practices linking current-period income and dividends

Accounting income is influenced, in varying degrees across countries, by firms' current dividend decisions. One influence results from laws on the taxation

---

[20] In response to a prior draft of this paper, Pope and Walker (1999) claim that the UK income before extraordinary items appears less conservative than US because UK firms enjoy greater discretion in reporting economic losses as extraordinary items. They use data from *Datastream* whereas we use the Compustat Global Vantage database. Reconciliation of the differences between the two studies is beyond the scope of our research.

R. Ball et al. / Journal of Accounting and Economics 29 (2000) 1–51 31

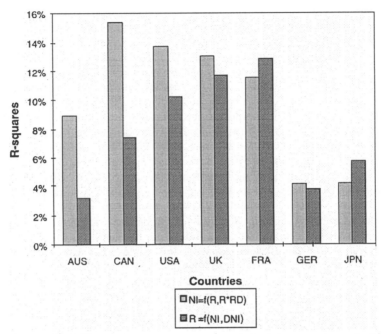

Fig. 3. International differences in the contemporaneous relation between earnings and returns; R-squares from (1) the pooled reverse regressions of earnings against (a) annual return and (b) Annual return times negative return dummy and (2) annual return against NI and ΔNI.

of corporate income and of dividend distributions.[21] We address these linkages in code and common-law countries separately.

5.1.1. Code-law links between dividends and accounting income

In the code-law 'stakeholder' corporate governance model, governments frequently are viewed as stakeholders, and tax payments are viewed as government's share of the same income 'pie' from which dividends and bonuses are paid. Politics requires reported and taxable incomes to converge, particularly since the government is responsible for both tax and accounting codes. Tax rules in the three sample code-law countries allow a deduction against taxable income only if also taken against reported accounting income (Choi and Mueller, 1992, p. 104). In code-law countries generally, it thus is considered imprudent to report income in excess of that required to justify dividends and bonuses, to minimize corporate tax. The consequence is that accounting income is influenced by short-term dividend policy.

---

[21] Except as indicated, taxation facts are from annual editions of Coopers & Lybrand *International Tax Summaries*.

The influence is particularly strong in Germany, where (Nobes and Parker 1995, pp. 269–272) the *Handelsgesetzbuch* ('commercial code') includes the *Massgeblichkeitsprinzip* ('authoritative principle') that tax accounting be based on the firm's *Handelsbilanz* ('commercial balance sheet'). Choi and Mueller (1992, p. 96) conclude of Germany: 'The dominance of tax accounting rules means that there is literally no difference between financial statements prepared for tax purposes and financial statements published in financial reports. ... Financial reports reflect tax laws – not primarily the information needs of investors and other financial market participants.' The relation between income and dividends is tightened in Germany by two additional institutional factors. First, Federal law forbids management from paying dividends less than 50% of income without stockholders voting approval. Second, undistributed profits are taxed at a higher rate than distributed profits (currently 45% versus 30%, excluding the 'solidarity surcharge').

These code-law institutional factors impose an additional role on the (already reduced) public-disclosure role of accounting income: corporate policy on current payouts to 'stakeholders,' including governments (via taxation), shareholders (via dividends), and managers and employees (via bonuses). If these distributions per se are uninformative, then the testable implication is that code-law accounting income is noisier and less oriented to incorporating current economic income, relative to dividends, than common-law income.

H_4: *Code-law accounting income is less timely relative to dividends than common-law.*

Table 5 reports the contemporaneous association between returns and dividends, for the same sample of firm-years as for accounting income in Table 2.

Table 5
Contemporaneous association between dividends and returns[a]
   Statistics are from regressions using the pooled cross-section and time-series of firm/year observations for each country. Intercepts are not reported.

Panel A: DIV = β_0 + β_1 RD + β_2R + β_3R*RD + ε

	β_2	$t(\beta_2)$	β_3	$t(\beta_3)$	$Adj.R^2$(%)	N	Ratio
Australia	0.00	− 1.85	0.06	8.67	11.1	1,321	0.82
Canada	− 0.01	− 9.06	0.04	11.26	7.3	2,901	2.34
USA	− 0.02	− 26.54	0.05	34.24	9.2	21,225	1.60
UK	0.01	8.69	0.02	9.25	9.7	5,758	1.42
France	0.01	4.22	0.02	3.90	8.8	1,054	1.43
Germany	0.02	6.66	0.01	0.99	9.6	1,245	0.56
Japan	0.00	2.28	0.01	9.72	5.5	6,855	0.78
Common	− 0.01	− 25.23	0.05	35.67	8.4	25,447	1.70
UK	0.01	8.69	0.02	9.25	9.7	5,758	1.42
Code	0.01	10.08	0.01	3.78	5.5	9,154	0.96

Table 5 (continued)

Panel B:

	$DIV = \beta_0 + \beta_1 R + \varepsilon(R \geq 0)$					$DIV = \beta_0 + \beta_1 R + \varepsilon(R < 0)$				
	β_1	Adj.R²(%)	N	Ratio	Vuong	β_1	Adj.R²(%)	N	Ratio	Vuong
Australia	0.00	0.2	813	−0.36	0.65	0.06	18.3	508	0.55	2.41
Canada	−0.01	3.8	1,688	−0.02	5.22	0.03	7.9	1,213	2.26	−3.69
USA	−0.02	4.4	12,721	0.18	9.67	0.04	10.4	8,504	1.12	−1.48
UK	0.01	1.9	3,612	1.73	−1.74	0.03	9.3	2,146	1.24	−1.48
France	0.01	2.2	611	4.12	−2.46	0.03	9.5	443	0.49	1.88
Germany	0.02	4.8	712	0.50	1.43	0.02	3.8	533	1.31	−0.6
Japan	0.00	0.1	3,141	11.00	−2.74	0.01	4.5	3,714	0.19	6.06
Common	−0.01	3.4	15,222	0.13	8.71	0.04	10.3	10,225	1.19	−2.45
UK	0.01	1.9	3,612	1.73	−1.74	0.03	9.3	2,146	1.24	−1.48
Code	0.01	1.5	4,464	2.17	−2.87	0.01	2.7	4,690	0.62	1.89

[a]Sample consists of 40,359 firm-year observations selected from the Global Vantage industrial/Commercial and Issue files over 1985–95, using the following procedure. First, for each variable (see below) we eliminate the two extreme percentiles of firm-year observations. Second, we eliminate all firm-year observations with missing values for one or more variables, to facilitate comparability with results in previous tables. Third, we eliminate all firm-year observations from countries with less than 1,000 observations, leaving seven countries represented. Australia, Canada, United States, and the United Kingdom are the common-law countries, the rest are code-law countries. However, the common law country category in the third row from the bottom excludes the UK.

R = buy-and-hold security return inclusive of dividends over the fiscal year;

$RD = 1$ if $R = 0$ and $RD = 0$ if $R > 0$;

DIV = annual dividends per share deflated by beginning of period price;

N = the number of firm/year observations.

$Ratio$ = in panel A, the ratio of the R^2's of the equivalent earnings (Table 2) and dividends (this table) regressions, in panel B, the ratio of the R^2's of the equivalent earnings (Table 3) and dividends (this table) regressions.

Vuong statistic is a likelihood ratio statistic that compares the fit of the return/dividend model in this table in panel B against the return/earnings model in Table 3, both estimated separately using the good news and bad news return observations. The Vuong statistic is distributed unit-Normal, i.e., a Z-statistic.

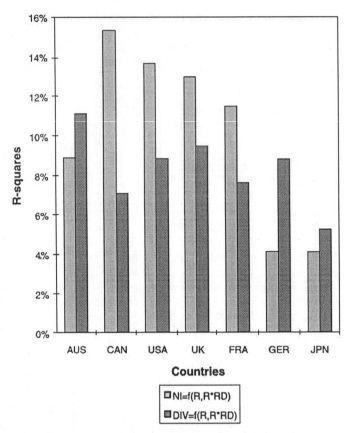

Fig. 4. Earnings versus dividends; R-squares from the individual country reverse regressions of (1) NI and (2) DIV against (a) annual return and (b) annual return times negative return dummy.

Fig. 4 depicts comparative R^2's for income and dividends. Results generally support the hypothesis that common-law accounting income is more timely relative to dividends than code-law. In the last column of panel A, the ratio of the returns/income R^2 to the returns/dividends R^2 exceeds unity for three of the four common-law countries. For the pooled common-law countries, the ratio is 170%. In contrast, dividends are *more* timely than income in two of the three code-law countries (Germany and Japan). In Germany, where there are particularly binding institutional links between them, accounting income captures only 56% as much current value relevant information as dividends. The equivalent ratio for Japan is 78%. For the pooled code-law group, the ratio is 96%, meaning current-year income and dividends capture approximately the same

R. Ball et al. / Journal of Accounting and Economics 29 (2000) 1–51   35

amount of current-year economic income. These results are consistent with the timeliness of code-law accounting income being constrained by its direct role in determining current-year dividend payouts.

Panel B of Table 5 reports separate dividend/return relations in positive and negative return years, comparable to Table 3 for accounting income. Since these are univariate regressions, we can report Vuong's (1989) likelihood ratio statistic for selection among non-nested models in which the dependent variable is the same, but the independent variables differ. We calculate the Vuong statistic with a common dependent variable (returns) but competing independent variables (accounting income and dividends). The results from the Vuong test in panel B of Table 5 are weakly consistent with Hypothesis 4. For example, for the bad news or negative returns sample, the Vuong test statistic (distributed as unit-Normal, i.e., a Z-statistic) shows that common-law accounting income explains returns significantly more than dividends, but that the opposite is true for code-law countries. We also estimate, but do not report, a linear relation model with dividends levels and changes, comparable to panel B of Table 2. These results also support Hypothesis 4.

5.1.2. Common-law tax imputation link between dividends and accounting income

Among common-law countries, there is considerable variation in the taxation of dividend distributions. We focus on 'imputation,' which penalizes corporations for reporting taxable income in excess of distributed dividends. There is an incentive to structure transactions and use accounting standards that make taxable income conform to dividend policy, which affects accounting income because it is correlated with taxable income. Australia, Canada and the UK operate imputation systems (Coopers & Lybrand, 1982–95), but not the US.[22] Provided dividends per se are uninformative, the testable implication is that accounting income in the US exhibits greater timeliness relative to dividends than it does in Australia and Canada.[23]

H₅: *The differential timeliness of accounting income relative to dividends is greater in the US than in common-law countries with dividend imputation (Australia, Canada, UK).*

There are mixed results for this hypothesis as seen from the 'ratio' reported in the last column of panel A of Table 5. The results for Australia and UK reported

---

[22] The Australian imputation system is described in Hamson and Ziegler (1990). The Canadian system is dividend credits, not full imputation; and the marginal Canadian investor could pay US tax and thus not receive credits.

[23] We expect this to be reinforced in US by stock repurchases to distribute cash to investors. Repurchases contain information about future income (Dann et al., 1991), likely reducing information in dividends.

are consistent with the hypothesis (the ratios are less than that for USA), but those for Canada are not. One conjecture is that the marginal investor in Canada is a US resident and does not receive imputation credits, so that Canada effectively is in the same tax category as the US.

5.2. Accounting income and cash flows from operations

We propose that cash flows are noisier than accounting income in reflecting contemporaneous value-relevant information (Dechow, 1994) in all countries. Provided there is no new information in managers' current financing and investment decisions, accruals are expected to make accounting income incorporate economic income in a more timely basis than cash flows. This logic holds under the accrual-accounting systems of all countries.

Table 6 and Fig. 5 report results for the contemporaneous association between returns and operating cash flow, for the same sample of firm/years as for income and dividends in Tables 2, 3 and 5. In all countries, the income R^2's are higher than those of operating cash flow, the ratio ranging from 2.10 (Germany) to 4.78 (US). This result would be obtained in less than 1% of cases by chance, assuming independence across the seven countries. The Vuong statistic and the ratio of explanatory powers of the income/return and cash flow/return relations reported in panel B indicate that the greater timeliness of accounting income than operating cash flow is due largely to bad news years. These findings generalize well-known US results on timeliness of accounting income compared to cash flow (Ball and Brown, 1968; Dechow, 1994; Basu, 1997), and contrast sharply with results reported above for dividends.

Table 6
Contemporaneous association between cashflows and returns[a]

Statistics are from regressions using the pooled cross-section and time-series of firm/year observations for each country. Intercepts are not reported.

Panel A: $OCF = \beta_0 + \beta_1 RD + \beta_2 R + \beta_3 R*RD + \varepsilon$

	β_2	$t(\beta_2)$	β_3	$t(\beta_3)$	Adj. R^2(%)	N	Ratio
Australia	0.07	2.74	0.16	2.11	2.4	1,321	3.80
Canada	0.02	1.07	0.25	5.28	3.6	2,901	4.75
USA	0.04	7.81	0.10	7.39	3.1	21,225	4.78
UK	0.11	11.40	− 0.02	− 0.87	3.7	5,758	3.69
France	0.19	4.78	− 0.16	− 1.39	3.3	1,054	3.79
Germany	0.16	4.28	− 0.04	− 0.37	2.6	1,245	2.10
Japan	0.01	1.17	0.08	7.18	1.7	6,855	2.49
Common	0.04	8.04	0.12	9.19	3.0	25,447	4.79
UK	0.11	11.40	− 0.02	− 0.87	3.7	5,758	3.69
Code	0.08	8.92	0.00	− 0.04	2.2	9,154	2.34

Table 6 (continued)

Panel B:

	OCF = $\beta_0 + \beta_1 R + \varepsilon(R \geq 0)$					OCF = $\beta_0 + \beta_1 R + \varepsilon(R < 0)$				
	β_1	Adj. R^2(%)	N	Ratio	Vuong	β_1	Adj. R^2(%)	N	Ratio	Vuong
Australia	0.07	0.9	813	0.25	0.92	0.23	1.4	508	12.88	− 3.38
Canada	0.02	0.0	1,688	384.00	0.42	0.27	2.8	1,213	2.82	− 6.23
USA	0.04	0.5	12,721	9.34	− 1.51	0.14	1.4	8,504	7.31	− 12.88
UK	0.11	3.4	3,612	0.55	0.18	0.09	0.7	2,146	13.85	− 6.93
France	0.19	2.9	611	0.76	− 2.12	0.03	− 0.2	443	− 47.40	− 1.67
Germany	0.16	2.2	712	2.22	− 0.16	0.13	0.3	533	13.96	− 2.18
Japan	0.01	0.0	3,141	10.00	− 2.79	0.09	2.2	3,714	2.07	2.61
Common	0.04	0.4	15,222	8.12	− 0.13	0.16	1.6	10,225	6.45	− 14.62
UK	0.11	3.4	3,612	0.55	0.18	0.09	0.7	2,146	13.85	− 6.93
Code	0.08	1.3	4,464	1.20	− 3.10	0.08	0.5	4,690	5.49	− 2.18

[a]*Sample* consists of 40,359 firm-year observations selected from the Global Vantage industrial/Commercial and Issue files over 1985–95, using the following procedure. First, for each variable (see below) we eliminate the two extreme percentiles of firm-year observations. Second, we eliminate all firm-year observations with missing values for one or more variables, to facilitate comparability with results in previous tables. Third, we eliminate all firm-year observations from countries with less than 1,000 observations, leaving seven countries represented. Australia, Canada, United States, and the United Kingdom are the common-law countries, the rest are code-law countries. However, the common law country category in the third row from the bottom excludes the UK.

R = buy-and-hold security return inclusive of dividends over the fiscal year;

$RD = 1$ if $R \leq 0$ and $RD = 0$ if $R > 0$;

OCF = annual operating cash flow per share, where operating cashflow is defined as earnings plus decrease in non-cash current assets plus increase in non-debt current liabilities plus depreciation;

N = the number of firm/year observations.

Ratio = in panel A, the ratio of the R^2's of the equivalent earnings (Table 2) and operating cash flow (this table) regressions, in panel B, the ratio of the R^2's of the equivalent earnings (Table 3) and operating cash flow (this table) regressions.

Vuong statistic is a likelihood ratio statistic comparing the fit of the return/operating cash flow model in this table with the return/earnings model in Table 3, both estimated separately from the good news and bad news observations in panel B.

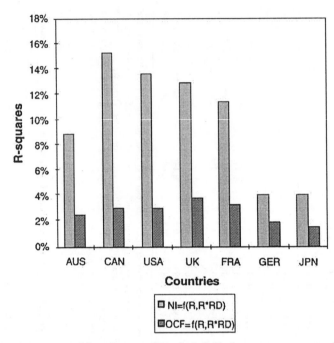

Fig. 5. Earnings versus cashflows R-squares from the individual country reverse regressions of (1) NI and (2) OCF against (a) annual return and (b) annual return times negative return dummy.

The incremental timeliness of accounting income (relative to cash flows) measures the extent to which accruals under a particular country's accounting rules are oriented toward timely incorporation of economic income. We hypothesize that common-law accruals reflect a greater demand for timely accounting income, and hence predict that common-law accounting income has more incremental timeliness (relative to cash flows) than code-law accounting income.

H_6: *Common-law accounting income is more timely relative to operating cash flows.*

Results generally support Hypothesis 6. In panel A of Table 6, three of the top four ratios of return/income R^2 to return/cash flow R^2 are common-law countries. Accounting income in Germany and Japan incorporates the least amount of current-period economic income, relative to cash flows. Thus, the greater timeliness of common-law income is not due entirely to underlying transactions.

R. Ball et al. / Journal of Accounting and Economics 29 (2000) 1–51   39

6. Specification tests: income and returns

The relation between accounting income and stock returns is robust with respect to a variety of specification tests, reported in Tables 7 and 8.

6.1. Variation in expected returns

When economic income is the independent variable, a possible misspecification arises from variation in expected returns (across time, countries and firms). Assume the true model for accounting income incorporates only the component of ΔV_t due to information about future cash flows a, and not due to variation in expected returns r. Assume these components are independent, both of each other and over time. Our model (2) then can be simplified as

$$NI_t = h(a_t, \zeta_t) \tag{6}$$

where the disturbance term ζ_t now incorporates expected return effects, in addition to lagged information about cash flows and accounting noise. Using ΔV_t as a proxy for a_t then would introduce measurement error in the independent variable, due to variation in expected returns.

Table 7 reports pooled regressions with two alternative controls for market-wide expected return effects. In column (2) the independent variable, annual return, is defined relative to the mean return for the firm's country/year. In column (3) the dependent variable, accounting income, is scaled by the country/year long-term interest rate. In both cases, results are similar to those in column (1), which repeats the results from Table 4 for comparison. We conclude market-wide effects do not substantially influence our results.

6.2. Consolidated versus parent income and control for special items

In countries where parent companies are not required to 'equity account' their share of affiliated-company income, their accounting income omits a component that accrues to their stockholders. This could be viewed as introducing measurement error that likely is positively correlated with parent-company income, thereby biasing the regression slopes downward. A counter-argument is that we are interested in properties of accounting income *as reported* under different countries' accounting rules, including any omission of affiliate income. Nevertheless, we replicate column (1) results for the 33,441 total firm/years for which Periodic Descriptor Array No. 13 on Global Vantage specifically labels income as 'fully consolidated,' thus including parent companies' proportional shares of affiliates' incomes. The sample size reduction is due almost entirely to Japan,

Table 7

Comparative asymmetry in the contemporaneous returns-earnings relation: alternative specifications[a]

Reported statistics are for the following model using the pooled cross-section and time-series of firm/year observations for all countries:

$$NI = \beta_0 + \sum_j \beta_{0j} CD_j + \beta_1 RD + \sum_j \beta_{1j} RD CD_j + \beta_2 R + \sum_j \beta_{2j} R CD_j + \beta_3 R RD + \sum_j \beta_{3j} R RD CD_j$$

Results are not reported for the intercept, the negative return intercept, and their respective country dummies. The country category models use the common law countries of Australia, Canada and the US as the base category; dummies are used for (1) the UK and (2) the code law countries of France, Germany and Japan.

Model Y Control	(1) NI Coeff.	t-Stat.	(2) NI R_{jt} Coeff.	t-Stat.	(3) NI/R_F Coeff.	t-Stat.	(4) NI2yr Coeff.	t-Stat.	(5) NI SIC Coeff.	t-Stat.
Panel A: country dummies model										
Earnings 'good news' sensitivity										
β_2 *(Return)*	0.03	9.88	0.01	3.96	0.36	9.88	−0.05	−84.24	0.04	10.25
β_{2j} *(Return∗Cntry Dums):*										
Australia	−0.03	−3.95	−0.04	−3.17	−0.48	−4.24	−0.02	−3.02	−0.04	−4.15
Canada	−0.03	−3.80	−0.01	−1.63	−0.32	−3.54	0.06	10.03	−0.02	−3.28
UK	0.02	2.40	0.03	3.74	0.14	1.57	0.09	2.92	0.01	1.57
France	0.05	4.16	0.06	3.48	0.65	3.86	0.55	21.28	0.05	3.69
Germany	0.03	1.57	0.04	1.81	0.55	2.54	0.21	19.32	0.02	1.42
Japan	−0.02	−2.64	0.00	−0.51	−0.17	−1.69	0.07	6.82	−0.02	−3.12
F-stat for Country Return Dummies	11.35 p < 0.01		7.73 p < 0.01		10.28 p < 0.01		164.13 p < 0.01		9.75 p < 0.01	

Incremental 'bad news' sensitivity

β_3 (Rdum*Return)	0.29	39.21	0.29	47.25	3.66	38.11	0.43	26.13	0.29	31.04
β_{3j} (Rdum*Ret*Cntry Dums):										
Australia	0.07	2.64	0.01	0.37	0.19	0.50	0.12	1.85	0.08	2.89
Canada	0.11	5.28	0.05	2.92	0.45	1.70	0.12	2.43	0.11	5.25
UK	−0.14	−8.26	−0.17	−11.11	−2.05	−9.10	−0.24	−2.47	−0.14	−7.96
France	−0.22	−5.81	−0.14	−4.40	−2.87	−5.99	−0.68	−7.40	−0.21	−5.54
Germany	−0.19	−4.41	−0.24	−5.74	−2.49	−4.55	−0.31	−7.48	−0.20	−4.73
Japan	−0.29	−15.74	−0.29	−16.80	−3.43	−14.90	−0.42	−10.70	−0.28	−15.16
F-stat: Country Negative Ret Dums	67.44 $p<0.01$		72.74 $p<0.01$		54.55 $p<0.01$		37.81 $p<0.01$		63.43 $p<0.01$	

Regression

N	40,359		40,359		39,240		33,082		40,359	
Adj. R²	15.4%		16.8%		13.8%		22.5%		16.2%	
F	272.98		303.32		234.19		410.56		117.16	

Panel B: country category dummies model

Earnings 'good news' sensitivity

β_2 (Return)	0.02	8.36	0.01	2.82	0.26	8.22	−0.05	−83.70	0.03	8.99
β_{2j} (Return*Cntry Dums):										
UK	0.02	3.52	0.04	4.35	0.23	2.75	0.20	19.12	0.02	2.58
Code	0.01	2.37	0.02	2.87	0.24	2.99	0.15	15.26	0.01	1.53
F-stat for Cntry Cat Return Dums	7.94 $p<0.01$		12.24 $p<0.01$		7.20 $p<0.01$		297.97 $p<0.01$		3.98 $p<0.01$	

Table 7 (continued)

Incremental 'bad news' sensitivity

Model Y Control	(1) NI Coeff.	t-Stat.	(2) NI R_{jt} Coeff.	t-Stat.	(3) NI/R_F Coeff.	t-Stat.	(4) NI2yr Coeff.	t-Stat.	(5) NI SIC Coeff.	t-Stat.
β_3 (RDum*Return)	0.31	46.23	0.30	53.64	3.76	43.28	0.46	30.27	0.31	36.68
β_{3j} (RDum*Ret* Cntry Cat Dums):										
UK	-0.16	-9.50	-0.17	-11.72	-2.14	-9.69	-0.34	-8.14	-0.16	-9.25
Code	-0.30	-19.00	-0.28	-18.82	-3.47	-17.41	-0.48	-13.65	-0.29	-18.31
F-stat: Cntry Cat Negative Ret Dums	200.92 p < 0.01		218.66 p < 0.01		174.82 p < 0.01		111.56 p < 0.01		187.17 p < 0.01	
Regression										
N	40,359		40,359		39,240		33,082		40,359	
Adj. R²	14.9%		16.2%		13.5%		21.3%		15.7%	
F	642.07		711.90		557.84		938.83		148.07	

[a]*Sample* consists of 40,359 firm-year observations selected from the Global Vantage industrial/Commercial and Issue files over 1985–95, using the following procedure. First, for each variable (see below) we eliminate the two extreme percentiles of firm-year observations. Second, we eliminate all firm-year observations with missing values for one or more variables, to facilitate comparability with results in previous tables. Third, we eliminate all firm-year observations from countries with less than 1,000 observations, leaving seven countries represented. Australia, Canada, United States, and the United Kingdom are the common-law countries, the rest are code-law countries. The sample sizes for model (3) that uses NI/R_F as the dependent variable and model (4) that uses only the two-year NI values are 39,240 and 33,082 respectively.

R = buy-and-hold security return inclusive of dividends over the fiscal year;

NI = annual earnings per share before extraordinary items deflated by beginning of period price;

NI/R_F = earnings deflated by the long-term interest rate;

$NI2yr$ = the sum of net income over the two years t and $t + 1$;

RD = the proxy for bad news = 1 if $R < 0$ and = 0 otherwise;

CD_j = country identifier = 1 for firm/years in country j and = 0 otherwise. USA is the 'base country' with $CD_j = 0 \forall j$.

In model (2) the regression is controlled for mean annual country return by scaling NI and by redefining RD; in model (5) the regression is controlled for the 10 most prevalent 2-digit SIC code by creating the appropriate dummy variables based on these SIC codes.

Interest rates: R_F is measured as the longest term bond yield available in the IMF's International Financial Statistics for the calendar year most coincident with the firm's fiscal year [-11,0]. Rates for the individual countries are for: treasury bonds 2 years (Australia); govt. bond yield > 10 yr (Canada); govt. bond yield (Germany); govt. bond yield, moyens (France); long term govt. bond yield (UK); govt. bond yield (Japan); govt. bond yield 10 yr (USA).

which loses most of its observations.[24] Results (unreported) are almost identical except for Japan (due to the small sample size).

The reported results in the paper are based on using accounting income before extraordinary items. Special items, which are included in calculating accounting income, have characteristics similar to extraordinary items, in that they tend to be negative and transitory (e.g., Collins et al., 1997). We repeat the analysis using accounting income net of special items and obtain qualitatively similar results.

6.3. Extending the lag in accounting income

Column (4) of Table 7 reports results with the dependent variable $NI2_{yr} = NI_t + NI_{t+1}$, allowing an additional year to incorporate economic income in accounting income. As expected, the coefficients generally increase: the median two-year coefficient is 1.6 times its one-year equivalent.[25] Accounting income thus incorporates economic income over time (it is 'smoothed,' and has 'momentum' or 'persistence').

6.4. Control for industry composition

Another concern is correlated omitted variables. For example, if the proportion of growth options relative to assets in place varies across countries, then common application of the *revenue realization rule* will cause accounting income to vary internationally in timeliness, due to 'real' rather than 'accounting' effects. This concern is reduced by our result that international differences in timeliness are due in part to accounting accruals and not entirely to differences in timeliness of cash flows. A related concern is that our sample contains only listed corporations. Public corporations are less prevalent under code-law systems probably because the latter do not facilitate public disclosure and public capital markets (see La Porta et al., 1997) to the same extent as common-law systems. For example, UK has approximately four times as many listed corporations as Germany. To alleviate concern that our results are due to different sample composition across countries, column (5) reports results after controlling for industry effects, in the form of interactive dummy variables for the ten most

---

[24] Excluding these observations is not clearly necessary because Japanese rules require equity accounting in the parent's books (Nobes and Parker, 1995, Chapter 13). Few observations are excluded for Germany where public companies have issued consolidated income since the European Union's Seventh Directive.

[25] The exception is the positive-return slopes for the US and Australia. The sample size decreases, due mainly to losing one year. Results are for overlapping samples.

Table 8

Contemporaneous association between earnings, dividends, cash flows and returns sub-period analysis[a]

Analysis: Statistics are from regressions using the pooled cross-section and time-series of firm/year observations for each country. Intercepts are not reported.

Panel A: $NI = \beta_0 + \beta_1 RD + \beta_2 R + \beta_3 R*RD + \varepsilon$

	1985–90						1991–95					
	β_2	$t(\beta_2)$	β_3	$t(\beta_3)$	Adj. R^2(%)	N	β_2	$t(\beta_2)$	β_3	$t(\beta_3)$	Adj. R^2(%)	N
Australia	0.02	1.04	0.26	5.31	13.0	500	−0.02	−0.99	0.48	7.55	9.4	1,821
Canada	0.00	−0.23	0.38	12.94	19.8	1,594	0.01	1.30	0.44	11.63	15.8	1,307
USA	0.03	6.14	0.28	26.79	17.3	11,978	0.03	6.54	0.33	22.14	12.9	9,247
UK	0.04	7.49	0.09	6.92	13.7	2,682	0.06	9.02	0.19	11.64	17.4	3,076
France	0.09	5.96	0.04	1.09	19.1	466	0.06	3.15	0.22	4.24	10.5	588
Germany	0.05	3.86	0.04	0.97	6.1	488	0.04	1.95	0.19	4.08	5.3	757
Japan	0.01	5.21	0.02	4.96	7.0	3,460	0.00	0.16	0.01	1.56	1.0	3,395
Common	0.02	5.64	0.29	30.12	17.3	14,071	0.02	5.32	0.36	26.22	12.7	11,374
UK	0.04	7.49	0.09	6.92	13.7	2,682	0.06	9.02	0.19	11.64	17.4	3,076
Code	0.03	10.97	0.00	0.42	5.3	4,413	0.05	8.05	0.01	1.38	4.4	4,739

Panel B: $DIV = \beta_0 + \beta_1 RD + \beta_2 R + \beta_3 R*RD + \varepsilon$

	β_2	$t(\beta_2)$	β_3	$t(\beta_3)$	Adj. R^2(%)	N	β_2	$t(\beta_2)$	β_3	$t(\beta_3)$	Adj. R^2(%)	N
Australia	0.00	−0.36	0.06	5.09	14.4	500	−0.01	−1.89	0.07	7.30	10.3	821
Canada	−0.01	−5.37	0.04	8.12	7.4	1,594	−0.01	−6.60	0.05	7.69	7.0	1,307
USA	−0.02	−18.02	0.05	25.51	9.8	11,978	−0.01	−19.45	0.05	23.09	8.9	9,247
UK	0.00	2.40	0.03	7.80	8.1	2,682	0.01	8.64	0.02	5.99	11.3	3,076
France	0.01	4.03	0.02	2.02	13.7	466	0.01	1.42	0.04	4.24	6.7	588
Germany	0.02	5.40	0.01	1.00	10.7	488	0.01	3.69	0.01	1.34	8.2	757
Japan	0.00	6.61	0.00	5.16	9.2	3,460	0.00	−0.61	0.01	7.81	7.2	3,395
Common	−0.01	−17.25	0.05	26.29	9.2	14,071	−0.01	−18.40	0.05	24.33	8.0	11,374
UK	0.00	2.40	0.03	7.80	8.1	2,682	0.01	8.64	0.02	5.99	11.3	3,076
Code	0.01	9.31	0.00	−0.51	4.2	4,413	0.01	9.99	0.00	1.88	9.7	4,739

R. Ball et al. / Journal of Accounting and Economics 29 (2000) 1–51 45

Panel C $OCF = \beta_0 + \beta_1 RD + \beta_2 R + \beta_3 R*RD + \varepsilon$

Australia	0.01	0.21	0.14	1.31	1.0	500	0.09	3.02	0.23	2.07	3.3	821
Canada	-0.02	-0.73	0.29	4.62	3.4	1,594	0.04	2.07	0.22	3.03	3.9	1,307
USA	0.03	3.82	0.09	5.13	2.5	11,978	0.05	7.15	0.13	5.99	3.8	9,247
UK	0.11	7.24	-0.02	-0.55	3.1	2,682	0.12	9.05	-0.03	-0.78	4.5	3,076
France	0.20	3.42	-0.15	-0.96	2.6	466	0.23	3.95	-0.17	-1.00	4.3	588
Germany	0.12	2.40	0.12	0.87	2.4	488	0.25	4.08	-0.19	-1.40	3.0	757
Japan	0.03	4.99	0.03	1.54	1.9	3,460	-0.01	-0.75	0.12	6.72	3.8	3,395
Common	0.02	2.87	0.12	6.88	2.5	14,071	0.05	8.13	0.15	6.98	3.7	11,374
UK	0.11	7.24	-0.02	-0.55	3.1	2,682	0.12	9.05	-0.03	-0.78	4.5	3,076
Code	0.08	7.30	-0.07	-2.34	1.6	4,413	0.21	11.49	-0.08	-2.39	6.3	4,739

[a] *Sample* consists of 40,359 firm-year observations selected from the Global Vantage industrial/Commercial and Issue files over 1985–95, using the following procedure. First, for each variable (see below) we eliminate the two extreme percentiles of firm-year observations. Second, we eliminate all firm-year observations with missing values for one or more variables, to facilitate comparability with results in previous tables. Third, we eliminate all firm-year observations from countries with less than 1,000 observations, leaving seven countries represented. Australia, Canada, United States, and the United Kingdom are the common-law countries, the rest are code-law countries. However, the common law country category in the third row from the bottom in each panel excludes the UK.

R = buy-and-hold security return inclusive of dividends over the fiscal year;

$RD = 1$ if $R \leq 0$ and $RD = 0$ if $R > 0$;

NI = annual earnings per share before extraordinary items deflated by beginning of period price;

DIV = annual dividends per share deflated by beginning of period price;

OCF = annual operating cash flow per share deflated by beginning of period, where operating cashflow is defined as earnings plus decrease in non-cash current assets plus increase in non-debt current liabilities plus depreciation;

N = the number of firm/year observations.

prevalent 2-digit SIC codes. Little change is apparent. The regression adjusted R^2 rises slightly and the F-statistic falls. The F-statistics for the countries' dummy slopes fall slightly. All remain significant at the 0.01 level. There is little change in the coefficients for both individual countries and country groups.

6.5. Subperiod results

Splitting the sample into two subperiods, 1985–90 and 1991–95, reveals three interesting results, reported in Table 8. First, the incremental coefficients on negative economic income increase in the second subperiod for six of the seven individual-country regressions (4), the exception being Japan. Several countries exhibit statistically significant increases, including Australia (0.48 versus 0.26), UK (0.19 versus 0.09), France (0.22 versus 0.04) and Germany (0.19 versus 0.05). The coefficient on negative economic income for US increases, but not significantly (0.33 versus 0.28). These results suggest Basu (1997) might have erred in attributing increased asymmetry over time in US accounting income to changes in US litigation rules, since similar increases have occurred in France and Germany. An intriguing possibility is that timely incorporation of economic losses has become a more important corporate governance mechanism over time worldwide (if not in Japan), and that pressure to adopt it has come from increased international product market competition (if not from changes in the policies of standard-setters around the world). Under this explanation, timely incorporation of economic losses in accounting income is an efficient governance mechanism that reduces managers' incentives to continue with loss-making investments and strategies, thereby reducing agency-related negative NPVs. We believe this phenomenon is worthy of further study.

Second, despite increased sensitivity to economic losses, the R^2's in six of seven country regressions (4) decreased between subperiods, generalizing the US result (Ramesh and Thiagarajan, 1995; Lev, 1997). Third, the results for cash flow from operations, reported in panel C, contrast unexpectedly with those for accounting income. Between subperiods, the point estimates of the slopes on positive returns *increased* for six of seven countries, the incremental slopes on negative returns show no systematic change, and the R^2's in all of the individual-country cash flow regressions *increase*. We have no explanation for these apparently systematic cash flow changes.

7. Conclusions, implications, and limitations

The worldwide trend toward 'internationalization' of markets, especially capital markets, in which accounting information is used has rekindled academic and professional interest in different national accounting models. The properties of accounting information prepared under common-law accounting

R. Ball et al. / Journal of Accounting and Economics 29 (2000) 1–51   47

standards are of particular contemporary interest because the International Accounting Standards Committee (IASC) recently completed a set of 'international' accounting standards widely viewed as reflecting a largely common-law approach of 'transparent,' timely disclosure.

We show that common-law accounting income does indeed exhibit significantly greater timeliness than code-law accounting income, but that this is due entirely to greater sensitivity to economic losses (income conservatism). This result has important implications for corporate governance. We conjecture that early incorporation of economic losses, as distinct from gradual incorporation over time, increases managers' incentives to attend to the sources of losses more quickly. It brings more and quicker pressure from security analysts, makes leverage and dividend restrictions binding more quickly, and affects current managers' and employees' bonuses. It also makes excessively optimistic statements by managers less credible. Conservative accounting thus facilitates monitoring of managers and is an important feature of common-law corporate governance. In contrast with Roe (1994), we conclude that enhanced common-law disclosure standards reduce the agency costs of monitoring managers, thus countering the advantages of closer shareholder-manager contact in code-law countries.

Our results suggest an explanation for the emergence of a largely common-law model in international transacting, and in particular for the IASC adoption of a more 'transparent' common-law approach to disclosure. The cost of cross-border transacting by parties who are geographically, culturally and linguistically separated from the firm's management presumably is greater in a system that assumes they are informed insiders than in one with more timely public disclosure. Timely disclosure of economic losses is particularly important to cross-border lenders. Whether this model will prevail in international transacting depends on whether high disclosure-quality firms (i.e., firms known a priori as likely to recognize economic losses in a timely fashion) can signal their quality effectively to users, or equivalently on whether low-quality firms can be excluded from false signaling. In the absence of common-law penalties to false signaling, it is difficult to see how high-quality firms in code-law countries will be able to reduce contracting costs through improved financial reporting, other than by listing in a common-law jurisdiction and exposing themselves to common-law penalties for low-quality disclosure.

Greater common-law income conservatism should be no surprise, considering the use of accounting income in common-law arm's-length debt and equity markets, and especially considering common-law litigation. Nevertheless, German accounting in particular is widely presumed to be more conservative, because German managers have unusual discretion to reduce reported income during good years. However, they also have unusual discretion to delay recognition of economic losses, and thus to increase reported income in bad years. This was a common UK practice at the beginning of the twentieth century (Yamey,

48   *R. Ball et al. / Journal of Accounting and Economics 29 (2000) 1–51*

1962), but effectively was extinguished in common-law countries by the Royal Mail case.[26] Similar observations can be made about accounting in Japan.

Our research design is subject to several limitations. The most obvious concern is the validity of stock returns as a proxy for economic income, particularly in code-law countries, which have endogenously lower liquidity and public disclosure standards. 'Noise' in annual stock returns as a measure of market-valued income could be a correlated omitted variable. We counter with three observations. First, poor public disclosure does not necessarily impede the flow of information into stock prices, since the information flow can occur instead via the trading of informed insiders. In the absence of effectively enforced insider-trading laws, which in many ways are fundamentally incompatible with code-law governance, corporate insiders' incentives are to trade on information and thereby incorporate it into prices. This, Ramseyer (1993) conjectures, explains the practice of Japanese banks trading in their clients' stock. To some degree, equating poor public disclosure with uninformed stock prices involves projecting common-law precepts onto code-law institutions, which are more likely to solve information asymmetry by private rather than public communication. Second, our results seem inconsistent with the hypothesis that stock returns reflect poor information flows in code law countries, which would imply less anticipation of accounting income, a stronger income 'surprise' effect, and a stronger return-income association. We observe the opposite. Third, we study stock returns over intervals of one and two years, not over short 'event windows,' which is long enough for international differences in liquidity, market microstructure and disclosure timing effects to have minimal impact.

Correlated omitted variables are another obvious concern. For example, if the proportion of growth options relative to assets in place varies across countries, then common application of the revenue realization rule will cause income to vary internationally in timeliness, due to 'real' rather than 'accounting' effects. Similarly, our results hold only for listed corporations. The number of listed code-law corporations is endogenously small compared with common-law countries, in part because code-law systems are not designed for the demands of public disclosure, so private corporations are comparatively more efficient and consequently more prevalent. Thus, our sample is less representative of code-law accounting in general. This concern is addressed to a degree in the Table 7 control for SIC codes. Another concern is whether the sample period is representative. Japan, for example, went through boom and bust during

---

[26] *Rex v. Lord Kylsant* 1932 1 KB 442. This case-law was codified in the 1948 UK Companies Act, which required companies to distinguish reserves from provisions, 'making the creation of secret reserves more difficult.' (Nobes and Parker, 1995, p. 103). The case can lay claim to be the legal genesis of the Rule 10b-5 in the US. US German practice is exemplified by the notorious Daimler-Benz case (Ball, 1998).

1985–95. Specification tests in Table 7 address this concern, where the results change little when annual firm return is defined relative to the mean return for that country/year, and when income is scaled by the country/year interest rate.

Another concern is our characterization of the relevant institutional features of the seven countries in our primary sample. In particular, the code/common law categorization is a proxy for an underlying economic construct, the extent to which accounting is determined by market supply and demand relative to political forces. The categories overlap, as is obvious from the roles of the Companies Acts in the UK and the SEC in the US. To some degree, this concern is alleviated by the consistent evidence we report from our primary sample. In addition, we report consistent evidence from a secondary sample of eighteen countries, suggesting that our results are generalizable.

A final concern is that institutional determinants of financial reporting vary over time. For example, shareholder lawsuits are reported as rising in Japan (*Wall Street Journal*, January 7, 2000, p. A13), which could signal a change in governance or incentives of financial statement preparers. While we have mechanically divided the 1985–95 period into approximately equal sub-periods and have thereby observed a systematic increase in conservatism, a finer partitioning based on changes in institutional determinants of accounting might obtain clearer results.

The research design also has its strengths. It studies the incorporation of economic income into accounting income over time, under different international institutions, using a model of accounting income determination that is based on fundamental properties of accounting. We believe the results to be of interest to accountants, analysts, standard-setters, regulators and students of corporate governance.

References

Alchian, A., 1984. Specificity, specialization, and coalitions. Journal of Institutional and Theoretical Economics 140, 34–49.

Alchian, A., Demsetz, H., 1972. Production, information costs and economic organization. American Economic Review 62, 777–795.

Alford, A., Jones, J., Leftwich, R., Zmijewski, M., 1993. The relative informativeness of accounting disclosures in different countries. Journal of Accounting Research 31 (Suppl.), 183–223.

American Accounting Association, 1977. Report of the Committee on International Accounting. Supplement to Accounting Review 52.

Amir, E., Harris, T., Venuti, E., 1993. A comparison of the value-relevance of U.S. versus non-U.S. GAAP accounting measures using form 20-F reconciliations. Journal of Accounting Research 31 (Suppl.), 230–264.

Ball, R., 1998. Daimler-Benz AG: evolution of corporate governance from a code-law 'stakeholder' to a common-law 'shareholder value' system. Unpublished manuscript, University of Rochester.

Ball, R., Brown, P., 1968. An empirical evaluation of accounting income numbers. Journal of Accounting Research 6, 159–178.

Bandyopadhyay, S., Hanna, D., Richardson, G., 1994. Capital market effects of U.S.-Canada GAAP differences. Journal of Accounting Research 32, 262–277.

Barth, M., Clinch, G., 1996. International accounting differences and their relation to share prices: evidence from U.K., Australian, and Canadian firms. Contemporary Accounting Research 13, 135–170.

Basu, S., 1997. The conservatism principle and the asymmetric timeliness of earnings. Journal of Accounting and Economics 24, 3–37.

Baums, T., Buxbaum, R., Hopt, K. (Eds.), 1994. Institutional Investors and Corporate Governance Walter de Gruyter, Berlin.

Beaver, W., Lambert, R., Morse, D., 1980. The information content of security prices. Journal of Accounting and Economics 2, 3–28.

Choi, F., Mueller, G., 1992. International Accounting. Prentice-Hall, Englewood Cliffs, NJ.

Coopers & Lybrand, 1982–95. International Tax Summaries, Annual Editions. Wiley, New York.

Collins, D., Maydew, E., Weiss, I., 1997. Changes in the value-relevance of earnings and book values over the past forty years. Journal of Accounting and Economics 24, 39–67.

Cramer, J., 1987. Mean and variance of R^2 in small and moderate samples. Journal of Econometrics 35, 253–166.

Dann, L., Masulis, R., Mayers, D., 1991. Repurchase tender offers and earnings information. Journal of Accounting and Economics 14, 217–251.

David, R., Brierley, J., 1985. Major Legal Systems in the World Today. Stevens & Sons, London.

Dechow, P., 1994. Accounting earnings and cash flows as measures of firm performance: the role of accounting accruals. Journal of Accounting and Economics 18, 3–42.

Dechow, P., Kothari, S., Watts, R., 1998. The relation between earnings and cash flows. Journal of Accounting and Economics 25, 133–168.

Easton, P., Harris, T., Ohlson, J., 1992. Aggregate accounting earnings can explain most of security returns. Journal of Accounting and Economics 15, 119–142.

Elliott, J., Hanna, J., 1996. Repeated write-offs and the information content of earnings. Journal of Accounting Research 34, 135–155.

Fama, E., MacBeth, J., 1973. Risk, return, and equilibrium: empirical tests. Journal of Political Economy 81, 607–636.

Financial Accounting Standards Board (FASB), 1985. Statement of financial accounting concepts no. 6. FASB, Stamford, Connecticut.

Gray, S., 1980. International accounting differences from a security analysis perspective. Journal of Accounting Research 18, 64–76.

Hamson, D., Ziegler, P., 1990. The impact of dividend imputation on firms' financial decisions. Accounting and Finance 30, 29–53.

Harris, T., Lang, M., Möller, H., 1994. The value relevance of German accounting measures: an empirical analysis. Journal of Accounting Research 32, 187–209.

Healy, P., 1985. The effect of bonus schemes on accounting decisions. Journal of Accounting and Economics 7, 85–107.

Hicks, J.R., 1946. Value and Capital 2nd edition. Clarendon Press, Oxford.

Hughes, J., Snyder, E., 1995. Litigation and settlement under the English and American rules: theory and evidence. Journal of Law and Economics 38, 225–250.

Jacobsen, R., Aaker, D., 1993. Myopic management behavior with efficient, but imperfect, financial markets. Journal of Accounting and Economics 16, 383–405.

Joos, P., Lang, M., 1994. The effects of accounting diversity: evidence from the European Union. Journal of Accounting Research 32 (Suppl.), 141–168.

Katz, A., 1987. Measuring the demand for litigation. Journal of Law, Economics, & Organization 3, 143–176.

Köndgen, J., 1994. Duties of banks in voting their clients' stock. In: Baums, Buxbaum, Hopt (Eds.), (Chapter 18). Institutional Investors and Corporate Governance Walter de Gruyter, Berlin.

Kothari, S., Lys, T., Smith, C., Watts, R., 1988. Auditor liability and information disclosure. Journal of Accounting, Auditing and Finance 3, 307–339.

Kothari, S., Sloan, R., 1992. Information in earnings about future earnings: implications for earnings response coefficients. Journal of Accounting and Economics 15, 143–171.

La Porta, L., Lopez-de-Silanes, F., Shleifer, A., Vishny, R., 1997. Legal determinants of external finance. Journal of Finance 52, 1131–1150.

Lintner, J., 1956. Distribution of incomes of corporations among dividends, retained earnings, and taxes. American Economic Review 46, 97–113.

Miceli, T., 1997. Economics of the Law. Oxford University Press, Oxford.

Miwa, Y., 1996. Firms and Industrial Organization in Japan. New York University Press, New York.

Mueller, G., Gernon, H., Meek, G., 1997. Accounting: An International Perspective. Richard D. Irwin, Chicago, IL.

Nobes, C., 1992. International Classification of Financial Reporting. Routledge, London.

Nobes, C., Parker, R., 1995. Comparative International Accounting 4th Edition. Prentice-Hall, Englewood Cliffs, NJ.

Ohlson, J., 1988. Accounting earnings, book value and dividends: the theory of the clean surplus equation. Unpublished manuscript, Columbia University.

Peltzman, S., 1976. Toward a more general theory of regulation. Journal of Law and Economics 19, 211–240.

Pope, P., Walker, M., 1999. International differences in the timeliness, conservatism, and classification of earnings. Journal of Accounting Research 37 (Suppl.), 53–87.

Posner, R. A., 1986. Economic Analysis of Law, 3rd Edition. Little, Brown, Boston, MA.

Posner, R.A., 1996. Law and Legal Theory in the UK and USA. Clarendon Press, Oxford.

Radebaugh, L., Gray, S., 1997. International Accounting and Multinational Enterprises, 4th Edition. Wiley, New York.

Ramesh, K., Thiagarajan, R., 1995. Inter-temporal decline in earnings response coefficients. Unpublished manuscript, Northwestern University.

Ramseyer, J., 1993. Columbian cartel launches bid for Japanese firms. Yale Law Journal 102, 2005–2020.

Roe, M., 1994. Some differences in corporate governance in Germany, Japan and America. In: Baums, Buxbaum, Hopt (Eds.), (Chapter 2). Institutional Investors and Corporate Governance Walter de Gruyter, Berlin.

Shavell, S., 1982. Suit, settlement and trial: a theoretical analysis under alternative methods for the allocation of legal costs. Journal of Legal Studies 11, 55–81.

Standish, P., 1997. The French *Plan Comptable*. Expert Comptable Média, Paris.

Vuong, Q., 1989. Likelihood ratio tests for model selection and non-nested hypotheses. Econometrica 57, 307–333.

Watts, R., Zimmerman, J., 1986. Positive Accounting Theory. Prentice-Hall, Englewood Cliffs, NJ.

Yamey, B., 1962. Some topics in the history of financial accounting in England, 1500-1900. In: Baxter, W.T., Davidson, S. (Eds.), Studies in Accounting Theory. Sweet & Maxwell, London.

[9]

Accounting and Business Research, Vol. 28. No. 3. pp. 173–188. Summer 1998

International Variations in the Connections Between Tax and Financial Reporting

Margaret Lamb, Christopher Nobes and Alan Roberts*

Abstract—This paper constructs a method for assessing the degree of connection between tax rules and practices and financial reporting rules and practices in a country. Five types of connection and disconnection are suggested, and 15 arenas of accounting are proposed for assessment on this basis. The method is applied to four countries, partly in order to test the claim of a clear distinction between Anglo-Saxon and continental European countries.

1. Introduction

A number of papers have begun to investigate the relationship between taxation and financial reporting in a comparative international context (e.g. Haller, 1992; Walton, 1993; Radcliffe, 1993; Quéré, 1994). Hoogendoorn (1996:793) suggests a seven-category classification of 13 European countries based on the relative independence or mutual dependence of tax and financial reporting. However, this was a brief editorial based on a summary of papers by different authors from different countries, writing without a standard approach to assessment of independence or dependence. The classification also gives equal weight to two quite separate issues: the financial reporting treatment of deferred tax and the connection between tax and financial reporting. Consequently, there remains a need for a systematic approach to assessing international variations in the connection between tax and financial reporting. This paper suggests one. It also tests the claim (e.g. Nobes and Parker, 1995, ch. 1) that there is a clear distinction between Anglo-Saxon countries[1] and some continental European countries.

*Margaret Lamb is at the University of Warwick; Christopher Nobes and Alan Roberts are at the University of Reading. They thank the following for their valuable comments on earlier drafts of this paper: Rob Bryer, Michel Couzigou, Axel Haller, Jean Harris, Liesel Knorr, Alain Le Deudé, Yannick Lemarchand, Dieter Ordelheide, Dieter Pfaff, Bernard Sauvée, Jim Schweikart, Anne Semler, Peter Walton, David Wilde, and two referees and the editor of this journal. They also thank participants in the following seminars for good discussion that has helped to clarify the analysis: the EIASM Workshop on Accounting in Europe: 4 (Geneva, June 1995); and the Fifth ICAEW Tax Research Workshop (Lancaster, September 1995). Any errors of interpretation or omission remain the responsibility of the authors. Correspondence should be addressed to Professor C.W. Nobes, Department of Economics, University of Reading, PO Box 218, Whiteknights, Reading RG6 2AA. This paper was first submitted in October 1996; the final version was accepted in March 1998.

Two aspects of this issue can be separated: taxation as an historical reason for accounting, and the degree of contemporary separation or connection between financial reporting[2] and tax for purposes of profit measurement. The first of these includes the effect of tax considerations on rule-making in financial reporting. Rule-makers and corporate taxpayers will have been alert to potential effects of financial reporting on tax liabilities. A few recent examples of this are mentioned in the text below. However, these issues are largely beyond the scope of this paper and are covered elsewhere (Lamb et al., 1995). This paper concentrates on the second aspect: connections and influences between tax and accounting practice in the

[1] 'Anglo-Saxon' is used here in its European sense to mean those countries, generally English-speaking, where accounting is seen as market-driven and where rules are made by non-governmental bodies. The UK and the US are examples.

[2] Our study considers connections between taxation and financial accounting (and its output, published financial reporting). It is beyond the scope of our study to consider connections between taxation and other functional parts of accounting practice.

[3] Radcliffe (1993:1) distinguishes 'financial conformity' from 'tax conformity': 'Financial conformity implies substantial reliance on the principle that choice of a particular accounting practice in the financial report is conclusive for tax purposes and that inclusion of particular items therein is a necessary precondition for the grant of tax relief; tax conformity implies the adoption of a general presumption that taxable profit is computed on the basis of generally accepted accounting principles'. (Radcliffe's categorisation is a broader representation of what we have referred to below as Case II and Case III connections between tax and accounting). The existence of either conformity condition is evidence of a strong link between tax and accounting. The dynamic nature of the link, as Radcliffe (1993) demonstrates through his legal study and as we discuss below, makes the observable patterns of influence reciprocal. The Haller (1992) and Ordelheide & Pfaff (1994) discussion of reverse 'congruence' (or 'authoritativeness') in the German context is a broader representation of what we have referred to below as Case IV and Case V connections.

context of existing sets of tax and financial reporting rules.

The argument proceeds as follows. First, we suggest a method of assessing the degree of linkage between tax and financial reporting. Then, we apply this to four countries: the UK, the US, France and Germany. Finally, we ask whether there is a clear distinction between the countries.

2. A method of assessing linkage

We examine here the degree of connection or conformity[3] between (i) tax rules[4] and practices and (ii) financial reporting and practices. It is suggested that five cases[5] of connection or disconnection for any particular accounting 'arena' (e.g. depreciation of fixed assets) can be distinguished, as in Table 1.

The issue here is not whether the economic decisions of management are affected by tax. We presume that this is the case for many decisions in all countries. The issue is the degree to which financial reporting practice and tax practice are connected in an operational sense. The cases in Table

---

[4] 'Rules' refer to authoritative practice. By far the most common source of rules in the analyses that follow is legislation: primary, secondary or tertiary. However, rules which govern practice may also be drawn from case law or extra-statutory guidance, produced by tax authorities. The key to our recognition of a 'rule' is whether or not it governs observable practice in the majority of cases. We have endeavoured to consider the rules in effect at 1 January 1996 and to base our comparative analysis on this date. Changes in details and shifts in patterns of interrelations between tax and accounting since that date are inevitable, and, where significant, have been noted.
[5] The classificatory scheme rests upon the authors' judgments concerning interrelationships. For a review of methodological issues in international accounting classification, and the importance of judgment, see Roberts (1995).

1 are presented in increasing order of the influence of tax on financial reporting decisions (the latter are also referred to below as accounting policy choices). Case I is disconnection of tax rules and practice from financial reporting rules and practice. This suggests lack of influence of tax on financial reporting decisions.

The other four cases involve various forms of connection. Case II is where there are tax rules and financial reporting rules without major options, and the rules are the same. This suggests that there is limited room for tax considerations to affect accounting policy choice by managers. In Case III, the accounting rules are more detailed than the tax rules, and tax practice is to follow accounting practice. Initially, this suggests the influence of accounting on tax. However, where the accounting rule allows choice or is vague, there may be a 'reverse effect' whereby the financial reporting rules (or options in them) are chosen, interpreted or shaped with the tax effect in mind. Examples of Case III where such a reverse effect seems most likely are shown as 'III†' in Table 2.

Cases IV and V are clearer examples of tax influence on accounting policy choice. In Case IV, there is no precise financial reporting rule, so a tax rule is followed for convenience or a tax option is chosen in order to reduce tax liabilities. In Case V, financial reporting rules are overridden.

We suggest a number of accounting arenas which can be assessed to determine the cases of linkage for any particular country.[8] The first col-

---

[8] More accurately, this could be applied to any particular combination of tax system and accounting system. Some countries have more than one accounting system. For example, group accounts may use different rules from individual accounts.

Table 1
Cases of linkage between tax and financial reporting

Case I	Disconnection	The different tax and financial reporting rules (or different options) are followed for their different purposes.[6]
Case II	Identity	Identity between specific (or singular) tax and financial reporting rules.
Case III	Accounting leads	A financial reporting rule or option is followed for financial reporting purposes, and also for tax purposes. This is possible because of the absence of a sufficiently specific (or singular) tax rule.[7]
Case IV	Tax leads	A tax rule or option is followed for tax purposes, and also for financial reporting purposes. This is possible because of the absence of a sufficiently specific (or singular) financial reporting rule.
Case V	Tax dominates	A tax rule or option is followed for tax and financial reporting purposes instead of a conflicting financial reporting rule.

[6]Such disconnection will be recognised when distinct, independent and detailed tax and financial reporting operational rules exist. Even if measurement outcomes are essentially the same, the particular arena may still be characterised as Case I; the independence and completeness of the sets of rules 'disconnects' tax and accounting in an operational sense.
[7]This case may be either *de facto* identity or an instance where financial reporting is the 'leader'. It may be difficult to distinguish between the two circumstances. However, both indicate a *prima facie* financial reporting influence on tax.

Table 2
Tax linkage in material arenas of financial reporting

Arena		Connection or disconnection case			
		UK	*US*	*France*	*Germany*
1	Fixed asset recognition and valuation	I	II (possibly IV)	II*	III, IV (and sometimes V)
2	Financial and operating leases	III†	Small operating lease payments: II Other lease payments: I	II*	IV
3	Depreciation (a) normal (b) excess	I n/a	I n/a	IV V*	IV V
4	Contingencies, provisions	I (possibly III)	I	II*	III†
5	Grants and subsidies	I	II	III	IV
6	Research and development costs	I	III	III†	III†
7	Inventory valuation: (a) flow assumptions (b) other areas	II III†	IV III†	II* II	IV IV
8	Long-term contracts	III in most cases	I (possibly IV in elements of details)	IV	III
9	Interest expense (a) capitalisation (b) other	I II	I I**	IV* III	III III
10	Foreign currency transactions	I**	I**	I	III
11	Non-consolidation purchased goodwill	I	I (IV may become the norm under new rules)	I	V
12	Pensions	I	I	IV	IV
13	Policy changes and fundamental errors	I	I	III, I	III
14	Scope of the group	I	I	I	I
15	Fines, charitable donations, entertaining expenses	I	I	I	I

Key: Cases I–V	As defined in Table 1.
*	Case I is specifically allowed or required for group accounts.
**	Strictly Case I, but measurements are identical in normal circumstances.
n/a	Not applicable, because there is no distinction for accounting or tax between normal and excess depreciation.
†	Examples of Case III where a reverse effect (i.e. tax considerations influencing financial reporting) seem particularly likely.

umn of Table 2 lists these arenas, which were chosen on the basis that they were sufficiently important[9] to warrant coverage[10] by an International Accounting Standard.

The discussion is set primarily in the context of listed companies, which encompass a large proportion of the economic activity of the four countries considered. As Walton (1993) notes, smaller companies' accounts may present information with tax users primarily in mind. In general, the comparative international issues discussed here apply to both listed and other companies. We concentrate on the rules in force in 1996.

The focus of most of our discussion is individual company financial statements, as these are the basis for tax computation[11] in each of the four countries. However, we will also highlight the relationship between taxation and financial reporting in the context of consolidated accounts. In the UK and the US, one would generally expect the same accounting policies to be used for parent and consolidated financial statements. This is not the case for some large French and German groups.

3. Application to four countries

Our classification of arenas by country into the five cases are, of course, subjective in the sense that judgment is required; first, in deciding how rules of accounting and taxation will normally be applied, and second, in deciding to which case the manner of application best corresponds. In the first sense, we are doing nothing more than replicating the application of professional judgment in practice. We have ensured the realism of our professional judgments of rule application and case classification by (i) extensive research in primary and secondary sources of tax and accounting rules; (ii) discussion among the three authors and reference to the original sources; and (iii) consultation with a minimum of two experts in each country to confirm our replication of professional judgments and subsequent case analysis. We explain the clas-

---

[9] This may not mean that all these differences between tax and accounting rules are material in size. This will vary by sector, country, etc. Nevertheless, we hope that this method will include most material issues.

[10] We have eliminated those International Accounting Standards (IASs) which seem irrelevant for our thesis because they do not affect the profit measurement of individual companies in the countries studied: those on disclosure (IASs 1, 7, 14, 15, 24, 30, 32 and 33); associates and joint ventures (IASs 28 and 31); IAS 26 on accounting by pension plans; and IAS 29 on hyperinflation. We have also left out IAS 12 on taxation (in order to avoid circularity) but have added the arena of fines, donations, etc. as a catch-all for tax/accounting disconnections which are common in all four countries. We use IASs as at the end of 1997.

[11] Very limited exceptions to this generalisation may apply in relation to groups of companies. However, rules of tax consolidation exist where appropriate. See Lamb (1995: 38–9) for a discussion of this aspect of group taxation.

sifications in the text below, providing references for the rules.

Given the general reliance of tax rules on accounting practice for all the countries covered by this study, it is not surprising that there are many examples of Case II and Case III conformity; to this extent, we could regard such conformity as the 'normal' state of affairs in any country. For example, on the whole, the tax rules do not specify treatments for such issues as sales, wages and most business overheads, so Case III conformity is normal.

3.1. The UK

A distinction between accounting profit and taxable profit—caused largely by definitions and distinctions incorporated into tax law—has been recognised since the late nineteenth century (Freedman, 1987; Lamb, 1996). Where there is no specific tax law to the contrary, recent UK case law has helped to clarify that modern accountancy practice will apply in normal circumstances. Despite the possibility that established legal concepts could overrule accountancy practice, a judge's ruling 'will not override a generally accepted rule of commercial accountancy which (a) applies to the situation in question[,] (b) is not one of two or more rules applicable to the situation[,] and (c) is not shown to be inconsistent with the true facts or otherwise inapt to determine the true profits or losses of the business' (Freedman, 1993:477). Therefore, net profit before taxation as shown in the published accounts of limited companies is the usual starting place for tax computations, but many adjustments in theory and in practice can be made.

An example of an unusually complex Case III relationship is the current treatment of lease accounting. The capitalisation of leases was unusual in the UK before the passage of Statement of Standard Accounting Practice (SSAP) 21 in 1984.[12] The Accounting Standards Committee (ASC) confirmed with the tax authorities that the application of SSAP 21 would not alter the tax position, i.e. rental payments under all leases[13] would remain deductible expenses for tax purposes (a Case I disconnection). However, a subsequent Inland Revenue Statement of Practice (confirmed by case law)[14] requires the tax basis to follow the accounting basis in normal circumstances (a Case III relationship). Accounting leadership is established by reference to the categorisation of leasing agreements as 'operating leases' or 'finance leases'.

---

[12] SSAP 21 applied to accounting periods beginning on or after 1 July 1987.

[13] Provided, in general, that the leases themselves, and the profile of payments, conformed to normal commercial practice.

[14] SP 3/91 and *Gallagher v. Jones, Threlfall v. Jones* (1993) STC 537.

Rental payments for operating leases are deductible in arriving at profit measured for financial reporting and tax purposes. In contrast, under new Inland Revenue practice 'inspectors will normally be prepared to accept that the properly computed commercial depreciation of the asset which is charged to the profit and loss account in the period' represents, together with the finance charge element of finance lease rentals, the appropriate tax deduction.[15] In principle, there are no major choices in the accounting rules. However, given the amount of judgment required to distinguish an 'operating lease' from a 'finance lease' under the terms of SSAP 21, there may be a reverse effect (as for many other Case III areas), in that the directors may wish to capitalise or not for tax purposes and therefore may seek to apply SSAP 21 in particular ways.

In the field of inventory valuation, LIFO is not acceptable for tax purposes in the UK,[16] nor generally for accounting purposes[17] (i.e. a Case II relationship). Other aspects of inventory valuation—recognition and categorisation of costs and lines of inventory—are generally subject to Case III conformity.[18] A reverse effect—application of the financial reporting rule with a tax effect in mind—may apply to such aspects of inventory valuation. Given the flexibility of SSAP 9's criteria for the use of the percentage-of-completion method, a reverse effect may also apply to long-term contract accounting. However, Case III conformity (and the scope for reverse effects) is limited by the Revenue's reluctance to accept provisions for foreseeable losses on long-term contracts as calculated in accounts; Inland Revenue guidelines[19] have been provided to deal with such provisions.

The UK treatment of provisions is an arena generally characterised by Case I disconnection. Tax law tends to distinguish between 'general provisions', which are not deductible for tax purposes, and 'specific provisions', which are. A combination of specific legislation and case law has established the clear distinction between 'general' and 'specific' in relation to provisions for bad debts[20] and repairs.[21]

The position for other sorts of provisions is less clear. In a recent case[22], Britannia Airways' provision for future aircraft engine overhaul was accepted as tax deductible, even though the costs had not been incurred, nor the time for overhaul arrived. The High Court's decision rested on the facts that (i) there was no specific tax law that dealt with this type of provision and (ii) that commercial accounting, as reflected in the company's audited accounts, accepted the provisions as accounting expenses. In other words, the Court accepted that a Case III connection existed. However, the strength of the Britannia Airways precedent for law and practice is not yet clear: the case sits somewhat uneasily with the tax treatment of other types of provisions. The extension of the Case III 'imperative' beyond the facts of the particular case is not yet clear;[23] and certain UK accounting standard setters seem unconvinced that Britannia's accounting treatment is an acceptable form of commercial accounting.[24] All in all, it is considered that Case I best characterises the current disconnection of tax and accounting rules in this arena.

Most other material arenas in UK financial reporting (see Table 2) involve quite separate rules for tax and financial reporting (Case I). Fixed assets and their depreciation provide good examples of this. It is provided in law[25] that fixed assets may be revalued in various ways, and this is common practice in the UK, particularly when property prices are rising. Revaluation (upward or downward) is ignored for tax purposes.[26] Similarly, depreciation for financial reporting purposes is controlled by company law and accounting

---

[15] SP 3/91, paragraph B 10–11.

[16] SP 3/90 and *Minister of National Revenue v. Anaconda American Brass Ltd.* (1956) AC 85.

[17] SSAP 9 suggests that LIFO will not normally give a true and fair view.

[18] 'The Revenue accepts any method of computing the value of stocks, which is recognised by the accountancy profession, so long as it does not violate the taxing statutes as interpreted by the Courts' (SP 3/90, paragraph 2).

[19] SP 3/90, paragraph 7.

[20] ICTA 1988, s. 74(1)(j); *Anderton and Halstead Ltd v. Birrell* (1931) 16 TC 200; and *Dinshaw v. Bombay Commissioner of Taxes* (1934) 13 ATC 284. Inland Revenue Interpretation,

Tax Bulletin: 12, August 1994 concerns the evidence required to justify the deduction of a bad debt provision.

[21] ICTA 1988, s.74(1)(d) for the basic legislation.

[22] *Johnston v. Britannia Airways Ltd.* (1994) STC 763.

[23] Clarification of the Revenue's views was sought by the Tax Faculty of the ICAEW in early 1995. For provisions such as warranty claims and closure costs, the Revenue made clear that normal practice would be to follow commercial accounting principles, but subject to judicial tests established by case law and in statute. The suggestion that a taxpayer might be able to claim a more prudent deduction than shown in commercial accounts was dismissed. (*Taxes*, 1995: 513–4 summarises the Inland Revenue guidance.)

[24] The Britannia Airways overhaul provision is, *prima facie*, inconsistent with the definition of 'liability' included in the ASB's draft *Statement of Principles* (see Chapter 3). Instead, the original purchase of the 'asset', the new aircraft, may in substance be better represented as the purchase of the aircraft (with a long useful life) and the purchase of a right to fly the aircraft (with a useful life that will expire after a much shorter period of flying) until the first overhaul. See Green (1995) and Whittington (1995) for summaries of these issues.

[25] CA 1985, Sch. 4, para. 31.

[26] Taxable capital gains or losses are calculated by reference to purchase cost, revaluation at particular dates and a form of indexation unrelated to financial reporting; TCGA 1992, Ss. 35, 38, 272.

standards,[27] but is not deductible against taxable income.[28] Instead, a scheme of capital allowances sets out the available tax depreciation.[29]

Case I disconnection also operates in the following arenas:

(i) *grants and subsidies*: tax treatment starts from general tax principles to distinguish 'capital' from 'revenue',[30] rather than by using the accounting rules in SSAP 4;

(ii) *research and development expenses*: tax rules[31] specify expensing even if development expenditure is capitalised under the rules of SSAP 13;

(iii) *non-consolidation purchased goodwill*: tax rules preclude an expense for amortisation of goodwill;

(iv) *pension costs*: tax allowances are calculated on a different basis[32] from that used by SSAP 24; and

(v) *fines, charitable donations, entertaining expenses*: tax rules very substantially restrict deduction for such expenses.

Two further Case I arenas are worth comment: foreign currency and changes in accounting policy. For foreign currency transactions, the tax rules[33] have recently been changed to bring them more into line with the financial reporting rules dealing with foreign exchange (SSAP 20).The method of this attempt to create greater conformity was to recreate a parallel set of 'commercial accounting rules' for tax purposes. Certain parts of the new legislation have been written in such a way that crucial measurement variables may be chosen in a manner that will permit compliance with both sets of rules: this is the case with Section 150, Finance Act 1993 which allows sufficient flexibility in the choice of translation rates for accounting/tax mismatches to be avoided (Muray and Small, 1995:19). Such provisions would suggest a Case III relationship between accounting and tax rules. However, the differences in detail remain so extensive that it still seems reasonable to describe this arena as Case I.[34]

The arena of changes in accounting policy and correction of fundamental errors also provides an example of Case I. For accounting purposes (FRS 3), these items are treated as prior year adjustments (i.e. the opening balance sheet is adjusted), whereas for tax purposes prior year assessments are amended or, in the case of acceptable[35] changes in accounting policy, are absorbed in the year.[36]

Historically, another example of Case I was that the UK tax system operated on a cash basis for interest and similar receipts or payments,[37] whereas financial reporting worked on an accruals basis. However, new rules for interest introduced in 1996 better align the tax rules with the accounting rules (i.e. establish a Case II relationship). Identity of measurement rules is achieved, but the new tax rules are very detailed as far as the tax categorisation of debits and credits related to 'loan relationships' are concerned; it is not a simple matter of tax rules being required to follow the accounting requirement.[38] Capitalisation of interest on construction projects is not followed for tax purposes (Case I).

As with the other countries considered here, group structures for tax purposes (e.g. loss reliefs, ACT surrender, chargeable gains)[39] are quite different from those for financial reporting as in the Companies Act and FRS 2.

In summary, the UK has many arenas characterised by Case I disconnection, despite general

---

their detail. Although there was an intention at the time of the creation of the new tax legislation that it should recreate existing accounting rules, there is no in-built mechanism for that substantial measure of congruence to be, of necessity, maintained in the future; accounting and tax rules can develop in their own separate ways in the future. This is the characteristic structure of traditional tax rule setting in the UK. As Muray and Small (1995: 19) explain, the complexity arises because 'a modern and sophisticated tax régime had to be laid over the top of an archaic and excessively complex framework.....Without the schedular system, the distinction between [types of taxable income] would have been unnecessary and no special loss relief rules would have been needed. The extraordinary contortions demanded by the regulations dealing with deferral calculations...could have been dispensed with'. As will be discussed below in connection with the US, such complex detail of tax rules, even when intended to replicate in substance commercial accounting rules, may lead to moves over time to a Case IV relationship between accounting and tax.

[35] 'Acceptable' generally means in accordance with the law and accounting standards.

[36] *Pearce v Woodall-Duckham Limited* (1978) CA, 51 TC 271.

[37] ICTA 1988, Ss. 337–338; IR Int. 3.

[38] A company has a 'loan relationship' if it is a debtor or creditor with regard to any debt which is a loan under general law, e.g. gilt-edged securities, corporate bonds, bank loans and overdrafts. Normally amounts payable and receivable are included in the tax computation on an accruals basis. However, if the relationship has been entered into for trade purposes, then the income or expense is treated as part of taxable trading income; otherwise, the income or expense is dealt with under other tax recognition rules (Melville, 1997: 364, 427).

[39] For example, ICTA 1988, Ss. 240, 402, 413, 770; and TCGA 1992, Ss. 170, 171, 175.

---

[27] CA 1985, Sch. 4, paras. 17-19, 32; SSAP 12.

[28] Save in respect of finance lease assets capitalised in conformity with SSAP 21. See above.

[29] CAA 1990, Ss. 24, 25, 159.

[30] Accounting and tax will almost always distinguish the general nature of government grants and subsidies in the same way. There is a substantial degree of accord concerning what is 'capital' in this context. However, SSAP 4 treatment of a capital grant is irrelevant to its tax treatment which depends on the type of asset to which it relates and the tax depreciation rules, if any, that apply. Revenue grants and subsidies will effectively be treated in the same way for tax and accounting.

[31] CAA 1990, part VII.

[32] ICTA 1988, Ss. 74, 592.

[33] SP 1/87 until April 1995; then FA 1993, Ss. 125–170, Schs. 15–17 and FA 1994, Ss. 114–116, Sch. 18.

[34] The different vocabulary, definitions and statements of rules create distinct sets of references that are disconnected in

principles of judicial tax law that tend toward 'tax conformity' (Radcliffe, 1993) and that emphasise the importance of commercial accounting in 'leading' tax treatment.

3.2. The US

Under the current Internal Revenue Code (IRC), there is no general requirement of conformity between taxable profit and financial statement profit. However, there is an apparently strong link between tax law and accounting in Section 446(a) IRC 1986 which states: 'taxable income shall be computed under the method of accounting on the basis of which the taxpayer regularly computes his income in keeping his books'. Most companies adopt the accruals method as their 'method of accounting' and GAAP for tax profit calculations. Relatively recent changes make clear that the phrase 'method of accounting' may be defined in such a way as to permit divergence from financial accounting in a number of circumstances.[40]

Although there is an absence of 'presumptive equivalency'[41] between accounting and tax measurement of profits, and although the opportunities for permissive disconnection of accounting and tax measurements have increased over time, US recognition of taxable profits rests on a bedrock of *de facto* conformity with commercial accounting. Therefore, we should not be surprised to find examples of Case II identity between tax and accounting rules in important areas of measurement. In most circumstances, such identity exists in the arena of fixed asset valuation (other than depreciation—see below).[42] However, as the tax rules[43] for the valuation of tangible fixed assets are often more specific and detailed than accounting GAAP,[44] a number of Case IV (tax leader) rela-

tionships may operate to support the identification and categorisation of historical costs for tax purposes. For example, uniform capitalisation rules for tax purposes[45] require direct costs and some indirect costs of fixed assets produced by the taxpayer to be capitalised, not expensed; categorisation for accounting purposes will provide *prima facie* evidence concerning the nature of costs.

Perhaps more characteristic, given the detailed nature of tax regulation, are those arenas characterised by Case III or Case IV conformity. In Case III examples, the detailed tax regulations outline a number of acceptable approaches, whereas the financial reporting rules are more constrained and will tend to be adopted for both purposes. In Case IV examples, the detailed tax guidelines will tend to be followed (or may have to be followed) rather than a more general, or an alternative, financial reporting rule.

In the arena of research and development expenditure, the accounting rule[46] is clear: research and development expenditure should be treated as an expense. The tax rules are more permissive: research and development expenditure incurred may be expensed, but if not, depreciation or amortisation over a specified period is possible.[47] Although the detailed accounting and tax rules are written without reference to one another, this arena seems characterised by a Case III relationship, without room for much reverse effect: if research and development expenses are written off in accounts in accordance with SFAS 2, then for tax purposes Section 174(a)(1) IRC 1986 will apply and will give the same treatment.

Inventory valuation is an arena where tax rules[48] state explicitly that 'best accounting practice' should be adopted to find appropriate valuation rules, provided 'income is clearly reflected'. In normal circumstances, therefore, tax and accounting valuations are identical. Both sets of rules[49] permit companies to choose a valuation method from a range of options—FIFO and LIFO are within the range of acceptable flow assumptions. However, given that the tax rules normally require conformity of flow assumption with financial reporting,[50] the tax option that has the most beneficial tax effect (e.g. LIFO in periods of rising inventory costs)

---

[40] Reg. § 1.446-1(a)(1) defines 'method of accounting' as 'not only the overall method of accounting of the taxpayer but also the accounting treatment of any item'. The taxpayer adopts an overall method of accounting and methods of accounting for particular items when first filing a tax return. The method(s) must thereafter be applied consistently, unless IRS approval is obtained for a change in overall method of accounting or for the method of accounting of a 'material item used in such overall plan' (Reg. § 1.446-1(e)(2)(ii)(a)). With some exceptions, the IRS no longer imposes 'a financial statement conformity condition on proper to proper changes in accounting method'; a year-end reconciliation is the only requirement (Godshalk, 1994: 159). Thus, financial accounts and tax computation 'methods of accounting' are permitted to diverge. Such a divergence does not apply to the LIFO choice; see footnote 50.

[41] *Thor Power Tool Co. v. CIR* (1979) 58L Ed. 2d 785.

[42] The same analysis applies to the treatment of grants and subsidies under tax and accounting rules. Neither system of rules deals with the impact of grants and subsidies on profit as an explicit subject. Instead, historical cost measurement takes this aspect into account. If grants or subsidies were not capital in nature, general principles of income recognition would apply for tax and accounting purposes.

[43] Sections 263A, 1011–1013, IRC 1986; Regs. § 1.1012–1.

[44] SEC rules and Accounting Principles Board Opinion (APBO) 6 (1965).

[45] Section 263A IRC 1986.

[46] Statement of Financial Accounting Standards (SFAS) 2 (1974).

[47] Section 174 IRC 1986.

[48] Section 471 IRC 1986; Regs. § 1.471–1; Regs. § 1.471–2.

[49] Inventory accounting is governed by Accounting Research Bulletin (ARB) 43: 4 (1953).

[50] Section 472(e) IRC 1986 requires that taxpayers who adopt LIFO methods must use the same method in their financial reports. Regs. § 1.472–2(e) deals with this LIFO 'report rule' in more detail.

will tend to be adopted for financial reporting,[51] to the exclusion of other options. Therefore, characterisation of the tax/accounting relationship as Case IV, rather than Case II, seems appropriate. The close link between accounting and tax in this arena is made clear by the requirement that taxpayers must obtain tax authority approval for any change in method of valuing inventory.[52]

In other respects, tax and accounting rules detail the types of inventory costs to be taken into account and the methods for reaching appropriate measures of cost. Despite the detail, the method of measurement advocated in each set of rules is consistent and, therefore, the financial reporting treatment normally leads the tax treatment (Case III): that this should be so seems clear from the reference to 'best accounting practice' in tax rules.

The distinct and separate purposes of tax and accounting rules (Case I) were clearly evident in the arena of long-term contracts until changes to tax law introduced in 1986: accounting rules[53] permitted the completed-contract or percentage-of-completion methods to be used (depending on the circumstances), while the tax rules required the use of the completed-contract method. The 1986 tax change[54] requires the percentage-of-completion method, defined in detail in the tax law, to apply to most long-term contracts.[55] As the choice for financial reporting does not depend on the tax rules, and *vice versa*, this remains a Case I relationship. However, when the percentage-of-completion method is applicable under both sets of rules, the more detailed tax basis of calculation is likely to be adopted, too, for financial reporting purposes. A secondary Case IV relationship may, therefore, apply to elements of measurement.

The fact that there is no presumptive equivalence in the US between tax and financial reporting, together with an institutional recognition of the separate, distinct purposes of tax accounting and financial reporting,[56] means that Case I disconnection of tax and financial reporting is likely to be an important feature of the US system. We find Case I disconnection in a number of arenas:

(i)   *Fixed asset depreciation*: The accounting rules[57] are distinct and separate from the tax rules.[58] The latter are very detailed and specify, *inter alia*, the method of depreciation to be used; guidelines for the length of useful life; salvage value should be equal to zero; and the convention of depreciation to apply in years of acquisition and disposal.

(ii) *Non-consolidation purchased goodwill*: Accounting rules[59] require amortisation over an expected useful life of no more than 40 years. Until 1993 the tax/accounting relationship was Case I because no tax deduction was available for goodwill. Under new rules introduced in 1993[60], certain non-consolidation purchased goodwill may be amortised over 15 years. The tax/accounting relationship remains, strictly, Case I but it is possible that a reverse effect will become evident to make the choice of useful life for accounting purposes tend to be at or near 15 years for reasons of simplicity.[61]

(iii) *Accounting for leases*: Accounting and tax rules are detailed and apply for their distinct purposes.[62] The accounting treatment of payments under leases depends, under SFAS 13, on whether or not the lease is classified as a capital lease. The tax rules do not recognise the concept of capital lease, but are concerned with ascertaining the permissible de-

---

[51] There is, of course, a trade-off between tax savings and reported earnings. A large literature exists concerning the implications of the choice of LIFO by management (e.g. Sunder, 1973, 1975; Ricks, 1982).

[52] Section 446(e) IRC 1986 and Regs. § 1.446–1(e). A number of other changes in method of accounting require prior Internal Revenue Service (IRS) approval. However, most of the other circumstances have greater impact on unincorporated businesses or small companies and are likely to have an impact on financial statements prepared for tax accounting purposes only. Special notice provisions apply to the adoption of LIFO.

[53] ARB 45 (1955). Both methods are acceptable, but the percentage-of-completion method is preferable when costs to completion estimates are reasonably reliable. Otherwise, the completed-contract method should be used.

[54] Bittker and Loklan (1989, ¶106.2.1) explain that the purpose of the 1986 change was to eliminate the deferral of taxable income permitted by adoption of the completed-contract method. They quote (fn. 3) a Congressional report as saying 'corporations had large deferred taxes attributable to this accounting method and low effective tax rates. Annual reports for the large defense contracts indicate extremely low (or negative) tax rates for several years due to large net operating loss deductions arising from the use of the completed-contract method' (H.R. Rep. No. 426, 99th Cong., 1st Sess. 625–26).

[55] Section 460 IRC 1986.

[56] *Thor Power Tool Co v CIR* (1979) 58L Ed. 2d 785.

[57] ARB 43, Chapter 9A (1953); ARB 44 (revised 1958).

[58] Sections 167, 168, 197 IRC; Regs. 1.167(a); Regs. 1.446–1(a). Nevertheless, the 1913 income tax law defined the depreciation rules that were then widely adopted for accounting purposes (Watts and Zimmerman, 1979).

[59] APBO 17 (1970).

[60] Section 197 IRC 1986. An 'amortisable section 197 intangible' means, broadly, purchased business 'goodwill', 'going concern value', business records (including customer lists and market intelligence), intellectual property and know-how, and 'workforce in place including its composition and terms and conditions...of its employment'. Self-created 'goodwill' will normally fall outside the definition of an 'amortisable section 197 intangible'; the exceptions are, broadly, property rights that have been legally documented (e.g., as a licence, trademark or covenant agreement). Detailed rules make clear that recognition of 'amortisable section 197 intangibles' will normally occur in connection with the purchase of assets amounting to a going concern.

[61] While a longer useful life may be justified and permissible for financial accounting purposes, equal amortisation for tax and accounting reduces the complexity of deferred tax calculations.

[62] SFAS 13 (1976); Section 467 IRC 1986; Regs. § 1.446–1(a).

duction of rent accrued under the lease for the period in question. Small operating lease payments (aggregate payments up to $250,000) will be presumed to follow the normal accounting method; other lease rentals will be deductible according to specific tax rules and calculations.

(iv) *Provisions and contingencies*: Accounting rules[63] require recognition of liabilities (and any consequential expense) where it is probable that losses have been incurred at the financial statement date and the amount can be reasonably estimated. Tax rules permit an expense deduction only when 'incurred', a concept defined by reference to specific statutory tests which take into account financial reporting treatment,[64] but must conform to a judicial test of appropriate accrual (the 'all events' test). The effect of the combined tax rules tends to make the tax concept of accrual more restricted than the accounting concept, which is defined in probabilistic terms to a far greater degree. Despite the explicit influence of the accounting treatment on the tax treatment, this remains an area best described as Case I because of the independence of the tests of judgment reserved to the distinct tax and accounting purposes.

(v) *Interest expense*: Tax rules[65] permit a deduction for interest accrued, but numerous special rules apply to deal with, *inter alia*, interest on indebtedness to fund corporate investment[66] and capitalised interest.[67]

(vi) *Foreign currency gains/losses*: Tax rules[68] will, in general, permit the gain or loss associated with accrued income and expenses to be recognised or deducted from ordinary income. Such treatment is consistent with the accounting rules[69] applicable to individual company accounts.[70] However, detailed rules exist to govern the tax treatment of foreign dividend flows.[71]

(vii) *Pension costs*: Accounting for employers' pension costs is an arena where tax and accounting rules diverge in their detail, impact on profit measurement, and intention. Ac-

counting rules[72] aim to ensure full recognition (using an actuarial method of calculation) of the pension costs and allocation to the periods in which they accrue. Tax rules[73] are more concerned to ensure that tax deductions are given for contributions made at an acceptable level to an acceptably constituted plan (e.g. a Section 401 qualified pension plan).

(viii) *Accounting policy changes and correction of fundamental errors*: The accounting rules[74] require prior year adjustment in certain cases. Tax rules require that certain accounting policy changes ('changes in accounting method' for 'material items' as defined in regulations) should be approved by the IRS in advance and, once approved, should be reflected in the year of the change.[75] Taxpayers may be able to take advantage of an option to reconstruct earlier years' calculations of taxable income to reflect the change of policy.[76] Fundamental errors will generally be corrected by adjustment of earlier years' taxable income.

(ix) *Group recognition*: The consolidated income tax return rules are defined in a manner entirely distinct from the accounting rules governing the recognition of an accounting group for consolidated accounts purposes.[77]

(x) *Fines, charitable donations, entertaining*: Accounting rules apply the general matching principle to recognise such expenses. Tax rules restrict the deductibility of these expense categories: in general, fines are disallowed; charitable contributions are restricted to 10% of a corporation's taxable income;[78] and many business entertaining expenses are disallowable or restricted by a 50% limitation.[79]

Although its volume and detail suggests the separateness of the tax accounting regime (and creates a number of Case I disconnections), US tax officials are free to observe, choose and adapt practices and rules from commercial accounting and financial reporting regulation[80] to suit tax pur-

---

[63] SFAS 5 (1975).

[64] Section 461(h)(3)(B) IRC 1986.

[65] Section 162(a) IRC 1986.

[66] Section 279 IRC 1986.

[67] Section 460 IRC 1986. Accounting rules would permit an interest deduction on an accruals basis, subject to special treatment for interest capitalised—SFAS 34 (1979).

[68] Sections 985–988 IRC 1986.

[69] SFAS 52 (1981).

[70] The translation of the results of overseas subsidiaries' accounts in consolidated group accounts has no applicability for tax purposes.

[71] The calculation of earnings and profits under Section 986 IRC 1986.

[72] SFAS 87 (1985); SFAS 88 (1985).

[73] Section 404 IRC 1986.

[74] APBO 9 (1966) and APBO 20 (1971); SFAS 16 (1977).

[75] Section 446, IRC 1986 and Regs. § 1-446-1(e).

[76] Section 481(a), IRC 1986 and Regs. § 1-481-1 and § 1-481-2.

[77] Sections 1501 and 1504 IRC 1986; ARB 51 (1959).

[78] But the excess may be carried forward.

[79] Sections 162, 170 and 274 IRC 1986 respectively.

[80] As many of the tax rules detailed above apply equally to companies that publish financial reports, companies not subject to public reporting requirements, and unincorporated businesses, detailed tax rules will define the primary accounting rules for many enterprises. It is unsurprising that tax authorities adopt sound financial reporting principles when trying comprehensively to define adequate standards of accounting.

poses. An indicator of the responsiveness of tax authorities to, and their awareness of, changing commercial accounting circumstances is the frequency and volume of changes in tax statutes and regulations.[81] Such frequency and volume constitutes part of a plausible explanation of the persistence of Case III and Case IV connections in the context of a tax accounting regime seemingly predisposed to disconnection. Further, the reliance on very detailed income tax regulations to articulate and clarify applications of primary legislation permits the tax authorities to rationalise circumstances when accounting is permitted to lead tax (Case III) and to specify those conditions when tax requirements should lead accounting (Case IV). The balance of influence in the relationship (i.e. should it be seen as Case III or Case IV?) may depend on the extent to which tax accounting detail overwhelms—for relative simplicity or to save effort—the rules in financial reporting standards.

3.3. France

A key requirement of the *Code Général des Impôts* (General Tax Code—CGI)[82] is that, for tax purposes, businesses must respect the definitions set out in the *Plan Comptable Général* (General Accounting Plan—PCG) to the extent that they are not incompatible with the tax base (*l'assiette d'impôt*). This emphasises the significance of accounting for tax purposes.

The many Case II connections between tax and accounting reflect the historical development of tax and accounting rules in France (Frydlender and Pham, 1995; Mikol, 1995). Tax influence on company financial reporting can be illustrated by a consideration of the rules concerning accounting for tax-deductible or regulatory provisions (*provisions reglementées*) and the difference between economic and fiscal depreciation (*amortissements dérogatoires*).

Regulatory provisions are defined in the PCG as provisions which do not correspond to the usual object of a provision[83] and are accounted for as a result of statutory regulations. In effect, these provisions are created for purely tax reasons; they include provisions for price increases in stocks, for exchange rate fluctuations relative to stocks (until 1998), for investment arising from employee share ownership, and for allowable industry-specific provisions. If a business wishes to claim the benefits of these provisions (and fiscally-calculated depre-

ciation), the CGI[84] requires that entries must be made within the financial accounting system of the business. That is, in order to claim accelerated depreciation, the business has to charge it in the profit and loss account (i.e. Case V).

The total depreciation is split between an economic charge to operating expenses and an excess fiscal charge to extraordinary expenses. The 1983 PCG recognised this fiscal occupation of the space of financial accounting by creating a set of account codes to handle these tax requirements. The bookkeeping involves a debit to the extraordinary items caption in the profit and loss account and a credit to a regulatory provisions caption on the capital and liabilities side of the balance sheet.

For normal depreciation expenses, there is also a connection between tax and accounting. The tax rules incorporate a number of specific requirements: the use of zero disposal values; guidelines on useful lives; and pro rata charges for assets bought or sold in the year. These rules seem to be derived from generally accepted commercial practice. Now that they have become tax rules, accountants tend to follow them for convenience; thus, the treatment of normal depreciation is an example of a Case IV tax/accounting relationship.

The general rules for asset valuation in individual company accounts are a clear *de jure* connection (Case II) between tax and accounting rules. The accounting rules[85] set out the general historical cost basis for the valuation of assets, and the wording used is effectively the same in the relevant section of the CGI.[86] However, there are nuances to this general identity. For example, there is a potential divergence between tax and accounting practice in the treatment of interest on borrowings used to finance fixed assets under construction. The accounting rule[87] permits companies to capitalise such interest into the cost of the fixed asset,[88] but such financial costs are excluded for tax purposes. They are to be treated as an expense in the determination of taxable profit[89] and thus an adjustment to accounting profit would be required[90] if a company opted for capitalisation. However, capitalisation is rare in practice (Case IV).

Case II identity exists, for individual company accounts, in the field of inventory valuation. The governing accounting rule[91] allows either FIFO or

---

[81] There are other reasons for the frequent and detailed changes in tax statute and regulation: for example, pursuit of socio-economic incentives or broader aims; political aims; control of certain kinds of avoidance activities or multinational commercial behaviour.

[82] CGI, Ann. III, art. 38 *quater*.

[83] Defined by CNC Terminology Commission as 'precise in its nature but uncertain as to its impact'.

[84] CGI, art. 39-1-2°.

[85] C. Com. art. 12; *Décret* 83-1020, art. 7; PCG *Titre* II, *Chapitre* III, Section IA.

[86] CGI, Ann. III, art. 38 *quinquies* and *nonies*.

[87] *Décret* 83-1020, art. 7-2°.

[88] A rule extended for consolidated accounts to permit capitalisation into the cost of production of a current asset: *Décret* 86-221, art. D248-8(d).

[89] CGI, Ann. III, at. 38 *quinquies*.

[90] On form N°2058-AN.

[91] C. Comm art. 12.

weighted average cost as methods of stock valuation and these methods are also those allowed for tax purposes.[92] Other situations exist where the tax/accounting identity may be said to derive from general principles. Accounting rules for individual company accounts do not permit the capitalisation of finance leases; indeed, a whole sub-section of the PCG[93] is devoted to accounting for leases which sets out the particular accounting codes to be used. There is no explicit provision in the CGI which considers the issue of capitalisation, and lease payments would thus be classified as an expense, recognised by the PCG, to be deducted in arriving at accounting and taxable profit.[94]

A more complicated relationship exists in circumstances where both accounting rules and tax rules contain options for treatment. Accounting for research and development provides one example. The accounting rules of the Commercial Code and the PCG[95] require such costs to be expensed, although exceptionally (and under certain conditions) applied research and development may be capitalised. The option provided in the Tax Code[96] is expressed slightly differently: at the choice of the enterprise, research and development costs may be either charged against profit or capitalised and then amortised. In this case the tax treatment seems to follow the accounting treatment of the expenditure (Case III). However, the possibility of a reverse effect seems equally to result: the accounting treatment may be chosen with the tax effect in view.

Another example of the complications for the tax/accounting relationship created by options in accounting treatment is accounting for long-term contracts. The accounting rules appear to admit both the completed-contract and percentage-of completion methods, although there are caveats. According to the general rule set out in the Commercial Code,[97] only realised profits can be recognised in the annual accounts, but a 1985 amendment to the rule[98] permits the inclusion of profit taken on work completed under certain conditions. The PCG[99] has particular accounting requirements when this percentage-of-completion method is used. The tax rules are not clear in this area. The main rule[100] appears to align taxable profit on long-term contracts with the completed-contract method; there seems to be no official consideration of the percentage-of-completion

method, which would generally accelerate tax liabilities. This appears to be a Case I. However given the indeterminacy of both sets of rules, this suggests a Case IV relationship in practice.

There are other instances that more clearly illustrate Case I in that, for tax purposes, adjustments are made to the profit declared in the company's annual accounts. One example has already been mentioned: capitalisation of interest. Similar divergences exist in the treatment of foreign exchange transactions where the provision for transaction losses arising on unsettled foreign currency debtors and creditors required by the PCG[101] is disregarded under the relevant tax rule,[102] and the unsettled transaction loss itself is included in arriving at taxable profit.

Another example which illustrates the struggle for the 'nerve centres' of accounting in France is pension provisions (Mikol, 1995). The central accounting rule contained in the Commercial Code requires pension commitment totals to be included in the notes to the annual accounts. Businesses can decide to make a provision for all or some of these commitments in the balance sheet.[103] However, the relevant provision of the CGI[104] specifically forbids the deduction of provisions relating to pensions; indeed, at one stage the tax authorities sought to bar the creation of pension provisions within company accounts (Scheid and Walton, 1992:223–4). Given the current divergence of accounting and tax rules, an adjustment for tax purposes is made to accounting profit where such provisions have been created. In practice, French companies do not generally make pension provisions in their accounts (Case IV).

The accounting treatment of changes in accounting policy or the correction of errors is to absorb the changes in the current year's income.[105] The tax treatment, however, is a little more complicated. For changes in accounting policy made in accordance with accounting law by managerial decision (*décisions de gestion régulières*) it appears that tax treatment follows accounting treatment (Case III), although it should be noted that the force of the accounting principle of the permanence of accounting methods in France[106] may, in practice, restrict the possibilities for companies to change their accounting policies. For the correction of errors, the situation is a little different. The

---

[92] D. adm. 4A-252 § 6.
[93] PCG, *Titre* II, *Chapitre* III, *Section* IIA4.
[94] CGI, art. 39-1.
[95] C. Com. art. D.19. PCG, *Titre* II, *Chapitre* III, *Section* IA (Code 203).
[96] CGI, art. 236-1.
[97] C. Com. art. 15.
[98] L85-31.
[99] PCG, *Titre* II, *Chapitre* III, *Section* IIB4.
[100] CGI, art. 38-2-*bis*.

[101] PCG, *Titre* II, *Chapitre* I, *Section* IC. The loss is shown in the balance sheet as an 'asset'.
[102] CGI, art. 38-4. Table 2058-A requires cancellation of the provision and substitution of the unsettled loss.
[103] C. com. art. 9, modified by L85-695.
[104] CGI, art. 39-1-5°.
[105] C. Com. art. 13; PCG, *Titre* II, *Chapitre* I, *Section* II. A recent CNC opinion (June 1997) has suggested that such changes and corrections should be treated as a prior period adjustment.
[106] C. com. art. 11.

impact of such corrections upon accounting profit must be eliminated in arriving at taxable profit (Case I);[107] adjustments would be made to earlier years' assessments.

For the most part the above discussion has focused on the tax/accounting relationship in French individual company accounts. However, a different kind of relationship exists for consolidated accounts. Statutory requirements for the publication of consolidated accounts only arrived in France with the enactment of the EU Seventh Directive—much later than in the UK or Germany. Although the French tax system has special tax *régimes* available for groups (e.g. *régime de l'integration fiscale*) the constitution of these groups is different from the requirements for the establishment of consolidated accounts. The French legislation enacting the Seventh Directive[108] took the opportunity to permit a flexibility of accounting rules for consolidation which removed the intimate tax/accounting relationship required for individual company accounts, and recognised the benefits for large multinational French companies of having internationally-comparable consolidated financial reports (*Gardes des Sceaux*, quoted by Corre, 1987:47).

Individual company accounts prepared according to the rules and definitions of the PCG, not consolidated accounts, are the starting point for the calculation of taxable profit. This flexibility and 'international orientation' are possible because no tax implications flow from consolidation for financial reporting purposes. Disconnections possible under the legislation are several:

(i) tangible fixed assets and inventories may be valued at replacement cost;
(ii) inventories may be valued using the LIFO method;
(iii) capitalised interest may be included in the cost of current assets under construction;
(iv) finance leases may be capitalised;[109] and
(v) unsettled gains on foreign currency monetary balances may be recognised as income.

In addition, the legislation requires the elimination of the effect of fiscal intrusions into the preparation of company annual accounts (specifically, in connection with investment grants, regulatory provisions and depreciation).[110] In practice, a number of large French groups do take advantage of these specific disconnections in order to move their groups accounts approximately or completely in accordance with US rules or international ac-

counting standards (Cauvin Angleys Saint-Pierre, 1996:177–182).

In summary, there are many examples of strong tax influences upon accounting for individual companies in France, but these influences can be substantially modified in the construction of consolidated financial reports.

3.4. Germany

As noted in the introduction, the context of this paper is largely the statutory annual accounts of individual tax-paying companies. For Germany, as for France, special comments for consolidated financial statements are relevant, and these are made at the end of this section.

The formal relationship between German tax and accounting rules is that the former rest on the latter (Ordelheide and Pfaff, 1994:81). There are many instances of this Case III conformity: for example, sales, wages, interest payments, research and development costs, and the compulsory accrual for repairs in the first three months of the following year.[111] Another example of Case III is the tax treatment of changes in accounting policy and the correction of fundamental errors. This follows the accounting treatment, which is to absorb the changes in the year's income. This conforms to the *Handelsgesetzbuch* (HGB) principle[112] that the opening balance sheet should be last year's closing balance sheet. In some arenas (e.g. long-term contracts and foreign currency transactions), the accounting rule is derived from the principles of the HGB, and then Case III follows.

However, it is also easy to find instances of Cases IV and V, where accounting practice chooses to follow tax rules for various reasons:

(a) for simplicity, in order to have a unified tax and accounting statements (*Einheitsbilanz*);
(b) for simplicity, to reduce the differences between the tax and accounting statements;
(c) following an option in the HGB, in order to gain tax relief;
(d) following a tax rule in the absence of other rules, in order to gain tax relief; or
(e) breaking *Grundsätze ordnungsmässiger Buchführung* (GoB),[113] with the permission of the HGB, in order to gain tax relief.

Areas of practice illustrating types (a) and (b) above include asset and liability recognition options in the HGB where there is no option for tax purposes. These accounting options might be considered as examples of 'disconnections', except that in practice most German companies choose to fall under (a) and nearly all the rest choose to fall under (b) for their individual company ac-

---

[107] C.E. 17 *mai* 1982, n°23559.
[108] *Loi* 85-11, *Décret* 86-221.
[109] *Décret* 86-221, art. D248-8.
[110] *Décret* 86-221, art. D248-6(c). This specific mention in legislation of the need to correct tax intrusions into consolidated accounts reflects the provisions of Article 29(5) of the EC Seventh Directive.

[111] HGB § 249(1).
[112] HGB § 252(1)1.
[113] Principles of proper accounting.

counts. In more detail, decisions of the highest tax court, the *Bundesfinanzhof* (BFH) (in 1969) hold that various HGB options to capitalise assets must be taken for tax purposes and various options for the recognition of liabilities must not be. An example of the former is discount on a debt,[114] which must be capitalised for tax purposes. An example of the latter is accruals for repairs to be carried out between three and 12 months after the year end,[115] which cannot be recognised for tax purposes. An exception to the asset rule relates to business start-up expenses, which must be expenses for tax purposes and are therefore generally treated as expenses for accounting purposes, although they do not have to be.[116]

Similarly, in practice, many companies adhere to the tax rules for financial reporting purposes in the following areas:
(i)   use of the tax law's 15-year write-off period for non-consolidation purchased goodwill, rather than the four-year period found in commercial rules (unless a longer period can be justified);[117]
(ii)   the tax law's maximum rate of 30% for declining balance depreciation is in practice not usually exceeded for accounting purposes;
(iii)   the use of inventory flow assumptions (e.g. average cost, FIFO or LIFO)[118] generally coincide for tax and accounting, although they do not have to;[119]
(iv)   the accounting option to include production overheads[120] is generally taken up following the tax requirement to include them;
(v)   the accounting option to provide for pension commitments relating to the period before 1987 is generally not taken up; and
(vi)   the tax decrees of the Ministry of Finance are followed for determining if a lease should be capitalised (Ordelheide and Pfaff, 1994:124).

An example of type (c) (following an HGB option in order to get tax relief) is the writing down of an asset below cost.[121]

Examples of type (d) (following a tax option in the absence of other rules, in order to get tax relief) include the common accounting practices of:
(i)   the use of maximum depreciation rates allowed by tax law;

(ii)   changing depreciation method[122] from reducing balance to straight-line for an asset when this would increase the expense;
(iii)   expensing items that cost less than DM800;[123]
(iv)   charging six months' depreciation on assets bought in the first half of the year and a full year's depreciation on assets bought in the second half;[124]
(v)   discounting of non-interest-bearing long-term debtors;
(vi)   calculation of pension expenses on the basis of interest rates and other assumptions in tax rules (Seckler, 1992: 238–9); and
(vii)   taking federal grants to income immediately because they are not taxable, whereas other grants are deducted from the related assets and therefore taken to income (and taxable income) more slowly.

Examples of type (e) (breaking GoB in order to gain tax relief) include:
(i)   the lack of re-instatement of historical cost[125] even when a previous write-down is no longer necessary; and
(ii)   using accelerated depreciation as allowed for certain assets or in certain regions.[126]

In terms of the five cases, types (a) to (d) seem to be examples of Case IV (tax rules followed instead of other acceptable financial reporting rules). However, type (e), although 'voluntary', seems to be an example of Case V (tax rule followed instead of a conflicting financial reporting rule). One could argue that the arena of lease accounting (as noted above) is another example of Case V. The HGB is unclear but the decrees of the Ministry of Finance are followed rather than the guidance of the *Institut der Wirtschaftsprüfer*. However, classification as Case V would rely on treating the *Institut*'s guidance as an accounting 'rule' which may be inappropriate. Therefore, we retain the Case IV classification.

By contrast, there are some specific disconnections between German accounting and tax rules where practice actually does diverge (Case I). These might be split into those instances where practice *sometimes* diverges and those where it *must*. The examples of types (a) to (e) above are not included here because practice tends not to diverge. However, an example where it sometimes

---

[114] HGB § 250(3).
[115] HGB § 249(1).
[116] HGB § 269.
[117] EStG § 7(1) as opposed to HGB § 255(4).
[118] HGB § 240(4) and § 256.
[119] Brooks and Mertin (1993: E13) suggest that, when prices rise, companies might use average cost for tax purposes and FIFO for financial reporting.
[120] HGB § 255(2).
[121] Allowed by HGB § 253(2) and EStG § 6.

[122] Incidentally, the BFH held in 1990 that conformity between tax and accounting was required for the method of depreciation, not merely the amount (BStB1, 1990 s. 681).
[123] See § 6, para. 2 of EStG.
[124] Art. 44, para. 2, *Einkommensteuer-Richtlinien*.
[125] With the permission of HGB § 280.
[126] There is an option to show the credit entry for this not against the asset but in a special balance sheet caption called *Sonderposten mit Rücklageanteil*, which might be interpreted as partly reserves and partly deferred tax.

does diverge is where a company feels obliged to make certain provisions which are not sufficiently concrete to be deductible for tax purposes. Instances where tax and accounting *must* diverge include expenses which are not tax deductible, including (i) certain fines, (ii) 20% of entertainment expenses, (iii) charitable and political donations above certain maxima, and (iv) half the fees of members of the supervisory board.

In summary, there are many examples of the influence of tax on accounting in Germany. However, some large companies choose to use different accounting policies in their consolidated financial statements in order to reduce this influence. Major examples of this are the annual reports of Bayer and Schering for 1994 onwards, where International Accounting Standards (IASs) have been followed by choosing appropriate options from the HGB. Other companies (e.g. Hoechst) have subsequently adopted this practice for 1995 onwards. A further development is that Deutsche Bank used IASs for a supplementary set of group accounts for 1995, and Daimler-Benz used US rules for a supplementary set in 1996.

Clearly, the choice of accounting policies for the group accounts of certain large German companies is driven by factors which override the influence of taxation. However, in some cases, these effects are seen particularly in non-statutory supplementary accounts (e.g. Deutsche Bank, Daimler-Benz) and, in other cases, the effects are not typical of German accounting in general (e.g. Bayer, Hoechst). As in the case of France, these effects are only apparent in the group accounts of certain large companies, although (at the time of writing)[127] there is no formal mechanism in Germany for the use of different rules.

4. Comparative analysis

In the opening section of this paper we set ourselves the task of investigating the claim that there is a clear distinction between Anglo-Saxon countries and some continental European countries with respect to the degree of connection between taxation and financial reporting. In this final section, we summarise our comparative analyses of the degree of linkage between tax rules and financial reporting in our four countries, and suggest some ways in which our analysis could be applied and extended.

Cases I and II have been defined as those where tax rules or considerations do not determine financial reporting practice in the sense of accounting

policy choices by managers. The Cases are distinguishable in that Case I involves different tax and financial reporting practices whereas Case II involves the same practices. Case III (accounting leads) is less clear. Where the financial reporting rule is precise, there may be little room for tax influence, but where there is vagueness or an option, then tax considerations may dominate. Cases IV and V involve clearer tax prominence. Table 3 summarises by country the distinct Cases of linkage previously reported in detail in Table 2. There are, of course, other areas of accounting where all four countries would score III. For example, the German requirement for *Massgeblichkeit* means that Case III applies in principle.

In Table 3 we see relatively numerous Case I disconnections between tax and financial reporting in the UK and the US, and relatively numerous Case IV and Case V relationships for Germany. The suggestion is clear that the influence of tax on operational accounting policy choice is least in the UK and the US and greatest in Germany, with France in between. This is supported by more Cases II and fewer Cases III for the UK and the US than for Germany. If the uncertainty of Case III is addressed by adding it to Cases IV and V, then the conclusion remains the same. Of course, the scoring in Table 3 assumes an equal weight for the 18 arenas or sub-arenas, and rests upon the particular arenas chosen. However, inspection reveals that assigning any other reasonable weightings would make little difference to the order of countries. Further, as noted above, adding more arenas would generally add more Cases III rather than more Cases I, IV or V, which are the clearest arenas of international variation. This assessment has been made at a particular point in time. Variations in the assessment over time could also be measured.

In summary, it is possible to distinguish our two Anglo-Saxon countries from our two continental European countries on the grounds of relatively low and relatively high tax influence on financial reporting in a contemporary operational sense. Consequently, we find some support for the hypothesis that it is possible to distinguish 'Anglo-Saxon' from 'continental European' countries according to the relative strength of tax influence on accounting policy choice. However, France, too may be clearly distinguished from Germany, and US and UK patterns of influence may be distinguished from one another.

This distinct modelling of tax-accounting inter-relations—'Anglo-Saxon' and 'continental European'—is also in concurrence with a number of German and French commentators (e.g. Quéré, 1994:71; Haller, 1992:321; Gélard, 1990:15), that German accounting is especially tax-influenced. However, the recognition of such models should not be allowed to obscure the complex pattern of

---

[127] In 1996, draft laws were in preparation in both Germany and France to allow the group accounts of certain companies to depart from national laws in order to follow other approved rules (e.g. US or IASC principles). In early 1998, laws were passed in both cases.

reciprocal influence between taxation practice and financial reporting practice in all four countries studied. In Section 3, we noted some examples of the changes in the relationship between tax and accounting practice over time. More examples are given in a paper which concentrates on this historical relationship (Lamb et al., 1995). More generally, focus on national models draws attention away from the richness and variety of changing patterns of tax influence.[128] Despite this caveat and the shifting nature of the relationships in the various countries, a stable pattern seems to be clear in each country and therefore comparatively.

The main change in the pattern relates to group accounting in France and Germany. Table 3 does not record the more complex position for group accounting in France and Germany. In both countries, the law allows group accounts to use different accounting policies from those used by the parent. Further, the previous section records how French law allows specific changes from individual company accounting to consolidated accounting. As a result there have been examples in France over many years of reduction of tax influence in group accounts.[129] Such an approach is clear for a few German companies from the mid-1990s.

One policy implication arising from our studies is that accounting harmonisation efforts in the world or in the EU would be more likely to succeed if focused on group accounts (cf. FEE, 1993 and Biener, 1995). The deeply entrenched links between tax and accounting and the large number of Case IV and V arenas in certain countries seem to

make harmonisation more difficult for individual company accounts.

In conclusion, we suggest that it may be more fruitful to compare systems of financial accounting according to the reciprocal patterns of influence and interrelations between tax and accounting, rather than to label such systems according to national, and to some extent out-of-date, stereotypes. One thing that we have clearly observed is that the degree and nature of tax influence on accounting changes over time, as do international patterns of similarity and dissimilarity. The assessment method adopted in our analysis of the influence of taxation on accounting could be used in a historical context 'to trace patterns of divergence and convergence over time' (Roberts, 1995) and to better link 'cross-temporal and cross-spatial variance' in accounting practices (Christiansen and McLeay, 1995:7). The extension of our approach to a wider range of countries could, of course, increase the richness of the comparative analysis.

References

Biener, H. (1995). *Statement to the Board of the IASC.* Amsterdam, May.

Bittker, B. I. and Loklan, L. (1989). *Federal taxation of income, estates and gifts.* Boston: Warren, Gorham and Lamont.

Brooks, J. and Mertin, D. (1993). *Deutsches Bilanzrecht.* Düsseldorf: IDW-Verlag.

Cauvin Angleys Saint-Pierre (1996). *L'information Financière, 100 Groupes Industriels et Commerciaux.* Paris: CPC Meylan.

Christiansen, M. and McLeay, S. (1995). 'A prisoner of the state: comparative cross-national research in accounting'. Paper presented at the EAA Congress, Birmingham, May.

Corre, J. (1987). *Les Nouvelles Règles de la Consolidation des Bilans.* Paris: Dunod.

Fédération des Experts Comptables Européens (FEE) (1993). *The Seventh Directive and Harmonisation, Seventh Directive Options and Their Implementation.* London: Routledge.

Freedman, J. (1987). 'Profit and prophets—law and accountancy practice on the timing of receipts—recognition under the earnings basis (Schedule D, Cases I and II)'. *British Tax Review,* 2: 61–79; 3: 104–33.

Freedman, J. (1993). 'Ordinary principles of commercial accounting—clear guidance or a mystery tour?'. *British Tax Review,* 6: 468–78.

---

[128]Further, undue focus on models defined by reference to nations may obscure important patterns of international diffusion of practices. Christiansen and McLeay (1995: 7) argue that 'the central problem of comparative research [is] linking cross-temporal and cross-spatial variance'; 'encompassing comparisons' that allow comparative research to escape being the 'prisoner of the state' are likely to be most appropriate in their view.

[129] The survey of the practices of large French groups illustrates this. See Cauvin Angleys Saint-Pierre (1996).

Table 3
Cases of linkage in certain material arenas of financing reporting for individual companies

	UK	US	France	Germany
Case I	12	11.5	4.5	2
Case II	2	2.5	5	0
Case III	3	2	3.5	7.5
Case IV	0	1	4	6.5
Case V	0	0	1	2
N/A	1	1	0	0

Note: Each of the 18 arenas or sub-arenas is weighted as one. Therefore, the total for each country should, and does, equal 18

Frydlender, A. and Pham, D. (1996). 'Relationships between accounting and taxation in France'. *European Accounting Review*, 5, Supplement: 845–857.

Gélard, G. (1990). 'La prudence en droit comptable allemand, la notion d'actif et la possibilité d'activer des charges'. *Revue Française de la Comptabilité*, 216, October: 15.

Godshalk, R. (1994). 'Financial statement conformity no longer required in change in accounting method consent letter'. *Tax Adviser*, March: 159.

Green, S. (1995). 'Accounting standards and tax law: complexity, dynamism and divergence'. *British Tax Review*, 6: 445–51.

Haller, A. (1992). 'The relationship of financial and tax accounting in Germany: a major reason for accounting disharmony in Europe'. *International Journal of Accounting*, 27: 10–23.

Hoogendoorn, M. N. (1996). 'Accounting and taxation in Europe—a comparative overview'. *European Accounting Review*, 5, Supplement: 783–94.

Lamb, M. (1995). 'When is a group a group? Convergence of concepts of "group" in European Union corporate tax'. *European Accounting Review*, 4(1): 33–78.

Lamb, M. (1996). 'The relationship between accounting and taxation: the United Kingdom'. *European Accounting Review*, 5, Supplement: 933–49.

Lamb, M., Nobes, C. and Roberts, A. (1995). 'The influence of taxation on accounting: international variations'. University of Reading Discussion Paper, No. 46, first half.

Melville, A. (1997). *Taxation—Finance Act 1997*. London: Pitman.

Mikol, A. (1995). 'The history of financial reporting in France' in Walton, P. (ed.), *European Financial Reporting: A History*. London: Academic Press.

Muray, R. and Small, D. (1995). 'Welcoming the dawn'. *The Tax Journal*, 16 February: 18–9.

Nobes, C. W. and Parker, R. (1995). *Comparative International Accounting* (4th ed.). Hemel Hempstead: Prentice Hall.

Ordelheide, D. and Pfaff, D. (1994). *European Financial Reporting: Germany*. London: Routledge.

Quéré, B. (1994). ' Le principe allemand de préponderance du bilan commercial sur le bilan fiscal et ses effects comptable'. *Revue Française de da Comptabilité*, March: 64–71.

Radcliffe, G. (1993). 'The relationship between tax law and accounting principles in the United Kingdom and France'. *Irish Journal of Taxation*, 1: 1–20.

Ricks, W. (1982). 'The market's responses to the 1974 LIFO adoptions'. *Journal of Accounting Research*, Autumn: 367–87.

Roberts, A. (1995). 'The very idea of classification in international accounting'. *Accounting Organizations and Society*, 20, No. 7/8.

Scheid, J.-C. and Walton, P. (1992). *European Financial Reporting: France*. London: Routledge.

Seckler, G. (1992). 'Germany' in D. Alexander and S. Archer, *European Accounting Guide*. London: Academic Press.

Sunder, S. (1973). 'Relationship between accounting changes in stock prices: problems of measurement and some empirical evidence'. *Empirical Research in Accounting: Selected Studies*: 1–45.

Sunder, S. (1975). 'Stock price and risk related accounting changes in inventory valuation'. *Accounting Review*, April: 305–14.

Taxes (1995). 'Revenue provide guidance on acceptability of accounting practices'. 28 April: 513–14.

Walton, P. (1993). 'Links between financial reporting and taxation in the United Kingdom: a myth explored'. Paper presented at the EAA Congress, Turkü, April.

Watts, R. L. and Zimmerman, J. L. (1979). 'The demand for and supply of accounting theories: the market for excuses'. *Accounting Review*, April: 273–304. [Reprinted in Bloom, R. and Elgers, P. T., *Accounting Theory and Policy: A Reader*. New York: Harcourt Brace Jovanovich, 1987: 22–57].

Whittington, Geoffrey (1995). 'Tax policy and accounting standards'. *British Tax Review*, 5: 452–6.

[10]

ABACUS, Vol. 34, No. 2, 1998

CHRISTOPHER NOBES

Towards a General Model of the Reasons for International Differences in Financial Reporting

The article first examines the existing modelling literature, which contains a large number of suggested reasons for international differences in accounting. After examining terminological problems, a preliminary parsimonious model is developed to explain the initial split of accounting systems into two classes. The term 'accounting system' is used here to mean the financial reporting practices used by an enterprise. A country might exhibit the use of several such systems in any one year or over time. Consequently, it should be systems and not countries that are classified. The model proposes a two-way classification using two variables: the strengths of equity markets and the degree of cultural dominance. Implications for classifiers and rule-makers are suggested.

Key words: Classification; International accounting.

INTRODUCTION AND PREVIOUS MODELLING

Many reasons have been suggested in the literature for international differences in financial reporting. Some authors state that they are merely listing plausible reasons; few provide precise hypotheses or tests of them, as noted by Meek and Saudagaran (1990). Wallace and Gernon (1991) complain about the lack of theory in international comparative accounting. This article seeks to address this.

The literature (e.g., Choi and Mueller, 1992, ch. 2; Radebaugh and Gray, 1993, ch. 3; Belkaoui, 1995, ch. 2; Nobes and Parker, 1995, ch. 1) offers a large number of possible reasons for international differences (see Table 1) but no general theory linking the factors. Schweikart (1985) and Harrison and McKinnon (1986) provide some elements of a general theory, without specifying which factors are major explanatory variables for accounting practices. Two somewhat similar theoretical models of the reasons for accounting differences are those of Gray (1988) and of Doupnik and Salter (1995; hereafter DS). Gray suggests a model based on cultural factors, as examined later. DS provide a synthesis of previous discussions, leading to a framework, which is simplified here as in Figure 1 so that an alternative can

CHRISTOPHER NOBES is Coopers & Lybrand Professor of Accounting at the University of Reading. The author is grateful for helpful comments on earlier drafts from Michael Page, Bob Parker, Alan Roberts and Autar Singh, and from the editor and the referees of this journal.

INTERNATIONAL DIFFERENCES IN FINANCIAL REPORTING

TABLE 1

REASONS PREVIOUSLY PROPOSED FOR INTERNATIONAL ACCOUNTING
DIFFERENCES

1	Nature of business ownership and financing system
2	Colonial inheritance
3	Invasions
4	Taxation
5	Inflation
6	Level of education
7	Age and size of accountancy profession
8	Stage of economic development
9	Legal systems
10	Culture
11	History
12	Geography
13	Language
14	Influence of theory
15	Political systems, social climate
16	Religion
17	Accidents

FIGURE 1

A SIMPLIFICATION OF DS'S MODEL OF DEVELOPMENT

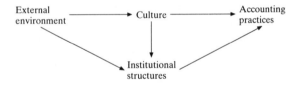

Source: Adapted from Doupnik and Salter (1995), exhibit 1.

be proposed later. One difficulty emerging from Figure 1 is that four of DS's ten variables (see Table 2) are cultural (based on Gray) and six are institutional, but culture is seen as giving rise to the institutions. This suggests the possibility of double counting. A related difficulty with DS is that there is no attempt to connect their six institutional factors to see whether they might cause each other. In particular, it is suggested later that four of the six (taxation, inflation, level of education and stage of economic development) are not necessary. DS thus have provided a mix of theories, not a general theory.

A number of terminological issues are raised by studying this literature. These need to be addressed before attempting to develop a general model.

TABLE 2

DS'S INDEPENDENT VARIABLES

Cultural	Institutional
Individualism	Legal system
Power distance	Capital market
Uncertainty avoidance	Tax
Masculinity	Inflation levels
	Level of education
	Level of economic development

SOME TERMINOLOGICAL ISSUES

One of the problems of identifying reasons for differences, and perhaps then classifying accounting systems, is a lack of clarity about what is being examined or classified. This article discusses accounting *practices*, using 'accounting' to mean published financial reporting. In some jurisdictions, the *rules* of financial reporting may be identical, or very similar, to the practices, but sometimes a company may depart from rules or may have to make choices in the absence of rules. The Price Waterhouse data, used by many researchers,[1] seem to contain a mix of *de facto* and *de jure* aspects 'in a perplexing way' (Rahman *et al.*, 1996).

Another difficulty concerns the word 'system' (Roberts, 1995). DS use it to cover such things as regulatory agencies. Others (e.g., Nair and Frank, 1980) have concentrated on a corpus of accounting rules or practices. This article follows the latter route, that is, an 'accounting system' is a set of practices used in a published annual report. Although this is a narrow definition, these practices will reflect the wider context in which they operate.

Another issue is whether to separate disclosure from measurement practices. Nair and Frank (1980) show that this can be important. Nobes (1983) looks at measurement practices only. DS acknowledge the distinction but add the categories together. It seems appropriate to include the presence or absence of certain key disclosures (e.g., earnings per share, cash flow statements) as elements of a system, and this is discussed later.

A further issue is to determine whose accounting practices are being examined. The Price Waterhouse data seem, in practice, to have reported on companies audited by Price Waterhouse (see Nobes, 1981). DS (p. 198) specify the measurement and disclosure practices of 'companies', which is vague, particularly for disclosure practices. Nobes (1983, p. 5) chose the measurement practices of 'public companies', which the context suggests meant those with securities which are traded publicly.

A related point is that all the researchers look at classifications of *countries* by their accounting environments or systems. Roberts (1995) highlighted this problem,

---

[1]   For example, Da Costa *et al.* (1978); Frank (1979); Nair and Frank (1980).

INTERNATIONAL DIFFERENCES IN FINANCIAL REPORTING

noting that a country could have more than one system, for example, one system for companies with publicly traded securities, and another for small private companies.[2] Similarly, some large public companies may adopt very different practices from what is 'normal' for most large companies in the country. This is becoming especially obvious in continental Europe, with the use of U.S. rules or International Accounting Standards (IAS) by some very large companies. Therefore, it may be useful to refer to a country's 'dominant accounting system', which might be defined as that used by enterprises encompassing the majority[3] of the country's economic activity. Hereafter, references to a country's 'system' should be taken to mean its dominant system.

In some countries, the law requires or commercial pressures dictate that a large number of companies use the same system. For example, in the U.K., most provisions of the Companies Act 1985 and of accounting standards apply to all companies. In other countries, a particular accounting system might be legally or commercially imposed on a small minority of companies, as in the U.S. where 'generally accepted accounting principles' are legally imposed on only that small proportion of companies registered with the Securities and Exchange Commission. In both these rather different cases, there is still clearly a dominant system as defined above.

Nevertheless, as there can be more than one system in a country it would be more useful to specify accounting systems, and then to note that particular companies in particular countries at particular dates are using them. Of course, for labelling purposes, it might be useful to refer, for example, to the system used in 1998 by U.S. public companies. With labels, it will then be possible to identify separate influences on, and to show separate places in the classification for, for example, 'normal' German public companies in 1998, compared to the group accounts of such companies as Daimler-Benz, Deutsche Bank and Bayer in 1998.

Also, a country's accounting system may change dramatically over time, for example, as a result of economic or political revolutions (c.f. China, Russia, Poland, etc.). Less dramatically, accounting in a country can change quite significantly as a result of new laws (e.g., Spain from the late 1980s as a consequence of EC Directives).[4]

Lastly, companies in two countries (e.g., the U.K. and Ireland) can use extremely similar accounting practices (i.e., perhaps the same 'system'). In a similar manner to the characteristics of human individuals, the detailed elements of a company's accounting practices can differ so much that the number of different sets of practices is effectively infinite. Nevertheless, it is useful for some purposes to recognize that humans all belong to the same species. The individual members

---

[2] I am grateful to my colleague, Autar Singh, for discussions that clarified my thoughts on this.

[3] Researchers would have to decide whether to start from the smallest enterprise or from the largest. Presumably, it would make sense to start from the largest, since this would involve far fewer enterprises, and since the small enterprises would not be publishing any financial reports in most countries.

[4] See, for example, Gonzalo and Gallizo (1992), ch. 3.

of the species are all different but have certain features in common. By analogy, a certain degree of variation among company practices may be allowed without having to abandon the idea that the companies are all using the same system.

AN INITIAL STATEMENT OF A GENERAL MODEL

The proposal here, which will be explained more fully later, is that the major reason for international differences in financial reporting is different purposes for that reporting.

Financing Systems

In particular, at a country level, it is suggested that the financing system is relevant in determining the purpose of financial reporting. Zysman (1983) distinguishes between three types of financing system: (a) *capital market based*, in which prices are established in competitive markets; (b) *credit-based system: governmental*, in which resources are administered by the government; and (c) *credit-based system: financial institutions*, in which banks and other financial institutions are dominant.

Zysman suggested that the U.K. and the U.S.A. have a type (a) system; France and Japan a type (b) system; and Germany a type (c) system. According to Zysman, in all systems companies rely considerably on their own profits for capital but their external sources of funds differ. Where external long-term finance is important, securities are the main source in the capital market system. In such countries, there is a wide range of capital instruments and of financial institutions, and the latter have an arm's-length relationship with companies. Investors change their holdings through the secondary securities markets, which are large. In credit-based systems, the capital market is smaller, so companies are more reliant on whoever grants credit. This usually means banks, whether under the influence of governments or not. Cable (1985) examined the importance of banks in the German economic system. In this system, investors will find it more difficult to adjust their holdings, so they may be more interested in long-run control of the management.

For the purposes of this article, a development of the Zysman classification is proposed, as in Table 3. For this, the concept of 'insider' and 'outsider' financiers needs to be developed. This idea of insiders and outsiders, which has its roots in the finance literature, has been used before for accounting purposes (e.g., see Nobes, 1988, p. 31), and to discuss contrasting corporate governance systems (e.g., Franks and Mayer, 1992; Kenway, 1994). 'Outsiders' are not members of the board of directors and do not have a privileged relationship with the company (e.g., such

TABLE 3

FINANCING SYSTEMS

	Strong credit	Strong equity
Insiders dominant	I	III
Outsiders dominant	II	IV

INTERNATIONAL DIFFERENCES IN FINANCIAL REPORTING

as that enjoyed by a company's banker who is also a major shareholder). They include both private individual shareholders and some institutions. For example, insurance companies and unit trusts normally have widely diversified portfolios, so that any particular holding does not constitute a large proportion of a company's capital. Therefore, such institutions should perhaps be counted as outsiders. By contrast, 'insiders' such as governments, banks, families and other companies are all likely to have close, long-term relationships with their investees. This will involve the private provision of timely and frequent accounting information.

Both of Zysman's credit-based systems fall into category I of Table 3. Category II (a credit-based system with a large amount of listed debt with outsider owners) is plausible but uncommon. A possible example is discussed near the end of this subsection. Category III is an equity-based system where most shares are owned by insiders. In Japan, for example, there are large numbers of listed companies and a large equity market capitalisation, but the shares are extensively owned by banks and other companies (Nobes and Parker, 1995, p. 9 and ch. 13).

Category IV systems involve important equity markets with large numbers of outsider shareholders. In these systems there will be a demand for public disclosure and for external audit because most providers of finance have no involvement in management and no private access to financial information. This is the classic setting of most of the finance literature (e.g., Jensen and Meckling, 1976; Beaver, 1989). More recently, a connection between more disclosure and lower cost of equity capital has been examined in such a context (Botosan, 1997). Pursuing this line, this article suggests that the key issue for financial reporting is the existence or otherwise of such Category IV financing. Ways of measuring this are proposed below.

In a particular country, there may be elements of several of these four systems. For example, small companies are unlikely to be financed by a Category IV system in any country. However, for the moment, let us assume that the economic activity in any country is dominated by one particular financing system. The hypothesis predicting a correlation between the style of corporate financing and the type of accounting system is that the rule-makers for, and the preparers of, financial reports in equity-outsider (Category IV) countries are largely concerned with the outside users. The conceptual frameworks used by the rule-makers of the U.S., the U.K., Australia and the IASC[5] make it clear that this is so. In particular, they state that they are concerned with reporting financial performance and enabling the prediction of future cash flows for relatively sophisticated outside users of financial statements of large companies. By contrast, credit-based countries (mostly Category I) will be more concerned with the protection of creditors and therefore with the prudent calculation of distributable profit. Their financiers (insiders) will not need externally audited, published reports. This difference of purpose will lead to differences in accounting practices. The less common categories (II and III) will be discussed later.

[5]   Statements of Financial Accounting Concepts of the FASB, particularly SFAC 1, *Objectives*; the similar chapter 1 of the ASB's draft *Statement of Principles; Statements of Accounting Concepts* of Australia; and the IASC's *Framework for the Preparation and Presentation of Financial Statements*, para. 15.

ABACUS

TABLE 4

EXAMPLES OF FEATURES OF THE TWO ACCOUNTING CLASSES

Feature	Class A	Class B
Provisions for depreciation and pensions	Accounting practice differs from tax rules	Accounting practice follows tax rules
Long-term contracts	Percentage of completion method	Completed contract method
Unsettled currency gains	Taken to income	Deferred or not recognised
Legal reserves	Not found	Required
Profit and loss format	Expenses recorded by function (e.g., cost of sales)	Expenses recorded by nature (e.g., total wages)
Cash flow statements	Required	Not required, found only sporadically
Earnings per share disclosure	Required by listed companies	Not required, found only sporadically

Empirical researchers would need to establish relevant measures to distinguish the categories (as done, for example, by La Porta *et al.*, 1997). These might include the number of domestic listed companies in a country (or this deflated by size of population), the equity market capitalization (or this deflated by GDP), and the proportion of shares held by 'outsiders'. Although the boundary between the types of financing system may sometimes be unclear (as in many of the classifications in social science, languages, law or, even, biology), the contrast between a strong equity-outsider system and other systems should be clear enough, as the Appendix demonstrates for some countries.

Financial Reporting Systems
It is proposed that financial reporting systems should be divided initially into two classes, for the moment labelled as A and B. Class A corresponds to what some have called Anglo-Saxon accounting and Class B to continental European. To assist researchers in measuring a system, some core features of the two systems are suggested in Table 4. For example, systems of Class A will share all, or a large proportion of, the practices shown for that class. Clear examples of actual systems exhibiting *all* of the features exist.[6]

It is proposed that, for developed countries,[7] the extent that a particular country is associated with Class A or Class B accounting is predictable on the basis of its position with respect to financing systems. If the present accounting system was developed in the past, then reference to the past importance of financing systems

---

[6] For example, Australia, the U.S. and the U.K. exhibit *all* the features of Class A, whereas the dominant systems in France, Germany and Italy exhibit *all* the features of Class B (although a few consolidated statements use a different system and depart from some aspects). Most items in Table 4 are covered by the relevant country chapters of Nobes and Parker (1995) or, for example, see Scheid and Walton (1992) for France, or Gordon and Gray (1994) for the UK.

[7] The idea of 'developed' or 'culturally self-sufficient' is examined further later.

INTERNATIONAL DIFFERENCES IN FINANCIAL REPORTING

will be relevant. Strong equity-outsider markets (Category IV) lead to Class A systems; otherwise Class B systems prevail.

Even if a particular country is traditionally associated with weak equity markets and therefore Class B accounting, the country might change. For example, China has been changing in the direction of a strong equity-outsider market and Class A accounting (Chow *et al.*, 1995). However, the accounting might remain stuck in the past for legal or other reasons of inertia. Nevertheless, in some countries, certain companies might be especially commercially affected. They might adopt Class A accounting by using flexibility in the national rules, by breaking national rules, or by producing two sets of financial statements. Some German examples of these routes can be given. Bayer's consolidated financial statements (for 1994 onwards) have used non-typical German rules, that are different from those used in its parent's statements, in order to comply with International Accounting Standards (IAS). Further, officials of the Ministry of Finance have announced that departure from German rules would be 'tolerated' for such group accounts.[8] In the case of Deutsche Bank (e.g., for 1995), two full sets of financial statements were produced, under German rules and IAS, respectively.

A related issue is that, as noted earlier, there are two aspects of financial reporting which can be separated: measurement and disclosure (e.g., Nair and Frank, 1980). Table 4 contains examples of both aspects. As explained below, the measurement issues seem to be driven by the equity/creditor split, and the disclosure issues by the outsider/insider split. The equity/creditor split leads to different kinds of *objectives* for financial reporting. As suggested earlier, systems serving equity markets are required to provide relevant information on performance and the assessment of future cash flows in order to help with the making of financial decisions. Systems in a creditor environment are required to calculate prudent and reliable distributable (and taxable) profit. By contrast, the outsider/insider split leads to different *amounts* of information: where outsiders are important, there is a demand for more published financial reporting.

It has been assumed here that equity financing systems are normally those which are associated with large numbers of outsiders, so that Class A systems are an amalgam of equity and outsider features. However, if there were countries (Category II of Table 3) with large markets for listed debt but not for listed equities, then one might expect a financial reporting system with the high disclosures of Class A but the measurement rules of Class B. Perhaps the closest example of a system with Class B measurement rules but high disclosures is the German system for listed companies.[9] Germany does indeed have an unusually large market in listed debt.[10]

[8] Herr Biener of the German Finance Ministry announced this at the board meeting of the International Accounting Standards Committee in Amsterdam in May 1996. In 1998, German law changed in order specifically to allow this.

[9] This feature of German accounting was highlighted by Nair and Frank (1980), who prepared separate classifications based on measurement and disclosure practices.

[10] For example, in 1993, the number of listed bonds in Germany was 13,309, whereas the number in France was 2,516 and in the U.K. 2,725 (data from *European Stock Exchange Statistics*, Annual Report, 1993).

ABACUS

This way of distinguishing between the forces acting on measurement and those acting on disclosure may help to resolve the difficulties of a cultural explanation as discussed by Baydoun and Willett (1995, pp. 82–8).

Category III (equity-insider) financing would not produce Class A accounting because published financial reporting is unimportant. The main financiers may be interested in performance and cash flows but they have access to private 'management' information.

Colonial Inheritance

Some countries are affected by very strong external cultural influences, perhaps due to their small size or underdeveloped state or former colonial status. Such culturally dominated countries are likely to be using an accounting system based on that of the influential country even if this seems inappropriate to their current commercial needs (Hove, 1986).

Colonial inheritance (Factor 2 in Table 1) is probably the major explanatory factor for the general system of financial reporting in many countries outside Europe (Briston, 1978). It is easy to predict how accounting will work in Gambia (British) compared to neighbouring Senegal (French).[11] The same general point applies to Singapore (Briston and Foo, 1990) or Australia (Miller, 1994). Colonial inheritance extends of course to legal systems and to other background and cultural factors, not just to direct imports of accounting (Parker, 1989). Allied to this are the effects of substantial investment from another country, which may lead to accountants and accounting migrating together with the capital.

Another influence is invasions (Factor 3) which may lead to major influence on accounting, as is the case with Japanese,[12] French,[13] and German[14] accounting. However, when the invader retires, any foreign accounting can be gradually removed if it does not suit the country: Japan closed down its Securities and Exchange Commission when the Americans left, whereas France retained its accounting plan in order to aid reconstruction after World War II (Standish, 1990).

WHY OTHER FACTORS MAY BE LESS USEFUL

If the above conclusions are accepted (i.e., that a general two-class model of financial reporting systems can be built which rests on only the importance of financing systems and colonial inheritance), then most of the seventeen factors listed in Table 1 seem unnecessary as explanatory independent variables, at least for the initial two-class classification. This section explains why, starting with DS's factors.

[11] An unpublished PhD thesis by Charles Elad (University of Glasgow, 1993) shows the colonial influences clearly.

[12] Japan's SEC, its structure of Securities Laws and its stock market owe much to U.S. influence during the occupation following World War II.

[13] The distinguishing feature of French accounting, the *plan comptable*, was first adopted in France while under German occupation (Standish, 1995).

[14] The German accounting plan, though copied in France, was abolished by the occupying Western powers after World War II. A version survived in the communist East Germany until reunification.

INTERNATIONAL DIFFERENCES IN FINANCIAL REPORTING

Tax

Previous writers (e.g., Nobes, 1983) have not been helpful by listing tax as one of the major causes of accounting differences. These writers have, in effect, suggested that Class A accounting systems are not dominated by tax rules whereas Class B systems are; and therefore, that the tax difference is one of the reasons for the difference in accounting systems. However, the disconnection of tax from accounting in Class A systems may be seen as a *result* of the existence of a competing purpose for accounting rather than the major cause of international accounting differences. Lamb *et al.* (1995) look at this in detail, concluding that:

1. Rules for the determination of the taxable profit of businesses will be important in all countries (assuming that taxation of profit is significant).
2. Without some major competing purpose for accounting for which tax rules are unsuitable, tax rules made by governments will therefore tend to dominate accounting, so that tax practices and accounting practices are the same (as in Class B).
3. In some countries (or for some companies), there is the major competing purpose of supplying financial reports to equity-outsider markets (for which tax rules are unsuitable). In this case, for many accounting topics, there will be two sets of accounting rules (and practices): tax rules and financial reporting rules (as in Class A).

Consequently, the tax variable is not needed to explain the difference between Class A and Class B systems. Nevertheless, for those systems where tax and accounting are closely linked (Class B), international differences in tax rules do create international accounting differences. However, these are detailed differences *within* a class of accounting systems which all share the major feature of being dominated by tax rules, which is one of the distinguishing marks of the class.

There is a further important connection here. The equity/credit split in financing, as discussed earlier, coincides with the proposed equity-user/tax-user split: accounting systems designed to serve creditors are systems dominated by tax rules. This is because the calculation of the legally distributable profit (to protect creditors) and the calculation of taxable profit are both issues in which governments are interested. The calculation of legally distributable profit is a different purpose from the calculation of taxable profit but it is not 'competing' in the sense of requiring a different set of rules because both calculations benefit from precision in the rules[15] and from the minimization of the use of judgment,[16] which is not the case for the estimation of cash flows.

---

[15] For example, in both the U.K. and Germany (typical Class A and Class B countries, respectively), there are large numbers of legal cases on the determination of taxable income and some on the determination of distributable income, but there are few or none on the determination of consolidated accounting profit (i.e., cases where there is no tax motivation).

[16] In the U.K., and recently in the U.S. with SFAS 115, certain assets are revalued above historical cost; and unsettled profits are taken to income (e.g., on long-term contracts and on foreign currency monetary balances). None of this is possible under German law.

Incidentally, DS follow previous writers and suggest that, 'In many countries, tax laws effectively determine accounting practice' (p. 196). However, they then find that tax is not a useful independent variable in explaining accounting differences. It is argued above that tax is not an independent variable for the main classificatory split. DS failed to find even a correlation, probably because they mis-specified the tax variable by using the marginal rate of corporate income taxes. This measure seems inappropriate for several reasons. First, tax rates change dramatically over time, without any obvious effect on accounting (e.g., the top U.S. rate fell from 46 per cent to 34 per cent in 1987; the main rate in the U.K. rose in 1973 from 40 per cent to 52 per cent, and then fell to 33 per cent in 1991). Second, many systems have more than one marginal rate (e.g., in Germany in 1995, 45 per cent for retained profit but 30 per cent for distributed profit; and, in the U.K., 33 per cent for large companies but 25 per cent for small). Third, the tax burden depends greatly on the definition of taxable income not just on the tax rate. More import-antly, in countries with a small connection between tax and accounting (typical of Class A), the tax rate will have little effect on accounting; and in countries with a close connection (typical of Class B), the effect of tax on accounting will be in the same direction and probably almost as strong whether the rate is 30 per cent or 50 per cent. For all these reasons, the level of the marginal rate of tax will not help to predict the financial reporting system.

Level of Education
DS's variable here is the percentage of population with tertiary education. It is hard to see how one could explain the major accounting differences on this basis. Can one explain the large accounting differences between, on the one hand, the U.K., the U.S. and the Netherlands (where Class A dominates) and, on the other hand, France, Germany and Italy (where Class B dominates) on the basis of the rather similar levels of tertiary education? Again, can one explain the remark-able similarities between accounting in Malawi, Nigeria and Zimbabwe (Class A countries) and the U.K. (also Class A) on the basis of the rather different levels of tertiary education? Instead there seems to be a connection with the 'colonial inheritance' point, as discussed earlier and as taken up again in the 'level of economic development' point below. Thus it is not surprising that the education variable did not help DS. Previous suggestions related to this factor (e.g., Radebaugh, 1975) seem, more plausibly, to involve the comparison of developed with less developed countries.

Different levels of professional accounting education might be relevant (Shoenthal, 1989), perhaps especially in developing countries (e.g., Parry and Grove, 1990). However, Nobes (1992) casts doubt upon the relevance of this type of factor for classification. To the extent that this is not another issue related to developed versus developing countries, differences in professional education might be covered by Factor 8 in Table 1 (age and size of accountancy profession) and may be a *result* of accounting differences rather than their cause.

INTERNATIONAL DIFFERENCES IN FINANCIAL REPORTING

Level of Economic Development
It is suggested that the key issue here is not the influence of the stage of economic development on financial reporting (as chosen by DS). Gernon and Wallace (1995, p. 64) agree that there is 'no conclusive evidence' about the relationship. The problem is that, while many African countries with a low level of development have accounting systems rather like the U.K.'s, some have completely different accounting systems rather like that in France. By contrast, the U.K. or the Netherlands have a rather similar level of economic development to that of Germany or Italy but completely different accounting systems.

It would seem plausible to argue that, if accounting systems were indigenously created in all countries, then they would develop differently in developed and undeveloped economies. However, it is suggested that this point is largely overridden by the proposition that developing countries are likely to be using an accounting system invented elsewhere. Perhaps the system has been forced on them, or they have borrowed it. Either way, it is usually possible to predict accounting in such countries by looking at the source of the external influences. Therefore, the level of development is not the key predictor for the split between Class A and Class B. Cooke and Wallace (1990) seem to support the distinction between developed and developing countries when it comes to the influence of various environmental factors on accounting.

Legal Systems
For developed Western countries and for many others (e.g., Japan, South America and most of Africa), it is possible to split countries neatly into codified legal systems and common law systems (David and Brierley, 1985). As DS note, this is of great relevance to the regulatory system for accounting. However, there is a high degree of correlation between equity-outsider financing systems and common law countries, and between credit-insider systems and codified law.[17] On the whole, therefore, the same groupings would result from using a legal system variable rather than from using a financing system variable, as DS find. This again suggests the possibility of double counting. The exception of the Netherlands, which raises further doubts about using the legal variable for accounting classification, is explained below.

For culturally dominated countries, both the legal and accounting systems are likely to have been imported from the same place, so the correlation between these two variables is unsurprising. Both factors can be explained by the colonial influence factor, so the legal factor is not needed. For other countries, there may be aspects of the common law system which predispose a country towards the creation of strong equity-outsider systems (La Porta *et al.*, 1997), but going that far back in the causal chain is not necessary for the present model. For present purposes, it may be more useful to specify the legal variable as the regulatory system for accounting rather than the more general legal system. The variable would be

[17]   This is examined in Nobes and Parker (1995, ch. 1).

measured by locating the source of the most detailed accounting regulations. A 0/1 variable would contrast (i) rules made by professional accountants, company directors, independent bodies, stock exchanges and equity market regulators, and (ii) rules made by tax authorities, government ministries (other than those concerned primarily with listed companies) and legal bureaucrats.

Once more, it could be argued that this version of the legal variable is not independent but is dependent on the financing variable. In strong equity-outsider systems, commercial pressure gives the strongest power over financial reporting to group (i) because, since the financial reporting for the equity/outsiders uses separate rules from tax rules, there is no need for group (ii) to control them. In particular, many of the disclosures (e.g., consolidated financial reports, cash flow statements, segmental reporting, interim reporting) are not relevant for tax or distribution purposes in most jurisdictions. Financial institutions and large companies are sufficiently powerful to persuade group (ii) to allow financial reporting to respond to commercial needs. In common law countries, the importance of group (i) creates no problems of jurisprudence because non-governmental regulation is commonplace. In the rare case of a codified law country with a strong equity market (e.g., the Netherlands), the regulatory system for financial reporting can still give prominence to group (i) although this creates tensions (Zeff *et al.*, 1992). In all systems, group (ii) retains full control over tax rules.

Inflation Levels
Another factor included by DS is the rate of inflation and, once more, previous writers have not been helpful here. For example, although Nobes (1983) did not include inflation as a key variable, Nobes and Parker (1995, p. 19) suggested that 'Without reference to this factor, it would not be possible to explain accounting differences in countries severely affected by it'. However, on reflection, the more important issue is illustrated by other points that they make in the same section:

1. 'accountants in the English-speaking world have proved remarkably immune to inflation when it comes to taking decisive action';
2. 'in several South American countries, the most obvious feature . . . is the use of methods of general price-level adjustment';
3. 'the fact that it was *governments* which responded to inflation in France, Spain, Italy and Greece . . . is symptomatic of the regulation of accounting in these countries'.

In other words, any accounting system would have to respond at some level of inflation sustained for a certain length of time.[18] The key points are who responds and how they respond. The nature of these responses to inflation is a good indicator of the regulatory system for accounting. In countries where Class A accounting is dominant, professional accountants respond; in countries where Class B accounting is dominant, governments respond within the framework of the tax

---

[18] From observation of Anglo-Saxon countries, it seems that inflation of above 10 per cent for several years will cause a response (e.g., in the U.K. in the early 1950s or early 1970s), and the same applies to some continental European countries in the 1970s (Tweedie and Whittington, 1984).

INTERNATIONAL DIFFERENCES IN FINANCIAL REPORTING

system.[19] Differential inflation does not cause the difference between Class A and Class B acounting, the regulators typical to the two classes respond differently to it. However, as with some other factors, differential inflation response may lead to differences between the systems *within* Class A or *within* Class B.

Culture

Culture (defined by Hofstede as 'the collective programming of the mind') is clearly a plausible cause of accounting differences as proposed by Gray's (1988) application of Hofstede's (1980) theory. DS's four culture variables (see Table 2) were drawn from Hofstede. However, the attempt to use cultural variables entails large problems (Gernon and Wallace, 1995, pp. 85, 90, 91). Baydoun and Willett (1995, p. 69) also suggest that the mechanisms of the effects are not obvious, and: 'such is the nature of the concepts involved and the state of the available evidence that it is questionable whether Gray's adaptation of Hofstede's theory can in fact be empirically validated in the usual scientific sense' (p. 72).

For the purposes of this article, one can agree with Gray that culture can at least be seen as one of the background factors leading to more direct causes of accounting differences (such as the financing system). Culture may be of more direct help when examining other issues, for example, differences in the behaviour of auditors (Soeters and Schreuder, 1988). It will also be useful later to divide countries into culturally self-sufficient and culturally dominated. As noted in the previous section, the latter countries (e.g., colonies or former colonies) might be expected to adopt practices from other countries. In this sense, culture might indeed overwhelm other factors for certain countries.

Broad Factors

Others of the seventeen factors of Table 1, not proposed by DS but elsewhere in the literature, are too wide to be useful and can be accommodated within more specific factors. On these grounds, history and geography (Factors 11 and 12) can be removed. In a sense, 'history' explains everything, but this is not helpful unless it is known which part of history. For example, colonial history and the history of the corporate financing system are likely to be particularly relevant, so other factors can cover this.

'Geography' is also too broad a factor to be useful. It seems unlikely that the physical nature of a country has a major effect on its dominant class of accounting. For example, the Netherlands and Belgium have very different accounting, although they are similar in physical environment. By contrast, the U.K. and Australia have similar accounting although they are dramatically different in climate, terrain and type of agriculture. A country's location may be relevant for other factors (such as colonial inheritance and invasions) or for certain aspects of its financial history (such as the fact that maritime countries may tend to develop

---

[19] For example, many South American countries respond with compulsory government-controlled systems of general price level adjusted accounting, whereas English-speaking countries responded with rules written by the profession (although there was government involvement) which required some supplementary disclosures (Tweedie and Whittington, 1984).

certain types of trading or markets). However, the relevant aspects of geography should be picked up by other factors. In the meantime, one merely notes that location seems to be overwhelmed by other factors in the sense that New Zealand has rather similar accounting to the distant U.K.; and the Netherlands has very different accounting from its neighbours, Germany and Belgium.

Covariation

Other factors may involve covariation rather than causation. For example, the fact that many English-speaking countries have similar accounting practices is probably not caused by their shared language (Factor 13): the language was inherited with the accounting or with other factors which affect accounting. Language similarities may contribute to the strength of cultural dominance, and language differences may slow down the transfer of accounting technology. However, these points do not make language a key independent variable.

Theory

Theory (Factor 14), in the form of an explicit or implicit underlying framework, is certainly of relevance in some countries.[20] However, there are always competing theories (as examined for accounting by Watts and Zimmerman, 1979). It is suggested here that the degree of acceptance of particular accounting theories within a country *depends upon* other factors, such as the strength of equity markets and the regulatory system.

Results Rather Than Causes

Some factors above have been seen as more results than causes of the major accounting differences. Similarly, the age and size of the accountancy professions (Factor 7) differ substantially around the world,[21] but this is likely to be the *result* of different accounting systems. For example, the comparatively small size of the German auditing profession seems to result from the comparatively small number of audited companies, which in turn results from comparative weakness of equity markets.

Factors More Relevant Outside the Developed World

Certain other factors might not discriminate between developed Western countries, on which most classifications have concentrated. For example, political systems (Factor 15), religion (Factor 16) and stage of economic development (Factor 8) are probably sufficiently homogeneous in these countries that they do not have major explanatory power. They might well be relevant for a broader study, and at levels of classification below the two major classes. For example, religion may have an effect on accounting in some countries (Gambling and Abdel-Karim, 1991; Hamid *et al.*, 1993). Of course, religion and culture may be closely related.

---

[20] For example, the Netherlands is often said to have been influenced by the current value theories of Limperg and the German business economist Schmidt (Zeff *et al.*, 1992; Clarke and Dean, 1990).

[21] For example, see Table 1.1 in Nobes and Parker (1995).

INTERNATIONAL DIFFERENCES IN FINANCIAL REPORTING

Accidents

Close examination of accidents (Factor 17) will generally reveal their causes. However, certainly at the level of detailed accounting practices within a class, 'accident' may be a useful summary explanation. For example, some of the largest differences between U.S. and U.K. accounting (LIFO, deferred tax and goodwill) could be said to have accidental causes.[22] However, it is not necessary to resort to 'accidents' as an explanation of the difference between Class A and Class B accounting. It is suggested that the model which is restated in more detail below is powerful enough without this feature. In the end the validity of this claim is an empirical matter.

Summary on Excluded Factors

Many of the factors which have been examined in this section may be contributory causes to accounting differences or may be *associated* with accounting differences. However, it has been suggested that each can be eliminated as a major reason for the differences identified at the first split of accounting systems into two classes. At lower levels in a classification, many of these factors may be useful explanations of relatively small differences between systems. Further, some of the factors, certainly 'culture', help to explain the different types of capital markets which, according to proposals here, do explain the major groupings.

THE PROPOSED MODEL

The proposed model consists of a number of linked constructs which will be expressed as propositions. Part of the model can be expressed in simplified form as in Figure 2, which amends DS's proposal (summarised in Figure 1). The variables needed have been introduced in the text above, but now need to be marshalled.

The first variable is the type of country culture and the second is the strength of the equity-outsider financing system. This article assumes that some cultures lead to strong equity-outsider markets, and others do not. However, this is an issue for economists and others and is not examined in detail here. The point of departure for the constructs and hypotheses explained below is the second variable: the nature of the equity markets. Suggestions have been made here about how empirical researchers could measure this variable, perhaps leading to a 0/1 (weak or strong equity-outsider market) classification.

A further variable is the type of company. For most companies (insider companies), a controlling stake is in the hands of a small number of owners. For a

FIGURE 2

SIMPLIFIED MODEL OF REASONS FOR INTERNATIONAL ACCOUNTING DIFFERENCES

External
environment ⟶ Culture, including
institutional structures ⟶ Strength of equity-
outsider system ⟶ Class of
accounting

---

[22] This is examined by Nobes (1996), where it is suggested that timing is a key factor. For example, the U.S. requirement to amortize goodwill was introduced earlier than U.K. standard setting on this issue, when goodwill was far less significant.

ABACUS

FIGURE 3

APPLICATION OF FIGURE 2 TO CULTURALLY SUFFICIENT COUNTRIES

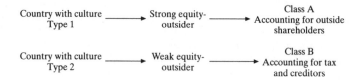

comparatively few companies (outsider companies), control is widely spread amongst a large number of 'outsider' equity-holders. Countries with strong equity-outsider systems generally have a large number of outsider companies which may comprise most of a country's GNP, but other countries may also have a few of these companies.

The fourth variable is the country's degree of cultural self-sufficiency. As discussed earlier, some countries have strong indigenous cultures whereas others have imported cultures which are still dominated or heavily influenced from outside. This dichotomy will be expressed by using the labels CS (for culturally self-sufficient) and CD (for culturally dominated). Researchers might wish to measure this in various ways, for example by the number of decades since a country gained political independence from another. Many developing countries are CD and many developed countries are CS, but there are exceptions. Again, the boundaries between CS and CD are unclear, but researchers should have little difficulty in classifying many countries. Concentration should be placed on aspects of business culture in cases where this may give a different answer from other aspects of culture.

The final variable is the type of financial reporting system (or, in short, 'accounting system') introduced earlier as Class A or Class B. Again, preliminary suggestions have been made about how researchers might measure and classify systems in this way.

The theoretical constructs which link these variables can now be brought together. It is relevant here to repeat the point that more than one accounting system can be used in any particular country at any one time or over time.

The model can be expressed in terms of propositions, which are then explained and illustrated:

P1: The dominant accounting system in a CS country with a strong equity-outsider system is Class A.

P2: The dominant accounting system in a CS country with a weak (or no) equity-outsider system is Class B.

P3: A CD country has an accounting system imported from its dominating country, irrespective of the strength of the CD country's equity-outsider system.

P4: As a country establishes a strong equity-outsider market, its accounting system moves from Class B to Class A.

P5: Outsider companies in countries with weak equity-outsider markets will move to Class A accounting.

INTERNATIONAL DIFFERENCES IN FINANCIAL REPORTING

FIGURE 4

A PROPOSED MODEL OF REASONS FOR INTERNATIONAL
ACCOUNTING DIFFERENCES

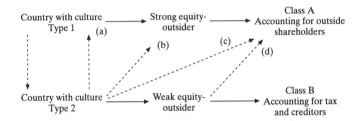

The analysis can begin with culturally self-sufficient (CS) countries (Propositions P1 and P2 above), as illustrated in Figure 3. For these countries, it is suggested that the class of the dominant accounting system will depend upon the strength of the equity-outsider market (or on its strength in the past, if there is inertia). Strong equity-outsider systems will lead to Class A accounting (see Table 4), whereas others will lead to Class B accounting. As explained earlier, the term 'dominant accounting system' is used to refer to the type used by enterprises representing the majority of a country's economic activity. For example, small unlisted enterprises in strong equity market countries might not practise Class A accounting or indeed any financial reporting at all.

Propositions P3 to P5 are now examined. Proposition P3 is that, in culturally dominated (CD) countries, accounting systems are imported. Sometimes a CD country will also have had time to develop the style of equity market associated with the culture. Therein, Propositions P1 or P2 will hold as in CS countries. However, sometimes a CD country may have imported its culture and its accounting system without establishing the related equity market. In this case the accounting system will seem inappropriate for the strength of the equity-outsider financing system. Proposition P4 is that, if either a CS or a CD country with a traditionally weak equity market gradually develops a strong equity-outsider system, a change of accounting towards Class A will follow. Also (P5), in a country with weak equity-outsider markets, there may be *some* 'outsider companies' (as defined earlier). Commercial pressure will lead these companies towards Class A accounting, even if the dominant system in the country is Class B. For such a company, there will be rewards in terms of lower cost of capital[23] from the production of Class A statements, particularly if there is an international market in the company's shares. If legal constraints hinder movement towards Class A accounting, then the company can use extra disclosures or supplementary statements.

Figure 4 shows some aspects of these constructs. The continuous arrows are those from Figure 3. Dotted arrows (a) and (c) concern aspects of Proposition P3.

---

[23] It is argued that equity investors and lenders will be persuaded to provide funds at lower returns to companies using more accepted, familiar and transparent financial reporting (see Botosan, 1997).

Arrow (b) relates to Proposition P4, and Arrow (d) Proposition P5. Some illustrations are:

1 (Arrow a) New Zealand is a CD country with wholesale importation of British culture and institutions (Type 1), including a strong equity-outsider system and Class A accounting. Whether the Class A accounting results from the equity market or from direct cultural pressure is not important to the model; it probably arises from both.

2 (Arrow b) China is a country without a strong equity-outsider tradition but which seems to be moving towards such a system. Class A accounting is following (Davidson *et al.*, 1995).

3 (Arrow c) Malawi is a CD country with very weak equity markets[24] but where the accountancy profession has adopted Class A accounting, consistent with its colonial inheritance from the U.K.

4 (Arrow d) The Deutsche Bank, Bayer and Nestlé are companies from countries with traditionally weak equity markets. These companies are now interested in world equity-outsider markets, so they are adopting[25] Class A accounting for their group accounts.

IMPLICATIONS FOR CLASSIFICATION

Discussions about the reasons for international differences in financial reporting are clearly related to the topic of classification of financial reporting 'systems'. Some implications of the above suggestions for classification researchers are examined here.

Before Darwin, the Linnaean classification was drawn up on the 'intrinsic' basis of observations about the 'essential' differences in the characteristics of species. Later, genetic and inheritance ('extrinsic') issues became the normal basis for classification, but largely came to the same conclusions. In accounting, one may also see both intrinsic and extrinsic classifications (Roberts, 1995), which may lead to similar conclusions. For example, one can extrinsically trace modern U.K. and modern New Zealand accounting back to a common ancestor; and one can intrinsically note many similarities in the accounting systems currently used. However, it is proposed here to discuss the classifications based on intrinsic factors. For this reason, the term 'species', to which Roberts (1995) objected, will be omitted.

It is not proposed here to re-work previous classifications but to suggest implications of the above conclusions for future classification work. Taking the classification by Nobes (1983), some improvements can be suggested, as shown in Figure 5. The two classes are shown, much as in the earlier classification, but the labels are sharper, following Propositions P1 and P2 above. The bottom level of classification is now a 'system' not a country. This accommodates P5 above. In order to make

---

[24]   These issues are discussed by Nobes (1996).

[25]   For example, Bayer adopted international accounting standards (IASs) for its group accounts for 1994, and Deutsche Bank produce supplementary IAS group accounts for 1995. Nestlé published IAS group accounts.

INTERNATIONAL DIFFERENCES IN FINANCIAL REPORTING

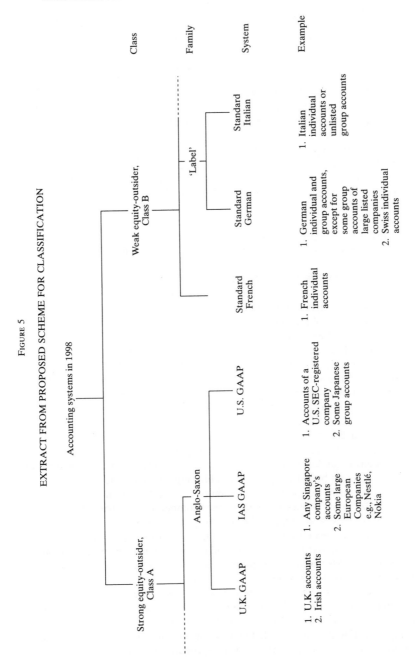

FIGURE 5

EXTRACT FROM PROPOSED SCHEME FOR CLASSIFICATION

the classification easier to use, the systems could be labelled (e.g., U.S. GAAP). The classification in Figure 5 is by no means complete, for it merely seeks to illustrate the type of amendments proposed for future classifiers.

Below each system, there are examples of users of the system. This accommodates the points made earlier about the meaning of the term 'dominant accounting system'. For instance, U.S. GAAP is used by SEC-registered companies but not by all U.S. companies. Similarly, some Japanese companies are allowed to follow U.S. GAAP for their group accounts for both U.S. and Japanese purposes. As another instance, the 'standard German' system is that used by German companies for individual company accounts and, by most of them, for group accounts. However, several German listed companies are now publishing group accounts in accordance with International Accounting Standards, either by carefully choosing unusual German options (e.g., Bayer for 1994) or by producing two sets of group accounts (e.g., Deutsche Bank for 1995).

Proposition P3 would be relevant for the inclusion of developing countries in a classification. The fourth proposition could be used to predict which countries would move their dominant systems towards Class A in the classification.

POLICY IMPLICATIONS FOR RULE-MAKERS

The import and export of accounting technology (Parker, 1989) seems to be accelerating as a result of globalization and the formation of economic blocs such as the European Economic Area and the North American Free Trade Area. Also, the World Bank has funded advice for China on reforming its accounting; the British Foreign Office for Romania; the European Union for Russia; and so on. This section examines some implications of the article's earlier sections for standard-setters and other rule-makers.

In a CD country, the rule-makers should note that the country's accounting system is likely to have been imported and may not be appropriate for the main purpose of accounting. For example, in a developing country with imported Class A accounting but with few or no listed companies, the paraphernalia of Class A (e.g., extensive disclosure, consolidation, external audit) may be an expensive luxury. Resources might be better spent on establishing a reliable and uniform bookkeeping system, partly for the purpose of improving the collection of tax.

A similar point applies to many former communist countries, where the introduction of Class A accounting for a large proportion of enterprises might be inappropriate. However, for some such countries (perhaps China) where an impression has been created that the population and the government seem keen on moving to an equity-outsider system, the introduction of Class A might be appropriate, at least for large or listed companies.

In CS countries with a credit-insider system, again the rule-makers should think carefully before a generalized introduction of Class A. For example, it is not at all clear that the benefits of Class A would exceed its cost for the bulk of German companies. It is also not clear that there would be much benefit in any improved ability to compare corner grocery shops in Stuttgart with those in Sydney. However,

INTERNATIONAL DIFFERENCES IN FINANCIAL REPORTING

German rule-makers should ask themselves (and are doing so) whether they should assist the large German companies who are being forced by commercial pressures towards Class A. One approach would be exemption from normal German rules for the preparation of consolidated financial statements by such companies.

There is another policy question for governments whose countries do not have equity-outsider financing systems but who wish to encourage them. Would the imposition of a Class A financial reporting system encourage a change in financing system? The thrust of this article is that the financial reporting *follows* from the financing system. This is reminiscent of the debate in the literature about the relationship between double-entry bookkeeping and the rise of capitalism (e.g., Sombart, 1924; Yamey, 1949; Yamey, 1964; Winjum, 1971). The weight of argument seems to rest with those who believe that double entry follows business developments rather than leading them. None of this proves that developments in accounting cannot assist in economic development. However, the *imposition* of Class A might be inappropriate, particularly if done for unlisted companies or within a detailed and slow-moving legal system, given that an important feature of Class A accounting is that it can adapt to commercial circumstances. It might be better to concentrate on making Class A *available* by removing any legal or economic barriers to its usage and by subsidizing education.

In CS countries with equity-outsider financing systems and Class A accounting, the rule-makers should ask whether the full panoply of Class A is necessary for smaller companies or whether a separate financial reporting system should be allowed for them. This issue has largely been resolved in the U.S.A., as discussed earlier, and recent moves in the U.K. have exempted some smaller companies from audit and from the disclosure rules of several standards.[26]

The International Accounting Standards Committee (IASC) does not impose its rules on any enterprises; it merely makes them available to companies or regulators. However, some regulators impose IASs on some or most enterprises in their countries.[27] Also, the World Bank requires its borrowers to use IASs. The IASC should consider whether it could make available some additional 'system' which might be more suitable for financial reporting by unlisted companies.

SUMMARY

This article proposes a general model of the reasons for international differences in accounting practices. Instead of dozens of potential independent variables, it proposes two explanatory factors for the first split of accounting systems into classes. For culturally self-sufficient countries, it is suggested that the class of the predominant accounting system depends on the strength of the equity-outsider market.

---

[26] In 1994, the audit requirement was removed or reduced for private companies with turnover under £350,000. The Accounting Standards Board published an exposure draft for a Financial Reporting Standard for Smaller Entities in 1996.

[27] This is approximately the position for Singapore, Hong Kong, and many other Commonwealth countries.

ABACUS

For culturally dominated countries, the class of the accounting system is determined by the cultural influence. However, sometimes an equity-outsider market may gradually develop, or certain companies may be interested in foreign equity markets. This will lead to the development of the appropriate accounting, and it is one of the reasons for the existence of more than one class of accounting in one country.

Many other factors, which had been suggested previously as reasons for accounting differences, result from or are linked to the equity market. Some factors are perhaps reasons for the differences in equity markets, but are too unclear to measure with any precision. A general theory previously proposed by Doupnik and Salter (1995) mixed several of these factors and mis-specified some of them.

Some improvements to the classification of accounting systems have been suggested, incorporating the idea that it is accounting practice systems, not countries, that should be classified. Some implications for rule-makers are suggested, warning against inappropriate transfers of technology.

REFERENCES

Baydoun, N., and R. Willett, 'Cultural Relevance of Western Accounting Systems to Developing Countries', *Abacus*, March 1995.

Beaver, W. H., *Financial Reporting: An Accounting Revolution*, Prentice-Hall, 1989.

Belkaoui, A., *International Accounting*, Quorum, 1995.

Botosan, C. A., 'Disclosure Level and the Cost of Equity Capital', *Accounting Review*, July 1997.

Briston, R. J., 'The Evolution of Accounting in Developing Countries', *International Journal of Accounting*, Fall 1978.

Briston, R. J., and Foo See Liang, 'The Evolution of Corporate Reporting in Singapore', *Research in Third World Accounting*, Vol. 1, 1990.

Cable, J., 'Capital Market Information and Industrial Performance: The Role of West German Banks', *Economic Journal*, March 1985.

Choi, F. D. S., and G. G. Mueller, *International Accounting*, Prentice-Hall, 1992.

Chow, L. M., G. K. Chau and S. J. Gray, 'Accounting Reforms in China: Cultural Constraints on Implementation and Development', *Accounting and Business Research*, Vol. 26, No. 1, 1995.

Clarke, F. L., and G. W. Dean, *Contributions of Limperg and Schmidt to the Replacement Cost Debate in the 1920s*, Garland, 1990.

Cooke, T. E., and R. S. O. Wallace, 'Financial Regulation and its Environment: A Review and Further Analysis', *Journal of Accounting and Public Policy*, Summer 1990.

Da Costa, R. C., J. C. Bourgeois and W. M. Lawson, 'A Classification of International Financial Accounting Practices', *International Journal of Accounting*, Spring 1978.

David, R., and J. E. C. Brierley, *Major Legal Systems in the World Today*, Stephens, 1985.

Davidson, R. A., A. M. G. Gelardi and F. Li, 'Analysis of the Conceptual Framework of China's New Accounting System', *Accounting Horizons*, March 1995.

Doupnik, T. S., and S. B. Salter, 'External Environment, Culture, and Accounting Practice: A Preliminary Test of a General Model of International Accounting Development', *International Journal of Accounting*, No. 3, 1995.

Federation of European Stock Exchanges, *Share Ownership Structure in Europe*, 1993.

Frank, W. G., 'An Empirical Analysis of International Accounting Principles', *Journal of Accounting Research*, Autumn 1979.

INTERNATIONAL DIFFERENCES IN FINANCIAL REPORTING

Franks, J., and C. Mayer, 'Corporate Control: A Synthesis of the International Evidence', working paper of London Business School and University of Warwick, 1992.

Gambling, T., and R. A. A. Abdel-Karim, *Business and Accounting Ethics in Islam*, Mansell, 1991.

Gernon, H., and R. S. O. Wallace, 'International Accounting Research: A Review of its Ecology, Contending Theories and Methodologies', *Journal of Accounting Literature*, Vol. 14, 1995.

Gonzalo, J. A., and J. L. Gallizo, *European Financial Reporting: Spain*, Routledge, 1992.

Gordon, P. D., and S. J. Gray, *European Financial Reporting: United Kingdom*, Routledge, 1994.

Gray, S. J., 'Towards a Theory of Cultural Influence on the Development of Accounting Systems Internationally', *Abacus*, March 1988.

Hamid, S. R., R. Craig and F. L. Clarke, 'Religion: A Confounding Cultural Element in the International Harmonization of Accounting?', *Abacus*, September 1993.

Harrison, G. L., and J. L. McKinnon, 'Culture and Accounting Change: A New Perspective on Corporate Reporting Regulation and Accounting Policy Formulation', *Accounting, Organizations and Society*, No. 3, 1986.

Hofstede, G., *Culture's Consequences: International Differences in Work-Related Values*, Stage Publications, 1980.

Hove, M. R., 'Accounting Practice in Developing Countries: Colonialism's Legacy of Inappropriate Technologies', *International Journal of Accounting*, Fall 1986.

Jensen, M. C., and W. H. Meckling, 'Theory of the Firm: Managerial Behavior, Agency Costs and Ownership Structure', *Journal of Financial Economics*, October 1976.

Kenway, P., 'The Concentration of Ownership and its Implications for Corporate Governance in the Czech Republic', University of Reading, Discussion Papers in Economics, Series A, No. 288, 1994.

Lamb, M., C. W. Nobes and A. D. Roberts, 'The Influence of Taxation on Accounting: International Variations', Reading University Discussion Papers, 1995.

La Porta, R., F. Lopez-de-Silanes, A. Shleifer and R. W. Vishny, 'Legal Determinants of External Finance', *Journal of Finance*, July 1997.

Meek, G., and S. Saudagaran, 'A Survey of Research on Financial Reporting in a Transnational Context', *Journal of Accounting Literature*, No. 9, 1990.

Miller, M. C., 'Australia', in T. E. Cooke and R. H. Parker (eds), *Financial Reporting in the West Pacific Rim*, Routledge, 1994.

Nair, R. D., and W. G. Frank, 'The Impact of Disclosure and Measurement Practices on International Accounting Classifications', *Accounting Review*, July 1980.

Nobes, C. W., 'An Empirical Analysis of International Accounting Principles: A Comment', *Journal of Accounting Research*, Spring 1981.

——, 'A Judgmental International Classification of Financial Reporting Practices', *Journal of Business Finance and Accounting*, Spring 1983.

——, Ch. 1 in C. W. Nobes and R. H. Parker (eds), *Issues in Multinational Accounting*, Philip Allan, 1988.

——, 'Classification of Accounting Using Competencies as a Discriminating Variable: A Comment', *Journal of Business Finance and Accounting*, January 1992.

——, 'Corporate Financing and its Effect on European Accounting Differences', Reading University Discussion Papers, 1995.

——, *Compliance with International Standards*, UNCTAD, 1996.

Nobes, C. W., and R. H. Parker (eds), *Comparative International Accounting*, Prentice-Hall, 1995.

Parker, R. H., 'Importing and Exporting Accounting: The British Experience', in A. G. Hopwood (ed.), *International Pressures for Accounting Change*, Prentice-Hall, 1989.

Parry, M., and R. Grove, 'Does Training More Accountants Raise the Standards of Accounting in Third World Countries? A Study of Bangladesh', *Research in Third World Accounting*, Vol. 1, 1990.

Radebaugh, L. H., 'Environmental Factors Influencing the Development of Accounting Objectives, Standards and Practices in Peru', *International Journal of Accounting*, Fall 1975.

Radebaugh, L. H., and S. Gray, *International and Multinational Enterprises*, Wiley, 1993.

Rahman, A., H. Perera and S. Ganeshanandam, 'Measurement of Formal Harmonization in Accounting: An Exploratory Study', *Accounting and Business Research*, Autumn 1996.

Roberts, A. D., 'The Very Idea of Classification in International Accounting', *Accounting, Organizations and Society*, Vol. 20, Nos 7/8, 1995.

Scheid, J.-C., and P. Walton, *European Financial Reporting: France*, Routledge, 1992.

Schweikart, J. A., 'Contingency Theory as a Framework for Research in International Accounting', *International Journal of Accounting*, Fall 1985.

Shoenthal, E., 'Classification of Accounting Systems Using Competencies as a Discriminating Variable: A Great Britain–United States Study', *Journal of Business Finance and Accounting*, Autumn 1989.

Soeters, J., and H. Schreuder, 'The Interaction between National and Organizational Cultures in Accounting Firms', *Accounting, Organizations and Society*, Vol. 13, No. 1, 1988.

Sombart, W., *Der Moderne Kapitalismus*, 6th edn, Duncker & Humblot, Vol. 2.1, 1924.

Standish, P. E. M., 'Origins of the *plan comptable général*: A Study in Cultural Intrusion and Reaction', *Accounting and Business Research*, Autumn 1990.

——, 'Financial Reporting in France', Ch. 11 in C. W. Nobes and R. H. Parker (eds), *Comparative International Accounting*, Prentice-Hall, 1995.

Tweedie, D. P., and G. Whittington, *The Debate on Inflation Accounting*, Cambridge University Press, 1984.

Wallace, R. S. O., and H. Gernon, 'Frameworks for International Comparative Financial Accounting', *Journal of Accounting Literature*, Vol. 10, 1991.

Watts, R., and J. Zimmerman, 'The Demand for and Supply of Accounting Theories: The Market for Excuses', *Accounting Review*, April 1979.

Winjum, J. O., 'Accounting and the Rise of Capitalism: An Accountant's View', *Journal of Accounting Research*, Vol. 9, 1971.

Yamey, B. S., 'Scientific Bookkeeping and the Rise of Capitalism', *Economic History Review*, 2nd ser, Vol. 1, 1949.

——, 'Accounting and the Rise of Capitalism: Some Further Notes on a Theme by Sombart', *Journal of Accounting Research*, II, 1964.

Zeff, S. A., F. van der Wel and K. Camfferman, *Company Financial Reporting: A Historical and Comparative Study of the Dutch Regulatory Process*, North-Holland, 1992.

Zysman, J., *Government, Markets and Growth: Financial Systems and the Politics of Industrial Change*, Cornell University Press, 1983.

INTERNATIONAL DIFFERENCES IN FINANCIAL REPORTING

APPENDIX

This appendix contains an example (relating to 1995) of the measures that could be used to distinguish between strong equity markets and others. The data in Table A relate to the eight largest economies in Europe, which are probably all CS countries.

TABLE A

EQUITY MARKET MEASURES

	Domestic equity market capitalization/GDP	Domestic listed companies per million of population
U.K.	1.34	30.2
Netherlands	0.99	14.4
Sweden	0.76	24.4
Belgium	0.50	14.3
France	0.40	12.4
Spain	0.36	9.3
Germany	0.31	8.4
Italy	0.18	4.3

Sources: European Stock Exchange Statistics, Annual Report 1995, Federation of European Stock Exchanges; and *Pocket World in Figures 1995*, The Economist.

In order to identify a Category IV financing system, it would also be necessary to establish that strong equity markets (e.g., U.K. and Netherlands) had a high level of 'outsiders'. This could be done using statistics of ownership of shares (e.g., Federation of European Stock Exchanges, 1993).

[11]

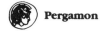 **Pergamon**

Accounting, Organizations and Society, Vol. 20, No. 7/8, pp. 639–664, 1995
Copyright © 1995 Elsevier Science Ltd
Printed in Great Britain. All rights reserved.
0361–3682/95 $9.50+0.00

0361–3682(95)00008–9

THE VERY IDEA OF CLASSIFICATION IN INTERNATIONAL ACCOUNTING

ALAN ROBERTS
Department of Economics, University of Reading

Abstract

The paper discusses some issues and problems associated with attempts to classify national systems of accounting. Attention is given to classification experiences in other disciplines. The analysis aims to show the incoherence of taxonomies which rely upon appeals to objectivity and tries to present a case for the development of classifications which explicitly focus on the concept of an "accounting system".

The history of attempts at taxonomy in the field of comparative international accounting reveals some contrasting methodological approaches. The earliest attempt was by Hatfield (1966, reprinted from a paper of 1911) who, on the basis of some observations about differences in accounting practices in four countries, suggested a three-group classification: U.S., U.K. and Continental Europe. In more recent times, one set of approaches has relied on extrinsic classifications of accounting, i.e. accounting in different countries was classified in terms of factors which influence the nature and practice of accounting in those countries. Thus, Mueller (1967) produced a four-group classification in terms of "patterns of accounting development" followed (Mueller, 1968) by another classificatory attempt based on business environments. Other examples of classification relying on extrinsic factors would include Seidler (1967) and the AAA (1977) whose classifications in international accounting were based upon "spheres of influence" and "zones of influence", respectively. More recent examples are provided by Gray (1988) who, using a research paradigm of Hofstede (1980, 1983), proposes "culture area classifications in the context of combinations of accounting values" (p. 11) and Shoenthal (1989) who

considers classifications in terms of professional competencies.

A second approach to classifying international differences in accounting has used intrinsic tests of divergence and resemblance; accounting in different countries is classified in terms of the nature of accounting practices in those countries. A number of researchers (da Costa *et al.*, 1978; Frank, 1979; Nair & Frank, 1980; Goodrich, 1982) have applied factor analysis to Price Waterhouse data (1973, 1975, 1979) on accounting practices to produce clusters or groupings of countries. In the Nair & Frank study, for example, consideration of measurement practices was separated from that of disclosure practices. In the former case, a four-country grouping was obtained which was broadly similar to the groups obtained by Frank in 1979; in the latter case, a seven-country classification was proposed. Following these classifications, Nair & Frank tried to associate economic and cultural variables with the groupings obtained, with mixed results (Gray, 1988).

A further approach to classification in the field of comparative international accounting is that of Nobes (1984). Nobes focuses on the measurement practices used in the financial reporting of public companies based in countries in the developed Western world in 1980, and, inspired by the example of biological classification and its methods of numerical taxonomy, takes 9 factors which might provide discriminating features of those practices in 14 countries which were then scored on a scale of 0–3 in order to construct a morphology. A variety of techniques, relying on concepts of taxonomic distance, were used to produce clusters of countries labelled as "species"; further levels of clustering led to the creation of a family tree hierarchy (Fig. 1). Significantly, in view of earlier criticisms of the use of Price Waterhouse data for classification purposes (Nobes, 1981), the scoring of the nine factors was made on the basis of information from a number of sources including works of reference, financial reports, detailed questionnaires and personal knowledge obtained from working in the countries concerned. In distancing himself from previous intrinsic classifiers, Nobes emphasized the need for judgement (Nobes, 1984, pp. 31–32) in attempting to derive classifications in international accounting.

This paper sets out, on the basis of these various taxonomic attempts, to explore some abstract issues about the derivation of classifications in comparative international accounting and to suggest some approaches which might be developed in the future. Attention is placed upon the experience of other disciplines in terms of dealing with the taxonomic process; in particular, debates about classification in biology are used to highlight a number of perspectives on the past development of international accounting classifications. The paper has a specific focus upon the Nobes model for a number of reasons. Firstly, unlike previous classifications, this model has not been the subject of major review and comment. Secondly, its development followed an explicit consideration of general issues in classification, including a review of attempts to classify in other disciplines. A third reason is that it represents a research paradigm in the field and has spawned, to use Kuhn's terminology (Kuhn, 1970), at least one working out of "normal science" (Al Najjar, 1987).

The structure of the paper is one which starts with a general review of the nature of the taxonomic process itself and, within this

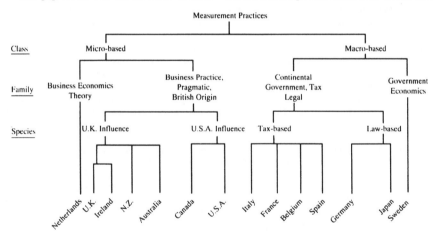

Fig. 1. Tested hypothetical classification of measurement practices of listed companies in the Developed countries in 1980 (after Nobes, 1984, p. 94).

review, argues that all classifications rely, implicitly or explicitly, upon a principle for attribute choice. The paper then considers a number of taxonomic approaches in international accounting and other disciplines in terms of the ways in which such attributes have, or have not, been selected. Five main approaches are identified: essentialist; phenetic; diachronic; set theoretical; and archetypal. The central purposes of the paper are, through a consideration of the implications of these approaches for international accounting, to show the incoherence of taxonomies which rely upon appeals to objectivity; to suggest that teleological concerns should be dominant in attempting to construct classifications in the discipline and to present a case for the development of classifications which explicitly focus on the concept of an "accounting system". But in making such a suggestion, it should be recognized that behind the issue of classification lies a more fundamental question: what is accounting? For the construction of taxonomies reflects our own prejudices about the discipline and, in so doing, imposes a way of thinking about accounting which is implicitly ethnocentric.

The nature and purposes of classification
What do we do when we classify? A simple, and seemingly obvious, answer to this question is that classification is based upon a recognition of difference and similarity between objects in any particular set under consideration. Objects which are similar to one another are classified into a group and distinguished from other objects which are dissimilar. However, this response is not very helpful unless we can specify in what respect(s) those objects might be similar or different. Objects may have a number of attributes any one of which will define a group but there is no reason why different attributes will all define the same group. This fact poses an immediate problem for classifiers, the problem of attribute choice, and demands that, for any classification, a principle or basis be established for the selection of attribute(s) which can be used to establish resemblance and difference and so define groupings. Consid-

erations of such a principle may well lead to the idea that some groupings are more "real", "objective", or "natural" than others but that idea, again, has to be justified in some way or another. One approach to the problem of attribute choice is to relate it to the purpose that the classification is intended to serve. We might ask what the classification will be used for so that a sensible procedure would be firstly to agree on the aims of any classification and then to choose that principle of attribute choice which would lead to a classification best suited to those aims (Pratt, 1976).

This teleological dimension of classification has found explicit consideration in Nobes (1984) where four main purposes were identified for international accounting classifications. Broadly, these purposes could be summarized as descriptive and comparative; developmental; pedagogic and predictive.

The first purpose would appear to be uncontroversial: a classification "may be used as a way of describing and comparing accounting systems" with the classifier being led "to examine the exact nature and importance of the differences and similarities between accounting systems of different countries." Furthermore, a classificatory exercise would aid in the appreciation of the classifier's own system since it would help to uncover "the essential structure of a system from the mass of practical details" (Nobes, 1984, p. 28). Such a perspective echoes earlier comments about classification helping to reveal "underlying structures" (p. 26) and, indeed, the notion that classification serves a descriptive purpose in outlining essential or underlying facts about accounting systems is implicit in other approaches to international accounting classifications. Thus, Goodrich (1983), in commenting upon Nobes' criticism of an earlier work (Nobes, 1983; Goodrich, 1982), suggests that both he and Nobes "would like to rely on 'descriptions' of national accounting systems as the basis for proceeding" (p. 56); the whole approach of intrinsic classification relies implicitly upon the notion that statistical analyses provide parsimonious descriptions of the differences and similarities in accounting practices of different countries; and, in a different context, Smith and Shalchi suggest that past research efforts in the field of international accounting could be characterized as efforts where "the descriptive approach has been dominant" (Smith & Shalchi, 1981, p. 26).

But problems come in trying to make sense of the idea that classifications can describe things and, in so doing, reveal underlying or essential facts. Nobes emphasizes, in the review of what he calls "empirical" classification in international accounting, the idea that brute manipulation of data without "judgement" is empty: "a classification is by no means theory-free. A sensible classification is not produced by a summarization of a mass of facts. It involves preconceptions, judgements and weightings" (Nobes, 1984, p. 32). There is however, a tension between this position about the need for subjective intervention in the taxonomic process and the view that classification, through parsimonious description, can uncover essential structures or facts. An essentialist classification presupposes, on the basis of some principle, a selection of certain attributes of objects which are judged to be essential to them; we cannot from the achieved classification then argue that we can uncover or describe what is essential without indulging in some kind of circularity.

The idea that a classification can nakedly describe the real essences of those objects around which the classification is built would appear to be a difficult one to hold but, equally, the notion that we can describe objects without classification is incoherent. To be able to describe something must involve an issue about the criteria for being able to identify that thing and therefore, directly or indirectly, implies a question as to what kind of thing it is. Describing things then implies a prior classification as to the different kind of things there are; classification is the fundamental process that allows us to make sense of objects in the world. Classification is not therefore ready made but results from a way of thinking; in classifying we do no less than engage in

"ways of world making" (Goodman, 1978) and in creating a classification, our descriptions of things are always relative to that classification (Goodman, 1976). The conclusion here then would be that description of something presupposes prior classification of it so that description is not so much a purpose of classification as a direct consequence of it.

The extreme relativism implied by the previous paragraph might appear to sit uncomfortably with ideas that classifications in some other disciplines are, in some sense, "real" or objective. Thus, for example, we might suggest that the Mendeléèv periodic table of chemical elements constitutes a classification that, is in some way, objective. Mendeléèv discovered a periodic pattern between the atomic weights of chemical elements and the chemical and physical properties of those elements (Kneen *et al.*, 1972). The classification is treated as fundamental by chemists and has proved its worth in a number of ways: it has been confirmed by subsequent theory and experiment deriving from the electronic structure of matter; it has been useful in predicting successfully the existence of elements "missing" from the original table. Should we therefore not conclude that this classification does objectively describe what is true, that it captures the essence of chemistry? Whatever our intuitions on the issue, it still remains the case that the periodic table is only one possible classification of matter out of many, its truth is relative to the classification. To take such a position does not imply that we should not prefer it to other possible classifications. But to prefer it does not necessarily rely upon appeals to objectivity; we might just prefer it because it meets criteria that we set in terms of judging classifications: we might prefer it because it is coherent, simple, parsimonious, because it has initial credibility, wide scope or "rightness of fit" (Goodman, 1978).

The consequence of this position for international accounting classifications is that, in attempting to justify them, we do not need to appeal to notions of real descriptions of what is; we might be better advised to focus on the criteria, the principles, which allow us to judge various taxonomic versions and, in so doing, relate them to the purposes to which the classifications are to be put. Perhaps we should, rather than aim "at empirically assessing the validity of international classifications proposed repeatedly in the accounting literature" (Nair & Frank, 1980, p. 93), pay rather more attention to what our classifications are intended to achieve.

The idea that classification can be used for a descriptive purpose was linked by Nobes to the notion that classification can be used for a comparative purpose as well. This is a familiar idea in the social sciences. Thus Smelser (1972) quotes Kalleberg (1966) with approval:

> Truly comparative concepts . . . can only be developed after classification is completed. Classification is a matter of "either-or", comparison is a matter of "more or less". Two objects being compared must already have been shown to be of the same class.

But is the relationship between classification and comparison as clear cut as this? If the process of classification involves the selection of attributes of objects in a particular set which are used to identify resemblance and divergence between those objects and then lead to some objects being classified into one group and others into other groups, then it would appear that the process of comparison has already taken place in the act of classification. It is not even possible to identify comparability with similarity, as Kalleberg would imply, because to say that two objects are dissimilar is still to have compared them. So, the argument here is that it is not that classification begets comparison but the reverse; in this sense, it could be said that it is not a purpose of classification to provide a means of comparing accounting in different countries but, rather, that comparing accounting is a requirement for the creation of classifications.

The pedagogic purpose of classification in international accounting would appear rather easier to deal with than the descriptive or comparative purpose. A classification can, through

its imposition of a way of thinking, have an educative purpose for students and accountants by providing a frame of reference from which to view accounting diversity across the world. But what can we say about the developmental and predictive purposes claimed for classifications in international accounting? It has been suggested that a classification can help in the harmonization process by highlighting significant divergence and similarity in accounting across different countries; it can help legislators and the profession in one country to predict problems that may have to be faced in the future by considering the experience of countries that are "near" to it in the classification. Such claims are well made but they do depend upon what is adjudged to be significant, upon the criteria or principles we use to say that one country is "near" to another in any particular classification. We need to be able to say that a classification has been drawn up in order to show, for example, policy-makers where difficulties might exist in attempting to harmonize accounting across different countries; the classification would then be constructed on the basis of attributes of accounting in those countries which would have a bearing on the harmonization process (although it should be added that there is no evidence that accounting classifications have, in the past, been used by accounting regulators).

It is in the context of this issue of relating classification to purpose that we might consider a question which has particular importance for attempts to classify in international accounting: what are the objects which are to be classified? The periodic table in chemistry has a clearly defined set of objects which are classified, the chemical elements; biological classifications are clearly focused on living things. It is not clear, however, what we are, or should be, classifying in the field of international accounting. It appears from the proposed classifications that we can choose a variety of objects: "accounting development patterns"; business environments, culture areas; measurement and disclosure practices; and measurement practices alone. And the literature talks about the idea of different "accounting systems" so we may ask questions about what such a concept includes and how the proposed classifications relate to it.

This central issue can be illustrated by means of a single example. The Nobes classification permits us to take at least two positions on what the objects are that are classified:

Narrow: The measurement practices are themselves objects of the classifications and the attributes of those objects are the nine factors which provide discriminating features of those measurement practices.

Broad: The measurement practices are the attributes the ordering of which allows us to classify objects which are some other kind of entity such as "accounting systems" or, indeed, countries.

From the heading shown in Fig. 1, it rather looks as if the classification proposed should be interpreted from the viewpoint of the narrow position. If this is the case, the country labels shown in the figure are a shorthand: "U.S.A.", for example, does not denote the country U.S.A., but rather "the measurement practices used in financial reporting by public companies in the U.S.A." However, we might take a different view: the original hypothesis of a classification advanced by Nobes was in terms of "Accounting Systems by Practices" (Nobes, 1984, p. 67); this would tend to suggest a perspective from the broad position.

How might these two perspectives be reconciled? One strategy would be to adopt an essentialist stance and say that measurement practices represent the substance of an accounting system, its most significant component, and so we can say that in providing a classification of measurement practices, we are also, by proxy, as it were, providing a classification of accounting systems. But there are immediate problems: we have not provided any principle or justification for measurement practices being the "essence" of an accounting system and anyway, it is not clear that we could provide such a principle until we were able to

articulate what we might deem an "accounting system" to be. A second strategy would be to say that the concept of an accounting system is just too nebulous and ungrounded for a sensible classification of such objects to be produced; we would be better advised to focus on objects such as measurement practices to which we can apply objective statistical techniques and so allow any classifications to be checked scientifically. But to adopt such a stance is to appeal to a notion of objectivity which is neither necessary nor justified; we have already noted that classifications are irredeemably subjective. Furthermore, it is not obvious that, even if such classifications were objective, they would meet the purposes for which they were intended. Why should a classification of measurement practices used in financial reporting obviously aid the harmonization process? It might, indeed, mislead policy makers if there is, for example, a lack of congruence between how such practices ought to be (legal and professional norms) and how they actually are.

The third strategy is simply to recognize the plasticity which is inevitable in the discipline. It may be that classifications in terms of accounting systems, nebulous and vague though they might be, can be helpful in meeting certain purposes. But if we are to create and develop such classifications, we should have a clear idea of what we deem an accounting system to be; we need to specify its elements and their relationship, one to another, and to the system as a whole. This does not mean that we must attempt to find out what an accounting system "really" is; it does, however, mean that we should relate our conceptions of accounting systems to the purposes to which the classification is to be put.

APPROACHES TO CLASSIFICATION

Nobes (1984) outlines, as a prelude to the development of his classification, a number of ways of classifying. His typology of taxonomic methods includes dichotomous grouping, rank ordering, dimensioning, systematizing, multidimensional scaling and morphological structuring (p. 30). These are, indeed, all ways of classifying a set of objects. A more fundamental question, however, involves a consideration of the principle(s) that should be used to select the attributes of objects which produce the classification. Taxonomic attempts throughout history and across disciplines have indicated that there is a variety of approaches to this question of what principle to use and this section of the paper reviews a number of such approaches (Pratt, 1976; Ridley, 1986) as a backdrop against which international accounting classifications might be viewed.

Essentialist approaches

Although Plato did concern himself with issues in classification (Balme, 1987), it was his pupil, Aristotle, who, through his interest in natural history, was, perhaps, the first to explore the nature of classification and to establish some rules for its use (Barnes, 1982). His philosophical works were complemented by biological treatises (some 25% of the surviving corpus) and, although the principles which formed his classificatory scheme are well established, the detailed rules and techniques for classification are tantalizingly fragmentary (Balme, 1961, rev. 1975, 1987).

The themes which find their place in Aristotle's approach to classification arise out of his conception of what it is to be an object. A definition in the Aristotlean framework of, say, an object like a dog would not be a proposition about what the word "dog" means; rather, it would say what the "essence" of a dog is, what it is to be a dog: "the essence of a thing is that which it is said to be *per se*" (*Metaphysics* Z.4; trans. Waddington, 1956, p. 173). Once we can identify the essence of an object, we can distinguish those attributes of it which are fundamental to it from those that are not. In Aristotle's axiomatic scheme of things, a classification would start from the principle of identifying essences and then successively set out what are the derivative attributes. For ani-

mals, species would be classed into a genus if they possessed shared essences.

Taking such a view raises two immediate questions: what are the "essences" of objects, and how do we discover them? For Artistotle, the question of what is the essence of an object is linked to another question about change: what is it about an object that persists through time? A dog is born, lives and dies; it may change in all sorts of ways over time; its size and shape will change. His conclusion was that the essence of a dog cannot be located in those changing attributes, its essence is what it does, its function (*ergon*) which in turn is related to its purpose (*telos*). So essentialism in Aristotle in teleological and in classifying objects, we should look to the function of the objects as the underlying principle upon which the classification should be based. The way in which the purpose of objects such as animals is linked to their physical attributes is by taking the view that those attributes depend on the activities and functions of the objects and not the other way round (Ridley, 1986). Thus the approach to be adopted in producing a classification for living animals is to look for the homologues, that is, those attributes between animals which are similar, not because they arise out of a similar way of life (analogues), but because they possess similar structures which are related to the purposes or functions of those animals.

These themes in Aristotle provide an approach to classification which has had an appeal throughout history. The idea that we should look for the essence of objects, as implying the selection of attributes of those objects which locate their functional necessity, has been used, explicitly or implicitly, by a number of taxonomists in various disciplines.

One clear example of a classification based implicitly upon Aristotlean essentialism is Linnaeus' taxonomy of living things (the inspiration of Nobes' family tree model), although it could be argued that it owes as much to the theological essentialism of Thomas Aquinas (Ridley, 1986). Linnaeus' classification, which assumed that species were both constant and sharply delimited (Mayr, 1976), was recognized as essentialist by the Swedish Academy who honoured him in saying "He discovered the essential nature of insects" (quoted in Flew, 1984). In his botanical classification, plants were grouped on the basis of something which could be seen to go to the essence of those objects: the nature and attributes of their reproductive systems. Those systems might be seen in a teleological light as well: reproduction represents the purpose of those objects. But the themes of essentialism and functionality are not restricted to classifications in the natural sciences; there are echoes of this approach to classification in the social sciences also.

In the field of comparative law, Zweigert & Kötz (1977) suggest that, in attempting to create a classification of legal systems, the critical or essential attribute is a system's "style" and, in a different context, they argue that the principle of functionality is "the starting point and basis" for legal comparison. Equally, the concept of functionalism is well established in social theory (the idea that social processes, practices and institutions can be seen in terms of meeting society's needs) and this functionalist approach has been used in the field of political science to produce classifications adapted for comparative politics (Almond, 1956).

What implications are there of this approach for the field of comparative international accounting? We might sketch a few responses. Insofar as judgement about proposed classifications in the discipline should be made in terms of their usefulness in meeting the purposes of classification, it matters not whether there is an essence of accounting in different countries. But if we are to suggest that a set of purposes for classifications in the field are to be made on the basis of some identified essence, then we need some principle for distinguishing it. The idea that classification could be based on the notion of function or purpose of accounting in different countries represents an interesting possibility for taxonomic attempts in the field. It might be possible to view accounting systems as performing different functions in different countries, the sys-

tems responding to different needs and users, and in the light of these different functions, developing particular accounting institutions, practices and processes. A functionalist classification would, inevitably, rely on the creation of models which typify the nature of accounting systems and would focus on how such systems can be grouped together across countries in terms of whether they have shared particular functions or are intended to meet particular needs. Such a framework, inevitably subjective, might allow accounting classifications to be extended, using a common principle, across a wider range of countries than in many past classifications attempted in international accounting; in particular, including accounting systems in socialist countries. But could such a functionalist approach be justified in terms of meeting particular purposes for accounting classifications? If we take, say, the purpose of classifications as being one to aid policy-makers in the harmonization or standardization process, then it could be argued that understanding the differences and similarities that exist in the objectives and purposes of accounting in different countries is of prime importance (McComb, 1979).

Overall similarity approaches

At the other extreme to essentialist classifications lies a set of taxonomic approaches which reject the whole notion of essentialism in classification, either implicitly or explicitly. One response to the problem of attribute choice is to circumvent it by using techniques which focus on "overall similarity" between objects, i.e. to use all of the attributes, whether they are homologues or analogues, in the classification. Such an approach is then critically dependent upon the set of techniques which are used to measure overall similarity, techniques which are statistical in nature.

One example of this kind of approach in international accounting is the work of Nair & Frank (1980), who, in common with most other intrinsic classifiers, used the technique of factor analysis applied separately to accounting measurement and disclosure practices across countries. Factor analysis has been used in a number of disciplines to produce classifications (perhaps of particular interest are attempts by economists to group countries according to socioeconomic attributes using this technique (Adelman & Morris, 1965, 1967; Ram, 1982, Abizadeh & Basilevsky, 1986)). The technique relies basically on the idea of reducing a system of correlations between attributes into fewer dimensions; it factors a matrix of correlation coefficients to produce factors which can then be used to account for the main variations in the patterns of those attributes and thus allow groupings or classifications of attributes to be created. In the Nair and Frank study factor analysis was applied, on the basis of 1973 Price Waterhouse data, to 147 accounting measurement practices in 38 different countries. Four factors were used to provide a four-group patterning of the 38 "countries" and these were characterized as four models (as shown in Table 1): British Commonwealth, Latin America, Continental Europe and the U.S.

As has been mentioned already, the classification does critically depend on the quality of data that are used but there are other issues that arise from this approach to classification. One might argue that some attributes are more important than others (as in the Nobes' case for the need for judgement) in which case, some

weighting of the attributes might be required, or, indeed, some attributes might not be included. But this notion immediately raises a question about the criteria to be used for the judgement to be made. If the notion of equal weighting is rejected, then there must be some principle which underlines the weighting scheme and, if weighting is to be used in statistical classifications of this kind, then the whole approach to classification collapses into an essentialist approach, distinguished from it only by an appeal to statistical technique. We might also ask a question about the objects of the classification provided and relate it to the problem that was introduced earlier of interpretation from the broad and narrow positions in classification. What are the objects of the classification in the Nair and Frank study? Throughout the article, the researchers appear to say that they were classifying countries — albeit by or based upon their accounting practices. But this does not seem right: in a fundamental sense we don't know what the object "country" is, or might be taken to be; even if we did, it is not clear what accounting measurement practices have to do with it. Perhaps a better view would be to take the objects as being "accounting practices in different countries". But even this is difficult to grasp because what the study is doing, through the factor analysis technique, is producing classifications

TABLE 1. Four-group measurement practices classification (after Nair & Frank, 1980, p. 77)

Group I (British Commonwealth Model)	Group II (Latin American Model)	Group III (Continental European Model)	Group IV (U.S. Model)
Australia	Argentina	Belgium	Canada
Bahamas	Bolivia	France	Japan
Fiji	Brazil	Germany	Mexico
Jamaica	Chile	Italy	Panama
Kenya	Colombia	Spain	Philippines
Netherlands	Ethiopia	Sweden	United States
New Zealand	Paraguay	Venezuela	
Republic of Ireland	Peru		
Rhodesia	Uruguay		
Singapore			
South Africa			
Trinidad and Tobago			
United Kingdom			

of statistical abstractions of accounting practices in different countries. It is possible to go further and ask a question about the significance of the four groupings which are characterized as "models". How should we, for example, interpret the term "Continental European model" derived from the study of accounting measurement practices? It is very tempting to interpret this as meaning that there is a Continental European model of accounting measurement practices but to do so is to indulge in the "reification fallacy". All that the grouping actually tells us is that there is a class of statistical abstractions of accounting measurement practices in countries which is defined by statistical attributes that the members of that class share; it is a true universal and we have no obvious warrant to reify it.

One response to this kind of perspective upon classifications using statistical techniques is to argue that they do, at least, represent an advance on more subjective taxonomies because they are empirical in nature; the classifications can be checked by other researchers using the data and applying the techniques. But it is difficult to see, assuming that the data is appropriate, how a classification can be justified by a simple appeal to technique. Furthermore, there is not just one statistical technique: factor analysis has bred a number of offshoots and, indeed, there are other techniques such as those applied in the field of biological taxonomy.

The rise of the methods of phenetic taxonomy in biology in the 1960s arose, in part, out of a desire also to avoid the problem of attribute choice linked to practical problems of detecting evolution through the identification of homologues in living things. Phenetic taxonomy relies, for a principle, upon the idea that, in biology, living things should be classified on the basis of their overall similarity. Instead of relying upon weightings of characters (attributes) as did traditional evolutionary taxonomists, the programme of phenetic taxonomy suggested equal weighting with the desired classification being based upon those characters which recognize "the resemblance exist-

ing now in the material at hand" (Sohal & Sneath, 1963, p. 55).

Ridley (1985, 1986) presents an eloquent case against the agenda of the numerical taxonomists in biology and this case echoes many of the comments already made about statistical classifications in international accounting. In biology, two advantages have been claimed for the overall resemblance approach based on statistical technique: repeatability and objectivity. In the sense that researchers may be able to check each other's manipulations of data to produce statistical abstractions which are then used to produce groupings, then the claim to repeatability is well made. But what of the claim to objectivity, of producing "real" or "natural" classifications? Johnson (1970) provides a powerful critique of this claim and identifies a number of sources of subjectivity in phenetic taxonomy. Firstly, he argues that there is a subjectivity in the choice of attributes to be measured. At first sight this might appear to raise a contradiction: if the whole point of the overall similarity approach is to reject the idea of attribute choice and to take all of the attributes of objects into account when classifying, how is it that pheneticists in biology (or in international accounting) make choices of attributes? The resolution of this contradiction lies in the fact that "there is no such number as the number of (attributes) than an (object) has" (Pratt, 1976, p. 383). If we take any set of objects there is an infinity of attributes that those objects may have or that we might choose to give to them and, in choosing a particular number upon which to base a classification, subjectivity inevitably enters into the classification. Johnson identifies other sources of subjectivity, most notably, in the choices that have to be made in deciding how taxonomic distance is to be measured and which cluster statistic is to be used. The issue of subjectivity in the measurement of taxonomic distance is most obviously shown in international accounting in the method used to score the more discriminating factors against measurement practices to produce the classification of Nobes (who makes, it should be added, no claims for objectivity). Each factor was scored on a scale of 0–3 on the basis of studies of works of references, financial reports and of the use of questionnaires and personal knowledge. But the notion of subjectivity attached to a cluster statistic is, perhaps, more fundamental since it goes to the heart of claims about objectivity, the "naturalness" of phenetic classifications. The first point is simply that there are many different types of cluster statistic that can be used and a choice of one or some of those statistics has to be made. The second point is that the subjectivity inherent in choosing the appropriate cluster statistic is not just a practical problem: if a classification produced through the use of a cluster statistic is to be objective, then there must be an objective criterion for deciding which statistic to use; there is, however, no such criterion. The third point is that (to echo an earlier argument) it is not obvious that a classification can be justified by a technique. The whole rationale of phenetic taxonomy is that a cluster statistic can be used to show overall similarity between a number of objects and so produce a classification; we have, however, no conception of overall similarity which is not dependent on that statistic. If it is the case that overall similarity is statistic-dependent, then we cannot use the statistic to show that overall similarity without collapsing into circularity.

The conclusion which might be drawn from this foray into the notion of producing overall similarity classifications based on statistical technique is that the approach promises more than it can deliver. Claims, explicit or implicit, to overcoming the problem of attribute choice are spurious; the objects of the created classifications are nothing but mathematical abstractions; taxonomies produced rely on an inherent circularity; and the idea that such classifications are, in some sense, objective or natural cannot be justified. We might also ask how such classifications in international accounting might be useful for developmental or harmonization purposes. The answer is not clear, because for some researchers, the focus appears to be on some kind of testing of

"more" subjective classifications without direct consideration of policy issues (Nair & Frank, 1980, p. 93). But if phenetic taxonomy is itself subjective then such testing is specious and, again, even if claims to objectivity were granted, it is not obvious that phenetic classifications would necessarily meet any particular purpose of those classifications.

Diachronic approaches

Another way of dealing with the problem of attribute choice is to approach it indirectly. If we consider a set of objects (like living things) which now possess an infinity of attributes, we might try to posit some kind of connection or relationship between those objects over time which would allow us to identify attributes now as being particularly important in the light of that connection and which would allow us to classify the objects into groups. The approach relies upon the identification of a time relationship (itself an attribute) in which we might have particular confidence to provide the linking principle for selecting other attributes in order to create the classification. For biology, that relationship is one of evolution, the idea that living things have evolved from earlier living things through a process of natural selection; certain of the attributes that living things possess now are similar because those objects are interconnected in a network of relationships with earlier common ancestors. In a sense, this approach is essentialist; in Aristotelan terms, the essence of an object is no longer what it is in itself but rather how it came to be what it is. We should not think that such an approach to classification is limited to natural history; classifications in linguistics of the different languages of the world have a long tradition of being based upon an identification of how those languages have evolved from earlier ones. And the notion that the history of objects is of first importance in being able to compare them (and by extension, classify them) has formed expression in the social sciences as well: "if we wish to have a science of comparative policies, one first step is the writing of a series of comparative histories;

comparative history is a more fundamental discipline than comparative politics" (MacIntyre, 1978, p. 182).

To suggest that a time relationship between objects can provide a principle upon which to found classifications is not necessarily to claim that the classifications are objective; it has already been argued that the process of classification imposes its own relativity. But to say that they are not necessarily objective does not mean that we should not prefer them. We might be attracted by a certain coherence about the principle; in biology, the pattern of the fossil record might help us to believe in a certain "rightness of fit".

For the purposes of this paper, such approaches which rely upon the identification of a time relationship between objects are called diachronic. This word, along with the term synchronic, was introduced into the study of linguistics by Saussure (1916) who made the distinction between the study of language in terms of its history (diachronic analysis) and the study of language as it is at any point in time (synchronic analysis).

Diachronic approaches to classification have been most obviously developed in the field of biology and subject to wide debate in that discipline. Darwin himself recognized the significance of his discovery of evolution to the issue of taxonomy in biology (Darwin, 1859, p. 455). The curious feature, however, is that, although the significance was recognized, it has had very little impact on traditional Linnaean classifications in the discipline (Dobzhansky, 1937) until relatively recent times; indeed, de Queiroz (1988) argues that biological taxonomy has yet to undergo its Darwinian revolution.

To understand this contention it is necessary to consider how the principles of biological taxonomy work. The first point to note is the subtle shift in the meaning of the terms homologues and analogues. In the Linnaean system of taxonomy mentioned earlier, the assumption made was that the species were fixed; there is no diachronic dimension. Taxonomy then relied upon the examination of the attributes of living things at a point in time in order to distinguish those attributes shared by living things by reason of similar structure (homologues; Nobes quotes the example of human feet and dolphins' flippers (1984, p. 31)) and those shared attributes which arise from sharing environments (analogues; an example being bees' wings and birds' wings). The imposition of an evolutionary framework upon this distinction would have the effect of changing the principle upon which homologues and analogues are identified. Evolutionary taxonomists look for homologues because they might provide good evidence of the living things having evolved from a recent common ancestor (in this sense it matters not whether they perform the same functions in different environments as do flippers in water and feet on land); analogues are rejected because they do not indicate recent common ancestry but simply represent a process of convergence in terms of performing similar functions within the same environment, as do the wings of birds and bees. The reason, therefore, why the Linnaean taxonomy has been so little changed in the post-Darwinian era is that the search for homologues remains the same although the reason for that search is now principled on evolution.

This serendipity in biological taxonomy, however, does pose problems because the diachronic dimension provides two main aspects; these two aspects do not obviously imply common classifications. Evolution of living things can arise firstly because some things have split off from a common ancestor at different times but it can also arise through the fact that those things can evolve at different rates. The implications of these dual processes can be illustrated by an example taken from Ridley (1986, chaps 1, 2 & 4). The pattern of evolution for three types of living things, birds, crocodiles and lizards is shown in Fig. 2. All three types have evolved from a common ancestor with the order of evolution being shown: birds split off from crocodiles at a later date than did crocodiles (or their most recent ancestor) from the common ancestor of crocodiles and lizards. But, in addition, birds have evolved at such a rate that crocodiles now look more like lizards

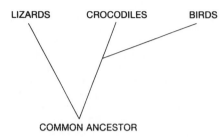

Fig. 2. The pattern of evolution among birds, crocodiles and lizards (after Ridley, 1986, p. 5).

than they do birds. The problem now arises as to how we should proceed in classifying these three types of living things on the basis of evolution.

There are two central approaches here (if we discount the previously identified overall similarity approach; this would simply group lizards and crocodiles together without taking into account the evolutionary principle because those two types are phenetically close). One approach might be called Mainstream Evolutionary Taxonomy (MET) (Simpson, 1961; Mayr, 1969). This approach would recognize the process of evolution and the common ancestor, by grouping lizards and crocodiles and the ancestor together in one class. This class is a monophyletic group in that the group is defined by homologies possessed *both* by the ancestor and the descendents. The class, along with other descendents, is the class of Reptilia: living things which are scaly, ectothermic, amniotes. The implication of the MET approach is not to recognize birds in the group because although, for example, feathers in birds are homologies of scales in lizards and crocodiles, they are not possessed by the common ancestor. MET then allows a phenetic principle to become dominant once evolution has been traced.

The other approach is to recognize, in biological taxonomy, *only* the order of splitting in the process of evolution so that if two living things possess a recent common ancestor then they will be grouped together even if they do not obviously resemble each other. In the example this would mean that birds and crocodiles would form one class (a clade) which "nests" inside another clade made up of birds, crocodiles and lizards. Since phenetic arguments do not enter into the classification (although they may be used to identify how the living things may have evolved) there is no need to resort to any labelling of clades (with terms like Reptilia); evolutionary branching provides an unambiguous principle for classification. Such an approach to biological taxonomy is most closely associated with the work of Hennig (1966) and is known as cladism. (Cladism, as outlined by Hennig, should be sharply distinguished from the approach of "transformed" cladism (Nelson, 1978, 1979; Patterson, 1980; Platnick, 1979, 1982; Nelson & Platnick, 1981, 1984; Rieppel, 1984). This school of thought tries to separate out cladistic principles from an evolutionary basis, an approach which Ridley (1986) (from whom the above references are derived) convincingly shows as being incoherent.)

How are we to judge between the competing approaches of MET and cladism? Cladism provides an unambiguous principle on which to found biological taxonomy but MET does not. At a more technical level it can be shown that the methods of MET can produce groups which do not reflect evolutionary (phylogenetic) relationships (Ridley, 1986, p. 54); MET, by relying after a certain point in the process of classification upon phenetic similarity, falls into the trap of the overall similarity approaches. Cladism rejects any notion of overall similarity as founding a taxonomy and relies exclusively upon the principle of evolutionary (branching) relationships.

It should now be asked how and why these debates in biological taxonomy have a bearing upon classifications in international accounting. The first response is that the Nobes hierarchical classification was explicitly developed on the basis of the example of biological taxonomy using a mix of inspiration from Linnaean terminology and the methods of MET. Therein lies one of the difficulties of the model

(Fig. 1). On the one hand, the hierarchical classification mixes diachronic and synchronic aspects. At the "species" level of the hierarchy there is a diachronic aspect (U.K. influence and U.S. influence) but within the same classification there are species defined synchronically (tax- and law-based); the classification is hybrid. On the other hand, the methods of phenetic taxonomy (as measuring overall similarity) have been used for both the synchronic and diachronic elements. The classification is labelled (as for classifications produced by Linnaeus and MET) to describe groups defined by their overall similarity. If a cladistic approach were to be used, no such labelling would be necessary since, in principle, objects would simply be grouped into series of nesting clades which showed, over time, the order of splitting.

The second response is to use this backdrop of method and debate in biological taxonomy to argue that the discipline's approach to classification may not be appropriate for classifications in international accounting.

The idea of hierarchies and family trees, inspired from the example in biology, and of the processes of evolution, has exercised a powerful effect upon classifiers in other disciplines. As has already been mentioned, it has been used in the field of linguistics. Languages do evolve and change over time with modern languages deriving, in common, attributes from earlier languages. It is therefore a short step to try and construct language family trees which rely on a principle of evolution where languages are shown to derive successively from earlier versions and, indeed, where attempts might be made (on the basis of derived attributes) to posit the existence and form of an original language, an *Ursprache*, from which, for a particular group, all later languages have evolved (e.g. the concept of a proto Indo-European language). But such attempts have drawn sharp attack from some linguists and archaeologists (Lyons, 1981; Renfrew, 1987) and the reason for this attack is relevant for international accounting classifications. The criticism of the family tree model in linguistics

is made up of two interrelated strands. The first recognizes that, over time, objects like languages might change through two processes: divergence and convergence. However, in biology only one of these processes is recognized, that of divergence; the whole point of the homologue/analogue distinction within the evolutionary perspective is to reject analogues (which indicate convergence) because they do not indicate any common ancestry. But in viewing language-relatedness, there is another process of convergence which is of some significance; thus, Lyons (1981, p. 186) argues that family tree classifications of languages "tend to oversimplify the facts, if not distort them completely, by failing to give recognition to the phenomena of convergence and diffusion and by representing language-relatedness as being the result of necessary and continuous divergence." Both Lyons and Renfrew make the suggestion that linguistic change (and by implication, language classifications) should be viewed from the perspective of a wave model; language change spreads like a wave over different geographical areas with each change spreading at different rates and over areas which might intersect (an idea inspired by the German linguist of the 19th century, Johannes Schmidt). The second, related point concerns the notion of ancestry. In biological taxonomy, evolution is significant and determinative since living things have *unique* common ancestors; the diachronic process of divergence is all. For example, it is not possible for crocodiles and birds to interbreed to produce a new living thing (which would then have two ancestors). This is not the case for the evolution of languages; it is very common to find the superimposition upon a language of "loan words" and structures derived from languages used in neighbouring geographical territories. Languages which stem from different origins can, and do, "interbreed". The same point is equally true for the comparison and classification of law across different countries; indeed, the point is far more significant because the accidents of history have produced sharp discontinuities in the form of wholesale replacements of law in particular countries (e.g. the imposition of Napoleonic legal codes in countries such as The Netherlands).

These issues raise important implications for any attempt to create hierarchical classifications in international accounting. The diachronic dimension cannot be captured in a hierarchy because it involves not just the process of divergence but the process of convergence as well. Thus, in the Nobes model, we cannot (particularly, if we wish to classify objects such as "accounting systems") represent the patterning of influence and change in accounting in different countries. But to draw this implication is not to suggest that we should not attempt to recognize the pattern of history in international accounting. The conclusions which might be drawn here are that diachronic approaches might prove useful but that if they are to be developed, they should be used consistently, not mixed with synchronic approaches to produce hybrid classifications. And we might look at how diachronic approaches could help in meeting certain purposes in comparative international accounting. If harmonization is to take place or if countries are to develop their accounting on the basis of the experience of "near" countries, then it is important for policy-makers to understand the pattern of history, to be able to trace common roots, to identify common "styles" of accounting based on common history and to relate the processes of cleavage and assimilation to historical change. Perhaps before we start classifying in international accounting, we should write comparative history.

Set theory approaches

One way of dealing with the problem of attribute choice in classification is to avoid it and look for other means of guiding classifiers. Such an approach might be exemplified in the use of set theory to provide "criteria" for taxonomic procedures and for judging taxonomies. In the field of international accounting, the AAA (1977, pp. 77–78) drew inspiration from the ideas of set theory to identify four properties of a "good" classification: consistency;

exhaustibility; mutual exclusivity; and hierarchical integrity. These four properties were used by Nobes to provide a perspective upon earlier extrinsic and intrinsic classifications and to support the construction of the classification that he tested (Nobes, 1984, pp. 65–66).

Before consideration is given to the significance of these four properties, it may be worthwhile emphasizing that they provide no guidance for the establishment of a principle for attribute choice in a classification; in this sense, they simply avoid the problem. Beyond this point, we might ask a question about the status of these properties: to what extent are they necessary or sufficient, either jointly or severally, for the construction of classifications in general or in international accounting in particular?

The first property — that of consistency — is taken to mean that in any classification "the characteristics used as a means of differentiating one element from another should be the same" (Nobes, 1984, p. 33). In the history of taxonomies there would appear to be no reason why this property is necessary; it is certainly not a property of biological taxonomies. (Indeed, Nobes makes the point that this property might be "impractical" if there are different purposes for a classification.) Perhaps the argument for consistency in classification is a slightly different one, one which owes its origins to Aristotle *Metaphysics Z.XII* (trans. Waddington, 1956, p. 220). Aristotle points out that, if we are to create a hierarchical structure in a classification (through a process of successive division), "we must at each stage (in the process) divide by the *differentia* of the previous *differentia*", that is the classification must be internally consistent in terms of the division of attributes down the hierarchy. Aristotle provides an example of such a requirement of consistency for the classification of animals: if the attribute "footed" is a *differentia* of the object "animal", then further subdivisions of "animal" should not be in terms of whether that object is, say, "winged" or not but rather divided on the basis of whether it is "cloven-footed" or not

(Balme, 1961; rev. 1975, 1987; Ridley, 1986). It should be noted that this idea of consistency is premised on a process of successive division which leads to a hierarchy and therefore begs the question of whether hierarchies are a necessary feature of classifications.

But there might be another interpretation of the property of consistency in a classification and that concerns, as has already been mentioned, the issue of hybridity in a classification. In the Nobes model there is a tension in the labelling of groups which might indicate a certain inconsistency of terminology. At the hierarchical level of "family", for example, it appears that two clusters are differentiated from others primarily on the basis of diachronic or geographical grounds (U.K. and U.S. influences) whilst two further groups are differentiated on the grounds of some other features (tax- and law-based) (Fig. 1). The principle underlying the labelling is not consistent and the significance of this issue is related to the extensional power of that classification: if there is hybridity in the labelling, then how should we proceed in trying to extend the classification to other countries?

The second property suggested by the AAA, that of exhaustive subsets, would seem to be unexceptionable but it does raise the question as to what is the nature of the universe which is to be exhausted by the classification. One aspect of the richness of a classification is its capacity for extension to cover a greater universe than that exhausted in its present form. This raises the issue of how we are to understand the extensional power of the Nobes classification. If the object of the classification is accounting measurement practices of public companies in developed Western countries then how is it to be extended into, say, socialist countries? Nobes recognizes this point when he says "if one wished to include developing countries or Eastern bloc countries, it would be necessary to include other discriminating factors . . . but such a process might not be sensible . . . so that one would have to classify something other than published financial reporting" (Nobes, 1987, p. 19).

Mutual exclusivity, the idea that objects in a classification should be ordered in such a way that they fall into one, and only one, subset or class within the classification, is claimed as a third property of a "good" classification. In the absence of a principle for attribute selection, it is difficult to see how this property can be a criterion for a good classification: the restriction that object X can fall (on the basis of some arbitrary attribute(s)) into category Y in classification Z is to ignore other attributes of X in other classifications but also within classification Z itself. The problem is compounded by the issue of labelling of subsets. Thus in the Nobes classification (Fig. 1) "Germany" and "Japan" are classified at the "family" level as being "law-based" whilst "France" is not. On the basis of the scores given for the discriminating factor "Law", "France" and "Japan" score 1 and "Germany" 0 (Nobes, 1984, p. 82). So we might ask the question as to why "Germany" and "Japan" are characterized as law-based whilst France is not. The issue here is not whether Germany and Japan, on the basis of a cluster statistic, fall within a class defined by that statistic, but that the combination of the property of mutual exclusivity with the process of labelling different subsets of a classification may create the effect of divergence which could be misleading.

The final property, that of hierarchical integrity, might also bear some examination, particularly as the concept of a hierarchy is involved with other properties. Why does there need to be a hierarchy at all in a classification? What exactly is shown in a hierarchical classification and what is the significance of the labelling of the subsets which make up the hierarchy?

There is a number of responses to this set of questions. Firstly, we might note from earlier discussions that there are many ways of classifying, not all of which require a family tree hierarchy. Indeed using the example of linguistics, we might say that such hierarchies which emphasize the process of divergence in a diachronic sense fail to recognize the significance of convergence processes. Secondly, as for comments on previous properties, the concept of a hierarchy begs the important and fundamental question as to the selection of attributes which define the classes within the hierarchy. Thirdly, we should recognize that not all hierarchical classifications are family tree classifications which have labelled levels as does the Linnaean model (class; family; species; etc.). Thus the methods of phenetic taxonomy in biology can be used to produce a hierarchy known as a dendrogram which is constructed on a purely numerical basis through the percentage of similarities of attributes at each level of the hierarchy. Finally, we might note that there is no necessity within a hierarchy for the groups formed within it to be labelled. In earlier comparisons of the approaches of MET and cladistics in biology, the point was made that the former, in relying upon measures of overall similarity within an evolutionary framework, had to resort to labelling of classes, like Reptilia in order to identify them. Cladistic approaches, which relied upon a single principle of evolutionary order of splitting, could dispense with such labels and recognize simply a system of nesting clades which trace the order of evolution.

The Nobes hierarchical classification is a labelled one; indeed, there are two dimensions of labelling. The first is that the levels of the hierarchy are labelled as in the Linnaean system (class; family; species), and the second is that the groups within the classification itself are labelled (e.g. "tax-based" and "law-based" at the "species" level).

As mentioned earlier, it is important to be clear as to the relationship between object and attribute in any classification: in the Nobes classification the objects are the accounting measurement practices of public companies in different countries and the attribute chosen to judge similarity and difference between those objects is a statistical abstraction (or statistical abstractions) based upon nine discriminating features of those measurement practices. Working up the hierarchy, groupings of these objects are obtained by classing them together successively on the basis of similarities in their attributes. Each successive

group is then labelled; we might then ask a question about the significance of these labels.

This issue of what interpretation to put on a label attached to a classification is a complex one and perhaps, the easiest solution is not to provide labels at all but simply to show a network of linkages between the objects in the classification (as is the case for a dendrogram in phenetic taxonomy) which is unlabelled. If, however, labels are to be used, then it is important that we are clear about which position we take as to their interpretation and that the terms used do, as far as is possible, capture the commonality implied by the attributes shared by the objects of the classification.

In classifications which are internationally oriented there is also another problem related to linguistic labels of groups which is of some significance. Indeed, the problem is not just related to the issue of labelling; it is related to the general issue of conceptualization in comparative studies. The starting point of classifications in international accounting is that we can recognize differences and resemblances of "accounting" in different countries; there is then an issue of how we are to express that recognition. The issue is, perhaps, most acute in trying to express the recognition of differences and similarities between cultures across the world, because we have to face the problem of cultural relativism. At one level cultural relativism would not appear to present a problem because our being able to recognize that another culture (or "accounting system") differs from our own in certain respects presupposes an ability on our part to gain access to that alien culture and recognize differences as differences. But in comparative social science the issue of the translatability of concepts used for the analysis of such differences between different cultures has proved to be more problematic. Winch (1970), for example, has argued that any attempt to use one set of cultural views to analyze another will lead to a breakdown of anthropological and sociological understanding. (Perhaps more relevant to the field of international accounting is the Gluckman-Bohannon debate in comparative law where there was some controversy about whether it was possible to use the concept of "the reasonable man" in analyzing African legal systems (Krislov, 1985).) The problem of cultural relativism and concept formation is one that continues to haunt cross-cultural researchers with some taking an "etic" framework (the idea that cultural differences can be expressed and understood from a perspective outside any particular culture) and others focusing on an "emic" orientation (the idea that cultures must be understood only in terms defined by those cultures) (Belkaoui, 1985). (It is clear, for example, that Gray (1988) is working within an etic framework for his classification of culture areas.) The relevance of this issue for the Nobes classification is that the use of labels like "pragmatic" or "uniform" have a significant cultural loading that may be important in our understanding of difference and similarity. Perhaps the lesson to be drawn here is that if such labels are to be used, then an explicit explanation of the sense of those terms is required.

A second dimension of labelling in the Nobes classification is the use of Linnaean terminology to describe the various levels of the hierarchy. First level groupings are labelled "species", second level groupings are "families" and so on. Although it is clear that these labels are simply used as indicators of successive levels of generalization, we might ask a question about the suitability of using terminology drawn from biology to indicate groupings in international accounting. The question can be illustrated by considering the term "species". In biology the term and its meaning has, over history, been subject to wide debate (Mayr, 1976) and a number of interpretations of it have been made. In the absence of a clear interpretation of the term from biology, it may then be inappropriate to use a label such as "species" in accounting classifications. But even if we wish to continue to use the label, we should be aware that in the post-Darwinian period, the term species has a specific evolutionary connotation. Insofar as the Nobes clas-sification does not reflect for all its groupings a diachronic dimension, it may be that the use of the term cannot be justified because of this connotation.

There is one final point about the use of set theory to provide criteria for the creation of classifications and this concerns the issue of "monotypic taxa". It sometimes occurs in evolutionary classifications in biology that a living thing (such as an aardvark) is the only member of the species, the genus, the family and the order in the Linnaean system. (In the Nobes classification, "Netherlands" and "Sweden" would be examples of monotypic taxa since they are the only members of species and family levels of the hierarchy.) Monotypic taxa within biology can then indicate, from an evolutionary perspective, the idea that some living things are far removed from others (Ruse, 1973). However, set theory would reject the concept of monotypic taxa since it violates the axiom of extensionality: the idea that classes having the same members are, in fact, the same class (Gregg, 1954). The impasse here for the Nobes classification is that in the case of Sweden and The Netherlands the species/family distinction collapses and this might beg the whole question as to whether such hierarchical levels are necessary within a classification. The way out of Gregg's paradox is, within biology, not to use extensional definitions of membership of different taxa but rather to use intensional definitions. This requires that the levels of family and species, etc., are defined by a set of properties necessary for membership of those levels rather than a list of the members of those levels. That is, instead of saying that the family which includes the "Netherlands" is defined by the fact that the "Netherlands" is a member of that family, we would say that the family is defined by a set of properties that would also be the properties that are possessed by the object the "Netherlands". However, this neat resolution relies on the idea that the number of properties which define the level "family" would be less than the number of properties which define the level "species" (but be included in the properties which define "species") and it is difficult to see how this might be done in the Nobes classification.

This review of set theory approaches to classification has indicated that they are defective in terms of their guidance to classifiers about a principle for attribute choice; it has also raised questions about the necessity or relevance of criteria for good classifications and has considered a number of issues which are raised by the attachment of labels to groupings in a taxonomy. The focus for these discussions has been the Nobes' hierarchical classification and it may be appropriate at this stage to consider another aspect of that classification: this concerns the claim to test a "hypothetical" classification using the methods of numerical taxonomy.

Nobes' approach to the creation and testing of his classification is a sophisticated one: earlier subjective classifications in international accounting are held to be defective because, *inter alia*, they do not meet the criteria for "good" classifications; statistical classifications are shown to rely on specious notions of objectivity. Nobes then marries the recognition that classifications must inevitably be subjective with an attempt to use numerical taxonomy to test a suggested classification which meets the criteria implied by set theory. At no point is there any claim for objectivity. The nine discriminating factors which provide the basis for the statistical abstractions which are the attributes of accounting measurement practices in different countries are carefully distinguished one from another and related to an earlier analysis of the causes and nature of difference in accounting internationally. The justification of the scoring of the nine factors is that although it is subjective, it is also "open" and thus checkable by other researchers. The whole approach emphasizes the importance of common sense, the tracing of causal influences, the judgement of what is trivial from that which is significant and the fitness of the classification to the purposes to which it might be put.

Given this emphasis, it does appear, at first sight, to be odd to characterize the proposed classification as a "hypothesis" which can then be "tested". The invocation of terms like these would appear to appeal to a spirit of objectivity: the proposed classification may be constructed subjectively but it seems that there might be something about it which is testable or verifiable. The curiosity of the approach is underlined by the fact that the scoring of the nine discriminating factors is subjective, although it is made clear it is open and so verifiable by other researchers. But in what sense is the classification (as opposed to the scoring of factors or the statistical manipulation of those scores) an hypothesis and how can it be tested?

We might first consider what the "hypothesis" is. Nobes (1984, p. 66) makes it clear that the classification itself is the hypothesis. The hypothetical classification is one which is "a testable suggestion about how various elements in a system fit together". This phrasing is not transparent in its meaning. As has been indicated earlier, the classification which is regarded as a hypothesis is of "Accounting Systems by Practice" whereas Fig. 1 indicates that the "tested" hypothesis is a classification of "Measurement Practices of Listed Companies in 14 Developed Countries in 1980." It is unlikely that, as a result of the testing, the hypothesis has changed in terms of what it is and we should therefore take the hypothesis as being that indicated in Fig. 1. The reference to "elements in a system" presumably refers to the idea that the classification is a "system" with the objects and groupings within the classification being the "elements". The notion of elements "fitting together" again, presumably, refers to the network of lines and branches which connect the objects and groupings within the classification. If these interpretations are correct, then it would appear that the hypothesis to be tested is the set of relationships (indicated by lines and branches) that hold between the objects and groupings of objects as indicated in Fig. 1.

We might now ask what it is that is signified by this set of relationships. The problem here is that there is no obvious relationship between the objects and the grouping of objects in the classification. The hybridity of the classification is such that, in part, it does indicate some relationship between certain objects (e.g. U.K. and U.S. influence) but, in other cases (e.g. "tax-based" and "law-based") all that seems to be indicated is a linkage based on similarities.

The distinction between relationship and similarity in taxonomy has attracted the attention of a number of writers in biology. Thus, de Queiroz (1988), following Griffiths (1974) and Ghiselin (1985), has, on the basis of the distinction, identified two kinds of taxonomic process. The first is that of *classification* where objects are ordered into classes so that classes are defined simply by the attributes which are shared by the members of them. Classification then proceeds on a recognition of similarities and differences between objects; there is no relationship between those objects which is posited. The second kind of taxonomy is called *systematization*; this involves the ordering of objects on the basis of there being some kind of relationship or process which links those objects together. In the case of biology this relationship or process is that of evolution. Evolution provides a principle or hypothesis upon which systematization can proceed. This hypothesis can then be tested. We might, for example, from the fossil record, hypothesize that birds and crocodiles are related through having a common ancestor. We could then test this hypothesis by examining the attributes that birds and crocodiles possess in common. Our confidence in the hypothesis can be confirmed or not by similarities discovered by that testing. Confidence in the general hypothesis of evolution can be further strengthened by testing for other (related) objects which can be used to support the specific hypothesis about birds and crocodiles.

Two points should be made about this approach in biological taxonomy. The first is that, as discussed earlier, we do not need to resort to ideas of "objectivity" in evolutionary taxonomies in order to justify them; we might just be attracted by the criteria of mutual support, clarity, coherence, simplicity and "right-ness of fit". But if we were to claim an objectivity about a systematization of living things based on evolutionary relationships, we would have to face an objection that evolution cannot be an hypothesis (theory). Popper (1974) for example, argued that evolution cannot be a scientific theory because it is not falsifiable; he suggested that it was a "metaphysical research programme" (p. 134). For taxonomic purposes, it matters not whether evolution is a theory or such a "research programme"; it does at least posit a relationship between objects which can be tested and, if confirmed through that testing, increase our confidence in the taxonomy suggested by that relationship.

We might now consider the use of terms like "hypothesis" and "testing" in relation to a taxonomy which is based not on relationships between objects but upon similarities between those objects. The issue posed here is simple: if the "hypothesis" of the classification is that certain objects are similar (e.g. accounting measurement practices in certain countries), how can it be that such similarity is to be "tested" by an appeal to similarity? If we just say that two objects are similar, it is difficult to see how any "evidence" can reject our recognition of that similarity. This is, perhaps, the force of Wittgenstein's injunction: "don't think, but look!" (1953, p. 31e). All we can do is recognize similarity, we cannot analyse it or test it; we have to take it as it is.

Now it might be objected that there may be different senses of the term "similarity". We might recognize, broadly, that, say, accounting measurement practices in certain countries have particular attributes in common; we might just look and recognize similarities without being able to articulate that recognition. We could then try to formalize that recognition by a review of the attributes which could go to make up similarity, to use, for example, statistical technique and abstraction which will express, in a parsimonious form, the heart of that recognition. This approach is one which underlies Nobes' methodology: statistical manipulation of attributes provides an *expression* of similarity. The taxonomy suggested is not built upon an hypothesis of relationship between objects which can then be tested; it is built, in the main, upon a recognition of similarities between objects which cannot be tested but simply expressed in a more formalized way.

There is one final gloss to this discussion about the role of "hypothesis" in accounting classifications and this concerns the issue of the objects of taxonomies. If we were to consider the notion of creating a taxonomy of "accounting systems", we might posit a classification based upon our recognition of similarities and differences. We might go on to say that there is a central attribute of such systems which is the attribute of how they deal with the problem of accounting measurement. We would hold a view that there is an essential "relationship" between how systems measure accounting variables and our conception of what such systems might be. If we can then show that a classification of accounting measurement practices mirrors our suggested classification of accounting systems, then we might have greater confidence in our view of that relationship.

But perhaps, before following through this line of thought, we need to provide some initial justification for this relationship, and this requirement, in turn, leads us to try to articulate what an accounting system might be deemed to be. In so doing we can relate our conceptions of accounting systems to the purposes to which their classification might be put.

Archetypal approaches

Throughout this paper, reference has been made to the concept of an accounting system and the fact that taxonomists in the international accounting field have tended to shy away from the concept, preferring instead to focus their classifications upon other objects. One final approach to the classificatory process recognizes this notion of "system". It is a variant of essentialist approaches and takes its inspiration from the idea that, in classifying a set of objects, the principle which should

guide attribute selection is not similarity or difference between those attributes *per se*, but similarities or differences in the relationship of those attributes (again, an attribute itself). The idea that objects might be composed, that, as it were, "primary" attributes might be internally related or structured, could then be used to provide the basis of a taxonomic scheme. In this case it is the structuring of objects which is identified as the essence of them. If the object is a "system", then we would need to have some view of how the elements of that system relate one to another and to the system as a whole and classify according to resemblance in the patterning of these relationships between one system and another.

The notion that objects to be classified are composed of interlocking elements which bear a relationship to each other and to the object as a whole has exercised a powerful influence upon thinkers in a number of disciplines. Within biology itself one pre-Darwinian taxonomist, Cuvier (1829), used the notion of "archetypes" to build a classification of living things (Pratt, 1976; Ridley, 1986). Living things, on this view, were constructed according to an "archetype" or plan and, therefore, in trying to classify them we should do so by reference to their fundamental organization. Such an approach, in pre-Darwinian times, fitted well with a theological perspective: living things were constructed in accordance with a Divine plan and classification was just a matter of elucidating the plan of nature that patterned life. Equally, if living organisms were constructed in line with some plan or plans, then each element or attribute of the organism had some role within the plan, it had some function within the whole (an echo of Aristotlian essentialism).

The themes of system, function and archetype have, however, found their most detailed exploration in sociology. Drawing on analogies with biological organisms (and, it must be added, originally with an evolutionary perspective), a number of writers in the discipline have viewed society as a mechanism or system made up of a number of interrelated components which function for the good of the whole. Although the evolutionary framework has long been jettisoned, the system–function relationship has been, and is being, developed (for example, Parsons, 1951; Münch, 1987). Parsonian theory would see society as a system which is itself composed of sub-systems. Each sub-system, each social institution, practice and process, fulfils some function within the whole which ensures that the social needs of individuals in society are met in some way. Some of the functions that these component parts perform are manifest, i.e. they are explicitly recognized by individuals as performing a particular function; others might be latent, i.e. people may not realize their function in meeting the needs of society. (Parsonian theory was explicitly used by Almond (1956) to provide a classificatory framework for comparative studies in politics.) Equally, the sociological analogue of an archetype has also been suggested in the term "ideal type", a term coined by Weber (1949). An ideal type is a concept, a heuristic device, which can be used to classify sets of objects; it is constructed out of our recognitions of those objects, an extrapolation as it were, in the abstract, of certain features of those objects. Thus, in economics, the concept of a "market economy" is an ideal type and it can be used, not as an hypothesis, but as a taxonomic aid, to view and order our perceptions of resemblance and divergence between national economies in different countries. And, of course, the construction of ideal types can be influenced by the purposes to which any classification upon which they are based are to be put (although this was not part of Weber's argument).

The idea of using ideal types (or "system-types") which provide abstractions of the functioning of different systems has recently been suggested by Krislov (1985) for use in classifying legal systems. It may be that such an approach holds promise for classification in international accounting as well. If it were pos-

sible to articulate some structural features of accounting in different countries which had particular significance for policy-makers (for example, the workings and processes of accounting institutions like government regulatory bodies or professional bodies; the nature of users of financial statements; feedback mechanisms) and which had some kind of functional significance for the way that accounting operated in those countries, it might be possible to construct idealized system-types which could provide the basis of taxonomic schemes. The workings of those system-types could then be revealed in the way that accounting was practised, the measurement and disclosure practices used. The articulation of system-types might be further used to examine how accounting systems (in an idealized form) intermesh with economic, legal and social systems and so reveal latent functions within society as a whole. Such an extension could well be of use to policy-makers who require a broader perspective than one which merely focuses on manifest, explicitly recognized, functions of accounting. Different models, different versions of system-types might require different conceptual constructs with which to fashion the structure of them and could be used to serve different purposes.

It is no argument to say that classifications based upon such approaches will be too nebulous and ungrounded. There is sufficient justification for them if they are coherent and of use to policy-makers. The threads of this paper have indicated, *inter alia*, that it is not necessary to ground or objectify classifications and, indeed, attempts to do so will falter on the rock of subjectivity implicit in the process of classifying. An accounting system may be anything we take it to be and our recognition of its whole, of the functioning of its component parts and attributes, can serve as a basis for useful classifications. As long as our conceptions are made explicit, we may debate and change them to fit our purposes.

SUMMARY AND CONCLUSIONS

This paper, after a brief review of past attempts to create taxonomies in international accounting, has considered a number of abstract issues concerned with the process of classification. The nature of the taxonomic process has been examined and the critical issue of attribute choice in classifications has been identified. It has been argued that classification is a way of viewing the world, a *Weltanschauung*, with the "truth" of classifications being relativized. From the recognition of this idea, it has been suggested that classifications should be created in line with their purposes. These purposes are not so much of description or comparison, which are either presupposed or part of the taxonomic process, but rather ones, in international accounting, of aiding policymakers who can use recognitions of similarity and difference in accounting between countries for developmental, harmonization and standardization reasons. In the context of previous classifications in international accounting it has been noted that a variety of objects have been chosen to be classified, objects which beg the question of how they might relate to an accounting system and classifications which beg the question of a principle for attribute choice.

A number of approaches to classification have been identified over history and across disciplines. Aristotlean essentialism which influenced Linnaean classifications in biology was seen to provide functionalist perceptions of the essence of objects, an approach which might have some significance for the development of accounting classifications. Overall similarity approaches which relied on statistical techniques were, it was argued, spurious in their attempts to provide objectivity in taxonomy, potentially misleading if statistical abstractions were reified, and circular in their claims to measure similarity. Diachronic approaches to classification were outlined in the fields of biology and linguistics and it was suggested that taxonomies in international accounting should not be founded on the example from

biology. It was proposed that in creating accounting taxonomies, we could and should develop our understanding of comparative accounting history and trace patterns of divergence and convergence over time. The example of the Nobes hierarchical classification was used to illustrate the significance of set theory approaches to classification. It was suggested that set theory, in the absence of a principle for attribute choice, does not provide criteria which are jointly necessary or sufficient for a "good" classification. The issue of labelling taxonomies has been explored and the issue, at a philosophical level, was argued to be a complex one without easy solution, a complexity underwritten by a linguistic relativity. The example of the Nobes classification was used to analyse the nature of a hypothesis in taxonomy. The general conclusion reached was that, following a distinction between the processes of classification and systematization, taxonomic hypotheses can only be constructed and tested on the basis of a posited relationship between objects in a taxonomy; classifications based on perceived similarities between objects cannot be tested. The similarities recognized between objects in a classification can only be expressed in the form of statistical abstractions. Finally, the approach to classification based on archetypes or ideal types has been sketched and, drawing on the example from sociology, it has been suggested that the construction of classifications in international accounting of accounting systems, which rely on the articulation of system-types, could prove to be a useful development of taxonomy in the discipline.

The process of classification is one aspect of "our craving for generality" (Wittgenstein, 1958, p. 17). In recognizing this craving we should also recognize that its satisfaction can be met in a myriad of possible classifications. In judging different taxonomic schemes, we do not have to indulge in methodologies which conjure up the spectre of objectivity; we can just develop criteria which reflect the purposes to which taxonomy might be put. Within this perspective we can ask classifiers to be explicit in their taxonomic principles and assumptions and to be bold, where the occasion demands. That boldness in terms of creating both synchronic and diachronic taxonomies can always be justified through the use to which those taxonomies can be put.

Implicit in much of the discussion in this paper has been a key question which the process of classification poses: what is accounting? If we are to proceed with the classification of the attributes of accounting in different countries, then it is clear that we should be explicit about the nature of the object "accounting" which is the focus of that classification. In this sense we should be aware that there is a danger of ethnocentrism in taking the object "accounting" at its face value. Classification, because it describes, imposes its own world view and sets up patterns of thinking, characterization and influence which may mislead and veil the nature of accounting in different countries. How far, for example, does the taxonomic process structure an imperialism in the way that we think about accounting? Does classification act as a brake upon the notion that accounting internationally is a seamless web of which we risk fracturing our understanding if we categorize? Can we ever adequately describe the patterns of diversity, similarity and change that constitute accounting? And if we do attempt to describe those patterns, do we just simply exercise our power over what is taken to be accounting?

BIBLIOGRAPHY

AAA, Report of the American Accounting Association Committee on International Accounting Operations and Education 1975–76, *The Accounting Review*, Supplement to Vol. 52 (1977).

Abizadeh, S. & Basilevsky, A., Socioeconomic Classification of Countries: a Maximum Likelihood Factor Analysis Technique, *Social Science Research* (1986).

Adelman, I. & Morris, C. T., Factor Analysis of the Interrelationships Between Social and Political Variables and Per Capita GNP, *Quarterly Journal of Economics* (1965).

Adelman, I. & Morris, C. T., *Society, Politics and Economic Development: A Quantitative Approach* (Baltimore, John Hopkins Press, 1967).

Al Najjar, F., Standardization in Accounting Practices: a Comparative International Study, *International Journal of Accounting* (1987).

Almond, G. A., Comparative Political Systems, *Journal of Politics* (1956).

Balme, D. M., Aristotle's Use of Differentiae, in Zoology, in S. Mansion (ed.) *Aristotle et les Problèmes de Méthode*, Louvain. (Revised version, 1975) in J. Barnes, M. Schofield and R. Sorabji (eds), *Articles on Aristotle 1, Science*, (London: Duckworth, 1961).

Balme, D. M., Aristotle's Use of Division and Differentiae, in A. Gotthelf and J. G. Lennox (eds), *Philosophical Issues in Aristotle's Biology* (Cambridge: Cambridge University Press, 1987).

Barnes, J., *Aristotle* (Oxford: Oxford University Press, 1982).

Belkaoui, A., *International Accounting: Issues and Solutions* (London: Quorum Books, 1985).

da Costa, R. C., Bourgeois, J. C. & Lawson, W. M., A Classification of International Financial Accounting Practices, *International Journal of Accounting* (Spring 1978).

Cuvier, G., *La Règne Animal*, nouvelle edition: Paris, (Trans., 1834, as *The Animal Kingdom*, London, G. Henderson, 1829).

Darwin, C., *The Origin of the Species* (1859), J. B. Barrow (ed.), (London: Penguin Books, 1968).

Dobzhansky, I., *Genetics and the Origin of the Species* (New York: Columbia University Press, 1937).

Flew, A., *Darwinian Evolution* (London: Granada Publishing Ltd, 1984).

Frank, W. G., An Empirical Analysis of International Accounting Principles, *Journal of Accounting Research* (Autumn 1979).

Ghiselin, M. T., Narrow Approaches to Phylogeny: A Review of Nine Books of Cladism, *Oxford Surveys of Evolutionary Biology I* (Oxford: Oxford University Press, 1985).

Goodman, N., *Languages of Art* (Indianapolis: Hackett Publishing Co., 1976).

CLASSIFICATION IN INTERNATIONAL ACCOUNTING   663

Goodman, N., *Ways of Worldmaking* (Indianapolis: Hackett Publishing Co., 1978).

Goodrich, P. S., A Typology of International Accounting Principles and Policies, *AUTA Review* (Spring 1982).

Goodrich, P. S., A Typology of International Accounting Principles and Policies: A Reply to a Comment, *AUTA Review* (Spring 1983).

Gray, S. J., Towards a Theory of Cultural Influence on the Development of Accounting Systems Internationally, *Abacus* (1988).

Gregg, J. R., *The Language of Taxonomy* (New York: Columbia University Press, 1954).

Griffiths, G. C. D., On the Foundations of Biological Systematics, *Acta Biotheoretica* (1974).

Hatfield, H. R., Some Variations in Accounting Practices in England, France, Germany and the United States, *Journal of Accounting Research* (Autumn 1966).

Hennig, W., *Phylogenetic Systematics* (Urbana: University of Illinois Press, 1966).

Hofstede, G., *Culture's Consequences* (Beverley Hills: Sage Publications, 1980).

Hofstede, G., Dimensions of National Cultures in Fifty Countries and Three Regions, in J. B. Deregowski, S. Dzuirawiec and R. Armis (eds), *Expiscations in Cross-Cultural Psychology* (Swets and Zeitlinger, 1983).

Johnson, L. A. S., Rainbow's End: the Quest for Optional Taxonomy, *Systematic Zoology* (1970).

Kalleberg, A. L., The Logic of Comparison: a Methodological Note on the Comparative study of Political Systems, *World Politics* (1966).

Krislov, S., The Concept of Families of Law, in A. Podgorecki, C. J. Whelan & D. Khosla (eds), *Legal Systems & Social Systems* (London: Croom Helm, 1985).

Kneen, W. R., Rogers, M. J. W. & Simpson, P., *Chemistry: Facts, Patterns & Principles*, (London: Addison-Wesley, 1972).

Kuhn, T. S., *The Structure of Scientific Revolutions*, 2nd edn. (Chicago: University of Chicago Press, 1970).

Lyons, J., *Language & Linguistics* (Cambridge: Cambridge University Press, 1981).

MacIntyre, A., Is a Science of Comparative Politics Possible? in A. Ryan (ed.), *The Philosophy of Social Explanation* (Oxford: Oxford University Press, 1978).

Mayr, E., *Principles of Systematic Zoology* (New York: McGraw Hill, 1969).

Mayr, E., Species Concepts & Definitions, in M. Grene & E. Mendelsohn (eds), *Topics in the Philosophy of Biology* (Boston: D. Reidel Publishing Co., 1976).

McComb, D., The International Harmonisation of Accounting: a Cultural Discussion, *International Journal of Accounting: Education & Research* (1979), reprinted in S. J. Gray (ed.), *International Accounting & Transnational Decisions* (London: Butterworths, 1979).

Mueller, G. G., *International Accounting* (London: Macmillan, 1967).

Mueller, G. G., Accounting Principles Generally Accepted in the United States Versus Those Generally Accepted Elsewhere, *International Journal of Accounting: Education & Research* (Spring 1968).

Münch, R., Parsonian Theory Today: In Search of a New Synthesis, in A. Giddens & J. Turner (eds), *Social Theory Today* (Oxford: Basil Blackwell, 1987).

Nair, R. D. & Frank, W. G., The Impact of Disclosure & Measurement Practices on International Accounting Classifications, *The Accounting Review* (July 1980).

Nelson, G., Ontogeny, Phylogeny, Palaeontology & the Biogenetic Law, *Systematic Zoology* (1978).

Nelson, G., Cladistic Analysis & Synthesis: Principles & Definitions with a Historical Note on Adamson's *Famille des Plantes* (1763–64), *Systematic Zoology* (1979).

Nelson, G. & Platnick, N. I., *Systematics & Biogeography* (New York: Colombia University Press, 1981).

Nelson, G. & Platnick, N. I., Systematics & Evolution, in M.-W. Ho & P. T. Saunders (eds), *Beyond Neo-Darwinism* (London: Academic Press, 1984).

Nobes, C. W., An Empirical Analysis of International Accounting Principles: a Comment, *Journal of Accounting Research* (Spring 1981).

Nobes, C. W., Book Review of F. D. S. Choi's *Multinational Accounting: A Research Framework for the Eighties*, *The Accounting Review* (Spring 1983).

Nobes, C. W., *International Classification of Financial Reporting* (London: Croom Helm, 1984).

Nobes, C. W., Classification of Financial Reporting Practices, in *Advances in International Accounting* (JAI Press Inc., 1987).

Parsons, T., *The Social System* (Glencoe, IL: Free Press, 1951).

Patterson, C., Cladistics, *Biologist* (1980).

Platnick, N. I., Philosophy & The Transformation of Cladistics, *Systematic Zoology* (1979).

Platnick, N. I., Defining Characters & Evolutionary Groups, *Systematic Zoology* (1982).

Popper, K., An Intellectual Autobiography, in P. A. Schilpp (ed.), *The Philosophy of K. R. Popper, 2 vols.*, (La Salla, IL: Open Court 1974). Later published and reprinted as *Unended Quest*, (London: Fontana Collins).

Pratt, V., Biological Classifications, in M. Grene & E. Mendelsohn (eds), *Topics in the Philosophy of Biology* (Boston: D. Reidel Publishing Co., 1976).

Price Waterhouse, *Accounting Principles & Reporting Practices: A Survey in 38 Countries* (London: ICAEW, 1973).

Price Waterhouse, *Accounting Principles & Reporting Practices: A Survey in 46 Countries* (London: ICAEW, 1975).

Price Waterhouse, *International Survey of Accounting Principles & Reporting Practices* (London: Butterworths, 1979).

de Queiroz, K., Systematics & the Darwinian Revolution, *Philosophy of Science* (1988).

Ram, R., Composite Indices of Physical Quality of Life, Basic Needs Fulfillment & Income: a Principal Component Representation, *Journal of Development Economics* (1982).

Renfrew, C., *Archaeology & Language: The Puzzle of Indo-European Origins* (London: Johnathan Cape, 1987).

Ridley, M., *The Problems of Evolution* (Oxford: Oxford University Press, 1985).

Ridley, M., *Evolution & Classification: The Reformation of Cladism* (Harlow: Longmans, 1986).

Rieppel, O., Atomism, Transformism & the Fossil Record, *Zoological Journal of the Linnaean Society* (1984).

Ruse, M., *The Philosophy of Biology* (London: Hutchinson, 1973).

Saussure, F. de, *Cours de Linguistique Génèrale* (Lausanne: Payot, 1916).

Seidler, L. J., International Accounting — The Ultimate Theory Course, *The Accounting Review* (October 1967).

Shoenthal, E. R., Classification of Accounting Systems using Competencies as a Discriminating Variable: a Great Britain–United States Study, *Journal of Business Finance and Accounting* (1989).

Simpson, G. G., *Principles of Animal Taxonomy* (New York: Colombia University Press, 1961).

Smelser, N. J., *Comparative Methods in the Social Sciences* (New Jersey: Prentice-Hall, 1972).

Smith, C. H. & Shalchi, H., Multinational Accounting: Some Methodological Considerations, in F. D. S. Choi (ed.), *Multinational Accounting: A Research Framework for the Eighties* (Ann Arbor.: UMI Research Press, 1981).

Sohal, R. R. & Sneath, P. H. A., *The Principles of Numerical Taxonomy* (San Francisco: W. H. Freeman, 1963).

Waddington, J., *Aristotle's Metaphysics* (London: J. M. Dent & Sons Ltd., 1956).

Weber, M., *The Methodology of the Social Sciences* (New York: The Free Press, 1949).

Winch, P., *The Idea of a Social Science* (London: Routledge & Kegan Paul, 1970).

Wittgenstein, L., *Philosophical Investigations* (Oxford: Basil Blackwell, 1953).

Wittgenstein, L., *The Blue & Brown Books* (Oxford: Basil Blackwell, 1958).

Zweigert, K. & Kötz, H., *An Introduction to Comparative Law* (Amsterdam: North Holland Publishing Co., 1977).

[12]

The European Accounting Review 2001, **10:1**, 133–147

Accounting in Europe

European languages of account

R.H. Parker
University of Exeter

ABSTRACT

Choice of 'language of account' is not a trivial decision for many European companies. This exploratory paper examines this choice, distinguishing between official, statistically dominant and socio-politically dominant languages; dominant and minority languages; and local and foreign languages. The paper concludes with a discussion of the dominant foreign language of account in the early twenty-first century (English) in its British, American and (possibly) 'international' varieties; with the ways in which accounting English is disseminated; and resistance to its use in some countries.

1. INTRODUCTION

Without language, writing materials, numerals and aids to calculation, accounting could only exist in the most primitive form (Parker, 1989b). All are practical necessities, but language at least is more than this. The choice of a language of account, even when made unconsciously, is not neutral. Accountants live and work in a world of many languages and few countries are completely monolingual. This is true even of the UK and France despite the efforts of their rulers for several centuries and superficial appearances to the contrary. There are thus many languages of account, some of which (e.g. English and French), in part because of their role as instruments of political, economic and cultural imperialism, may (wrongly) be thought inherently superior for the task. Choice of a language of account, if unconstrained, may be used to signify belonging as well as to communicate data. But language choice is seldom completely voluntary: it may be imposed by regulation or by the market. If somebody else's language is thus imposed, this may provide access to a wider world but may also cut off an accountant from other theories and practices (contrast, for example, the experi-

---

Address for correspondence
School of Business and Economics, University of Exeter, Streatham Court, Exeter EX4 4PU, UK

ISSN 0963-8180 print/1468-4497 online   DOI: 10.1080/09638180020017087
Published by Routledge Journals, Taylor & Francis Ltd on behalf of the EAA

ences of English and French accountants in Africa) and from their own culture. Translation may be necessary from a 'minor' to a 'major' language of account, giving scope for misunderstandings as well as spreading information. Not all accountants may be willing to acknowledge their own language to be minor. In the present paper these themes are developed with reference to European companies.

In what language or languages do European companies publish their financial statements?

There are several possibilities (cf. Calvet, 1987: Ch. 3):

1   the language which is dominant statistically (i.e. spoken by the most people);
2   the language which is dominant socio-politically (i.e. the language spoken by the social and political elite);
3   the official language (i.e. the language used in government);
4   a foreign language (e.g. American or British English, French).

Table 1, based on Alexander and Archer's *European Accounting Guide* (1998), sets out what are there stated to be the official languages of the Member States of the European Union (EU), two other Member States of the European Economic Area (Iceland and Norway), and Switzerland.

In many European countries there is one language which is not only the official language but is also both statistically dominant and socio-politically dominant. This is so for Austria, Denmark, France, Germany, Greece, Italy, the Netherlands, Portugal, Sweden, Iceland and Norway. The remaining countries (Belgium,

Table 1 Official languages of European countries

Austria	German
Belgium	Dutch, French, German
Denmark	Danish
Finland	Finnish, Swedish
France	French
Germany	German
Greece	Greek
Italy	Italian
Luxembourg	French, German, Luxembourgish
Netherlands	Dutch
Portugal	Portuguese
Republic of Ireland	Irish, English
Spain	Spanish, Catalan (in Catalonia), Basque (in Basque Country), Galician (in Galicia)
Sweden	Swedish
UK	English, Welsh (in Wales)
Iceland	Icelandic
Norway	Norwegian
Switzerland	German, French, Italian

Source: Alexander and Archer (1998).

Finland, Luxembourg, Ireland, Spain, the UK and Switzerland) are more complicated linguistically. In Spain and the UK one language is statistically and socio-politically dominant at the national level but another language or languages has official recognition within particular autonomous or semi-autonomous regions. In Spain Catalan, Basque and Galician are so recognized; in the UK Welsh is so recognized. Note, however, that Breton is not recognized as an official language in France.

In the five remaining countries in Table 1, no one language is socio-politically dominant at the national level. Belgium has two languages (Dutch and French) which are both statistically and socio-politically dominant within their own regions. Before the Second World War French was dominant socio-politically at the national level, reflecting the then relative economic strength of Wallonia as against Flanders. Switzerland is superficially similar in that German, French and Italian are statistically and socio-politically dominant within their own regions, but German (in its spoken form Swiss German rather than High German) is dominant statistically taking the country as a whole. As is well known, Belgium is constantly at war with itself linguistically whereas Switzerland is not. In Finland, Finnish is the statistically dominant language but shares socio-political status with Swedish. In Luxembourg, French and German are the socio-politically dominant languages but the statistically dominant language is Luxembourgish. In Ireland, English is the statistically dominant language, but Irish has a ceremonial and symbolic role.

2. LANGUAGES OF ACCOUNT

A language of account may be defined as a language in which accounting records are commonly kept and financial statements drawn up and for which a vocabulary of 'words of account' exists.

Can any language become a language of account? Linguists are agreed that all languages can be made to serve any purpose if the need arises. This conclusion, perhaps surprising to some speakers of major European languages, is based on the following arguments (e.g. Harlow, 1998). All languages have a grammar. If a language currently lacks words to discuss a particular technical subject (e.g. accounting) it can borrow them from other languages or develop them from its own resources (as guardians of the 'purity' of a language may prefer). Thus any technical subject can be discussed in any language if that language adapts. Objectively, there is no 'best' language. What is regarded as best changes over time. For example, Greek was regarded as better than Latin; later Latin was regarded as better than English; later still English was regarded as better than, say, Maori.

Some languages may be dominant over others but dominance is better explained in terms of statistical and socio-political than linguistic factors. Calvet (1987: 249–51), for example, explains both the expansion and the fallback of the French language as due to three main factors: until the nineteenth century

French was the language in Europe spoken by the greatest number of people as their first language; until the nineteenth century much of Europe was divided into small rather undemocratic kingdoms whose elites preferred to speak French rather than a 'national' language; France was the most powerful country in Europe economically and politically and its literature the best known. In the twentieth century, when comparisons must be made worldwide rather than just within Europe, the number of persons speaking French as a first language has been overtaken by the number of persons speaking English as a first language; national languages have greatly increased in prestige; economic and political power has passed to English-speaking countries (first the UK, then the USA).

The borrowing of accounting words from other languages can be illustrated by the history of English accounting terminology. In medieval England the most common language of account – at least for governmental, ecclesiastical and manorial purposes – was Latin. English did not become established as the dominant language of account until the sixteenth century. As late as 1586 George Pettie complained (in a non-accounting context) that:

> There are some others yet who wyll set lyght by my labours, because I write in Englysh...they count [our Tongue] barren, they count it barbarous, they count it unworthy to be accounted of.
>
> (Quoted in Baugh and Cable, 1978: 206)

English was sufficiently dominant by this date, however, for the sixteenth-century texts on double entry to be written in that language, although the relative unimportance of English as a world language of accounting is demonstrated by the heavy reliance on Italian and Dutch texts and words as sources. The oldest surviving text on double entry in English (Ympyn's *New Instruction* of 1543) is a translation into English of a translation into French of a text originally written in Dutch. The English language in general has borrowed massively from French, Latin and Greek, significantly from other European languages (notably Italian in an accounting context) and in varying degrees from every other language with which it has come into contact. Such borrowings were explicitly recognized by Roger North in the 'Short and Easy Vocabulary of Certain Words, that in the Language of Accompting take a Particular Meaning', appended to his book *The Gentleman Accomptant* (1714). Words that he recognized as borrowed from Italian include cash, debtor, creditor, imprests, nett, posting and premio (Parker, 1997: 43). In more recent centuries 'just-in-time' and 'target costing' have been borrowed (and translated) from Japanese, and a number of new terms borrowed from French or German (e.g. 'provisions for liabilities and charges') were introduced by the English version of the EU Fourth Directive.

It is not only English which has borrowed words of account. Latin was Europe's principal language of account until the sixteenth century and from it languages such as English, French and Italian have borrowed directly or indirectly words such as receipt (Lat. *receptus*, Fr. *recette*, It. *ricevuto*), account (Lat. *compotus*, Fr. *compte*, It. *conto*), and debt (Lat. *debita*, Fr. *dette*, It. *debito*).

Several European languages have borrowed from French the terms *actif* and *passif* as general headings to a two-sided balance sheet. Scrutiny of the local language versions of the financial statements in the *European Accounting Guide* produces the following:

German	*aktiva, passiva*
Dutch	*activa, passiva*
Danish	*aktiver, passiver*
Italian	*attivo, passivo*
Portuguese	*activo, passivo*
Spanish	*activo, pasivo*
Polish	*aktywa, pasywa*

Notable absentees from this list are English and the Scandinavian languages other than Danish. The distribution is probably influenced by the boundaries of the Napoleonic Empire.

French is an example of a language which has preferred to generate new accounting words from its own resources. In particular in recent years English terms have often been translated rather than borrowed (e.g. *impôts différés* for 'deferred taxation') or replaced by neologisms (e.g. *ordinateur* for 'computer', *logiciel* for 'software'). An exception is *mercatique*, which has not replaced the English borrowing *marketing*. There has been less difficulty in adopting English terms, such as *audit* and *management*, which sound as if they have French or Latin origins. *Consolidation* is a slightly different example. Corre (1969) pointed out that *agrégation* would be more appropriate in French than *consolidation*, but in later editions omits this comment.

3. MINORITY LANGUAGES OF ACCOUNT

Minority languages may be defined as those with a relatively small number of speakers living within the domain of a much more widely spoken language, a command of which is generally felt necessary for the pursuit of a full economic and social life. These languages may not be languages of account. Breton is a possible example. Some minority languages, however, have a long history as languages of account. For example, accounting records in Catalan survive from the fourteenth century (Antoni, 1970).

Three examples of minority languages within the British Isles are Scottish Gaelic, Welsh and Irish. Their roles as languages of account are interestingly different. Scottish Gaelic appears not to be used as a language of account; Welsh to have established itself as a language of account; and Irish to be only ceremonially a language of account.

Welsh has become a language of account mainly by borrowing its accounting vocabulary from English. An analysis of Garrod's (1992) Welsh–English dictionary of accounting terms (*Termau Cyfrifeg*) suggests that Welsh borrowings from English (with appropriate changes in spelling and pronunciation) include:

amortization, appreciation, asset, bank, bill, bond, bonus, contra, cost, credit, creditor, data, debit, debtor, depreciation, dividend, equity, imprest, income, lease, par, patent, portfolio, premium, price, prospectus, risk, stock. It is possible that some of these borrowings owe more to Garrod than to everyday use. For example, Fuller-Love (1998: 271–2) cites three different Welsh expressions for the English term 'work in progress'. Most (but not all) of these words were borrowed by English from Latin, Italian and French. Some are included in North's 'vocabulary' of 1714.

Irish illustrates that although all languages are potential languages of account this does not mean that they will become so in practice, even if the national language academies and dictionary-makers provide the terms. The perceived costs may outweigh the perceived benefits. Hindley's (1990: 217) statement about Irish is probably true of other languages as well:

> Lack of modern technical vocabulary in Irish is often cited as a reason why people in 'practical' occupations turn from Irish. This is unjustified, for adequate vocabulary is constantly created.... Nevertheless [specialist vocabularies] are not owned or used by most native speakers, who get their English technical vocabulary through normal work channels and just 'pick them up on the job'. The Irish terms exist but are not familiar to ordinary people, who are far more likely (for basically economic reasons) to encounter their English equivalents.

Why, then, do some speakers of minority languages believe that their language deserves to be a language of account? Part of the answer is that language is about belonging as well as communicating. All use of language concerns communication but what is communicated may be more than facts about, say, accounting. By choosing one language or one variety of a language rather than another a person may communicate that he or she belongs to a particular community – a socio-political elite, a professional elite, a group opposed to existing elites.

Within the UK the language of the socio-political and professional elites is English, so to keep accounts in another language, especially if that language currently lacks an established accounting vocabulary and the accountant is bilingual, requires a conscious identification with a non-English-speaking community. Such appears to be the case with accounts in Welsh. Fuller-Love (1998: 272–3) reports that most organizations publishing financial statements in Welsh do so either because they operate in a Welsh language environment (e.g. in the media or in agriculture) or because they are public bodies obliged to do so by law. But, the law aside, factual accounting communication could just as easily – in the beginning at least, more easily – be achieved by using English. Thus, the use of Welsh as a language of account by some Welsh private companies may be partly as means of communication among Welsh speakers but also contains an element of 'belonging', of solidarity with the use of Welsh in other contexts. This is partly a reaction to the suppression of Welsh in the past (e.g. Wardhaugh, 1987: Ch. 4), although in the twentieth century there have been numerous regulations aimed at encouraging Welsh in education. The Welsh Language Act of 1993 gave equal validity to Welsh and English in the public sector. The Companies Act 1976 introduced the concept of Welsh companies which could file accounts in Welsh together with a certified translation into English. From 1992 a private company whose registered office is in Wales may file accounts in Welsh without a translation. Companies House (which is in the Welsh capital, Cardiff) will then arrange a translation at no cost to the company. Up to 200 companies file accounts in Welsh only, notably S4C, the Welsh-language television channel (Fuller-Love, 1998).

The advance of Welsh as a language of account has not been mirrored by Breton. The Ordinance of Villers-Cotterêts of 15 August 1539 aimed to replace Latin with French as the language of the law in France. For the many people in France who spoke languages such as Breton and Occitan it changed the law from one inaccessible language to another. In the 1790s the use of French rather than other languages was strongly encouraged by the politicians and administrators of the Revolution (especially the Jacobins). During the Third Republic, the school laws of Jules Ferry absolutely prohibited from 1886 the use of any other language than French for purposes of instruction in France. The law was not changed until 1951. But Breton and other languages are still tolerated only as regional languages, 'part of the colorful folklore of France'. They are not regarded as languages of civilization and education – or of account (Kuter, 1989: 87). The European Charter for Regional or Minority Languages adopted by the Council of Europe in 1992 has caused great controversy in France. The Constitutional Council ruled in 1996 that it was incompatible with the statement in Article 2 of the Constitution of 1958 that 'the language of the Republic is French'. France signed the Charter in 1999 with many reservations but ratification is by no means certain. The French State's opposition to the recognition of the minority languages within its borders detracts from the credibility of its resistance to languages from outside its borders.

4. MULTIPLE AND FOREIGN LANGUAGES OF ACCOUNT

Companies in multilingual countries sometimes publish their financial statements in more than one language. Some domestic Belgian companies, for example, publish statements in both French and Flemish; some Finnish companies in both Finnish and Swedish; some Luxembourg companies in both French and German (but not in Luxembourgish, the statistically dominant language); some Welsh companies in Welsh and English.

There is no reason why a domestic company should publish its accounts in a foreign language, i.e. one which although it may be widely understood is not native to the country concerned. Multinational companies, however, often publish in foreign as well as local languages, particularly if they wish to raise finance abroad. Table 2 provides some data on multiple reporting languages in continental European annual reports.

Some multinationals go even further and keep accounting records in a foreign language. Multinational companies based in countries in which, in global terms, a

Table 2 Reporting languages in continental European annual reports

Number of companies choosing as a secondary reporting language		
	English	42
	French	12
	German	6
	Spanish	4
	Italian	2
	Portuguese	1
	Swedish	1

Note: Sample consists of 42 positive responses to a request for annual reports.
Source: Calculated from Archer and McLeay (1989: Appendix).

minority language is spoken, e.g. Swedish, 'a small speech community on the periphery of Europe' (Hollqvist, 1984: 18–19, 143) may decide to keep accounting records in English, a language more likely to be familiar to their managers throughout the world, in order to communicate and compete internationally. English-speaking multinationals often use English to communicate to the rest of the world (Inman, 1978, cited in Hollqvist, 1984). The Swedish company SKF moved to English as the company's internal language worldwide in 1966 (Tugendhat, 1973: 147, 238); English is the language of the Dutch company Philips (Loonen, 1996: 6); English is not regarded as a foreign language at Sony (Japanese) or at Asea Brown Boveri (Swiss–Swedish) (Newman, 1996: 18).

5. WHOSE ENGLISH?

The foreign language most used in translations of financial statements and in accounting records is English. The question then arises: whose English? There are many varieties of English but in a European accounting context only British, US and, possibly, 'international' English are relevant. Whether or not there is an international accounting English in the sense that there is an international aviation English is a question for future research and is not discussed in the present paper.

Table 3 compares the accounting vocabulary of the English-language versions of the company financial statements in the *European Accounting Guide*, of the English-language versions of the EU Fourth and Seventh Directives, and of international accounting standards. It is possible of course that the English accounting terms in the table are not representative of the countries concerned.

The first interesting thing about this table is that it is possible to construct it. Almost all the country entries (except the UK and Ireland, of course) have been taken from translations made by companies who have thought it worthwhile to make them. Second, US English appears to be more popular than British English, although this may be because, apart from the term 'reserves' (for which close analogues exist in the Romance languages and in Dutch), the IASs use US not British terms. The choice between 'sales' and 'turnover' is especially interesting.

Table 3 British versus US English in Europe

Austria	inventories	accounts receivable	sales	reserves
Belgium	inventories	accounts receivable	sales	retained earnings
Denmark	stocks	debtors	turnover	reserves
Finland	stocks	debtors	turnover	reserves
France	inventories	current receivables	sales	reserves
Germany	inventories	accounts receivable	sales	reserves
Greece	inventories	debtors	turnover	reserves
Italy	inventories	receivables	sales	reserves
Netherlands	inventories	receivables	sales	reserves
Portugal	stocks	debtors	sales	reserves
Republic of Ireland	stocks	debtors	turnover	reserves
Spain	inventories	accounts receivable	sales	reserves
Sweden	inventories	accounts receivable	sales	reserves
UK	stocks	debtors	sales	reserves
Iceland	inventories	receivables	sales	other owners' equity
Norway	inventories	receivables	sales	reserves
Switzerland	inventories	accounts receivable	sales	reserves/surplus
4th and 7th Directives	stocks	debtors	turnover	reserves
IAS	inventories	receivables	sales	surplus/reserves

In the UK, unlike the US, 'turnover' (the term used in company legislation) is a synonym for 'sales'. The French equivalents of the UK terms are *chiffre d'affaires* and *ventes*. Note, however, that both the UK and the French companies prefer 'sales' to 'turnover'. Furthermore, the French company prefers US 'inventories' to UK 'stocks' even though the French word is *stocks*.

There can be considerable problems and difficulties in translating accounting terms (Archer and McLeay, 1991). Nobes (1993) provides an illustration of this in his discussion of the translation of the UK and Irish concept of a 'true and fair view' into the legislation of the other EU Member States. The financial statements in the *European Accounting Guide* provide an opportunity to look at how these terms have been translated back into English. The auditors' reports show that most companies have translated the terms (presumably with the agreement of the auditors concerned) as 'give a true and fair view', although the French company prefers 'present an accurate picture', and the Greek, Portuguese, Spanish and Norwegian companies prefer the US phrase 'present fairly'. The auditors' reports of the Swedish and Swiss companies make no reference to a true and fair view in either the source language or the English translation.

Speakers of English in all European countries may consider that they are entitled to 'appropriate' English accounting terminology, i.e. to modify it without reference to the original native speakers' claim of 'ownership'. For example, a German accountant writing in English in a French journal coined the happy phrase 'soft transformation' to describe the way in which the provisions of the EU

Fourth Directive were implemented in German legislation (Ordelheide, 1990). Increasingly, for speakers of 'Euro-English', the English language has become an 'open reservoir' (Carstensen, 1986), a 'language of the world, available to any country that uses it – not merely to fulfil linguistic needs but also to be used as a symbolic resource' (Cheshire and Moser, 1994: 469).

Does this mean that English as a language of account will break up into mutually incomprehensible dialects? In a wider context McArthur (1998: Ch. 8) refers to this as 'the Latin analogy' but quotes Görlach (1995: vii) as arguing that:

> New factors of electronic communication and air travel are likely to prevent the fracturing of English into mutually incomprehensible languages. Locally divergent forms of English may drift off into separate languages, but the core of English is likely to remain a varied, diversified, but recognizably 'same' language.

Modern technology means that the world's English-speaking accountants are constantly in touch with each other. Accounting terminology will change everywhere, and not always in the same way, but it seems highly unlikely that, say, US and British accounting English will become much more different from each other than they are now (which is quite a lot: see Nobes and Parker, 2000: Ch. 7.4). British and US terminology will continue to spread to other countries through the influence of professional qualifications and accounting literature (see next section).

Accounting is part of a wider world in which the monolingual nation state is under attack both from globalization and localization. English as a language of account is being affected by both. At one extreme it is increasingly the language in which multinational companies keep accounting records and publish financial statements. At the other extreme companies in one part of the UK have been given the right to file financial statements in Welsh without themselves providing an English translation. But at the first extreme it is US English which triumphs, and at the second it is UK English that gives way.

6. PROFESSIONAL QUALIFICATIONS AND ACCOUNTING LITERATURE

The major incentive to translation of financial statements into English is no doubt the dominance of that language in international capital markets, but the use of English is reinforced if English is the language in which the non-English accountant has learned to keep accounts. Preparers of accounts are likely to prefer the language in which they have been taught to keep accounts. Some countries rely wholly or partly on institutions in other countries to provide such a training.

The most accessible professional accounting qualifications worldwide today are those of two UK accountancy bodies: the Association of Chartered Certified Accountants (ACCA) and the Chartered Institute of Management Accountants (CIMA). Johnson and Caygill (1971) and Parker (1989a) have shown how these accountancy bodies, unable to challenge the supremacy of English and Scottish chartered accountants in the UK, deliberately sought to expand overseas. Such expansion was easiest not in Canada, Australia or New Zealand, where settlers of mainly British descent were establishing their own professional bodies, but in those parts of the British Empire under colonial rule. These were countries in which only a small elite spoke English, which was socio-politically but not statistically dominant. Briston and Kedslie (1997) show that, despite the demise of the British Empire, there has been a marked increase since the 1980s in the export of accounting qualifications by ACCA and CIMA. In 1995, 38.6% of ACCA's membership and 22.6% of CIMA's membership was outside the UK. Their membership was particularly strong in countries such as Malaysia, Singapore and Hong Kong, where formal links have been forged with local professional bodies.

Since the late 1980s, the ACCA has expanded into Central and Eastern Europe (Focus, 2000), sensing that 'there was a significant potential for ACCA to promote its own examinations to a new and well educated market eager to acquire internationally recognised qualifications'. The demand arose in part from the needs of the international accounting firms and multinational companies to recruit accounting and finance personnel trained in Western accounting practices. Examinations are in English, based on international accounting and auditing practices. ACCA sees it as a challenge for the future to offer testing in languages other than English.

With the end of Empire it might be thought that the UK bodies would face competition from the US. This has not happened because of the differences between the UK and US models of professional accountancy. In the US the right to practise public accountancy depends upon a licensing authority (normally one of the states) rather than membership of a professional body, thus creating for non-US citizens the barrier of a home-based licensing authority (Seidler, 1969: 44). US English has been spread not through the availability of professional qualifications but through the provision of an extensive accounting literature, which is easily accessible – once, of course, the local accountant has learned English. The international accounting firms are mainly of British and US origin, but probably perceived in most countries outside the UK as US rather than British.

Professional qualifications and accounting literature have combined to reinforce the dominance throughout much of the world of English as a language of account. This dominance has been much less marked, however, in continental Europe (at least until recently) and in the former French colonial empire. This is mainly due to the popularity of that very un-British, un-American form of accounting, the national accounting plan. The history of such plans has been well documented by Standish (1990) and by Richard (1995a, 1995b). Standish (1997: 273–6) claims that the terminology of the PCG (*plan comptable général*, national accounting plan) as to its charts of accounts, rules and recommendations for the functioning of accounts, and model formats for information outputs, has in effect created a national accounting language, and that the *Conseil national de la comptabilité* (National Accounting Council) plays a comparable role to the Académie Française. Countries wishing to operate a national accounting plan will find a helpful literature in French but not in English.

7. RESISTING ENGLISH

Despite the above, it remains true that the overwhelming majority of companies in countries in which English is not an official language do *not* produce financial statements in English. These include purely domestic companies in countries such as Germany and Spain. They do not need to use English if they do not raise money on the international capital market. Less powerful countries, however, and especially those which are used as tax havens, may allow foreign companies to use English. In the Netherlands foreign companies may file financial statements in Dutch, English, French or German; in Luxembourg, the stock exchange accepts financial statements in English as well as in French and German (Clark, 1994: 113).

France is the best-known country in which there has been resistance to the encroachment of accounting English. This is, of course, part of a more general concern at competition from English, especially American English. This concern has resulted in legislation, although it has not always been fully complied with. For example, the Loi Bas-Lauriol of 31 December 1975 prescribed that French must be used when describing, offering or presenting goods or services for sale, in describing their use, defining their guarantee, in any advertising, written or oral, and also in invoices and receipts (Thody, 1995: 10–11). There have been several other such laws and decrees (Calvet, 1987: 257–8), particularly the Loi Toubon of 4 August 1994. A *Dictionnaire des termes officiels de la langue française* was published in 1994 (Thody, 1995: 21).

A ministerial Commission of Economic and Financial Terminology was created in 1985 and has produced lists of French terms to be used in place of American English terms. Some examples are: *cession-bail* for lease back; *coefficient de capitalisation des résultats* for price–earnings ratio; *coentreprise* for joint venture; *dernier entré, premier sorti* for last-in, first out; *écart d'acquisition* for goodwill on acquisition; *marge brute d'autofinancement* for cash flow; *titrisation* for securitization. The imposition by regulation of the *plan comptable général* has helped to ensure the dominance of French as the language of the accounts of individual enterprises in France, as has also the close links between taxation and accounting. This means that Breton, unlike Welsh and Irish, faces a standardized national accounting vocabulary.

Hoarau (1995) has protested that solutions arrived at internationally by predominantly English-speaking accountants may be inappropriate in a French context. It can, of course, be counter-argued that these solutions are the appropriate ones for French-based multinationals in international capital markets and that they need not affect domestic French accounting, especially for individual enterprises as distinct from groups (Nobes, 1995).

Speakers of dominated languages are always likely to feel oppressed by speakers of dominant languages and more especially if a previously dominant language loses ground against others. Perhaps in a Europe in which French not English was the dominant language of account, the *European Accounting Review* would be published in French and British accountants would happily borrow accounting terms from French. As Shakespeare might have written: 'What's in a name? That which we call *cash flow* by any other name would smell as sweet'.

8. SUMMARY AND CONCLUSIONS

This paper represents a preliminary and exploratory survey of the choice of languages of account by European companies. It is argued that all languages in Europe are potentially languages in which accounts can be kept, and that the reason for the dominance of some languages (e.g. English and French) is socio-political not linguistic. The main themes of the paper have been the increasing dominance of English (but US English rather than British English and thus to some extent a foreign language to *all* European accountants); and, at the other end of the spectrum, the development of some minority languages (e.g. Welsh) but not others (e.g. Breton) as languages of account.

There are several directions in which research into accounting and language could be pursued more deeply than has been attempted here. Collaborative research between accountants and linguists would be especially useful, perhaps taking the form mainly of surveys and case studies. The suggestions given below are not intended to be exhaustive.

In multilingual countries empirical research is needed to establish in what languages accounting records are kept and financial statements prepared. For example, a comparative study of account keeping in, say, Welsh, Irish, Catalan and Breton would throw light on the extent to which devolution, decentralization and the gaining of independence has had an impact on the relatively private act of keeping accounts and the more public act of filing them with a state authority. Similarly, a comparative study of published financial statements in Belgium and Switzerland would demonstrate the effects of language diversity in countries where no one language is dominant.

What reporting languages are currently used by continental European companies? The research of Archer and McLeay (published in 1989 but carried out several years before) badly needs updating. Case studies are needed of the translation of financial statements. A comparative study of the attitudes of French and German legislators and accountants to the introduction of English-language accounting terms would also be useful.

Another area of research is accounting terminology. To what extent have the languages of Europe directly borrowed their accounting terms, acquired them by translation, or developed their own? Has the adoption of other people's terms (e.g. English 'consolidation', French '*actif*' and '*passif*') also meant acceptance of their concepts and practices? How does the International Accounting Standards Committee choose its terminology?

Finally, this paper has deliberately not discussed the idea that accounting itself is a language. This is an area of research where the concepts of linguistics could most fruitfully be applied.

REFERENCES

Alexander, D. and Archer, S. (1998) *European Accounting Guide*. San Diego: Harcourt Brace.
Antoni, T. (1970) 'Il "Lou dels Pizans' del 1303"', *Bolletino Storico Pisano*, 39.
Archer, S. and McLeay, S. (1989) 'Financial reporting by interlisted European companies: issues in transnational disclosure', in Hopwood, A. G. (ed.) *International Pressures for Accounting Change*. London: Prentice Hall.
Archer, S. and McLeay, S. (1991) 'Issues in transnational financial reporting: a linguistic analysis', *Journal of Multinational and Multicultural Development*, 12(5).
Baugh, A. C. and Cable, T. (1978) *A History of the English Language*. London: Routledge & Kegan Paul.
Briston, R. J. and Kedslie, M. J. M. (1997) 'The internationalization of British professional accounting: the role of the examination exporting bodies', *Accounting, Business and Financial History*, July.
Calvet, L. J. (1987) *La guerre des langues et les politiques linguistiques*. Paris: Payot.
Carstensen, B. (1986) 'Euro-English', in Kastovsky, D. and Szwadek, A. (eds) *Linguistics Across Historical and Geographical Boundaries*. Berlin: Mouton de Gruyter.
Cheshire, J. and Moser, L.-M. (1994) 'English as a cultural symbol: the case of advertisements in French-speaking Switzerland', *Journal of Multilingual and Multicultural Development*, 15(6).
Clark, P. (1994) *European Financial Reporting. Luxembourg*. London: Routledge.
Corre, J. (1969) *La consolidation des bilans*. Paris: Dunod.
Focus (2000) 'Focus on Central and Eastern Europe', *ACCA Students' Newsletter*, April.
Fuller-Love, N. (1998) 'Accounting in a European minority language: accounting in Welsh', *European Accounting Review*, 7(2).
Garrod, N. (1992) *Termau Cyfrifeg*. Cardiff: University of Wales Press.
Görlach, M. (1995) *More Englishes: New Studies in Varieties of English, 1988–1994*. Amsterdam: John Benjamins.
Harlow, R. (1998) 'Some languages are just not good enough', in Bauer, L. and Trudgill, P. (eds) *Language Myths*. London: Penguin Books.
Hindley, R. (1990) *The Death of the Irish Language. A Qualified Obituary*. London: Routledge.
Hoarau, C. (1995) 'International accounting harmonization: American hegemony or mutual recognition with benchmarks', *European Accounting Review*, 4(2).
Hollqvist, H. (1984) *The Use of English in Three Large Swedish Companies*. Uppsala: Acta Universitatis Upsaliensia, Studia Anglistica Upsaliensia 55.
Inman, M. (1978) *Foreign Languages, English as a Second/Foreign Language, and the U.S. Multinational Corporation*. Arlington, VA: Center for Applied Linguistics.
Johnson, T. J. and Caygill, M. (1971) 'The development of accountancy links in the Commonwealth', *Accounting and Business Research*, Spring.
Kuter, L. (1989) 'Breton vs French: language and the opposition of political, economic, social and cultural values', in Dorian, N. C. (ed.) *Investigating Obsolescence. Studies in Language Contraction and Death*. Cambridge: Cambridge University Press.
Loonen, P. (1996) 'English in Europe: from timid to tyrannical?', *English Today*, 12(2).

McArthur, T. (1998) *The English Languages*. Cambridge: Cambridge University Press.

Newman, B. (1996) 'Global chatter: the reality of "business English"', *English Today*, 12(2).

Nobes, C. (1993) 'The true and fair view requirement. Impact on and of the Fourth Directive', *Accounting and Business Research*, Winter.

Nobes, C. (1995), 'International accounting harmony: a commentary', *European Accounting Review*, 4(2).

Nobes, C. and Parker, R. (2000) *Comparative International Accounting*. Hemel Hempstead: Prentice Hall Europe.

Ordelheide, D. (1990) 'Soft transformation of accounting rules of the 4th Directive in Germany', *Les cahiers internationaux de la comptabilité*, 3.

Parker, R. H. (1989a), 'Importing and exporting accounting: the British experience', in Hopwood, A. (ed.) *International Pressures for Accounting Change*. Hemel Hempstead: Prentice Hall.

Parker, R. H. (1989b) 'Accounting basics: language, writing materials, numerals and calculation', in Macdonald, G. and Rutherford, B. A. (eds) *Accounts, Accounting and Accountability*. London: Van Nostrand Reinhold.

Parker, R. H. (1997) 'Roger North: gentleman, accountant and lexicographer', *Accounting History*, 2(2).

Richard, J. (1995a) 'The evolution of accounting chart models in Europe from 1900 to 1945: some historical elements', *European Accounting Review*, 4(1).

Richard, J. (1995b) 'The evolution of the Romanian and Russian accounting charts after the collapse of the communist system', *European Accounting Review*, 4(2).

Seidler, L. J. (1969) 'Nationalism and the international transfer of accounting skills', *International Journal of Accounting*, Fall.

Standish, P. E. M. (1990) 'Origins of the plan comptable général: a study in cultural intrusion and reaction', *Accounting and Business Research*, Autumn.

Standish, P. E. M. (1997) *The French Plan Comptable*, Ordre des experts comptables and The Institute of Chartered Accountants in England and Wales (Paris).

Thody, P. (1995) *Le Franglais*. London: Athlone.

Tugendhat, C. (1973) *The Multinationals*. Harmondsworth: Penguin.

Wardhaugh, R. (1987) *Languages in Competition: Dominance, Diversity and Decline*. Oxford: Blackwell.

[13]

The International
Journal of
Accounting

The Determination of a Group for Accounting Purposes in the UK, Poland, and the Czech Republic in a Supranational Context

John Craner,* Danuta Krzywda,† Jiri Novotny,‡ and Marek Schroeder*
* University of Birmingham, Birmingham, UK, †Krakow Academy of Economics, Krakow, Poland, and ‡Prague University of Economics, Prague Czech Republic

Key Words: Groups; United Kingdom; Poland; Czech Republic

Abstract: A detailed cross-national and supranational comparison of the de jure requirements for the determination of a group for accounting purposes in the United Kingdom (UK), Poland, and the Czech Republic establishes differences at both levels. The analysis identifies cross-national differences that cannot be fully explained by non-equivalencies between relevant International Accounting Standards (IAS) and the European Commission (EC) 7th Directive on consolidated accounts. These differences are non-trivial and more numerous than the research literature suggests and provide evidence of the prolonged nature of the accounting reforms in economies in transition. In the absence of a theoretical framework for determining the content and sequence of accounting reform in transition, accounting change defaults to an iterative process of learning by doing.

The article compares *de jure* requirements for the determination of a group for accounting purposes cross-nationally among the United Kingdom (UK), Poland, and the Czech Republic and supranationally with reference to International Accounting Standards (IAS) and the European Commission (EC) 7th Directive.[1] The cross-national comparison provides evidence of diversity in group accounting requirements. The supranational comparison indicates that not all the differences revealed by the cross-national comparison can be explained by differences between the supranational requirements, especially for Poland and the Czech Republic. Differences remain that are country-specific and attributable to the prolonged and different transition routes from a command to a market economy.

A focus on *de jure* requirements is relevant to accounting regulators. Poland and the Czech Republic are negotiating accession to the European Union (EU) and compliance

Direct all correspondence to: John M. Craner, Department of Accounting and Finance, University of Birmingham, Edgbaston, Birmingham, B15 2TT UK; E-mail: J.M.Craner@bham.ac.uk.

The International Journal of Accounting, Vol. 35, No. 3, pp. 355–397   ISSN: 0020-7063.

356   THE INTERNATIONAL JOURNAL OF ACCOUNTING   Vol. 35, No. 3, 2000

with EC Directives is a priority. Both countries wish to encourage foreign direct investment and compliance with IAS will lift a barrier to cross-border investment. National regulators will need to perform a detailed supranational comparison when designing *ab initio* or reforming existing consolidation requirements. They may turn to the example of a well-developed market economy and current EU member (e.g., the UK) for guidance and may monitor developments in other transition economies; hence, the cross-national comparison. The study of the consolidation issue is both timely and relevant because Poland plans a reform of its accounting legislation in 2000 (Misinska, 1998) and the Czech Republic plans an earlier reform (Schroll, 1995).

De jure requirements set the parameters for *de facto* practice and a thorough knowledge of the former is indispensable for multinational companies (preparers) and multinational firms of auditors. National consolidation regulations will affect foreign direct investment in terms of amount, financing, and the form it takes (e.g., branch, subsidiary, associate, joint venture). Multinational companies and their auditors may consider familiar consolidation requirements as less of a barrier to entry into a particular national market. They may also use "accounting arbitrage" to exploit differences to their advantage (Johnson, 1999).

The focus on a narrow area of consolidation is justified by its complexity and by the fact that it is the obvious starting point for both regulators and preparers: the group must first be defined before measurement and disclosure requirements may be applied. Only a detailed comparison of the relevant requirements for the determination of a group is sufficient: regulators must pay attention to the detail of the legislation and the substantial expenditure on technical accounting departments by multinational audit firms testifies to the importance of an attention to detail.

Poland and the Czech Republic have been neglected in comparative international accounting research. More attention has been paid to these countries subsequent to 1989 but the focus has been on accounting in a national context excluding consolidation. Moreover, compliance of national requirements with supranational rules (a surrogate measure for the progress of accounting transition) has been merely asserted or studied at a general level.[2]

The article proceeds as follows. The next section reviews the literature and distinguishes previous work in the area. This is followed by the outline of the research method and the data used in the comparison. This is followed by the political and economic backgrounds to the consolidation regulations in Poland and the Czech Republic. The next sections deal with the actual comparisons in terms of: objectives and contents of consolidated accounts; requirements for the determination of a group; exemptions from the consolidation requirement; bases for exclusion from consolidation. The final sections discuss the results and present the conclusions.

LITERATURE REVIEW

The international accounting literature on Poland in transition initially focused on issues of reform (Jaruga, 1991; Lisiecka-Zajac, 1991) and on accounting in the privatization process (UNESCO, 1992; Organization for Economic Co-operation and Development (OECD), 1993). Subsequently, accounting developments were placed both in an historical context and in relation to macroeconomic transition policies (Jaruga, 1993a,b, 1996; Dixon and Jaruga, 1994; Krzywda et al., 1994, 1995, 1996). More descriptive studies concentrated on *de jure* accounting change in general (Jaruga, 1995; Parker and Nobes, 1998) or addressed specific issues such as accounting for goodwill (Kamela-Sowinska, 1995), the relationship between accounting and taxation (Jaruga et al., 1996), stock exchange regulation (Sochacka and Malo, 1996), and charts of accounts (Jaruga and Szychta, 1997). The studies focused on *de jure* change and with few exceptions (Krzywda et al., 1994; Kamela-Sowinska, 1995; Jaruga et al., 1996) contained no comparative analysis.

The literature on the Czech Republic evolved similarly. A focus on reform and privatization (Langr, 1991; Craner, 1993; OECD, 1993) was superseded by contextual studies (Schroll, 1995; Seal et al., 1995, 1996; Zelenka et al., 1996). The descriptive literature (Dolezal, 1995) was supplemented by studies on particular areas: the relationship between accounting and taxation (Holeckova, 1996); Czech perceptions of the "true and fair view" (Sucher et al., 1996); disclosure determinants of Czech listed company annual reports (Patton and Zelenka, 1997). As with Poland, the focus was on *de jure* accounting and the studies were not comparative.

The cited studies did not compare in detail national accounting regulations with supranational rules published by the International Accounting Standards Committee (IASC) or the EC. The specialist studies did not focus on consolidation. This study rectifies these omissions.

Overviews of accounting change in Central and Eastern Europe have been published as introductions to country studies (Alexander and Archer, 1995; Garrod and McLeay, 1996) or as summaries of policy issues in accounting reform (OECD Secretariat, 1991; OECD, 1993). Due to the lack of specialist academics (Meek and Saudagaran, 1990), comparative analyses of accounting in transition are rare (Bailey, 1995; Jaruga, 1996; Richard, 1998) despite early recognition of the importance of the issue (Shama and McMahan, 1990; Gray and Roberts, 1991).

Although in general no studies analyze *de jure* accounting rules in Poland and the Czech Republic in a supranational context, there are two exceptions. Jermakowicz and Rinke (1996) compared accounting requirements in the Czech Republic, Hungary, and Poland with IAS and EC Directives. However, the high level of aggregation in their comparative table (Jermakowicz and Rinke, 1996) failed to capture essential details. In the item "consolidated accounts" in Table 1 (Jermakowicz and Rinke, 1996) with reference to the Czech Republic, the authors correctly state that "Consolidated accounts are required for 20 percent ownership interest" but fail to distinguish between ownership and voting rights, a distinction crucial in terms of the supranational comparison because both the EC 7th Directive and the relevant IAS specify voting rights but the Czech requirements do not, referring only to majority share ownership.[3] This analysis does not support the conclusion reached by Jermakowicz and Rinke (1996) that "(a)lthough the standard-setting bodies of these countries were confronted with choosing from sometimes conflicting accounting standards, they appear to have taken views consistent with those of the IASC and EU." This study of consolidation requirements identifies country-specific differences not consistent with either set of supranational rules.

The second exception is Adams and McMillan (1997) who compared Polish requirements with those of the EC and the IASC but on a general level that failed to capture essential details. A comparative table under the heading "Consolidation" (Adams and

Table 1. Objectives and Contents of Consolidated Accounts

(a) UK, Poland, Czech Republic

Reference	UK	Reference	Poland	Reference	Czech Republic	Item
	Objectives					
FRS 2, paragraph 1	The objective of this FRS is to require parent undertakings to provide financial information about the economic activities of their groups by preparing consolidated financial statements. These statements are intended to present financial information about a parent undertaking and its subsidiary undertakings as a single economic entity to show the economic resources controlled by the group, the obligations of the group and the results the group achieves with its resources.	AA 1994, Article 55(1)	A capital group, consisting of the holding entity and the entities subsidiary to or associated with it, prepares, on the basis of the financial statements of the entities that comprise the group, consolidated financial statements presented in such a way that the group forms a single entity.	CM 1993, App. 1, Article I, paragraphs 1 (1), 1(2)	By consolidated financial statements are meant the financial statements of a group of entities (an economic grouping of accounting entities) that unify the asset and liability (debt) positions and the attained economic results of the holding entity with its participating interest in the rest of the entities that it controls or over that it has significant influence. The consolidated financial statements serve to inform the shareholders and partners of the accounting entity that controls or that exercises a significant influence over the commercial activities of other accounting entities. They do not serve for tax purposes or for the appropriation of economic results.	1

	CA 1985, S227(2)	AA 1994, Article 55(1)	CM 1993, App.1, Article I, paragraph 1(3)
Contents	Group accounts shall be consolidated accounts comprising:	Consolidated financial statements consist of: a consolidated balance sheet, a consolidated profit and loss account, a consolidated statement of cash flows, the notes in the accounts and a report on the activities of the financial group for the financial year.	Consolidated financial statements consist of: [2]
	a. a consolidated balance sheet dealing with the state of affairs of the parent company and its subsidiary undertakings, and		a. a balance sheet,
	b. a consolidated profit and loss account dealing with the profit or loss of the parent company and its subsidiary undertakings.		b. a profit and loss account,
FRS 1, paragraph 5	FRS 1 (cash flow statements) applies to all financial statements intended to give a true and fair view of the financial position and profit or loss (or income and expenditure) (…).		c. notes on the accounts.

(continued on next page)

Table 1. (*continued*)

Reference	UK	Reference	Poland	Reference	Czech Republic	Item
CA 1985, S227(4)	A company's group accounts shall comply with the provisions of Schedule 4A as to the form and content of the consolidated balance sheet and consolidated profit and loss account, and additional information to be provided by way of notes to the accounts.					
CA 1985, S234(1)	The directors of a company shall for each financial year prepare a report a. containing a fair review of the development of the business of the company and its subsidiary undertakings during the financial year and their position at the end of it, (...).					
CA 1985, S227(3)	*Conceptual basis* The accounts shall give a true and fair view of the state of affairs as at the end of the financial year, and the profit or loss for the financial year, of the undertakings included in the consolidation as a whole, so far as concerns members of the company.	CD 1995, Article 1(2)	The consolidated financial statements should ensure the correct and faithful presentation of the asset and financial situation and the financial result of the capital group.	AA 1991, Article 7(1)	Accounting units shall keep their accounting records in a complete manner, with proper support and correctly, so that they fairly present the accounting events that are the object of accounting.	

CA 1985, S23(1)	CD 1995, Article 12(5)	CM 1993, App. 1, Article IV, paragraph 1	CM 1993, App. 1, Article VI, paragraph 2(7)	
Cross shareholdings Except as mentioned in this section, a body corporate cannot be a member of a company that is its holding company and any allotment or transfer of shares in a company to its subsidiary is void.	Own shares of the holding entity held by another entity included in the consolidation are disclosed in the consolidated balance sheet as own shares.	During the process of consolidation it is necessary to respect the current accounting principles established by the act on accounting and the accounting system and accounting procedures for entrepreneurs.	Where they were acquired for the short term with a view to resale, they are shown in the consolidated balance sheet as short-term financial assets.	Where they were acquired for the purpose of a long term holding, these shareholdings are shown in the consolidated balance sheet as a decrease of equity under the item "Reserves (derived from profit)" and disclosed in the notes on the accounts.

(continued on next page)

Table 1. (*continued*)

(b) IAS and the 7th Directive

Reference	IAS	Reference	7th Directive	Item
	Objectives			
IAS 27, paragraph 9	Users of the financial statements of a parent are usually concerned with, and need to be informed about, the financial position, results of operations, and changes in financial position of the group as a whole. This need is served by consolidated financial statements, which present financial information about the group as that of a single enterprise without regard for the legal boundaries of the separate legal entities.	Preamble	(…); whereas many companies are members of bodies of undertakings; whereas consolidated accounts must be drawn up so that financial information concerning such bodies of undertakings may be conveyed to members and third parties; (…). Whereas consolidated accounts must give a true and fair view of the assets and liabilities, the financial position and the profit and loss of all the undertakings consolidated taken as a whole; whereas, therefore, consolidation should in principle include all of those undertakings; whereas such consolidation requires the full incorporation of the assets and liabilities and of the income and expenditure of those undertakings and the separate disclosure of the interests of persons out with such bodies; (…).	1
	Contents			
Preface, paragraph 5	The term "financial statements" (…) covers balance sheets, income statements or profit and loss accounts, statements of changes in financial position, notes and other statements and explanatory material that are identified as being part of the financial statements.	Article 16.	(1) Consolidated accounts shall comprise the consolidated balance sheet, the consolidated profit and loss account, and the notes on the accounts. These documents shall constitute a composite whole.	2

Framework, paragraph 46

Conceptual basis

Financial statements are frequently described as showing a "true and fair" view of, or as presenting fairly, the financial position, performance, and changes in financial position of an enterprise. Although this framework does not deal directly with such concepts, the application of the principal qualitative characteristics and of appropriate accounting standards normally results in financial statements that convey what is generally understood as a true and fair view of, or as presenting fairly, such information.

Article 16

(2) The consolidated annual report must include at least a fair review of the development of business and the position of the undertakings included in the consolidation taken as a whole.

(3) Consolidated accounts shall give a true and fair view of the assets, liabilities, financial position, and profit or loss of the undertakings included therein taken as a whole.

McMillan, 1997) stated that "(c)ompanies under common ownership required to prepare consolidated financial statements." In fact, Polish requirements with respect to the control of subsidiaries are in accordance with the EC 7th Directive and IAS in providing for control through provisions in the subsidiary's deed (or statute) or by virtue of a control contract. In addition, the criterion for control is not "common ownership" but control of voting rights.[4]

Over a decade ago, Nobes (1983) stated that "the real problem in international accounting is ... (that) there is too much *inaccurate* descriptive work." Meek and Saudagaran (1990) state "(a)t a minimum one should consult more than one source as a test for both accuracy and up-to-dateness. Better yet is consulting original documents and other sources from the country of interest." There is a danger that the errors of the past identified by Nobes (1983) and highlighted by Meek and Saudagaran (1990) will be repeated with reference to emerging market economies of Central and Eastern Europe whose accounting histories have been a neglected area of international accounting study. In performing its comparisons, this study has followed the advice of Meek and Saudagaran (1990) and has used original legislative sources.

The consolidation issue has been a focus of comparative research in a Western European context (FEE, 1993; Gray et al., 1993) due to harmonization pressures at the European level (European Commission, 1978, 1983) that have in turn impacted on the specification of international rules contained in IAS (Cairns, 1995). *De jure* compliance with EC Directives is a condition of accession to the EU for the associated countries of Central and Eastern Europe as detailed in the *White Paper: Preparation of the Associated Countries of Central and Eastern Europe for Integration into the Internal Market of the Union* (European Commission, 1995) (hereafter, *White Paper 1995*). Studies of *de jure* or formal harmonization in a comparative context (Rahman et al., 1996; Richard, 1998) are a necessary step prior to an empirical analysis of *de facto* harmonization (Tay and Parker, 1990) and especially appropriate with reference to neglected countries such as Poland and the Czech Republic that have not featured in either European (FEE, 1991, 1992) or international (Ordelheide and Semler, 1995) comparative surveys. More recently, the IASC has adopted a proposal to consider whether separate accounting standards may be appropriate for countries in transition (IASC, 1998). A focus on consolidation is therefore timely from both a European and an international perspective.

RESEARCH METHOD AND DATA

The choice of countries for comparative study can be criticized for reflecting the predilections of the researchers rather than the rigor of a research design but inevitable resource constraints—financial and human—have limited the article's scope.

The environmental differences among the countries are obvious from the indicators in Fig. 1 but both Poland and the Czech Republic are candidates for fast-track EU membership. The UK is a member and a potential model. EC Directives apply to each and UK influence was especially strong in the development of the 7th Directive. Accounting solutions embodied in IAS are influenced by Anglo-American principles and most IAS treatments are adopted by the UK rendering its accounting a useful embodiment of supranational rules.

Indicators (all data 1994 unless indicated)	UK	Poland	Czech Republic
World Bank classification of income status	High	Lower-middle	Upper-middle
Population (m)	58.4	38.5	10.3
Area (thousands of sq.km)	245	313	79
Urban population as a % of total population	89	64	65
GNP per capita (US dollars)	18,340	2,410	3,200
PPP estimates of GNP per capita (US=100)(%)	69.4	21.2	34.4
Average annual inflation 1990-94 (%)	4.0	36.9	21.3
GDP (million$)	1,017,306	92,580	36,024

Figure 1. Selected Development Indicators: UK, Poland, Czech Republic.
Source: International Bank for Reconstruction and Development (The World Bank) (1996), World Development Report 1996: From Plan to Market.

Poland and the Czech Republic share similar histories in that both were among the more economically developed socialist states with Soviet-installed, rather than home-grown, socialist regimes and in each country democratization proceeded via peaceful elections in which the opposition to the socialist regime gained immediate government control to set in train a transition that has not been reversed. Other transition advantages included a history of previous reforms (Poland); a history of past resistance (Czech Republic and Poland); a history of a mixed economy during the inter-war period (Czech Republic and Poland).

In terms of cumulative inflows of foreign direct investment between 1989 and 1996 in Eastern Europe and the Baltic States as a whole, the Czech Republic and Poland rank second and third, respectively (behind Hungary) (EBRD, 1997). Both countries have experienced international pressures for accounting change emanating from foreign multinationals and the multinational audit firms, the latter having well-established offices in each country. Both countries have signed Europe (Association) Agreements with the EU as part of their pre-accession strategies and will need to comply with the accounting requirements of the EC's *White Paper 1995*. The European and international pressures on each country to harmonize their accounting with supranational requirements are comparable.

The comparison was undertaken in three stages. The first stage was a cross-national comparison to identify differences (Tables 1(a) and 2(a)).[5] The second stage was a comparison of supranational requirements (Tables 1(a) and 2(a)).[5] The third stage identified the extent to which national differences were explained by reference to supranational differences and identified country-specific differences, i.e., those that could not be explained by supranational differences (Table 3(a) and (b)). The latter have been characterized as differences of commission or omission. Country-specific differences of commission occur when a stated requirement in the national legislation

366   THE INTERNATIONAL JOURNAL OF ACCOUNTING   Vol. 35, No. 3, 2000

Code	Explanation
A	Equivalent to 7th Directive and IAS.
B	Equivalent to 7th Directive only.
C	Equivalent to IAS only.
X	Country-specific difference of commission.
N	Country-specific difference of omission.

Figure 2.   Analytical Coding of National Requirements in a Supranational Context.

is *different* from corresponding supranational requirements. A country-specific difference of omission occurs when national requirements are *silent* in respect of a requirement of the supranational bodies (Fig. 2).

The approach identifies equivalencies across requirements (Code A) and when a country's requirements have been influenced by one or other set of supranational requirements (Codes B or C). Non-equivalence is defined as a situation where a supranational requirement differs or exists in one set of supranational rules but not the other. This approach identifies the relative influence of each set of supranational requirements on each country. The extent of non-equivalence with supranational requirements is illustrated by the identification of country-specific differences of commission and omission (Codes X and N).

The study identifies the frequency of equivalence or non-equivalence. The number of such differences will be influenced by the degree of disaggregation adopted in the analysis, e.g., the requirement for a management/directors' report could be disaggregated into its required contents. Despite this limitation, the level of disaggregation adopted has not been previously attempted in the literature and is within relevant parameters. The distinction between country-specific differences of commission and omission is an analytical approach that has not been attempted previously but is relevant to regulators assessing compliance with supranational requirements in context of the potential amendments and to other users wishing to assess the extent of accounting policy choice available nationally: country-specific differences of omission (silence in national requirements in respect of supranational requirements) are less of a barrier to *de jure* or *de facto* harmonization than county-specific differences of commission (explicit differences between corresponding national and supranational requirements).

The data consist of consolidation requirements for each country and for supranational bodies. Original sources in the native language have been consulted for both Czech and Polish requirements. The multinational nature of the research team, consisting of at least one member from each country, ensures that translations of relevant requirements are accurate.

The Czech requirements exist in separate sets of regulations with different authority. General provisions, limited to the establishment of a consolidation requirement per se, are contained in the Zakon c. 563/1991 *Sb. o ucetnictvi* (Act no.563/1991 on accounting, hereafter *Accounting Act 1991*) an act of parliament passed in December 1991. The detailed requirements are contained in the *Opatreni kterym se stanovi postupy pro provedeni konsolidace ucetni zaverky* Cj. 281/73 570/93 (Measure that determines the procedures for preparing consolidated financial statements no. 281/73 570/93, hereafter *Consolidation Measure 1993*) issued in 1993 by the Ministry of Finance on the basis of derogation contained in Article 4, paragraph 2 of the *Accounting Act 1991*.

The Polish requirements have similar authority. The *Ustawa z dnia 29 wrzesnia* 1994 *r. o rachunkowosci* (Act of 29 September 1994 on accounting, hereafter *Accounting Act 1994*) is a parliamentary act effective from 1 January 1995. On the basis of derogation contained in Article 81, paragraph 3(2) of the act, the Ministry of Finance issued the *Rozporzadzenie Ministra Finansow z dnia 14 czerwca 1995 r. w sprawie szczegolowych zasad sporzadzania przez jednostki inne niz banki skonsolidowanych sprawozdan finansowych* (the Decree of the Minister of Finance of 14 June 1995 on the specific principles for the preparation of consolidated financial statements by entities other than banks, hereafter *Consolidation Decree 1995*). The decree contains more detailed guidance and similar to the Czech *Consolidation Measure 1993* specifies group-reporting formats in an appendix.

In the UK group accounting legislation is contained in parliamentary acts devoted to the regulation of joint-stock and limited liability companies specifically the *Companies Act 1985* as amended by the *Companies Act 1989*, the latter introducing the provisions of the EC 7th Directive. However, they have a similar legislative status as the Czech and Polish acts. At this point, the form of UK requirements begins to differ in that more detailed requirements not necessarily fully consistent with the provisions contained in company law are to be found in Financial Reporting Standards (FRS) issued by the Accounting Standards Board (ASB). Although standards are not identical to regulations issued by Ministries of Finance for the purposes of comparison they are treated as equivalent. The relevant standards are *FRS 2 Accounting for Subsidiary Undertakings* (ASB, 1992) and *FRS 9 Associates and Joint Ventures* (ASB, 1997).

Supranational requirements exist at the European and the international level. The European requirements are contained in the 7th EC Directive on consolidated accounts. The international requirements are those of the IASC, mainly *IAS 27 Consolidated Financial Statements and Accounting for Investments in Subsidiaries* (IASC, 1989b) and *IAS 28 Accounting for Investments in Associates* (IASC, 1989c).

THE POLITICAL AND ECONOMIC BACKGROUND

Of particular interest in the comparison is the fact that the UK is a mature market economy while Poland and the Czech Republic are in the process of a prolonged socioeconomic transformation from a command to a market economy. The differences revealed by the cross-national comparison and by the supranational comparison with IAS and the EC Directive (both designed for implementation in well-developed market economies) need to be understood within the transition context. Initial attempts at regulation in Poland and the Czech Republic may exhibit more differences with supranational requirements than the provisions of the UK with a longer tradition of consolidation. This section outlines why this may be the case. Furthermore, the different transition routes adopted by the two countries will explain the particular configuration of consolidation rules adopted. The issue here, not addressed elsewhere in the literature, concerns the impact upon the nature and extent of the differences in *de jure* consolidation rules that may be expected given the

368   THE INTERNATIONAL JOURNAL OF ACCOUNTING   Vol. 35, No. 3, 2000

transition to a market economy in general and the transition routes adopted by each country in particular.

Although Poland and the Czech Republic achieved a peaceful transition from Soviet-imposed single-party socialist rule to government by freely elected liberal democratic regimes, their political experiences after 1989 were very different. These different political experiences are important because fundamental economic initiatives such as privatization involve issues of both economic efficiency and social equity and the balance struck between the two is inevitably a political decision. This point is illustrated by the Czechoslovakian Federation split into the separate countries of the Czech Republic and Slovakia with effect from 1 January 1993. The rapid liberalization and privatization policies pursued by the Federal government from 1 January 1991 were controversial and perceived to have a more socially detrimental effect (specifically in terms of unemployment) on the Slovak as opposed to the Czech part of the Federation. The June 1992 national elections saw Slovakia electing a government with a more gradualist and socially oriented approach to economic transformation while the Czech Republic elected a government committed to the existing policy of speedy socio-economic transformation in which the priority remained the achievement of economic efficiency. The Polish political situation had been more volatile, characterized by frequent elections and more frequent changes of government. Partially free elections in June 1989 had ushered in a reforming Solidarity government that had initiated macroeconomic liberalization and privatization policies but the subsequent fall of the Berlin Wall in November 1989 had rendered the Polish constitutional arrangements, in which the former socialist government had been guaranteed a majority of the seats in deference to perceptions of continuing Soviet influence, both anachronistic and devoid of legitimacy. Fully free elections in October 1991 resulted in a fragmented parliament in which government was by increasingly unstable coalitions. Further elections in 1993, called to resolve the political uncertainty, brought into power a more socially minded left-wing coalition of parties that had its roots in the socialist parties of the pre-1989 political era. As a result, the pace of socioeconomic transformation slowed until subsequent elections saw the return of a more reform-minded right-wing government. The Polish experience illustrates that the balance between the political goals of economic efficiency and social equity had been much more difficult to achieve: there would appear to have been less consensus over the direction and pace of socioeconomic transformation in the early years of transition than in the Czech Republic.

The contrast between the two countries arises from their different experiences of previous reform. In Czechoslovakia, limited political and economic reform based on the Hungarian model had been brutally suppressed using Soviet military force in 1968. In the aftermath, classical command economy structures had been re-imposed and these had persisted relatively unchanged until 1989. The commitment in the new Czech Republic to rapid economic reform needs to be understood against this background. The Polish experience is one of failed reforms from the 1970s onwards that provoked social discontent and that led to the initial formation, subsequent suppression and ultimate political victory of the Solidarity movement. Post-1989 Polish governments had to take into account the aspirations of this strong trade union based constituency in the formulation of socioeconomic transformation policies. As a result, the Polish privatization strategy contained methods of transferring ownership that favored management and employee buy-outs and the consequent establishment of insider control in newly privatized firms.

Fig. 3 compares the main privatization methods in Poland and the Czech Republic. Management and employee buy-outs are a primary feature of the privatization process in Poland and the Czech Republic remains the primary example of the mass privatization route in which the public are allocated vouchers for a nominal fee that are subsequently invested in privatized firms either directly or, more commonly, through the medium of intermediate investment funds. Although such an approach was advocated in Poland as early as 1991, legislation on mass privatization did not reach the statute book until 1993, was much smaller in scale than the Czech approach and in any case did not begin to be seriously implemented until 1995 as a result of the delays caused by the election in 1993 of a social democratic government more skeptical of privatization. In the Czech Republic, the first mass privatization wave occurred in 1992–1993 and the second in 1993–1994 and neither was interrupted by a change in the political persuasion of the government. Direct sale of enterprises to outside owners (usually via a public share issue) did not feature strongly in the Czech Republic but was an important initial privatization route (based on the UK model) in Poland: practical experience with the process revealed it to be a costly and time-consuming privatization method and ultimately led to its demise and the adoption of the mass privatization legislation.

The Polish and Czech mass privatization programs embody substantially different approaches. The Czech route emphasizes early privatization and leaves the necessary operational and financial restructuring of the newly privatized state-owned enterprises to the new private owners, relying on market pressures (e.g., hard budget constraints and competition) to establish good corporate governance practice. The danger that dispersed ownership structures will inhibit the emergence of corporate governance patterns that would facilitate restructuring was obviated by the Czech Republic's laissez faire approach to the establishment of privately owned investment funds (over 200 subsequently appeared) to act as intermediaries between voucher holders and firms. The Czech approach embodies a belief in the efficiency of rapidly established markets to solve the restructuring problems of the former command economy. The Polish approach differed in that comprehensive financial restructuring of the entities to be privatized was undertaken prior to their allocation to one of 15 state-established investment funds. The process was much slower and revealed a more skeptical attitude to the ability of the emerging market to pick privatization winners and losers correctly. For example, while Czech investment funds were initially limited to a maximum 20 percent stake in any one enterprise, each Polish privatized enterprise was to have a more influential stake (about 33%) held by one of the 15 investment funds. The Polish funds were designed to have a substantial interest in

	Sale to outside owners	Equal access voucher privatization	Management-employee buy-outs
Czech Republic	Secondary	Primary	
Poland	Tertiary	Secondary	Primary

Figure 3. Methods of Privatization of Medium-Sized and Large Enterprises in the Czech Republic and Poland.
Source: Table 5.7, EBRD, Transition Report (1997).

370   THE INTERNATIONAL JOURNAL OF ACCOUNTING   Vol. 35, No. 3, 2000

ensuring the successful operational and financial restructuring of the firms allocated to their portfolio irrespective of the strength of external market pressures.

Four basic patterns of enterprise ownership and governance emerged in Poland and the Czech Republic (EBRD, 1995):

1. continued state ownership for unprivatized firms with control exercised by insiders (managers and employees);
2. insider ownership with control exercised by employees and managers;
3. domestic outsider ownership with control exercised by domestic investment funds and individual voucher holders; and
4. foreign outsider ownership (individual, firm or investment fund).

The privatization strategies and the nature of the ownership and governance structures in enterprises that have arisen as a result have implications for the financial reporting and consolidation. Continued state or insider ownership by employees and managers (the primary privatization route in Poland) result in corporate governance structures that do not stimulate a demand for external financial reporting nor in an active market for corporate control requiring consolidation rules to facilitate its efficient and transparent operation. Enterprises in state ownership will not be permitted to expand through merger or acquisition. Firms owned and controlled by insiders will be concerned with maximizing employees' job security and wage levels and will not have access to the necessary finance (due to the lack of a track record of successful performance) to fund expansion through acquisition. The fact of insider control and the lack of alternative opportunities in the labor market also make such firms difficult takeover targets for outsider control firms whether domestic or foreign.

Extensive outsider ownership characterized the Czech mass privatization program and under these conditions the demand for external financial reporting is maximized and consolidation rules will be needed to cope with the emerging market for corporate control. Against this background, the Czech *Accounting Act 1991* (Section 22), which came into force on 1 January 1992, contained a legal requirement for the preparation and audit of consolidated financial statements. The equivalent Polish requirement appeared much later in the *Accounting Act 1994*, which came into force on 1 January 1995. Up to this date, Polish privatization had been dominated by management and employee buy-outs and the mass privatization program had not yet been implemented. The timing of the incorporation of the consolidation requirement into law in each of the countries is the result of the adoption of a different dominant method of privatization.

By mid-1996, the market capitalization of the Prague Stock Exchange amounted to 42 percent of Czech gross domestic product; the equivalent figure for the Warsaw Stock Exchange was 5 percent (EBRD, 1996). This disparity had arisen despite the fact that the Warsaw Stock Exchange was reactivated in 1991, 2 years prior to its Czech counterpart in Prague and is entirely attributable to the different privatization strategies adopted: initial company listings in Poland were entirely the result of a slow stream of public offers for sale of attractive state-owned enterprises (and the mass privatization program was delayed) while in the Czech Republic the mass privatization route had resulted in numerous listings. Nevertheless, neither country could point to the emergence of an active market for corporate control. While in Poland the creation of such a market had not been a priority, in the Czech Republic such market forces were integral to the effective corporate governance and restructuring of enterprises. The market's emergence in the Czech case was hampered by the predominance of investment fund intermediaries. The funds proved a popular intermediate investment location for voucher holders because of the benefits of diversification and their investment expertise. The more popular funds were set up and owned by banks that in fact, combined with the 20 percent investment limit in any one enterprise, limited the efficiency of the funds as primary agents of operational and financial restructuring. A recent amendment to Czech legislation allows investment funds to own controlling stakes in enterprises but in order to be effective the funds themselves need to be effectively governed, however, examples exist of such funds converting from joint-stock companies to unit trusts to prevent takeover. *De facto*, therefore, the expected demand for effective external financial reporting has not materialized in the Czech Republic and the early enactment of the consolidation requirement may prove to have been premature.

Although the consolidation requirement in the Czech Republic was in force for the 1992 calendar year, the detailed technical rules did not appear until the issue by the Ministry of Finance of the *Consolidation Measure 1993*, applicable for the first time to the 1993 calendar year. The delay between the enactment of the consolidation requirement and the issuance of detailed procedures is explained by the technical complexity of the subject area and by the fact that such procedures were not encountered under the command economy. In any case, Czech technical guidance on the preparation of consolidated financial statements came into force 2 years earlier than in Poland. The later Polish legislation will exhibit fewer differences with supranational rules given the greater amount of time allowed for the assimilation of the subject matter by regulators and because the requirements were drafted and enacted subsequent to the country's application for membership of the EU. The Czech requirements were a temporizing measure (Schroll, 1995) promulgated prior to application for EU membership and exact compliance with the 7th Directive was not a political priority.

A distinction needs to be drawn between regulations requiring the preparation, audit, and publication of consolidated financial statements and rules that establish the existence of group relationships per se. For example, the Polish *Ustawa z dnia 22 marca 1991 r.: Prawo o publicznym obrocie papierami wartosciowymi i funduszach powierniczych* (Act of 22nd March 1991: The law on public trading in securities and trust funds, hereafter *Securities Act 1991*), which reestablished the Warsaw Stock Exchange, contained definitions of subsidiary and associate companies without the requirement to prepare consolidated financial statements. Such provisions ensure the transparency of trading on the emerging securities exchange by preventing undeclared takeovers by concert parties of firms under common ownership. The Czech consolidation requirements need to be seen similarly in the context of the reestablishment of the Prague Stock Exchange in 1993 except that legislation went much farther in specifying the production of consolidated financial statements in line with the more rapid path of socioeconomic transformation adopted. Even the EC *White Paper 1995* recognized that compliance with the 7th Directive was a second stage measure, compared to the implementation of the 4th Directive, in the overall program of compliance with EC Directives (EC, 1995).

General features of the consolidation regulations in Poland and the Czech Republic are attributable directly to the transition. In each country macroeconomic liberalization began

372   THE INTERNATIONAL JOURNAL OF ACCOUNTING   Vol. 35, No. 3, 2000

and a small number of acquisitions took place prior to the establishment of the consolidation requirement, resulting in the necessity for the regulations in both countries to contain provisions specifying the accounting rules for such circumstances. In the early years of the transition, in the Czech Republic by design and in Poland by default, positive and negative goodwill on consolidation were calculated by reference to book values and not the market or fair values of the net assets acquired (in Poland the use of market values was introduced in the *Accounting Act 1994*). The establishment of reliable market values in a transition economy is both difficult and costly and legislation did not impose this burden on newly privatized firms but the consequences for the goodwill on consolidation figure need to be born in mind: the resulting number is a difference on consolidation devoid of the economic significance attached to the figure in well-developed market economies. Further aspects of the regulations attributable to the transition are discussed in the following sections.

COMPARISON OF OBJECTIVES AND CONTENTS OF CONSOLIDATED FINANCIAL STATEMENTS

The objectives of consolidated financial statements may be defined in terms of the representation of the activities of an economic or legal "reality" ("the group") or in terms of the needs of users or by a combination of these approaches. The Czech requirements exclude the use of group accounts as a basis for determining tax liabilities and dividend distribution policy. This exclusion is not found in other requirements and is a country-specific difference of commission. The objective of group accounts in the Czech requirements is "... to inform the shareholders and partners ...," however, it is clear that a focus on an "economic grouping" underlies the requirements that combine the economic and user needs approaches consistent with the aims of the mass privatization strategy. Polish legislation has no user emphasis that is consistent with the more insider-oriented privatization strategy but employs the idea of a capital (not economic) group. This is a country-specific difference of commission with reference to the IAS emphasis on a single economic entity. The UK standard specifies "single economic entity" and stresses the economic nature of a group. The IAS combines approaches by referring to both (unspecified) users and a non-legal single enterprise. The 7th Directive takes a user emphasis, referring to members and third parties. It is clear that there exists an array of differently phrased objectives.

In terms of content all requirements specify a balance sheet, profit and loss account, and notes on the accounts. In the Czech Republic, the management report and the cash flow statement are constituent parts of the notes. In Poland and the UK, they are primary statements. The 7th Directive does not require a cash flow statement. The IAS do not apply to management reports (IASC Framework, 1989). Despite the differences in supranational requirements, consolidated financial statements in all three countries effectively comprise the same principal documents.

All countries and the supranational rules acknowledge some notion of fair presentation, albeit phrased differently. The concepts underlying these phrases have defied unambiguous interpretation (Alexander, 1993). A debate as to the meaning of "true and fair" in the UK, "correct and faithful" in Poland and "fairly present" in the Czech Republic is outside

Table 2. (Extract) The Determination of a Group

(a) UK, Poland, Czech Republic

Reference	United Kingdom	Reference	Poland	Reference	Czech Republic	Item
FRS 2, paragraph 14. CA 1985, S258(2), (4)	*Parent/subsidiary relationships* An undertaking is the parent undertaking of another undertaking (a subsidiary undertaking) if any of the following apply: (a) It holds a majority of the voting rights in the undertaking. (b) It is a member of the undertaking and has the right to appoint or remove directors holding a majority of the voting rights at meetings of the board on all, or substantially all, matters.	AA 1994, Article 3(1)(4)	Holding entity—by this is meant a joint-stock company, a company with limited liability or any other share capital company: (a) that holds a majority of the total number of votes in the bodies of another (subsidiary) entity, including on the basis of agreements with others entitled to vote, or (b) that is entitled to take decisions concerning the financial policies and current operating activities of this other (subsidiary) entity on the basis of the Act, a company deed or contract, or	CM 1993, App. 1, Article 1, paragraphs 4,5; paragraph 2(1)	By a holding entity is understood a subject that exercises either directly or indirectly a dominant influence over subsidiary entities or a significant influence over associated entities. By subsidiary entity is understood a subject over which another entity exercises directly or indirectly a dominant influence. That subject is also considered a subsidiary entity in the case where the holding entity has more than a 50 percent share (participation) in its basic assets either directly or indirectly through one or more subsidiary entities over which the holding entity exercises a dominant influence. The amount of the share (participation) of the holding entity in the basic assets of that subject is made up of the direct share of one or more subsidiary entities in the basic assets of that subject and the direct share (participation) of the holding entity in the basic assets of that subject.	5

(continued on next page)

Table 2. *(continued)*

(a) UK, Poland, Czech Republic

Reference	United Kingdom	Reference	Poland	Reference	Czech Republic	Item
	(c) It has the right to exercise a dominant influence over the undertaking:		(c) which as a shareholder is entitled to appoint or dismiss the majority of the members of the management or supervisory bodies of another (subsidiary) entity, or		The dominant influence of one accounting entity (the holding entity) over another (the subsidiary entity) is understood to be a degree of dependence (influence) characterized by:	
	(i) by virtue of provisions contained in the undertaking's memorandum or articles; or		(d) whose management board members or the persons fulfilling management roles, or the members of the management board or persons fulfilling such management roles in a subsidiary entity, constitute at the same time more than half of the management board of another (subsidiary) entity.		(a) direct or indirect ownership of more than a 50 percent share (participation) in the basic assets of the subsidiary entity, as long as other arrangements do not apply as a result or written contracts or provisions in the articles of the company's statue.	
	(ii) by virtue of a control contract. The control contract must be in writing and be of a kind authorized by the memorandum or articles of the controlled undertaking. It must also be permitted by the law under which that undertaking is established. (d) It is a member of the undertaking and controls alone, pursuant to an agreement with other shareholders or members, a majority of the voting rights in the undertaking.				(b) a written contract or provisions in the articles of the company's statue whereby the holding entity governs the financial and operating policies of the subsidiary entity and is also a shareholder or partner in the given entity.	

Reference	Provision	Reference	Provision	Reference	Provision	
CA 1985, S258(5)	(e) It has a participating interest in the undertaking and: (i) it actually exercises a dominant influence over the undertaking; or (ii) it and the undertaking are managed on a unified basis. (f) A parent undertaking is also treated as the parent undertaking of the subsidiary undertakings of its subsidiary undertakings.	AA 1994, Article 55(2)	Holding entities (…), are obliged to prepare, each year, consolidated financial statements to include the holding entity and entities subsidiary to or associated with it at all levels, (…).			
Parent/associate relationships						
CA 1985, Sch4A, S20	(1) An "associated undertaking" means an undertaking in which an undertaking included in the consolidation has a participating interest and over whose operating and financial policy it exercises a significant influence, and that is not	AA 1994 Article 3(1)(4)	(Holding entity …)	CM 1993, App. 1, Article 1, paragraph 6; paragraph 2(2)	By associated entity is meant a subject over which another exercises, directly or indirectly through a subsidiary or subsidiary entities, a significant influence.	6

(continued on next page)

Table 2. *(continued)*

(a) UK, Poland, Czech Republic

Reference	United Kingdom	Reference	Poland	Reference	Czech Republic	Item
	(a) a subsidiary undertaking of the parent company, or		(e) that holds in another (associated) entity not less than 20 percent and not more than 50 percent of the votes at the general meeting of shareholders,		By the significant influence of one accounting entity (the holding entity) over another accounting entity (the associated entity) is understood to be that degree of dependence (influence) in which the holding entity owns directly or indirectly at least 20 percent and not more than 50 percent of the share (participation) in the basic assets of another entity, as long as written contracts or the provisions in the articles of the company's statute do not provide otherwise.	
	(b) a joint venture dealt with in accordance with paragraph 19.		(f) that in some way other than that specified under letter (e), exercises a significant influence on the financial policies and current operating activities of another (associated) entity.			
	(2) Where an undertaking holds 20 percent or more of the voting rights in another undertaking, it shall be presumed to exercise such an influence over it unless the contrary is shown.					

(b) IAS and the 7th Directive

Reference	IAS	Reference	7th Directive	Item
	Parent/subsidiary relationships			
IAS 27 paragraph6	A parent is an enterprise that has one or more subsidiaries.	Article 1	(1) A member state shall require any undertaking governed by its national law to draw up consolidated accounts and a consolidated annual report if that undertaking (a parent undertaking):	5
IAS 27, paragraph 6	A subsidiary is an enterprise that is controlled by another enterprise (known as the parent).		(a) has a majority of the shareholders' or members' voting rights in another undertaking (a subsidiary undertaking); or	
IAS 27, paragraph 12	Control is presumed to exist when the parent owns, directly or indirectly through subsidiaries, more than one half of the voting power of an enterprise unless, in exceptional circumstances, it can be clearly demonstrated that such ownership does not constitute control.		(b) has the right to appoint or remove a majority of the members of the administrative, management or supervisory body of another undertaking (a subsidiary undertaking) and is at the same time a shareholder in or member of that undertaking; or	
	Control also exists even when the parent owns one half or less of the voting power of an enterprise when there is:		(c) has the right to exercise a dominant influence over an undertaking (a subsidiary undertaking of which it is a shareholder or member, pursuant to a contract entered into with that undertaking or to a provision in its memorandum or articles of association, where the law governing that subsidiary undertaking permits its being subject to such contracts or provisions. A member state need not prescribe that a parent undertaking must be a shareholder in or member of its subsidiary undertaking. Those member states the laws of which do not provide for such contracts or clauses shall not be required to apply this provision; or	
	(a) power over more than one half of the voting rights by virtue of an agreement with other investors;		(d) is a shareholder in or member of an undertaking; and	

(continued on next page)

Table 2. *(continued)*

(b) IAS and the 7th Directive

Reference	IAS	Reference	7th Directive	Item
	(b) power to govern the financial and operating policies of the enterprise under a statute or an agreement;		(aa) a majority of the members of the administrative, management or supervisory bodies of that undertaking (a subsidiary undertaking) who have held office during the financial year, during the preceding financial year and up to the time when the consolidated accounts are drawn up, have been appointed solely as a result of the exercise of its voting rights; or	
	(c) power to appoint or remove the majority of the members of the board of directors or equivalent governing body;		(bb) controls alone, pursuant to an agreement with other shareholders in or members of that undertaking (a subsidiary undertaking), a majority of shareholders' or members' voting rights in that undertaking. The member states may introduce more detailed provisions concerning the form and contents of such agreements.	
	(d) power to cast the majority of votes at meetings of the board of directors or equivalent governing body.		The member states shall prescribe at least the arrangements referred to in (bb) above. They may make the application of (aa) above dependent upon the holding's representing 20 percent or more of the shareholders' or members' voting rights. However, (aa) above shall not apply where another undertaking has the rights referred to in subparagraphs (a), (b) or (c) above with regard to that subsidiary undertaking.	
			(2) Apart from the cases mentioned in paragraph 1 above and pending subsequent coordination, the member states may require any undertaking governed by their national law to draw up consolidated accounts and a consolidated annual report if that undertaking (a parent undertaking) holds a participating interest as defined in Article 17 of Directive 78/660/EEC in another undertaking (a subsidiary undertaking), and:	
			(a) it actually exercises a dominant influence over it; or	

Article 12	(b) it and the subsidiary undertaking are managed on a unified basis by the parent undertaking. (1) Without prejudice to Articles 1 to 10, a member state may require any undertaking governed by its national law to draw up consolidated accounts and a consolidated annual report if: (a) that undertaking and one or more other undertakings with which it is not connected, as described in Article 1 (1) or (2), are managed on a unified basis pursuant to a contract concluded with the undertaking or provisions in the memorandum or articles of association of those undertakings; or (b) the administrative, management or supervisory bodies of that undertaking and of one or more other undertakings with which it is not connected, as described in Article 1 (1) or (2), consist for the major part of the same persons in office during the financial year and until the consolidated accounts are drawn up.
IAS 27 paragraph 11 Article 3	A parent that issues consolidated financial statements should consolidate all subsidiaries, foreign and domestic, other than those referred to in paragraph 13. (1) Without prejudice to Articles 13, 14 and 15, a parent undertaking and all of its subsidiary undertakings shall be undertakings to be consolidated regardless of where the registered offices of such subsidiary undertakings are situated. (2) For the purpose of paragraph 12 above, any subsidiary undertaking of a subsidiary undertaking shall be considered a subsidiary undertaking of the parent undertaking that is the parent of the undertakings to be consolidated.

(continued on next page)

Table 2. *(continued)*

(b) IAS and the 7th Directive

Reference	IAS	Reference	7th Directive	Item
	Parent/associate relationships			
IAS 28, paragraph 3	An *associate* is an enterprise in which the investor has significant influence and that is neither a subsidiary nor a joint venture of the investor.	Article 33	(1) Where an undertaking included in a consolidation exercises a significant influence over the operating and financial policy of an undertaking not included in the consolidation (an associated undertaking) in which it holds a participating interest, as defined in Article 17 of Directive 78/660/EEC, that participating interest shall be shown in the consolidated balance sheet as a separate item with an appropriate heading. An undertaking shall be presumed to exercise a significant influence over another undertaking where it has 20 percent or more of the shareholders' or members voting rights in that undertaking. Article 2 shall apply.	6
IAS 28, paragraph 4	If an investor holds, directly or indirectly through subsidiaries, 20 percent or more of the voting power of the investee, it is presumed that the investor does have significant influence, unless it can be clearly demonstrated that this is not the case. Conversely, if the investor holds, directly or indirectly through subsidiaries, less than 20 percent of the voting power of the investee, it is presumed that the investor does not have significant influence, unless such influence can be clearly demonstrated. A substantial or majority ownership by another investor does not necessarily preclude an investor from having significant influence.			

the scope of this article but has been addressed elsewhere in the literature (Sucher et al., 1996). Legal rules regarding cross-shareholdings significantly impact upon comparative group structures. Although cross-shareholdings are prohibited in the UK, they are allowed (or not prohibited) in Poland and the Czech Republic but there is a requirement to disclose such holdings. In Poland, such shareholdings are separately disclosed. In the Czech Republic the accounting treatment differs according to whether the holding is long- or short-term. This issue is not addressed in either IAS or the 7th Directive and has not been included in the supranational comparison in Table 3(a).

COMPARISON OF RELEVANT REQUIREMENTS FOR THE DETERMINATION OF A GROUP

Table 2(a) schedules the relevant requirements for the determination of a group for the three countries and Table 2(b) schedules the supranational requirements.

In the UK, consistent with the IAS and the 7th Directive, a group consists of the parent and its subsidiary undertakings. In the Czech Republic it is clear from Article 22(2) of the *Accounting Act 1991* that a group may comprise a holding entity with associates only.[6] In the Polish requirements a capital group consists of the parent company and *either* subsidiaries *or* associates (*Accounting Act 1994*, Article 55(1)). In fact, Polish legislation exempts a parent with only associates from consolidation unless the parent is a listed company, in which case consolidation using the equity method is required. The Czech and Polish requirements define a group in a manner not recognized by supranational requirements and this results in country-specific differences of commission. The wider Czech and Polish definitions are appropriate given the shareholdings held by privatization investment funds as a result of mass privatization program.

Legally in the UK the parent is necessarily a limited liability company but the relevant FRS applies to any parent undertaking regardless of legal form or whether it is operating with or without a view to profit. In Poland, the holding entity must be a share capital company. The requirements are silent on the profit objective but a share capital company incorporated under the provisions of commercial law will be operating with a view to profit. The Czech requirements specify a business company that may include a partnership but that excludes operations without a view to profit. The IAS apply to any "enterprise" regardless of legal form but which operates with a view to profit. The 7th Directive is silent on the profit objective and is primarily directed at limited liability companies although unincorporated parent undertakings are also required to draw up consolidated accounts if any of their subsidiaries are a limited liability company but there is an option to exempt them. These different positions are summarized in Fig. 4.

The Czech Republic and Poland have limited their legislation to entities trading with a view to profit, in line with the IAS rather than the wider scope of the 7th Directive. Polish requirements are further limited to share capital companies and this, combined with the view to profit orientation, represents a country-specific difference of commission. In the transition from a command to a market economy, it is logical for new legislation to deal first with the newly emerging, profit-orientated business sector. However, a consequence of the Polish regulations is that existing state-owned enterprises whose legal form has not been changed to that of a share capital company do not fall within the scope of the

382   THE INTERNATIONAL JOURNAL OF ACCOUNTING   Vol. 35, No. 3, 2000

	Profit orientation	
	View to profit only	Any orientation
Limited liability/share capital companies	Poland.	7th Directive & option (art.4(2)). UK (Companies Act).
Legal form · All entities	IAS. Czech Republic.	7th Directive + no option (art.4(1)). UK (FRS2).

Figure 4.   Scope of Consolidation: Legal Form and Profit Orientation of Parent/Holding Company.

consolidation regulations. Important intercompany links in the still substantial state-owned sector of the Polish economy remain obscured and there is no level playing field for market transactions among state-owned and share capital (mainly private) enterprises. With respect to the legal form and profit orientation of subsidiary companies in all requirements the definitions are drafted to include all entities, regardless of legal form or profit orientation.

In terms of the parent/subsidiary relationship, a country-specific difference of commission arises only in the Czech Republic where there is no explicit mention of voting rights but reference is made to a share in the "basic assets."[7] A provision in the Czech requirements deals with consolidation by more than one holding entity but does not cover the situation where one holding entity owns more than 50 percent of the equity share capital but another entity holds more than 50 percent of the voting rights. The focus on shares not votes is outdated and the temporizing Czech measures may have been modeled on out-of-date legislation.

All requirements specify a right to exercise control by virtue of a company deed or a contract. A related issue is whether the controlling company is required to be a member of the controlled undertaking. Under the UK and Polish rules, membership is not a requirement. In the Czech requirements, the *Accounting Act 1991* and the *Consolidation Measure 1993* differ. The former (Article 22(2)) uses the phrase "... regardless of the level of its ownership interest." The latter states "... and is also a shareholder or partner in the given entity." The 7th Directive allows either approach but to incorporate both is inconsistent. The relevant IAS does not require membership of the controlled undertaking ("... owns one-half or less ...") as long as the text bears the interpretation that ownership of nothing is still ownership. Cairns (1995) takes this view.

The Czech requirements for determining the parent/subsidiary relationship contain no further criteria. The UK and IAS criterion, control of the board, specifies the appointment and removal of directors holding a majority of the voting rights and not, as in Poland and the 7th Directive, the appointment and removal of a simple majority of the directors. The national differences are explained by differences in supranational requirements except for the country-specific difference of omission in the Czech Republic. Article 1.1(d) of the 7th Directive is an option whereby an entity may be considered *de facto* a subsidiary if the parent is a member and the majority of directors have been appointed solely as a result of the exercise of voting rights but this option has not been taken up in any of the requirements (including IAS).

The fourth criterion in Polish legislation, i.e., companies sharing a common board membership, has no equivalent in UK legislation. The Polish criterion applies whether or not the parent is itself a member of the subsidiary entity. A difficulty in the application of this rule in the absence of a uni-directional or any shareholding occurs where two companies have common majority board membership: which is the parent and which is the subsidiary given the absence of *de facto* criteria for determination of the relationship in Polish legislation? This criterion is equivalent to the option contained in Article 12 (1)(b) of the 7th Directive. The UK did not take up this option; the IAS and Czech requirements are silent. In respect of control through agreements with others entitled to vote the UK, Polish, and supranational requirements are equivalent. The Czech Republic exhibits a country-specific difference of omission in having no equivalent criterion. The UK requirement regarding *de facto* control originates as a 7th Directive option and has not been taken up by the Polish legislators. The decision by Poland not to incorporate the option leaves its criteria for determining the parent/subsidiary relationship more consistent with IAS that similarly have no overriding *de facto* criteria. By default the Czech Republic is also in this position. The UK and the 7th Directive require consolidation with respect to groups with subsidiaries and the intention of the Polish and Czech legislation and the IAS is identical. Neither the countries nor IAS contain a provision equivalent to that in Article 12(1)(a) of the 7th Directive.

Further differences arise in the definition of a parent/associate relationship. The Czech requirements use numerical thresholds of more than 20 percent and less than 50 percent but stated in terms of share ownership and not voting rights. The issue of ownership within the relevant parameters but with no exercise of significant influence is dealt with only in terms of written contracts or provisions in the entity's statute. The Czech definition of significant influence presumes the existence of a shareholding. The Polish legislation requires that an entity in which the parent holds between 20 and 50 percent of the voting capital be treated as an associate. An additional requirement indicates that a significant influence may exist in situations other than that of holding this specified level of voting capital. Both the UK and the IAS stress the exercise of significant influence and the 20 percent threshold is a rebuttable presumption of the existence of significant influence. The 7th Directive uses the term "presumed" but without further explanation. Country-specific differences of commission in the Czech Republic and Poland are observable from this comparison. The Czech Republic does not recognize the possibility of significant influence where share ownership is less than the 20 percent threshold. In circumstances where voting rights are between 20 and 50 percent, the UK, IAS, and 7th Directive requirements acknowledge that significant influence may not exist. The Czech regulations provide that the parent/associate relationship based on the thresholds may not subsist only in the presence of statutory or contractual provisions. In Poland, it would appear that there is no acknowledgment of ownership within the thresholds without significant influence. The Czech and Polish decisions to eschew *de facto* significant influence criteria are attributable to the short period of transition during which track records of the exercise of de facto significant influence will be difficult to establish hence regulations that emphasize legal criteria. The exercise of de facto significant influence is a more subtle form of control that requires the operation of a sophisticated market economy to appreciate.

In the UK, the *Companies Act 1985* dealt with joint venture relationships and required inclusion using proportional consolidation unless the joint venture was a corporate body. In the latter case, joint ventures were treated as either associates or subsidiaries depending upon the circumstances. *FRS 9 Associates and Joint Ventures* (ASB, 1997) has now clarified the treatment of joint ventures. The "gross equity method" is required for joint ventures by the standard. This is an expanded form of equity accounting. As regards supranational rules, the IAS allow use of either the proportional method or the equity method. The 7th Directive specifies proportional consolidation as an option otherwise equity accounting is used. The national requirements exhibit country-specific differences of omission: neither Poland nor the Czech Republic regulates the consolidation of joint ventures.

COMPARISON OF EXEMPTIONS FROM THE CONSOLIDATION REQUIREMENT

In all requirements, an exemption exists for small-/medium-sized groups. In the UK, Poland, and the 7th Directive, the size criteria are specified in terms of balance sheet total, turnover, and number of employees and the exemption relates to two of these three thresholds. The Czech Republic specifies balance sheet total and turnover only and both thresholds apply. In each of the countries exemptions on the grounds of size do not apply if any member of the group is a listed company. The IAS do not include any specific size criteria but are not intended to apply to immaterial items. The supranational rules are effectively equivalent in that both address the problem of size criteria and no country-specific differences arise.

In each country the consolidation requirement applies not only to the direct subsidiaries of the parent but also to sub-subsidiaries of the parent, i.e., where the subsidiary of a parent company is itself a parent. As a result, national requirements address the problem of exempting parent undertakings that are themselves subsidiaries. The shareholding in the exempted parent must exceed 90 percent in the Polish requirements and 95 percent in the UK. The Polish exemption requires the prior agreement of the minority whereas in the UK the minorities must request preparation of the consolidated accounts in the absence of which agreement to the exemption is assumed. In the Czech requirements a level of shareholding exceeding 90 percent automatically exempts the sub-group. If the holding is between 50 and 90 percent then the minority may request group accounts in the absence of which agreement to the exemption is assumed.

Unlike Polish requirements the UK allows UK-established wholly owned parents of companies registered in EU member states exemption from consolidation. This is unsurprising, as Poland cannot be expected to favor members of a club to which it does not belong. The Czech Republic, not a member of the EU, exempts sub-groups with foreign (not just EU) parents from consolidation if ultimate parent's accounts are prepared in accordance with the 7th Directive. The IAS and the 7th Directive exempt wholly owned parents. Neither Polish nor Czech requirements distinguish between wholly owned and virtually wholly owned parents. Both the IAS and the 7th Directive exempt virtually wholly owned parents and both indicate 90 percent as the appropriate virtual threshold and require some form of minority approval.

The 7th Directive extends this exemption for the wholly owned and virtually wholly owned parents of ultimate parents where the latter are governed by the law of a Member State. However, the 7th Directive contains an option allowing Member States to extend this exemption to non-EU ultimate parents conditional upon the ultimate parent's consolidated accounts being drawn up in accordance with the 7th Directive or in an equivalent manner. The IAS, unsurprisingly, do not specify any jurisdictional boundaries on the exemption. Each of the countries adopts a different approach within the parameters of the supranational rules. Poland adopts the IAS approach; the UK adopts the 7th Directive without the option to extend to non-EU ultimate parents; the Czech Republic adopts the 7th Directive with this option. There are no country-specific differences despite the diversity.

COMPARISON OF BASES FOR EXCLUSION FROM CONSOLIDATION

Next to be considered are the bases upon which it is permitted to exclude subsidiaries from the group accounts. Polish regulations and IAS require exclusion of subsidiaries and associates acquired exclusively with a view to resale. The Czech requirements adopt the permissive approach of the 7th Directive: the decision is at the discretion of the holding entity. In the UK the exclusion is with reference to subsidiaries held with a view to resale *and* that have not previously been consolidated. A difference within UK requirements, however, can be observed between the *Companies Act 1985* and *FRS 2 Accounting for Subsidiary Undertakings* (ASB, 1992). The former states that the subsidiary may be excluded, the latter that it should be excluded. The approach of the standard is considered best practice. Each set of requirements seems to allow such a subsidiary to be excluded from consolidation for a number of successive years. In the UK, however, *FRS 2* establishes that there should be a reasonable expectation of disposal within 1 year of acquisition as in the IAS that refers to "... disposal in the near future." There is no such condition attached to the Polish or Czech requirements nor in the 7th Directive.

The UK devolves the decision on materiality levels to the entity and, effectively, its statutory auditors consistent with the approach of the 7th Directive. The Polish and Czech requirements exhibit country-specific differences of commission in specifying thresholds of insignificance. In Poland, the thresholds are 10 or 20 percent of balance sheet or revenue totals of the holding company and the group (before exclusions), respectively. The Czech requirements refer to balance sheet and revenue totals without numerical thresholds. IAS do not apply to immaterial items.

There is a Polish requirement for exclusion on the basis that control is expected to last for less than 1 year from the balance sheet date. There is no equivalent basis in any other requirements. The Polish requirement requires the de-consolidation of a subsidiary where disposal is expected within 1 year of the balance sheet date. In the UK it is a requirement that any subsidiary previously consolidated will continue to be so up until the date of disposal.

All requirements recognize restrictions on control as a basis for exclusion. Differences exist in terms of whether the exclusion is obligatory or permissive, the way restrictions are characterized and the extent to which there is explanation of the effect of the restrictions on control. The obligatory nature of the exclusion is found in the IAS, in FRS 2 in the UK and in the Polish legislation. The permissive approach is adopted by the 7th Directive, UK law, and the Czech requirements. The restrictions

386   THE INTERNATIONAL JOURNAL OF ACCOUNTING   Vol. 35, No. 3, 2000

are characterized in the IAS, the 7th Directive, and the UK as having to be both severe and long-term. The Polish legislation is brief in the extreme: the exclusion applies to control that is restricted in a material way. The Czech requirement specifies "long-term" but does not specify nor define the degree of restriction. It does, however, specify a cause for the restrictions, i.e., political reasons. These are country-specific differences of commission.

Neither the Polish nor Czech requirements contain any explication of the effect of the restrictions on control and these represent country-specific differences of omission. In the UK and the 7th Directive restrictions are explained in terms of the exercise of rights over assets or management of the subsidiary. The IAS explains the restrictions in terms of the ability to transfer funds to the parent. None of the explanations of what contributes restrictions are identical. The extent to which they are equivalent is more problematic. The UK and 7th Directive requirements are clearly equivalent. The IAS criterion would appear to be more restrictive in its emphasis on rights of repatriation of funds. The brevity of the Polish requirement means that it may bear any interpretation including those not meeting supranational criteria. The phrase "political reasons" in the Czech requirements either subsumes all of the above criteria or is different from them depending upon its interpretation.

The IAS prohibits dissimilar activities as a basis for exclusion of a subsidiary. In the UK exclusion on this basis is seen as so exceptional that it is not possible to identify circumstances in which it may occur. In the Polish requirements "production, construction, and service activities" are dissimilar to the provision of "banking or insurance." The Czech requirements are drafted strangely, however, the effect is to exclude on the basis of dissimilar activities the entities identified in Article I (2) of the *Chart of Accounts Decree 1992*, e.g., banks, insurance companies, national property funds and state budget entities. The UK requirements follow the 7th Directive in that dissimilarity of this type is not considered sufficient grounds for the exclusion of subsidiaries. Exclusion on this basis is mandatory in Poland, the UK, and the 7th Directive but is permissive in the Czech Republic that represents a country-specific difference of commission. The Czech Republic and Poland exhibit country-specific differences of commission in the treatment of banking and insurance subsidiaries.

Disproportionate expense and undue delay are not recognized as bases for exclusion in Poland or the IAS and although they are reasons for exclusion in UK company law and the 7th Directive, they are not permitted under the UK's *FRS 2 Accounting for Subsidiary Undertakings* (ASB, 1992). The Czech requirements allow exclusion on the basis of disproportionate expense but only if the subsidiary is based abroad. Once more, the Czech requirements are the most permissive and represent a country-specific difference of commission.

The Czech requirements permit two further bases for exclusion: the first basis permits the exclusion of partnerships and the second basis permits the exclusion of subsidiaries in liquidation. These bases for exclusion represent a country-specific difference of commission. Article 15(1) of the 7th Directive contains an option permitting the omission from consolidation of any parent undertaking not carrying on any industrial or commercial activity that holds shares in a subsidiary undertaking on the basis of a joint arrangement with one or more undertakings not included in the consolidated accounts. This option has not been taken up in any of the countries and does not feature in the IAS.

DISCUSSION OF RESULTS

Table 3(a) summarizes the equivalence or non-equivalence of national requirements. Table 3(b) quantifies their frequency. Table 3(b)(i) focuses on requirements where the 7th Directive and the IAS are equivalent and Table 3(b)(ii) on non-equiva-lent requirements.

An important result is the identification of a number of non-equivalencies between IAS and the 7th Directive. This result conflicts with previous work in the area. While Cairns (1995) states that "(t)he tests for the existence of control in IAS 27 are virtually the same as in the Seventh Directive" this study has identified three differences relating to: tests for control of the board; common board membership; de facto control. The interpretation of "virtually the same" is subjective and depends upon the level of detail compared as illustrated in the approach taken by the EC Contact Committee on the Accounting Directives (European Commission, 1996):

> One approach would be to compare systematically the two accounting systems (IAS and Accounting Directives) and highlight the existing differences. However, this approach was dismissed because of the substantially different way in which accounting is dealt with in the Accounting Directives and in the IAS. (. . .) For the above reasons, a systematic comparison between IAS and the Accounting Directives would result in the collection of a huge amount of differences. However, only a limited part of this information would be useful for the objective of the analysis. The Contact Committee has therefore not entered into a detailed examination of those issues which are logically dependent on the fundamentally different nature of the two systems (Accounting Directives and IAS).

That the majority of non-equivalencies are systematic is not borne out by the analysis in this article that identifies 15 non-equivalencies. Perhaps four issues (single economic entity, management report, parent undertaking, and the exclusion of financial subsidiaries) may be attributed to systematic differences. The other 11 non-equivalencies cannot be explained away in this manner. The Contact Committee identifies exclusion on the basis of dissimilar activities as one unsystematic difference (European Commission, 1996). The approach adopted by the Committee is less rigorous than this study as it involves an a priori judgment as to which differences are systematic and which are not. For transition economies these supranational non-equivalencies provide an impediment to smooth accounting reform. On the one hand, the political goal of EU membership requires compliance with the 7th Directive; on the other hand the economic imperative of attracting foreign direct investment favors compliance with IAS. It has been reported that the EC has proposals in process that will allow listed companies in EU member states to use IAS in their main accounts (Kelly, 1999). It is not clear how these proposals will affect the requirements of the *White Paper 1995*. In terms of compliance with supranational requirements, transition countries have to aim at a constantly moving target.

The cross-national data were compared to equivalent (Table 3(b)(i)) and non-equivalent supranational requirements (Table 3(b)(ii)). The UK complies fully with equivalent requirements that are unsurprising given that it is a mature market economy closely involved in the development of the supranational requirements. Both Poland and the Czech Republic, however, are in transition. The 7th Directive (1983) and the relevant IAS (1989) pre-date the transition. The requirements of both countries were promulgated after

388   THE INTERNATIONAL JOURNAL OF ACCOUNTING   Vol. 35, No. 3, 2000

Table 3.   *De Jure* Comparison in a Supranational Context

(a) Analysis of de jure comparison in a supranational context

Item	Issue	UK	Poland	Czech Republic
1.	Objective:			
	single economic entity,	C	X	C
	excluded uses (dividend and taxation purposes).	A	A	X
2.	Contents:			
	profit and loss account, balance sheet, and notes on the accounts,	A	A	A
	management report/review,	B	B	B
	cash flow statement.	C	C	C
3.	Definition of a group:			
	parent and subsidiaries	A	A	A
	parent with associates only	A	X	X
4.	Undertaking/entity:			
	parent (legal form and profit orientation)	B	X	C
	subsidiaries (legal form and profit orientation).	A	A	A
5.	Parent/subsidiary relationships:			
	majority of voting rights,	A	A	X
	control by deed or contract,	A	A	A
	control of the board,	C	B	N
	common board membership,	C	B	C
	control through agreements with others entitled to vote,	A	A	N
	de facto control,	B	C	C
	control of sub-subsidiaries (vertical groups).	A	A	A
6.	Parent/associate relationships:			
	20 to 50 percent threshold, plus rebuttable presumption,	A	X	X

7.	Joint venture relationships: joint control		
	definition	A	N	N
8.	Exempt parent undertakings:		
	size criteria,	A	A	A
	90 percent threshold, plus minority agreement,	A	A	A
	jurisdictional boundaries.	B	C	B
9.	Bases for exclusion from consolidation:		
	view to resale,	C	CB
	materiality,	B	XX
	control not for the long term,	A	A	XA
	restrictions on control:		
	permissive exclusion,	C	CB
	nature of restrictions,	A	A	XX
	explication of restrictions;	B	B	NN
	dissimilar activities:		
	permissive exclusion,	B	B	BX
	exclusion of financial subsidiaries;	B	B	XX
	disproportionate expense or undue delay,	C	C	CX
	other bases.	A	A	AX

(continued on next page)

Table 3. *(continued)*

(b) Summary of de jure comparison in a supranational context

Equivalence/non-equivalence with:	Category	UK	Poland	Czech Republic
(i) Equivalent supranational requirements				
7th Directive and IAS	A	17	12	8
Country-specific difference of commission	X	0	4	7
Country-specific difference of omission	N	0	1	2
(ii) Non-equivalent supranational requirements				
7th Directive only	B	8	4	4
IAS only	C	7	6	5
Country-specific difference of commission	X	0	4	4
Country-specific difference of omission	N	0	1	2

Key: A = Equivalent to 7th Directive and IAS. B = Equivalent to 7th Directive only. C = Equivalent to IAS only. X = Country-specific difference of commission. N = Country-specific difference of omission.

these dates but the timescale for full assimilation of the issues has been relatively short resulting in the observable differences. Poland exhibits greater equivalence than the Czech Republic but this may be explained by its earlier adoption of an EU accession strategy and later regulation (Fig. 5). The Czech Republic exhibits a higher number of country-specific differences and thus the rules are more idiosyncratic which result is attributed to earlier relevant legislation (1993). Other inaccuracies due to the hasty introduction of simplified consolidation rules in the Czech Republic are especially visible in the (lack of) criteria specifying the parent/subsidiary relationship. Failure to re-specify ownership in terms of voting rights and to add other criteria will leave Czech consolidation requirements open to abuse through creative accounting techniques as well as deficient in respect to compliance with the 7th Directive. These differences provide evidence of the effects of adopting different methods of privatization as discussed above.

Where no supranational equivalencies exist (Table 3(b)(ii)) a difference between the UK and the transition economies is again observable. In respect of the 15 non-equivalencies, the UK has complied with either the 7th Directive or the IAS. Further analysis of the country-specific differences of commission reveals few in the more fundamental requirements, e.g., contents of the financial statements, the parent/subsidiary relationship (Table 3(a)). More frequent are country-specific differences of commission in issues such as the parent/associate relationship and bases for exclusion. An important country-specific difference of omission is the absence of requirements on consolidation accounting for joint ventures in Poland and the Czech Republic. This absence may be compensated by the country-specific differences of commission on accounting for associated companies that define a group in terms of a parent and associate only (for listed companies in Poland; for all companies in the Czech Republic). This may be a transitional solution but given the development of innovative trading and investment relationships it will be necessary in the future to devise accounting methods to which distinguish between associates and joint ventures. That the transition economies favor legal criteria for defining the parent/associate relationship over the criterion of *de facto*

Event	UK	Poland	Czech Republic
Date of Europe (Association) Agreement	Not applicable	1 February 1994	1 February 1995
Date of application for European Union membership	10 May 1967	5 April 1994	17 January 1996
Date of accession	1 January 1973	To be agreed	To be agreed
Date of relevant consolidation legislation (7th Directive : 1983)	1989	1994	1993

Figure 5. Chronology of Events Relevant to EU Accession and Consolidation Requirements. Source: Adapted from Avery and Cameron, 1998.

392   THE INTERNATIONAL JOURNAL OF ACCOUNTING   Vol. 35, No. 3, 2000

significant influence preferred by the UK and supranational rules is attributable to the short period of existence and emerging nature of the market economy.

The differences with respect to bases for exclusion from consolidation are more difficult to explain systematically except in terms of the timescale for full assimilation. The Polish criterion that excludes subsidiaries from consolidation on the grounds that control is not for the long term falls into this category, as does the Czech basis for exclusion on the grounds of political restrictions on control. Both of these idiosyncratic provisions need to be revised to achieve compliance with supranational requirements. In contrast, the exclusion of financial subsidiaries from consolidation is a systematic difference that reflects a greater need for separate regulation of the reforming financial sector given the adverse consequences of banking collapse for the socioeconomic transformation process as a whole.

The analysis of the data in Table 3(b) is performed in terms of the supranational comparison and does not highlight where national equivalencies with supranational requirements coincide, i.e., to what extent do the 8 equivalencies with supranational rules for the Czech Republic identified in Table 3(b)(i) match the 12 equivalencies identified for Poland? Table 4(a) lists patterns of compliance and their incidence for equivalent supranational requirements and Table 4(b) for non-equivalent supranational requirements. The results indicate that the analysis in Table 3(b) implicitly overstates the extent of uniformity, especially in relation to non-equivalent supranational requirements. Polish and Czech equivalencies with the 7th Directive (code B) each number a total of four (compared to the UK's total of eight), however, Table 4(b) lists only one case where these equivalencies coincide (i.e., in a BBB pattern as in Table 3(a)). Also, there is only one instance of a CCC pattern despite the fact that the number of matches from Table 3(b)(ii) could number as many as five, the total number of Czech equivalencies with IAS. In terms of equivalent supranational requirements (Table 4(a)) there is a better cross-

Table 4.   Cross-National Patterns of Compliance with Supranational Requirements

Pattern	Incidence
(a) Equivalent supranational requirements	
AAA	7
AAX	5
AXX	3
AAN	1
ANN	1
Total	17
(b) Non-equivalent supranational requirements	
BBB	1
CCC	1
BBX	1
BXX	2
BNN	1
CCX	2
BBC	1
BCC	4
BCX	1
BCN	1
Total	15

national match with seven from a possible eight AAA patterns occurring. Nevertheless, the analysis confirms the existence of substantial cross-national diversity in the application of supranational *de jure* requirements among the three countries.

CONCLUSIONS

The article presents a comparative analysis of *de jure* consolidation requirements in the UK, Poland, and the Czech Republic highlighting the existence of non-equivalencies cross-nationally and supranationally that are non-trivial and more frequent than the previous research suggests. In particular, the differences exhibited by the economies in transition provide evidence of the prolonged but different nature of the accounting reforms. A number of these differences detailed above arise from the incomplete or inaccurate incorporation of supranational provisions into national requirements and because of this, their planned revision will not be problematic. Other differences will be more difficult to eliminate as they are attributable to the prolonged transition and the nature of privatization strategies: the wider definition of a group; the legal form and profit orientation of the parent; the avoidance of *de facto* significant influence tests for associates; the lack of specific joint venture consolidation rules; the exclusion of financial subsidiaries from consolidation. These differences may or may not become permanent as the transition economies of the Czech Republic and Poland mature.

    In the absence of a theoretical framework for determining the content and sequence of accounting reform in transition, accounting change defaults to an iterative process of learning by doing. On this basis, further research may reveal that the experiences of Poland and the Czech Republic are representative of other economies in transition.

NOTES

1.   The study is part of a larger comparative research project on the accounting and taxation aspects of groups within the three countries sponsored by the UK's Economic and Social Research Council (ESRC) whose generous financial support is gratefully acknowledged by the authors (R000222118).
2.   The larger research project referred to in footnote 1 above will subsequently deal with group accounting requirements, a de facto comparative analysis of published group financial statements and a comparison of requirements for tax, as opposed to accounting, groups.
3.   In the same table, Jermakowicz and Rinke (1996) state that "Czech law does not require Statement of Cash Flows," which would not seem to be consistent with Article 5 of the Decree on Financial Statements for Entrepreneurs, No. 281/71 701/1995, which states that a cash flow statement is required as a component part of the notes to the accounts. With reference to Poland, Jermakowicz and Rinke (1996, p. 80) that consolidated accounts are required if a company holds 50 percent of the equity or controlling interest, when in fact it is clear from the relevant Polish requirements that, unlike the Czech Republic, the share of voting rights is the criterion. Additionally, Polish law does require consolidated accounts to be prepared for groups consisting of a holding company and associates only, as in the Czech Republic, but that unlisted groups are exempted from this requirement (see main text below). It is also not the case that the reporting period in Poland is required to be the calendar year (*Accounting Act 1994*, Article 3 (1)(8)) although this is the case for the Czech Republic (*Accounting Act 1991*, Section 3(2)).

394   THE INTERNATIONAL JOURNAL OF ACCOUNTING   Vol. 35, No. 3, 2000

4. With respect to the cash flow statement in Poland, Adams and McMillan (1997) state that there is a requirement to produce a cash flow statement according to one of three templates. However, given that one of the templates is designed for insurers, another for banks, and the third for all other companies, the implication that companies have some sort of choice as to template is misleading.

5. Due to limitations of space, only extracts from Tables 1 and 2 are reproduced here. Full versions of the tables are available from the authors upon request.

6. Article 22(2) of *Accounting Act 1991*: Consolidated financial statements shall be prepared by a company (entity) having at least a 20 percent ownership interest in another company, or being authorized to manage another company (entity) on the basis of a contract or company statutes (articles of association), regardless of the level of its ownership interest.

7. Zelenka (1995) translates this as:"... direct or indirect holding of more than 50 percent of the subsidiary's equity share capital, ..." This translation does not mention voting rights and therefore does not alter the analysis.

REFERENCES

Accounting Standards Board (ASB). 1992. *Financial Reporting Standard No. 2 Accounting for Subsidiary Undertakings.* London: ASB.

Accounting Standards Board (ASB). 1997. *Financial Reporting Standard No. 9 Associates and Joint Ventures.* London: ASB.

Adams, Carol A. and Katarzyna M. McMillan. 1997. "Internationalizing Financial Reporting in a Newly Emerging Market Economy: The Polish Example." *Advances in International Accounting, 10:* 139–164.

Alexander, David. 1993. "A European True and Fair View?" *European Accounting Review, 2*(1): 59–60.

Alexander, David and Simon Archer. 1995. "Eastern Europe: Overview." In Alexander, David and Simon Archer, eds. *"European Accounting Guide,"* 2nd edn. New York: Harcourt Brace and Company, pp. 1371–1377.

Avery, Graham and Fraser Cameron. 1998. *The Enlargement of the European Union.* Sheffield, UK: Sheffield Academic Press.

Bailey, Derek. 1995. "Accounting in Transition in the Transitional Economy." *European Accounting Review, 4*(4): 595–623.

Cairns, David. 1995. *A Guide to Applying International Accounting Standards.* Milton Keynes, UK: Institute of Chartered Accountants in England and Wales.

"Companies Act 1985." In *British Companies Legislation 1997.* Oxford: CCH Editions, pp. 101–759.

"Companies Act 1989." In *British Companies Legislation 1997.* Oxford: CCH Editions, pp. 2201–2313.

Craner, John. 1993. "Privatisation in Czechoslovakia and the EC Harmonisation of Financial Reporting: A Problem of Matching." *European Business and Economic Development, 1*(4) (January): 7–15.

Dixon, Rob and Alicja Jaruga. 1994. "The Changing Face of Accountancy in Poland." In *The New Europe: Recent Political and Economic Implications for Accountants and Accounting.* University of Illinois: Centre for International Education and Research in Accounting, pp. 233–252.

Dolezal, Jan. 1995. "The Czech Republic." In Alexander, David and Simon Archer, eds. *"European Accounting Guide",* 2nd edn. New York: Harcourt Brace and Company, pp. 1465–1484.

European Bank for Reconstruction and Development (EBRD). 1995. *Transition Report.* London: EBRD.

European Bank for Reconstruction and Development (EBRD). 1996. *Transition Report.* London: EBRD.

European Bank for Reconstruction and Development (EBRD). 1997. *Transition Report.* London: EBRD.

European Commission. 1978. "Fourth Council Directive of 25 July 1978 on the Coordination of National Legislation Governing the Annual Accounts of Certain Types of Companies (78/660/EEC)." *Official Journal of the European Communities, No. L222/11–31.*

European Commission. 1983. "Seventh Council Directive of 13 June 1983 Based on the Article 54(3)(g) of the Treaty on Consolidated Accounts (83/349/EEC)." *Official Journal of the European Communities, No. L193/1–17.*

European Commission. 1995. *White Paper: Preparation of the Associated Countries of Central and Eastern Europe for Integration into the Internal Market of the Union.* 1983 COM(95) 163 final (3 May 1995). Brussels: European Commission.

European Commission. 1996. *Contact Committee on the Accounting Directives: An Examination of the Conformity Between the International Accounting Standards and the European Accounting Directives.* Luxembourg: European Commission.

Federation des Experts Comptables Europeens (FEE) 1991. *European Survey of Published Accounts.* 1991. London: Routledge.

Federation des Experts Comptables Europeens (FEE). 1992. *Analysis of European Accounting and Disclosure Practices.* London: Routledge.

Federation des Experts Comptables Europeens (FEE). 1993. *Seventh Directive Options and their Implementation.* London: Routledge.

Garrod, Neil and Stuart McLeay, eds. 1996. *Accounting in Transition: The Implications of Political and Economic Reform in Central Europe.* London: Routledge.

Gray, Sidney J. and Clare B. Roberts. 1991. "East–West Accounting Issues: A New Agenda." *Accounting Horizons,* 5(1) (March): 42–50.

Gray, Sidney J., Adolf Coenenberg, and Paul Gordon. 1993. *International Group Accounting: Issues in European Harmonization.* London: Routledge

Holeckova, Jaroslava. 1996. "Relationship Between Accounting and Taxation in the Czech Republic." *European Accounting Review,* (Supplement) 5: 859–869.

International Accounting Standards Committee (IASC). 1989. *Framework for the Preparation and Presentation of Financial Statements.* London: IASC.

International Accounting Standards Committee (IASC). 1989. *International Accounting Standard No. 27 Consolidated Financial Statements and Accounting for Investments in Subsidiaries.* 1989. London: IASC.

International Accounting Standards Committee (IASC). 1989. *International Accounting Standard No. 28 Accounting for Investments in Associates.* London: IASC.

International Accounting Standards Committee (IASC). 1998. *Current Project: Developing Countries and Countries in Transition.* 1989 Online at http://www.iasc.org.uk/frame/cen3_23.htm.

International Bank for Reconstruction and Development (The World Bank). 1996. *World Development Report 1996: From Plan to Market.* 1998. New York: Oxford University Press.

Jaruga, Alicja. 1991. "Accounting Issues Arising in the Context of the Transition to Market Economies: The Experience of Poland." In *OECD. Accounting Reform in Central and Eastern Europe.* Paris: Centre for Co-operation with European Economies in Transition, pp. 39–41.

Jaruga, Alicja. 1993a. "Changing Rules of Accounting in Poland." *European Accounting Review,* 2(1): 115–126.

Jaruga, Alicja. 1993b. "New Accounting Regulation in Poland: Current Issues." *Research in Third World Accounting,* 2: 856–896.

Jaruga, Alicja. 1995. "Poland." In Alexander, David and Simon Archer, eds. *"European Accounting Guide"*, 2nd edn. New York: Harcourt Brace and Company, pp. 1465–1484.

Jaruga, Alicja. 1996. "Accounting in Socialist Countries: The Beginnings of Reform." In Garrod, Stuart and Stuart McLeay, eds. *Accounting in Transition*. London: Routledge, pp. 12–27.

Jaruga, Alicja and Anna Szychta. 1997. "The Origin and Evolution of Charts of Accounts in Poland." *European Accounting Review, 6*(3): 509–526.

Jaruga, Alicja, Ewa Walinska, and Andrzej Baniewicz. 1996. "The Relationship Between Accounting and Taxation in Poland." *European Accounting Review,* (Supplement) *5*: 883–897.

Jermakowicz, Eva and Dolors F. Rinke. 1996. "The New Accounting Standards in the Czech Republic, Hungary, and Poland vis-a-vis International Accounting Standards and European Union directives." *Journal of International Accounting and Taxation, 5*(1): 73–87.

Johnson, Todd. 1999. "Levelling the Playing Field." *Accountancy, 123*(1270).

Kamela-Sowinska, Aldona. 1995. "Goodwill in the Process of Privatization in Poland." *European Accounting Review, 4*(4): 765–776.

Kelly, Jim. 1999. "Brussels Pushes for Changes on Company Reports." *Financial Times,* (February) *19*: 1.

Krzywda, Danuta, Derek Bailey, and Marek Schroeder. 1994. "Financial Reporting by Polish Listed Companies for 1991." *European Accounting Review, 3*(2): 311–328.

Krzywda, Danuta, Derek Bailey, and Marek Schroeder. 1995. "A Theory of European Accounting Development Applied to Accounting Change in Contemporary Poland." *European Accounting Review, 4*(4): 625–657.

Krzywda, Danuta, Derek Bailey, and Marek Schroeder. 1996. "The Impact of Accounting Regulation on Financial Reporting in Poland." In: Garrod, Neil and Stuart McLeay, eds. *"Accounting in Transition."* London: Routledge, pp. 61–92.

Langr, Ladislav. 1991. "Income Statement and Profit Allocation in the Czech and Slovak Federal Republic." In *OECD. Accounting Reform in Central and Eastern Europe*. Paris: Centre for Co-operation with European Economies in Transition, pp. 67–70.

Lisiecka-Zajac, Bozena.. 1991. "The Reform of Accountancy in Poland." In *OECD. Accounting Reform in Central and Eastern Europe*. Paris: Centre for Co-operation with European Economies in Transition, pp. 139–142.

Meek, Gary K. and Shahrokh M. Saudagaran. 1990. "A Survey of Research on Financial Reporting in a Transnational Context." *Journal of Accounting Literature, 9*: 145–182.

Ministry of Finance. 1993. Opatreni kterym se stanovi postupy pro provedeni konsolidace ucetni zaverky. Cj. 281/73, 570/1993.

Misinska, Danuta. 1998. "Przeslanki Przestrzegania Prawa Bilansowego Przez Podmioty Gospodarcze." In *Rachunkowosc w Progu XXIw*. Warsaw: Fundacja Rozwoju Rachunkowosci w Polsce, pp. 173–178.

Nobes, Christopher. 1983. "Review of Multinational Accounting: A Research Framework for the Eighties, by F. D. S. Choi." *Accounting Review, LVIII*(2) (April): 464–465.

Ordelheide, Dieter and Anne Semler. 1995. *Transnational Accounting: A Reference Matrix*. London: Macmillan.

Organization for Economic Co-operation and Development (OECD). 1993. *Valuation and Privatisation*. Paris: Centre for Co-operation with European Economies in Transition.

Organization for Economic Co-operation and Development (OECD) Secretariat. 1991. "Accounting Reforms in Central and Eastern Europe: Main Issues." In : *OECD. Accounting Reform in Central and Eastern Europe*. Paris: Centre for Co-Operation with European Economies Transition, pp. 11–21.

Parker, Robert and Christopher Nobes. 1998. "Financial Reporting in Central and Eastern Europe and China." In Nobes, Christopher and Robert Parker, eds. *Comparative International Accounting*, 5th edn. Hemel Hempstead, UK: Prentice-Hall Europe, pp. 292–304.

Patton, James and Ivan Zelenka. 1997. "An Empirical Analysis of the Determinants of the Extent of Disclosure in Annual Reports of Joint Stock Companies in the Czech Republic." *European Accounting Review, 6*(4): 605–626.

Rahman, Asheq, Hector Perera, and Siva Ganeshanandam. 1996. "Measurement of Formal Harmonisation in Accounting: An Exploratory Study." *Accounting and Business Research, 26*(4): 325–339.

Richard, Jacques. 1998. "Accounting in Eastern Europe: From Communism to Capitalism." In Walton, Peter and Axel Haller, and Bernard Raffournier, eds. *International Accounting*. London: International Thomson Business Press, pp. 295–323.

Rozporzadzenie Ministra Finansow z dnia 14 czerwca 1995 r. w sprawie szczegolowych zasad sporzadzania przez jednostki inne niz banki skonsolidowanych sprawozdan finansowych. *Dziennik Ustaw*, 1995, No.71, item 355.

Schroll, Rudolf. 1995. "The New Accounting System in the Czech Republic." *European Accounting Review, 4*(4): 827–832.

Seal, Willie, Pat Sucher, and Ivan Zelenka. 1995. "The Changing Organisation of Czech accounting." *European Accounting Review, 4*(4): 659–681.

Seal, Willie, Pat Sucher, and Ivan Zelenka. 1996. "Post-Socialist Transition and the Development of an Accountancy Profession in the Czech Republic." *Critical Perspectives on Accounting, 7*: 485–508.

Shama, Avraham and Christopher G. McMahan. 1990. "Perestroika and Soviet Accounting: From a Planned to a Market Economy." *International Journal of Accounting, 25*: 155–169.

Sochacka, Renata and Jean-Louis Malo. 1996. "Emerging Capital Markets, Securities Regulation and Accounting: A Systems Perspective." In Garrod, Neil and Stuart McLeay, eds. *Accounting in Transition*. London: Routledge, pp. 28–42.

Sucher, Pat, Willie Seal, and Ivan Zelenka. 1996. "True and Fair in the Czech Republic: A Note on Local Perceptions." *European Accounting Review, 5*(3): 545–557.

Tay, Judith S. W. and Robert Parker. 1990. "Measuring International Harmonization and Standardization." *Abacus, 26*(1): 71–88.

United Nations Economic and Social Council (UNESCO). 1992. *Accounting Problems Arising During Privatization in Poland. London: Commission on Transnational Corporations, Tenth Session* E/C.10/AC.3. Paris: UNESCO.

Ustawa z dnia 22 marca 1991 r.: Prawo o publicznym obrocie papierami wartosciowymi i funduszach powierniczych, *Dziennik Ustaw*, 1991, No. 35, item 155.

Ustawa z dnia 29 wrzesnia 1994 r. o rachunkowosci. *Dziennik Ustaw*, 1994, No. 121, item 591.

"Zakon c. 563/1991 Sb. o ucetnicvi." *Accounting Legislation in 1997*. 1992. Prague: Trade Links.

Zelenka, Vladimir. 1995. "Legal framework for consolidated financial statements in the Czech Republic compared with international practice." *Paper presented at the 18th Annual Congress of the European Accounting Association, Birmingham, UK, 10–12 May.*

Zelenka, Ivan, William Seal, and Pat Sucher. 1996. "The Emerging Institutional Framework of Accounting in the Czech and Slovak Republics." In Garrod, Neil and Stuart McLeay, eds. *Accounting in Transition*. London: Routledge, pp. 93–115.

[14]

ABACUS, Vol. 38, No. 1, 2002

CHRISTOPHER NOBES

An Analysis of the International Development of the Equity Method

The equity method was used as an early form of consolidation for all sub-sidiaries in the U.K. and for certain subsidiaries in the U.S. Another use of the method in some countries, even in the era of full consolidation, has been in the financial statements of investor legal entities. This seems to result from using the equity method as a technique for valuation or as an aid in the preparation of consolidated statements rather than as a form of consolidation. The method has also been used as a substitute for consolidation for excluded subsidiaries or for controlled companies not included in the definition of subsidiaries. Later, the equity method was introduced for joint ventures and then for other forms of 'strategic alliance', but the latter bring definitional problems, which have led to a consensus around an arbitrary threshold of 20 per cent of voting rights. This article traces these developments across time and space, and criticizes several of the past and present applications of the equity method. There is also an examination of the development of the terms 'equity method' and 'associated company'.

Key words: Accounting; Equity; International.

Across time and across countries, the equity method has been used for different types of investees, and it has also been used in both unconsolidated and con-solidated statements. The present international consensus about its use in con-solidated statements for certain non-subsidiary investees is hard to defend on the basis of extant accounting conceptual frameworks or of legal concepts. The consensus about the threshold (20 per cent shareholding) connected to the use of the equity method seems to have arisen by accident. The spread of the equity method is another example of the international transfer of accounting technology, as

CHRISTOPHER NOBES is PricewaterhouseCoopers Professor of Accounting at the University of Reading. The author is grateful for comments on an earlier draft and for other assistance from David Cairns, Janie Crichton (Accounting Standards Board, London), Sigvard Heurlin (Öhrlings Coopers & Lybrand, Stockholm), Jan Klaassen (KPMG and Free University, Amsterdam), Liesel Knorr (Deutsches Rechnungslegungs Standards Committee), Pat McConnell (Bear Stearns and Co., New York), Malcolm Miller (University of New South Wales), Michael Mumford (University of Lancaster), Christopher Napier (University of Southampton), Dieter Ordelheide (formerly of Goethe University, Frankfurt), Paul Pacter (IASC), Bob Parker (University of Exeter), Alan Roberts (University of Reading), Rolf Rundfelt (KPMG, Stockholm), Michael Wallace (Listing Department, London Stock Exchange), Stefano Zambon (University of Ferrara), Peter van der Zanden (Moret Ernst & Young, Eindhoven), Steve Zeff (Rice University), and to the editor and a referee of this journal. The author is particularly indebted to Malcolm Miller for information on Australia and on empirical studies, to Alan Roberts for information on European regulations, and to Steve Zeff for suggesting a study of early textbooks and for providing photocopies of some relevant parts of them.

INTERNATIONAL DEVELOPMENT OF THE EQUITY METHOD

outlined by Parker (1989) for double-entry bookkeeping and for the true and fair view requirement (see also Nobes, 1993, for the spread of the latter in Europe).

There are several forms of the equity method (e.g., see Ma *et al.*, 1991, p. 188), but the common feature is the inclusion in the investor's income statement of the appropriate proportion of the investee's earnings rather than merely the dividends flowing to the investor or, at the other extreme, rather than the investee's detailed revenues and expenses. In the investor's balance sheet, there is also 'one-line consolidation' of the net assets of the investee rather than merely the cost of the investment and rather than line-by-line consolidation of assets and liabilities. As will be clear to users of American English, the term 'equity method' implies a measurement at the investor's proportion of equity (subject in some versions to adjustment for goodwill), which is equal to net assets. This article does not deal with the technical details of the equity method except when there are underlying theoretical issues of relevance to the paper's theme.

To begin, there is a description of the use of the equity method early in the twentieth century as a form of consolidation used before full consolidation had developed (called 'proto-consolidation', below). Its use in parent company statements (pseudo-consolidation) is also a long established treatment of subsidiaries. Another early use was in consolidated statements for excluded subsidiaries (substitute-consolidation). The next three sections below deal with these uses relating to subsidiaries.

In the 1960s, the equity method began to be recommended also for investments in certain non-subsidiaries: as a form of pseudo-consolidation in investor statements and as a form of semi-consolidation in consolidated statements. It is possible to see pseudo-consolidation and semi-consolidation as techniques of valuation rather than of consolidation. For all these uses, there has been opposition, concentrated in a few countries.

This article pieces together the above history, analyses the reasons for the rise of the equity method and assesses the strength of the criticisms. The threshold for the use of the equity method is also examined. One conclusion is that the forces of accounting harmonization might have overcome logic and law, and that the equity method is inappropriate for most, if not all, of its present uses; a point noted earlier by, for example, Chambers (1974) and Miller and Leo (1997). There is also a summary of previous academic research and a look at the development of the terms used in the context of the equity method in various countries.

Thus, the aim is to contribute to the literature on the international transfer of accounting technology, but there are also major policy implications for standard setting in an area of financial reporting where further developments can be expected soon (Milburn and Chant, 1999). The concentration is on major countries in the English-speaking world and Continental Europe. In the topic areas considered here, the rest of the world has probably derived its practices from these countries. For example, for Japan, there are many consolidation practices similar to those of the U.S.A., including the 20 per cent threshold for equity accounting (Sawa, 1998). Issues of special relevance to group structures in the Far East (e.g., the Keiretsu in Japan or the Chaebol in Korea) are not examined here.

17

PROTO-CONSOLIDATION

In the U.K., the earliest use of the equity method appears to be for the purposes of including subsidiaries in the financial statements of investors as an alternative to consolidation. This method was more common than full consolidation in the 1910s and was still used in the 1920s (Edwards and Webb, 1984, Table 1); for example by Lever Brothers (Edwards, 1989, p. 229). On the whole, the equity method was superseded, in the 1930s, by full consolidation or no consolidation; predominantly the latter (Bircher, 1988, p. 7). Another approach was to treat subsidiaries as though they were branches of the parent. This was still practised in the 1930s in such companies as Unilever (Hodgkins, 1979, p. 45). Only with the Companies Act 1947 did 'branching' finally disappear.

Walker (1978a, pp. 99, 117) suggests that the equity method became less popular because, in the context of the conservative mood following the Royal Mail case, it was interpreted as recognizing unrealized profit. However, Edwards and Webb (1984, p. 40) point out that the equity method is more conservative in the sense that it does not ignore losses of subsidiaries as the cost-based method can. As another part of the explanation, they note that the Greene Committee on law reform and the Companies Act 1928 provided no support for the equity method. The Act required holding companies to show shares in subsidiaries, which would not be shown naturally by the equity method. Counsel's opinion[1] suggested that the balance sheet of the legal entity should be the one filed and presented to the shareholders.

In the U.S., a more full-blooded approach to consolidation was taken at the beginning of the century, without much need for partial steps such as the equity method. This seems to be due to fewer legal problems in the U.S., less conservatism of practice, and to acceptance of consolidation for certain purposes by the tax authorities and the New York Stock Exchange (Edwards and Webb, 1984, pp. 41–7; Walker, 1978a, Section III). Nevertheless, the equity method was used in parent company statements for certain subsidiaries. For example, Kester (1918, p. 261) distinguished between parents which had 'substantially full ownership' of subsidiary companies and cases where 'ownership is not complete but still controlling'. For the latter, the equity method in parent statements was seen as a reasonable alternative to the preparation of consolidated statements.

PSEUDO-CONSOLIDATION

The early use of the equity method for subsidiaries in the financial statements of holding companies before the full development of consolidation is considered above under 'proto-consolidation'. However, its use has continued in parent statements in some jurisdictions despite inclusion of the subsidiaries in consolidated statements. In the U.S., a long line of textbooks describe and recommend the use of the

---

[1] Edwards and Webb (1984) refer to *The Accountant*, 31 August 1929, p. 281.

INTERNATIONAL DEVELOPMENT OF THE EQUITY METHOD

equity method in this context. Until the 1960s, there was little promulgated GAAP[2] in this area, so textbooks and monographs contributed to unpromulgated GAAP.

As noted above, Kester (1918) recommended use of the equity method in parent statements early on for certain purposes, but was still recommending it in his 1933 edition and the 1945 reprint of that (pp. 194–5), when consolidated statements had become fully developed. Perhaps because of the comparative lack of legal restraints, Kester (1918, p. 262) had no qualms about the resulting profit, suggesting that 'the profit taken onto the books of the holding company by the above method is a real, not a book, profit', given that the parent controls the subsidiary's dividend policy. A similar view was taken by Finney (1922, p. 42) for the investment account in the holding company's books, even though there would also be a consolidated balance sheet.

Moonitz (1944, p. 49) also advocated the use of the equity method in the parent's books for several reasons:

1. The cost method makes sense when there is uncertainty but that does not apply to subsidiaries (p. 48) over which there is full control of dividend policy (p. 49).
2. The status of the investments varies with the fortunes of the investees not with the movements of cash (p. 49). Income accrues as the investments increase in value. Income accrues to the parent when it accrues to the subsidiary (p. 52).
3. The validity of the subsidiary's profit calculation is as well established as the parent's (p. 49).
4. Because companies plough back part of their profits, the cost rule will probably understate parent income in prosperous periods (p. 53).

Incidentally, Carman (1932, p. 103) and Dickerson and Weldon Jones (1933, p. 200) also propose the method for the treatment of subsidiaries in the investment account of the parent. However, they see it as a useful arithmetic device for preparing consolidated balance sheets when there are several layers of subsidiaries. They seem to regard the resulting balance sheet of the parent as not important in its own right, so that they should not be seen as proposers of pseudo-consolidation.

The contrary point of view to that of Kester and Moonitz is argued by Kohler (1938) who suggests that 'no practical benefits are derived from accruing profit and loss of subsidiaries on the books of the controlling company'. This is strongly supported by Paton (1951), who specifically opposes Moonitz' arguments: 'He is recommending, in effect, that the parent company keep its own accounts from the consolidated point of view, and were his recommendation adopted there would be little excuse left for preparing consolidated statements' (p. 46).

Despite this disagreement, it is clear that the method was acceptable where it really mattered. Kester (1945, pp. 211–12) wrote that: 'The Securities and Exchange Commission considers the equity of a holding company in subsidiary profits and losses sufficiently important to require disclosure . . . if such equities are not taken up on the books of the holding company'.

---

[2] That is, 'generally accepted accounting principles' as adopted by a body approved by the SEC (e.g., currently, the Financial Accounting Standards Board).

Finney (1946) illustrates the use of the equity method and calls it the 'economic basis' of parent company accounting, but notes that it does not conform 'strictly to the legal realities' (p. 299). As a compromise, Finney recommends the equity method with the undistributable earnings shown separately in shareholders' equity (p. 301). The matter of whether equity-accounted profit was distributable seems not to have constrained the debate.[3]

When GAAP was promulgated in 1971 by APB Opinion 18 (para. 14), the equity method was required in parent statements. Although the requirement was subsequently removed by SFAS 94 (of 1987, para. 15), there is no replacement instruction, so the equity method can still be used in parent statements. The lack of U.S. interest in this area is because parent statements are not generally required to be filed. This is unlike the position in most countries, where the law deals with parent statements, sometimes clearly as less important than consolidated statements (as in the U.K.) and sometimes as more important (as traditionally in some other European countries).

There was no equivalent U.K. discussion, let alone advocacy, of the equity method for use in parent statements in the days before accounting standards, presumably for the legal reasons noted earlier. For example, Cropper's *Accounting* (Cropper *et al.*, 1932, p. 316) recommends that subsidiaries should be accounted for either at cost with attached statements or by consolidation. Similar recommendations come from Garnsey (1923 and 1931, ch. VI); and others are silent on the issue (e.g., Pixley, 1910; Dicksee, 1927; Dicksee and Montmorency, 1932; Bogie, 1949, 1959; Castle and Grant, 1970). Subsequently, the method was prohibited in the U.K. by accounting standard.[4] It is also not allowed for this purpose in Australia[5] (AASB 1016).

However, in the Netherlands, subsidiaries (and joint ventures and associates; see later) are reported by using the equity method in the unconsolidated financial statements of the investor (Art. 389 (1–3) Book 2, Title 9 of the Civil Code; Dijksma and Hoogendoorn, 1993, p. 132). This use of the equity method in parent statements is long-standing practice. For example, it can be found in the parent statements which accompanied one of the earliest examples of Dutch consolidation: that by Philips[6] in 1931. The treatment generally enables the equity of the parent to be equal to that of the group. The equity-accounted share of profit (in excess of dividends) is, under certain conditions,[7] shown as undistributable reserves (Art. 389 (4)). In order to allow such practices, an option was written into

---

[3] The notion of distributable profit was discussed early on (e.g., Hatfield, 1918, pp. 205–31) but the rules vary from state to state (e.g., Littleton, 1934, pp. 140–8).

[4] SSAP 1, para. 18; FRS 9, para. 26.

[5] Except where there are no consolidated statements.

[6] I am grateful, for this information, to Professor H. L. Brink, a former Philips executive. He writes, on 20 March 1999 to Peter van der Zanden, that 'The equity per the company only and the consolidated balance sheets was exactly the same' (translation by Peter van der Zanden).

[7] The elements for which the parent cannot control the distribution of profits.

INTERNATIONAL DEVELOPMENT OF THE EQUITY METHOD

the EC Fourth Directive (Article 59, as amended by Article 45 of the Seventh Directive). Consequently, the Netherlands and some other member states have enacted legal permission for this practice. For example, it is allowed and common in Denmark (Christiansen and Elling, 1993, p. 136), where the practice began in the 1970s (before the Directive). It is also allowed in France (Art. L340–4, Law of 3.1.1985) and in Italy (Civil Code, Art. 2426(4)), but is seldom used. Such permission is not granted in law in the U.K. or in Germany, where equity accounting is restricted to consolidated statements. Given this international difference, it is not surprising that IAS 3 deliberately excluded this issue (para. 3), and that its replacement (IAS 27) allows, but does not require, equity accounting for subsidiaries in an investor's financial statements (para. 29).

This use of the equity method in investor financial statements could be seen as an example of attempts by accountants to express commercial substance over legal form. Since an investor could usually obtain its share of profits in a subsidiary merely by requesting them, to recognize only dividends might seem like a legal nicety. A clue to another rationale for the use of equity accounting in investor statements can be found in the Dutch term for the method: *intrinsieke waarde* (intrinsic value). That is, this may be seen as a method of valuation rather than as a method of consolidation. Further, the consolidated statements are treated in Dutch law (Art. 406) as a note to the legal entity's statements, which raises an expectation of consistency of valuation, which is also encouraged by the Seventh Directive (Art. 292 (a)). These rationales are examined later.

SUBSTITUTE-CONSOLIDATION

Another use of the equity method, this time in consolidated statements, was as a back-up in cases where certain subsidiaries were not consolidated. For example, in the U.S., Accounting Principles Board Opinion No. 18 (of 1971) required the equity method for unconsolidated subsidiaries. The reasons for lack of consolidation in the rules of the 1950s onwards (Accounting Research Bulletin No. 51, para. 2; Accounting Research Bulletin No. 43, ch. 12, para. 8) include temporary control, control being with non-majority owners, large minority interest and foreign subsidiaries (particularly those subject to restrictions on the transfer of funds).

However, the AICPA proposed that, in those cases where there was lack of control or there were foreign exchange restrictions, the cost method would be more suitable (AISG, 1973, para. 50). More recently, SFAS 94 (of 1987) requires all subsidiaries to be included except when control is temporary or when significant doubt exists about ability to control. SFAS 94 removes the APB 18 requirement to use equity accounting for unconsolidated subsidiaries, although such treatment seems still to be allowed (Williams, 1996, p. 6.05).

One important piece of context is that the U.S. definition of a subsidiary seems to be based in practice on ownership of a majority of voting shares rather than on *de facto* control. Although ARB 51 refers to 'controlling financial interest', the usual condition for this is said to be a majority voting interest, and no other examples are given (paras 1 and 2). This is reinforced by the title of SFAS 94,

Consolidation of All Majority Owned Subsidiaries. As a result, certain[8] controlled investees are not seen as entities to be consolidated. Here, the equity method seems a useful fallback position.

In Australia, the matter of equity accounting was first officially raised by the accountancy bodies in 1970 in the context of the de-consolidation of loss-making subsidiaries (Zeff, 1973, p. 39; Walker, 1978b, p. 107; Gordon and Morris, 1996, p. 161). The equity method is not now used as a substitute for consolidation, because no exclusions from consolidation are allowed[9] (AASB 1024). Its use for other purposes in Australia is examined later.

The original International Accounting Standard in this area (IAS 3 of 1976) derives from a study by the Accountants' International Study Group (1973) which noted (para. 47) the use of the equity method for excluded subsidiaries. The IASC's E3 (of 1974) had proposed (para. 31) to require the method for exclusions on the ground of temporary control, but IAS 3 required its use instead as a substitute for consolidation where dissimilar subsidiaries were optionally not consolidated (para. 40). The current standard (IAS 27) no longer allows dissimilar subsidiaries to be unconsolidated. However, it does continue to require (para. 13) exclusion from consolidation when (and only when) control is temporary (and the investee has never been consolidated) or when there are severe long-term restrictions on the transfer of funds to the parent. In such cases, reference should be made to IAS 25 on investments (or from 2001 to IAS 39), which does not allow the equity method. Perhaps this is reasonable, as there is no long-term significant influence.

In the U.K., SSAP 14 (of 1978) contained the earliest requirement for the use of the equity method for subsidiaries excluded from consolidation for reasons of dissimilarity or lack of effective control (paras 23 and 24). Subsequent law[10] confirmed this. Thus, the equity method acted as a safety net for the partial inclusion of companies that were controlled but were 'off balance sheet' due to the lax U.K. definition[11] of a subsidiary in the U.K. until the Companies Act 1989. The requirement is retained by FRS 2 (of 1992) for subsidiaries excluded on the grounds of dissimilarity (para. 30), although such cases are said to be exceptional (para. 25(c)). Support for this exclusion and for the concomittant use of the equity method seems to come from the EC Seventh Directive.[12] Consequently, it can be found in

---

[8] The SEC has a somewhat broader notion, including special purpose entities. EITF 90–15 also goes somewhat further.

[9] 'Temporary' exclusions are not allowed; the existence of severe restrictions on ability to control implies that the investee is not a subsidiary.

[10] Companies Act 1981; re-enacted as Sch. 4, para. 65(1) to the 1985 Act; then, in 1989, relating to dissimilarity, as Sch. 4.A, para. 18.

[11] The definition was expressed (Companies Act 1985, s. 736) in terms of control of the composition of the board (not votes on the board), or ownership of the majority of equity (not of voting equity). This gave rise to the possibility of 'controlled non-subsidiaries'.

[12] Reference in Article 14 (1) (on exclusion) is made to Article 33 (on the equity method).

INTERNATIONAL DEVELOPMENT OF THE EQUITY METHOD

the laws of other member states (e.g., Germany: *HGB*, §295 (1)[13]; Italy: *Decreto Legislativo 127*, Art. 36; Sweden: Annual Accounts Act 1995, Chapter 7, Section 23).

SEMI-CONSOLIDATION

So far, there has been concentration on three types of use of the equity method for the treatment of subsidiaries, as summarized in the first column of Table 1. Another use of the equity method is in consolidated statements (and sometimes in investor statements) for certain investees other than subsidiaries. Here the rationale for the equity method as a form of semi-consolidation or of valuation is less clear than above, as will be explored in a later section, after a discussion of some definitional points and an outline of international practice.

Scope
The major issue here is to identify the nature of the non-subsidiary investees for which equity accounting would be a suitable treatment. It is clear that, in the U.K. and the U.S., joint ventures were originally much in mind. The first exposure draft (in 1970) of the U.K.'s Accounting Standards Steering Committee (ASSC)[14] was on the subject of equity accounting, for reasons explored below. It defined an associated company as a joint venture or a company in which there is a substantial interest '(i.e. not less than approximately 20 per cent of the equity voting rights)' (para. 6).

TABLE 1

USES OF EQUITY METHOD

	Subsidiaries	Joint ventures	Associates
Investor statements	I *Proto-consolidation* (e.g., U.K. and U.S., early 20th century) II *Pseudo-consolidation* (e.g., Netherlands)	III *Pseudo-consolidation* (e.g., Netherlands)	IV *Pseudo-consolidation* (e.g., Netherlands)
Consolidated statements	V *Substitute consolidation* (e.g., U.S. if no majority votes; formerly for foreign subsidiaries and dissimilar subsidiaries)	VI *Semi-consolidation* (e.g., U.S.; and EU Directive and IAS 31 when not using proportional consolidation) (Note the use of gross equity method in U.K.)	VII *Semi-consolidation* (e.g., U.S. and EU) (Note former Australian use of disclosures based on equity method for this Case and Case VI)

[13]   Ordelheide and Pfaff (1994, p. 177) suggest that it is also appropriate for optionally excluded subsidiaries (e.g., limitations on control).

[14]   Established in 1970 and later re-named the Accounting Standards Committee.

Commenting on the development of the U.K. standard, Leach (1981, p. 6) states that 'the existence of consortium companies, controlled by no single corporate body, was very much in point' and that the definition 'emerged as the concept of partnership, recognition of substantial interest . . . and ability to exercise substantial influence'.

The U.S. statement of 1971 on the equity method referred to 'joint ventures and certain other investments in common stock' (APB Opinion 18, para. 1). Thus, there are two categories in the original U.K. and U.S. statements, but joint ventures come first, and the others are to be treated in the same way.

In some other jurisdictions (e.g., Australia, France and now in the U.K.), a clear separation of joint ventures from associates is made. It leads to the possibility or the requirement that joint ventures and associates are treated differently. The rest of this section considers the use of the equity method for associates in consolidated and investor statements. In the following two sections, more detail is added to the above outline of the definition of an associate, and the special treatments for joint ventures are considered.

Recommendations and Requirements for Consolidated Statements
This subsection looks at the treatment of associates in consolidated financial statements. It is followed by a note on treatments in investor statements. The requirement to use the equity method for associates (defined then as including joint ventures) in consolidated statements can be found in the U.K.'s SSAP 1 (of January 1971). This followed 'extensive developments' in the 1960s of holdings in associates (Shaw, 1973, p. 176) and a brief period of experimentation with the method by some British companies (Accountancy, 1970b). Tweedie (1981, p. 171) reports that the ASSC stated that only nine out of a survey of 300 major companies for 1968[15] went beyond accounting for dividends received. However, this had risen to twenty for 1969 (ICAEW, 1971); and it included some very important companies (e.g., GEC and Dunlop). Incidentally, Tweedie suggests that the equity method was therefore 'not a subject of great controversy' (p. 171) and that it was chosen as the ASSC's first topic partly because the ASSC had inherited work-in-progress for a draft Recommendation from the Institute of Chartered Accountants in England and Wales. By contrast, the first chairman of the ASSC suggested that the topic was 'a highly controversial one', chosen because of varied practice (Leach, 1981, p. 6). The controversial aspect is backed up by an editorial in *The Accountant* (1970) and, in retrospect, by Sharp (1971). Perhaps these views are reconcilable by noting that the subject was not controversial *before* ED 1 but that the ASSC's proposal *caused* a controversy.

Of relevance here are several observations by Napier (1999). There are at least two reasons why the ASSC's first chairman (Sir Ronald Leach) would have been interested in this topic. First, Leach was one of the inspectors appointed by the government in September 1969 to investigate Pergamon Press which had not shown

---

[15]   Tweedie and the survey's title refer to 1968–9, but that is largely to include a few companies with year ends in early January 1969.

INTERNATIONAL DEVELOPMENT OF THE EQUITY METHOD

its share of a large 1968 trading loss in its consolidated profit and loss account because it was not using equity accounting for its 50 per cent interest in a company (Napier, 1999, pp. 6, 12, 14, 17). Second, Leach's most important audit client, Rank Organisation, had a 49 per cent interest in a company that carried out the group's most important operations, Rank Xerox.

Similar U.S. requirements on equity accounting date from very slightly later: APB Opinion 18 of March 1971. In some other countries, recommendations can be found in the 1960s. In France, a ministerial decree of 20 March 1968 (Beeny, 1976, p. 147) referred to methods used in group accounts, including full consolidation (*intégration globale*), proportional consolidation (*intégration proportionnelle*) and equity accounting (*mise en équivalence*). The equity method was recommended for companies in which the investee held more than 33.3 per cent of the equity and which were neither subsidiaries nor joint ventures. There was further official encouragement from the Conseil National de la Comptabilité (CNC, 1973).

In the Netherlands, the non-governmental[16] Hamburger Report of 1962 recommended a version of the equity method ('intrinsic value', see above) for 'participations' (*deelnemingen*), which are long-term significant holdings where the business of the investor and investee are similar (Zeff *et al.*, 1992, p. 135). This would include joint ventures. The governmental Verdam Commission reported in 1964, recommending particular disclosures (although no particular accounting method) for such investments, defined as holdings of 25 per cent or more (Zeff *et al.*, 1992, p. 154). The first exposure draft of the Tripartiete Overleg[17] in 1971, following soon after U.K. and U.S. drafts, also preferred a version of the equity method for participations (Zeff *et al.*, 1992, p. 207).

This growing international consensus led to the inclusion, in the IASC's E3 (of 1974) and IAS 3 (of 1976) and in the EC Seventh Directive (drafts of 1976 and 1978, and Article 33 of the final version of 1983), of requirements for the use of equity accounting for associates in consolidated statements. The requirement in the Directive also explicitly covers joint ventures unless proportionally consolidated (see later). Some European countries had held out against the equity method until they were overwhelmed by the Seventh Directive. For example, in Germany, the concept of the group in the 1965 *Aktiengesetz* was based on uniform direction (*einheitliche Leitung*), which survives as an optional basis for the definition of a subsidiary in the Seventh Directive (Art. 1 (2)). On this conceptual basis, since associates are not managed on a unified basis with the investor (because they are not controlled) and so they are not group companies, they had to be accounted for on a cost basis. Although German influence was clear on many issues in the first draft of the Seventh Directive, the Germans had little support on this point and the equity method for associates was proposed as compulsory from the beginning (Diggle and Nobes, 1994, p. 324).

---

[16] Set up by the Council of Dutch Employers' Federations.

[17] Tri-partite committee; the predecessor of the Council for Annual Reporting (Raad voor de Jaarverslaggeving).

ABACUS

In Sweden, the equity method was regarded with suspicion from a legal stand-point in the early 1980s. The doubt concerned whether the equity method was a legally acceptable valuation method.[18] A few large groups used it in consolidated statements but most did not (Cooke, 1988, p. 62). Legal doubts were partially resolved by considering the equity method as a form of consolidated rather than as a valuation method. The equity method was proposed for consolidated statements by the then standard-setting body (FAR) in 1986 (Heurlin and Peterssohn, 1995, p. 1997) before becoming legally required on implementation of the Seventh Directive in the Swedish Annual Accounts Act of 1995 (Chapter 7, Article 24).

Outside of Europe, the most sceptical country has been Australia. A series of exposure drafts (1971, 1973 and 1979) recommending equity accounting began to be issued soon after those in the U.K. and the U.S. However, these met problems. First there was an impediment arising from a legal interpretation of the Victorian Companies Act 1971 that group accounts should encompass only the holding company and subsidiaries and therefore not equity-accounted earnings. Gordon and Morris (1996, p. 166) explain how the legal debate began in 1972 and continued for years. The legal impediment is also discussed by Eddey (1995, p. 303) and Vallely *et al.* (1997, p. 17). There were also, in the 1980s, abuses of the equity method. For example, some effectively controlled entities were equity-accounted instead of being consolidated, and some investees not subject to significant influence were equity-accounted (Ma *et al.*, 1991, pp. 204–8). Consequently, the standard setters eventually limited the use of the equity method to disclosures based on it (Ma *et al.*, 1991, p. 191). Some Australian groups showed an extra column in their consolidated financial statements on an equity-accounted basis (Deegan *et al.*, 1994).

Just as the legal and conceptual doubts of Germany and Sweden seem to have been swept aside by majority international practice rather than by clear arguments, even Australia amended AASB 1016 in 1998 to require equity accounting, following the removal of the legal impediment and a commitment to harmonization with IASC standards (Peirson and McBride, 1997). To avoid a conflict with the Australian conceptual framework (which clearly places associates outside the group reporting entity) and the consolidation standard, equity accounting is said to be a valuation method rather than a consolidation technique (Miller and Leo, 1997). This is up-side down compared to the reasoning in Sweden (noted above), although it fits the Dutch view.

Associates in Investor Statements

In most countries examined here, associates (like subsidiaries) are valued at cost in investor financial statements. However, in those countries where pseudo-consolidation (or valuation) is used for subsidiaries in an investor's statements, it is generally extended to associates and joint ventures. Otherwise, the objective of making the group equity equal to the investor's equity is not achieved.

For example, in Denmark and the Netherlands, the equity method is used in the investor's statements for associates and joint ventures. This appeared to be in conformity with the Fourth Directive, where Article 59 allowed such treatment for

---

[18] I am grateful, here, to Rolf Rundfelt of KPMG, Sweden.

INTERNATIONAL DEVELOPMENT OF THE EQUITY METHOD

an undefined category of 'affiliated undertakings'; and this was clarified by an amendment in Article 45 of the Seventh Directive which refers to significantly influenced undertakings. In the U.S., the equity method was also originally required in parent statements for those investments that were equity accounted in consolidated statements (APB Opinion 18, para. 17). It is presumably now allowed despite the amendments to SFAS 94 (see the earlier section on pseudo-consolidation). It is also allowed by IAS 28 (paragraph 12). In the same way as for subsidiaries, the method is allowed for associates in France and Italy (but not used), and is not allowed in the U.K. or Germany.

MORE ON THE DEFINITION OF AN ASSOCIATE

The UK Origins of the 20 Per Cent Threshold
U.K. and U.S. rules (SSAP 1 and APB Opinion 18, both of 1971) basically defined associates[19] as those over which the investor exercises a significant influence over operating and financial policies (SSAP 1, para. 13; APB Opinion 18, para. 17). This is the definition followed by the EC Seventh Directive of 1983 (Article 33 (1)), and therefore found in many European national laws.

However, this is a much vaguer concept (and more difficult to audit) than even the concept of 'control' which is the basis of the definition of a subsidiary in many jurisdictions. Consequently, it is difficult to operationalize (Chambers, 1974) and guidance is needed if standardized practice is to result. Part of the guidance comes in the form of a numerical threshold of the percentage of shares (or voting shares) to be held. In some jurisdictions, the threshold appears to be of a mechanical nature; in others it is hedged around with rebuttable presumptions. This point will be considered after the *size* of the threshold has been examined. The emergence of an internationally agreed threshold of 20 per cent of voting shares seems to have been accidental, as will now be charted.

There is a long history of separately identifying non-subsidiary investments above a certain size of holding. For example, in the U.K., the Companies Act 1947[20] designated certain holdings as 'trade investments'. According to Shaw (1973, p. 175), these: 'may be taken to be investments made to cement a trading relationship or for specific purposes associated with the trade of the investing company'.

Recommendation N 20 (ICAEW, 1958, para. 41) also required disclosures relating to material, but undefined, 'associated companies'. The Companies Act 1967 (s. 4) was more precise and required some non-financial disclosures where an individual investor held more than 10 per cent of equity[21] in an investee. Also, the London Stock Exchange Listing Agreement required, at least from the first 'Yellow Book' of 1966, disclosures about so called 'associated companies', defined

---

[19] APB Opinion 18 does not use this term, although it can be found in U.S. literature (e.g., Neuhausen, 1982, p. 55).

[20] Consolidated as paras 8(1)(a) and 12(1)(g) of Schedule 8 to the 1948 Act.

[21] Or where the book value of the shares was more than 10 per cent of total assets.

originally as those in which the investing group held more than a certain threshold level of equity. Shaw (1973, p. 176) suggests that this was a significant precedent for the ASSC's work because of the use of the term 'associated company' and the reference to total group holdings rather than to investor holdings. These two points distinguish the Stock Exchange's requirement from previous company law or tax law. Shaw (1973, p. 176) also states that the Listing Agreement uses a 20 per cent threshold, which would seem to clinch the argument about the source of the definition. However, the Yellow Books of June 1966 and of April 1969 use 25 per cent in their definitions.[22] This threshold is noted in the ICAEW's survey of 1970–71 (ICAEW, 1972, p. 13). An amendment to the Yellow Book, to reduce the threshold from 25 per cent to 20 per cent holdings, was published in June 1972, which puts it *after* SSAP 1, suggesting that the latter influenced the stock exchange, rather than the other way round.

In the U.K., the ASSC's first exposure draft (ED 1) of June 1970 had already used a threshold of 20 per cent (para. 7). No explanation is given for this level in the exposure draft.[23] There are no references to the origins of the 20 per cent threshold in the archives[24] of the ASSC or in the current memories of participants[25] in the debates. There are several comments on equity accounting in the accountancy journals[26] of the day (Titcomb, 1970; Goch, 1972), but only one can be found with any explanation of the 20 per cent: MacNair (1970, p. 367) notes that, under tax law of the time, a consortium that could share tax losses was one where equity participation was held by five or fewer companies. It was suggested that 'common interest' would be implied where such consortium relief was used.

A survey of tax and company law literature fails to reveal any other convincing source of the 20 per cent threshold. In U.K. tax law, thresholds of 10, 50 and 75 per cent can be found (Lamb, 1995, p. 37). The Companies Act 1948 had contained various thresholds other than 20 per cent; for example, 10 per cent relating to an extraordinary general meeting (s. 132(1)), 15 per cent relating to variation in rights and alteration of memorandum (ss. 72(1) and 5(2)), and 75 per cent for special resolutions (s. 141(1)).

The practices of the few British companies who used equity accounting before ED 1 may have been influential. Grand Metropolitan in its 1967 accounts reported on a number of associates held from 28 per cent to 50 per cent. A comment in

---

[22] Schedule VIII, part A, para. 6(c), note (i): 'For the purpose of this Undertaking "associated company" means a company which is not a subsidiary but in which 25% or more of the equity is held by the company or, if the company has subsidiaries, by the group companies collectively (i.e. before excluding any proportion attributable to interests of outside shareholders in the subsidiaries).'

[23] Reprinted in *Accountancy*, July 1970, pp. 496–8.

[24] I am very grateful to Michael Mumford (letter to me of 29 June 1998) for examining the relevant minutes of the ASSC in the John Rylands Library.

[25] I have corresponded with Harold Edey, Michael Renshall and Chris Westwick.

[26] The author has examined contemporary issues of *Accountancy, The Accountant's Magazine, The Accountant* and *The Journal of Accountancy*.

INTERNATIONAL DEVELOPMENT OF THE EQUITY METHOD

Accountancy (1970a) presumed a threshold of 25 per cent, which had been used by Dunlop and by William Cory in their 1969 accounts. Other companies stressed a relationship rather than a specific threshold (Holmes, 1970, pp. 514–18). However, British Ropes adopted a specific 20 per cent threshold for the first time in its accounts issued in early 1970, before ED 1 (Holmes, 1970, p. 515). Other companies (e.g., Delta Metal; see ICAEW, 1971) used the term 'associated' for holdings of above 10 per cent, but only for disclosures not for equity accounting. It seems that the ASSC chose the lowest threshold actually used in practice for equity accounting, beginning its tradition of accommodating companies' wishes.

The Spread of the Threshold
In the U.S., the APB's sub-committee on this subject initially favoured a 10 per cent threshold on the basis of what it called an 'economic interest' interpretation.[27] Some members of the sub-committee[28] and the SEC staff preferred a 25 per cent threshold on the basis of 'presumption of control', particularly over dividend payments. The board, at its meeting of March 1970, changed its position from favouring 10 per cent to 25 per cent. However, at the July meeting, it was noted[29] that the U.K.'s ED 1 proposed 20 per cent and that international coordination would be beneficial (Defliese, 1981, p. 110; Journal, 1970, p. 12). It seems that, even in the first year of operations of the U.K. standard-setter, there was an exchange of exposure drafts with the APB; and in the following year, the APB chairman was in London for discussions (Accountancy, 1971). In October 1970, the board decided on 20 per cent as an internationally coordinated compromise between its two previous views, although the SEC still did not agree.

Thus, on the basis of no clear arguments, the foundations for the eventual worldwide triumph of 20 per cent were laid. In January 1971, SSAP 1 was issued, retaining the 20 per cent. In March 1971, APB Opinion 18 (also containing 20 per cent) was issued. The U.K. press had noted[30] the earlier U.S. change to 25 per cent and then noted[31] the change to 20 per cent. However, in neither case was there any comment about the comparison with the British exposure draft's 20 per cent. This Anglo-American agreement is mirrored in a reference to a 20 per cent threshold in IAS 3 (para. 4) of 1976.

In the meantime, many other thresholds were in use internationally. As explained earlier, 25 per cent was to be found in Dutch proposals from at least 1964, and 33.3 per cent was preferred in France from 1968. However, another strand of

---

[27] I am most grateful to Steve Zeff for the information in this paragraph. Professor Zeff writes in a letter to me of 8 July 1996 that he has based the information on minutes of the APB sub-committee and reports of Big 8 firms to partners after meetings of the sub-committee.

[28] The sub-committee was chaired by George R. Catlett of Arthur Andersen, but those preferring 25 per cent included representatives from Arthur Young and from Lybrand.

[29] See note 26.

[30] News section of *Accountancy*, November 1970, p. 759.

[31] News section of *Accountancy*, August 1971, p. 431.

French thinking relevant to this issue is the concept of participating interests (*participations*). From the 1966 Companies Law, these are investments of 10 per cent and above, which reminds one of the 10 per cent threshold in the U.K.'s 1967 Act noted earlier. Such investments were, and still are, to be shown separately in an investor's balance sheet in France, and one of the *régimes*[32] for group taxation treats income from such investments favourably. In Italy, a remnant of this survives, in that investments of 10 per cent or more in *listed* companies are treated as associates (Civil Code, Article 2359). This seems to accord with the APB's 'economic interest' concept.

Given the diversity of European views and the ascendancy of Anglo-American practices in the field of consolidation (Diggle and Nobes, 1994), it is not surprising that the EC Seventh Directive contained a 20 per cent threshold from its earliest published version (Article 1 (2) of the 1976 draft). This threshold has now been implemented into the laws of most of the 15 EU member states, and elsewhere in Europe (e.g., Norway, as a member of the European Economic Area). In these cases, previous thresholds for other issues have been ignored. For example, many thresholds are found in tax legislation in Europe, including 5, 10, 25 and 95 per cent (Lamb, 1995, pp. 62–73). The predominant thresholds are 10 and 25 per cent, with 20 per cent appearing rarely.[33] On other issues, German law contained a threshold of 25 per cent for blocking changes to a company's constitution and for the existence of a mutual participation (*wechselseitige Beteiligung*).[34] However, as noted above, the Italian implementation (of 1991) refers to holdings of 10 per cent in the case of listed investees. The Spanish implementation (of 1989) refers to holdings of 3 per cent in the case of listed investees (Article 185 (2), Decree 1564/ 1989; Gonzalo and Gallizo, 1992, p. 167). These lower thresholds are not mentioned in the Seventh Directive. However, since the Directive states that significant influence is presumed where the investor 'has 20% or more of the . . . voting rights' (Article 33 (1)), a lower threshold is not specifically ruled out.

Further afield, 20 per cent is recommended in Switzerland by the standard-setters (ARR 2 of FER), and it is required in Japan by the rules of the Ministry of Finance (Financial Accounting Standards, IV, 5, 2) and in Korea (Financial Accounting Standards App. II, Art. 15(a)). Although Australia held out for years against the use of the equity method as a valuation or consolidation practice, the 20 per cent threshold was in the first exposure draft of 1971 and continued through to the eventual disclosure standard of 1988 (ASRB 1016). Turning to international standards, IAS 28 (originally of 1988) naturally followed the international consensus of 20 per cent (now in IAS 28, para. 4). Table 2 summarizes the exceptions from the 20 per cent threshold; the last two of which are extant.

---

[32] The *régime des sociétés mères et filiales*.

[33] For example, the draft EC Parent/Subsidiary Directive of 1969 would relieve withholding taxes at a 20 per cent threshold, although this was changed to 25 per cent in the directive of 1990.

[34] I am grateful to Dieter Ordelheide for pointing out the blocking percentage. The mutual participation is to be found in s. 19 of Aktiengesetz 1965.

INTERNATIONAL DEVELOPMENT OF THE EQUITY METHOD

TABLE 2

SOME EXCEPTIONS FROM THE 20% FOR THE DEFINITION OF ASSOCIATES

Netherlands	25% in a government report of 1964
France	33$^1/_3$% in CNC recommendation of 1968
U.S.	10% and 25% in APB discussions in early 1970
Spain	3% for listed holdings in 1989 law
Italy	10% for listed holdings in 1991 law

Rebuttable Presumption

As noted above, the numerical threshold is stated baldly in some rules, particularly those flowing from the Seventh Directive. For example, in Germany (HGB §311 (1)) and in Italy (Civil Code, Art. 2359 (3)), the assumption of significant influence rests squarely on the numerical thresholds, and no qualitative indications are given. In other jurisdictions, the rule-makers appear to have attempted to ensure that financial reporting choices rest on something less mechanical. As noted later, the problem then becomes the vagueness of the rationale for equity accounting. Some rule-makers are clear, at least, that an investor should not be able to treat an investee differently from year to year by buying and selling a few shares around the 20 per cent threshold. Consequently, in the U.S., APB Opinion 18 discusses this in terms of 'considerations' (e.g., representation on the board, and the concentration of other shareholdings) and 'presumptions' (para. 17). The same applies to IAS 3 (para. 4) and IAS 28 (para. 4).

Despite the U.S. attempt to make the threshold less stark, Mulford and Comiskey (1985) found a high concentration of investments in the 16–24 per cent range. Further, affiliates in the 19–19.99 per cent range of ownership reported losses far more often than those in the 20–20.99 per cent range.

The U.K.'s ED 1 (para. 6) contained the threshold of 'approximately 20 per cent'. The 'approximately' was removed for the original SSAP 1 (para. 6), presumably on the grounds of reducing vagueness. However, the 'rebuttable presumption' basis was introduced later (in 1982, para. 14), along U.S. lines. This was strengthened in FRS 9, where there is an extensive discussion of 'significant influence' and it is made clear that this overrides the numerical threshold (paras. 4 and 14–19). Indeed, the 20 per cent is referred to as part of 'companies legislation', suggesting that the reference to a numerical threshold would have been removed but for this. The irony here is that the 20 per cent threshold in the British law was based on the Seventh Directive which was based on the Anglo-American practice which can be traced to a British exposure draft of 1970.

WHAT'S IN A NAME?

It is now appropriate to address a related issue: the origins of the terms 'equity method' and 'associated company'.

31

Equity Method

'Equity method' is clearly an American coinage, and can be traced back at least to the early 1930s in the context of the arithmetic used for the preparation of consolidated balance sheets (Carman, 1932, p. 103; Dickerson and Weldon Jones, 1933, p. 200). The term can also be found later in the context of 'pseudo-consolidation' in investor statements. This is the case in Noble *et al.* (1941, p. 581) and in Finney and Miller (1952, pp. 343–5); although not in the previous edition of the latter book (Finney, 1946, p. 297). Other terms for the equity method in this context were also in use: for example, 'book value' (Paton, 1943, p. 1073; and Moonitz, 1994, p. 51), 'economic basis of accounting' (Finney, 1946, p. 297); 'book value change basis' (Moonitz and Staehling, 1950, p. 184).

In promulgated GAAP, the term was not initially used; that is, it cannot be found in ARB No. 51 of 1959 (see para. 19). However, it was employed in APB Opinion 10 of 1966: 'This practice is sometimes referred to as the "equity" method' (para. 3). By APB Opinion 18 of 1971 (para. 6), the quotation marks have disappeared. The term was then frequently used by the IASC in IAS 3 of 1976.

In the U.K., acceptance of the term is much more recent. It was not to be found in SSAP 1 (of 1971 and subsequent amendments to 1990). It does, however, appear in the EC Fourth Directive (Article 59 of the 1978 final version, but not the drafts of 1971 and 1974). Since, as noted earlier, the U.K. did not take up the Directive's option in Article 59 to use the equity method in the investor's accounts, the term was not used in the Companies Act 1981 which implemented the Directive. It is used in the Companies Act 1989,[35] though not in the EC Seventh Directive which preceded it (see Article 33). In FRS 9 of 1997 it is well established (e.g. para. 4). In Australia, the term appeared in the two exposure drafts in 1971 and 1974 (see Chambers, 1974).

The terms in French (*mise en équivalence*) and in Dutch (*intrinsieke waarde*) appear to have other origins. The French term seems to refer to the fact that the parent's and group's equity are made equal. The Dutch term refers to the valuation aspect of the method, as noted earlier. Terms in some other languages seem likely to be derived from the American (e.g., the unofficial German terms, *Equitykonsolidierung* and *Equitymethode*).

Associated Company

The term 'associate' (used here to include 'associated company' and similar expressions) is not in universal use in the English-speaking world. For example, it is not to be found in U.S. authoritative literature, which refers to such enterprises elliptically.[36] The term seems to be of British origin but was originally undefined. For example, it was used by Lever Brothers in the 1920s to include subsidiaries. It also has such a meaning in British tax law.[37] It was used vaguely in the ICAEW's

---

[35] Now paragraph 22 of Schedule 4A to the 1985 Act.

[36] For example, APB Opinion 18 (para. 17) refers to significant influence over an investee. In practice, the equivalent to 'associated undertaking' is an expression such as 'equity accounted investee'.

[37] For example, in the Income and Corporation Taxes Act 1970, s. 302(1), a company is associated with another if one of the two controls the other or both are under the control of the same person.

INTERNATIONAL DEVELOPMENT OF THE EQUITY METHOD

Recommendation N 20 and precisely (for disclosures) in the Stock Exchange listing requirements of 1966 (see earlier discussion). Companies used the term; for example, Grand Metropolitan in its 1967 accounts (*Accountancy*, 1968) and several others by 1970 (Holmes, 1970; ICAEW, 1971). The term then arrived in accounting standards in 1971 (international standards in 1976) and law in 1989.[38]

The term is not to be found in the Fourth Directive (where the vague 'affiliated undertakings' includes subsidiaries; and 'participating interests' includes those not significantly influenced), but 'associated undertaking' does appear in the Seventh Directive (Art. 33). The English origin seems clear enough in other language versions of the Directive; for example, *geassocieerde onderneming* in Dutch, *enterprise associée* in French, *assoziertes Unternehmen* in German, *impresa associata* in Italian and *sociedad asociada* in Spanish.

The Directive's terms survive into some EU national laws (e.g., German[39] and Spanish[40]) but not all. For example, the Italian code[41] uses *società collegata*, and no terms are used in Dutch[42] or French[43] law, merely references to significant influence.

JOINT VENTURES

Definition
It was noted above that 'semi-consolidation' was initially seen in the U.S. and the U.K. as particularly appropriate for joint ventures, with other associated investees also mentioned. Originally in the U.K. the category 'associate' included the joint venture. However, most jurisdictions now define the terms exclusively, even where the accounting treatment is to be the same.

Early French definitions of the joint venture, including that in a report of the CNC of March 1968 (CNC, 1973; Beeny, 1976, p. 47) refer to a *société fermée* (i.e., one where no shares are held outside of a group of venturers). For an investee to be a joint venture, the investor would have to hold a *participation* (i.e., at least 10 per cent of the shares). Once more, the 10 per cent threshold arises. In APB Opinion 18 (para. 3) the relevant joint venture is 'a corporation owned and operated by a small group of businesses . . . as a separate and specific business or project for the mutual benefit of the members of the group'.

The EC Seventh Directive depicts joint ventures as separate from associates, partly because different treatments are allowed (see below). The Directive's definition of joint venture (Article 32) rests on 'jointly managed'. British law (1985 Act,

---

[38] The Companies Act 1981 used 'related companies' (e.g., Schedule 4, part I, B) whereas the 1989 Act has 'associated undertakings' (now para. 20 etc. of Schedule 4A to the 1985 Act).

[39] HGB § 311.

[40] Real Decreto 1815/1991, Cap. 1, art. 5.

[41] Codice civile, Art. 2359.

[42] Art. 389.

[43] Art. L357–1.

33

Sch. 4A, para. 19) follows these words but in FRS 9 'jointly controlled' is used, as follows: 'An entity in which the reporting entity holds an interest on a long-term basis and is jointly controlled by the reporting entity and one or more other venturers under a contractual arrangement' (para. 4).

A similar interpretation has occurred in France, where the Directive says *dirige, conjointement* but the law refers to *contrôle conjoint* (amendment in 1985 to Article 357-1 of the Law of 1966).

In what follows, joint ventures will be assumed to be entities separate from the venturers. For example, IAS 31 (para. 3) distinguishes between jointly controlled 'entities', 'operations' and 'assets'. The latter two categories create few accounting problems because the various assets and liabilities belong to the venturers, so they are included in the financial statements of the venturer (both in the individual entity statements and in the consolidated).

Treatment of Joint Ventures
As noted earlier, in cases where equity accounting is used in an investor's unconsolidated financial statements for subsidiaries and associates (e.g., in Denmark and the Netherlands), then it is also used for joint ventures. This seems to create no difficulty for the Fourth Directive and various laws in the EU because joint ventures fall within the broad categories of 'affiliated' or significantly influenced undertakings. However, there is a difficulty in IAS 31, which specifically deals with joint ventures rather than associates. Strangely, IAS 31 gives no direct consideration[44] to the treatment of joint ventures in the unconsolidated statements of a venturer. That is, there is no equivalent of paragraph 29 of IAS 27 or paragraph 12 of IAS 28. Consequently, although IASs allow subsidiaries and associates to be held by the cost method in investor statements, it appears[45] that IAS 31 does not allow this for joint ventures. This seems to be an oversight.[46]

In consolidated financial statements, the treatment of joint ventures now differs internationally. U.S. and U.K. practice[47] (at least for joint ventures that are incorporated entities) is to use equity accounting on the grounds that there is significant influence but no control. In effect, joint ventures are still seen as a special case of associates, or associates are seen as a less formal type of joint venture. Consistently with this, the equity method is allowed in consolidated statements by the Seventh

---

[44]   Paragraph 38 is deliberately non-committal. David Cairns (IASC Secretary General at the time of IAS 31) confirms that the IASC could not agree on a single practice (letter to me of 7 July 1999). Paragraph 41, despite its heading, relates to particular joint ventures where an investor is not a venturer.

[45]   Paragraph 39 requires profit made by selling from an investor to a joint venture (including a joint venture entity) to be eliminated. In practice, this requirement means that the cost method cannot be used. There is no similar requirement in IASs 27 or 28 for an investor selling to a subsidiary or an associate.

[46]   The author contacted the IASC on this (9 February 1999), and there is informal acceptance of the problem. But as yet there is no action to amend the IASs.

[47]   APB Opinion 18 (para. 16); the Companies Act 1985 (as amended in 1989), Sch. 4A, paras 19–22; and FRS 9 (para. 20) cover this.

INTERNATIONAL DEVELOPMENT OF THE EQUITY METHOD

Directive and by IAS 31. However, proportional consolidation is also allowed by the Directive (Article 32); and in IAS 31 (paras 25 and 33) it is *preferred* on the grounds that it 'better reflects the substance and economic reality of a venturer's interest in a jointly controlled entity, that is control over the venturer's share of the future economic benefits'. This is despite the fact that the IASC's Framework (para. 49) defines assets in terms of control over the resources not control over the benefits from the resources. It is clear that the venturer does not *control* any of the resources. Consequently, neither the resources nor part of them are assets of the venturer. The same conclusion would be arrived at even if the definition of asset had referred to control over benefits.[48]

The response to the Seventh Directive in France was to *require* proportional consolidation, which was previous French practice. In most EU member states proportional consolidation is allowed. However, this is not the case in Greece, nor in Ireland and the U.K. for corporate joint ventures. It is also not allowed for joint venture entities in Australia (AASB 1006 and 1024 and AAS 19).

In some jurisdictions where proportional consolidation is not allowed, there is nevertheless some concern about the potentially misleading nature of equity accounting for joint ventures. For example, a group would not be required to recognize its share of the liabilities of a 50 per cent held joint venture. One way of responding to this is now used in the U.K., where FRS 9 requires the use of the 'gross equity method' for joint venture entities (paras 20–1). This method, which has a precedent in FASB discussion papers,[49] involves extra disclosures on the face of the consolidated financial statements, including the investor's share of the joint venture's turnover, gross assets and gross liabilities.

The Reporting Entity

This international lack of agreement on the treatment for joint ventures illustrates the need for greater clarity in some conceptual frameworks. The EC Seventh Directive has no explicit framework. The U.S. and IASC frameworks do not discuss the boundary of the reporting entity, and therefore have nothing directly to offer on consolidation issues, although the definition of asset seems relevant, as noted above. By contrast, the U.K.'s later *Statement of Principles* covers the 'reporting entity'. The boundary of the group rests on control (para. 2.6) which puts joint venture entities outside the group and therefore proportional consolidation should not be used (para. 8.9). There was a similar conclusion on the status of joint venture entities in the earlier Australian concepts statement, SAC 1.

RATIONALES FOR THE EQUITY METHOD

Although the equity method is now used for various purposes in much of the world, the rationales for this are not well explained. The seven cases in Table 1 are examined here.

---

[48]   Because the definition would mean control over the services provided by the asset, not control over a share of net profit. A venturer does not control these services.

[49]   I am grateful to Janie Crichton (the ASB's project director on FRS 9) for this information.

In the context of the treatment of subsidiaries in an investor's unconsolidated financial statements, the rationale for proto-consolidation (Case I) has been over-taken by the development of full consolidation. Possible rationales for pseudo-consolidation (Case II) include that the equity method is a form of accruals accounting rather than the cash accounting used by the cost method (Neuhausen, 1982, p. 62). This seems inconsistent with the realization convention but, given that Case II relates to subsidiaries, one could try to support it with a substance over form argument. Several such arguments of U.S. writers were examined earlier. A doubt, which did not concern early U.S. writers, could be raised for foreign investees where there might be uncertainties connected to the transfer of funds and the exchange rate.

A similar rationale for the equity method is that it is a form of valuation. The link is made in an Australian exposure draft where equity accounting is seen as 'a method of accounting, on an accrual basis, . . . thereby ensuring improved report-ing on the worth of particular investments to the investor' (ASA/ICAA, 1973, para. 19). This seems to be inconsistent with the historical cost convention used in most countries, though not uniformly in some countries (e.g., Australia and the Netherlands).

For investees other than subsidiaries, pseudo-consolidation in investor state-ments (Cases III and IV) seems even less convincing. The substance over form argument no longer applies, as the investor controls neither the assets of the investee nor its dividend decisions. The profits of the investee (in excess of dividends) are not within the control of the investor. The basis for a threshold at 20 per cent is also unclear, particularly since the 'intrinsic value' of all investments changes as profits are made. Further, as pointed out by Paton (1951, p. 46) and discussed (along with other criticisms of the equity method) by Zambon (1996, pp. 220–5), there seems little economic significance in the 'values' arrived at by the equity method. So, the method is not a conceptually impressive way of valuing, and 'fair value' would now seem more relevant (e.g., IASC, 1997). Nevertheless, a possible defence of the method in the context of the general use of fair values would be that fair value cannot always be reliably measured (e.g., for some unlisted securities) and that large blocks of shares could not be sold at apparent market value. Of course, a large block of shares does have a fair value, although it may be more difficult to identify.

For the above Cases II to IV, the usefulness of making the parent's income and equity the same as the group's is unclear, unless the parent statements are merely unpublished worksheets.

Turning to consolidated statements, the rationale for substitute-consolidation (Case V) has also been overtaken by events in jurisdictions where all controlled investees must be consolidated. For uncontrolled investees (Cases VI and VII), the equity method could be seen again as a method of valuation, whereupon the above points on that topic apply. It could also be seen as a form of semi-consolidation. However, just as the investor does not control the investee's assets, profits or dividend decisions, neither does the group. A basic question here is: Are such investees part of the investor's group? As noted above for joint venture entities,

INTERNATIONAL DEVELOPMENT OF THE EQUITY METHOD

the answer in the Australian and British frameworks is that they are clearly not. Elsewhere, the answer should be the same if the scope of the group is either based on control or majority ownership, as is the case in the U.S. (ARB 51, para. 2), the European Union (Seventh Directive, Article 1) or the IASC (IAS 27, para. 6). It seems difficult, then, to support the equity method as semi-consolidation on the basis of substance over form.

However, perhaps a rationale can be built around the idea that, above a certain threshold level of interest, the investor is in some form of special relationship with the investee. This approach, which regards associates and joint ventures as much the same, survived into the U.K. Discussion Paper in this area (ASB, 1994) which treated them both as 'strategic alliances' (para. 2.3) to be accounted for by the equity method. Later, FRS 9 (of 1997) rephrases this as follows:

> The investor needs an agreement or understanding, formal or informal, with its associate to provide the basis for its significant influence. An investor exercising significant influence will be directly involved in the operating and financial policies of this associate. Rather than passively awaiting the outcome of its investee's policies, the investor uses its associate as a medium through which it conducts a part of its activities. . . . Over time, the associate will generally implement policies that are consistent with the strategy of the investor and avoid implementing policies that are contrary to the investor's interests. (para. 14)

This clearly interprets the equity method as semi-consolidation, and it rests on joint control of the dividend decision even in those cases where there is not joint control of the individual assets and liabilities. It seems to suit Case VI the best, but might be extended to some associates in Case VII.

TECHNICAL PROBLEMS RAISED BY LACK OF FRAMEWORK

Since the concept behind the equity method and the purpose of its use are unclear, it also becomes difficult to resolve technical issues. Three examples are examined: elimination of profits, presentation in income and cash flow statements, and discontinued operations.

First, when an investor makes a profit by selling to an associate which retains the goods (downstream sales), should some or all of the profit be eliminated from the investor's and the consolidated statements? The profit in the hands of the investor results form an arm's length transaction. It is realized and legally distributable, and therefore should presumably not be eliminated. The same could be said of a profit arising from a sale from a parent to a subsidiary. On consolidation, this latter profit would be eliminated because the subsidiary is part of the group, and the price (and therefore profit) of the sale was controlled by the group. Neither of these points applies to a sale to an associate, which might suggest no elimination, even in consolidated statements.

The Seventh Directive (Article 33 (7)) appears to require elimination but either total or proportional elimination seem to be allowed. In the U.K., FRS 9 (para. 31) states that there should be proportional elimination. The IASC has also recently concluded (SIC Interpretation No. 3) that there should be proportional elimination.

ABACUS

The problem is that, since the theory supporting the equity method is unclear, the theoretical answer on elimination is also unclear.

Another technical point is the location of the equity-accounted elements in income and cash flow statements. The basic issue is whether the amounts are to be classified as operating or as financial. In the EC Fourth Directive (e.g., Article 23, line 9), the profit from participating interests is shown after operating items and as the first financial item. This allows companies to draw the operating line above or below equity-accounted profits. In the U.K., for example, SSAP 1 did not specify the treatment, but FRS 9 (para. 27) requires equity-accounted operating profits to be shown immediately after group operating profit. For U.K. cash flow statements, dividends from associates were originally to be shown as returns on investments (FRS 1 of 1991, para. 19), then as operating activities (FRS 1 as revised in 1996, paras. 11, 14), then as a separate item between the two (FRS 1 as revised again by para. 61 of FRS 9).

The EC Seventh Directive (Article 33 (6)) could be interpreted as allowing a different position for equity-accounted income in consolidated income statements from that required under the Fourth Directive. In France, advantage has been taken of this, so that such amounts are shown after consolidated profit and before minority interests (*Plan comptable général*, p. 11.168). This suggests that such profit is neither operating nor financial.

In the U.S., APB Opinion 18 (para. 19 (c)) is unclear on the location of equity-accounted income. Burnett *et al.* (1979) found that, for twenty-two finance subsidiaries excluded from consolidation, there were five different presentations of the equity-accounted income in consolidated income statements. Modern practice still ranges from presentation as 'other income' before various operating expenses to presentation after minority interests.[50] In U.S. cash flow statements, dividends received form equity-accounted companies are generally included in operating activities (Williams, 1996, p. 4.23).

IAS 1 (para. 75, and appendix) shows equity-accounted profits after operating and financial items in income statements, whereas IAS 7 (paras 31 and 37) allows dividends from equity accounted companies to be treated as either operating or investing items in cash flow statements.

A third technical issue is the presentation of discontinued operations. There are U.S., U.K. and IASC rules in this area. The relevant issue relates to the disposal of some shares in a major subsidiary such that it becomes an associate. Assuming that the subsidiary were large enough to satisfy the size criterion for being a discontinued operation (e.g., FRS 3, para. 4), would the disposal of the shares amount to a discontinuance of the operation by the reporting entity? This issue was a matter for international debate[51] when IAS 35 was agreed in 1998. Since the reporting

---

[50]   For example, General Electric (1996, p. 49) do the former, and General Motors (1997, p. 50 in a supplementary statement) do the latter.

[51]   The author was the chairman of the IAS 35 steering committee, and chaired the IASC Board discussion leading to approval of IAS 35 in April 1998.

INTERNATIONAL DEVELOPMENT OF THE EQUITY METHOD

entity is the group, it would seem that the group has disposed of the operation, and it no longer consolidates any individual assets, liabilities, revenues or expenses. However, the IASC Board decided that is would be consistent with other equity accounting practices to regard the operation as continuing within the sphere of the group's interests. The issue is not directly addressed in IAS 35.

SOME EMPIRICAL FINDINGS

In addition to the many writings referenced above, there has been some empirical research related to the use of the equity method. Mulford and Comiskey (1985) and Burnett *et al.* (1979) have already been mentioned. Another U.S. paper is by Ricks and Hughes (1985) who found a positive market reaction to the first publication of U.S. financial statements using the equity method. The reaction was positively correlated with size of equity earnings and degree of previous underestimate by analysts. This suggested that 'the equity method provided information concerning affiliate earnings not previously available from other sources' (p. 50).

Vallely *et al.* (1997) survey eight studies on equity accounting in Australia. Most of these examine whether management adopts aspects of equity accounting for particular reasons (e.g., attempting to increase management compensation). Mazay *et al.* (1993) suggest that the equity method may be useful in controlling management's behaviour where a material proportion of a firm's assets is in the form of investments in associates. Without the equity method, management might be able to manipulate profit by influencing dividend decisions or by non-arm's length transactions with investees. Similarly, lenders cannot reliably assess borrowers who have material investments in unlisted associates.

Another Australian paper (Czernkowski and Loftus, 1997) suggests that, in the period 1983 to 1990, the equity method provided useful information, particularly when cost-based information was also available.

SUMMARY AND POLICY IMPLICATIONS

The equity method arose as a form of proto-consolidation for inclusion of subsidiaries (or less than fully owned subsidiaries) in parent's financial statements before the practice of consolidation was fully established. Later, the equity method was seen to be unnecessary in some jurisdictions for parent statements. However, in other jurisdictions its sporadic or generalized use is still found, such that the parent's statements contain technically unrealized profits. This pseudo-consolidation can be seen instead as a method of valuation. The term 'equity method' is an American coinage used originally in this context of investor statements. Another formerly widespread use (substitute-consolidation) relates to the treatment in consolidated statements of certain subsidiaries or controlled non-subsidiaries excluded from full consolidation.

These three uses of the equity method for the treatment of subsidiaries (Cases I, II and V of Table 1) seem to be unnecessary or unsuitable:

1. proto-consolidation, because it has been replaced by consolidation;

2. pseudo-consolidation in investor's financial statements, because any form of consolidation seems inappropriate or unhelpful and because there are convincing arguments against using the equity method as a valuation method; and

3. substitute-consolidation, because a control-based concept of the group means that all controlled enterprises should be fully consolidated.

The equity method has also been used for inclusion of joint ventures and associates in investor statements (Cases III and IV: more pseudo-consolidation or valuation) or in consolidated statements (Cases VI and VII: semi-consolidation or valuation). These uses seem to have arisen with little theoretical justification and no prior research into their usefulness. Cases III and IV seem inappropriate for the same reasons as apply to pseudo-consolidation of subsidiaries, and for some extra reasons related to lack of control. This leaves semi-consolidation, which can be divided into two categories: joint ventures (Case VI) and less formal partnerships and other holdings of 20 per cent or more (Case VII). In the U.K. and the U.S., the context for the method originally stressed joint ventures, but other associated enterprises were also included, leading to definitional problems. Terms such as 'associated company' were U.K. inventions of the 1920s onwards.

The arguments for Case VII seem the weaker of the two, particularly where there is no sense of partnership. The concept of 'significant influence' is vague and not easily operationalized; and the 20 per cent threshold is unsupported by argument, having apparently arisen pragmatically in the U.K. and been accepted in the U.S. as a compromise. Where an arbitrary threshold has to be invented in order to operationalize an accounting rule, two features generally occur in conjunction. First, there is a lack of convincing theory and, second, management will try to avoid unattractive financial reporting by making arrangements that fall above or below the threshold, as noted earlier.

An analogy to this aspect of equity accounting for associates is the capitalization of finance leases. The U.S. and U.K. rules[52] contain, *inter alia*, a threshold of 90 per cent of fair value. The German tax rules[53] (and therefore accounting practice) also contain numerical thresholds. These various rules enable management to select leases below the thresholds, which the leasing industry is happy to provide. The U.S. and U.K. thresholds can be seen as an attempt to operationalize the 'substantially all of the risks and rewards of ownership of an asset to the lessee' concept (e.g., SSAP 21, para. 15). However, this has no theoretical basis in any published conceptual framework. When the frameworks' definitions of asset and liability are applied, it becomes clear that all non-cancellable leases meet the definitions, so the arbitrary thresholds are not needed (McGregor, 1996). The U.K. standard setter, in conjunction with others, has begun a project to move in this direction (Nailor and Lennard, 1999).

Applying this analogy to equity accounting, the 'significant influence' concept is difficult to operate, which is why an arbitrary threshold (of 20 per cent) arose.

---

[52]   SFAS 13 (para. 7) and SSAP 21 (para. 15).

[53]   See Nobes (1997, p. 64).

INTERNATIONAL DEVELOPMENT OF THE EQUITY METHOD

However, the concept is not found in the frameworks (except for the U.K.'s recent *Statement of Principles*). Further, it is clear that an application of the frameworks' definitions suggests that an associate is not part of the group and that its profits (in excess of dividends) are not group profits. This all suggests that equity accounting has little theoretical support. If equity accounting were not allowed, we would not need non-operational concepts or arbitrary thresholds. We would also not need to worry about technical problems such as the treatment of profits made on selling to associates.

Overriding all this must be a consideration of the objectives of financial statements. If one accepts the frameworks' objectives, then the issue becomes largely an empirical matter of the best prediction of future cash flows (subject to reliability). In academic writings, there is some justification for the equity method as an approximate valuation method, as a way of reducing agency problems or as a way of providing more information on earnings. However, more research is needed here.

One conclusion is that standard setters should not perpetuate operationally difficult concepts and arbitrary thresholds or group concepts which seem inconsistent with their frameworks unless they can produce evidence that the prediction of future cash flows is enhanced. One way forward would be to require all investments to be shown at fair value, taking gains and losses to comprehensive income.[54] This would replace the equity method with a more honest valuation approach and would remove arbitrary thresholds.

In practice, recent moves towards the use of fair value for investments have deliberately excluded investments in subsidiaries, joint ventures and associates (e.g., SFAS 115, para. 4; and IAS 39, para. 1a). This leads to such delicious ironies as that, under IAS accounting, a 10 per cent holding in a listed company would be held at fair value in the investor's statements, whereas a 25 per cent holding would generally[55] be valued at cost. In the group's statements, the 10 per cent holding would again be fair valued, whereas the 25 per cent holding would be equity accounted. If the latter were seen as a valuation method, it would not be a serviceable one.

Most of the above arguments also apply against using the equity method in the final remaining case: for the treatment in consolidated statements of joint ventures (Case VI) and perhaps other 'partnerships' (those associates most like joint ventures). Theoretical support has to rest on the idea that the investor exercises long-run control over its share of the profits. Another form of support comes from concern that any alternative to the equity method is worse. For example, full consolidation or proportional consolidation of individual assets of a 20 per cent holding in a joint venture or other partnership would be inconsistent with the frameworks' concept of control. At the other extreme, a cost-based method seems to be misleading as a group presentation of an interest in a 50 per cent-held joint venture. Consequently, this last case seems to be the least objectionable use of

[54] 'Comprehensive income' is the term now to be found in SFAS 130. In U.S. terms, whether such gains and losses should be shown in 'income' or 'other comprehensive income' may become a relatively trivial issue as moves are made towards a single income statement.

[55] Assuming, as in many countries, that equity accounting is not used in investors' statements.

equity accounting, and could be seen as semi-consolidation rather than valuation. The U.K.'s 'gross equity method' addresses some of the disclosure problems caused by the netting off involved in the equity method. A report of six English-speaking standard setters (the G4 + 1) concluded in a similar way about the treatment of joint ventures (Milburn and Chant, 1999, p. 25) and makes a supporting reference[56] to an earlier (1998) draft of this article.

The spread of the equity method from one use to another can be seen as part of the response of pragmatic accountants to a series of technical problems: the lack of consolidated statements, then the complications of preparing such statements, then the lack of consolidation of certain subsidiaries, then the lack of consolidation of those jointly controlled investees that were rather like subsidiaries, and so on. The spread of the equity method internationally, despite good arguments against it in several countries, should warn us that the pressures for international harmonization (that are now even stronger than in the period covered in this article) can lead to world-wide use of bad methods as well as good ones. Similarly, the international spread of the 20 per cent threshold illustrates how a pragmatically neat number, once it is supported by the two strongest accounting nations, can prosper in a theoretical vacuum.

REFERENCES

Accountancy, 'Editorial Comment', *Accountancy*, March 1968.

——, 'Editorial Comment', *Accountancy*, June 1970a.

——, 'First Proposal from Accountancy [*sic*] Standards Committee', *Accountancy*, July 1970b.

——, 'APB Chairman in London', *Accountancy*, July 1971.

Accountant, 'A Revolutionary Proposal', *The Accountant*, 25 June 1970.

Accountants International Study Group, *Consolidated Financial Statements*, AISG, 1973.

Accounting Standards Board, *Associates and Joint Ventures*, Discussion Paper, Accounting Standards Board, 1994.

ASA/ICAA, Second Exposure Draft, ASA and ICAA, 1973.

Beeny, J. H., *European Financial Reporting: France*, Institute of Chartered Accountants in England and Wales, 1976.

Bircher, P., 'The Adoption of Consolidated Accounting in Great Britain', *Accounting and Business Research*, Winter 1988.

Bogie, D. J., *Group Accounts*, Jordon & Sons, 1949.

——, *Group Accounts*, 2nd ed., Jordon & Sons, 1959.

Burnett, T., T. E. King and V. C. Lembke, 'Equity Method Reporting for Major Finance Company Subsidiaries', *Accounting Review*, October 1979.

Carman, L. A., 'Intercorporate Relationships', *American Accountant*, April 1932.

Castle, E. F., and A. J. C. Grant, *Practical Bookkeeping and Accounts (Advanced Stage)*, University Tutorial Press, 1970.

Chambers, R. J., 'The Use of the Equity Method in Accounting for Investments in Subsidiaries and Associated Companies', *The Chartered Accountant in Australia*, February 1974.

---

[56] See Milburn and Chant (1999), note 21. This refers to the 1998 draft in the form of a University of Reading discussion paper in accounting, No. 59.

INTERNATIONAL DEVELOPMENT OF THE EQUITY METHOD

Christiansen, M., and J. O. Elling, *European Financial Reporting: Denmark*, Routledge, 1993.

Conseil National de la Comptabilité, *Consolidation des Bilans et des Comptes*, CNC, 1973.

Cooke, T. E., *European Financial Reporting—Sweden*, Institute of Chartered Accountants in England and Wales, 1988.

Cropper, L. C., F. D. Morris and A. K. Fison, *Accounting*, 5th ed., Macdonald and Evans, 1932.

Czernkowski, R., and J. Loftus, 'A Market-Based Evaluation of Alternative Methods of Reporting on Investments in Associated Entities', paper presented at the European Accounting Association annual congress, Graz, 1997.

Deegan, C., P. Kent and C.-J. Lin, 'The True and Fair View: A Study of Australian Auditors' Application of the Concept', *Australian Accounting Review*, Vol. 4, No. 1, 1994.

Defliese, P., 'British Standards in a World Setting', in Leach and Stamp (1981).

Dickerson, W. E., and J. Weldon Jones, 'Observations on "the Equity Method" and Intercorporate Relationships', *The Accounting Review*, September 1933.

Dicksee, L. R., *Published Balance Sheets and Window Dressing*, Gee, 1927.

Dicksee, L. R., and J. E. G. Montmorency, *Advanced Accounting*, 7th ed., Gee, 1932.

Diggle, G., and C. W. Nobes, 'European Rule-Making in Accounting: The Seventh Directive as a Case Study', *Accounting and Business Research*, Autumn 1994.

Dijksma, J., and M. N. Hoogendoorn, *European Financial Reporting: The Netherlands*, Routledge, 1993.

Eddey, P., *Accounting for Corporate Combinations and Associations*, Prentice-Hall, 1995.

Edwards, J. R., *A History of Financial Accounting*, Routledge, 1989.

Edwards, J. R., and K. M. Webb, 'The Development of Group Accounting in the UK to 1933', *Accounting Historians Journal*, Spring 1984.

Finney, H. A., *Consolidated Statements*, Prentice-Hall, 1922 (reprinted, Arno Press, 1982).

——, *Principles of Accounting, Advanced*, 3rd ed., Prentice-Hall, 1946.

Finney, H. A., and H. E. Miller, *Principles of Accounting, Advanced*, Prentice-Hall, 1952.

Garnsey, G., *Consolidated Accounts*, Gee, 1923.

——, *Consolidated Accounts*, 2nd ed., Gee, 1931.

Goch, D., 'Accounting for Associated Companies', *The Accountant*, 1 June 1972.

Gonzalo, J. A., and J. L. Gallizo, *European Financial Reporting: Spain*, Routledge, 1992.

Gordon, I., and R. D. Morris, 'The Equity Accounting Saga in Australia: Cyclical Standard Setting', *Abacus*, September 1996.

Hatfield, H. R., *Modern Accounting*, Appleton, 1918.

Heurlin, S., and E. Peterssohn, 'Sweden', in D. Alexander and S. Archer (eds), *European Accounting Guide*, Harcourt Brace, 1995.

Hodgkins, P., 'Unilever—the First 21 Years', in T. A. Lee and R. H. Parker (eds), *The Evolution of Corporate Financial Reporting*, Nelson, 1979.

Holmes, G., 'Associated Companies', *Accountancy*, July 1970.

International Accounting Standards Committee, *Accounting for Financial Assets and Financial Liabilities*, Discussion Paper, IASC, 1997.

Institute of Chartered Accountants in England and Wales, *Recommendation N 20, Treatment of Investments in the Balance Sheets of Trading Companies*, ICAEW, 1958.

——, *Survey of Published Accounts, 1969–70*, ICAEW, 1971.

——, *Survey of Published Accounts, 1970–71*, ICAEW, 1972.

Journal, 'Three Nations Join in Common Standards', *Journal of Accountancy*, October 1970.

Kester, R. B., *Accounting Theory and Practice*, Vol. II, Ronald Press, 1920 (year of printing; 1918 year of copyright and publication).

Kohler, E. L., 'Some Tentative Propositions Underlying Consolidated Reports', *Accounting Review*, March 1938.

43

ABACUS

Lamb, M., 'When is a Group a Group? Convergence of Concepts of "Group" in European Union Corporation Tax', *European Accounting Review*, Vol. 4, No. 1, 1995.

Leach, Sir R., 'The Birth of British Accounting Standards', in Leach and Stamp (1981).

Leach, Sir R., and E. Stamp (eds), *British Accounting Standards: The First 10 Years*, Woodhead-Faulkner, 1981.

Littleton, A. C., 'The Dividend Base', *The Accounting Review*, June 1934.

MacNair, H. S. A., 'A Practitioner's View', *The Accountant's Magazine*, September 1970.

McGregor, W., *Accounting for Leases: A New Approach*, Financial Accounting Standards Board, 1996.

Ma, R., R. H. Parker and G. Whittred, *Consolidation Accounting*, Longman Cheshire, 1991.

Mazay, V., T. Wilkins and I. Zimmer, 'Determinants of the Choice of Accounting for Investments in Associated Companies', *Contemporary Accounting Research*, Vol. 10, No. 1, 1993.

Milburn, J. A., and P. D. Chant, *Reporting Interests in Joint Ventures and Similar Arrangements*, Financial Accounting Standards Board for the G4 + 1, 1999.

Miller, M. C., and K. Leo, 'The Downside of Harmonisation Haste: The Equity Accounting Experience', *Australian Accounting Review*, Vol. 7, No. 2, 1997.

Moonitz, M., *The Entity Theory of Consolidated Statements*, American Accounting Association, 1944 (reprinted, Foundation Press, 1951).

Moonitz, M., and C. C. Staehling, *Accounting: An Analysis of its Problems*, Foundation Press, 1950, (printed in 1952).

Mulford, C. W., and E. Comiskey, 'Investment Decisions and the Equity Accounting Standard', *The Accounting Review*, July 1985.

Nailor, H., and A. Lennard, *Leases: Implementation of a New Approach*, Accounting Standards Board, 1999 (and published by other G4 + 1 bodies in 2000).

Napier, C. J., 'Scandalous Accounts: Robert Maxwell and the British Accounting Crisis of 1969', paper revised after *Accounting History* conference, Melbourne, August 1999.

Neuhausen, B. S., 'Consolidation and the Equity Method—Time for an Overhaul', *Journal of Accountancy*, February 1982.

Nobes, C. W., 'The True and Fair View Requirement: Impact on and of the Fourth Directive', *Accounting and Business Research*, Winter 1993.

——, *German Accounting Explained*, Financial Times Reports, 1997.

Noble, H. S., W. E. Karrenbrock and H. Simons, *Advanced Accounting*, South-Western Publishing Co., 1941.

Ordelheide, D., and D. Pfaff, *European Financial Reporting: Germany*, Routledge, 1994.

Parker, R. H., 'Concepts of Consolidation in the EEC', *Accountancy*, February 1997.

——, 'Importing and Exporting Accounting: The British Experience', in A. G. Hopwood (ed.), *International Pressures for Accounting Change*, Prentice-Hall, 1989.

Paton, W. A., 'Editorial Note' in Moonitz (1951).

Peirson, G., and P. McBride, 'More on International Harmonisation in Australia', *CPA Communiqué*, 75, 1997.

Pixley, F. W., *Auditors' Duties and Responsibilities*, Henry Good, 1910.

Ricks, W. E., and J. S. Hughes, 'The Case of Long-Term Investments', *The Accounting Review*, January 1985.

Sawa, E., 'Accounting in Japan', in P. Walton, A. Haller and B. Raffournier (eds), *International Accounting*, Thomson, 1988.

Sharp, K., 'Accounting Standards After 12 Months', *Accountancy*, May 1971 (reprinted and added to in S. A. Zeff, *Forging Accounting Principles in Five Countries*, Stipes, 1972).

Shaw, J. C. (ed.), *Bogie on Group Accounts*, 3rd ed., Jordon & Sons, 1973.

Titcomb, S. J., 'A Stockbroker's View', *The Accountant*, 17 September 1970.

Tweedie, D. P., 'Standards, Objectives and *The Corporate Report*', in Leach and Stamp (1981).

INTERNATIONAL DEVELOPMENT OF THE EQUITY METHOD

Vallely, M., D. Stokes and P. Liesch, 'Equity Accounting: Empirical Evidence and Lessons From the Past', *Australian Accounting Review*, Vol. 7, No. 2, 1997.

Walker, R. G., *Consolidated Statements*, Arno Press, London, 1978a.

——, 'International Accounting Compromises: The Case of Consolidation Accounting', *Abacus*, December 1978b.

Williams, J. R., *GAAP Guide 1996*, Harcourt Brace, 1996.

Zambon, S., *Entità e Proprietà nei Bilanci di Esercizio*, Cedam, 1996.

Zeff, S. A., *Forging Accounting Principles in Australia*, Australian Society of Accountants, 1973.

Zeff, S. A., F. van der Wel and K. Camfferman, *Company Financial Reporting: A Historical and Comparative Study of the Dutch Regulatory Process*, North Holland, 1992.

Part II
The Measurement and Effects of Diversity

Accounting and Business Research, Vol. 23, No. 92, pp. 460–476, 1993

The Impact of Accounting Principles on Profits: The US versus Japan

T. E. Cooke*

Abstract—Weetman and Gray (1991) sought to add quantitative information to the extant qualitative literature on differences in profits reported under US GAAP with those in the Netherlands, Sweden and the UK. This paper introduces Japanese companies to such analysis and seeks to add to both the qualitative and quantitative literature on profit comparisons. In attempting to undertake such work, the paper serves to highlight the difficulties of trying to compare financial statements in Japan with those published in the US and as a consequence the problem of undertaking quantitative analysis. On the basis of a case study approach, there is some evidence that the profits of companies prepared in accordance with Japanese GAAP are considerably more prudent than if prepared in accordance with US GAAP for companies operating in the financial sector. Such differences may not be so pronounced in the non-financial sector.

Weetman and Gray (W&G) (1991) investigated the extent to which there are material differences in reported profits based on US Generally Accepted Accounting Principles (GAAP) with profits prepared in accordance with GAAP in the UK, the Netherlands and Sweden. This paper introduces Japanese companies to a similar analysis based on 20-F filings with the SEC and additional information supplied by companies themselves. The object is to add to both the qualitative and quantitative literature on profit comparisons but the paper also highlights the difficulties of trying to compare financial statements in Japan with those published in the US.

At the outset it must be recognised that, even if accounting measurement rules and disclosure were identical in two countries, this does not mean that accounting reports would be '... universally understood and interpreted unambiguously. Unfortunately, countries also exhibit substantial economic and cultural differences that preclude accounting figures from having the same interpretation, even if they were generated using the same accounting principles' (Choi and Levich, 1990, p. 2). This paper does not consider environmental factors influencing financial reporting in Japan since these are covered in some detail by Cooke and Kikuya (1992).

The focus of this paper is to compare US GAAP with Japanese GAAP. This topic is of interest because international accounting differences have implications for both users and preparers of corporate annual reports located in countries with the world's two largest stock exchanges in terms of both turnover and market capitalisation. For investors and investment analysts there is the problem of comparing investment opportunities between enterprises. Over the last 20 years the capital markets have undergone great changes including product innovation, securitisation, liberalisation, globalisation and greater competition. These changes have provided new opportunities for international investment. However, comparing the financial statements produced in one country with those of another country is often problematical, even though the International Accounting Standards Committee (IASC) uses its best endeavours to reduce these differences. Thus, international accounting differences present problems for capital market regulators and as a consequence accounting regulators.

Companies that raise money and have their securities traded on international stock exchanges face a problem because of accounting diversity. Without reciprocal agreements between the issuer's home country and other countries, substantial costs are involved in restating or reconciling profits based on one country with those based on another.[1] Fortunately reciprocal arrangements

---

*The author is professor of accounting at the University of Exeter, England and visiting professor at the Free University Amsterdam, The Netherlands. He would like to thank P. A. Collier and A. Gregory of the University of Exeter, E. Sawa of the Japanese Institute of Certified Public Accountants, and the referees for their helpful comments.

[1]These costs form part of what has been referred to as information preparation costs as opposed to competitive costs which refer to the costs borne by a company that provides disclosures which are advantageous to a competitor to the detriment of the discloser (Gray, 1984; Choi and Levich, 1990).

exist between a number of countries, with the major exception of the US.

As far as the London Stock Exchange is concerned, Japanese companies may file consolidated accounts that comply with Japanese, US or UK GAAP although the financial statements are scrutinised for acceptability on a company by company basis each year. In contrast, the Securities and Exchange Commission (SEC) requires all foreign companies that wish to have their securities traded in the US to file a 20-F report which either reconciles or restates profits in accordance with US GAAP. For many Japanese companies this cost, particularly the associated competitive cost, is too great and is one reason why they have traditionally avoided a quotation in the US in favour of the more liberal European capital markets. Evidence on this issue is shown in Table 1. It is noticeable that Frankfurt and Luxembourg are the most popular stock exchanges for Japanese companies outside Japan. To a large extent the reason for this is historical in that the disclosure requirements of the exchanges in Frankfurt and Luxembourg have been less extensive than in London. The extent to which these differences are now significant, bearing in mind attempts at accounting disclosure harmonisation in the European Community, is beyond the scope of this paper but worthy of assessment.

Another trend revealed in Table 1 is that Japanese companies have been increasing their presence in Europe, particularly on the exchanges in Paris and London. One explanation for this is that the Japanese have been concerned about the possibility of 'fortress Europe' after the implementation of the single market at the end of 1992. As a consequence, the Japanese have been making substantial investments in Europe, especially in the UK whose government is seen by the Japanese as protecting their interests in Europe. Another recent change is that the seven Japanese companies that had a listing on the Hong Kong stock exchange in 1987 are no longer listed on that market. The reason for this is clearly political as Hong Kong moves from being a colony of the UK towards integration with China in 1997.[2] It is noticeable that all seven Japanese companies (Kumagai Gumi, Toray Industries, Asahi Chemical, Kubota, Hitachi, Omron, and Sony) withdrew from the Hong Kong market but did not seek alternative listings in the region or indeed a substitute listing elsewhere.

---

[2]The extent to which changes in country risk ratings influence multinational enterprises to list or delist on international capital markets is an interesting research question that is beyond the scope of this paper.

Table 1.
Listing of Japanese Companies (First Section only)

Stock exchange (ranking based on 1991)	Number of Japanese companies listed	
	1991	1987
Tokyo	1,223	1,089
Osaka	851	794
Nagoya	435	406
Frankfurt	56	52
Luxembourg	53	51
Paris	37	16
London	29	9
Amsterdam	24	20
Zurich	15	7
Basle	11	7
Dusseldorf	10	10
Geneva	10	7
New York	9	7
Singapore	6	4
Brussels	5	4
Antwerp	4	4
Pacific (San Francisco)	2	2
Hong Kong	0	7
Number of listings in Europe	254	187
Number of listings in the rest of the world	17	20
Number of companies	1,294	1,154

Source: The table was constructed from data in the *Japan Company Handbook* Winter 1987 and 1991 and information supplied by the Tokyo Stock Exchange.

Detailed requirements in Japan

Accounting Regulatory Framework in Japan

An unusual feature of the post-war accounting regulatory framework in Japan is its dual nature (Oguri and Hara, 1990) in which listed companies produce one set of accounts based on the requirements of the Commercial Code (CC) and a second set based on the provisions of the Securities and Exchange Law (SEL). The important difference is that the CC accounts are primarily to protect creditors and current investors whereas the SEL accounts are more shareholder oriented (JICPA, 1991). The requirements of the SEL apply to all companies that have issued securities to the public (in the main those corporations with a listing on a Japanese stock exchange) and they affect about 3,000 corporations out of a total of about 1.1 million joint stock corporations. Corporations subject to the requirements of the SEL represent a significant proportion of economic activity.

Table 2.
20-F Filings by Japanese companies with the SEC

Company No. and Name	Stock Exchange Listing	Industry Type	Consolidated Japanese Accounts?	JAP/US %, 1989, 1990, 1991	Quantified Analysis?
1. Canon	NMS	Precision machinery	No		DT
2. Hitachi	NYS	Heavy electrical machinery	No		DT, FC
3. Honda Motor	NYS*	Motor vehicles	No		DT, FC
4. Ito-Yokado	NMS	Retailing	No		DT, L
5. Komatsu	OTH	Industrial machinery	No		DT, FC
6. Kubota	NYS	Industrial machinery	No		DT
7. Kyocera	NYS	Electrical products etc	No	72,77,92	Profits
8. Makita	NMS	Electrical machinery	No	79,122,73	Profits
9. Matsushita	NYS	Consumer electronics etc	No		DT, FC
10. Mitsubishi Bank	NYS*	Banking	Yes	n/a,103,88	Profits
11. Mitsui	NMS	Commerce (general trading)	No		DT, FC
12. NEC	NMS*	Communications equipment	No		DT, FC
13. Nippon Telegraph and Telephone	OTH	Communications	No		DT, FC, L
14. Pioneer Electronic	NYS	Consumer electronics	No		DT, L
15. RICOH	OTH	Precision machinery	No		DT, FC
16. Sony	NYS*	Consumer electronics	No		DT, FC, L
17. TDK	NYS*	Consumer electronics	No		DT, L
18. Tokio Marine and Fire Insurance	NMS	Nonlife insurance	No	n/a,48,50	Reconciliation
19. Wacoal	OTH	Textiles	No		DT, L
Company without a 20-F filing					
20. Orix	n/a	Financial sector	Yes	n/a,38,36	Profits etc

Key:
Stock exchange codes:
NYS = New York Stock Exchange
NMS = NASDAQ, National Marketing System
OTH = Over-The-Counter
* = Listing on the London Stock Exchange
Quantified analysis:
DT = Deferred tax
FC = Foreign currency
L = Lease capitalisation
Source: SEC Filing Companies, Disclosure Inc.

Some[3] major listed companies in Japan produce an English annual report in addition to their reports that comply with the requirements of the CC and SEL. As far as the Japanese are concerned the reports in English are for the 'international' reader where 'international' is defined as US. These accounts are *not* translations of either the CC or SEL accounts but are accounts that are in a US format which comply to some degree with US GAAP. Those Japanese companies with a listing in the US or with American Depositary Receipts (ADRs) must file Form 20-F with the SEC. At 30 October 1991 there were 19 Japanese companies

that filed a 20-F report with the SEC (see Table 2), including nine that were listed on the New York Stock Exchange and six with ADRs traded on the National Marketing System (NASDAQ). Of the 19, five had a listing on the London Stock Exchange. Table 2 also summarises the quantified analysis reported on later in this paper.

Qualitative differences in Japanese and US GAAP

Accounting standards in Japan are issued by the Business Accounting Deliberation Council (BADC) under the authority of the Ministry of Finance. Membership of BADC comes from business, academe, and the professional accounting communities as well as the Ministry itself. In contrast, the Japanese Institute of Certified Public

---

[3]In addition to those companies that are required to file a 20-F report, a number of other Japanese companies produce English annual reports. The exact number is not known because these voluntary statements are not filed with any regulatory authority.

Accountants (JICPA) offers a sort of administrative guidance to the standards in the form of statements, opinions and working rules.

The essential difference between GAAP in the US and in Japan is that accounting standards are set, in the main, in the private sector (FASB) in the US whereas they are prepared in the public sector in Japan (principally the Ministry of Finance). For a review of the historical development of Japan's regulatory framework see Cooke (1991). The form of regulatory framework helps explain some of the differences between the two countries.

The following represent major differences between the US and Japanese GAAP that have been identified in the literature (see for example, Cooke and Kikuya, 1992):

Tax

In Japan, income for taxation purposes is based on the published financial statements. Deferred taxation is not normally practised in Japan and is in fact not permitted in the CC accounts. In the main company accounts prepared in accordance with the SEL, deferred taxation is not provided for but in the supplementary consolidated financial statements deferred taxation is permitted although is not common in practice. However, deferred taxation is provided for in the English language financial statements prepared in accordance with US GAAP.

In contrast to Japan, deferred taxes, based on the deferral method, must be provided in the US where there are timing differences between book and taxable income (APB Opinion 11). However, in December 1987 the Financial Accounting Standards Board issued SFAS No. 96, *Accounting for Income Taxes*, which requires an asset and liability approach in the measurement of deferred taxes rather than the deferred method. SFAS No. 103 amended SFAS No. 96 so that the effective date for implementation became 15th December 1992, although earlier application was permitted. (The more recent introduction of SFAS 109 in February 1992 does not affect the period reviewed in this research.) Early implementation was not adopted by Japanese companies and therefore the change does not affect the results under review. As a consequence, for the period under review all Japanese companies filing 20-F reports provided for deferred taxes using the deferral method.

Differences also exist in the presentation of taxes between the two countries. In Japan, the enterprise tax, which is a local tax on taxable net income, is treated as a selling, general and administrative expense whereas in the US such taxes are included in the tax charge for the year.

Foreign Currency Translation

In Japan, it is normal for the temporal method to be used in translating the foreign currency

financial statements of a foreign branch. Long-term monetary items are translated at the historical rates and exchange differences are included in current income. In contrast, the modified temporal method is used for a foreign subsidiary or associate with any exchange gain or loss on long-term monetary items treated as deferred assets/liabilities. Under the modified temporal method, net income and retained earnings are translated at the closing rate and exchange differences resulting from the translation of balance sheet items are charged or credited to assets or liabilities as appropriate. There is no equivalent to the requirements of IAS 21 which stipulate that either the restate-translate method should be used for the financial statements of a foreign entity which is affected by high rates of inflation or, alternatively, the temporal method may be used. Thus, foreign currency financial statement translation in Japan is similar to SFAS 8 whereas in the US it is based on SFAS 52.

Notes with Detachable Warrants

In Japan the face amount of the note with detachable warrants is recognised at the time of issuance whereas in the US the estimated fair value of the warrants at the time of issue is considered to represent a discount on the face value of the notes and is amortised as an interest expense over the life of the notes. Consequently, in Japan the transaction is dealt with as a capital item whereas in the US the discount has an impact on the profit and loss account.

Consolidations

The US requires that all subsidiaries should be consolidated whereas in Japan only material subsidiaries need be included. In Japan, the Ministry of Finance has made a pronouncement on the scope of consolidation for the purpose of audits undertaken by Certified Public Accountants in accordance with the SEL. The pronouncement introduces a 10% materiality rule which permits exemption from consolidation in the following circumstances:

(1) where total assets of the subsidiaries are less than 10% of the total assets of the parent company and other consolidated subsidiaries, and

(2) aggregate sales of the subsidiaries are less than 10% of the total sales of the parent company and other consolidated subsidiaries.[4]

---

[4]This means that it is possible to organise subsidiaries so as to exclude some from consolidation.

In addition to the materiality concept, subsidiaries may be exempt from consolidation if they are:

(1) not part of the group because of a loss of effective control;
(2) not a going concern;
(3) the investment is only held for the short-term;
(4) inclusion of the results of the subsidiary would mislead interested parties.

As a result of the above, it is likely that some subsidiaries may be exempt from consolidation in Japan but would need to be included to comply with US GAAP.

Equity Accounting

In 1983 it became compulsory in Japanese consolidated accounts to apply the equity method of accounting for investments to both unconsolidated subsidiaries and affiliates, where the latter are defined in terms of ownership of between 20 and 50 per cent. In the parent only company accounts, such investments are stated at cost or, where there has been a permanent reduction in value, written down value. In contrast, under equity accounting the carrying value is normally cost plus a share of the undistributed profits. This disparity in valuation and the fact that intercompany profits or losses are not eliminated from the parent company accounts, may lead to material differences between the operating results of the parent company and the consolidated financial statements.

The Japanese requirements may be contrasted with those in the US. In the US, the equity method is applied in accounting for affiliates with all subsidiaries being consolidated. Thus, some subsidiaries may be consolidated in accordance with US GAAP but would be subject to the equity method under Japanese GAAP. Also, in accordance with US GAAP, unrealised profits or losses on intercompany transactions should be eliminated on the parent only financial statements which is not the case in Japan.

Leases

In the US, finance leases should be capitalised by the lessee whereas in Japan it is permissible either to capitalise the asset or, alternatively, to disclose the amounts involved. In practice, Japanese companies do not capitalise their leased assets but treat the obligation as a rental fee that is included in expenses.

Pensions

It is now common for Japanese companies to provide for employee retirement and severance benefits. In general, employees are entitled to a lump-sum payment based on the current rate of pay and length of service. In practice, it is normal to use base pay to apply the service multiple since this excludes various allowances and any bonuses. Many schemes for employees have not been fully funded although in recent years some companies have decided partially to fund their schemes. Where schemes do exist, it is common to try to obtain the maximum tax advantage on the unfunded element which is set at 40 per cent of the voluntary retirement and severance liability as at the balance sheet date rather than at retirement date. Contributions to the pension fund are charged to income as incurred whereas those costs that relate to past service are treated as a liability and amortised.

It is more common in the US for pension schemes to be fully funded and therefore the stated liability appears much greater than for Japanese companies.

Marketable Securities

In Japan, the general rule for valuing marketable securities (classified as both current and non-current assets) is the same as for inventories: cost or the lower of cost and market value. In practice, securities are often stated at acquisition cost, which includes commissions and any other incidental charges. The moving average approach is a popular method of cost determination since profit can be recognised on an individual security basis. In contrast, FASB Statement No. 12 requires the carrying amount of marketable securities to be valued at the lower of the portfolio's aggregate cost and market value as at the balance sheet date. Thus, in the US a portfolio approach is adopted whereas in Japan securities are valued on an individual security basis.

Accounting for Stock Dividends

In Japan, a bonus issue should normally be accounted for by a transfer of an amount equal to the par value of the shares from additional paid-in capital, legal reserve or retained earnings to the capital stock account. In the US the transfer is at market value rather than par value and is from retained earnings. Expenses involved in such issues are deducted from stockholders' equity in the US whereas in Japan they may be expensed immediately or over a period of three years.

Instalment Sales on Accruals Basis

Where uncertainties exist it is possible in Japan to record revenues on an instalment basis. Since this approach is allowed for tax purposes it is quite common for revenue to be accounted for in this way. In contrast, in the US transactions should be accounted for at the time of the sale and a provision made for doubtful debts where appropriate.

Inventories

Considerable flexibility is offered to Japanese companies in valuing inventories, in terms of both accounting and tax regulations. Unit cost, FIFO, LIFO, weighted average cost, moving average cost, straight average cost, latest purchase price, and the retail inventory cost method are all acceptable methods of valuing inventories. In the US, cost is determined by FIFO, LIFO, standard cost or weighted average and a combination of approaches is permissible.

When valuing stocks at the year-end the rule in Japan is either cost or the lower of cost (applying one of the above methods) and market value. Companies may interpret market value to be either current replacement cost or net realisable value. Where market price is significantly less than cost, stocks must be written down to market value unless the recovery of the shortfall is certain. In contrast, ARB No. 43 in the US stipulates the lower of cost or market value where market value is usually current replacement cost but market value cannot exceed net realisable value.

In Japan, where there is a substantial and irrevocable decline in the market value of inventories it is necessary to value inventories on the basis of the new market value, in accordance with the provisions of the CC.

Goodwill

Consistent with international practice, internally generated goodwill is not accounted for in Japan. However, purchased goodwill should be valued at acquisition cost and amortised to income on a systematic basis over its estimated useful life. The CC states that goodwill should be written off over a period not exceeding five years whereas in the US goodwill may be written off over 40 years. With respect to goodwill arising on consolidation (referred to in Japan as a consolidation adjustment) it is normal for the amortisation period to be five years although it is accepted that a longer period may be appropriate in exceptional circumstances.

Dividends, Auditors' Remuneration and Bonuses to Directors

In Japan, all these items are deemed to be appropriations of profit and are dealt with on a cash basis. While dividends are treated on a cash basis in both Japan and the US they are dealt with on an accruals basis in the UK. In the US, auditors' remuneration and all payments to directors are considered to be selling, general and administrative expenses whereas in Japan only the non-bonus element of remuneration to directors is considered to constitute selling, general and administrative expenses.

Depreciation

There is no requirement in Japan for the useful lives of assets to be reviewed periodically whereas in the US such a review should be undertaken and depreciable rates adjusted for the current and future periods if expectations are significantly different from previous estimates.

In Japan, a company may elect to use either the straight-line or declining-balance method (or other method approved by the Ministry of Finance) for calculating depreciation on tangible fixed assets, but intangibles should be amortised by the straight-line method (although again it is possible for other methods to be used subject to approval). The amount of depreciation or amortisation allowable for tax purposes is also determined by ministerial ordinance. In exceptional circumstances, such as the severe decline in value of an asset, the useful life may be shortened by approval from the tax authorities. In practice, companies try to obtain the maximum immediate benefit and typically use the declining-balance method (Cooke and Kikuya, 1992, p. 47).

In contrast, in the US the depreciation rates used for tax purposes need not be the same as those for financial statement purposes (Cooke, 1988, p. 431).

Capitalisation of Borrowing Costs

In the US, interest should be capitalised in certain specified circumstances whereas in Japan capitalisation is not mandatory and may only be undertaken for borrowing costs in relation to tangible depreciable assets.

Research and Development Expenditure

In Japan, research and development costs may be capitalised and amortised over a period not exceeding five years for both accounting and tax purposes whereas in the US, SFAS 2 stipulates that such costs should be expensed in most circumstances. For tax purposes in the US, research and development expenditure may be either capitalised or deducted against income, regardless of where the expenses were incurred. A taxpayer may elect to amortise any research and development costs that have been capitalised on an equitable basis over 60 or more months.

Quantitative differences in Japanese and US GAAP

The criterion for comparison is the 'conservatism' index (I) used by Gray (1980) which in the case of Japan is as follows:

$$I = 1 - \frac{(\text{Profits US} - \text{Profits Japan})}{|\text{Profits US}|}$$

Provided the figure for 'Profits US' is positive, the index is a simple relative of 'Profits Japan'

466   ACCOUNTING AND BUSINESS RESEARCH

divided by 'Profits US'. For partial indices (P) the
formula is:

$$P = 1 - \frac{\text{(partial adjustment)}}{|\text{Profits US}|}$$

The Research Data

The SEC requires all foreign companies that are
obliged to report to it to file a 20-F report. The
report should include a set of consolidated financial statements that either complies with US
GAAP or is reconciled to US GAAP. W&G used
the 20-F reports to analyse the profit reconciliations of UK, Swedish and Dutch companies. The
situation as far as Japanese companies is concerned
is rather different, presenting great problems in
attempting to undertake such work.

The main problem is that consolidated financial
statements are relatively new to Japan and are still
considered to be supplementary to the main accounts that are based on a single company. Consolidated accounting was introduced in Japan
when the Ministry of Finance issued the Regulations Concerning Consolidated Financial Statements in 1976 and the related interpretative rules
in 1977. As a result, consolidated financial statements became a requirement for listed companies
for the financial year beginning on or after 1 April
1977. However, the Ministry of Finance permits
Japanese companies that prepare 20-F reports to
file them also with the Japanese Ministry. As a
result, there is no obligation for those companies
that prepare their financial statements in accordance with US GAAP to prepare consolidated
accounts in accordance with Japanese GAAP. If
this option is adopted a Japanese company is not
disclosing consolidated accounts prepared in accordance with Japanese GAAP, thus making it
extremely difficult for an investor or analyst to
compare Japanese companies.[5] Since Japanese
companies have a history of being somewhat resist-
ant to disclosure (Ballon *et al.*, 1976; Someya,
1989; Cooke, 1991; Cooke and Kikuya, 1992) then,
a priori, Japanese companies are unlikely to produce consolidated financial statements on the basis
of both US and Japanese GAAP since they are not
required to do so.

All 19 companies shown in Table 2 were
contacted by letter[6] and additional information
was obtained from the JICPA, the publishers
of the Japan Company Handbook, the Tokyo
stock exchange and Disclosure Inc. (a company
search agency). The analysis was based on the
latest available information as at 31st December
1991.

---

[5]This assumes that consolidated financial statements contain
information value.
[6]The letter enquired as to the availability of a reconciliation
statement between Japanese GAAP and US GAAP.

Of the 19 companies, only the Mitsubishi Bank
Ltd prepares consolidated accounts that conform
with the requirements of both US and Japanese
GAAP. In addition, a second Japanese company,[7]
Orix Ltd, which does not have any overseas
listings and therefore does not file a 20-F report,
also produces financial statements that conform
with the requirements of both US and Japanese
GAAP. These statements were scrutinised and the
reconciliations are provided in the next section.
Additional useful information was supplied by
The Tokio Marine and Fire Insurance Company.
The company provided a reconciliation and gave
permission for the information to be disclosed
despite the fact that not all the details were available in the financial statements. Further useful
information was obtained from the financial statements of the Kyocera Corporation since their
account notes discussed differences in the total
level of profits drawn up in accordance with
Japanese GAAP from those based on US GAAP.
The account notes also mentioned how the differences arose but did not identify the individual
components.

Given the lack of information, statistical analysis involving 'conservatism' indices was not possible. Consequently, a case study approach was
adopted using the US as the reference point in a
manner similar to W&G for Sweden and the
Netherlands. However, since deferred taxation is
rarely practised by Japanese companies in Japan
but is obligatory under US GAAP and as this
information is disclosed by all 19 companies, it was
possible to calculate a partial index of deferred
taxes.

Case study material

The case study material covers five of the 19
companies that file 20-F reports with the SEC and
Orix, a company without any overseas listings but
one that prepares consolidated accounts in accordance with both US and Japanese GAAP. These
case studies serve to highlight some of the interesting information disclosed. Companies are identified by name with the number in parentheses
referring to those used in Table 2. With the exception of the companies dealt with immediately
below, the companies are dealt with in the order
stated in Table 2. All figures are in millions of yen.
The following companies identified differences between US GAAP and Japanese GAAP but are not
identified in the case material: Komatsu (5), Kubota (6), Mitsui (11), NEC (12), RICOH (15), Sony
(16), and Wacoal (19).

---

[7]This information was supplied by the Tokyo stock exchange
and the Japanese Institute of Certified Public Accountants.

Table 3
Differences between US GAAP and Japanese GAAP: Ito-Yokado

	1991	1990	1989
Net income for domestic reporting purposes (parent company only)	44,101	39,919	36,305
Net increase to reflect US accounting principles	25,121	18,546	15,281
Consolidated net income	69,222	58,465	51,586

Canon (1), *Hitachi* (2), *Honda Motor* (3), *Matsushita* (9), *Nippon Telegraph and Telephone* (13), *Pioneer Electronic* (14), *TDK* (17)

All these companies state that the English version accounts reported in their 20-F filings are prepared in accordance with US GAAP but none of them discloses differences with Japanese GAAP and none discloses the aggregate effect of the differences. As a result, all seven companies are excluded from the analysis provided in Table 9.

It is noticeable that all seven companies are organisations well known in the West, six of them being in the manufacturing sector and the seventh, NTT, in the communications sector. One explanation is that these companies suffer from 'disclosure shyness', but since they are well-known firms this appears unlikely. An alternative explanation is that because they are well-known in the West they are more anglicised in their financial reporting and consequently differences between profits drawn up on US GAAP compared with those based on Japanese GAAP are not as significant as in other industrial sectors. No information is available on these companies to make that judgement but the following cases may provide some pointers.

Ito-Yokado (4)

Ito-Yokado's business operations are in retail stores, franchised convenience stores and restaurants. The accounting principles stated in the notes to the consolidated financial statements identify the major differences between US GAAP and Japanese GAAP that affect the company (see Table 3).

This note is potentially misleading because a comparison is made between the net income of the parent company based on Japanese GAAP (in accordance with the requirements of the CC and

the SEL) and the consolidated net income based on US GAAP. Much more helpful for users making and advising on investment decisions would be a comparison between consolidated net income based on Japanese GAAP with consolidated net income based on US GAAP.

Kyocera (7)

Kyocera is a high technology company operating in electronics, metal processing, automobiles, communications, optics, medicine and energy. The annual report shows the effect on profits of the differences between US GAAP and Japanese GAAP that have affected the company. Using this information the conservatism index was calculated (see Table 4).

It is noticeable that net profits prepared in accordance with Japanese GAAP are more conservative than those prepared in accordance with US GAAP but that the differences have diminished over time.

Makita Corporation (8)

Makita is a designer and producer of portable electric power tools. Its consolidated accounts include a comparison of its profits prepared in accordance with both US and Japanese GAAP. The comparison over time is made difficult because of the change in year end date from February to March and because of the 'abnormal' deferred tax charge over the six months ending 31 March 1990. In addition, the stock market decrease in 1990 and 1991 has had an effect on the valuation of marketable securities and consequently on deferred taxation. The aggregate market value of the current and non-current marketable equity securities exceeded aggregate cost in the year to 30 September 1989 but subsequently the reverse occurred as

Table 4
Differences between US GAAP and Japanese GAAP: Kyocera Corporation

	31 March 1991	31 March 1990	31 March 1989
Japanese GAAP	29,558	26,062	23,891
US GAAP	32,250	33,827	33,293
Japanese/US =	91.65%	77.05%	71.76%

Table 5
Differences between US GAAP and Japanese GAAP: Makita Corporation

	Year ended 31 March 1991	Six months ended 31 March 1990	Seven months and eight days ended 30 September 1989	Year ended 20 February 1989
Japanese GAAP	9640	5567	6433	9085
US GAAP	13271	4555	8122	11364
Japanese/US =	72.6%	122.3%	79.2%	80%

security market values fell sharply. This was reflected in the deferred tax account by debits to the income statement prior to 31 December 1989 and substantial credits to the profit and loss account in later periods.

A summary of the comparison between profits on the basis of US and Japanese GAAP is shown in Table 5.

Mitsubishi (10)

Mitsubishi Bank[8] is one of the top five commercial banks in the world and specialises in providing banking services to domestic companies, small business enterprises and consumers in Japan. In addition, it provides banking services including corporate and personal banking, trade financing, specialised project and asset-based finance, cash management and foreign exchange to customers in 24 foreign countries.

Mitsubishi Bank prepares consolidated accounts based on both US and Japanese GAAP enabling conservatism indexes to be calculated. The conservatism indexes for 1990 and 1991 do not give a consistent message but the mean of the two indexes, which is only a mild indicator, is 95.56%, perhaps showing a greater degree of conservatism in reported revenue and profits in banking in Japan compared with US GAAP (see Table 6). Indeed, the 12 month forecast shows that expected profits prepared in accordance with Japanese GAAP are 90.9% of US profits. The accounts do not explain why these differences arise.

Tokio Marine and Fire Insurance (18)

Tokio Marine and Fire Insurance is Japan's largest non-life insurance company. In reply to a letter sent to the company enquiring about differences between US GAAP and Japanese GAAP, the accounting administrator supplied a reconciliation statement for the two years ending 31st March 1991. Not all the information is available in the accounts but permission has been granted for publication of the statement (see Table 7). The

reconciliation statement highlights the level of prudence in the insurance industry in Japan compared with US GAAP, although, over the three years scrutinised, there was a marginal reduction in the extent of conservatism.

The summary of significant accounting policies states that:

The financial statements of the Company are presented herein in accordance with United States generally accepted accounting principles, which vary in certain respects from Japanese accounting principles. In the financial statements distributed by the Company to its stockholders (which have been prepared in conformity with Japanese accounting principles), the Company reported net income of ¥77,031 million ($264,507 thousand) in 1991, and ¥40,253 million ($287,521 thousand) in 1990, and stockholders' equity of ¥528,303 million ($3,773,593 thousand) at March 31, 1991, and ¥502,672 million ($3,590,514 thousand) at March 31, 1990.

Deferred policy acquisition costs in Japan refer to commissions and brokerage costs of acquiring insurance policies on which the premiums will accrue in the future. The unearned premiums are deferred and amortised over the term of the policies so that the premiums are matched with the related acquisition costs.

It is clear from the above that this company adopts accounting policies that conform with Japanese GAAP that are extremely prudent compared with those reported under US GAAP.

Orix (20)

Orix is a financial company with its main interests in the leasing industry. The company does not have any overseas listings but produces consolidated accounts prepared on the basis of both Japanese GAAP and US GAAP. The information shown in Table 8 is disclosed and filed with the Ministry of Finance in Tokyo.

This statement reveals that profits are much lower under Japanese GAAP than under US GAAP showing a much greater degree of conservatism in reported profits in Japan in this area of

---

[8]Based on assets held at the end of 1988, de Carmoy (1990, p. 123) places Mitsubishi Bank as the fourth largest in the world.

Table 6
Differences between US GAAP and Japanese GAAP:
Mitsubishi Bank

	31 March 1991	31 March 1990
Japanese GAAP		
Ordinary revenue	4,341,609	3,859,224
Ordinary profit	180,332	270,173
Current profit	90,053	142,593
US GAAP		
Ordinary revenue	4,341,609	3,809,152
Ordinary profit	224,619	301,258
Current profit	102,186	138,451
Japanese/US =	88.13%	102.99%

Estimated result for next year

	Japanese GAAP	US GAAP
Ordinary revenue	4,700,000	4,700,000
Ordinary profit	190,000	230,000
Current profit	100,000	110,000
Japanese/US = 90.91%		

N.B. Ordinary or operating profits are obtained by deducting operating expenses from sales (ordinary revenue). Current profits are obtained by deducting items such as interest and foreign exchange gains/losses from operating profit. Extraordinary profits/losses are then added/deducted along with income tax to obtain net profit.

the financial sector. In addition to information on current levels of profits, the company prepares a 12 month forecast which again emphasises the conservative nature of Japanese financial reporting, with profits based on Japanese GAAP being about 35% of those reported in accordance with US GAAP. The reason why profits and sales differ so significantly is primarily due to the way in which lease contracts are accounted for. In the Japanese accounts the 'operating method' of accounting for direct financing leases is used whereas the 'financing method' is used in the consolidated accounts prepared in accordance with US GAAP. The result is that income is concentrated towards the latter part of the lease term using Japanese GAAP whereas, under US GAAP, income is recognised over the lease term so as to yield a constant rate of return on the unpaid balance of the lessee's obligation under the lease.

Table 7
Reconciliation statement: the Tokio Marine and Fire Insurance Company

	31 March 1991	31 March 1990
Net income (Japanese GAAP)	40,253	37,031
Add:		
Excess of change in underwriting reserves in report to stockholders over change in unearned premiums in the financial statements	32,379	33,934
Deferred policy acquisition costs	19,576	13,973
Other	7,540	5,552
Deduct:		
Additional provision for losses incurred but not reported	(2,593)	(6,380)
Income taxes (deferred taxation)	(9,300)	(2,200)
Other	(4,619)	(7,969)
Net income (US GAAP)	83,236	73,941
Japanese/US =	48.36%	50.08%

N.B. A reconciliation was not provided for 1989 although the net income reported to shareholders using Japanese GAAP was ¥44,092m and the comparable figure based on US GAAP was ¥92,978m. The Japan/US comparison is 47.41%.

Table 8.
Differences between US GAAP and Japanese GAAP: Orix

	31 March 1991	31 March 1990
Japanese GAAP		
Operating revenues (sales)	973,949	848,299
Operating profit	29,372	27,823
Ordinary profit	21,261	25,378
Current profit (net income)	7,244	7,240
US GAAP		
Operating revenues (sales)	445,384	316,042
Profit before tax	40,482	40,006
Current profit (net income)	20,109	19,307
Current profit Japanese/US =	36.02%	37.50%

Estimated result for next year	Japanese GAAP	US GAAP
Ordinary profit	21,500	43,000
Current profit (net income)	7,300	21,000
Current profit Japanese/US = 34.76%		

N.B. Under Japanese GAAP, operating profit represents the results of deducting cost of sales and selling, general and administrative expenses from operating revenues. Ordinary profit is the result of adding or subtracting other income and expenses (such as gains from the sale of securities) to or from operating profit. Current profit is calculated by adding/subtracting gains/losses on the sale of fixed assets, taxes, minority interests, goodwill amortisation, and equity earnings from affiliates, from operating profit.

Analysis and results

Table 9 summarises the major differences between US and Japanese GAAP highlighted by the 12 entities disclosing such information. The qualitative differences already outlined are those that may be important in comparing consolidated accounts prepared in accordance with US GAAP and Japanese GAAP. However, all the companies filing 20-F reports follow US GAAP and, with the

Table 9
Company identification of accounting policy differences between US and Japanese GAAP

Number of companies recognising differences	12
Provision for deferred taxes	12
Foreign currency translation	11
Recognition of warrant value	7
Accruals for certain expenses	7
Consolidation of subsidiaries and implementation of equity accounting	6
Accounting for leases	4
Treatment of pensions	3
Appropriation for special allowances	3
Valuation of marketable securities	2
Stock issue expenses	2
Accounting for stock dividends	1
Accounting for business combinations	1
Recognition of expected losses on purchase and sale of commissions	1
Instalment sales on accruals basis	1
Inventory valuation	1
Excess of change in underwriting reserves	1
Deferred policy costs	1
	64

exception of Mitsubishi, do not prepare consolidated financial statements in accordance with Japanese GAAP. Thus, the characteristics highlighted by the companies themselves represent the intermingling of differences: first, those that may result in comparing consolidated accounts prepared in accordance with US GAAP with those that may have arisen if prepared in accordance with Japanese GAAP; secondly, those differences that arise from a comparison of GAAP used in preparing the parent company accounts in Japan with principles used to prepare consolidated accounts in accordance with US GAAP. As a result, the qualitative differences already discussed may differ somewhat from those identified by the companies themselves.

Table 10 summarises differences that have either been identified by the companies themselves or else may be deduced from the financial statements. For example, while only 12 companies identified deferred taxation as a major difference between Japanese GAAP and US GAAP, all 19 companies provided sufficient disclosure for the difference to be apparent. The discussion that follows is based on accounting policy differences shown in Table 10 and serves to relate the earlier discussion on qualitative differences with the research findings. The order of discussion is on the basis of frequency of differences that may be identified in the financial statements.

Deferred Taxes

For the period being considered SFAS 96 was optional and was not applied by Japanese companies. As a consequence all the companies under review used the deferral method of accounting for deferred taxes, as required by APB Opinion No 11, in their annual reports filed with the SEC. Since deferred taxation is not accounted for in Japan it is possible that this may be an important difference, in terms of frequency of occurrence, in accounting principles for the period under review. Indeed, every Japanese company filing a 20-F report with the SEC referred to this as a component part of significant differences between the two countries. However, the fact that Japanese financial reporting is substantially influenced by taxation requirements is likely to reduce the significance of deferred taxation. Table 11 shows that the difference in the accounting principle between the two countries is not significant in any of the three years scrutinised. For example, in 1991 Japanese profits were 3.27% higher than the US profits; in 1990 Japanese profits were 0.89% higher; and in 1989 they were 1.84% lower. In all of the three years the difference was not significant at either the 5% or 10% levels. The Wilcoxon test confirms this finding.

These results, based on deferred taxes introduced by Japanese companies in their 20-F reports, contrasts sharply with those for UK companies established by W&G. They found that for each of the years 1986 to 1988 the differences were significant at the 10% level and for 1987 and 1988 significant at the 5% level.

The distribution of indices classified by level of materiality is shown in Table 12. As W&G found for the UK, the indices are concentrated in the +5% of US profit category. However, whilst W&G found that outliers were a problem, it is noticeable that the standard deviation of the deferred tax indices for Japanese companies was lower in each of the three years considered here compared with the indices on UK companies.

W&G found that there was a significant difference between the partial provision for deferred taxation in the UK and comprehensive tax allocations as in the US. However, that difference is more substantial than that between (i) Japanese financial accounts that are based, to a large extent, on tax requirements but with no provision for deferred taxes, and (ii) financial accounts based more on economic substance with comprehensive tax allocations as in the US.

Makita provides an illustration of deferred tax disclosure and the reasons for the incidence of timing differences.

Makita

The fall in the Japanese stock market in 1990 and 1991 had an effect on the valuation of marketable securities and consequently on deferred taxation. The aggregate market value of the current and non-current marketable equity securities exceeded aggregate cost in the year to 30 September 1989 but subsequently the reverse occurred as security market values fell sharply. This was reflected in the deferred tax account by debits to the income statement prior to 31 December 1989 and substantial credits to the profit and loss account in later periods (see Table 13).

Foreign Currency Translation

Seventeen of the 19 companies identified their accounting policy with respect to foreign currency translation and 11 stated that this was an area in which there was a material difference between Japanese GAAP and US GAAP. Nine companies quantified the extent of the gains/losses on foreign currency translation, including Honda which disclosed the accounting policy followed by the following information:

Foreign currency translation gains/(losses) included in the determination of net income for

Table 10
Differences between US and Japanese GAAP

Company number	1	2	3	4	5	6	7	8	9	10	11	12	13	14	15	16	17	18	19	Total
Provision for deferred taxes	q	q	q	q	q	q	q	q	q	q	q	q	q	q	q	q	q	q	q	19
Foreign currency translation/hedging operations[a]		q	q	x	q	x	x	x	q	x	q	q	q	x	q	x	q	q	x	17
Accounting for leases			x	q				x			x				q	q		q		7
Recognition of warrant value							x			x	x	x	q	q	x	x	x	q	x	10
Accruals for certain expenses						x	x	x		x	x	x			x	x			x	7
Treatment of pensions												x	x		x					7
Consolidation of subsidiaries				x	x	x	x				x				x		x			5
Implementation of equity accounting				x	x										x	x			x	4
Valuation of marketable securities				x	x		x	x		x	x									4
Appropriation for special allowances				x	x						x					x				4
Stock issue expenses							x			x	x	x				x			x	3
Accounting for stock dividends						x		x												2
Accounting for business combinations							x	x												2
Recognition of expected losses on purchase and sale commitments											x									1
Instalment sales on accruals basis											x									1
Excess of change in underwriting reserves																		x		1
Deferred policy costs																		x		1
Total	1	2	3	6	6	5	7	7	2	5	9	5	4	3	7	7	4	6	7	96

Key: a = hedging operations were often linked with information on foreign currency translation
q = difference in accounting policy quantified in a disclosure note
x = different accounting policy identified by the company but not quantified

Table 11
Descriptive statistics on deferred taxation

Year	N	Mean	St dev	SE mean	t	P value (2-tailed)
1991	19	1.0327	0.172	0.039	0.83	0.418
1990	19	1.0089	0.209	0.048	0.19	0.855
1989	19	0.9816	0.101	0.023	−0.79	0.438

Year	N for test	Wilcoxon statistic	P value	Estimated median
1991	19	112.5	0.247	1.033
1990	19	102.0	0.397	1.013
1989	19	76.5	0.778	0.9842

each of the years in the three-year period ended March 31, 1991 were as follows:

	Yen m		US dollars (thousands) note 2
1989	1990	1991	1991
¥12,167	¥(24,126)	¥9,320	$66,099

In addition, seven companies provided information on foreign currency hedging activities and four identified the amount involved at the year-end. In general, hedging was undertaken against foreign currency receivables and payables and the resulting gains or losses were credited or charged to income in the current period. Thus, some companies provided information on foreign currency transactions although none quantified the difference between implementing Japanese GAAP and US GAAP in this area.

Accounting for Leases
Ten companies identified that leased assets were capitalised to conform with US GAAP. In practice, Japanese companies do not capitalise finance leases in their Japanese corporate annual reports

(Cooke and Kikuya, 1992, p. 230) and capitalisation is a major difference between Japan and the US. Seven companies quantified the extent of leased assets.

Recognition of Warrant Value and Accruals for Certain Expenses
Seven companies identified the treatment of warrants and the accrual for certain expenses to be material differences between US and Japanese GAAP but none provided any useful information on these issues in either descriptive or numerical form.

Treatment of Pensions
Five companies identified compliance with US GAAP in this area and while there was some quantified disclosure of pension obligations the information was not useful in determining differences between US and Japanese GAAP.

Consolidation of Subsidiaries
None of the four companies that identified this as an important difference between the US and Japan provided any quantification of those

Table 12
Partial index of conservatism: deferred taxation

Level of materiality	Index values	1991	1990	1989
Japanese profits 10% or more below the US profit	0.9000 and below	3	4	4
Japanese profits 5% or more below the US profit but less than 10% below	0.9001–0.9500	3	2	3
Japanese profit within +5% of US profit	0.9501–1.0499	7	7	7
Japanese profit 5% or more above the US profit but less than 10% above	1.0500–1.0999	2	0	2
Japanese profit 10% or more above the US profit	1.1000 and above	4 / 19	6 / 19	3 / 19
Range: Lowest value		0.716	0.501	0.784
Highest value		1.491	1.419	1.141

Table 13
Disclosure of deferred income taxes: Makita Corporation

	Year ended 31 March 1991	*Six months ended 31 March 1990*	*Seven months and eight days ended 30 September 1989*	*Year ended 20 February 1989*
Estimated retirement and termination allowances and other accrued expenses	(448)	472	(156)	(757)
Valuation of inventories	(35)	(20)	(4)	157
Intercompany profits	649	(511)	(810)	109
Undistributed earnings of overseas subsidiaries	871	674	114	342
Valuation of marketable securities	(1100)	(1976)	893	293
Other	(690)	(47)	(50)	133
Deferred taxes	(753)	(1408)	(13)	277
Of which deferred tax:				
Domestic	(406)	(1219)	(95)	(101)
Foreign	(347)	(189)	82	378
	(753)	(1408)	(13)	277

differences. This is because the companies involved did not prepare consolidated accounts in accordance with Japanese GAAP and therefore had not considered the impact of differences in this area. Rather the accounts revealed that the preparers were comparing the parent company accounts filed in Japan with the consolidated accounts filed in the US. Thus, statements of elimination of inter-company transactions were made.

Implementation of Equity Accounting
As with the consolidation of subsidiaries, companies seem to be comparing Japanese parent company accounts with consolidated accounts prepared in accordance with US GAAP. As a result there is likely to be a material difference between cost, as recorded at the parent company level, and equity accounting, as recorded in the consolidated accounts. Highlighting equity accounting as a material accounting difference between the two countries is somewhat misleading because equity accounting would have to be applied to affiliates if consolidated accounts were prepared in accordance with Japanese GAAP.

Appropriation for Special Allowances
None of the three companies identifying this as an area of difference between the US and Japan provided any details of what the allowances constitute.

Valuation of Marketable Securities
Makita demonstrates the importance of the valuation of marketable securities to deferred taxation and highlights one important difference between

Japanese GAAP and US GAAP.[9] Prior to 31 December 1989 losses from the valuation of marketable equity securities for tax and financial accounting purposes in Japan were greater than those recognised under US GAAP. This probably arose because the lower of cost or market method is applied on an individual security basis in Japan, whereas in the US a portfolio basis is applied. This means that during a period of rising stock prices, the aggregate market value is usually greater than the aggregate cost and therefore there is no need for a valuation allowance according to SFAS No. 12. However, for Japanese tax and financial accounting purposes write-downs would be necessary for some securities as even during a general increase in security prices some securities would suffer price falls that bring the valuation below cost. As a result, such write-downs would be introduced into the financial statements in accordance with Japanese GAAP but would be reversed to comply with US GAAP because unrealised gains would exceed unrealised losses on a portfolio basis, given a rising market. Since this is a timing difference under APB Opinion No. 11 (the loss for tax purposes was recognised earlier than for US reporting purposes, i.e. pre-tax accounting income is greater than taxable income), a deferred tax liability would need to be provided with a deferred tax expense in the profit and loss account.

After 31 December 1989 the decline in the aggregate market value below aggregate cost led to the valuation allowance computed on an individual

---

[9]See the deferred tax illustration shown in Table 13.

420 Developments in International Accounting – General Issues and Classification

basis being in excess of the valuation based on a portfolio basis. This led to the reversal of the deferred tax liability to income and, in the case of Makita, the reversing effects for the six months ended 31 March 1990 and for the year ended 31 March 1991 were greater than the originating effects of the previous two periods.

Stock Issue Expenses

Two companies identified this as an area of difference between the US and Japan but no further information was supplied.

Accounting for Stock Dividends

Makita notes the difference in accounting treatment of stock dividends between Japan and the US. However, the company did not comply with the US requirement to transfer an amount equal to the market value of the shares issued. 'Had such free distributions been accounted for in this manner, additional paid-in capital as of March 31, 1991, would have increased by approximately ¥115,072 million (US$816,113 thousand), with a corresponding decrease in retained earnings; total shareholders' equity would have remained unchanged'. Since there was no mention in the audit report of lack of compliance with US GAAP in this respect it may be assumed that the auditors considered this to be immaterial.

Accounting for Business Combinations

Kyocera was the only company that stated that accounting for business combinations was a major adjustment to the parent company accounts. However, if the company had prepared consolidated accounts in accordance with Japanese GAAP a decision would have to be made as to how such transactions should be accounted for in the same way that a decision had to be made to comply with US GAAP. For the period under review, Kyocera acquired two companies: one was accounted for as a purchase and the other using the pooling of interests approach. Both approaches are permitted in Japan although the purchase method is more common.

Recognition of Expected Losses on Purchase and Sale Commitments

Mitsui identified this as a material difference but no information was supplied on what these losses involve and how the accounting treatment differs between the two countries.

Instalment Sales on Accruals Basis

In Japan, it is usual to recognise sales when the goods are delivered, but where a business is subject to particular uncertainties revenue may be recognised when the instalment payments are either due or are received. Such an approach is backed up by tax regulations which permit profit recognition on an instalment basis for contracts that have a completion date of at least two years. Under US GAAP, it is usual to account for revenues from instalment sales at the transaction date with a provision for uncollectible items. Only in exceptional circumstances may revenues be treated on an instalment basis. Mitsui identified this as a material difference between Japan and the US but did not provide any quantified information.

Excess of Change in Underwriting Reserves and Deferred Policy Costs

These accounting issues relate to specialist companies in the insurance sector and are not cited in the literature as being areas of major differences between Japan and the US. These issues were highlighted by Tokio Marine and Fire Insurance and covered in the above case study material.

Inventory Valuation

While the valuation of inventories is cited in the literature as a difference between Japan and the US none of the companies filing a 20-F report made this point.

Goodwill

While goodwill was not mentioned by any of the companies as representing a material difference between US and Japanese GAAP it is noticeable that some of the companies extended the amortisation of goodwill on consolidation beyond the five years normally allowed under Japanese GAAP. Sony states that goodwill is amortised over 40 years, Kyocera uses a period not exceeding 20 years, Mitsui periods of between five and 20 years, TDK 10 years, Pioneer between five and 10 years, whereas NEC uses a five year amortisation period.

Other Issues

The following accounting issues, which were raised in the early section on qualitative differences, were not raised as important considerations by Japanese companies: dividends; auditors' remuneration; directors' bonuses; depreciation; capitalisation of borrowing costs; and research and development expenditure. It appears that either the differences in accounting policies in these areas were not material or that the Japanese companies followed US GAAP.

Discussion and summary

This paper has sought to add to the qualitative and quantitative literature on profit comparisons between the US and Japan. International accounting differences may present problems, not only for investors, but also for capital market and accounting regulators. Historically, differences in the extent of disclosure between the US and Japan have meant that the majority of Japanese companies seeking an overseas listing has avoided the US because of the consequential competitive costs.

Only two Japanese companies prepare and publish consolidated accounts in accordance with both US and Japanese GAAP and only one of these files a 20-F report with the SEC. This presents a problem for investment analysts who wish to compare Japanese companies that prepare their accounts on different bases. This occurs because those companies that prepare consolidated financial statements in accordance with US GAAP and file them with the SEC are allowed also to file them with the Ministry of Finance in Tokyo instead of consolidated accounts prepared in accordance with Japanese GAAP. This problem has been recognised by the Ministry of Finance in Ordinance No. 41 issued on 25 December 1990.[10] From 1 April 1995 Japanese companies must file consolidated accounts prepared in accordance with Japanese GAAP with the appropriate stock exchange and the Ministry of Finance. Unless the SEC allows Japanese companies to file consolidated accounts prepared in accordance with Japanese GAAP, which seems unlikely, it will be necessary for those filing 20-F reports to prepare consolidated accounts on both bases. Those companies involved opposed the change, principally because it would increase preparation costs.

It is difficult to generalise with such a small population but it is possible that there is a pronounced difference in profit comparisons in the financial sector between the US and Japan that is not so acute in the manufacturing sector. Of the seven Japanese companies that did not specifically identify any differences, six are in manufacturing and the seventh, NTT, is in the communications sector. One explanation is that the accounting

differences between the two countries are less pronounced in these sectors than in others. This seems a more plausible theory than the alternative: that these well-known Japanese companies suffer from 'disclosure shyness'. Testing these alternative theories will be possible after 1995. Another way of considering the problem is to ask why the Mitsubishi Bank is the only Japanese company that produces consolidated accounts in accordance with both Japanese and US GAAP and files a 20-F report with the SEC. It is possible that a bank operating in the investment markets in both Japan and the US feels that the political pressures to disclose are more acute than for other industrial sectors.

References

Ballon R. J., Tomita I. and Usami H. (1976), *Financial reporting in Japan*, Kodansha International

Choi F. D. S. and Levich R. (1990), 'Behavioral effects of international accounting diversity', *Accounting Horizons*, June.

Cooke T. E. (1988), *International Mergers and Acquisitions*, Blackwell Publishing.

Cooke T. E. (1991), 'The evolution of financial reporting in Japan: a shame culture perspective', *Accounting, Business and Financial History*, Vol. 1, No. 3.

Cooke T. E. and Kikuya M. (1991), *Accounting in Japan: an International Perspective*, Teihan.

Cooke T. E. and Kikuya M. (1992), *Financial Reporting in Japan: Regulation, Practice and Environment*, Blackwell Publishing and the Institute of Chartered Accountants in England and Wales.

de Carmoy H. (1990), *Global Banking Strategy*, Blackwell Publishing.

Japanese Institute of Certified Public Accountants (1991), *Corporate Disclosure in Japan—Reporting*, Japanese Institute of Certified Public Accountants.

Oguri T. and Hara Y. (1990), 'A critical examination of accounting regulation in Japan', *Accounting, Auditing and Accountability Journal*, Vol. 3, No. 2.

Someya K. (1989), 'Accounting "revolutions" in Japan', *Accounting Historians Journal*, June.

Weetman P. and Gray S. J. (1991), 'A comparative international analysis of the impact of accounting principles on profits: the USA versus the UK, Sweden and the Netherlands', *Accounting and Business Research*, Autumn.

---

[10]'Regulations concerning the terminology, forms and preparation methods of the consolidated financial statements.'

[16]

European Accounting Review 1993, 3, 495–530

A comparative analysis of the impact of accounting differences on profits and return on equity

Differences between Swedish practice and US GAAP

Niclas Hellman
Stockholm School of Economics

ABSTRACT

The purpose of this paper is to make a quantitative comparative analysis of differences between Swedish accounting practice and US GAAP. The empirical data consisted of eighty-four US GAAP reconciliations of income statements and shareholders' equity, disclosed in Swedish annual reports during 1981–90. Prior qualitative research has suggested that Swedish accounting practice is conservative compared with that in the USA. However, the empirical analysis of profits and return on equity provided little support for this hypothesis. Instead, there were indications of a less conservative accounting treatment in the Swedish accounts compared with US GAAP. The most material differences between Swedish profits and those calculated using US GAAP were caused by differences in treatment of foreign currency translation, income taxes, sale and leaseback transactions and business combinations.

INTRODUCTION

The main objective of accounting is that accounting information should be *decision relevant* to a wide range of users. However, there are measurement constraints, such as the principles of objectivity and conservatism, that prevent accounting from fully complying with this objective. Furthermore, there is also an important user constraint on the relevance objective, namely *consistency*.

Hendriksen refers to consistency as

the use of the same accounting procedures by a single firm or accounting entity from period to period, the use of similar measurement concepts and procedures for related items within the statements of a firm for a single period, and the use of the same procedures by different firms.

(Hendriksen, 1982: 73)

Address for correspondence
Stockholm School of Economics, Box 6501, S–113 83 Stockholm, Sweden.

In this paper, the focus will be on the *comparability* aspects of consistency.

During the 1980s, there was a growing internationalization of capital markets. This has led to an increased need for making comparative international analysis of financial statements, and thus an increased need for comparability across countries. Accounting differences within countries are often considerable. If there are international differences as well, the analysis becomes even more complex. In recent years, the impact of international accounting differences has been subject to several studies. Two main types of studies can be identified:

(1) *qualitative analysis*, showing the accounting differences between countries, for example, Nobes (1988) on UK/USA, Cooke (1988) on Sweden/UK, and Nobes (1990) on Europe/UK;

(2) *quantitative analysis*, showing the overall impact of accounting differences between countries, on profits and financial ratios. Examples are Gray (1980), who analysed the impact of accounting principles on profits, in UK, France and Germany; Weetman and Gray (1990), who analysed differences between US GAAP and UK GAAP; Weetman and Gray (1991), who compared profits in UK, Sweden and the Netherlands with US GAAP; and Choi *et al.* (1983), who analysed quantitative differences between the USA, Korea and Japan.

The overall purpose of this paper is to make a quantitative comparative analysis of company profits and return on equity between Swedish accounting practice and US GAAP. In the case of company profits, comparative analysis will be conducted for profits *per se*, and for important accounting items. In the case of return on equity, the analysis will be conducted at an aggregate level. Since the sample is rather small (eighty-four observations distributed among thirteen companies), the study should be regarded as *a pilot project*.

There were two main reasons for choosing to compare Swedish practice with US GAAP. Firstly, there has been an increased international interest in Swedish accounting in recent years (Cooke, 1988, 1989; Weetman and Gray, 1991). These authors have had various reasons for choosing Sweden. Cooke writes:

> Sweden is of interest because of the rapid growth in the Stockholm stock exchange and because of the country's disproportionate number of multinational enterprises.

> (Cooke, 1989: 113)

Weetman and Gray (1991) refer to Nobes (1989), who claims that Swedish accounting is somewhat extreme, compared with countries like the Netherlands, the USA and the UK. The suggested reason for this is the strong government influence on accounting principles in Sweden.

Secondly, the interest in international accounting within Sweden seems to have increased over the last few years. Studies by Rundfelt (1988, 1990), on Swedish companies' use of, and adjustments to, international accounting principles, is a good example of this increase in interest.

In the next section, prior research is examined. Special emphasis is put on how different accounting items affect profits in accordance with Swedish accounting practice versus US GAAP. This section is followed by the research methodology section, which includes sampling and data analysis considerations. Thereafter, the findings are presented, and a tentative explanation for them proposed. The paper closes with suggestions for future research on these issues.

PRIOR RESEARCH

Differences in profits

For the purpose of making quantitative analysis of differences in accounting practices at the aggregate level, Gray (1980) developed a so-called 'index of conservatism'. The purpose of the index is to measure the extent to which disclosed profits in a country are more or less conservative than in other countries on the basis of differences in accounting principles. Principally, the index of conservatism is calculated as: $1 - [(R_A - R_D)/|R_A|]$, where R_A = adjusted profits and R_D = disclosed profits. In this formula, R_A is *the yardstick*, the norm used to make comparisons. The yardstick used in this study is US GAAP (Generally Accepted Accounting Principles in the USA), which makes the results comparable with Weetman and Gray (1991) who used US GAAP in their evaluation of Swedish accounting practice.

It should be emphasized that the degree of conservatism that the index measures is *relative*, i.e. the degree of conservatism depends on how conservative the norm is considered to be. Prior research has indicated that Swedish accounting is more conservative than US accounting (see discussion below). For the purpose of this study, the index of conservatism is calculated as follows:

$$\text{Index of cons.} = 1 - \left(\frac{\text{US GAAP profits} - \text{Swedish profits}}{|\text{US GAAP profits}|} \right)$$

An index value *greater than* 1 means that the Swedish profits are higher (*less* 'conservative') than the US measure would have been. An index value *less than* 1 means that the Swedish profits are lower (*more* 'conservative') than the US measure would have been. An index value exactly *equal to* 1 indicates neutrality in comparison with US GAAP.

Weetman and Gray (1991) used this index of conservatism in their study of overall differences between Swedish accounting practice and US GAAP. They used a sample of eight Swedish companies, which they analysed for a period of three years (1986–8). The data used were the Form 20-F reconciliations filed with the Securities and Exchange Commission (SEC) as a requirement by companies having a stock exchange listing in the USA. As very few Swedish companies have USA listings, the sample was necessarily small. This made it impossible to conduct any statistical analysis, and was why only mean values were calculated.

Adjustments to income	*1986*	*1987*	*1988*
(A) Total index for Swedish net profit after appropriations and tax	0.92	1.20	0.85
(B) Appropriation net of deferred tax provision	*0.11*	*0.21*	*0.12*
(C) Total index for Swedish net profit after tax but before appropriations, compared with US GAAP	1.03	1.41	0.97

Source: Weetman and Gray (1991: 372)

Figure 1   Index of conservatism; results in Weetman and Gray (1991)

Figure 1 shows some of the results of the Weetman and Gray study. Measure A is net income in Swedish income statements. This measure does not include the share of the appropriations that is not deferred tax. Therefore, Weetman and Gray put back the share of the appropriations they considered not to be deferred tax (measure B). Weetman and Gray used the 'separate figure for the tax effect of allocations to [untaxed] reserves [which is given in] the note to the accounts' (p. 371), to calculate this appropriation net. According to Weetman and Gray, the outcome (measure C) is a more relevant and comparable measure of income under Swedish generally accepted accounting principles (GAAP)[1] than measure A.

Unfortunately, the empirical results of the comparison with US GAAP were inconclusive. The application of US GAAP seemed neither to increase nor to decrease Swedish profits in any consistent way. Clearly, this result was not fully in line with Weetman and Gray's expectations:

> Taken overall, the impact on profits of Swedish accounting principles seems likely to be more 'conservative' than US GAAP with particular reference to taxation effects, the amortisation of goodwill and the treatment of associated companies.
>
> (Weetman and Gray, 1991: 364)

Such a priori expectations are also common in comparative international studies of different accounting regimes. In such studies Sweden is often referred to as a country with very conservative accounting rules, belonging to the continental Europe tradition, rather than to that of the United Kingdom or the United States. Nobes and Parker state:

> This greater conservatism in continental Europe seems to be a long-run phenomenon. Davidson and Kohlmeier (1966) and Abel (1969) noted that profit figures would be consistently lower in France, Sweden, Germany and the Netherlands ... if similar companies' accounts were merely adjusted for differences in inventory and depreciation practices from those used in the United States or the United Kingdom.
>
> (Nobes and Parker, 1991: 26)

Nair and Frank (1980) reached a similar conclusion. They used factor analysis to classify countries into different 'accounting models'. As it turns out, Sweden fits into the 'Continental European model', together with countries like Belgium, France, Germany and Switzerland. The other three models were named the 'British Commonwealth model', the 'Latin American model' and the 'United States model'. In Nobes (1983) Sweden was classified as a government-driven and tax-dominated country, together with continental European countries and Japan, but clearly separated from the UK and the USA.

Thus, a hypothesis based on prior research would be that Swedish accounting is *more conservative* than US accounting. In other words, we would expect profits adjusted to US GAAP to be *higher* than profits in accordance with Swedish accounting practice. The hypothesis was tested in this research.

Adjustment items: qualitative research

The focus of this study is on actual practice and the term 'Swedish accounting practice' will be used throughout the paper to denote the object of study. In most cases actual practice will be equivalent to Swedish GAAP (see note 1), but not always. A reason for discrepancy during the period studied was that Swedish GAAP was not clear-cut regarding some accounting items, and, as a consequence, companies chose different accounting treatments.

Qualitative differences between Swedish accounting practice and US GAAP have been studied by Cooke (1988) and Rundfelt (1988, 1990). According to Rundfelt (1988), the most *common* adjustments which have to be made to bring Swedish accounts into line with US GAAP are:

1. *Fixed Assets (Revaluation).* Companies who in their Swedish accounts have written up fixed assets must, under US GAAP, put the revaluation and the excess depreciation back.
2. *Interest Expenses.* In Sweden, interest expenses are normally charged to expenses immediately, while, under US GAAP, such expenses may be subject to capitalization and depreciation.
3. *Goodwill (Business Combinations)* includes two kinds of adjustments. Firstly, goodwill depreciations in Swedish accounts could be reduced in some cases, due to a longer maximum amortization

period under US GAAP (forty years). On the other hand, if good-will has been written off against equity in the Swedish accounts, it must be recognized as an asset under US GAAP, and depreciated. Secondly, due to more restrictive requirements for the pooling method under US GAAP versus Swedish practice, some acquisitions may have to be reclassified, from mergers (the pooling method) to ordinary acquisitions. This could lead to the recognition of goodwill under US GAAP.

4.   *Associated Companies*. In Swedish practice, the acquisition cost method was a common accounting method for associated companies during the studied period. This method implies that the owner company is not credited/charged for the share of profits/losses that is not distributed to the owners through dividends. US GAAP require that the equity method is used for associated companies.

In further research Rundfelt (1990) found two additional adjustments which could be classified as *common*.

5.   *Sale and Leaseback*. In Swedish practice, sale and leaseback transactions have often been treated as sales. The Swedish treatment implies that profits from the sale may be recognized immediately. Under US GAAP, sale and leaseback transactions are treated as financing arrangements, which means that profits from the sale are deferred and amortized over the leasing period.

6.   *Pensions*. In 1985, the FASB issued a new accounting recommendation regarding pension costs (FAS 87). Swedish practice differs from this recommendation in two fundamental ways: (1) no increases in the employees' salaries are assumed to occur in the future; (2) on the other hand, the interest rate is assumed to be only 4 per cent, which compensates for the unchanged salaries. FAS 87 requires more realistic assumptions, in both these cases.

Rundfelt (1988) also gives some examples of adjustments that are *less common* than the six items mentioned so far. Two of them could perhaps be seen as more important than the others.

7.   *Foreign Currency Translation*. In Sweden, receivables and payables in foreign currencies are normally translated at the lower/higher of transaction date rate and current rate. US GAAP require current rates to be used. Since 1 January 1990, a recommendation from Bokföringsnämnden (The Swedish Accounting Standards Board) requires current rates to be used also in Swedish financial statements.

8.   *Other Expenses Subject to Capitalization*. In Sweden, financial leasing contracts, tooling costs and forestry costs are normally charged to expenses. US GAAP require such costs to be capitalized.

According to Rundfelt, adjustment is made, but much less frequently, for negative goodwill, future restructuring costs, revenue recognition for long-term contracts, acquired deductions for loss, low interest rate receivables, and research and development expenses.

Cooke (1988) perceives six accounting differences between Sweden and the USA to be of special interest: taxation, legal reserves, fixed assets, goodwill, associated companies and foreign currency translation. Two of these items, legal reserves and taxation, have not been discussed so far. Rundfelt (1988, 1990) mentions taxation differences but does not classify the putting back of allocations to untaxed reserves under US GAAP as an accounting difference, since Swedish readers normally make this adjustment themselves (see the quotation from Föreningen auktoriserade revisorer (The Swedish Institute of Authorized Public Accounts) in the section on 'Data analysis' below).

'Legal reserves' refer to the fact that the Swedish Companies Act requires 10 per cent of net income to be transferred to a legal reserve until it represents 20 per cent of the issued par value of share capital. This legal reserve only affects the amount available for dividends and it has no effect on profits or the total amount of shareholders' equity.

> 9. *Income Taxes.* Swedish companies are allowed to make allocations to untaxed reserves. Such appropriations are not permitted under US GAAP and they have to be put back. Furthermore, until 1992 it was not Swedish accounting practice to make provisions for the deferral of income taxes. US GAAP require that every year is charged with the tax costs that can be allocated to that year (the deferral method). This means that deferred tax must be calculated for all material items that carry tax payments forward (so-called *timing differences*). For Swedish companies most of the timing differences should concern allocations to untaxed reserves.

In 1987, the FASB issued a new recommendation (FAS 96), which stated that from 1989 at the latest, the liability method should be used to calculate deferred taxes. The FASB has later postponed the effective adoption date (FAS 103). In Sweden, Redovisningsrådet (The Swedish Financial Accounting Standards Board) has issued a recommendation concerning group accounts, which requires the liability method to be used (Jonnergård, 1992). The recommendation has been in force since 1 January 1992.

The nine adjustment items briefly described in this section will be examined empirically in the section on 'Findings', which also includes a detailed list of Swedish companies' US GAAP adjustments 1981–1990.

Adjustment items: quantitative research

Weetman and Gray (1991) developed a 'partial index of conservatism', which allows a more detailed analysis of the factors underlying the overall index. The partial index is calculated as follows:

$$\text{Partial index of conservatism} = 1 - \left(\frac{\text{Partial adjustment}}{|\text{US GAAP profits}|}\right)$$

An example of how the partial index could be used is shown in Figure 2.

Example:	MSEK
'Swedish' earnings	700
Adjustments for US GAAP:	
Appropriations to reserves	200
Sale and lease back transaction	−100
Adjusted earnings per US GAAP	800
Overall index of conservatism	0.875
Partial index: appropriations	$1 - \left(\dfrac{200}{|800|}\right) = 0.750$
Partial index: sale and lease back	$1 - \left(\dfrac{-100}{|800|}\right) = 1.125$

Figure 2   Partial index of conservatism: example

The interpretation of the partial index is in line with the overall index of conservatism. In other words, an index value *greater than* 1 means that the US GAAP adjustment will decrease Swedish profits (the Swedish accounting practice is *less* 'conservative' than its US counterpart). An index value *less than* 1 means that the US GAAP adjustment will increase Swedish profits (the Swedish accounting practice is *more* 'conservative' than its US counterpart). An index value exactly *equal to* 1 indicates neutrality in comparison with US GAAP.

Using the partial index, Weetman and Gray (1991: 372–4) found the following *major differences* between Swedish practice and US GAAP (emphasis added).

> Special tax allowances and *transfers to untaxed reserves* . . . were by far the most significant adjustments in the reconciliation of Swedish net profit after appropriations.

> *Increased depreciation through revaluation of fixed assets* . . . was found in four out of the six companies . . . the reduced depreciation charge . . . was material at the 10% level on only two occasions.

Accounting for *business combinations* led to significant differences in two cases. One of these cases concerned *pooling of interests*, where the adjustment caused deductions from the Swedish profit.

Failure to use *equity accounting* for associated companies, *capitalization of interest* as a US requirement, and *currency translation*, all caused significant differences in one instance for each item.

RESEARCH METHODOLOGY

Sample

Some of the big Swedish companies disclose a restatement of their Swedish accounts to US GAAP in their annual reports. This 'US GAAP footnote' describes what adjustments are necessary in the income statement and in the shareholders' equity, in order to reach compliance with US GAAP. Many of these companies also disclose balance sheet adjustments (50 per cent of the companies in 1990) and earnings per share under US GAAP (100 per cent in 1990).

Rundfelt (1990) made a descriptive analysis of Swedish accounting practice in 111 Swedish companies quoted at the Stockholm Stock Exchange at the end of 1989 (banks, insurance companies and most investment companies were excluded). Among these 111, he found, in total, twelve companies which disclosed US GAAP reconciliations. Out of these twelve companies, eleven disclosed US GAAP footnotes in their annual reports and one company disclosed a US GAAP footnote in a US prospectus. By the end of 1989, nine of these companies were listed on some US Stock Exchange, thus required to submit a Form 20-F reconciliation.

For the purpose of this paper, seventy-two Swedish companies were selected to find out what companies disclosed US GAAP reconciliations in their Swedish annual reports, in 1990. The selection criterion, apart from being Swedish, was quotation on the Stockholm Stock Exchange's 'A:I list'[2] during 1990. Some industries were excluded, namely insurance, banking and investment companies. In total, there were ten companies disclosing US GAAP footnotes. None of these were 'new', compared with the companies Rundfelt found for 1989. To get a larger sample of company years, Rundfelt's twelve companies were examined for years prior to 1989.

In total, eighty-one cases of US GAAP reconciliations in Swedish annual reports were found. In addition, Asea Brown Boveri was found to disclose US GAAP footnotes for 1988–90. Since Asea referred to the ABB footnote in their adjustments, ABB was also included in the sample (see Table 1). Thus, the final sample consisted of eighty-four observations.

Table 1 Sample of companies who make US GAAP adjustments

Company	Disclosure period	Number of years
ABB	1988–1990	3
Asea	1983–1990	8
Atlas Copco	1985–1990	6
Electrolux	1985–1990	6
Ericsson	1982–1990	9
Gambro	1982–1990	9
Inter Innovation	1987–1990	4
Pharmacia	1981–1989	9
Procordia	1987–1989	3
Sandvik	1987–1990	4
SCA	1983–1990	7
SKF	1984–1990	7
Volvo	1982–1990	9

Data analysis

The *overall index of conservatism* was used to analyse possible significant differences and trends at the aggregate level. To make a comparison between Swedish net income and US GAAP net income meaningful, the Swedish measure initially had to be adjusted for deferred tax in allocations to untaxed reserves. The reasons for doing this are summarized by Föreningen auktoriserade revisorer (FAR – The Swedish Institute of Authorized Public Accountants) as follows:

> Swedish law and practice has so far not recognized deferred tax accounting except in the case of untaxed reserves in acquired subsidiaries. . . . This results in Swedish financial statements being totally silent on the existence of considerable deferred tax liabilities relating to the untaxed reserves found in practically every balance sheet. Swedish readers are naturally aware of the situation and automatically make the necessary adjustments in their head (using a 30% tax rate) as they read the statements.

> (1992: 6)

The measure of Swedish net income used in this study was *Profit after full tax* (PAFT), which is calculated as follows:

Net income under Swedish GAAP
+ (1-standard tax rate) * Allocations to untaxed reserves

= Profit after full tax

This set-up is in line with the recommendation of Näringslivets börskommitté (1983) (The Swedish Business Community's Stock Exchange Committee). The standard tax rates used were: for 1981–8: 50 per cent; for 1989: 40 per cent; and for 1990: 30 per cent. These standard tax rates are considered to be in line with Swedish financial statement analysis practice during the period studied. Weetman and Gray (1991) did not use such standardized tax rates. Instead, they used the effective tax rate for allocations. However, for the purpose of this study, it was considered to be of interest to compare all companies using the same norm, the advantage being that the comparability of profits increases, the disadvantage being that PAFT will not reflect the specific company's tax situation.

Since 1987, some companies have begun to account for deferred tax in allocations to untaxed reserves. This way of calculating net income is in line with international practice. The measure will be referred to as 'Profits disclosed in accordance with international practice' (PDIP). These observations will be analysed both in combination with PAFT observations and separately, in the subsequent analysis. The rationale for making a joint analysis of PAFT and PDIP observations is that, in most cases, PDIP is calculated by the companies in the same way as 'Profits after full tax'. This is indicated in Table 9 in the 'Findings' section, where the US GAAP income tax adjustments are shown to have very similar statistical characteristics: the adjustment is based on either a case where net income in the Swedish income statement can be used directly (PDIP) or a case where Swedish net income has to be adjusted for the profit proportion in appropriations, as described earlier (PAFT). In total, there were sixty-six PAFT observations and eighteen PDIP observations. Fifty per cent of the latter type of observations occurred in 1990.

The partial index of conservatism was used to identify significant differences and trends for specific accounting items. The nine items described in the 'Prior research' section will be analysed in detail. In addition, the 'residual' of the adjustments will be analysed. These have been classified as either 'other adjustments', if the company has specified what the adjustments consist of, or as 'non-specified adjustments', if the company has not specified the adjustments. 'Other adjustments' do not include any of the nine items in the 'Prior research' section. 'Non-specified adjustments' could possibly include such items.

Return on equity was calculated in the following way:

$$\text{Swedish ROE}_1 = \frac{\text{PAFT}_t}{[E_{t-1} + (1-t_t) * UR_{t-1} + E_t + (1-t_t) * UR_t]/2}$$

$$\text{Swedish ROE}_2 = \frac{\text{PDIP}_t}{[E(DIP)_{t-1} + E(DIP)_t]/2}$$

$$\text{US ROE} = \frac{P(\text{US GAAP})_t}{[E(\text{US GAAP})_{t-1} + E(\text{US GAAP})_t]/2}$$

where
PAFT = Swedish net profit after full tax
E = Shareholders' equity in the Swedish accounts
t = Standard tax rate
UR = Untaxed reserves

PDIP = Swedish profits, disclosed in accordance with international practice
E(DIP) = Shareholders equity in the Swedish accounts, disclosed in accordance with international practice
P(US GAAP) = Profits, adjusted to US GAAP
E(US GAAP) = Shareholders' equity, adjusted to US GAAP

The calculation of 'Swedish' ROE_1 could be seen as the standard way of calculating ROE in Sweden, It should be noted that the same standard tax rate is used both in the numerator and in the denominator, to achieve consistency. ROE_2 is used if a company has chosen the international method of disclosing profits, discussed earlier. The same type of measure is used in both the numerator and the denominator, for ROE_1 and ROE_2 respectively. Therefore, ROE_1 and ROE_2 have been considered to be fully comparable, and the ratios have not been separated in the subsequent analysis.

As mentioned at the beginning of this paper, the sample is rather small, and the study should be regarded as a pilot project. Thus, the statistics calculated are very basic: average, standard deviation and median. The Wilcoxon test for small samples (< 25) was applied to examine differences in net income and return on equity. The Wilcoxon test ranks absolute differences in order of size, disregarding sign. The smallest difference gets the lowest rank. Ideally, the Wilcoxon test requires a random sample. This criterion was considered to be met to a reasonable extent, by analysing each year separately.

FINDINGS

Differences in profits

As a first step in the analysis, the index of conservatism was used to measure differences in the overall profit between Swedish accounting practice and US GAAP. It was noted earlier, that in several previous studies Sweden has been classified as a country with conservative accounting rules. Weetman and Gray's (1991, see Figure 1), empirical results neither corroborated nor rejected the hypothesis that Swedish accounting practice was more conservative than US GAAP. With respect to these previous results, *the hypothesis that Swedish accounting practice is more conservative than US GAAP* was tested. In terms of a one-tailed Wilcoxon test, the hypothesis is expressed as:

H_1: Sum of negative ranks (index < 1) >
  > Sum of positive ranks (index > 1)

The sums of positive and negative ranks are shown in Table 2, and the significant years are also indicated. Table 2 also includes median values for the overall index of conservatism each year.

Averages and standard deviations are shown in Table 3. For the calculation of averages and standard deviations, two outliers were excluded.[3, 4]

Table 2 Overall index of conservatism: Wilcoxon sum of ranks and medians

Years	N	Index of cons. Sum of positive ranks (> 1.000)	Index of cons. Sum of negative ranks (< 1.000)	Median index
1982	4	8	2	1.072
1983	6	13	8	1.014
1984	7	17	11	0.929
1985	9	16	29	0.940
1986	9	24	21	1.032
1987	12	56*	22	1.059
1988	13	57	34	1.035
1989	13	75**	16	1.082
1990	10	39	16	1.078
All	84			1.028
87 PAFT	11	44	22	1.057
88 PAFT	10	30	25	0.995
89 PAFT	8	22	14	1.012
90 PDIP	9	30	15	1.021

* significantly higher than 1.000 at the 10% level.
** significantly higher than 1.000 at the 2.5% level.

Table 3 Overall index of conservatism: averages and standard deviations

Years	N	Min.	Max.	Average	Standard deviation
1982	4	0.976	1.377	1.124	0.181
1983	6	0.861	1.179	1.023	0.119
1984	7	0.894	1.515	1.090	0.252
1985	9	0.173	1.770	0.960	0.410
1986	8	0.847	1.501	1.124	0.261
1987	12	0.821	2.632	1.272	0.626
1988	13	0.421	1.364	1.029	0.233
1989	13	0.884	1.542	1.113	0.187
1990	9	0.903	2.107	1.289	0.457
All	82	0.173	2.632	1.115	0.359
87 PAFT	11	0.821	2.566	1.154	0.498
88 PAFT	10	0.421	1.309	0.995	0.241
89 PAFT	8	0.884	1.542	1.093	0.215
90 PDIP	8	0.903	2.107	1.296	0.488

There is not much support for the hypothesis that Swedish accounting practice is more conservative than US GAAP. The negative sum of ranks was higher than the positive sum of ranks only in one year (1985). The median values of the overall index of conservatism were below 1.000 during two years, 1984 and 1985, and the averages were lower than 1.000 only once (1985). If only PAFT observations are included, the median and average for 1988 were also lower than 1.000.

Only for two years (1987 and 1989) were there statistically significant differences between Swedish profits and US GAAP profits, but the difference was opposite to the one expected. Swedish profits were significantly *higher* than US GAAP in these two years. In addition, the sum of positive ranks exceeded the sum of negative ranks in seven out of nine years, and both the median and the average for all years were higher than 1.000. The average index of conservatism for the whole period was 1.115, which implies that on average Swedish profits in the companies studied were 11.5 per cent higher than the same profits measured in accordance with US GAAP. Thus *the results indicate that, for the sample studied, Swedish accounting practice was less conservative than US GAAP.*

The fact that the averages were generally higher than the medians

Table 4 Total index of conservatism: observations classified according to level of materiality

Index of conservatism (level of materiality)	1981	1982	1983	1984	1985	1986	1987	1988	1989	1990
Swedish profit 10% or more below the US profit	1		1	1	4	4	1	1	1	1
Swedish profit 5% or more below the US profit but less than 10% below			1	3	1		1	3	1	1
Swedish profit within ±5% of US profit		2	2		2	1	3	3	4	3
Swedish profit 5% or more above the US profit but less than 10% above				1			4	2	1	
Swedish profit 10% or more above the US profit		2	2	2	2	4	3	4	6	5
N	1	4	6	9	9	9	12	13	13	10

implies a size effect. That is, there must be some observations of material size that increase the average index. In Table 4 all observations have been classified in terms of their level of materiality.

Table 4 shows that for the period 1981–90, there was some variety between companies and years. There was a growing proportion of companies that made material adjustments that increased Swedish profits. At the same time, there were always some companies each year who measured Swedish net income more conservatively compared with US GAAP. For the whole period, a rather large proportion of the observations (54 per cent) were material in either direction (exceeding 10 per cent). It should be mentioned that in the only two cases where companies showed a negative Swedish net income, profits seem to have been rather conservatively measured. That is, the US GAAP adjustment led to very material improvements (see note 6).

The impact of different adjustment items

In almost every case, the companies examined made qualitative and quantitative specifications of how different accounting items were affected by the application of US GAAP. Following the classification into nine adjustment items made in the 'Prior research' section, Figure 3 describes in detail the observed adjustments of Swedish net income. A tenth type of adjustments, 'other adjustments', is also added, including items occurring less frequently. In Figure 3, each Swedish accounting treatment that caused an adjustment under US GAAP is specified. Most of the ten adjustment items have sub-items. For example, number (2) 'Interest expenses' has two sub-items: (2a) 'Property plant' and (2b) 'Book inventory'. The column 'Number of observations' shows the number of observations where the accounting treatment of a sub-item has been referred to in the US GAAP reconciliation text. Since different sub-items are often combined in the quantitative adjustment, it was not always possible to separate the quantitative effect of each sub-item. However, to the extent such specifications were possible, they are shown in the last two columns. The cases where different sub-items were combined in the quantitative adjustment are also included in the figure.

Tables 5–8 include quantitative examinations of eleven classes of accounting adjustment items (the ten classes described in Figure 3 plus 'Non-specified adjustments'). Table 5 shows the frequency of these adjustment items over time. Tables 6–8 provide some descriptive statistics (median, average and standard deviation) for the same adjustment items, based on the partial index of conservatism, described earlier. For the calculation of averages and standard deviations, two outliers were excluded (see note 6).

The figure and tables described here will be referred to in the following presentation of each adjustment item.

1. Fixed assets (revaluation)

We would expect the lower depreciation costs under US GAAP to lead to *higher* US GAAP profit. In forty-six out of forty-eight cases, the adjustments actually caused *higher* profits under US GAAP (see Figure 3). However, in two cases the adjustments led to *lower* profits under US GAAP: ABB 1988 and Volvo 1986. ABB was founded in 1988, and perhaps this reversed effect on profit had something to do with the fusion of Asea and Brown Boveri. For ABB 1989 and ABB 1990 the expected effect could be observed. In the case of Volvo 1986, Volvo wrote down the book value of the share holdings in Hamilton and Saga by MSEK 500. At the same time they wrote up the book value of the share holdings in Catena by the same amount. The revaluation of Catena was not in line with US GAAP, and therefore Volvo increased their costs with MSEK 500, when calculating US profit. No other company seems to have applied Volvo's way of adjusting for revaluation of fixed assets. Instead, the other companies have eliminated the revaluation in the balance sheet and decreased depreciations by the amount caused by the revaluation.

From Table 5 it can be seen that a decreasing proportion of the companies have made US GAAP adjustments for revaluation of fixed assets since 1982. Tables 6–8 show that, in general, the impact of the revaluation adjustments is rather small, and decreasing over time.

2. Interest expenses

During the period studied a large share of the companies made adjustments for capitalization of interest expenses (see Table 5). The trend is that the proportion of companies that make such adjustments is decreasing.

Figure 3 illustrates that there are two different kinds of Swedish accounting treatments of interest expenses that cause US GAAP adjustments. Interest expenses incurred in connection with financing the construction of properties and plant (2a) are charged to expenses immediately. Under US GAAP, such interest expenses are required to be capitalized and depreciated according to plan. This would lead to *higher* profits under US GAAP during a period of construction which follows a period of no construction, and a somewhat *lower* US GAAP profit when periods of no construction follow periods of construction. In thirty-four out of forty-six pure cases concerning interest expenses in property/plant, the US GAAP adjustment led to higher profits.

The other Swedish accounting treatment that caused adjustment concerned interest expenses incurred in connection with financing products

Adjustment item	Swedish accounting treatment that caused adjustment	US GAAP adjustment	Observed adjustm. effects (No. of company years) Number of observ.	Higher US profit	Lower US profit
1. Fixed assets	Revaluation	Revaluation is not permitted	48	46	2
2. Interest expenses	a) *Property/plant:* charged to expenses	Capitalization	55	34	12
	b) *Book inventory:* capitalization	Charged to expenses	9		
Combination: 2a–2b			9	5	4
3. Business combinations	a) *Goodwill:* progressive depreciation	Linear depreciation	1		
	b) *Goodwill:* direct write-off against equity	Linear depreciation; max. depr. period = 40 years	8		7
	c) *Goodwill:* direct write-off against profits	Linear depreciation; max. depr. period = 40 years	1		
	d) *Goodwill:* unspecified adjustment	Not specified	6	1	
	e) *Pooling method applied*	More restrictive criteria for applying the pooling m.	11		6
	f) *Negative goodwill:* deferred credit released as income over max. 10 years	Reduces noncurrent assets; amortized over economic lifetime	20	3	4
	g) *Acquisition analysis*	Excess values are allocated to different and more assets with other amortization periods	12	2	3
	h) *Low interest rate loans:* the loan amount is not adjusted	The loan amount is adjusted for the interest discount	5		

Adjustment item	Swedish accounting treatment that caused adjustment	US GAAP adjustment	Observed adjustm. effects (No. of company years)		
			Number of observ.	Higher US profit	Lower US profit
	i) *Share issue*: cost of acquisition = par value	Cost of acquisition is determined with reference to market price	3		2
	j) *Acquired deductions for loss*: reduce tax cost in the year of the acquisition	The tax credit is recorded as an asset	15		
	k) *Acquisitions of associates*: no consolidation	Consolidation; recognition of excess values	3		2
Combination: 3a-e-f-g			1	1	
Combination: 3b-g-h			1	1	
Combination: 3c-e-g			1	1	
Combination: 3d-3j			5	4	1
Combination: 3e-3g			2	2	
Combination: 3e-f-g			1	1	
Combination: 3f-3g			1	1	
Combination: 3f-3j			6	2	4
Combination: 3f-h-j			4	1	3
Combination: 3i-3k			1	1	

continued overleaf

4. Associated companies	Investments are carried at cost and dividends are included in income	The equity method	55	34	21
5. Sale and lease back	Accounted for as sales	Accounted for as financing arrangements	24	9	15
6. Pensions	a) Certain *assumptions* regarding future salary level and interest rate	Different assumptions (FAS 87)	9	6	3
	b) *Early retirement pension costs* allocated over several years	Accounted for in the year of the agreement	7	3	4
7. Foreign currency translation	a) *Receivables and payables*: in accordance with FAR's Recommendation Proposal	In accordance with FAS 52	21	5	13
	b) *Foreign subsidiaries*: translation differences charged to expenses	In accordance with FAS 52	2		
	c) *Foreign subsidiaries*: change from FAS 8 to FAS 52	In accordance with FAS 52	1		1
	d) *Foreign subsidiaries*: highly inflationary economies: year-end exchange rates; no effect on income	The temporal method	6		3
	e) *Forward contracts*: gains and losses are not accounted for over the income statement	In accordance with FAS 52	1	1	
Combination: 7a–7d			1	1	
Combination: 7a-b-d			2	1	1

Adjustment item	Swedish accounting treatment that caused adjustment	US GAAP adjustment	Observed adjustm. effects (No. of company years)		
			Number of observ.	Higher US profit	Lower US profit
8. Other expenses subject to capitalization under US GAAP					
i) Capital leases	Charged to expenses	Capitalization	2	2	
ii) Tooling costs	Charged to expenses	Capitalization	9	9	
iii) Forestry costs	Charged to expenses	Capitalization	1	1	
9. Income taxes	a) *Allocations to untaxed reserves*	Not permitted	*66	54	12
	b) No provision made for the *deferral of income taxes*	The deferred method (APB 11)	66	5	57
	c) Provisions made in accordance with *the liability method*	The deferred method (APB 11)	11	4	7
	d) Provisions made in accordance with *the deferred method*	The liability method (FAS 96)	2	2	
	e) Provisions made in accordance with *US GAAP*	Tax provision for other US GAAP adjustments	5	2	3
	f) *Associated companies*: no tax provision when the equity method is applied	Adjustment for tax effects resulting from the distribution of earnings	9	4	5

* In four cases the adjustment effects were zero.

continued overleaf

10. 'Other adjustments'

i) Taxes paid on intercompany transactions	No deferral	Deferred as a prepaid tax	8	6	2
ii) Revenue recognition for long-term contracts	At the completion of the contract or defined phases thereof	The percentage-of-completion method	5	3	2
iii) Research and development	Capitalization	Charged to expenses	2	1	1
iv) Future restructuring costs	Not specified	Not specified	3	1	2
v) Interest expenses on convertible loans	Not specified	Not specified	4	4	
vi) Inventories in foreign subsidiaries	Change from LIFO to FIFO accounted for as an extraordinary revenue	Recalculation of the inventory values for earlier years	2		2
vii) New issue of shares	a) *Expenses for share issues* are accounted for over the income statement	Charged to a capital account	3	3	
	b) *New issue in subsidiary:* premium over par value increases equity	Accounted for over the income statement	1	1	
viii) Options	The issued options are not accounted for over the income statement	Recognized as an expense	1	1	

Adjustment item	Swedish accounting treatment that caused adjustment	US GAAP adjustment	Observed adjustm. effects (No. of company years)		
			Number of observ.	Higher US profit	Lower US profit
ix) Oil and gas activities	The full cost method	The successful efforts method	3	1	2
x) Minority interest		Minority interest in US GAAP adjustments	9	3	6

Note
* In four cases the adjustment effects were zero.

Figure 3 Observed US GAAP adjustments of Swedish profits 1981–1990

Table 5 Proportion of companies (%) that adjust for different adjustment items

Years	Revaluation	Interest expenses	Business comb.	Associated companies	Sale and lease back	Pensions	Foreign currency transl.	Other exp. subj. to cap. taxes	Income taxes	'Other' adjustments	Non-specified adj.
				Adjustment items							
				% of companies making adjustments							
1981									100	100	100
1982	25	50	50	50			50	25	100	50	50
1983	33	83	54	83			50	17	100	33	50
1984	43	86	43	86	14	14	43	14	100	29	29
1985	56	67	44	89	11	11	33	11	100	44	22
1986	78	67	44	89	22	11	33	11	100	33	22
1987	75	75	67	67	25	8	25	17	100	58	25
1988	62	62	77	54	46	8	23	15	100	39	31
1989	62	62	77	54	54	46	23	15	100	46	31
1990	50	50	70	40	50	30	20	10	100	40	40
All*	57	65	61	65	30	17	30	14	100	43	32

* Weighted average.

Table 6 Partial index of conservatism: median values for different adjustment items

								Adjustment items			
							Partial index of conservatism: median				
Years	Revaluation	Interest expenses	Business comb.	Associated companies	Sale and lease back	Pensions	Foreign currency transl.	Other exp. subj. to cap.taxes	Income taxes	'Other' adjustments	Non-specified adj.
1981	0.96	0.98	1.09	1.06			1.00	0.92	1.00	0.89	0.92
1982	0.98	0.99	1.01	1.00			1.01	0.89	1.06	1.06	0.98
1983	0.96	0.97	1.02	0.95	1.06	0.93	0.96	0.93	1.06	1.04	0.98
1984	0.98	0.97	1.01	0.99	0.99	0.90	1.18	0.93	1.03	0.89	1.14
1985	0.94	0.96	0.97	0.98	1.14	1.00	1.18	0.96	1.06	0.88	0.99
1986	0.99	0.99	1.00	0.99	1.20	0.99	1.13	0.98	1.07	1.01	1.03
1987	1.00	1.00	1.06	0.99	1.00	1.00	1.01	0.98	0.99	1.05	0.98
1988	1.00	1.00	1.05	0.99	1.07	0.99	1.01	0.93	1.03	0.98	1.00
1989	1.00	1.00	1.08	0.99	1.00	0.95	2.13	-30.22	1.04	0.98	1.02
1990									1.00	0.99	1.18
All	0.99	0.99	1.02	0.99	1.05	0.99	1.02	0.94	1.04	0.99	1.00

Table 7 Partial index of conservatism: mean values for different adjustment items

Adjustment items
Partial index of conservatism: averages

Years	Revaluation	Interest expenses	Business comb.	Associated companies	Sale and lease back	Pensions	Foreign currency transl.	Other exp. subj. to cap.	Income taxes	'Other' adjustments	Non-specified adj.
1981	0.96	0.98	1.09	1.06				0.92	1.00	0.89	0.92
1982	0.98	0.99	1.02	0.99			1.00	0.89	1.07	1.06	0.98
1983	0.95	0.98	1.00	0.99			0.96	0.93	1.08	1.04	0.97
1984	0.96	0.96	0.97	1.00	1.06	0.93	1.10	0.93	1.09	0.89	1.14
1985	0.97	0.96	0.98	0.97	0.99	0.90	1.24	0.96	1.16	0.55	0.99
1986	0.98	0.99	1.23	0.99	1.14	1.00	1.20	0.98	1.09	1.03	1.03
1987	0.99	0.99	0.93	0.97	1.34	0.99	1.12	0.93	0.92	1.20	1.04
1988	0.98	0.99	1.05	0.98	1.26	1.00	1.00		1.09	0.71	1.05
1989	0.99	1.00	1.09	0.99	1.09	0.99	1.00		1.03	1.03	1.08
1990					1.15	0.96	1.05		1.01	1.06	1.33
All	0.98	0.98	1.04	0.99	1.17	0.98	1.08	0.95	1.05	0.95	1.08

Table 8   Partial index of conservatism: standard deviations for different adjustment items

Years	Revaluation	Interest expenses	Business comb.	Associated companies	Sale and lease back	Pensions	Foreign currency transl.	Other exp. subj. to cap.	Income taxes	'Other' adjustments specified	Non-specified adj.
1982	0.00	0.02	0.08	0.08			0.04		0.07	0.09	0.00
1983	0.05	0.01	0.01	0.06			0.15		0.11	0.21	0.06
1984	0.04	0.02	0.03	0.14			0.31		0.18	0.02	0.15
1985	0.11	0.05	0.12	0.09			0.49		0.19	0.73	0.05
1986	0.03	0.03	0.02	0.04	0.13		0.17		0.13	0.06	0.02
1987	0.02	0.02	0.57	0.08	0.45		0.15	0.01	0.16	0.38	0.19
1988	0.03	0.02	0.43	0.04	0.42		0.03	0.01	0.18	0.52	0.11
1989	0.01	0.01	0.08	0.05	0.12	0.02	0.01	0.04	0.07	0.09	0.13
1990			0.09	0.01	0.20	0.02			0.09	0.11	0.46
All	0.05	0.03	0.31	0.07	0.28	0.03	0.21	0.03	0.15	0.39	0.22

Adjustment items
Partial index of conservatism: standard deviations

that are manufactured 'by routine' (2b). There were nine observations where such interest expenses had been capitalized. We would expect the US GAAP prohibition of this treatment to cause *lower* US profits. Unfortunately, there were no pure observations, only cases where (2a) and (2b) had been combined. Tables 6–8 show that US GAAP adjustments for the Swedish treatment of interest expenses were not a material adjustment item. However, on average, the US GAAP adjustments caused higher US profits.

3. Business combinations

In Figure 3 some different types of business combinations adjustments are distinguished. It turns out that companies, in many cases, do not separate the effects of goodwill amortization, pooling of interests and other types of business combination adjustments.

With respect to goodwill amortization, the impression was that companies tended to make such adjustments only when they had written off goodwill against equity or, in one case, when a company had used progressive depreciation (Atlas Copco 1990). When the companies already used linear depreciation under Swedish GAAP, they did not make any explicit changes of the amortization period, even though a longer maximum amortization period is allowed under US GAAP (forty years).[5] As one might expect, the pure cases of adjustments for direct write-off of goodwill against equity and for pooling caused *lower* profits under US GAAP. It should be emphasized that business combination adjustments included no less than eleven different types of sub-items. Perhaps somewhat surprisingly, the sub-items most frequently referred to in the US GAAP footnote texts were negative goodwill, acquired deductions for loss and acquisition analysis.

Tables 6–8 indicate that the business combination adjustments have often been material. On average, the US GAAP adjustments caused lower US profits. A case where Swedish net income was adjusted downward was Pharmacia 1988, who wrote off a large goodwill amount against net income in their Swedish accounts. Table 5 shows that business combination adjustments have occurred quite frequently during the observed period. During 1988–90, it was the most common adjustment item.

4. Associated companies

There were a large number of equity accounting adjustments (fifty-five) during the period 1982–90 (see Table 5). In most cases this resulted in *higher* US GAAP profits (Figure 3), but the adjustments were seldom material (see Tables 6–8). In 1987, FAR published a recommendation draft, where the equity method is permitted in the consolidated statements.

Since then, a larger share of the companies have begun to apply the equity method in their Swedish accounts.

5. Sale and leaseback

The Swedish treatment of sale and leaseback transactions as sales instead of financing arrangements was observed in twenty-four cases. As illustrated in Tables 6–8, the adjustments have often been material, causing *lower* US GAAP profits on average. The results may be interpreted by saying that, on average, Swedish net income was 17 per cent higher than US GAAP net income because of the differences in treatment of sale and leaseback transactions.

Figure 3 shows that in nine out of the twenty-four observations, the US GAAP adjustment caused *higher* US profits. The reason for this has to do with profits from sales, recognized in the Swedish accounts. Under US GAAP, such profits are put back and depreciated over the leasing period. The US GAAP adjustment of a sale and leaseback arrangement in Gambro illustrates the effects on Swedish profit. In 1986, Gambro recognized a profit from the sale of a real estate of MSEK 16.2. Under US GAAP this profit was distributed over the leasing period, fifteen years (MSEK 1.1 per year). Therefore, Gambro reduced their profits in 1986 with MSEK 16.2, but they increased their profits with MSEK 1.1 in 1987 and onwards.

The proportion of companies that make sale and leaseback adjustments has increased over the years (see Table 5).

6. Pensions

Adjustments concerning pension costs were made in fourteen cases. Nine of these observations occurred in 1989 or 1990, and concerned how the application of FAS 87 would affect the pension cost. SKF also made adjustments concerning early retirement pensions during 1984–90. SKF have spread such costs over several years, while the US GAAP requirement is that the cost should be charged to expenses in the same year as the early retirement pension has been agreed. In Figure 3, the effects of both these kinds of adjustments are illustrated.

So far, the frequency of pension adjustments has not been very high (see Table 5). However, in 1990 five more companies mentioned pension costs in their qualitative description of adjustment items, without making any quantitative adjustments.

On average, the adjustments for pensions have led to lower profits under US GAAP, but the effects have seldom been material (see Tables 6–8).

7. Foreign currency translation

Three different causes for foreign currency translation adjustments were identified (see Figure 3). The most common one concerned the Swedish treatment of receivables and payables under FAR's Recommendation Proposal, which requires translation at the lower/higher of transaction rate and current rate. Under US GAAP, current rates should be used.

Out of the four other sub-items that led to US GAAP adjustments, three concerned consolidation of foreign subsidiaries, and one concerned forward contracts.

Different types of foreign currency translation adjustments caused quite material adjustments during the period studied, especially in the mid–1980s (see Tables 6–8). In most cases, Swedish net income was *lowered* under US GAAP. One example where the adjustments caused much lower profits under US GAAP, is SKF 1984–6.[6] During these years SKF used the current-rate method when translating accounts of foreign subsidiaries located in high-inflation countries. Under US GAAP, the temporal method is required. SKF began to apply the latter method in their Swedish accounts in 1987.

It appears that the differences between Swedish practice and US GAAP have become smaller during the period (1982–90). The proportion of companies that make adjustments for foreign currency translation has decreased (see Table 5). In addition, the impact of the adjustments has become smaller. One explanation of this development is that some Swedish companies began to apply a new Swedish recommendation regarding receivables and payables in foreign currency (see 'Prior research' section), before it came into force.

8. Capitalization of other expenses

In total, there were twelve observations of capitalization of financial leases, tooling expenses or forestry expenses (see Figure 3). In all cases, the adjustments caused *higher* profits under US GAAP, which is in line with what one would expect. The adjustments were sometimes quite material (see Tables 6–8). For example, in nominal terms Volvo's adjustment in 1990 was MSEK 718. However, the number of companies that make these kind of adjustments have decreased over time (see Table 5).

9. Income taxes

In the analysis of differences in profits, standardized tax rates were used to calculate profits after full tax (PAFT). As a consequence, this approach is also used for income taxes (see also 'Research methodology' section):

US GAAP adjustment for income taxes (9a, b, f in Fig. 3)

–(1-standard tax rate) * Allocations to untaxed reserves

= Net adjustment for income taxes under US GAAP

As discussed earlier in the paper, some Swedish companies have begun to disclose profits in accordance with international practice (PDIP), excluding untaxed reserves and appropriations from the financial statements. In these cases (9c–9e), the adjustments for income taxes need not be recalculated. In Table 9, such adjustments are referred to as 'adjustments for income taxes, disclosed in accordance with international practice (DIP)'.

Table 9   Partial index of conservatism: income taxes

Income taxes	N	Min.	Max.	Average	Std. dev.
Net adjustment for income taxes	65	0.642	1.510	1.056	0.147
Adjustment for income taxes (DIP)	17	0.778	1.594	1.041	0.168

Table 9 shows that the two types of adjustments have similar statistical characteristics, in terms of average and standard deviation. In other words, the technique just described for calculating the 'net adjustment of income taxes under US GAAP' seems to be a reasonable approximation for how the Swedish companies that account for deferred taxes actually do so in practice.

All eighty-four observations of US GAAP reconciliations include some kind of income tax adjustment. On average, the adjustments led to a *decrease* in profits under US GAAP. The effects were in some cases material, but the differences between Swedish accounting treatment and US GAAP have decreased over time (see Tables 6–8).

All adjustment items perceived by Rundfelt (1988, 1990) and Weetman and Gray (1991) to be important have now been dealt with. To complete the analysis of different adjustment items it is useful to discuss the *residual adjustment items*. These have been divided into two groups: '*other adjustments*' and '*non-specified adjustments*'.

10. 'Other' adjustments

Figure 3 shows the ten different items that were identified: taxes paid on intercompany transactions, revenue recognition for long-term contracts, research and development, future restructuring costs, interest expenses on convertible loans, inventories in foreign subsidiaries, new issues of shares, options, oil and gas activities and minority interests. As illustrated in Tables 6–8, the adjustments have in many cases been material. On average, US

GAAP profits have become *lower* compared to Swedish profits as a consequence of the 'Other adjustments', described in Figure 3. On average, 43 per cent of the companies made these kind of adjustments during the period studied, but there is no clear trend (see Table 5).

Non-specified adjustments are simply adjustments that the companies make without specifying what they contain. Non-specified adjustments were observed in twenty-seven cases. On average, the non-specified adjustments caused *lower* profits under US GAAP. The level of materiality was quite high, especially during 1987–90 (see Tables 6–8). Table 5 indicates that the number of companies that make non-specified adjustments have gradually increased since 1985.

Return on equity

No prior empirical studies were found that indicated whether return on equity under US GAAP could be expected to be higher or lower than the Swedish counterpart. Theoretically, a more conservative accounting regime (Sweden) should cause both lower profits and lower equity values, compared with a less conservative accounting regime (the USA). Thus, at the ROE-level one would expect any differences between Swedish accounting practice and US GAAP to tend to smooth out. Because of this a two-tailed Wilcoxon test was conducted, where the hypothesis was stated as:

H_1: Sum of positive ranks ($ROE_{Sw} > ROE_{US}$) $\neq$
    $\neq$ Sum of negative ranks ($ROE_{Sw} < ROE_{US}$)

In total, there were seventy observations of return on equity, ranging between 1983 and 1990. There were no outliers. The sums of positive and negative ranks are shown in Table 10. Medians, averages and standard deviations are shown in Table 11.

Table 10   Return on equity: Wilcoxon sum of ranks

Years	N	ROE Sum of positive ranks ($ROE_{Sw} > ROE_{US}$)	ROE Sum of positive ranks ($ROE_{Sw} < ROE_{US}$)
1983	4	3	7
1984	6	1	20*
1985	7	7	21
1986	9	25	20
1987	9	33	12
1988	12	40	38
1989	13	63	28
1990	10	40	15

* ROE_{Sw} significantly lower at the 5% level.

Table 11   Return on equity: medians, averages and standard deviations

Years	N	Median ROE_{Sw}	Median ROE_{US}	Average ROE_{Sw}	Average ROE_{US}	Std. dev. ROE_{Sw}	Std. dev. ROE_{US}
1983	4	14.73	15.19	15.50	15.99	3.79	3.87
1984	6	15.51	19.49	14.62	17.26	9.50	11.65
1985	7	12.00	14.41	12.73	13.90	8.11	8.90
1986	9	11.90	11.22	11.45	11.29	7.02	6.82
1987	9	14.29	14.37	14.52	12.77	5.31	6.73
1988	12	16.94	16.03	16.53	15.76	5.47	5.05
1989	13	16.76	16.57	17.54	15.91	3.17	5.60
1990	10	13.79	8.05	12.61	10.51	7.64	7.58
All	70	15.27	14.39	14.64	14.03	6.37	7.09

In one single year (1984), there was a significant difference between 'Swedish ROE' and 'US ROE' at the 5 per cent level (see Table 10). During the first three years of the period studied (1983–5), the sum of negative ranks was greater than the sum of positive ranks ($ROE_{Sw} <$ ROE_{US}.) During the last five years (1986–90) the differences between the sum of ranks had reversed signs ($ROE_{Sw} > ROE_{US}$). If we also look at medians and averages the same trend can be observed (see Table 11). The median and average for the whole period were higher for 'Swedish ROE' compared to 'US ROE'. Standard deviations were 0.72 per cent units higher for ROE_{US} compared with ROE_{Sw}.

Table 12   Return on equity: observations classified according to level of materiality

Return on equity (Level of materiality)	1983	1984	1985	1986	1987	1988	1989	1990
ROE_{Sw} 1.5% units or more below ROE_{US}	1	4	4	4	2	3	3	2
ROE_{Sw} 0.75% units or more below ROE_{US} but less than 1.5% units below	1		1			2		1
ROE_{Sw} within ±0.75% units of ROE_{US}	2	2	1	2	3	3	5	2
ROE_{Sw} 0.75% units or more above ROE_{US} but less than 1.5% units above					1			1
ROE_{Sw} 1.5% units or more above ROE_{US}			1	3	3	4	5	4
N	4	6	7	9	9	12	13	10

In Table 12 all observations have been classified in terms of their level of materiality.

Table 12 illustrates that, although the differences between ROE_{Sw} and ROE_{US} were significant for only one year, the observations are not clustered in the middle rows in Table 12 (differences within 0.75 per cent units). Instead, a rather large proportion of the observations (61 per cent) could be seen as material in either direction (differences exceeding 1.5 per cent units).

DISCUSSION

The results from the analysis of overall differences in profits between Swedish accounting practice and US GAAP indicate that, for the sample studied, Swedish practice was slightly *less* conservative than US GAAP during the period 1981–90. Stated somewhat differently, the adjustments for US GAAP requirements, on average, caused *lower* profits under US GAAP, compared with profits in accordance with Swedish accounting practice. With respect to return on equity, the US average and median return on equity was slightly *lower* than 'Swedish ROE', during the period studied (1983–90).

These results were *not* in line with expectations. On the contrary, many of the prior comparative accounting research studies on Sweden have suggested that Sweden is a quite conservative accounting regime (see 'Prior research' section). That is, Sweden is often associated with countries in continental Europe (for example, Germany and France), rather than the United Kingdom or the USA.

What then could explain the somewhat contradictory results? Some answers could be found by examining the different accounting items. The adjustment items that earlier caused *higher* profits under US GAAP have had a reduced impact on profits over time. These items include fixed assets (revaluation), interest expenses, associated companies and other expenses subject to capitalization under US GAAP. At the same time, income taxes and foreign currency translation, which earlier in the period often caused *lower* profits under US GAAP, have also become less material. In most of these accounting areas, Swedish regulations have approached US GAAP. The items 'left', still causing material adjustments, are business combinations, sale and leaseback transactions, and residual adjustments. *A tentative explanation* of the contradictory results is that the companies in the sample, to a varying extent, have utilized the Swedish accounting rules that have favourable effects on profits. Business combinations and sale leaseback transactions are two items where the Swedish accounting recommendations seem very favourable. In the case of business combinations, the accounting practices for goodwill have been very flexible during the 1980s, ranging from direct write-off against equity to direct write-off against earnings. In the case of sale and leaseback transactions, Rundfelt writes:

> [Swedish] accounting for sale and leaseback transactions is controversial. On one side we find merchant banks and a majority of the representatives of the business world. They consider the current accounting practice to be good, and it facilitates the companies' raising of funds. This side is also supported by FAR. . . . On the other side, we have those who wish to see a harmonisation to international accounting practice, and some of the analysts.
>
> (Rundfelt, 1988: 49, trans.)

This quotation indicates that the accounting rules for sale and leaseback transactions are more favourable in Sweden than in other countries.

Finally, a question that also must be discussed is: to what extent *are these companies representative of Swedish accounting practice*? Most of the companies studied were rather large multinational companies, whose shares are listed in the US and are traded internationally. They could be expected to compete for capital in international capital markets. Therefore, a suggestion could be that *these companies, compared to other Swedish companies, may have been quicker to adjust to, or move ahead of, new Swedish regulation in line with international recommendations.*[7] As a consequence, the results in this paper cannot automatically be generalized to domestic companies. Furthermore, it should be emphasized that within the sample there was much variation between companies (see Tables 4 and 12). For practical financial statement analysis purposes, this is important to keep in mind.

Given the 'international' characteristics of the sample used in this study, an interesting subject for future research would be to investigate the behaviour of MNCs versus domestic companies, with respect to the choice of accounting methods.

NOTES

The author gratefully acknowledges the helpful comments of Sidney Gray, Anne Loft, Walter Schuster, Stuart Turley and two anonymous reviewers. The research was funded by Lars Erik Lundberg's Scholarship Fund.
 1 Swedish companies must follow Swedish accounting laws. These laws require compliance with Swedish generally accepted accounting principles (GAAP). Swedish GAAP are generally defined as the actual accounting practices performed by a picked group of qualitatively representative Swedish companies. In practice, accounting recommendations from different Swedish standard-forming organizations have much impact on the interpretation of Swedish GAAP.
 2 The requirements for quotation on the A:I list are mainly a shareholders' equity equal to or greater than MSEK 20, and a minimum number of shareholders, holding at least one unit of trade each, of 1,000.
 3 The two cases were Pharmacia 1986 (index of conservatism (IC) for PAFT = −4.52) and Volvo 1990 (IC for PDIP = −42.35). In these two cases the profits

under US GAAP were near zero. Since 'US profits' is the denominator in the formula for calculating the index of conservatism, such index values become inappropriate. Pharmacia 1986 and Volvo 1990 were the only two cases where PAFT/PDIP were negative. It should be noted that in both cases there was a reduction of loss under US GAAP [(Pharmacia 1986; PAFT = MSEK –48.9; P(US GAAP) = MSEK –7.5); (Volvo 1990; PDIP = MSEK –1,020; P(US GAAP) = MSEK –23)].

4   SEK 100 is approximately equal to DEM 20, FFR 70, GBP 8 and USD 12.

5   There were six observations of non-specified goodwill adjustments that possibly could include an extension of the amortization period.

6   In nominal terms, the adjustments were for 1984 MSEK –308, for 1985 MSEK –421 and for 1986 MSEK –220.

7   As described earlier, Swedish regulation has moved closer to US GAAP for some items (associated companies, foreign currency translation and income taxes).

REFERENCES

Choi, F. D. S. *et al.* (1983) 'Analyzing Foreign Financial Statements: The Use and Misuse of International Ratios Analysis', *Journal of International Business Studies*, Spring/Summer: 113–31.

Cooke, T. E. (1988) *European Financial Reporting: Sweden*, Institute of Chartered Accountants in England and Wales.

Cooke, T. E. (1989) 'Disclosure in the Corporate Annual Reports of Swedish Companies', *Accounting and Business Research*, Spring: 113–24.

Föreningen Auktoriserade Revisorer FAR (1992) *Key to Understanding Swedish Financial Statements*, Stockholm.

Gray, S. J. (1980) 'The Impact of International Accounting Differences from a Security-Analysis Perspective: Some European Evidence', *Journal of Accounting Research*, Spring: 64–76.

Hendriksen, E. (1982) *Accounting Theory*. Irwin.

Jonnergård, K. (1992) 'Latenta skatter – en Knäckfråga för 90-talet' ('Deferred Taxes – A Key Question in the 90s'), *Balans*, 8–9: 45–50.

Nair, R. D. and Frank, W. G. (1980) 'The Impact of Disclosure and Measurement Practices on International Accounting Classifications', *Accounting Review*, July: 426–50.

Näringslivets Börskommitté (1983) *Rekommendation om ändrad resultaträkning, nyckeltalsberäkning m m* (Recommendation Regarding Changed Income Statement, Key Ratio Calculation etc.). Stockholms Handelskammare and Sveriges Industriförbund.

Nobes. C. W. (1983) 'A Judgemental International Classification of Financial Reporting Practices', *Journal of Business Finance and Accounting*, Spring: 1–19.

Nobes, C. W. (1988) *Interpreting US Financial Statements*. London: Butterworths.

Nobes, C. W. (1989) *Interpreting European Financial Statements: Towards 1992*. London: Butterworths.

Nobes, C. W. (1990) *Accounting Comparisons: UK/Europe*, Vol. 1. London: Coopers & Lybrand Deloitte.

Nobes, C. W. and Parker R. (1991) *Comparative International Accounting*, 3rd edition. Englewood Cliffs, NJ: Prentice-Hall.

Rundfelt, R. (1988) *Tendenser i börsbolagens årsredovisningar 1988* (Tendencies in Swedish Quoted Companies' Annual Reports 1988). Stockholm Stock Exchange and Bokföringsnämnden.

Rundfelt, R. (1990) *Tendenser i börsbolagens årsredovisningar 1990* (Tendencies in Swedish Quoted Companies' Annual Reports 1990). Stockholm Stock Exchange and Bokföringsnämnden.

Stockholm Stock Exchange (1990) *Annual Report.*

Weetman, P. and Gray, S. J. (1990) 'International Financial Analysis and Comparative Corporate Performance: The Impact of UK versus US Accounting Principles on Earnings', *Journal of International Financial Management and Accounting*, 2(2) and 2(3): 111–30.

Weetman, P. and Gray, S. J. (1991) 'A Comparative International Analysis of the Impact of Accounting Principles on Profits: The USA versus the UK, Sweden and The Netherlands', *Accounting and Business Research*, Autumn: 363–79.

[17]

ABACUS, Vol. 31, No. 2, 1995

JULIE NORTON

The Impact of Financial Accounting Practices on the Measurement of Profit and Equity: Australia Versus the United States

The purpose of this paper is to make a quantitative comparative analysis of differences between Australian financial reporting practices and U.S. GAAP. The empirical data consist of Form 20-F filings for thirteen Australian incorporated companies for the period 1985–93. Based on prior research, there is a test of the hypothesis that U.S. GAAP is more conservative than Australian financial reporting practice. The results of the empirical analysis offer little support for this hypothesis in the context of the reporting of profit. However, the hypothesis is supported for the reporting of shareholders' equity. The most frequent and material differences in profits relate to asset measurement, equity consolidation and accounting for intangible assets. Generalizations relating to differences in shareholders' equity are more difficult to make.

Key words: Accounting practices; Accounting procedures; Measurement; Profit.

A major element of international financial accounting research has been attempts to quantify the effects of different GAAP regimes, particularly on the measurement of income. A number of these studies have involved a degree of artificiality or subjectivity, by requiring the interpretation and application of differing national GAAP by the researchers themselves or by users with particular information needs (see, e.g., Davidson and Kohlmeir, 1966; Gray, 1980; Choi *et al.*, 1983; Simmonds and Azières, 1989; Brunovs and Kirsch, 1991; and Rees, 1993).

Other recent research, however, has used data from overseas incorporating companies that have securities traded in the U.S. The Securities and Exchange Commission (SEC) requires those companies to file annual financial statements through Form 20-F. Companies have the option of reporting under U.S. GAAP or another comprehensive body of accounting principles. Those reporting their financial statements other than in U.S. GAAP are, however, required to reconcile reported net income and equity to net income and equity under U.S. GAAP, with a

JULIE E. NORTON is lecturer in Accounting, University of Reading, United Kingdom.

The author gratefully acknowledges the helpful comments of Professor C. W. Nobes, Dr S. Greenblatt, Mr S. Burke and Mr A Roberts (Reading University), Professor G. Carnegie (Deakin University) and two anonymous referees.

ACCOUNTING   PRACTICES: AUSTRALIA   V.   U.S.A.

separate quantification of the effect of each accounting policy which differs materially from U.S. GAAP. The accounting policies, as they affect the company, also must be explained by way of a note. There is no requirement for any of this information to be disclosed to domestic shareholders.

Walton and Wyman (1990), Weetman and Gray (1990, 1991), Goldberg and Goodwin (1992), Hellman (1993) and Cooke (1993) have studied the financial statements of companies from the United Kingdom, the Netherlands, Sweden, the Republic of Ireland, Denmark, France and Japan using the reported reconciliations in Form 20-F. In all cases, save Sweden (where results were mixed) and Japan (where Japanese GAAP were identified as possibly more prudent), companies were identi-fied as reporting lower earnings under U.S. GAAP than their 'home' GAAP. Walton and Wyman identified similar reported equity under U.S. and U.K. GAAP. Consistent and frequent adjustments to income and equity have been identified for the U.K. as relating to accounting for goodwill and accounting for deferred taxes, although researchers have also highlighted the importance of individual company differences in terms of the magnitude, frequency and direction of accounting effects.

This article entails a qualitative and quantitative comparative analysis of the differences between Australian financial reporting practice and U.S. GAAP and their effects on company-reported net profit and shareholders' equity. The next section discusses prior qualitative and quantitative work in this area in order to identify the significant differences between Australian financial reporting practice and U.S. GAAP and to produce testable hypotheses. Following sections detail the research data and methodology, and discuss the findings. Some conclusions are then drawn.

PRIOR RESEARCH

Qualitative Differences in Profits and Equity
The Australian Accounting Research Foundation (AARF) has recently published a paper explaining its views on the subject of international comparability (AARF, 1994). Chapter 4 discusses comparability of existing Australian standards with those of the major standard-setting jurisdictions of the U.S., Canada, the U.K., New Zealand and with the pronouncements of the International Accounting Standards Committee. Comparisons indicated that generally there existed more differences between Australian accounting standards and U.S. GAAP than between Australian accounting standards and those of the other jurisdictions reviewed.

The AARF paper also reproduced an extract from the SEC's 1993 'Survey of Financial Statement Reconciliations by Foreign Registrants'. Analysis of this and individual accounting standards identified a number of important qualitative differences between Australian accounting standards and U.S. GAAP which would affect reported financial position and performance. As a contrast to this cross-sectional analysis, Norton (1994) provides a longitudinal study of the differences between Australian financial accounting practices and U.S. GAAP for one SEC-registered Australian incorporated company, The News Corporation (TNC).

ABACUS

Although neither the AARF nor the SEC detail the names of the companies surveyed it is likely that TNC was included in the SEC's 1993 survey.

The qualitative differences between Australian financial reporting requirements and practice and U.S. GAAP[1] identified by these two studies, together with further differences identified from an examination of the Forms 20-F of the Australian registrants studied here are combined and detailed in Table 1.

TABLE 1

QUALITATIVE ACCOUNTING DIFFERENCES
AUSTRALIA VERSUS THE UNITED STATES

Qualitative difference	Mandatory Australian reporting requirements	Mandatory U.S. GAAP
1 Asset valuation		
a Revaluation	Revaluation of tangible and intangible non-current assets (excluding goodwill) allowed.	Historical cost convention upheld; revaluation not allowed.
b Depreciation on revalued assets	Depreciation is based on the revalued carrying amount of the assets.	Depreciation is based on historical carrying amounts.
c Sale of revalued assets	Gains (losses) on the sale of assets calculated from the revalued carrying amount.	Gains (losses) calculated from the historical carrying amount.
d Permanent impairment	Permanent impairments in individual asset values may be taken through the revaluation reserve where there is a net credit balance for any class of assets. Only any excess will be debited to the profit and loss account.	Permanent impairments of individual assets are directly expensed to the profit and loss account.
e Marketable equity securities	Provision for unrealised losses on marketable equity securities held as non-current assets is not required, provided the diminution in value is considered to be temporary. Disclosure may be required.	Such assets must be carried at the lower aggregate cost or market value with accumulated provision deducted in shareholders' equity.
	Source: AAS 10/AASB 1010; AASB 1013 *Corporations Law.*	Source: APB 6; CON 5; FAS 12.
2 Intangible assets		
a Goodwill amortization	Goodwill amortized over a period not exceeding twenty years.	Goodwill amortized over a period not exceeding forty years.
b Identifiable intangible assets	Recognition allowed at purchase price or production cost; amortized over the asset's useful life: certain interpretation would allow for no amortization.	Recognition of acquired assets at cost allowed; amortization over a period not exceeding forty years.
	Source: AAS 18/AASB 1013; AAS 4/AASB 1021.	Source: APB 16; APB 17.

[1] The terminology 'financial reporting requirements' is used to encompass regulation by both accounting standards and *Corporations Law*. 'U.S. GAAP' is normally taken to represent all regulatory requirements.

A C C O U N T I N G   P R A C T I C E S :   A U S T R A L I A   V .   U . S . A .

TABLE 1 (contd)

Qualitative difference	Mandatory Australian reporting requirements	Mandatory U.S. GAAP
3 Business combinations and intercompany investments		
a Purchase versus pooling	Purchase method of accounting must be applied to all business combinations.	Pooling of interests method must be applied to certain business combinations.
b Identification of subsidiaries	Based on control, defined as the capacity to dominate decision-making, rather than purely ownership levels. (Mandatory for reporting periods ending on or after 31 December 1991.)	Usual condition for control is a majority voting interest.
c Equity-accounted results	Not allowed to be incorporated into the main statutory financial statements but to be additionally disclosed in the accounts.	Required to be incorporated into statutory accounts.
d Minority interests	Included in shareholders' equity.	Not considered part of shareholders' equity.
	Source: AAS 21/AASB 1015; AASB 1024; *Corporations Law*.	Source: APB 16; APB 18; FAS 94; S-X 5-02; S-X 5-03.
4 Cost Recognition		
a Research and development	Costs may be deferred under certain circumstances and amortized upon commercial production.	Such costs are expensed immediately.
	Source: AAS 13/AASB 1011.	Source: FAS 19.
b Exploration expenditure	Certain exploration costs in defined areas of interest may be capitalized.	Such costs are expensed immediately.
	Source: AAS 7/AASB 1022.	Source: FAS 19.
c Petroleum amortization	Amortization of costs is determined by calculating production over proven and probable reserves.	Only proven reserves are to be used in the calculation.
	Source: AAS 7/AASB 1022.	Source: FAS 19.
d Business start-up costs	Expenditure may be deferred under certain criteria.	Expenditure may be deferred under certain criteria. These are much tighter than in Australia.
	Source: Accounting practice supported by AAS 9 (non-mandatory).	Source: FAS 7.
e Refinancing costs	Charged as abnormal expenses.	Deferred and amortized over the life of the refinancing agreement.
	Source: Accounting practice supported by taxation regulations (non-mandatory).	Source: FAS 15.
f Superannuation benefits	Contributions are normally expensed as incurred.	Expensed on an accruals basis.
	Source: Accounting practice — no standard (non-mandatory).	Source: FAS 87.
5 Share compensation plans	Compensation cost element is not recognized in the accounts.	Compensation element recognized and expensed

A B A C U S

TABLE 1 (contd)

Qualitative difference	Mandatory Australian reporting requirements	Mandatory U.S. GAAP
		over the periods in which the employee performs the related services.
	Source: Accounting practice — no standard (non-mandatory).	Source: APB 25.
6 Taxation	More stringent in relation to the recognition of deferred tax assets.	
	Deferred income tax is accounted for according to the liability method, that is:	Liability method now required. However, during the period investigated, the deferral method was allowed, i.e. change in statutory tax rate not recognized.
	Change in the statutory tax rate is taken to income immediately.	Not recognized.
	Change in law recognized immediately.	Change in law not recognized.
	Source: AAS 3; AASB 1020.	Source: APB 11; FAS 96; FAS 109.
7 Cash dividend	Recognized on an accrual basis in the year to which they relate.	Recognized in period declared.
	Source: AASB 1018; *Corporations Law*.	Source: Accounting practice— no standard.
8 Preference share classification	Included in shareholders' equity.	Where subject to mandatory redemption or where redemption is outside the control of the issuer, then not considered part of shareholders' equity.
	Source: *Corporations Law*.	Source: S-X 5-02; ASR 268.

Note. For references to the authoritative literature, see Appendix.

Table 2 identifies the likely directional effect that these qualitative differences would have on Australian reported profit and equity on reconciliation to U.S. GAAP. In respect of the number of differences that affect reported figures, most of these would lead to lower reported profit and equity after reconciliation to U.S. GAAP (see 'Total' line), although this is less pronounced for profit than for equity. The actual effect of these differences depends of course on the particular mix of accounting policies adopted by companies and the magnitude of the figures involved. The extent to which these accounting policies represent timing differences is also important as the directional effects will be reversed at future dates.

Quantitative Differences in Profits and Equity
The AARF's extract from the SEC's survey showed that eighteen Australian

A C C O U N T I N G   P R A C T I C E S :   A U S T R A L I A   V .   U . S . A .

TABLE 2

DIRECTIONAL EFFECT OF QUALITATIVE ACCOUNTING DIFFERENCES
AUSTRALIA VERSUS THE UNITED STATES

Qualitative difference	Effect on Australian profit of adoption of U.S. GAAP				Effect on Australian equity of adoption of U.S. GAAP			
	Increase	Decrease	Variable	No effect	Increase	Decrease	Variable	No effect
1 Asset Valuation								
a Revaluation	✓	–	–	–	–	✓	–	–
b Depreciation	✓	–	–	–	✓	–	–	–
c Sale of assets	–	✓	–	–	–	–	–	✓
d Permanent impairment	–	–	–	✓	–	–	–	✓
e Marketable equity securities	–	–	–	✓	–	✓	–	–
2 Intangible assets								
a Goodwill amortization	✓	–	–	–	✓	–	–	–
b Identifiable intangible assets								
(i) with amortization	✓	–	–	–	✓	–	–	–
(ii) without amortization	–	✓	–	–	–	✓	–	–
3 Business combinations and inter-company investments								
a Purchase verus pooling	✓	–	–	–	–	–	✓	–
b Identification of subsidiaries	–	–	✓	–	–	–	✓	–
c Equity accounted results	–	–	✓	–	–	–	✓	–
d Minority interests	–	–	–	✓	–	✓	–	–
4 Cost recognition								
a Research and development	–	✓	–	–	–	✓	–	–
b Exploration expenditure	–	✓	–	–	–	✓	–	–
c Petroleum amortization	–	✓	–	–	–	✓	–	–
d Business start-up costs	–	–	✓	–	✓	–	–	–
e Refinancing costs	✓	–	–	–	–	–	✓	–
f Superannuation benefits	–	✓	–	–	–	✓	–	–
5 Share compensation plans	–	✓	–	–	–	–	✓	–
6 Taxation	–	–	✓	–	✓	–	–	–
7 Cash dividend	–	–	–	✓	–	✓	–	–
8 Preference share classification	–	–	–	✓	–	✓	–	–
Total	6	7	4	5	5	10	5	2

A B A C U S

registrants presented financial statements in accordance with Australian financial reporting requirements and, therefore, also provided a reconciliation to U.S. GAAP within Form 20-F. Six of these companies reported profit greater under U.S. GAAP (ranging from an increase of 2 per cent to an increase of 709 per cent), nine reported lower profit (ranging from a decrease of 1 per cent to a decrease of 111 per cent) and three reported the same profit. Three companies reported equity greater under U.S. GAAP (ranging from an increase of 2 per cent to an increase of 37 per cent), thirteen companies reported equity less (ranging from a decrease of 6 per cent to a decrease of 117 per cent) and two reported the same equity. Table 3 provides further details of these reconciliations.

The effect of reconciliation to U.S. GAAP for TNC over eight years is summarized in Table 4. Profit was lower under U.S. GAAP for six of the years examined, and reported equity was lower for all eight years. The directional effect of the quantitative differences in profit and equity support the directional effect of the qualitative differences, that is, that both profit and equity are lower according to U.S. GAAP than according to Australian financial reporting requirements.

Measuring Differences in Profits and Equity
Prior research using data filed with the SEC has made use of the 'index of conservatism' as developed by Gray (1980) for analytical purposes. For the purpose of this study the index is calculated as follows:

$$\text{Index of conservatism} = 1 - \left[\frac{\text{Profits (or equity) U.S. - Profits (or equity) Aust.}}{|\text{Profits (or equity) U.S.}|} \right]$$

where profits (or equity) US relates to profit (or equity) under U.S. GAAP, and profit (or equity), and Aust. relates to profit (or equity) under Australian financial reporting requirements (this approach is adopted to allow comparison with previous work using the index).

The greater the index value the less conservative is reported Australian profits (or equity) relative to U.S. GAAP. An index measure greater (less) than 1 indicates that Australian profits (or equity) is higher (lower) or less (more) conservative than U.S. GAAP profits (or equity). An index value exactly equal to 1 indicates neutrality in comparison to U.S. GAAP.

Having established an overall index of conservatism it is then possible to establish the relative effects of the various individual adjustments by constructing partial indices of conservatism using the formula developed by Weetman and Gray (1991):

$$\text{Partial index of conservatism} = 1 - \left[\frac{\text{Partial adjustment}}{|\text{Profits (or equity) U.S.}|} \right]$$

The interpretation of the partial index corresponds with that of the overall index of conservatism. For example, an index measure greater than 1 indicates that the particular GAAP adjustment will increase Australian profits (or equity) — that is, Australian financial reporting requirements are less conservative than U.S. GAAP.

ACCOUNTING PRACTICES: AUSTRALIA V. U.S.A.

TABLE 3

SEC REGISTERED AUSTRALIAN COMPANIES' RECONCILIATION VARIANCES
Net profit

Profit under U.S. GAAP greater than profit under Aust. requirements	Number of registrants	Variance range % of Aust. requirements
More than 100%	2	279.47%, 708.82%
50.01% – 100%	0	–
25.01% – 50%	0	–
10.01% – 25%	1	22.39%
0.01% – 10%	3	1.97% – 8.86%

Profit under U.S. GAAP less than profit under Aust. requirements	Number of registrants	Variance range % of Aust. requirements
More than 100%	1	(111.13)%
50.01% – 100%	1	(51.97)%
25.01% – 50%	1	(31.67)%
10.01% – 25%	1	(16.44)%
0.01% – 10%	5	(6.13)% – (0.70)%

Shareholders' equity		

Equity under U.S. GAAP greater than equity under Aust. requirements	Number of registrants	Variance range % of Aust. requirements
25.01% – 50%	1	36.81%
10.01% – 25%	0	–
0.01% – 10%	2	1.69%, 1.33%

Equity under U.S. GAAP less than equity under Aust. requirements	Number of registrants	Variance range % of Aust. requirements
More than 100%	1	(117.06)%
50.01% – 100%	4	(90.75)%–(61.59)%
25.01% – 50%	1	(34.98)%
10.01% – 25%	2	(21.72)%, (17.56)%)%
0.01% – 10%	5	(8.80)%–(5.88)%

Source: AARF (1994) Appendix 2, p. 108.

Based on the prior qualitative and quantitative research examined above, and using the terminology of conservatism analysis, the hypothesis to be tested is:

H1: U.S. GAAP is more conservative than Australian financial reporting requirements.

A B A C U S

TABLE 4

THE NEWS CORPORATION'S RECONCILIATION VARIANCES
Net profit

Profit under U.S. GAAP greater than profit under Aust. requirements	Number of years	Variance range % of Aust. requirements
10.01% – 25%	2	19.00%, 20.00%
0.01% – 10%	0	–

Profit under U.S. GAAP less than profit under Aust. requirements	Number of years	Variance range % of Aust. requirements
50.01% – 100%	1	(56.00)%
25.01% – 50%	0	–
10.01% – 25%	3	(17.00)%–(21.00)%
0.01% – 10%	2	(3.00)%,(10.00)%

Shareholders' equity		

Equity under U.S. GAAP less than equity under Aust. requirements	Number of years	Variance range % of Aust. requirements
50.01% – 100%	6	(52.00)%–(69.00)%
25.01% – 50%	1	(49.00)%
10.01% – 25%	0	–
0.01% – 10%	0	–

Source: Norton (1994), adapted.

However, it should perhaps be made clear that prior research, by using actual data from company accounts, is in fact comparing domestic financial reporting *practice* with U.S. GAAP. That reporting practice and reporting requirements might differ has not previously been considered an issue. Yet, on reconciliation to U.S. GAAP, company accounts may continue to be influenced by older, presently unacceptable, accounting policies. Furthermore, companies may adopt a policy of non-compliance in relation to reporting requirements. In such cases reporting practice will differ from reporting requirements. To reflect this the hypothesis to be tested is restated as follows:

H2: U.S. GAAP is more conservative than Australian financial reporting practice.

RESEARCH DATA AND METHODOLOGY

As with other studies using actual data, this survey draws its information from the

ACCOUNTING PRACTICES: AUSTRALIA V. U.S.A.

accounts of Australian incorporated companies that are also quoted on U.S. stock exchanges. A total of nineteen such companies were identified.[2]

For the purposes of this study, four companies in the banking and financial services sector were excluded as reporting under different regulations. Two further companies chose to report results in conformity with U.S. GAAP, and therefore provided no reconciliation information. The remaining thirteen companies are examined here. Reconciliation information was available for these companies for between three and nine years. Table 5 identifies the final sample of seventy-six profit observations and sixty-eight equity observations.[3]

The number of companies examined compares favourably with most other surveys: Weetman and Gray (1991) included only eight Swedish and eight Dutch companies; Goldberg and Godwin (1992) included three Dutch, one Irish, one Danish and one French company; Cooke (1993) examined five Japanese companies; and Hellman (1993) examined ten Swedish companies. The data used do, however, mean that this survey, as with those others, suffers from the same lack of control over basic issues, such as whether companies listed overseas are representative of all quoted companies; industry specific accounting distortions; and the degree to which the accounting principles applied by the examined companies are typical of their 'home' GAAP. Furthermore, the narrow window of analysis (at most, nine years) may not allow for the timing differences involved in differing accounting policies to be completely resolved. Nor may the period covered reflect a 'typical' economic environment and, therefore, 'typical' accounting policies. Use of the index of conservatism itself is also problematic (see Rees, 1993, who favours a regression approach). However, as this paper seeks comparability with prior work, the index's role in the analysis was retained.

The index of conservatism was used to analyse possible significant differences and trends in reported profit and equity at the aggregate level, and the partial index of conservatism was used to identify significant differences and trends for specific accounting items. As the sample is small, basic statistics are used: median, mean and standard deviation. The Wilcoxon test for small samples of matched pairs was applied to examine differences in net profit and shareholders' equity.[4]

---

[2] As at 30 June 1994 by Disclosure Ltd., London, U.K. As neither the AARF nor the SEC provide details, it is not possible to describe how the nineteen companies here relate to the eighteen in the SEC's 'Survey'.

[3] Within Form 20-F companies provide income and equity reconciliation figures for the current year and the preceding two years. However, in this sample seven companies provided equity reconciliations for the current year and only one preceding year (these companies were Boral Limited, The Broken Hill Proprietary Company Limited, Coles Myer Ltd, Great Central Mines N.L., The News Corporation Limited, Trans Global Resources N.L. and Western Mining Corporation Holdings Limited). This resulted in one less equity observation for these companies. In all cases this equity observation related to the first year of the disclosure period. Boral did not provide equity reconciliation figures for 1993.

[4] The Wilcoxon test ranks absolute differences in order of size, disregarding sign, with the smallest difference allocated the lowest rank. The sums of the ranks corresponding to positive and negative differences are calculated. The smaller of these sums is the Wilcoxon test statistic T, used to test the null hypothesis.

A B A C U S

TABLE 5

SAMPLE COMPANIES

Company	Disclosure period	Number of years	
		Profit and loss	Balance sheet
Amcor Limited	1991–93	3	3
Boral Limited	1988–93	6	4
The Broken Hill Proprietary Company Limited	1985–93	9	8
Coles Myer Ltd	1988–93	6	5
CRA Limited	1990–93	4	4
Great Central Mines N.L.	1990–93	4	3
Mayne Nickless Limited	1989–93	5	5
The News Corporation Limited	1986–93	8	7
Orbital Engine Corporation Limited	1989–93	5	5
Pacific Dunlop Limited	1985–93	9	9
Ramtron Holdings Limited	1988–91	4	4
Trans Global Resources N.L.	1987–93	7	6
Western Mining Corporation Holdings Limited	1988–93	6	5
Total observations		76	68

ANALYSIS AND RESULTS

Differences in Profits and Equity
In terms of a one-tailed Wilcoxon test, the conservatism hypothesis is expressed as:

H3: Sum of positive ranks (index > 1) > Sum of negative ranks (index < 1).

The sums of positive and negative ranks for profit observations are shown in Table 6, and the significant years are also indicated. Table 6 also includes median values, means and standard deviations of the index of conservatism for each year. For calculation purposes, two outliers were excluded.[5]

There is little support for the hypothesis that U.S. GAAP is more conservative than Australian financial accounting practice in the reporting of profit. For only one year (1987 — with only four observations) was there a statistically significant difference between Australian profits and U.S. GAAP profits, but the difference was in the opposite direction to that expected: U.S. GAAP profits were significantly greater than Australian profits. In addition, the positive sum of ranks was higher

---

[5] Observations were classified as outliers where the index of conservatism was above 10.00 or below –9.00. All outliers related to observations where U.S. GAAP profit was less than Australian profit. The two cases were Orbital Engine Corporation Limited 1989 (index of 60) and Pacific Dunlop Limited 1992 (index of 186). In both cases profits under U.S. GAAP were near zero. Given the construction of the index of conservatism, index values in these circumstances become inappropriate.

ACCOUNTING PRACTICES: AUSTRALIA V. U.S.A.

TABLE 6

INDEX OF CONSERVATISM—NET PROFIT
Wilcoxon sum of ranks and medians

Years	N	Index of cons. Sum of positive (ranks (>1.00)	Index of cons. Sum of negative (ranks (<1.00)	Median index
1985	2	0	3	0.855
1986	3	2	4	0.962
1987	4	1	9[a]	0.805
1988	8	10	26	0.955
1989	8	11	25	1.000
1990	10	32	23	1.010
1991	11	41	25	1.009
1992	10	21	34	0.966
1993	11	35	30	1.020
All	67			

Note. For seven observations index of conservatism = 1.
[a] significantly lower than 1 at the 10% level.

		Means and standard deviations			
Years	N	Min.	Max.	Mean	SD
1985	2	0.767	0.945	0.854	0.085
1986	3	0.714	1.113	0.929	0.165
1987	4	−3.500	1.112	−0.195	1.912
1988	8	−0.875	1.122	0.581	0.700
1989	9	−0.556	1.261	0.641	0.620
1990	12	0.181	1.602	1.010	0.312
1991	13	0.198	2.375	1.126	0.515
1992	11	−2.889	2.249	0.465	1.521
1993	12	−4.000	2.688	0.645	1.656
All	74				

than the negative sum of ranks in only three of the nine years; the median values of the overall index of conservatism were above 1 for only four of the nine years; and, the mean was higher than 1 for only two of the nine years. The index of conservatism for total profits for the period was 0.673. This implies that for the period 1985–93 Australian profits for the companies studied were 32.7 per cent lower than the same profits measured in accordance with U.S. GAAP.

It would appear that the mix of accounting policies adopted and their frequency and magnitude outweighs the simplistic directional effects, identified in Table 2.

A B A C U S

Significant policies, reducing Australian reported profits, for example, may be the increased depreciation charges on revalued assets and the shorter (twenty years rather than forty years) amortization period of goodwill. The exclusion of profitable equity-accounted results may also be important. Later analysis, using the partial index of conservatism, will attempt to identify these significant policies.

Incidentally, the fact that the median was higher than the mean for six of the nine years implies that there must be some large observations that decrease the mean index (i.e., cases where Australian profits are lower than under U.S. GAAP). Table 7 classifies all observations in terms of their level of materiality. For the period 1985–93, a large proportion of the observations (62 per cent) were material (difference exceeding 10 per cent). However, 55 per cent of material observations

TABLE 7

INDEX OF CONSERVATISM — NET PROFIT

Index of conservatism (level of materiality)	1985	1986	1987	1988	1989	1990	1991	1992	1993
Profit under U.S. GAAP greater than profit under Australian requirements									
Over 100%	–	–	1	2	2	–	–	2	2
50.01%–100%	–	–	–	–	1	1	1	–	–
25.01%–50%	–	1	–	1	–	–	–	–	–
10.01%–25%	1	–	2	1	1	2	2	2	1
5.01%–10%	1	–	–	–	–	1	1	1	1
0.01%–5%	–	1	–	–	–	–	–	1	1
Number	2	2	3	4	4	4	4	6	5
Profit under U.S. GAAP equal to profit under Australian requirements:	–	–	–	–	1	2	2	1	1
Profit under U.S. GAAP less than profit under Australian requirements									
0.01%–5%	–	–	–	–	2	1	2	1	1
5.01%–10%	–	–	–	3	1	2	1	–	–
10.01%–25%	–	1	1	1	–	1	1	1	1
25.01%–50%	–	–	–	–	1	1	1	1	2
50.01%–100%	–	–	–	–	–	1	1	–	1
Over 100%	–	–	–	–	1	–	1	2	1
Number	–	1	1	4	5	6	7	5	6
Total number	2	3	4	8	10	12	13	12	12

Note. Observations classified according to level of materiality.

related to an increase in profits under U.S. GAAP which confirms their relevance in reducing the mean index.

The sums of positive and negative ranks for shareholders' equity observations are shown in Table 8, and the significant years are indicated. Table 8 also includes median values, means and standard deviations for the index of conservatism each year. For calculation purposes three outliers were excluded.[6]

There is much stronger support for the hypothesis that shareholders' equity is more conservative under U.S. GAAP than under Australian financial accounting practice. Statistically significant differences between Australian and U.S. shareholders' equity occurred in the years 1990–93. Those differences were all in the hypothesized direction and related to years with a greater number of observations. In addition, the positive sum of ranks was higher than the negative sum of ranks in eight of the nine years; the median values of the overall index of conservatism was greater than 1 for seven of the nine years; and the mean was greater than 1 again for eight of the nine years. The index of conservatism in respect of total equity for the period 1985–93 was 1.534, indicating that Australian shareholders' equity in the companies studied was 53.4 per cent greater than the same shareholders' equity measured in accordance with U.S. GAAP.

The fact that the mean was higher than the median for six of the nine years again implies an effect as before, and Table 9 classifies all observations in terms of their level of materiality. For the whole period, again a rather large proportion of the observations (63 per cent) were material (exceeding 10 per cent). Eighteen per cent of material observations related to an increase in equity under U.S. GAAP. Forty-six per cent of material observations related to a reduction in equity and 50 per cent of these related to a reduction of over 100 per cent. This confirms that relatively few individual equity observations were highly material in decreasing equity under U.S. GAAP.

The Impact of Different Adjustment Items
To analyse further these total index values, a partial analysis was undertaken in order to confirm and quantify the principal differences between Australian financial accounting practice and U.S. GAAP. Tables 10 and 11 detail the occurrence and impact of these on profit and shareholders' equity as reported in the reconciliations. The frequency of the adjustments is measured as the number of companies making the adjustment and the number of company years the adjustment was observed. The effect of the adjustment is recorded, first, in terms of its direction on reported profits and shareholders' equity and, second, in terms of descriptive statistics (median, mean and standard deviation) based on the partial index of conservatism described earlier.

---

[6] All outliers related to observations where U.S. GAAP equity was less than Australian equity. The three cases were Ramtron Holdings Limited 1988 (index of 39) and Orbital Engine Corporation Limited for 1989 and 1990 (indices of 20.380 and 10.850).

A B A C U S

TABLE 8

INDEX OF CONSERVATISM – SHAREHOLDERS' EQUITY
Wilcoxon sum of ranks and medians

Years	N	Index of cons. Sum of positive ranks (>1.00)	Index of cons. Sum of negative ranks (<1.00)	Median index
1985	1	0	1	0.955
1986	2	2	1	1.020
1987	3	5	1	1.164
1988	4	7	3	1.425
1989	8	25	11	1.000
1990	9	35*	10	1.044
1991	11	53**	13	1.040
1992	10	45**	10	1.036
1993	8	31**	5	1.031
All	56			

Note. For nine observations index of conservatism = 1.
* significantly higher than 1 at the 10% level.
**significantly higher than 1 at the 5% level.

		Means and standard deviations		
Years	N	Min.	Max.	Mean	SD
1985	1	0.955	0.955	0.955	0.000
1986	2	0.923	1.123	1.023	0.100
1987	3	0.912	1.954	1.342	0.443
1988	4	0.418	2.194	1.366	0.785
1989	9	0.673	2.358	1.291	0.543
1990	10	0.726	5.865	1.765	1.530
1991	13	0.753	7.956	2.105	2.189
1992	12	0.831	8.200	1.898	2.000
1993	11	0.836	9.000	2.058	2.291
All	65				

For the calculation of means and standard deviations a number of outliers were excluded.[7]

[7] Outliers relate to the following:

Adjustment	*Partial index of conservatism*
Net profit	
Amortization of reinstated goodwill	15.000
Other intangible asset adjustment	–135.000

ACCOUNTING PRACTICES: AUSTRALIA V. U.S.A.

The nature of the adjustment is described in the same terms as in Table 1. However, some additional explanation of the items in Tables 10 and 11 is required:

(i)   Item 2b: The adjustment recorded here arises from the adoption in the accounts of Australian companies of a policy of capitalization of intangible assets without any amortization. This has been achieved through particular interpretations of the depreciation standards AAS 4/AASB 1021. These standards 'require amounts relating to the depreciation of non-current assets with limited useful lives to be recognized' (AAS 4.4). On this basis depreciation may be avoided where assets are deemed to have unlimited useful lives. For example, The News Corporation's accounting policies relating to publishing rights, titles and television licences stated that 'no amortization is provided ... since, in the opinion of the Directors, they do not have a finite useful economic life'.

Furthermore, the Australian standard defines 'depreciable amount' as 'the historical cost of a depreciable asset, or other revalued amount ... less in either case the net amount expected to be recovered on disposal of the asset at the end of its useful life' (AAS 4.7). Therefore, where the carrying value of the asset is no greater than its realizable value there may also be no requirement to amortize that asset.

In response to this practice the AARF issued Accounting Guidance Release (AGR) No. 5, *Accounting for Intangible Assets*, which affirmed the requirement that identifiable intangible assets should be depreciated. However, this release is non-mandatory and, for the companies surveyed here, non-compliance is evident in a number of instances. Non-compliance in this area appears to have been widespread throughout the Australian corporate sector (Wines and Ferguson, 1993).

(ii)   Items 2c and 2d: Prior to the issue of AAS 18 (1984) and AASB 1013 (1988) a number of Australian companies adopted a policy of writing-off goodwill either against profits as an extraordinary item (2c) or against reserves (2d). In some cases these policies continued until 1989, a further example of non-compliance on the part of the Australian corporate sector (Wines and Ferguson, 1993).

Reconciliation to U.S. GAAP requires the reinstatement of this goodwill amount and its subsequent amortization. The first adjustment has the effect of increasing profits or shareholders' equity (depending on the location of the write-off), while amortization reduces reported profit.

(iii)   Item 3b: Prior to 1991 the *Corporations Law* (or its antecedents) had not encouraged the use of other than 'shareholding' control as the basis for identifying subsidiaries, with the result that accounting practice adopted an ownership criterion similar to that of APB 18 and FAS 94. However, in its ruling on consolidation policy the SEC emphasizes the need to consider control, risk and substance over form

Research and development	20.000
Petroleum amortization	60.000
Share compensation plan	13.000
Shareholders' equity:	
Write-off of intangible assets	10.190 & 19.385
Research and development	31.500

193

A B A C U S

TABLE 9

INDEX OF CONSERVATISM – SHAREHOLDERS' EQUITY

Index of conservatism (level of materiality)	1985	1986	1987	1988	1989	1990	1991	1992	1993
Equity under U.S. GAAP greater than equity under Australian requirements:									
Over 100%	–	–	–	–	–	–	–	–	–
50.01%–100%	–	–	–	1	–	–	–	–	–
25.01%–50%	–	–	–	–	1	1	–	–	–
10.01%–25%	–	–	–	1	1	1	2	2	2
5.01%–10%	–	1	1	–	2	–	–	–	–
0.01%–5%	1	–	–	–	–	–	1	–	–
Number	1	1	1	2	4	2	3	2	2
Equity under U.S. GAAP equal to equity under Australian requirements:	–	–	–	–	1	1	2	2	3
Equity under U.S. GAAP less than equity under Australian requirements:									
0.01%–5%	–	–	–	–	–	3	3	3	1
5.01%–10%	–	–	–	–	–	–	–	–	–
10.01%–25%	–	1	1	–	1	1	1	1	1
25.01%–50%	–	–	–	–	–	–	1	1	1
50.01%–100%	–	–	1	1	2	1	–	–	–
Over 100%	–	–	–	2	2	3	3	3	3
Number	–	1	2	3	5	8	8	8	6
Total number	1	2	3	5	10	11	13	12	11

Note. Observations classified according to level of materiality

(S-X1, S-X3). In practice, therefore, differences in the classification of investments and the identification of subsidiaries in this paper are only likely to be apparent prior to 1991 when Australian companies were reporting under the older Australian rules emphasizing ownership.[8]

---

[8] Broken Hill Proprietary (BHP) was affected by this. In its Australian accounts for the period 1988–90, BHP accounted for a 50 per cent owned investment at cost. Under U.S. GAAP this investment was fully consolidated. The company reported that the main effect on its Australian accounts of reconciliation to U.S. GAAP was for shares in BHP held by the investee to be treated as similar to authorized but unissued shares and deducted from shareholders' equity. From 1991 the investment was fully consolidated in both sets of accounts.

ACCOUNTING PRACTICES: AUSTRALIA V. U.S.A.

(iii)   Item 3c: Australian financial reporting regulations do not allow equity-accounted results to be incorporated into the main statutory accounts, whereas U.S. GAAP requires their inclusion. Adjustments to Australian profit and shareholders' equity are, therefore, of two kinds: the inclusion of the results of such investments (item 3c(i)), and their adjustment to conformity with U.S. GAAP (item 3c(ii)).

The most frequent adjustments to profit relate to the reversal of depreciation charges on revalued assets (recorded by 10 companies with 52 observations), consolidation and adjustment of equity-accounted investments (7 companies and 34 observations), the recording of superannuation benefits (7 companies and 32 observations), the amortization of separable intangible assets (6 companies and 28 observations) and taxation adjustments (6 companies and 24 observations).

Three of these are also material in terms of the magnitude of their effect. The mean values indicate Australian profits are 15 per cent lower as a result of higher depreciation charges on revalued assets and also 15 per cent lower as a result of the exclusion of equity-accounted results. However, Australian profits are 22 per cent higher as a result of the non-amortization of separable intangible assets. The median effects in all three cases, however, are less significant. Other material effects arise from a goodwill write-off to the profit and loss account, resulting in 68 per cent lower Australian profits (although this relates to one company only); and the capitalization of research and development costs recorded by four companies, which has a mean effect producing a 35 per cent higher Australian profit.[9]

The most frequent adjustments to shareholders' equity relate to the elimination of the revaluation reserve (recorded by 10 companies with 51 observations), taxation adjustments (7 companies and 29 observations), the recording of superannuation benefits (7 companies and 28 observations) and the consolidation and adjustment of equity-accounted investments (6 companies and 27 observations).

However, generalizations regarding the effect of different accounting policies are problematic given that the adjustments to shareholders' equity with the greatest frequency were not the adjustments with the greatest effect. Adjustments relating to the classification of investments (Australian equity 122 per cent higher), research and development costs (89 per cent higher), preference share classification (24 per cent higher) and intangible asset write-off (20 per cent lower) being more material to the companies recording those adjustments.

The investment reclassification by Mayne Nickless Limited was different. In its accounts for 1989–91 the company equity accounted for a major investment, based on circumstances other than percentage ownership. Under U.S. GAAP this investment was accounted for at cost, which had the effect of reducing shareholders' equity on reconciliation to U.S. GAAP. The investment was disposed of in 1992.

[9] Accounting for non-current assets, an adjustment recorded by six companies, also appears material, resulting in Australian profits 67 per cent lower than U.S. However, generalizations are difficult as this difference is attributed to a number of differing policy adjustments under this heading, including: (a) individual asset revaluations below cost being taken through the profit and loss account under U.S. GAAP; (b) the reversal of provisions for the diminution in value of investments not recognized under U.S. GAAP until the investment is sold; and (c) the revision of asset values on the acquisition of an investment coupled with the reversal of a translation adjustment. This reversal was particularly material in producing lower Australian profits for one company.

A B A C U S

TABLE 10

IMPACT OF ADJUSTING ITEMS — NET PROFIT

Adjustment (see Table 1 for more detail of items)	Frequency		Effect		Partial index of cons.		
	Nos. of cos. (max. 13)	Nos.of observ. (max. 76)	Higher U.S. profits	Lower U.S. profits	Median	Mean	SD
1 Asset valuation							
b Depreciation reversal	10	52	49	3	0.969	0.845	0.237
c Sale of asset adjustment	5	30	27	3	0.974	0.948	0.133
d Adjustment to non-current asset values	6	8	4	4	0.609	0.425	0.697
2 Intangible assets							
a Change in rate of goodwill amortization	1	8	8	–	0.962	0.962	0.000
b Amortization of separable intangible assets	6	28	–	28	1.047	1.220	0.307
c Reversal of goodwill extraordinary write-off	1	5	5	–	0.318	0.318	0.000
d Amortization of reinstated goodwill	3	18	2	16	1.036	1.044	0.025
3 Business combinations and inter-company investments							
c (i) Equity consolidation	4	21	16	5 }	0.946	0.849	0.378
c (ii) Adjustment to U.S. GAAP	7[a]	34	20	14 }			
4 Cost recognition							
a Research and development	4	19	2	17	1.230	1.348	0.353
b Exploration expenditure	2	15	5	10	1.018	1.018	0.017
c Petroleum amortization	1	4	1	3	1.062	1.062	0.000
d Business start-up costs	2	7	1	6	1.102	1.102	0.057
e Refinancing costs	1	3	1	2	1.002	1.002	0.000
f Superannuation benefits	7	32	20	12	1.074	1.056	0.158
5 Share compensation plans	4	28	–	28	1.019	1.024	0.016
6 Taxation	6	24	17	7	0.984	0.931	0.167

[a] Three companies included both equity consolidation and adjustment under this heading.

Two issues require further emphasis. First, differences in accounting for intangible assets appear to be more important than suggested by the AARF (1994) due to the continuing influence on reconciliations of older, but now unacceptable, policies in the case of goodwill and the lack of a specific accounting standard for separable intangible assets. Second, differences in accounting for research and development expenditure need to be considered within a wider context of cost recognition. The elements of cost recognition identified in this study suggest that U.S. GAAP are much stricter than Australian financial reporting requirements in disallowing the deferral of costs.

Not only is generalization problematic due to the varied effect of accounting policy differences, but also due to important individual company differences. The

A C C O U N T I N G   P R A C T I C E S :   A U S T R A L I A   V .   U . S . A .

TABLE 11

IMPACT OF ADJUSTING ITEMS – SHAREHOLDERS' EQUITY

Adjustment (see Table 1 for more detail of items)	Frequency		Effect		Partial index of cons.		
	Nos of cos. (max. 13)	Nos.of observ. (max. 68)	Higher U.S. equity	Lower U.S. equity	Median	Mean	SD
1 Asset valuation							
a Revaluation reserve reversal	10	51	–	51	1.091	1.160	0.175
e Market equity securities provision	3	5	1	4	1.029	1.029	0.002
2 Intangible assets							
b Amortization of intangible assets	5	23	–	23	1.066	1.092	0.046
d Reinstatement of goodwill written-off	3	16	16	–	0.796	0.796	0.047
3 Business combinations and inter-company investments							
b Investment reclassification	2	6	–	6	2.221	2.221	0.824
c (i) Equity consolidation	4	20	16	4 }	1.054	1.073	0.093
c (ii) Adjustment to U.S. GAAP	7[a]	27	11	16 }			
d Reclassification of minority interests	5	22	–	22	1.076	1.081	0.042
4 Cost recognition							
a Research and development	4	18	–	18	1.323	1.893	1.050
b Exploration expenditure	2	12	–	12	1.026	1.026	0.009
c Petroleum amortization	1	5	–	5	1.009	1.009	0.000
d Business start-up costs	2	6	–	6	1.034	1.034	0.003
e Refinancing costs	1	3	3	–	0.973	0.973	0.000
f Superannuation benefits	7	28	22	6	0.994	0.991	0.007
5 Share compensation plans	5	18	–	18	1.016	1.077	0.096
6 Taxation	7	29	6	23	1.010	1.029	0.049
7 Cash dividend	5	19	19	–	0.957	0.963	0.016
8 Preference share reclassification	1	7	–	7	1.239	1.239	0.000

[a] Three companies included both equity consolidation and adjustment under this heading.

results of Orbital Engine and Ramtron are materially affected by different policies relating to research and development; Pacific Dunlop's results have been materially affected by its policies in respect of accounting for goodwill, and Western Mining's results are materially affected by the differing policies relating to equity consolidation. Table 12 provides details of the individual companies surveyed.

SUMMARY

Prior work examining the differences between Australian financial reporting practice and U.S. GAAP suggests that the latter are likely to be more conservative. This study has attempted to assess the quantitative impact of these differences on the

A B A C U S

TABLE 12

INDEX OF CONSERVATISM – COMPANY PROFILE
Net profit

Company	Index of conservatism		
	Median	Mean	SD
Amcor Limited	0.902	0.897	0.102
Boral Limited	0.990	0.990	0.061
The Broken Hill Proprietary Company Limited	1.069	1.002	0.109
Coles Myer Ltd	1.045	1.045	0.066
CRA Limited	0.990	1.175	0.448
Great Central Mines N.L.	1.000	1.000	0.000
Mayne Nickless Limited	0.876	0.960	0.189
The News Corporation Limited	1.155	1.290	0.459
Orbital Engine Corporation Limited	1.910	1.955	0.591[a]
Pacific Dunlop Limited	0.767	0.651	0.655[a]
Ramtron Holdings Limited	1.231	0.956	0.711
Trans Global Resources N.L.	–0.875	–1.113	2.411
Western Mining Corporation Holdings Limited	0.400	–0.511	1.231

Shareholders' equity

Company	Index of conservatism		
	Median	Mean	SD
Amcor Limited	1.028	1.033	0.005
Boral Limited	1.036	1.015	0.043
The Broken Hill Proprietary Company Limited	1.305	1.510	0.354
Coles Myer Ltd	1.213	1.190	0.038
CRA Limited	1.015	1.018	0.018
Great Central Mines N.L.	1.000	1.000	0.000
Mayne Nickless Limited	1.000	0.992	0.028
The News Corporation Limited	2.358	2.566	0.493
Orbital Engine Corporation Limited	3.045	3.857	1.477[b]
Pacific Dunlop Limited	0.862	0.829	0.097
Ramtron Holdings Limited	5.865	5.200	2.566[a]
Trans Global Resources N.L.	1.000	3.437	3.664
Western Mining Corporation Holdings Limited	0.818	0.824	0.010

[a]One outlier excluded.
[b]Two outliers excluded.

ACCOUNTING PRACTICES: AUSTRALIA V. U.S.A.

measurement of profit and shareholders' equity for Australian companies reporting on Form 20-F to the SEC. The results indicate that, for the sample and time period studied, the hypothesis that U.S. GAAP is more conservative than Australian financial reporting practice is not supported in terms of the impact on profits, but is supported in terms of the impact on shareholders' equity. Important differences were identified in relation to asset valuation, accounting for intangible assets, equity accounting, and elements of cost recognition and taxation. The results demonstrate that the overall quantitative impact is highly material for several of these differences, particularly in individual company cases. However, generalization relating to the impact of different accounting adjustments is difficult due to the varied impact of the adjustments on what is a small sample size.

Other limitations should also be reiterated. The data lack control over basic issues, such as whether companies listed overseas are representative of all quoted companies, industry-specific accounting distortions, and the degree to which the accounting principles applied by the examined companies are typical of Australian practice or reflect a 'typical' economic environment. Furthermore, the narrow window of analysis (at most, nine years) may not allow for the timing differences involved in differing accounting policies to be completely resolved.

The quantitative and qualitative literature now available relating to differences in international financial reporting is, however, sufficient to inform future research addressing related topical issues. These include, for example, the economic consequences of international differences in financial reporting; the extent to which such differences inform capital markets for investment-decision purposes and debt markets for contracting purposes; and the process of international harmonization of accounting standards.

REFERENCES

Australian Accounting Research Foundation, *Towards International Comparability of Financial Reporting*, Australian Accounting Standards Board, 1994.

Brunovs, R., and R. J. Kirsch, 'Goodwill Accounting in Selected Countries and the Harmonization of International Accounting Standards', *Abacus*, September 1991.

Choi, F. D. S., H. Hino, S. K. Min, S. O. Nam, J. Ujiie and A. I. Stonehill, 'Analysing Foreign Financial Statements: The Use and Misuse of International Ratio Analysis', *Journal of International Business Studies*, Spring/Summer 1983.

Choi, F. D. S., and C. Lee, 'Merger Premia and National Differences in Accounting for Goodwill', *Journal of International Financial Management and Accounting*, Vol. 3, No. 3, 1991.

Cooke, T. E., 'The Impact of Accounting Principles on Profits: The U.S. Versus Japan', *Accounting and Business Research*, Vol. 23, No. 92, 1993.

Davidson, S., and J. M. Kohlmeir, 'The Measure of the Impact of Some Foreign Accounting Principles', *Journal of Accounting Research*, Autumn 1966.

Goldberg, S. R., and J. H. Godwin, 'Differences between U.S. and non-U.S. GAAP and the Quality of Earnings', XV Conference of the European Accounting Association, 1992.

Gray, S. J., 'The Impact of Comparative Accounting Differences from a Security-Analysis Perspective: Some European Evidence', *Journal of Accounting Research*, Vol. 18, No. 1, 1980.

Hellman, N., 'A Comparative Analysis of the Impact of Accounting Differences on Profits and Return on Equity – Differences Between Swedish Practice and U.S. GAAP', *The European Accounting Review*, Vol. 2, No. 2, 1993.

A B A C U S

Norton, J. E., 'Comparative Accounting and the Rise to Globalism – the Case of The News Corporation', XVII Conference of the European Accounting Association, 1994.

Rees, W., 'Measuring Conservatism – the Case of Published and DVFA/SG Adjusted Earnings for German Firms', *Working Paper 93/059*, University of Strathclyde Department of Accounting and Finance, 1993.

Simmonds, A., and O. Azières, *Accounting for Europe*, Touche Ross, 1989.

Walton, P., and H. E. Wyman, 'Anglo-American Accounting Differences and Their Effects on the Accounting Measurements of Inter-Listed British Companies', XIII Conference of the European Accounting Association, 1990.

Weetman, P., and S. J. Gray, 'International Financial Analysis and Comparative Corporate Performance: The Impact of U.K. Versus U.S. Accounting Principles on Earnings', *Journal of International Financial Management and Accounting*, Vol. 2, Nos 2, 3, 1990.

———, 'A Comparative International Analysis of the Impact of Accounting Principles on Profits: The U.S.A. Versus the U.K., Sweden and the Netherlands', *Accounting and Business Research*, Vol. 21, No. 84, 1991.

Wines, G., and Ferguson, C., 'An Empirical Investigation of Accounting Methods for Goodwill and Identifiable Intangible Assets: 1985 to 1989', *Abacus*, March 1993.

APPENDIX
REFERENCES TO AUTHORITATIVE LITERATURE

Australia:
  AAS   Australian Accounting Standards
  AASB Australian Accounting Standards Board
USA:
  APB   Opinion of the APB
  ASR   Accounting Series Release (SEC)
  CON   Statement of Financial Accounting Concepts (FASB)
  FAS   Statement of Financial Accounting Standards (issued by the Financial Accounting Standards Board)
  S-X   Regulation S-X (issued by the SEC)

[18]

Journal of Accounting Research
Vol. 37 Supplement 1999
Printed in U.S.A.

International Differences in the Timeliness, Conservatism, and Classification of Earnings

PETER F. POPE* AND MARTIN WALKER†

1. Introduction

In this paper, we analyze differences in the timeliness of income recognition between the U.S. and U.K. *GAAP* financial reporting regimes. Building on previous work in the area we focus on the links between current reported earnings and current and past changes in market value. In the light of Basu [1997] we present a formal model in which the response of reported earnings to changes in market value varies according to whether the value change is good news or bad. This model yields a number of insights with regard to the definition and measurement of earnings conservatism. We also report evidence indicating that controlling for cross-jurisdictional classification differences affects comparisons of earnings timeliness and earnings conservatism; specifically, we find that apparent differences in conservatism between the U.S. and U.K. accounting regimes are sensitive to the inclusion or exclusion of extraordinary items in U.K. accounting earnings.

Recent research documents significant variation in the information content of earnings across international *GAAP* regimes (e.g., Alford et al.

*Lancaster University; †University of Manchester. The research support of the Economic and Social Research Council (award R000237663) is gratefully acknowledged. The authors wish to thank Mary Barth, Sudipta Basu, Peter Joos, Steve Lin, Stuart McLeay, Jim Ohlson, Ken Peasnell, Norman Strong, Shyam Sunder, Eamonn Walsh, and seminar participants at Copenhagen Business School, University College Dublin, and the 1998 Financial Accounting and Auditing Research Conference for helpful comments on earlier drafts.

54   CREDIBLE FINANCIAL REPORTING: 1999

[1993], Amir, Harris, and Venuti [1993], Bandyopadhyay, Hanna, and Richardson [1994], Barth and Clinch [1996], Harris, Lang, and Möller [1994], Jacobson and Aaker [1993], Joos and Lang [1994], and Pope and Rees [1992]). Differences in information content have been associated with institutional and capital market characteristics that might imply differences in fundamental earnings measurement attributes. However, comparative analysis of such attributes is scarce.[1]

Our paper extends and formalizes Basu's [1997] observation that conservative accounting should induce asymmetry in earnings timeliness: "bad news" is reflected in earnings faster than "good news." We introduce a model designed to capture Basu's intuition, and we use this model to develop new measures of earnings conservatism. In addition we present new results on the sensitivity of our parameter estimates to the choice of earnings measure, and the inclusion of proxies for prior period news as explanatory variables in the analysis.

Ball, Kothari, and Robin [1997] (hereafter BKR) extend the Basu [1997] analysis to seven international *GAAP* regimes. They document substantial variation in asymmetric earnings timeliness across regimes and attribute this variation to jurisdiction-specific legal and institutional factors. BKR report that the earnings before extraordinary items of U.K. firms are approximately half as sensitive to the arrival of bad news as are the earnings before extraordinary items of U.S. firms. Given institutional similarities between U.S. and U.K. financial reporting and stock market environments, BKR attribute this result to higher regulatory and litigation costs in the United States. We show that BKR's conclusions about the relative conservatism of U.S. and U.K. *GAAP* are sensitive both to the measurement of conservatism and to the components of earnings examined.

Specifically, we examine both earnings before extraordinary items (ordinary earnings) and earnings after extraordinary items for large samples of U.S. and U.K. listed firms during 1976–96. We show that U.S. *GAAP* earnings, measured both before *and* after extraordinary items, exhibit similar timeliness properties. In contrast, U.K. *GAAP* earnings before extraordinary items are significantly less timely with respect to bad news than earnings after extraordinary items. Our comparative results based on earnings before extraordinary items confirm those of BKR: U.S. *GAAP* earnings are more timely with respect to bad news than U.K. *GAAP* earnings. However, we reach very different conclusions when the comparison is based on earnings after extraordinary items. In this case, U.K. *GAAP* earnings are significantly more timely in the recognition of bad news than U.S. *GAAP* earnings. Our results suggest that U.K. firms *recognize* bad news faster than U.S. firms, but that they *classify* the bad news

---

[1] A notable exception is Alford et al. [1993] who examine *intra*-year timeliness of earnings across various *GAAP* regimes. In contrast, this paper examines timeliness over longer horizons.

differently. This is consistent with the greater latitude in the accounting for extraordinary items under U.K. *GAAP* being used to smooth ordinary earnings, as predicted by Gonedes [1978] and Ronen and Sadan [1981]. We further show that the timeliness of earnings with respect to good news is significantly lower under U.S. *GAAP* than under U.K. *GAAP.*

Prior research by Collins, Kothari, and Rayburn [1987], Collins et al. [1994], Kothari and Sloan [1992], and Kothari and Zimmerman [1995] for the United States, Donnelly and Walker [1995] for the United Kingdom, and Jacobson and Aaker [1993] for Japan suggests that earnings lag returns by up to three years. However, such studies have not considered the links between timeliness and the application of the conservatism principle in income recognition rules. Therefore, we examine the sensitivity of our main results to proxies for three years of prior period news and present new results on the relative speeds with which good news and bad news are reflected in earnings. The findings show that, while our parameter estimates are sensitive to proxies for prior period news, our main qualitative conclusions are not affected. We also find that most, but not all, of the delayed recognition of good news is captured in earnings with a lag of one year.

In section 2, we compare the treatment of extraordinary items under U.S. *GAAP* and U.K. *GAAP.* Section 3 presents a model that captures the intuition underpinning Basu's [1997] empirical tests and serves as a basis for our own empirical analysis. Section 4 explains the research design of the study, describes the data, and reports the main empirical results. Section 5 reports additional findings, including the sensitivity of the main results to the treatment of prior period news. Finally, we present our main conclusions in section 6.

2. *Extraordinary Items under U.S. GAAP and U.K. GAAP*

The development of accounting standards on extraordinary items has followed similar patterns in the U.S. and the U.K., but U.K. practice has tended to lag U.S. practice by about twenty years. The adoption of the all-inclusive income concept (*Accounting Principles Board Opinion No. 9* (*APB No. 9* [1966])) led to most losses in the U.S. being reported in the income statement. Subsequently, growing concern (especially from the SEC) over possible abuse of extraordinary items[2] led to *Reporting the Results of Operations—Reporting the Effects of Disposal of a Segment of a Business, and Extraordinary, Unusual and Infrequently Occurring Events and Transactions* (*APB No. 30* [1973]). This opinion reduced managers' reporting discretion and created a "below-the-line" extraordinary items category to include discontinued operations and other items that are both unusual

---

[2] Elliott and Shaw [1988] discuss the U.S. treatment of extraordinary items. Eskew and Wright [1976] present evidence on the market response to U.S. extraordinary items for the period 1967 to 1975.

56   PETER F. POPE AND MARTIN WALKER

in nature and infrequent in occurrence. Under *APB No. 30* gains and losses on sales of assets were to be reported above the line as part of income from continuing operations.

The development of U.K. *GAAP* with respect to extraordinary items also originated in the 1970s. *Statement of Standard Accounting Practice No. 6 (SSAP No. 6)* was issued in 1974 to eliminate the practice of accounting for extraordinary items and prior year adjustments directly through reserves. *SSAP No. 6* required the separate classification and disclosure of extraordinary items in the income statement,[3] after profit or loss on ordinary activities.[4] However, *SSAP No. 6* was ambiguous about the definition of extraordinary items, leading to inconsistent treatments. In 1986, a revision of *SSAP No. 6* defined extraordinary items as material items deriving from events or transactions outside the ordinary activities of the business and not expected to recur frequently or regularly. It also defined ordinary earnings as relating to activities that are usually, frequently, or regularly undertaken by the company. Items which, though exceptional on account of size or incidence, derived from the ordinary activities of the business were defined as exceptional items, not extraordinary items.

While the recommended treatment of extraordinary items by U.K. *GAAP* and U.S. *GAAP* may appear to have been similar since 1986, there were significant differences in application. Ambiguity and lack of precise guidance in *SSAP No. 6* concerning the definition of extraordinary items results in U.K. companies defining ordinary activities differently from U.S. companies (Pereira, Paterson, and Wilson [1992]).[5] In particular, rationalization, reorganization, and redundancy costs associated with the discontinuance of a business segment could be classified as extraordinary items under *SSAP No. 6*, as could profits and losses on disposals and expropriation of assets and the sale of long-term investments, and provisions for permanent diminution in the value of fixed assets. Under *APB No. 30* such items could not be classified as extraordinary. Further, although *SSAP No. 6* defined extraordinary items as nonrecurring, in practice many firms classified items such as restructuring and termination costs as extraordinary, even though such items do recur.

Financial Reporting Standard No. 3: Reporting Financial Performance superseded *SSAP No. 6 (Revised)* as of June 1993.[6] The motivation for *FRS No. 3* was to address concerns over possible abuse of extraordinary

---

[3] The profit and loss account, in the terminology of U.K. *GAAP.*

[4] The requirements of *SSAP No. 6* were subsequently given statutory backing in the Companies Act of 1981.

[5] In the U.S., *APB No. 30* provides examples of items that would and would not be regarded as extraordinary. U.S. *GAAP* explicitly rules out certain items being treated as extraordinary, where they would commonly have been treated as extraordinary under U.K. *GAAP* before 1993.

[6] Firms with accounting year-ends falling between 29 October 1992 and 21 June 1993 could elect to implement the new standard immediately but were not required to do so.

items. *FRS No. 3* gave greater emphasis to all-inclusive income by requiring the reporting of earnings per share using earnings after extraordinary items,[7] and narrowed the definition of extraordinary items to the point where they were eliminated from the income statements of U.K. firms. In contrast to *APB No. 30*, under *FRS No. 3* all gains and losses on discontinued operations are reported "above-the-line" as *exceptional* items, even if they arise from disposals of entire business segments. *FRS No. 3* also requires separate reporting of the contribution to operating profit of discontinued operations and of new acquisitions, and exceptional items relating to disposals, reorganization, and sales of fixed assets. All of these items could have been classified as extraordinary in the United Kingdom before the implementation of *FRS No. 3*.[8] Thus, since 1993, U.K. *GAAP* has apparently become more restrictive on the use of extraordinary items than U.S. *GAAP*, after two decades of relative permissiveness.

Ball, Kothari, and Robin [1997] argue that the incentives for timely recognition of bad news are weaker in the United Kingdom than in the United States, due to the U.K.'s relatively loose approach to accounting regulation and lower expected litigation costs. However, the relatively permissive and ambiguous definition of extraordinary items under U.K. *GAAP* before 1993 created opportunities for firms to manage ordinary earnings by taking large transitory write-offs, consistent with conservative income recognition, through extraordinary items. One effect of such an earnings classification strategy would be to produce more permanent reported ordinary earnings. In view of the role of ordinary earnings as the basis for calculating reported earnings per share, prior to the implementation of *FRS No. 3*, there would appear to have been strong incentives for firms to exploit the opportunity to classify transitory bad news as extraordinary, where permissible. Thus, we do not see strong reasons for predicting that bad news recognition will be faster in the United States than in the United Kingdom, once extraordinary items are taken into account. However, we do predict that the sensitivity to bad news of earnings after extraordinary items in the U.K. should be significantly higher than the sensitivity to bad news of ordinary earnings. We also predict that ordinary earnings in the United States will display greater sensitivity to bad news than ordinary earnings in the United Kingdom, irrespective of whether the overall degree of conservatism in income recognition is greater under U.S. *GAAP*.

---

[7] This measure of earnings per share is to be reported at least as prominently as any additional earnings per share measures that firms choose to report. According to Holgate and Roberts [1994], 54 of the U.K. top 100 companies disclosed one additional earnings per share number.

[8] *FRS No. 3* also introduced the "Statement of Total Recognized Gains and Losses," reflecting profit and loss for the period together with all other movements on reserves attributable to shareholders.

58   PETER F. POPE AND MARTIN WALKER

3. Modeling Conservative Income Recognition

3.1 THE BASIC MODEL

This section provides a model capturing the intuition behind the Basu [1997] empirical analysis. We assume that stock prices efficiently reflect publicly available, value-relevant information,[9] and define permanent earnings[10] as the perpetuity which, when capitalized at the firm's cost of capital, is consistent with the observed stock price. Permanent earnings (x_t) are defined by the identity:

$$p_t = kx_t \tag{1}$$

where p_t is the stock price at time t and k, the earnings multiple, is the reciprocal of the cost of equity. We further assume that dividends are equal to permanent earnings and that stock price, and hence permanent earnings, follow a random walk:

$$x_t = x_{t-1} + e_t \tag{2}$$

where e_t is the random shock to permanent earnings in period t. For the derivations below, note that equations (1) and (2) together imply:

$$\frac{e_t}{p_{t-1}} = \frac{1}{k}\left(\frac{p_t}{p_{t-1}} - 1\right). \tag{3}$$

We assume that reported earnings (X_t) are related to permanent earnings as follows:

$$X_t = x_t - \theta_0 e_t^+ + \gamma_0 e_t^- + V_t \tag{4}$$

where θ_0 is a parameter capturing under-recognition of good news in period t (i.e., $e^+ > 0$, $e^- = 0$), γ_0 reflects the over-recognition of period t bad news (i.e., $e^+ = 0$, $e^- < 0$), and $V_t = V_t(e_{t-\tau}^+, e_{t-\tau}^-; \forall \tau = 1, \ldots, T)$ represents the effects of prior period news on current period earnings. If wealth shocks are assumed to show up in earnings eventually, but contemporaneous reported earnings and permanent earnings differ, current earnings will also reflect prior period "accounting errors."

Equation (4) allows for two sources of deviation between reported earnings and permanent earnings. If the permanent earning shock is positive (i.e., if there is good news so that $e_t = e_t^+ > 0$), recognition of a proportion, θ_0, of the shock is delayed under conservative accounting. If the period t permanent earnings shock is negative (i.e., if there is bad

---

[9] We make no assumptions about the source of information used by the market. However, to the extent that reported earnings are used, we assume that allowance is made for lack of timeliness and for the relatively more timely reporting of bad news due to conservative accounting.

[10] The permanent earnings concept is consistent with the Hicks [1946] Income Concept No. 2.

news so that $e_t = e_t^- < 0$), a multiple, $\gamma_0 + 1$, of the shock is recognized in current period reported earnings. If $\gamma_0 > 0$, income recognition is conservative and reported earnings are less than permanent earnings. In the limit, if $\gamma_0 = k - 1$, the entire capitalized value of the permanent earnings shock is written off immediately against current period earnings. An unbiased, and perfectly timely, *GAAP* regime would be one in which θ_0 and γ_0 are both equal to zero.

The final term in equation (4), V_t, reflects the effects of prior period news on current period income recognition. V_t captures the multiperiod effects of delayed recognition and any reversal of accelerated recognition of bad news in earnings under conservative accounting.[11] Consistent with Basu [1997], we assume initially that the effects of prior period news on current period income are uncorrelated with the current period shock. A priori, this assumption seems reasonable since current shocks to permanent earnings are, by definition, uncorrelated with the prior period shocks.[12]

In order to apply equation (4) in empirical analysis, we first deflate all components by beginning-of-period price, and using equation (1) we obtain:

$$\frac{X_t}{P_{t-1}} = \frac{1}{k}\frac{P_t}{P_{t-1}} - \frac{\theta_0 e_t^+}{P_{t-1}} + \frac{\gamma_0 e_t^-}{P_{t-1}} + \frac{V_t}{P_{t-1}}. \tag{5}$$

Defining $R_t = (p_t/p_{t-1}) - 1$, equations (5) and (3) give:

$$\frac{X_t}{P_{t-1}} = \frac{1}{k} + \frac{1-\theta_0}{k} R_t + \frac{V_t}{P_{t-1}} \qquad \text{if } R_t \geq 0 \tag{6'}$$

and:

$$\frac{X_t}{P_{t-1}} = \frac{1}{k} + \frac{1+\gamma_0}{k} R_t + \frac{V_t}{P_{t-1}} \qquad \text{if } R_t \leq 0. \tag{6''}$$

---

[11] However, value changes may take several years to flow through the income statement. Also, if the firm's cash flows are independent of the cost of capital, changes in firm value associated with shifts in the discount rate will not flow through earnings. Finally, we should note that, relative to U.S. earnings, earnings in the U.K. tend to be higher because firms involved in takeover activity typically write off goodwill on acquisitions against reserves. This practice could induce a higher intercept in our model, but the slope parameters should not be materially affected.

[12] Basu [1997] suggests that, on average, V_t should be positive because of conservatism. This is correct with regard to the delayed reporting of good news. It is also correct with regard to the accelerated write-off of bad news, provided that the write-off is executed in a single period. In general, however, firms may write off bad news over more than one period, and so it is logically possible for V_t to be negative in some periods. In our empirical tests we attempt to decompose V_t to gain further insights into the timeliness of reported earnings.

60   PETER F. POPE AND MARTIN WALKER

For estimation purposes expressions (6') and (6″) can be combined by introducing a dummy variable, D_t, defined to have a value of one if R_t is less than zero, and zero otherwise, as follows:

$$\frac{X_t}{P_{t-1}} = \frac{1}{k} + \frac{1-\theta_0}{k} R_t + \frac{\gamma_0+\theta_0}{k} R_t D_t + \frac{V_t}{P_{t-1}}. \qquad (7)$$

Equation (7) can be used to interpret the main regression model estimated by Basu [1997], i.e.:

$$\frac{X_t}{P_{t-1}} = \alpha_1 + \alpha_2 D_t + \beta_1 R_t + \beta_2 R_t D_t + u_t \qquad (8)$$

where α_1, α_2, β_1, and β_2 are regression coefficients and u_t is the mean zero regression error. If equation (8) is estimated as a cross-sectional regression, comparison with equation (7) indicates that:

$$E(\alpha_1) = \frac{1}{k} + E\left(\frac{V_t}{P_{t-1}}\right) \qquad E(\alpha_2) = 0$$

$$E(\beta_1) = \frac{1-\theta_0}{k} \qquad E(\beta_2) = \frac{\gamma_0+\theta_0}{k}.$$

The coefficient β_1 reflects the responsiveness of earnings to contemporaneous good news, as indicated by positive returns. If good news is fully recognized without a lag, β_1 equals the cost of equity, $1/k$. If recognition of good news is partially deferred, β_1 is predicted to be positive but lower than the cost of equity. Given the cost of equity, we can estimate the proportion of good news not recognized in current period earnings as $\theta_0 = 1 - k\hat{\beta}_1$.

The sum of the coefficients β_1 and β_2 captures the responsiveness of earnings to contemporaneous bad news, as indicated by negative returns. Conservative accounting implies $\beta_2 > 0$. Again, given the cost of equity, we can estimate the parameter reflecting the speed of recognition of current period bad news as $\gamma_0 = k(\hat{\beta}_1 + \hat{\beta}_2) - 1$.[13]

3.2 MEASURING CONSERVATISM

This model yields the conservatism measures summarized in figure 1. Basu [1997] uses the related measures $C1$ and $C2$. $C1$ is the ratio of the sensitivities of deflated earnings to bad news (the numerator) and good

---

[13] In common with Basu [1997], we have made no attempt to correct for the potential simultaneity bias examined by Beaver, McAnally, and Stinson [1997]. The extension of our model to incorporate this possibility would be extremely complex, given the nonlinear nature of the main empirical relation. The work of Beaver, McAnally, and Stinson [1997] indicates that the parameter values tend to increase when one models earnings changes and returns in a simultaneous equations framework. However, we have no reason to expect such an extension to alter the main conclusions of this paper relating to the relative timeliness of earnings with respect to good and bad news.

INTERNATIONAL DIFFERENCES IN EARNINGS   61

---

1. Ratio of Bad/Good News Regression Model Slope Parameters

$$C1 \ = \ \frac{(1+\gamma_0)}{(1-\theta_0)}$$

2. Ratio of Adjusted R^2 Statistics for Bad/Good News Regression Models

$$C2 \ = \ \frac{R^2(Bad\ News)}{R^2(Good\ News)}$$

3. Sensitivity to Bad News less Sensitivity to Good News

Either: $$C3a \ = \ \frac{\gamma_0+\theta_0}{k}$$

Or: $$C3b \ = \ \gamma_0 + \theta_0$$

4. Sensitivity to Bad News

Either: $$C4a \ = \ \frac{1+\gamma_0}{k}$$

Or: $$C4b \ = \ 1 + \gamma_0$$

5. Average Earnings/(Lagged Price) Bias

$$C5(Total) \ = \ \frac{\theta_0}{k}\ E(R|Good)P(Good) \ - \ \frac{\gamma_0}{k}\ E(R|Bad)P(Bad)$$

$$C5(Good) \ = \ \frac{\theta_0}{k}\ E(R|Good)P(Good)$$

$$C5(Bad) \ = \ \frac{\gamma_0}{k}\ E(R|Bad)P(Bad)$$

FIG. 1.—Measures of conservatism. All conservatism measures except $C2$ are based on regression equation (7) as follows:

$$\frac{X_t}{P_{t-1}} \ = \ \frac{1}{k} + \frac{1-\theta_0}{k}\ R_t + \frac{\gamma_0+\theta_0}{k}\ R_t D_t + \frac{V_t}{P_{t-1}}$$

where $1/k$ is the cost of equity, θ_0 is the parameter capturing under-recognition of good news in contemporaneous earnings, and γ_0 is the parameter capturing over-recognition of bad news in contemporaneous earnings.

For measure $C2$: R^2 ($Good$) is the adjusted R^2 statistic of the good news regression (6′) as follows:

$$\frac{X_t}{P_{t-1}} \ = \ \frac{1}{k} + \frac{1-\theta_0}{k}\ R_t + \frac{V_t}{P_{t-1}} \qquad \text{if } R_t \geq 0.$$

R^2 (Bad) is the adjusted R^2 statistic of the bad news regression (6″) as follows:

$$\frac{X_t}{P_{t-1}} \ = \ \frac{1}{k} + \frac{1-\gamma_0}{k}\ R_t + \frac{V_t}{P_{t-1}} \qquad \text{if } R_t \leq 0.$$

For measures $C5$: $E(R|Good)$ is mean return in good news company-years, $E(R|Bad)$ is mean return in bad news company-years, $P(Good)$ is the sample proportion of good news company-years, and $P(Bad)$ is the sample proportion of bad news company-years.

62   PETER F. POPE AND MARTIN WALKER

news (the denominator). $C2$ is the ratio of the explanatory power of returns for deflated earnings in bad news company-years, relative to the explanatory power of returns for deflated earnings in good news company-years. The properties of least squares regression imply that:

$$R^2(Bad) = \left(\frac{1 + \gamma_0}{k}\right)^2 \mathrm{var}(R|Bad) \Big/ \mathrm{var}(X_t/P_{t-1}|Bad)$$

and:

$$R^2(Good) = \left(\frac{1 - \theta_0}{k}\right)^2 \mathrm{var}(R|Good) \Big/ \mathrm{var}(X_t/P_{t-1}|Good) .$$

It follows that:

$$\frac{C2}{C1^2} = \frac{\mathrm{var}(R|Bad)}{\mathrm{var}(X_t/P_{t-1}|Bad)} \Big/ \frac{\mathrm{var}(R|Good)}{\mathrm{var}(X_t/P_{t-1}|Good)} .$$

If earnings are more sensitive to bad news than good news, then $C2$ will typically be less than $C1^2$ because the ratio of the variance of returns to the variance of deflated earnings is greater for good news firm-years than it is for bad news firm-years.

Conservatism measures $C1$ and $C2$ are independent of $1/k$, so they can be compared across different *GAAP* regimes. However, the measures also produce extreme values when the proportion of contemporaneous good news reflected in earnings is low (i.e,. θ_0 is close to one). All accounting regimes with values of θ_0 equal to one will be judged equally conservative regardless of the responsiveness of earnings to bad news. Our results indicate that the U.S. accounting regime has, indeed, moved close to this extreme possibility in recent years.

Ball, Kothari, and Robin [1997] focus their discussion on measures $C1$, $C2$, and $C3$, paying close attention to $C3a$, which measures the difference between sensitivities of earnings to, respectively, bad news and good news.[14] They present evidence that $C3a$ is systematically greater in common law *GAAP* regimes than in code law *GAAP* regimes, consistent with income recognition rules in common law regimes being directed primarily toward incorporation of bad news. However, $C3a$ will not necessarily yield reliable inferences about the speed of recognition of bad news across *GAAP* regimes. For example, a *GAAP* regime might have $\theta_0 > 0$ and $\gamma_0 = 0$, implying a positive value for $C3a$, even though the accounting for bad news is unbiased. In addition, $C3a$ is potentially sensitive to the value

---

[14] Basu [1997] bases several of his formal hypothesis tests on $C3$.

of k. Given a country-specific estimate for k, measure $C3b$ would seem to be a more appropriate basis for cross-country comparisons.

If BKR are correct in their conjecture that the distinguishing feature of common law *GAAP* regimes is the treatment of bad news, then measure $C4b$, which captures bad news sensitivity after controlling for potential differences in k, may be an appropriate measure on which to base international comparisons. However, $C4b$ requires a precise estimate of k, so $C4a$ may be a more practical alternative.

An alternative approach to measuring conservatism is to estimate the average effect of asymmetric timeliness on the ratio of reported earnings to lagged stock price. Measures $C5(Total)$, $C5(Good)$, and $C5(Bad)$ capture this idea. Measure $C5(Total)$ calculates the combined effect of delayed recognition of good news and accelerated recognition of bad news. Measures $C5(Good)$ and $C5(Bad)$ show the separate effects of the good news and bad news biases respectively. The calculation of all three measures requires an estimate of k.

Under certain conditions, measure $C5(Total)$ will be directly related to the parameters of our model. Specifically, measure $C5(Total)$ will be equivalent to $E(V_t)/p_{t-1}$ in a long-run stationary state in which all firms live forever, no new firms are created, and the cost of equity is constant (or at least fluctuates around a long-run constant value). Given these conditions, the equivalence $C5(Total)$ to $E(V_t)/p_{t-1}$ should produce a superior estimate of $1/k$.[15]

In summary, each of the conservatism measures summarized in figure 1 has some limitation in making international comparisons across *GAAP* regimes. Measures $C1$ and $C2$ can produce extreme values. Moreover, if good news and bad news biases in fact reflect different features of the financial reporting system, then these aggregate measures should be supplemented by separate measures capturing bad news and good news effects.[16] Measures $C3$ to $C5$ provide separate estimates of good and bad news bias, but all require a cost of capital estimate.

3.3. SENSITIVITY OF MODEL COEFFICIENTS TO PROXIES FOR PRIOR PERIOD SHOCKS

Equation (7) contains the unobservable term V_t/p_{t-1}. Following Basu [1997], one could argue that *OLS* estimation of equation (7), treating V_t/p_{t-1} as part of the error term, should produce unbiased estimates because V_t is a function of prior period stock returns and current period returns are unlikely to be correlated with prior period returns. While we employ this assumption in our main analysis, we also present sensitivity results in

---

[15] Recall from equation (8) that $E(\alpha_1) = 1/k + E(V_t)/p_{t-1}$. Of course, these ideal conditions do not hold, but we would nevertheless expect use of this equivalence to produce a less biased estimate of $1/k$ than the value of α_1 generated by estimating equation (8).

[16] BKR [1997] and Basu [1997] both contain brief discussions of good news conservatism but it is not a prominent topic in either paper.

which we include lagged stock price changes, deflated by p_{t-1}, as proxies for V_t/p_{t-1}.[17] We estimate the following augmented regression:

$$\frac{X_t}{P_{t-1}} = \alpha_1 + \alpha_2 D_t + \beta_1 R_t + \beta_2 R_t D_t + \sum_{\tau=1}^{3} \lambda_\tau R_{t-\tau}$$

$$+ \sum_{\tau=1}^{3} \delta_\tau R_{t-\tau} D_{t-\tau} + u_t \qquad (9)$$

where $R_{t-\tau} = \dfrac{(p_{t-\tau} - p_{t-\tau-1})}{p_{t-1}}$ and $\alpha_1, \alpha_2, \beta_1, \beta_2, \lambda_\tau$ ($\tau = 1, \ldots ,3$), and δ_τ ($\tau = 1, \ldots ,3$) are regression coefficients, and $D_{t-\tau}$ is the bad news dummy for year $t - \tau$.[18]

3.4 THE RECOGNITION OF PRIOR PERIOD NEWS IN EARNINGS

While equation (7) provides a basis for analyzing the relation between current period earnings and current period shocks, it sheds no light on the speed with which *prior* period news is recognized in earnings. Since conservative accounting is expected to delay the recognition of good news, this issue is of specific interest in making *GAAP* regime comparisons.

Previous research has suggested that share prices anticipate earnings up to three years ahead. To represent this idea we rewrite equation (4) as follows:

$$X_t = x_{t-4} + \sum_{\tau=0}^{3} (1 - \theta_\tau) e_{t-\tau}^+ + \sum_{\tau=0}^{3} (1 + \gamma_\tau) e_{t-\tau}^- + V_{t/t-4}. \qquad (10)$$

In this model $V_{t/t-4}$ represents the component of V_t associated with shocks in years prior to $t - 4$. As before, we can move to an empirical version of this model by deflating (10) by the stock price at time $t - 4$, as follows:

$$\frac{X_t}{P_{t-4}} = \alpha_1 + \alpha_2 D_t + \sum_{\tau=0}^{3} \omega_\tau R_{t-\tau} + \sum_{\tau=0}^{3} \rho_\tau R_{t-\tau} D_{t-\tau} + u_t \qquad (11)$$

where $R_{t-\tau} = \dfrac{(p_{t-\tau} - p_{t-\tau-1})}{p_{t-4}}$ and ω_τ ($\tau - 0, \ldots ,3$) and ρ_τ ($\tau = 0, \ldots ,3$) are regression coefficients, and $D_{t-\tau}$ is the bad news dummy variable for year $t - \tau$. It can be shown that $k\omega_\tau$ captures the proportion of the period $t - \tau$ permanent earnings shock recognized in period t earn-

---

[17] Recall that, by definition, $e_{t-\tau} = \frac{1}{k}(p_{t-\tau} - p_{t-\tau-1})$.

[18] Basu [1997, p. 15] notes that his main results were insensitive to a similar (unreported) specification check involving lagged returns. Equation (9) uses lagged price differences scaled by p_{t-1} rather than lagged returns to maintain consistency with our theoretical model. We limit the number of lags to three years because of survivorship considerations. Previous research, such as Kothari and Sloan [1992], has found no evidence of share price anticipation earlier than three years ahead.

ings when there is good news in period $t - \tau$. Similarly, when there is bad news in period $t - \tau$, a multiple, $k(\omega_\tau + \rho_\tau)$, of the shock is reflected in period t earnings. If income recognition is unbiased and reported earnings equal permanent income, $k\omega_\tau = 1$ and $k\rho_\tau = 0$ for all values of τ. Deferred recognition of good news will reduce $k\omega_\tau$ below 1.0 for $\tau = 0$, increasing toward 1.0 as τ increases. Accelerated recognition of bad news implies $k\rho_\tau > 0$ for $\tau = 0$, and $k\rho_\tau$ will tend toward zero as τ increases.

4. Empirical Tests and Main Findings

4.1 RESEARCH DESIGN

We estimate the relative conservatism of ordinary earnings and earnings after extraordinary items, using equation (8). If extraordinary items are used to eliminate bad news from ordinary earnings, then earnings after extraordinary items should appear more sensitive to bad news. We assess differences in conservatism for similar earnings measures across *GAAP* regimes by analyzing comparable panels of data for the United States and the United Kingdom. We examine the conservatism measures presented in figure 1 for similar earnings measures across the two panels.

To enhance comparability with Basu [1997], we present pooled results. However, we also report annual cross-section results and base inferences on the time-series average values of the estimated parameters. Given the large sample sizes, it is reasonable to assume that annual cross-section parameter values will be approximately normally distributed. Further, since we use nonoverlapping data, the estimated parameters are independent across years, so inferences based on annual regressions are likely to have a higher degree of statistical integrity than inferences based on pooled regressions.

As we discussed earlier, *FRS No. 3* effectively eliminated extraordinary items in the United Kingdom from 1993 onward. U.K. firms are no longer required to publish any ordinary earnings per share number on a standardized basis. Therefore, our U.S. and U.K. *GAAP* comparisons report subperiod results for 1976–92 when appropriate. However, we examine estimates of ordinary earnings that would have been reported in the post-1992 period had *FRS No. 3* not been introduced. Estimated ordinary earnings are based on the approach recommended by the Institute of Investment Management and Research [1993] and used by investment analysts and by many companies reporting supplementary earnings per share numbers.[19]

4.2 DATA

The data are for all December fiscal year-end nonfinancial firms listed in the U.S. (*NYSE/AMEX*) and U.K. (London Stock Exchange) during

---

[19] Other companies report earnings per share numbers using earnings definitions similar, but not identical, to *IIMR*.

66   PETER F. POPE AND MARTIN WALKER

1976–96. Data for the U.S. sample for the period 1976 to 1992 (1993 to 1997) are from the active and research files of the 1993 (1997) version of *Compustat PC Plus*. For the U.S. sample, the relevant variables are defined as follows: *ORD*—earnings per share before extraordinary items and discontinued operations (*Compustat* item *EPSPX*); *EXT*—earnings per share after extraordinary items and discontinued operations (*Compustat* item *EPSPI*); *PRI*—fiscal year-end stock price (*Compustat* item *PRCCF*).

Data for the U.K. are from *Datastream*.[20] For the U.K. sample, the relevant variables are defined as follows: *ORD*—ordinary earnings per share (*Datastream* item #182 divided by the number of outstanding shares); *EXT*—ordinary earnings per share plus (after tax) extraordinary items per share, (*Datastream* item #182 plus item #193 divided by the number of outstanding shares); *PRI*—fiscal year-end stock price.

For the 1993–96 period, we use detailed information reported by U.K. firms under *FRS No. 3* to construct our own estimate of the *IIMR* earnings per share. We use this estimate as the proxy for ordinary earnings per share (*ORD*) for the last four years of the U.K. sample period. Earnings per share after extraordinary items (*EXT*) for this period are defined as the difference between *FRS No. 3* reported earnings per share and *IIMR* earnings per share.[21]

In both samples, extraordinary items (*EI*) are defined as $EXT - ORD$, and returns (*RET*) are defined as $(PRI_t - PRI_{t-1})/PRI_{t-1}$. All earnings variables used in the regression tests are deflated by lagged stock price. To control for the effects of outliers, we delete from each annual cross-section the top and bottom 1% of observations based on *RET*, *ORD*, and *EI*. Visual inspection of the data after this procedure revealed no further obvious outliers in the U.S. data. Four additional observations were deleted from the 1993 to 1996 U.K. sample.[22]

4.3 THE MAGNITUDE OF ORDINARY EARNINGS AND EXTRAORDINARY ITEMS

Figure 2 shows annual means of ordinary earnings (deflated by market value). U.K. ordinary earnings exceed U.S. ordinary earnings in 14 of the 21 sample years. The only interval in which U.K. earnings are materially lower than U.S. earnings is during the U.K. recession of 1980 to 1982. Figure 3 shows the annual mean values of extraordinary items (deflated by market value). On average, U.K. firms reported relatively large negative extraordinary items over the sample period, compared with their

---

[20] To ensure that the U.K. panel does not suffer from survivorship bias, the population of all listed U.K. firms was identified from the *London Share Price Database*. Data for 1993 onward were obtained using the *Datastream* current and dead company equity lists. *Datastream* identifies accounting line items by numeric codes. Share prices in *Datastream* are stored in a separate part of the database accessed by running a *Datastream* program.

[21] All per share data were adjusted for stock splits and other capital changes.

[22] Each of the four observations had a value of deflated ordinary earnings greater than 200%.

INTERNATIONAL DIFFERENCES IN EARNINGS   67

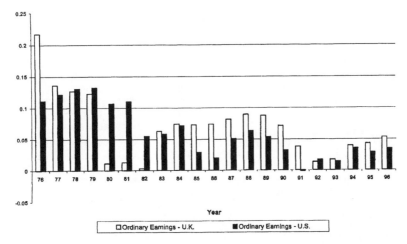

FIG. 2.—Average annual scaled ordinary earnings under U.S. and U.K. *GAAP*, 1976–96. Ordinary earnings are defined as earnings before extraordinary items scaled by market value at the end of the relevant fiscal year. The figure shows the average value of scaled ordinary earnings in each country for each year in the period 1976–96.

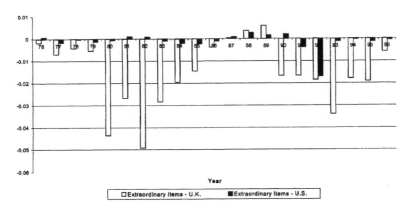

FIG. 3.—Average annual scaled extraordinary items under U.S. and U.K. *GAAP*, 1976–96. Extraordinary items are scaled by market value at the end of the relevant fiscal year. The figure shows the average value of scaled extraordinary items in each country for each year in the period 1976–96.

68   PETER F. POPE AND MARTIN WALKER

TABLE 1
Descriptive Statistics for U.S. and U.K. Samples, 1976–96

	Mean	SD	Min.	Q1	Median	Q3	Max.
Panel A: U.S. Sample (*n* = 18,380)							
ORD	0.068	0.129	−2.000	0.042	0.078	0.123	0.640
EXT	0.068	0.137	−2.000	0.040	0.079	0.125	0.819
EI	−0.001	0.035	−0.763	0.000	0.000	0.000	0.665
R	0.140	0.392	−0.875	−0.098	0.088	0.301	4.165
D	0.373	0.484	0	0	0	1	1
Panel B: U.K. Sample (*n* = 7,189)							
ORD	0.089	0.129	−1.311	0.054	0.088	0.137	1.178
EXT	0.077	0.158	−1.570	0.044	0.084	0.136	1.238
EI	−0.012	0.077	−1.290	−0.009	0.000	0.000	1.205
R	0.164	0.465	−0.856	−0.121	0.087	0.357	5.403
D	0.376	0.484	0	0	0	1	1

Variables are defined as follows: *ORD* is earnings before extraordinary items, *EXT* is earnings after extraordinary items, *EI* is extraordinary items, *R* is the price relative over the fiscal year minus one, and *D* is a dummy variable having a value of one if $R < 0$, and zero otherwise. All earnings variables are scaled by opening market value.

U.S. counterparts. For the U.K. (U.S.) the mean value of annual average extraordinary earnings is −1.6% (−0.1%). In all but three years, average extraordinary items in the U.K. are negative and greater in magnitude than extraordinary items in the U.S. The differences are especially marked for the recessions in the early 1980s and the early 1990s.

Table 1 reports descriptive statistics. The distributions of returns are similar in the two panels and in both cases just over 37% of returns are negative. While the mean value of ordinary earnings (*ORD*) is almost 30% higher in the U.K. than in the U.S., the mean values of earnings before and after extraordinary items (*EXT*) are much closer, reflecting the higher negative average value of U.K. extraordinary items. These results are consistent with the processes determining extraordinary items being substantially different in the two countries.

4.4 POOLED REGRESSION RESULTS: CONTEMPORANEOUS NEWS

Table 2 reports the pooled regression estimates of equation (8) for the entire sample period 1976–96, and for the subperiods 1976–92 and 1993–96 corresponding, respectively, to the periods before and after *FRS No. 3*. The reported regressions are based on reported earnings and raw returns. Further analysis (unreported) based on market-adjusted earnings and market-adjusted returns led to qualitatively similar results.[23] The main parameters of interest, β_1 and β_2, are consistently significant at

---

[23] As expected, the estimated values of the intercepts fell in the market-adjusted regressions, but the main relationships between the slope parameters were unaffected. The market-adjusted analysis provides a useful robustness check because it can be argued that market-adjusted returns may provide a more reliable indicator of good versus bad news. To explore this possibility further will require extending the model to distinguish the share price and accounting effects of market-wide and firm-specific shocks.

INTERNATIONAL DIFFERENCES IN EARNINGS   69

TABLE 2

Pooled Sample Regression Results for Tests of Asymmetric Timeliness of Earnings Pre- and Post-Extraordinary Items with Respect to Contemporaneous Information

Dependent Variable	α_1	α_2	β_1	β_2	Adj. R^2 (%)
1976–92					
U.S.					
ORD	0.093	0.008	0.033	0.308	12.9
	(49.58)	(2.34)	(8.49)	(26.09)	
EXT	0.092	0.007	0.039	0.302	11.8
	(45.48)	(2.030)	(9.30)	(23.84)	
U.K.					
ORD	0.092	0.008	0.103	0.141	19.3
	(32.17)	(1.49)	(20.26)	(8.58)	
EXT	0.086	0.008	0.098	0.201	16.4
	(24.83)	(1.29)	(16.07)	(10.15)	
1993–96					
U.S.					
ORD	0.052	0.000	0.010	0.199	7.2
	(19.57)	(–0.05)	(1.92)	(11.71)	
EXT	0.049	0.002	0.014	0.193	6.6
	(17.97)	(0.340)	(2.57)	(10.97)	
U.K.					
ORD	0.059	0.020	0.036	0.219	15.7
	(16.10)	(2.76)	(6.41)	(9.72)	
EXT	0.054	0.031	0.034	0.358	13.4
	(9.67)	(2.83)	(3.97)	(10.44)	
1976–96					
U.S.					
ORD	0.083	0.005	0.026	0.282	11.2
	(52.91)	(1.73)	(8.07)	(28.35)	
EXT	0.082	0.005	0.031	0.276	10.4
	(48.66)	(1.66)	(9.10)	(26.06)	
U.K.					
ORD	0.087	0.008	0.081	0.165	17.2
	(36.43)	(1.89)	(19.81)	(11.82)	
EXT	0.081	0.011	0.077	0.242	14.8
	(27.19)	(2.03)	(15.19)	(13.94)	

The pooled regression is of the form $\dfrac{X_t}{P_{t-1}} = \alpha_1 + \alpha_2\,D_t + \beta_1\,R_t + \beta_2 R_t D_t + u_t$, where X_t is earnings in year t and p_{t-1} is stock price at the end of year $t-1$. In panel A, $R_t = (p_t/\,p_{t-1} - 1)$ and D_t is a dummy variable taking a value of one if $R_t < 0$, and zero otherwise. t-statistics are in parentheses.

the 1% level with the predicted sign, and β_1 is consistently higher in the U.K. than in the U.S.. This provides an initial indication that U.K. earnings recognize a higher proportion of contemporaneous good news than U.S. earnings. The results also indicate that the sensitivity of earnings to bad news $(\beta_1 + \beta_2)$ is dependent on the definition of the earnings measure in the U.K. but not in the U.S.[24] Specifically, the bad news sensitivity

---

[24] This result appears to conflict with Basu [1997, p. 19], most likely because Basu's sample includes 1963–75. As discussed above, *APB No. 30* was implemented in 1974. We expect

70   PETER F. POPE AND MARTIN WALKER

of ordinary earnings is 0.308 in the U.S., compared to 0.246 in the U.K., but for earnings after extraordinary items the U.S. sensitivity is 0.307, compared to 0.319 in the U.K.. The R^2 statistics also show that ordinary earnings are more closely associated with returns than earnings after extraordinary items, reflecting the transitory nature of extraordinary items.

4.5 ANNUAL REGRESSION RESULTS: 1976 TO 1992

Table 3 summarizes the annual regression results for both samples. The mean value of the good news parameter (β_1) is 0.042 (0.053) for the *ORD (EXT)* regressions, both significant at the 0.01 level. The corresponding mean values of the bad news parameter ($\beta_1 + \beta_2$) are consistently higher, being 0.317 (0.319) for *ORD (EXT)*, with both significant at the 0.01 level. Similar analysis for the U.K. reveals a mean value of the good news parameter of 0.082 (0.082) for the *ORD (EXT)* regressions, with both significant at the 0.01 level. The corresponding estimates for the bad news parameter are 0.282 (0.382) for *ORD (EXT)*, with both significant at the 0.01 level. Again, these results are consistent with differences in the speed of recognition of good and bad news between the two earnings measures and across *GAAP* regimes. We quantify these differences in relation to the measures of conservatism in more detail in section 4.7.

We argued above that one would expect the increase in β_2 between *ORD* and *EXT* to be greater in the United Kingdom than in the United States. We used the annual regression estimates to test whether the increase in the mean value of the β_2 parameter between the *ORD* and *EXT* regressions conducted on the U.K. sample is greater than the increase in the mean value of β_2 for the U.S. regressions. The *t*-test of the null hypothesis that the increase in the U.K. was the same as in the U.S. was rejected at the 0.01 level.

4.6 ANNUAL REGRESSION RESULTS: 1993–96

Because we estimate ordinary earnings for the U.K. sample in the period after *FRS No. 3* was implemented, the results for U.K. ordinary earnings after 1993 are not directly comparable with the results for the previous 17 years. For the sake of completeness, and in order to gain some impression of trends in the post-*FRS No. 3* U.K. *GAAP* regime, we therefore consider the subperiod 1993–96 separately in table 3.

For the U.S., the β_2 parameter has remained significantly positive at the 0.01 level under both *ORD* and *EXT*, while the good news parameter estimate, β_1, has been very low. Furthermore, our annual results from

---

the classification of earnings in the U.S. in the period before 1974 to be similar to the U.K. in our sample period. In particular, we would expect earnings before extraordinary items to be less sensitive to bad news for this earlier period of the Basu [1997] sample.

INTERNATIONAL DIFFERENCES IN EARNINGS   71

TABLE 3

Annual Cross-Section Regression Estimates of Tests of Asymmetric Timeliness of Earnings Pre- and Post-Extraordinary Items with Respect to Contemporaneous Information

Dependent Variable	α_1	α_2	β_1	β_2	Adj. R^2 (%)
1976–92					
U.S.					
ORD	0.098	−0.006	0.042	0.275	17.8
	(9.80)	(0.92)	(3.95)	(9.07)	
EXT	0.097	−0.006	0.053	0.266	17.6
	(9.13)	(0.91)	(4.45)	(8.66)	
U.K.					
ORD	0.097	−0.002	0.082	0.200	22.01
	(8.19)	(0.38)	(6.70)	(6.97)	
EXT	0.090	0.000	0.082	0.300	19.79
	(6.71)	(0.01)	(6.01)	(6.17)	
1993–96					
U.S.					
ORD	0.052	−0.003	0.008	0.218	8.48
	(8.21)	(0.79)	(1.27)	(15.33)	
EXT	0.050	−0.002	0.009	0.212	8.00
	(6.75)	(0.48)	(1.00)	(11.43)	
U.K.					
ORD	0.059	0.017	0.038	0.241	20.05
	(5.46)	(3.82)	(4.90)	(5.62)	
EXT	0.052	0.034	0.040	0.449	19.35
	(4.59)	(1.96)	(5.54)	(2.67)	
1976–96					
U.S.					
ORD	0.089	−0.005	0.036	0.264	16.02
	(9.82)	(1.02)	(3.89)	(10.54)	
EXT	0.088	−0.005	0.044	0.255	15.78
	(9.21)	(0.97)	(4.26)	(10.08)	
U.K.					
ORD	0.090	0.001	0.073	0.208	21.64
	(8.72)	(0.30)	(6.91)	(8.49)	
EXT	0.082	0.007	0.074	0.329	19.71
	(7.23)	(0.95)	(6.34)	(6.56)	

For each separate sample, results are reported for two dependent variables, *ORD* and *EXT*. For the U.S. sample, *ORD* represents ordinary earnings scaled by price at the start of the year and *EXT* represents earnings after extraordinary items and discontinued operations scaled by price at the start of the year. For the U.K. sample, *ORD* represents ordinary earnings scaled by price at the start of the year (for 1993–96 ordinary earnings are defined as "headline" earnings) and *EXT* represents earnings after extraordinary items and discontinued operations scaled by price at the start of the year. For 1993–96, extraordinary earnings are defined as *FRS No. 3* reported earnings per share minus ordinary earnings per share.

The annual regressions are of the form: $\dfrac{X_{it}}{P_{it-1}} = \alpha_{1t} + \alpha_{2t} D_{it} + \beta_{1t} R_{it} + \beta_{2t} R_{it} D_{it} + u_{it}$, where X_t is earnings in year t, p_{t-1} is stock price at the end of year $t-1$, R_t is the price relative for period t, i.e., $R_t = (p_t/p_{t-1}) - 1$, and D_t is a dummy variable taking a value of one if $R_t < 0$, and zero otherwise. The average parameter values are the simple unweighted means for the respective periods. Values in parentheses are Z-statistics.

1988 onward (not reported) suggest that the reporting delay for good news has actually increased, extending the apparent trend of reduced sensitivity of earnings to good news first reported by Basu [1997] for the late 1980s. The 1993–96 results for the U.K. indicate that β_2 has remained significantly positive at the 0.01 level under the post-*FRS No. 3* regime, and that the β_2 parameter for *ORD* has remained lower than the β_2 parameter for *EXT.* It is too early to tell whether the post-*FRS No. 3* U.K. *GAAP* regime is more or less conservative than the previous regime.

4.7 COMPARATIVE MEASURES OF CONSERVATISM

In table 4 we report the various measures of conservatism defined in figure 1. The reported measures are based on the regression results summarized in tables 2 and 3 above, and on supplementary regressions based on equations (6′) and (6″) for subsamples of good news company-years and bad news company-years. The first entry in each cell of table 4 is the relevant conservatism measure derived from the average parameter values of the annual regression results for 1976–96, as summarized in table 3. The second entry, in parentheses, is based on the pooled regression parameter estimates reported in table 2 (1976–96). The "revised" estimates for measures *C3B*, *C4B*, and *C5* are calculated by assuming that the pooled estimate of α_1 is equal to $1/k + E(V_t)/p_{t-1}$, i.e., that all deviations of reported earnings from permanent income eventually reverse.

For the annual regressions, conservatism measures *C1* and *C2* indicate that the responsiveness of earnings to bad news relative to the responsiveness to good news was greater for the United States compared to the United Kingdom, consistent with the original findings of Basu [1997] and BKR [1997]. The measure *C3A*, the incremental bad news responsiveness measure emphasized by BKR, indicates that U.S. ordinary earnings were materially more conservative than U.K. ordinary earnings. However, using the same measure, earnings after extraordinary items were more conservative under U.K. *GAAP* than under U.S. *GAAP.* Similarly, measures *C4* and *C5(Bad)*, which focus on bad news responsiveness, indicate that U.S. ordinary earnings were more conservative than U.K. ordinary earnings. Again, the ranking of relative conservatism reverses for each measure when earnings after extraordinary items are considered: U.K. *GAAP* earnings after extraordinary items were more conservative than under U.S. *GAAP.*

Measure *C5* reflects the average effect of conservatism on the earnings-to-(lagged)-price ratios (a typical earnings-to-price ratio is of the order 0.08). Thus, a *C5* measure of 0.01 implies, approximately, that the earnings-to-price ratio is depressed by about 12.5%. The results for *C5(Total)* indicate that earnings under U.S. *GAAP* were more conservative than earnings under U.K. *GAAP*, both for ordinary earnings and earnings after extraordinary items. The measure of overall conservatism *C5(Total)* divides between conservatism due to low good news responsiveness, *C5(Good)*, and conservatism due to high bad news responsiveness, *C5(Bad)*. The results indicate that a major difference between U.S.

TABLE 4

Comparative Analysis of Conservatism Measures

Conservatism Measure	U.S.		U.K.	
	ORD	*EXT*	*ORD*	*EXT*
C1	8.33	6.81	3.85	5.45
	(11.83)	(9.91)	(3.04)	(4.15)
C2	4.03	3.17	1.71	2.12
	(19.00)	(14.37)	(1.29)	(2.02)
C3A	0.26	0.26	0.21	0.33
	(0.28)	(0.28)	(0.17)	(0.24)
C3B	3.04	3.00	2.30	3.84
	(3.17)	(3.14)	(1.83)	(2.95)
C3B(*revised*)	4.18	4.03	2.71	5.16
	(4.45)	(4.37)	(2.15)	(3.80)
C4A	0.30	0.30	0.28	0.40
	(0.31)	(0.31)	(0.25)	(0.32)
C4B	3.46	3.52	3.10	4.70
	(3.46)	(3.49)	(2.73)	(3.89)
C4B(*revised*)	4.75	4.74	3.66	6.31
	(4.87)	(4.86)	(3.21)	(5.01)
C5(*Total*)	0.024	0.022	0.013	0.019
	(0.029)	(0.028)	(0.015)	(0.021)
C5(*Total*)(*revised*)	0.021	0.020	0.013	0.018
	(0.026)	(0.025)	(0.013)	(0.018)
C5(*Good*)	0.010	0.008	0.000	−0.001
	(0.013)	(0.012)	(0.002)	(0.001)
C5(*Good*)(*revised*)	0.005	0.004	−0.001	−0.005
	(0.008)	(0.007)	(−0.001)	(−0.003)
C5(*Bad*)	0.014	0.014	0.013	0.020
	(0.016)	(0.016)	(0.013)	(0.020)
C5(*Bad*)(*revised*)	0.016	0.016	0.015	0.022
	(0.018)	(0.018)	(0.014)	(0.021)

(*i*) See figure 1 for definitions of the conservatism measures listed in column 1.

(*ii*) In columns 2 to 4 the first entry in each cell is the average value of the conservatism measure derived from the annual regressions from 1976 to 1996. The second entry in each cell (in parentheses) is the estimate derived from the 1976 to 1996 pooled regression.

(*iii*) Measures indicated as (*revised*) are calculated under the assumption that, on average, all deviations from permanent earnings fully reverse. To implement this idea using the parameter estimates from the pooled regression, we assume that the intercept from the pooled regression equals $1/k + C5(Total)$ (*revised*). This allows one to establish a set of three independent equations involving three unknowns ($1/k$, θ, γ) and three regression parameters. To derive the year-by-year (revised) conservatism measures we use the estimated value of $1/k$ from the pooled regression as the "cost of capital."

(*iv*) The C2 measure for the annual estimates is calculated as the cross-year average value of the adjusted R^2 statistics of the bad news regressions divided by the average of the adjusted R^2 statistics of the good news regressions.

GAAP and U.K. *GAAP* is the very low responsiveness of U.S. earnings to current period good news. For example, the C5(*Total*) measure for U.S. ordinary earnings, derived from the annual estimates, is the sum of two components: 0.014 due to bad news conservatism, i.e., C5(*Bad*), and 0.010 due to good news conservatism, i.e., C5(*Good*). For U.K. ordinary earnings, the entire value of 0.013 for $C5(Total)$ is attributable to bad news conservatism.

The entries in parentheses in table 4 report the values of the different conservatism measures derived from the pooled regression estimates. Results are qualitatively similar to those for the annual estimates. In particular, measures $C1$, $C2$, and $C3$ suggest a higher level of conservatism in the U.S. for both ordinary earnings and earnings after extraordinary items. They also confirm that earnings after extraordinary items were more conservative than ordinary earnings under U.K. *GAAP*. Measures $C4$ and $C5(Bad)$ again confirm that earnings after extraordinary items were more timely with respect to the recognition of bad news under U.K. *GAAP* than under U.S. *GAAP*. Again, although overall conservatism as measured by $C5(Total)$ is higher in the U.S., the difference across *GAAP* regimes is due to relatively slow recognition of good news under U.S. *GAAP*.

Table 4 also contains "revised" estimates for measures $C3B$, $C4B$, and $C5$, based on the assumption that all deviations from permanent earnings fully reverse.[25] It is interesting to note that measures $C3B$ and $C4B$ appear to be sensitive to the method of calculation, i.e., the revised values are materially larger than the original values. Measures $C5$, however, appear to be fairly robust to the method of calculation.

In summary, the results indicate that, over the sample period, the U.K. *GAAP* regime was ultra-conservative in the recognition of bad news. However, this property only becomes evident once extraordinary items are taken into consideration. With respect to good news, U.K. *GAAP* earnings were essentially unbiased. In contrast, earnings reported under the U.S. *GAAP* regime were conservative with respect to the recognition of both bad news and good news. While an explanation for these international differences in conservatism properties is beyond the scope of this paper, the results serve to demonstrate the importance of distinguishing between speeds of recognition of good news and bad news, and of allowing for the effects of classification differences, when making cross-regime comparisons.

5. Additional Findings and Sensitivity Analyses

5.1 SPECIAL ITEMS AND EXCEPTIONAL ITEMS

U.S. ordinary earnings are reported after accounting for special items. Supplementary analysis reveals that the pooled sample average value of special items per share scaled by stock price, for U.S. firms, was −0.007 and the standard deviation was 0.070.[26] Estimates of the pooled regression model, based on earnings before special items and extraordinary items, yielded similar results to those for ordinary earnings, except that

---

[25] The calculation is based on the following three equations: $\alpha_1 = \{(\theta_0/k)E(R|G)P(G) - (\gamma_0/k)E(R|B)P(B)\}$, $\beta_1 = (1 - \theta_0)/k$, and $\beta_2 = (1 + \gamma_0)/k$.

[26] Calculated after removing one obvious outlier from the original data set.

the estimated incremental bad news slope coefficient was 0.234, compared to value of 0.282 obtained from the ordinary earnings regression.[27] Annual cross-section regressions based on earnings before special items yielded results similar to those reported for ordinary earnings, except that the average incremental bad news slope coefficient was significantly lower (0.233 compared to 0.264).[28]

The annual descriptive statistics for special items suggest that U.S. *GAAP* could have changed in recent years. The value of special items per share as a proportion of stock price increased from an average value of −0.002 during 1976–89 to −0.014 during 1990–96. Annual regression results indicate that the difference between β_2 measured using ordinary earnings and β_2 measured using earnings before special and extraordinary items also increased from 0.018 pre-1989 to 0.056 in 1990 to 1996. Unfortunately we do not have enough annual cross-sections to assess the statistical significance of this increase.

Prior to 1993, U.K. ordinary earnings were reported after accounting for exceptional items. For the 1976 to 1992 sample period, the pooled average value of exceptional items scaled by stock price was −0.015 and the standard deviation was 0.084.[29] Pooled regression estimates based on earnings before exceptional and extraordinary items for 1976 to 1992 yielded similar results to those reported for ordinary earnings, except that the bad news slope coefficient was 0.088, compared to 0.141 for ordinary earnings. Annual cross-section regression estimates based on earnings before exceptional and extraordinary items yielded similar results to those reported in table 3 for ordinary earnings, except that the average incremental bad news slope coefficient was lower (0.168 compared to 0.200). These results indicate that U.K. earnings before exceptional items were slightly less conservative than ordinary earnings pre-*FRS No. 3*.

5.2 SENSITIVITY OF THE MAIN RESULTS TO PRIOR PERIOD NEWS

Interpretation of the results reported in tables 2, 3, and 4 depends on the assumed independence of V_t, the component of reported earnings associated with prior period shocks, and the current period shock. Violation of this assumption could lead to coefficient bias and incorrect inferences regarding the sensitivity of earnings to current period shocks. To test the robustness of our earlier results to the independence assumption, we estimate equation (9) based on pooled and annual regressions. We also estimate different versions of equation (9) to quantify the incremental explanatory power of returns for earnings when we allow for asymmetry with respect to contemporaneous and prior period shocks. In

---

[27] Special items in the U.S. and exceptional items in the U.K. are both reported on a pretax basis. Strictly, these items should be adjusted at the effective marginal tax rate for each firm. The results in this subsection should be interpreted with this caveat in mind.

[28] Basu [1997] reports a similar result for special items. Elliott and Hanna [1996] also find that the incidence of special items is materially greater after 1988.

[29] Calculated after removing three exceptional item outliers from the original data set.

model 1 we examine the bivariate relation between earnings in t and returns in t, with no control for asymmetry or prior period shocks. In model 2 we allow for contemporaneous asymmetry by including the contemporaneous slope dummy for bad news in t.[30] In model 3 we include three years of scaled lagged price changes, but we do not control for asymmetry in the response of earnings to good and bad news. Finally, in model 4 we include three years of lagged price changes and we do control for asymmetric responses. Table 5 contains the results for the pooled regressions and summary results from the annual regressions.

The results for model 1 show that the ability of returns in t to explain earnings in t is rather weak, in both *GAAP* regimes. The pooled R^2 statistic for U.K. ordinary earnings of 13.3% is almost double the corresponding U.S. value of 6.8%, and the U.K. contemporaneous slope parameters are also higher, consistent with prior research indicating stronger contemporaneous association between earnings and returns in the U.K. The results for earnings after extraordinary items are almost identical to those for ordinary earnings for the U.S., but there is a reduction in the R^2 statistic for the U.K. to 10.5%. The difference between the results for ordinary earnings and earnings after extraordinary items under U.K. *GAAP* is consistent with our earlier results, suggesting that the process determining extraordinary items is significantly different for the U.K.

The results for model 2 are consistent with those reported earlier in tables 2 and 3. In particular, the incremental bad news slope dummy is consistently positive and significant at the 0.01 level or better. Also, the bad news slope dummy increases materially between the *ORD* and the *EXT* regressions in the U.K. sample but not in the U.S. sample. These results confirm that asymmetry in the sensitivity of earnings to contemporaneous good and bad news is an important feature of both U.S. and U.K. *GAAP*.

The results for model 3 show the effect of including prior period returns in the model, without any distinction between the responsiveness of earnings to prior period good and bad news. These findings are consistent with prior research on stock price anticipation of earnings (see, e.g., Kothari and Sloan [1992] for the U.S. and Donnelly and Walker [1995] for the U.K.), suggesting that returns lead earnings overall. Relative to the benchmark model 1, allowing for the effects of lagged shocks on current period earnings increases the explanatory power of the pooled regressions. For example, based on earnings before extraordinary items, the regression adjusted R^2 statistic increases from 6.8% to 20.1% (13.3% to 19.8%) for the U.S. (U.K.). The R^2 statistics for the annual regressions also increase, on average, although the increases are not as large as those reported for the pooled regressions.

---

[30] The results for model 2 in table 5 are not identical to those reported in table 2 because the sample is required to have survived for four years, allowing comparability across models.

TABLE 5
Tests of Asymmetric Timeliness with Respect to Contemporaneous
News: Sensitivity to Prior Period Information

	α_1	α_2	β_1	β_2	λ_1	λ_2	λ_3	δ_1	δ_2	δ_3	Adj. R^2
Panel A: U.S. Data 1979 to 1996—Earnings before Extraordinary Items (ORD) (n = 12,785)											
Model 1 Pooled	0.055 (53.87)		0.083 (30.54)								0.068
Annual	0.062 (6.05)		0.102 (8.19)								0.113
Model 2 Pooled	0.078 (47.71)	0.005 (1.81)	0.026 (6.90)	0.269 (24.07)							0.117
Annual	0.084 (8.97)	0.001 (0.17)	0.034 (5.06)	0.293 (16.74)							0.167
Model 3 Pooled	0.049 (51.03)		0.088 (35.15)		0.098 (37.37)	0.063 (24.85)	0.037 (16.09)				0.201
Annual	0.062 (6.85)		0.101 (9.49)		0.068 (6.01)	0.038 (3.65)	0.025 (3.14)				0.224
Model 4 Pooled	0.093 (47.22)	0.005 (1.80)	0.047 (13.58)	0.202 (19.42)	-0.002 (0.33)	0.007 (1.28)	0.011 (2.23)	0.116 (14.07)	0.071 (8.94)	0.033 (4.70)	0.260
Annual	0.089 (9.71)	0.002 (0.43)	0.051 (7.04)	0.227 (13.37)	0.009 (0.69)	0.021 (1.55)	0.015 (1.18)	0.090 (5.44)	0.027 (1.86)	0.017 (0.89)	0.275
Panel B: U.K. Data 1979 to 1996—Earnings before Extraordinary Items (ORD) (n = 4,447)											
Model 1 Pooled	0.061 (37.72)		0.097 (26.16)								0.133
Annual	0.063 (9.17)		0.106 (11.05)								0.179

continued overleaf

TABLE 5 – *continued*

		α_1	α_2	β_1	β_2	λ_1	λ_2	λ_3	δ_1	δ_2	δ_3	Adj. R^2
Model 2	Pooled	0.081 (30.58)	0.005 (1.12)	0.058 (11.22)	0.197 (12.11)							0.167
	Annual	0.080 (11.32)	0.004 (0.98)	0.061 (8.11)	0.212 (7.81)							0.215
Model 3	Pooled	0.059 (37.02)		0.100 (27.77)		0.048 (12.62)	0.035 (10.47)	0.007 (2.78)				0.198
	Annual	0.064 (12.15)		0.105 (10.90)		0.039 (3.84)	0.027 (2.75)	0.006 (0.85)				0.237
Model 4	Pooled	0.075 (20.21)	0.004 (0.94)	0.072 (14.08)	0.147 (9.10)	0.020 (2.05)	0.041 (4.71)	0.009 (1.18)	0.036 (2.83)	-0.015 (1.37)	-0.005 (0.55)	0.217
	Annual	0.082 (11.08)	0.006 (1.33)	0.070 (6.28)	0.177 (7.55)	-0.001 (-0.10)	0.006 (0.41)	0.011 (1.45)	0.058 (7.55)	0.026 (2.19)	-0.044 (0.74)	0.285

Panel C: U.S. Data 1979 to 1996—Earnings after Extraordinary Items (*EXT*) ($n = 12{,}785$)

		α_1	α_2	β_1	β_2	λ_1	λ_2	λ_3	Adj. R^2
Model 1	Pooled	0.053 (49.02)		0.086 (30.06)					0.066
	Annual	0.060 (5.54)		0.108 (8.25)					0.115
Model 2	Pooled	0.076 (43.54)	0.005 (1.59)	0.030 (7.59)	0.263 (22.20)				0.108
	Annual	0.081 (8.18)	0.000 (0.05)	0.041 (5.00)	0.284 (16.04)				0.163
Model 3	Pooled	0.047 (45.76)		0.092 (84.38)		0.099 (35.45)	0.066 (24.60)	0.039 (16.13)	0.191
	Annual	0.060 (6.27)		0.106 (9.59)		0.069 (6.30)	0.036 (3.41)	0.026 (3.28)	0.215

		α_1	α_2	β_1	β_2	λ_1	λ_2	λ_3	δ_1	δ_2	δ_3	R^2
Model 4	Pooled	0.090 (42.59)	0.005 (1.56)	0.052 (13.90)	0.197 (17.62)	0.002 (0.29)	0.011 (1.88)	0.013 (2.45)	0.112 (12.66)	0.069 (8.19)	0.034 (4.50)	0.241
	Annual	0.085 (8.51)	0.001 (0.28)	0.058 (6.84)	0.220 (11.96)	0.015 (1.13)	0.028 (1.90)	0.018 (1.52)	0.085 (5.19)	0.015 (1.02)	0.014 (0.78)	0.260

Panel D: U.K. Data 1979 to 1996—Earnings after Extraordinary Items (EXT) (n = 4,447)

		α_1	α_2	β_1	β_2	λ_1	λ_2	λ_3	δ_1	δ_2	δ_3	R^2
Model 1	Pooled	0.045 (21.47)		0.111 (22.87)								0.105
	Annual	0.049 (5.12)		0.124 (8.89)								0.145
Model 2	Pooled	0.072 (21.09)	0.011 (1.74)	0.055 (8.32)	0.287 (13.62)							0.148
	Annual	0.071 (7.51)	0.011 (1.32)	0.065 (6.23)	0.314 (6.80)							0.191
Model 3	Pooled	0.042 (20.97)		0.114 (24.62)		0.077 (15.67)	0.043 (10.06)	0.008 (2.53)				0.187
	Annual	0.047 (5.93)		0.124 (9.18)		0.068 (4.84)	0.040 (3.79)	0.016 (1.64)				0.210
Model 4	Pooled	0.059 (12.32)	0.101 (1.61)	0.076 (11.59)	0.218 (10.55)	0.040 (3.12)	0.070 (6.19)	0.031 (3.02)	0.056 (3.45)	-0.042 (2.95)	-0.030 (2.51)	0.124
	Annual	0.068 (6.07)	0.012 (1.51)	0.076 (5.63)	0.266 (6.89)	0.017 (1.02)	0.029 (1.78)	0.041 (2.74)	0.083 (2.93)	0.028 (0.92)	-0.063 (-1.77)	0.260

Regressions are based on the following general model:

$$\frac{X_t}{P_{t-1}} = \alpha_1 + \alpha_2 D_t + \beta_1 R_t + \beta_2 R_t D_t + \sum_{\tau=1}^{3} \lambda_\tau R_{t-\tau} + \sum_{\tau=1}^{3} \delta_\tau R_{t-\tau} D_{t-\tau} + u_t$$

where X_t is earnings in year t, P_{t-1} is stock price at the end of year $t-1$, $R_{t-\tau} = \dfrac{(P_{t-\tau} - P_{t-\tau-1})}{P_{t-1}}$, D_t is a dummy variable taking a value of one if $R_t < 0$, and zero otherwise, and α_1, α_2, β_1, β_2, λ_τ ($\tau = 1, \ldots, 3$), and δ_τ ($\tau = 1, \ldots, 3$) are regression parameters. t-statistics are in parentheses.

80   PETER F. POPE AND MARTIN WALKER

The results for model 4 indicate that our main results are robust to the inclusion of prior period shocks. In all cases, earnings are more responsive to contemporaneous bad news than to good news and, for the U.K., earnings after extraordinary items are more responsive than ordinary earnings. The increase in the pooled β_2 parameter from 0.139 to 0.201 shows that the U.K. continues to exhibit greater responsiveness to contemporaneous bad news due to recognition of bad news through extraordinary items.

A comparison of models 4 and 2 indicates that the parameter estimates may be sensitive to the treatment of prior period news. In particular, the good news slope parameter for both countries is considerably higher under model 4 than under model 2, and the magnitude of the bad news slope dummy falls in all regressions when prior period news is incorporated. These results cast some doubt on the assumption underlying Basu [1997] and the earlier results in this paper that the components of earnings associated with prior period shocks are independent of the current period shock. In particular, the parameter δ_1, which captures the effect of bad news with a one-year lag, is consistently significant at the 0.01 level or better in all cases. Moreover, this is the only parameter associated with prior period shocks that is consistently significant in the annual regressions. Since we believe that the annual results provide the more reliable basis for statistical inference, we conclude that the independence assumption appears reasonable, except for bad news arising in year $t - 1$.[31]

5.3 RESPONSIVENESS OF EARNINGS TO PERIOR PERIOD NEWS

The results reported so far have indicated a substantial degree of deferred reporting of good news in reported earnings, especially under U.S. *GAAP.* In this section we assess the speed with which good news is eventually reflected in reported earnings, based on estimates of equation (11).

Table 6 reports the results of annual estimates of equation (11), along with the pooled results for 1979 to 1996. Our model predicts that the good news slope parameters ($\omega_0, \ldots, \omega_3$) should increase toward $1/k$ as the lag increases, and that the bad news incremental slope parameters ($\rho_0, \ldots, \rho_3$) should decrease toward zero as the lag increases. The results in table 6 are broadly consistent with these predictions, especially the average results from the annual regressions. In particular, the good news parameter increases sharply from lag zero to lag one, consistent with most of the good news being reflected in earnings with a lag of one

---

[31] The results in table 5 are based on a sample selected on the basis that returns are observable for each of four consecutive years and that earnings are also observable for the final year. It is possible that coefficient bias might arise as a result of the selection criteria, if the probability of inclusion in the sample is associated with the independent variables in equation (9) (see, e.g., Greene [1993, chap. 22]).

TABLE 6

Annual Cross-Section Regression Results for Tests of Asymmetric Timeliness of Earnings Pre- and Post-Extraordinary Items with Respect to Contemporaneous and Prior Period Information

	α_1	α_2	ω_0	ω_1	ω_2	ω_3	ρ_0	ρ_1	ρ_2	ρ_3	Adj. R^2
Panel A: U.S. Data 1979 to 1996—Earnings before Extraordinary Items (ORD)											
1979	0.136	-0.001	0.025	0.126	0.023	0.281	0.260	0.007	0.132	-0.242	0.476
1980	0.166	-0.006	0.013	0.071	0.077	0.083	0.217	0.105	0.093	0.118	0.401
1981	0.197	-0.029	0.022	0.071	0.016	0.135	0.041	0.102	0.269	0.019	0.373
1982	0.131	-0.059	0.016	0.090	0.112	0.005	0.060	0.002	-0.014	0.143	0.266
1983	0.119	0.018	0.054	0.088	-0.017	0.074	0.225	0.124	0.172	-0.001	0.464
1984	0.145	-0.033	0.062	0.109	0.088	0.051	0.063	0.145	0.118	0.135	0.602
1985	0.086	-0.025	0.031	0.065	0.129	0.111	0.293	0.165	-0.040	0.028	0.497
1986	0.073	-0.042	0.036	0.074	0.134	0.094	0.167	0.097	-0.005	-0.012	0.523
1987	0.082	0.072	0.003	0.129	0.088	0.103	0.403	-0.041	0.107	0.045	0.445
1988	0.100	-0.028	0.056	0.135	0.096	0.061	0.128	0.005	-0.015	0.199	0.413
1989	0.090	-0.033	-0.008	0.080	0.181	0.100	0.179	0.247	-0.095	-0.022	0.396
1990	0.095	-0.010	-0.055	0.067	0.112	0.117	0.219	0.149	0.048	0.012	0.297
1991	0.075	-0.061	0.027	0.005	0.095	0.034	0.169	0.138	0.022	0.080	0.345
1992	0.075	-0.017	0.032	0.047	0.032	0.065	0.120	0.091	0.132	0.005	0.396
1993	0.069	-0.016	0.026	0.060	0.061	-0.048	0.067	0.095	0.088	0.173	0.347
1994	0.070	-0.001	0.041	0.068	0.056	0.087	0.062	0.044	0.137	0.024	0.419
1995	0.077	-0.036	0.007	0.045	0.114	0.069	0.140	0.116	-0.005	0.061	0.263
1996	0.071	-0.007	0.035	0.038	0.047	0.070	0.060	0.104	0.066	0.052	0.336
Annual	0.103	-0.017	0.023	0.076	0.080	0.083	0.160	0.094	0.067	0.045	0.403
	(11.64)	(2.46)	(3.71)	(9.63)	(6.97)	(5.39)	(6.91)	(5.74)	(3.21)	(1.98)	
Pooled	0.102	-0.023	0.026	0.071	0.087	0.088	0.098	0.092	0.084	0.062	0.353
	(52.53)	(8.50)	(11.69)	(26.60)	(25.69)	(21.78)	(16.06)	(13.34)	(9.69)	(5.68)	
Panel B: U.K. Data 1979 to 1996—Earnings before Extraordinary Items (ORD)											
1979	0.157	-0.071	-0.019	0.173	0.220	0.076	0.254	0.130	-0.808	-0.035	0.511
1980	0.141	-0.071	0.026	0.121	0.006	0.173	0.196	0.166	0.312	-0.522	0.336
1981	0.099	-0.046	0.113	-0.006	0.079	0.138	0.074	0.245	0.137	-0.148	0.352

continued overleaf

TABLE 6 – *continued*

	α_1	α_2	ω_0	ω_1	ω_2	ω_3	ρ_0	ρ_1	ρ_2	ρ_3	Adj. R^2
1982	0.105	-0.070	0.006	0.161	0.014	0.085	0.101	-0.121	0.190	0.061	0.404
1983	0.114	-0.051	0.009	0.052	0.181	0.040	0.083	0.121	-0.134	0.059	0.486
1984	0.128	-0.053	0.066	0.043	0.045	0.135	0.066	0.127	0.091	-0.028	0.429
1985	0.120	-0.021	0.045	0.047	0.054	0.088	0.096	0.108	0.007	-0.031	0.466
1986	0.088	0.014	0.081	0.038	0.097	0.095	0.245	0.149	-0.073	-0.014	0.699
1987	0.084	-0.034	0.017	0.120	0.132	0.101	0.147	-0.341	-0.051	-0.055	0.682
1988	0.104	0.013	0.050	0.071	0.171	0.053	0.151	0.105	0.105	0.138	0.754
1989	0.113	-0.027	0.032	0.066	0.083	0.149	0.043	0.146	0.166	0.102	0.574
1990	0.111	-0.014	-0.039	0.031	0.080	0.108	0.101	0.110	0.107	-0.106	0.375
1991	0.088	-0.008	0.065	-0.059	0.070	0.042	0.057	0.164	0.057	0.082	0.603
1992	0.079	-0.024	0.042	0.061	0.027	0.051	0.006	0.049	0.058	0.017	0.654
1993	0.048	0.000	0.052	0.066	0.071	0.032	0.113	-0.013	-0.024	0.033	0.717
1994	0.059	-0.003	0.025	0.089	0.090	0.058	0.071	-0.052	-0.004	-0.005	0.645
1995	0.074	-0.019	0.019	0.089	0.093	0.080	0.065	0.007	0.004	-0.014	0.638
1996	0.068	-0.001	0.011	0.041	0.133	0.115	0.150	0.113	-0.048	-0.100	0.587
Annual	0.099	-0.027	0.033	0.067	0.091	0.090	0.112	0.067	0.005	-0.032	0.551
	(14.75)	(4.10)	(3.94)	(5.13)	(6.72)	(9.35)	(7.09)	(2.13)	(0.10)	(0.93)	
Pooled	0.106	-0.022	0.025	0.085	0.121	0.084	0.142	0.091	0.004	0.011	0.474
	(26.80)	(4.07)	(7.53)	(18.97)	(23.60)	(14.03)	(12.90)	(6.85)	(0.24)	(0.60)	
Panel C: U.S. Data 1979 to 1996—Earnings after Extraordinary Items (*EXT*)											
1979	0.139	-0.003	0.031	0.121	0.020	0.278	0.257	0.019	0.141	-0.280	0.477
1980	0.165	-0.007	0.012	0.075	0.080	0.085	0.230	0.105	0.084	0.111	0.395
1981	0.199	-0.032	0.026	0.071	0.023	0.140	0.041	0.118	0.256	0.003	0.357
1982	0.130	-0.057	0.012	0.095	0.116	-0.001	0.071	-0.008	-0.041	0.143	0.256
1983	0.111	0.023	0.059	0.095	-0.003	0.073	0.240	0.116	0.152	-0.018	0.488
1984	0.140	-0.034	0.066	0.111	0.093	0.062	0.063	0.139	0.072	0.132	0.563

Year											
1985	0.080	-0.036	0.033	0.056	0.140	0.116	0.276	0.188	-0.072	0.013	0.496
1986	0.071	-0.040	0.054	0.079	0.145	0.081	0.151	0.086	-0.012	0.010	0.473
1987	0.083	0.071	0.011	0.136	0.093	0.096	0.400	-0.040	0.067	0.051	0.426
1988	0.104	-0.028	0.070	0.123	0.079	0.077	0.109	0.021	0.007	0.145	0.356
1989	0.092	-0.030	-0.005	0.085	0.177	0.099	0.183	0.242	-0.085	-0.026	0.386
1990	0.094	-0.009	-0.058	0.074	0.118	0.113	0.226	0.140	0.035	0.015	0.297
1991	0.070	-0.065	0.028	0.007	0.099	0.031	0.164	0.134	0.006	0.075	0.323
1992	0.048	-0.015	0.038	0.053	0.059	0.064	0.118	0.074	0.094	0.011	0.278
1993	0.064	-0.014	0.026	0.049	0.061	-0.044	0.059	0.096	0.063	0.179	0.274
1994	0.070	-0.001	0.042	0.067	0.056	0.093	0.059	0.053	0.147	0.019	0.419
1995	0.075	-0.039	0.007	0.050	0.113	0.070	0.145	0.108	-0.002	0.056	0.264
1996	0.071	-0.007	0.039	0.040	0.035	0.066	0.052	0.099	0.076	0.070	0.332
Annual	0.100	-0.018	0.027	0.077	0.084	0.083	0.158	0.094	0.055	0.039	0.381
	(10.68)	(2.47)	(3.89)	(9.95)	(7.41)	(5.45)	(6.81)	(5.84)	(2.70)	(1.66)	
Pooled	0.101	-0.023	0.023	0.073	0.088	0.089	0.096	0.091	0.088	0.066	0.338
	(48.95)	(8.23)	(11.99)	(25.63)	(24.53)	(20.75)	(14.92)	(12.51)	(9.63)	(5.69)	

Panel D: U.K. Data 1979 to 1996—Earnings after Extraordinary Items (*EXT*)

Year											
1979	0.160	-0.069	-0.023	0.178	0.210	0.110	0.286	0.098	-0.597	-0.026	0.481
1980	0.138	-0.112	0.015	0.161	0.020	0.177	0.276	0.120	0.394	-0.338	0.314
1981	0.092	-0.065	0.110	0.003	0.018	0.166	0.148	0.206	0.255	-0.219	0.304
1982	0.087	-0.085	-0.003	0.155	0.038	0.149	0.142	-0.027	0.166	0.008	0.374
1983	0.089	-0.047	-0.005	0.076	0.132	0.030	0.077	0.173	-0.099	0.010	0.290
1984	0.098	-0.059	0.089	0.040	0.042	0.112	0.062	0.171	0.090	-0.017	0.325
1985	0.117	-0.018	0.051	0.049	0.041	0.058	0.122	0.120	0.002	0.047	0.384
1986	0.083	-0.021	0.086	0.011	0.091	0.120	0.139	0.231	-0.027	-0.178	0.513
1987	0.081	-0.050	0.017	0.120	0.120	0.150	0.201	-0.404	-0.053	-0.068	0.557
1988	0.112	0.024	0.050	0.080	0.181	0.017	0.173	0.109	0.105	0.213	0.695
1989	0.120	-0.056	-0.014	0.036	0.135	0.265	0.173	0.300	0.119	-0.159	0.416
1990	0.111	-0.008	-0.039	0.054	0.091	0.080	0.127	0.116	0.068	-0.054	0.333

continued overleaf

TABLE 6 – *continued*

	α_1	α_2	ω_0	ω_1	ω_2	ω_3	ρ_0	ρ_1	ρ_2	ρ_3	Adj. R^2
1991	**0.080**	0.001	**0.064**	-0.073	**0.086**	0.040	**0.086**	**0.201**	0.026	0.075	0.545
1992	**0.073**	-0.023	**0.043**	**0.072**	0.056	**0.042**	0.035	0.023	0.030	0.018	0.607
1993	**0.047**	-0.002	**0.056**	**0.071**	**0.073**	0.038	0.187	0.002	-0.004	0.037	0.557
1994	0.015	0.028	0.044	**0.114**	**0.110**	**0.060**	**0.098**	-0.040	-0.041	-0.014	0.428
1995	**0.067**	-0.034	0.015	**0.116**	**0.104**	**0.073**	0.064	-0.016	-0.026	0.015	0.530
1996	**0.061**	0.007	0.004	**0.039**	**0.165**	**0.119**	**0.202**	**0.163**	-0.079	-0.108	0.571
Annual	0.091	-0.033	0.031	0.072	0.095	0.100	0.144	0.086	0.018	-0.042	0.457
	(11.42)	(3.64)	(3.19)	(4.93)	(7.31)	(6.62)	(8.74)	(2.35)	(0.40)	(1.44)	
Pooled	0.100	-0.025	0.022	0.087	0.128	0.086	0.180	0.117	0.006	0.021	0.397
	(52.53)	(-8.50)	(11.69)	(26.60)	(25.69)	(21.78)	(16.06)	(13.34)	(9.69)	(5.68)	

Regressions are based on the following general model:

$$\frac{X_t}{P_{t-4}} = \alpha_{1t} + \alpha_{2t}D_t + \beta_{1t}R_t + \beta_{2t}R_tD_t + \sum_{\tau=1}^{3}\omega_{t}R_{t-\tau} + \sum_{\tau=1}^{3}\rho_{t}R_{t-\tau}D_{t-\tau} + u_t$$

where X_t is earnings in year t, P_{t-4} is stock price at the end of year $t-4$, $R_{t-\tau} = \dfrac{(P_{t-\tau} - P_{t-\tau-1})}{P_{t-1}}$, D_t is a dummy variable taking a value of one if $R_t < 0$, and zero otherwise; and u_t, α_{2t}, β_{1t}, β_{2t}, ω_{t} ($\tau = 1, \ldots, 3$), and ρ_{t} ($\tau = 1, \ldots, 3$) are regression parameters. Annual regression parameter estimates shown in boldface are significant at the 5% level.

year. As predicted, the incremental slope parameters for bad news decrease with the size of the lag, and the bad news parameter is not significantly different from zero at lag three in the average annual results. However, the contemporaneous incremental bad news parameters are materially lower than those reported in our main results, perhaps because the results are sensitive to the precise way in which the earnings dynamics related to prior period shocks are represented.[32]

6. Conclusions

This study compares conservatism of two measures of reported earnings across the U.S. and U.K. accounting regimes. Write-offs of large transitory losses through extraordinary items were tolerated, if not encouraged, in the United Kingdom before the introduction of *FRS No. 3* in 1993. In the United States, many such items would have been classified as components of ordinary earnings. Our results suggest that the incentives facing U.K. firms to classify bad news earnings components as extraordinary items were strong over the sample period. As a result, inferences regarding the relative conservatism of the U.S. and U.K. *GAAP* regimes are sensitive to the earnings measure analyzed.

Our model of earnings timeliness provides a formal representation of the differential speeds of recognition of good news and bad news, and suggests several ways of measuring conservatism in income recognition. In particular, the analysis suggests that when evaluating comparative conservatism, it is important to capture two distinct properties of conservative accounting: delays in reporting good news and early recognition of bad news.

Our results show that the degree of conservatism displayed by earnings before extraordinary items under U.S. *GAAP* was higher than under U.K. *GAAP.* However, examination of earnings after extraordinary items reveals that the sensitivity of earnings to bad news was higher under U.K. *GAAP* than under U.S. *GAAP.* Our results also indicate that an important distinguishing feature of U.S. *GAAP* conservatism is the relatively slow recognition of good news in earnings.

REFERENCES

ACCOUNTING PRINCIPLES BOARD. *Opinion No. 9: Reporting the Results of Operations.* New York: AICPA, 1966.

_____. *Opinion No. 30: Reporting the Results of Operations—Reporting the Effects of Disposal of a Segment of a Business, and Extraordinary, Unusual and Infrequently Occurring Events and Transactions.* New York: AICPA, 1973.

---

[32] Consideration of the earnings/return relation within a simultaneous equations framework could have implications for modeling the dynamics linking current earnings to prior period returns. As mentioned above, modeling the effects of simultaneity is beyond the scope of this paper.

86   PETER F. POPE AND MARTIN WALKER

ACCOUNTING STANDARDS BOARD. *Financial Reporting Standard No. 3: Reporting Financial Performance.* London: ASB, 1992.

ACCOUNTING STANDARDS COMMITTEE. *Statement of Standard Accounting Practice No. 6: Extraordinary Items and Prior Year Adjustments.* London: ASC, 1974.

_____. *Statement of Standard Accounting Practice No. 6 (Revised): Extraordinary Items and Prior Year Adjustments.* London: ASC, 1986.

ALFORD, A.; J. JONES; R. LEFTWICH; AND M. ZMIJEWSKI. "The Relative Informativeness of Accounting Disclosures in Different Countries." *Journal of Accounting Research* (Supplement 1993): 183–223.

AMIR, E.; T. S. HARRIS; AND E. K. VENUTI. "A Comparison of the Value-Relevance of U.S. versus Non-U.S. *GAAP* Accounting Measures Using Form 20-F Reconciliations." *Journal of Accounting Research* (Supplement 1993): 230–64.

BALL, R.; S. P. KOTHARI; AND A. ROBIN. "The Effects of Institutional Factors on Properties of Accounting Earnings: International Evidence." Working paper, University of Rochester, October 1997.

BANDYOPADHYAY, S. P.; J. D. HANNA; AND G. RICHARDSON. "Capital Market Effects of U.S.–Canada *GAAP* Differences." *Journal of Accounting Research* (Autumn 1994): 262–77.

BARTH, M., AND G. CLINCH. "International Accounting Differences and Their Relation to Share Prices: Evidence from U.K., Australian and Canadian Firms." *Contemporary Accounting Research* (Spring 1996): 135–70.

BASU, S. "The Conservatism Principle and the Asymmetric Timeliness of Earnings." *Journal of Accounting and Economics* (December 1997): 3–37.

BEAVER, W. H.; M. L. MCANALLY; AND C. STINSON. "The Information Content of Earnings and Prices: A Simultaneous Equations Approach." *Journal of Accounting and Economics* (May 1997): 53–81.

COLLINS, D. W.; S. P. KOTHARI; AND J. D. RAYBURN. "Firm Size and the Information Content of Prices with Respect to Earnings." *Journal of Accounting and Economics* (July 1987): 111–38.

COLLINS, D.; S. P. KOTHARI; J. SHANKEN; AND R. SLOAN. "Lack of Timeliness versus Noise as Explanations for Low Contemporaneous Return–Earnings Associations." *Journal of Accounting and Economics* (November 1994): 289–324.

DONNELLY, R., AND M. WALKER. "Share Price Anticipation of Earnings and the Effect of Earnings Persistence and Firm Size." *Journal of Business Finance and Accounting* (January 1995): 5–18.

ELLIOTT, J. A., AND J. D. HANNA. "Reporting Accounting Write-Offs and the Information Content of Earnings." *Journal of Accounting Research* (Supplement 1996): 135–55.

ELLIOTT, J. A., AND W. H. SHAW. "Write-Offs as Accounting Procedures to Manage Perceptions." *Journal of Accounting Research* (Supplement 1988): 91–119.

ESKEW, R. K., AND W. F. WRIGHT. "An Empirical Analysis of Differential Capital Market Reactions to Extraordinary Accounting Items." *Journal of Finance* (May 1976): 651–74.

GONEDES, N. J. "Corporate Signaling, External Accounting, and Capital Market Equilibrium: Evidence on Dividends, Income, and Extraordinary Items." *Journal of Accounting Research* (Spring 1978): 26–79.

GREENE, W. H. *Econometric Analysis.* 2d ed. New York: Macmillan, 1993.

HARRIS, T. S.; M. LANG; AND H. P. MÖLLER. "The Value Relevance of German Accounting Measures: An Empirical Analysis." *Journal of Accounting Research* (Autumn 1994): 187–209.

HICKS, J. R. *Value and Capital.* Oxford: Clarendon Press, 1946.

HOLGATE, P., AND H. ROBERTS. "FRS 3: The Results So Far." *Accountancy* (December 1994): 142–43.

INSTITUTE OF INVESTMENT MANAGEMENT AND RESEARCH. *Statement of Investment Practice No. 1: The Definition of Headline Earnings.* London: IIMR, 1993.

JACOBSON, R., AND D. AAKER. "Myopic Management Behavior with Efficient, but Imperfect Financial Markets: A Comparison of Information Asymmetries in the U.S. and Japan." *Journal of Accounting and Economics* (October 1993): 383–405.

Joos, P., and M. Lang. "The Effects of Accounting Diversity: Evidence from the European Union." *Journal of Accounting Research* (Supplement 1994): 141–76.

Kothari, S. P., and R. G. Sloan. "Information in Prices about Future Earnings." *Journal of Accounting and Economics* (June–September 1992): 143–71.

Kothari, S. P., and J. L. Zimmerman. "Price and Return Models." *Journal of Accounting and Economics* (September 1995): 155–92.

Pereira, V.; R. Paterson; and A. Wilson. *UK/US GAAP: A Comparison between U.K. and U.S. Accounting Principles*. London: Ernst & Young, 1992.

Pope, P. F., and W. Rees. "International Differences in GAAP and the Pricing of Earnings." *Journal of International Financial Management and Accounting* (Autumn 1992): 190–219.

Ronen, J., and S. Sadan. *Smoothing Income Numbers: Objectives, Means and Implications*. Reading, Mass.: Addison-Wesley, 1981.

[19]

The European Accounting Review 1999, **8:1**, 1–22

Reducing the burden of US GAAP reconciliations by foreign companies listed in the United States: the key question of materiality

Carol A. Adams
University of Glasgow

Pauline Weetman, Edward A. E. Jones
Heriot-Watt University

Sidney J. Gray
University of New South Wales

ABSTRACT

The European Commission has long been concerned over the extensive disclosures required by the Securities and Exchange Commission (SEC) in form 20-F. As the IASC moves towards completing its core standards programme to the satisfaction of IOSCO, the debate has centred around the likelihood of its acceptance by the SEC. This paper examines aspects of the reconciliations to US GAAP, provided by UK registrant companies, and proposes an approach of selective disclosure focusing on material items. We find that goodwill was the dominant adjustment prior to the implementation of FRS 10. When goodwill is excluded there were on average 4.9 adjustments to net income and 5.8 adjustments to shareholders' equity per company reporting. Defining materiality as 10% or more of the reported US net income or shareholders' equity and disregarding immaterial items reduces these to an average of only 1.6 adjustments to the income statement and 0.6 adjustments to shareholders' equity per company. We find that the majority of adjusting items in the reconciliations are not material, adding weight to arguments opposed to the reconciliation requirements. We consider the possibility of a more focused disclosure requirement for foreign companies reporting to the SEC.

Address for correspondence
Professor Carol Adams, University of Glasgow, Department of Accounting and Finance, 65–71 Southpark Avenue, Glasgow G12 8LE, Scotland. E-mail: c.adams@accfin.gla.ac.uk

0963-8180

INTRODUCTION

The Securities and Exchange Commission (SEC) in the United States requires all foreign companies seeking a listing to prepare a reconciliation from domestic to US GAAP on form 20-F. This places a costly obligation on European registrants to prepare two sets of accounts, an issue of great concern to the European Commission (European Commission, 1995) which has tried, unsuccessfully, to negotiate a mutual recognition agreement (Cairns, 1997; Flower, 1997). In addition, the requirement for reconciliation is an inhibiting factor for some foreign companies (Saudagaran and Biddle, 1992, 1995). At the end of 1997 the New York Stock Exchange (NYSE), by far the largest in the world, had only 356 international companies listed representing 13% of the total companies listed on that exchange. This compared with, for example, 526 (21%) on the London Stock Exchange, 163 (46%) on the Amsterdam Stock Exchange and 193 (26%) on the Paris Stock Exchange (London Stock Exchange, *Fact File* 1997). Table 1 shows the distribution of foreign registrant companies on the New York Stock Exchange at October 1997, highlighting the very low number of companies from continental Europe. It clearly indicates an Anglo-American bias, the largest single country group comprising Canadian companies and the second largest comprising UK companies. The UK is the only EU member state providing a group of sufficient size to permit quantitative analysis of differences.

Table 1 Foreign registrant companies on New York Stock Exchange

Canada	62
US or UK Anglo-influence	78
Latin American countries	73
Japan	11
China	8
UK	45
Netherlands	15
France	11
Italy	11
Germany	6
Ireland	4
Portugal	3
Sweden	3
Denmark	3
Belgium	1
Luxembourg	1
Norway and Finland	9
Switzerland	2
Russian Federation	1
	347

Source: Web page of New York Stock Exchange, October 1997.

Each 20-F registration form contains a reconciliation of the net income reported under domestic GAAP to the net income reported using US GAAP. The purpose of this paper is to assess the materiality of the reconciliation difference, and hence its relevance to US investors evaluating UK companies. We use our findings to identify those companies which have material differences in net income overall and those which have material adjustments within the component elements.

The paper addresses the literature which challenges the SEC disclosure requirements and then outlines the various regulatory differences between US and UK measurement rules and between EU and IAS measurement rules. The research questions are set in this context and are addressed by calculation of comparability index values for reported net income and shareholders' equity. The results are considered in relation to statistical significance and accounting materiality, leading to conclusions on the direct UK/US comparisons and the wider implications for European companies in relation to a US listing.

US financial disclosure levels

The financial disclosure levels required of foreign companies seeking a listing in the US have been shown to be the most onerous in the world (see, for example, Cairns *et al.*, 1984; Choi and Bavishi, 1982; Lafferty and Cairns, 1980; Saudagaran and Biddle, 1992, 1995) and their appropriateness has been questioned (see, for example, Bhushan and Lessard, 1992; Biddle and Saudagaran, 1989; Choi *et al.*, 1983; Saudagaran and Biddle, 1992, 1995). The various works of Biddle and Saudagaran have shown that the financial disclosure level required in any particular country is a major factor influencing stock exchange listing behaviour. The probability of a firm listing on a given foreign exchange has been found to be inversely related to the exchange's disclosure level (Biddle and Saudagaran, 1989; Saudagaran and Biddle, 1992, 1995). Thus the US disclosure requirements have had an important effect in limiting the number of foreign companies listing there. Consequently US investors have relatively limited access to foreign investment opportunities and US stock exchanges are potentially at a competitive disadvantage.

Usefulness of US GAAP reconciliations

Those in favour of the 20-F reconciliation argue that requiring foreign companies to be subject to almost the same listing and disclosure rules as domestic companies is the best way of protecting domestic investors from misleading financial statements. On the one hand the regulators must protect investors and on the other hand investors must be allowed access to foreign investments, thus ensuring the competitiveness of US stock exchanges. This has been a much debated issue in recent years. The SEC and NYSE have on occasions taken opposite sides (see, for example, Saudagaran and Biddle, 1995).

In their study of the behavioural effects of accounting diversity, Choi and Levich (1991) interviewed stock market participants in the UK and US and three countries (Japan, Switzerland and Germany) where reporting practices differ quite significantly from international norms. They found that only about half of those interviewed felt that accounting diversity affected their capital market decisions. The other half of the interviewees did not find accounting diversity to be a problem, either because successful coping mechanisms were used or because information less sensitive to accounting treatment was used.

Bhushan and Lessard (1992) found that, among US- and UK-based international investment managers, quantitative reconciliation to US GAAP was viewed as less important than either uniform disclosure or harmonization. Indeed, none of these options was viewed as critical in the investment process and it was suggested that a greater emphasis on mutual recognition, subject to certain minimum standards of disclosure and presentation, would be more effective.

A number of recent capital market studies in the US have attempted to assess the value relevance, i.e. the impact on share prices and returns, of non-US GAAP information and reconciliations to US GAAP. The research findings suggest that non-US GAAP accounting does have value relevance (Meek, 1983; Pope and Rees, 1992; Chan and Seow, 1996). However, the value relevance of the reconciliation to US GAAP is less clear with mixed results although a stronger case can be made for the shareholders' equity reconciliation compared to the earnings reconciliation (Amir *et al.*, 1993; Bandyopadhyay *et al.*, 1994; Rees, 1995, 1996; Barth and Clinch, 1996; Fulkerson and Meek, 1998).

Measurement differences: Fourth and Seventh Directives/IASs/US standards

When the European Commission announced in 1995 that it would look to the IASC to carry forward the work of harmonization, it was reported in the IASC Annual Review (1996) that a study had shown only two very minor conflicts between IASs and the rules contained in the European directives. In contrast a draft FEE study of conflicts between EC accounting directives and IASs (FEE, 1998) indicated potential for measurement differences in a number of potentially significant matters. Table 2 summarizes the main areas of difference indicated in the FEE study. In those accounting issues listed in section (a) of Table 2 the UK/US comparison studied in this paper provides a basis on which to consider EU/IAS measurement differences, particularly

Table 2

(a) Measurement issues where there are EU/IAS differences and where UK/US differences require reconciliation

Goodwill

EU	Directives require goodwill to be amortized, where capitalized, but elimination against reserves is not prohibited.
IASC	IAS 22 (1993): Capitalize and amortize, up to 20 years.
UK	FRS 10 (1997): From Dec. 1998 capitalize and amortize, normally up to 20 years. Previously SSAP 22 (1984): Dominant practice to eliminate against reserves.
US	Capitalize and amortize, up to 40 years.

Negative goodwill

EU	Article 31 of Seventh Directive does not specify how negative goodwill should be treated, except to restrict transfer to profit-and-loss account.
IASC	IAS 22 (1998): If related to expected future losses, recognize in income when future losses occur.
UK	FRS 10 (1997): Measurement not dependent on cause; deduct from positive goodwill. Previously SSAP 22 (1984): Required transfer to reserves only.
US	Proportionately write-down value of fixed assets acquired; classify residual negative goodwill as deferred credit and amortized to income statement.

Deferred income taxes liability

EU	Not a specific aspect of directives.
IASC	IAS 12 (1979, revised 1996): Full provision.
UK	SSAP 15 (1978): Partial provision.
US	SFAS 109 (1992): Broadly comparable to IAS.

Deferred tax asset

EU	Not in directives but do not appear to meet view of an asset as determined in practice.
IASC	IAS 12 (1979): Did not provide for capitalization of loss carried forward. Revised IAS 12 (1996): Requires recognition if recovery is probable.
UK	SSAP 15 (1978): Recognize deferred tax assets if recoverable without replacement by equivalent timing differences.
US	SFAS 109 (1992): Recognize deferred tax assets but apply valuation allowance if recovery is less than 50% likely.

Provisions for employees' benefits

EU	Article 42 of Fourth Directive – may not exceed in amount the sums which are necessary.
IASC	IAS 19 (1983, revised 1998): 1983 similar to UK; 1998 closer to US.
UK	SSAP 24 (1988): Accrue for cost of pensions: discount rate differs from US.
US	SFAS 87, 88 (1985) and 106 (1992): Accrue for cost of benefits as for pensions.

Property, plant and equipment

EU	Historical cost preferred. Article 33 has allowed alternative.
IASC	IAS 16: Use historical cost or revalued amount.
UK	Practice comparable to IAS 16, now described in FRS 15 (1999).
US	Various standards: Revaluations not permitted.

6   *The European Accounting Review*

Table 2 Continued

Investment properties
EU   Article 35(1) of Fourth Directive requires cost to be depreciated over useful life.
IASC   IAS 25 (1986): Treat either as investment or as property, plant and equipment.
UK   IAS 19 (1991): Carry at open market value without depreciation.
US   Various standards: Treat in same way as other properties – historical cost with depreciation.

Capitalization of expenses
EU   Must not be capitalized unless explicitly provided (e.g. formation costs, development cost) (Articles 4, 9 and 10 of Fourth Directive).
IASC   IAS 23 (1993): Permits but does not require capitalization of borrowing costs.
UK   Similar to IASs.
US   SFAS 34 (1978): Compulsory capitalization of borrowing costs when related to construction of specific types of asset.

Research and development costs
EU   Fourth Directive, Articles 37 and 34.1(a) requires that, where capitalized, research and development expenditure should be amortized over maximum 5 years.
IASC   IAS 38 (1998): Separates research from development; capitalization of development required under specified conditions.
UK   SSAP 13 (1989): Comparable to IAS except that capitalizing development costs is optional.
US   SFAS 2 (1974): Expense both research and development.

Fair value concepts for derivatives and other financial instruments
EU   Historical cost dominates Fourth Directive apart from Article 33. No specific permission or requirement to fair value financial instruments.
IASC   IAS 32 (1996): Disclosure only. IAS 39 (1999). Measurement at fair value.
UK   Measurement standard for fair value under development. Disclosure required by FRS 13 (1998).
US   SFAS 119 (1994); SFAS 133 (1999): Fair value disclosure required.

Foreign currency translation
EU   Not mentioned in directives.
IASC   IAS 21 (1993): Closing rate for balance sheet; average rate for profit-and-loss account. Report differences through equity and include in gains on disposal.
UK   SSAP 20 (1983): Closing rate for balance sheet; average rate for profit-and-loss account. Exchange difference through Statement of Total Recognised Gains and Losses. Not included in gains on disposal.
US   SFAS 52 (1981): Comparable to IAS 21.

(b) Measurement issues where there are EU/IAS differences but where UK/US practices do not require reconciliation

Provisions
EU   Fourth Directive, Article 20(1): Requires provision for future losses where nature is defined and they are likely to be incurred.
IASC   IAS 37 (1998): No provision for future losses.

Table 2 Continued

UK	FRS 12 (1998): There must be a present obligation, so generally no provision for future losses.
US	No standard on general issue of provisions, specific recommendations of the Emerging Issues Task Force (EITF) are various, e.g. restructuring costs in EITF 94-3; broadly the approach of the FASB and the EITF is similar to that of FRS 12.

Impairment of fixed assets

EU	Fourth Directive requires provision for diminution but does not specify the measurement of impairment.
IASC	IAS 36 (1998): Recoverable amount is higher of net selling price and value in use, based on discounted cash flows.
UK	FRS 11 (1998): Assess impairment by reference to discounted cash flows. Reversal allowed if economic conditions or usage change.
US	SFAS 121 (1995): Uses undiscounted cash flows to indicate impairment. No subsequent reversal of impairment allowed.

Leases: lessee accounting

EU	Not addressed in directives.
IASC	IAS 17 (1982): Record finance leases as asset and obligation.
UK	SSAP 21 (1984): Comparable to IAS.
US	SFAS 13 (1977): Comparable to IAS.

Construction contracts – percentage of completion method

EU	Percentage of completion method used within general rules of 'calculated accurately'.
IASC	IAS 11 (1993): Percentage of completion subject to 'measured reliably'.
UK	SSAP 9 (1988): Comparable to IAS.
US	ARB 45 (1955): Comparable to IAS, percentage of completion when estimates are 'reasonably dependable'.

Hybrid capital instruments – split presentation

EU	Not addressed in directives.
IASC	IAS 32 (1995): Debt and equity elements split.
UK	FRS 4 (1993): No split.
US	SFAS 125 (1996): No split.

Sources: FEE (1998), Price Waterhouse (1997), IASC *Insight*, various issues.

where the UK/US differences are reflective of the EU/IAS differences. For the issues listed in section (b) of Table 2 the UK and US practices are sufficiently similar to require no reconciling item.

Since 1995 the IASC has been working with the International Organization of Securities Commissions (IOSCO) to produce a set of core international standards which will be acceptable to major stock exchanges. The acceptability is to be considered towards the end of 1998. The SEC has indicated that, in deciding on acceptability, it will consider whether the standards constitute a comprehensive body of accounting; whether they are of high quality and result in comparability and transparency and provide for full disclosure; and whether they can and will be rigorously interpreted and applied (SEC, 1997).

This paper offers a direct quantification of UK and US accounting measurement practices which differ. Consideration of this quantitative evaluation in the context of Table 2 leads to an indication of the magnitude of reconciling items which would be most likely to affect other EU companies if the SEC persists in requiring foreign registrants to publish reconciliations to US GAAP but allows compliance with IASs to be regarded as equivalent to US GAAP.

RESEARCH QUESTION AND METHODOLOGY

The key question raised by this paper is:

- Would the SEC be justified in abandoning the requirement for a reconciliation from domestic GAAP to US GAAP, in the case of UK companies?

As subsidiary questions we ask:

- To what extent is the difference in reported net income material?
- To what extent is the difference in reported shareholders' equity material?
- To what extent are the various adjustments material?
- Does the presentation of the reconciliations detract from their usefulness?

Our findings with respect to materiality will enable us to determine whether the SEC would be justified in abandoning or significantly modifying the requirement for UK companies, as foreign registrants, to prepare a US GAAP reconciliation.

We examined the 20-F reports of all UK companies reporting to the SEC in December 1994 (or the closest year-end either side of that date – see the Appendix for a list of companies used). The date was chosen as marking the completion of the IASC Comparability Project but predating the start of the project to gain IOSCO support for a core set of standards. We considered both quantitative and qualitative aspects of the reconciliations of net income and of shareholders' equity. The quantitative impact of the reconciliations and of individual reconciling items was measured using an index of comparability (see Gray, 1980; Weetman and Gray, 1991; Adams *et al.*, 1993; Cooke, 1993; Hellman, 1993; Weetman *et al.*, 1993; Norton, 1995). Gray (1980) first used the 'index of conservatism' in comparing net income measurement practices of several countries. However, for the purposes of this paper, renaming the index as a measure of 'comparability' places clearer emphasis on relative accounting treatment without requiring a judgement as to which set of GAAP is more or less conservative.

Formulae for the index of comparability

Where UK reported net income or equity is being compared to that reported under US GAAP, the index may be expressed by the formulae:

$$1 - \left(\frac{\text{net income}_{USA} - \text{net income}_{UK}}{|\text{net income}_{USA}|} \right)$$

and

$$1 - \left(\frac{\text{equity}_{USA} - \text{equity}_{UK}}{|\text{equity}_{USA}|} \right)$$

The numerical value of the net income or equity in the USA is chosen as the denominator because the reconciliation is a report to US investors who will view the differences as departures from US net income or equity rather than departures from UK net income or equity. This particular denominator also provides a basis for inter-country comparisons. Net income or equity as the denominator is also consistent with the objective of evaluating materiality. Although there is no agreed guidance on materiality, those assessing materiality of accounting information will make reference in their work to percentage. (For example, Wolk and Tearney (1997) refer to a research study by Patillo (1976) in which it was found that among both users and preparers of financial statements many respondents used a range of 5% to 10% of net income as the boundary of materiality.) This study provides information based on bands at 5% and 10% of net income and equity.

The neutral value of 1.0 is used for consistency with prior literature. An index value greater than 1.0 means that the UK reported net income is greater than that reported under US GAAP (or a UK loss is not as large as a US loss). An index value less than 1.0 means that the UK reported net income is less than that reported under US GAAP (or a UK loss is larger than a US loss).

Because the reconciliations reported to the SEC contain considerable detail, it is also possible to present partial index values using the formulae:

$$1 - \left(\frac{\text{partial adjustment}}{|\text{net income}_{USA}|} \right)$$

$$1 - \left(\frac{\text{partial adjustment}}{|\text{equity}_{USA}|} \right)$$

These provide a relative measure of the contribution of each reconciling item. The neutral value is retained as 1.0 for consistency of interpretation. The indexes of partial adjustments add to the total index by the formula:

$$\text{Total index} = \sum_{1}^{n} \text{adjustment}_n - (n - 1)$$

Statistical tests

Statistical tests may be applied to the index measures. In order to test whether the US reported net income was significantly higher or lower than the UK reported net income, the non-parametric Wilcoxon signed rank test was applied (Siegel and Castellan, 1988). The Wilcoxon test is useful where the researcher is able to rank differences in order of absolute magnitude. It is also appropriate for situations of relatively small sample size. A parametric *t*-test was used for comparison but requires more cautious interpretation as the distributions may be skewed. The significance level chosen was the conventional level of 5%, although it should be noted that statistical significance of 5% and accounting materiality of 5% are quite different concepts.

RESULTS

The results are presented for net income and shareholders' equity before and after elimination of the adjustments for goodwill and other intangibles. Other major adjustments are discussed briefly and the limitations of the analysis are indicated.

Index of comparability for net income and shareholders' equity

The impact of the total adjustments to income and equity is shown in Table 3. UK reported net income was on average 12% higher than US reported net income (index 1.12). From the Wilcoxon test, the median index of 1.15 was significantly different from the neutral value of 1.0, although the *t*-test on the mean was inconclusive. UK reported shareholders' equity was on average 27% below that reported under US GAAP (index 0.73 in Table 3), showing statistical significance on both the Wilcoxon and the *t*-test. Outliers eliminated from the *t*-test are indicated at the foot of Table 3.

Goodwill and other intangibles

The most important individual adjustments were those relating to goodwill and intangibles. Continuing through Table 3, on average the effect of goodwill adjustments was such that UK reported net income was 21% greater

Table 3 Index of comparability for net income and shareholders' equity

Nature of adjustment	Net income			Shareholders' equity		
	Mean	Median	Companies	Mean	Median	Companies
Total adjustments to income/equity†	1.12	1.15*	41	0.73*	0.74*	41
Goodwill†	1.21*	1.14*	34	0.59*	0.67*	35
Intangibles	1.25	1.10	9	0.93	0.99	12
Total excluding goodwill and intangibles††	0.94	1.03	41	1.10*	1.05*	41
Deferred tax†	1.05	1.02	35	1.14*	1.04*	33
Pensions/post-retirement benefits†	1.00	1.00	29	1.01	1.00	28
Historic cost/revalued asset†	0.94	0.99	21	1.05*	1.04*	26
Restructuring‡	0.77	0.85*	9	0.98	0.99*	9
Various: asset/expense recognition	1.11	1.01	21	0.96	0.99	19
Foreign currency translation	0.96	0.99	6	1.00	1.00	2
Financial instruments	0.91	0.99	6	1.00	0.99	10
Leasing	1.16	1.15	4	0.98	1.01	5
Tax on adjustments	0.81	0.99	7	1.04	1.00	7
Dividends	–	–	–	0.96	0.96	30
Revenue recognition	0.95	0.99	3	1.01	1.00	4
Miscellaneous	0.81	1.01	19	0.97	1.00	17
Other taxation	−0.69	−0.69	2	0.98	0.98	2
Other	1.05	1.00	12	1.01	1.01	12

Notes:
† Tested for significance by *t*-test and Wilcoxon test.
‡ Tested for significance by Wilcoxon test only.
* Index is significantly different from 1.00 at the 5% level (tested where number of companies is greater than or equal to 20).
Net income mean excludes outliers as follows:
Total adjustments: co.10 (3.36), co.19 (10.77), co.30 (4.98), co.38 (4.98).
Goodwill: co.19 (9.02), co.38 (4.72).
Deferred tax: co.30 (3.07).
Pensions/post-retirement benefits: co.10 (3.07).
Asset/expense: co.33 (4.9).
Miscellaneous: co.30 (3.67).

than US net income (index 1.21) and UK shareholders' equity was 41% lower than shareholders' equity under US GAAP (index 0.59). Both the Wilcoxon test and the *t*-test indicated index values significantly different from 1.0. In 21 out of 34 cases, the goodwill adjustment caused UK net income to be 10% or more in excess of US net income. In 31 out of 35 cases, the goodwill adjustment caused UK shareholders' equity to be 10% (or more) less than the US reported equity. Adjustments reported separately for other intangibles are also included.

However, from December 1998, standard accounting practice in the UK will require the amortization of intangibles including goodwill over a maximum of twenty years, or application of an impairment test if it is argued that goodwill has a longer life or is expected to be maintained indefinitely (ASB, 1997). This brings the UK closer to the IAS requirement of amortization over a maximum twenty-year period. The SEC already allows foreign registrants to adopt the IAS treatment since it is within the US requirements which allow a maximum write-off period of forty years (Cairns, 1997). If the SEC finds the new UK practice acceptable, reconciliations prepared by UK companies will show only the adjustments other than those related to goodwill. Our data indicate the potential impact of this change.

From Table 3 it may be seen that all aspects of the accounting treatment of goodwill and other intangibles formed the most significant component of the difference in reported net income and equity, both in the magnitude of adjustment and frequency of occurrence.

In contrast, the difference in net income after *exclusion* of the adjustments for goodwill and intangibles showed that UK net income was, on average, 6% below the reported US net income. However, statistical tests indicated that the difference was not significant. The UK shareholders' equity was 10% above the reported US equity and the index was significantly greater than 1.0. Table 3 indicates the significance of further adjustments based on statistical tests, where these could be applied.

As an alternative presentation the accounting materiality of differences in net income is indicated in Table 4 showing bands of relative materiality. The final two columns show the distribution of the index of comparability when adjustments for goodwill and intangibles are eliminated. The distribution of the index values based on reported net income and equity is shown in parentheses in each column.

It may be seen that the number of companies reporting net income 10% or more above the US figures reduces from 25 to 16 when the adjustments for goodwill and other intangibles are eliminated but the number reporting equity 10% or more above the US figures increases from 4 to 14. These observations result from charging amortization to reported net income and restoring to an asset the goodwill previously written off against reserves. The number of companies reporting UK net income 10% or more below the US figures increases from 8 to 11 while the number reporting US equity 10% or more below the US figure reduces from 23 to 3. It is interesting to note that the number of index values within the 5% to 10% range is relatively low, indicating that a materiality decision based on 10% of the relevant US base may be a relatively safe cut-off point in practice. Of course, this can only be indicative of likely lack of materiality in the future but this finding is nevertheless significant.

Table 4 Frequency table of distribution of values of index of comparability for net income and shareholders' equity with goodwill adjustment eliminated (figures in parentheses show distribution with goodwill adjustment not eliminated)

Level of materiality	Index values	Adjustment to net income	Adjustment to shareholders' equity
Addition to UK net income/equity is 10% or more of the amount of US net income/equity	≤0.90	11 (8)	3 (23)
Addition to UK net income/equity is between 5% and 10% of the amount of US net income/equity	0.90–0.95	1 (1)	3 (3)
Adjustment to UK net income/equity is within ±5% of US net income/equity	0.95–1.05	11 (4)	15 (11)
Deduction from UK net income/equity is between 5% and 10% of the amount of US net income/equity	1.05–1.10	2 (3)	6 (0)
Deduction from UK net income/equity is 10% or more of the amount of the US net income/equity	≥1.10	16 (25)	14 (4)
Total		41	41

The most frequently occurring adjustments (see Table 3) are now discussed in more detail.

Deferred taxation

On average, the effect of deferred taxation was such that UK reported net income was 5% greater than US net income (index 1.05) and UK shareholders' equity was 14% higher than shareholders' equity under US GAAP (index 1.14). The statistical significance test indicates that if US investors are primarily concerned with net income then little would be lost by eliminating the requirement to report the adjustment. At the same time, the difference in reported shareholders' equity is significant. However, the adjustment from partial to full provision is already disclosed in notes to the UK balance sheet and notes within the form 20-F. This could be indicated to the reader of the accounting report rather than repeating the information.

Pension costs and post-retirement benefits

The mean adjustment to net income in respect of pension cost adjustments was very close to zero whilst the adjustment to shareholders' equity was 1% of the US reported figure. No statistical significance was found and it was noted that the majority of index values for pension costs and post-retirement benefits were clustered within the ±5% band around the US net income.

Although adjustments for pension costs and post-retirement benefits appear important because they occur so often, their magnitude is not on average significant. The UK and US approaches are broadly similar in impact on measurement.

Revaluation of fixed assets

The US insistence on historical cost accounting requires elimination of any element of depreciation based on replacement cost and of any revaluation of fixed assets. Depreciation adjustments to net income were not significant, with the majority of depreciation adjustments due to asset revaluation being clustered within the $\pm 5\%$ band apart from one large adjustment added back (1.48 times the US net income) caused by a major disposal. For the adjustment to shareholders' equity the mean of the partial index of comparability was 5% of US reported equity (index 1.05) and both the t-test and the Wilcoxon test indicated statistical significance. Thus while the US investor may not find particular interest in the depreciation adjustments to net income, the changes in shareholders' equity could have a significant impact on the calculation of return on capital employed.

Restructuring costs

Under US GAAP a number of specific criteria must be met before restructuring costs can be recognized as an expense in the income statement (EITF 94-3). The mean adjustment added back to UK net income was 23% of US reported net income (index 0.77) and 2% of US reported equity (index 0.98). The Wilcoxon test indicated that the adjustments to net income and shareholders' equity were statistically significant. This provides an example of an emerging cause of adjustment where relatively high magnitudes are involved and it might be expected that the US investor would wish to be informed.

Materiality considerations

Table 5 shows in panel (a) the total number of adjustments for goodwill and intangibles and in panel (b) the total number of adjustments for items other than goodwill and intangibles. When the adjustments for goodwill were eliminated from the analysis there remained 201 adjustments to net income and 239 adjustments to shareholders' equity. Of these, only 66 (32.8%) of the adjustments to net income and 25 (10.4%) of the adjustments to shareholders' equity were material at the 10% level. When the materiality threshold was reduced to 5%, 92 items of net income (45.8%) were material and 55 items of shareholders' equity (23.0%).

For an item-by-item analysis of materiality, the average number of 4.9 adjustments to net income and 5.8 adjustments to shareholders' equity could

Table 5 An overview of adjustments listed in reconciliations of UK/US net income and equity

Taking materiality as difference ≥5% and ≥10% of reported US net income or equity

	Net income		*Shareholders' equity*	
Panel a: Goodwill and intangibles				
Goodwill and intangibles adjustments, total number	51		52	
Materiality level	*≥10%*	*≥5%*	*≥10%*	*≥5%*
Goodwill and intangibles, material adjustments	29	37	35	40
Panel b: Other adjustments				
Total of other adjustments	201		239	
Average other adjustments per company	**4.9**		**5.8**	
Materiality level	*≥10%*	*≥5%*	*≥10%*	*≥5%*
Other adjustments, material	66 (32.8%)	92 (45.8%)	25 (10.4%)	55 (23.0%)
Other adjustments, not material	135 (67.2%)	109 (54.2%)	214 (89.6%)	184 (77.0%)
Average material adjustments across all companies	**1.6**	**2.2**	**0.6**	**1.3**
Panel c: Analysis of non-material adjustments				
Materiality level	*≥10%*	*≥5%*	*≥10%*	*≥5%*
Mean index	1.01	1.01	1.00	1.00
Median index	1.01	1.00	0.99	0.99
Minimum index	0.83	0.94	0.86	0.90
Maximum index	1.18	1.12	1.21	1.08

be reduced to disclosing an average of 1.6 adjustments to net income and 0.6 adjustments to shareholders' equity if the materiality level for each separate item of disclosure was set at 10%. Thus if the SEC were to accept that only material adjustments influenced the user, the number of companies producing reconciliations could be reduced and the number of reported line items per company could also be reduced. The comparison presented in panel (b) of Table 5 indicates the trade-off in terms of additional disclosures where the materiality limit is set at 5% rather than at 10%. This approach of concentrating on items which are likely to be material is reinforced by the index values for the non-material adjustments taken as a group (panel (c) of Table 5). The means and medians are close to 1.0, although the range shows the potential for materiality in specific cases.

The distribution of items is shown in Table 6, indicating that the location of a material adjustment is not readily predictable. Hence any recommendation for disclosure based on materiality must allow for this lack of predictability.

16   *The European Accounting Review*

Table 6 Frequency of occurrence of material adjustments, taking materiality as difference ≥10% and ≥5% of reported US net income or equity

	Net income		Shareholders' equity	
Nature of adjustment	*≥10%*	*≥5%*	*≥10%*	*≥5%*
Total adjustments to income/equity	66	92	25	55
Deferred tax	14	19	12	14
Pensions/post-retirement benefits	9	14	0	7
Historic cost/revalued asset	5	7	5	11
Restructuring	7	9	0	1
Various: asset/expense recognition	8	9	2	3
Foreign currency translation	2	3	0	0
Financial instruments	2	4	0	3
Leasing	4	4	2	2
Tax on adjustments	3	4	1	1
Dividends			0	6
Revenue recognition	1	2	0	0
Miscellaneous	9	15	3	7
Other taxation	2	2		
Other				

Wider EU implications

The findings of the analysis are summarized in Table 7, in terms of the accounting issues outlined in Table 2(a) where EU practice is said to be different from the requirements of US GAAP. To the extent that the UK information is relevant to the wider EU experience it would appear that the frequency and magnitude of adjustments will be reduced once FRS 10 is fully operational. A similar analysis for practice in other EU countries could indicate the *de facto* impact of the *de jure* differences analysed in the FEE document summarized in Table 2.

Limitations of analysis due to matters of presentation

There are some limitations on interpretation of the foregoing analysis, due to matters of presentation. In most cases, the reconciliation begins with UK net income after minority interests and preference shares but in some cases these are removed from US net income as an adjustment. One company separated discontinued operations and presented the effect of discontinued operations as an adjustment. Items were often combined and may also have been netted off. For example, some companies included goodwill and intangibles together. One company included a 'goodwill and trademarks' adjustment. Furthermore, goodwill adjustments often combined amortization with a write-off due to the sale of a business or US purchase accounting adjustments. In seven instances the tax consequences of adjustment to net income were reported

Table 7 Summary of findings for UK companies in this research, related to Table 2(a)

Subject	Findings
Goodwill and negative goodwill	Most significant and material source of UK/US difference. Should cease to be a cause of difference from 1998. Not possible to single out negative goodwill
Deferred income taxes liability and asset	Frequently occurring adjustment for UK companies; rarely significant for profit measurement but accumulated amount in balance sheet is significant over the sample and materially different in several cases. Not possible to separate asset and liability aspects
Provisions for employees' benefits	Frequently occurring adjustment; relatively few instances are material to reported profit
Property, plant and equipment, and investment properties	No significant impact overall on profit and loss; significant effect on balance sheet. Material adjustments are seen. Not possible to single out investment properties
Capitalization of expenses, particularly interest Research and development costs Fair value concepts for derivatives and other financial instruments Foreign currency translation	All have relatively few adjustments by number, any one could be material in a specific situation

separately and in two cases the description 'other taxation' was used without explanation. In the remaining cases the tax adjustments might have been made to each line item separately, or within the deferred taxation adjustment, or within the 'miscellaneous' category. Several companies made adjustments to shareholders' equity for the goodwill of associated undertakings. Reconciliations often included a category labelled 'other' or 'miscellaneous'. In general these appeared to be minor adjustments.

Finally, there is no requirement to make adjustments for areas where, in practice, UK and US companies follow different allowed practices. For example, both countries have regulations which in principle permit either LIFO or FIFO methods of inventory valuation. However, US companies commonly use LIFO because it is allowed for tax purposes and UK companies commonly use FIFO, because, although allowed by the Companies Acts, LIFO is not accepted by SSAP 9 (ASC, 1988) or the taxation legislation. Such *de facto* differences are not quantified in the reported reconciliations.

SUMMARY AND DISCUSSION

The key question raised at the start of the paper was:

- Would the SEC be justified in abandoning the requirement for a reconciliation from domestic GAAP to US GAAP, in the case of UK companies?

Our empirical study of US GAAP reconciliations revealed that the most frequently occurring items appearing in the reconciliations were adjustments for goodwill, deferred tax, pension costs and post-retirement benefits, asset revaluation and restructuring costs.

The most important adjustments related to goodwill and other intangible assets. These were statistically significant in relation to both net income and shareholders' equity. At the same time, adjustments for deferred tax and asset revaluation were statistically significant in relation to shareholders' equity but not in relation to net income. Adjustments for pension costs and post-retirement benefits were not statistically significant for either net income or shareholders' equity. Adjustments for restructuring costs were less frequent but were significant for both net income and shareholders' equity.

From the end of 1998 onwards, however, UK companies will apply FRS 10 which treats intangible assets, including goodwill, as a fixed asset with amortization. Consequently a more balanced view of the impact of the remaining adjustments is obtained if the starting point of the reconciliation is the UK reported net income *after* deduction of the goodwill adjustment. After removing the goodwill adjustment from the reconciliation in this manner, there is an average of 1.61 net income adjustments per company which are 'material' (measured as 10% or more above or below US net income) and 0.61 shareholders' equity adjustments per company which are 'material'.

Narrowing down the material elements in the manner indicated in this analysis leads us to propose that, until full agreement with IOSCO is achieved, the desire of US investors for access to foreign capital could be satisfied, with an acceptable level of protection, in terms of providing useful accounting information, if the SEC were to modify its reconciliation requirements for foreign registrants. We would argue that foreign registrants should be required to report adjusted profit and equity only where domestic standards and IASC standards differ and where the difference in *total* reported income and shareholders' equity is likely to be 10% or more of the US shareholders' equity. Material individual items of adjustment should also be reported by way of explanatory note where any one of these is 10% or more of US GAAP net income or shareholders' equity. Such a procedure would seem to meet the needs of US investors without inhibiting foreign companies from seeking a listing. While it could be argued that this will not save a substantial amount in terms of preparation costs, because the calculations must be undertaken to establish the materiality of adjustment, there will nevertheless be some savings in reporting costs and a reduction in uncertainty about the company's results. Selective reporting meets concerns over excessive disclosure levels but satisfies information needs related to diversity of practice. It would be a matter for further investigation to discover whether these benefits outweigh the costs of calculation of both material and non-material adjustments.

Our recommendation that the SEC regulation might concentrate on material items only is reinforced by our experience that the complexity and detail of the reconciliations as presently presented is potentially confusing and detracts from the key issues. Taking materiality as the trigger for disclosure of particular items in the financial statements affords flexibility to deal with the possible objection that observed lack of materiality in the past is no guarantee of lack of materiality in the future.

This recommendation is supported by the recent capital market studies in the US of the value relevance of non-US GAAP compared to US GAAP earnings, referred to earlier, which indicate that non-US GAAP reporting is relevant in valuing non-US firms but that the value of reconciliations from domestic to US GAAP is less clear (Fulkerson and Meek, 1998).

It could also be asked whether the SEC would unduly jeopardize the interests of investors if the quantitative reconciliations were abandoned altogether as suggested by the New York Stock Exchange (Cochrane, 1992). If the International Organization of Securities Commissions (IOSCO) accepts the result of the IASC core standards programme, a desirable outcome is that the SEC will no longer require reconciliations where International Accounting Standards are effective. However, currently, the UK treatment of deferred taxation and of pension costs and post-retirement benefits differs from that of the relevant IASs. While retaining reconciliation for these items would, based on our results, have no significant impact on net income they could be significant for the balance sheet. Revaluation of fixed assets is an allowed alternative under IAS 16 and therefore would not require a reconciling line item. Restructuring costs and some of the less frequently occurring items of adjustment might continue to require reporting where material.

In conclusion we believe that our recommendations are within the spirit of the SEC's concern to maintain the rigour, quality, comparability and transparency of US capital markets while at the same time making such markets more accessible to European companies in general.

ACKNOWLEDGEMENTS

The authors are grateful for comments received on an earlier draft of this paper from Bill Rees and Neil Garrod and to participants at the 21st Annual Congress of the European Accounting Association, particularly John Flower and Gary Meek, for their helpful comments. The comments of an anonymous reviewer are also acknowledged with thanks.

REFERENCES

Adams, C. A., Weetman, P. and Gray, S. J. (1993) 'Reconciling national with international accounting standards: lessons from a study of Finnish corporate reports', *European Accounting Review*, 2(3): 471–95.

Amir, E., Harris, T. S. and Venuti, E. K. (1993) 'A comparison of the value-relevance of U.S. versus non-U.S. GAAP accounting measures using form 20-F reconciliations', *Journal of Accounting Research*, Supplement: 230–75.

ASB (1997) *Financial Reporting Standard FRS 10: Goodwill and Intangible Assets*. London: Accounting Standards Board.

ASC (1988) *Statement of Standard Accounting Practice SSAP 9: Stocks and Long-term Contracts*. London: Accounting Standards Committee (standard issued 1975, revised 1988).

Bandyopadhyay, S. P., Hanna, J. D. and Richardson, G. (1994) 'Capital markets effects of U.S.–Canada GAAP differences', *Journal of Accounting Research*, Autumn: 262–77.

Barth, M. and Clinch, G. (1996) 'International accounting differences and their relation to share prices: evidence from U.K., Australian and Canadian firms', *Contemporary Accounting Research*, Spring: 134–70.

Bhushan, R. and Lessard, D. R. (1992) 'Coping with international accounting diversity: fund managers' views on disclosure, reconciliation, and harmonization', *Journal of International Financial Management and Accounting*, 4(2): 149–64.

Biddle, G. C. and Saudagaran, S. M. (1989) 'The effects of financial disclosure levels on firms' choice among alternative stock exchange listings', *Journal of International Financial Management and Accounting*, 1(1): 55–87.

Cairns, D. (1997) 'The future shape of harmonization: a reply', *European Accounting Review*, 6(2): 305–48.

Cairns, D. M., Lafferty, M. and Mantle, P. (1984) *Survey of Accounts and Accountants 1983–84*. London: Lafferty Publications.

Chan, K. C. and Seow, G. S. (1996) 'The association between stock returns and foreign GAAP earnings versus earnings adjusted to US GAAP', *Journal of Accounting and Economics*, 21: 139–58.

Choi, F. D. S. and Bavishi, V. B. (1982) 'Diversity in multinational accounting', *Financial Executive*, August: 45–9.

Choi, F. D. S. and Levich, R. M. (1991) 'Behavioural effects of international accounting diversity', *Accounting Horizons*, June: 1–13.

Choi, F. D. S., Hino, H., Min, S. K., Nam, S. O., Ujiie, J. and Stonehill, A. I. (1983) 'Analysing foreign financial statements: the use and misuse of international ratio analysis', *Journal of International Business Studies*, Spring/Summer: 113–31.

Cochrane, J. L. (1992) 'Helping to keep U.S. capital markets competitive: listing world-class non-U.S. firms on U.S. exchanges', *Journal of International Financial Management and Accounting*, 2: 165–70.

Cooke, T. E. (1993) 'The impact of accounting principles on profits: the US versus Japan', *Accounting and Business Research*, Autumn: 460–76.

Doupnik, T. S. and Salter, S. B. (1995) 'External environment, culture and accounting practice: a preliminary test of a general model of international accounting development', *International Journal of Accounting*, 30: 189–207.

European Commission (1995) *Accounting Harmonization: A New Strategy Vis-à-Vis International Harmonisation*, Communication from the Commission Internal Document, COM95(508).

FEE (1998) *FEE Study: Actual and Potential Conflicts between the EC-Accounting Directives and IASs*, Fédération des Experts Comptable Europééns (draft report at April 1998).

Flower, J. (1997) 'The future shape of harmonization: the EU versus the IASC versus the SEC', *European Accounting Review*, 6(2): 305–48.

Fulkerson, C. L. and Meek, G. K. (1998) 'Analysts' earnings forecasts and the value relevance of 20-F reconciliations from non-U.S. to U.S. GAAP', *Journal of International Financial Management and Accounting*, 9: 1–15.

Gray, S. J. (1980) 'The impact of international accounting differences from a security analysis perspective: some European evidence', *Journal of Accounting Research*, Spring: 64–76.

Hellman, N. (1993) 'A comparative analysis of the impact of accounting differences and return on equity', *European Accounting Review*, 2(3): 495–530.

International Accounting Standards Committee (1989) *E32 Comparability of Financial Statements: Proposed Amendments to International Accounting Standards 2, 5, 8, 9, 11, 16, 17, 18, 19, 21, 22, 23 and 25*. London: International Accounting Standards Committee.

Lafferty, M. and Cairns, D. (1980) *Financial Times Survey of Annual Reports*. London: Financial Times Business Information.

London Stock Exchange (1997) *Fact File 1997*, London: London Stock Exchange.

Meek, G. K. (1983) 'U.S. securities market response to alternative earnings disclosures of non-U.S. multinational corporations', *Accounting Review*, April: 394–402.

Norton, J. (1995) 'The impact of accounting practices on the measurement of profit and equity: Australia versus the United States', *Abacus*, 3(3): 178–200.

Patillo, J. W. (1976) *The Concept of Materiality in Financial Reporting*, Financial Executives Research Foundation. (Cited in Wolk and Tearney, op. cit.)

Pope, P. F. and Rees, W. P. (1992) 'International differences in GAAP and the pricing of earnings', *Journal of International Financial Management and Accounting*, Autumn: 190–219.

Price Waterhouse (1997) *International Accounting – Similarities and Differences: IAS, US GAAP and UK GAAP*, Price Waterhouse, December.

Rees, L. L. (1995) 'The information contained in reconciliations to earnings based on U.S. accounting principles by non-U.S. companies', *Accounting and Business Research*, 25: 301–10.

Rees, L. L. (1996) 'A comparison of investors' abilities to assimilate US GAAP disclosures', *Journal of Accounting and Public Policy*, 15: 271–87.

Saudagaran, S. M. and Biddle, G. C. (1992) 'Financial disclosure levels and foreign stock exchange listing decisions', *Journal of International Financial Management and Accounting*, 14(2): 105–48.

Saudagaran, S. M. and Biddle, G. C. (1995) 'Foreign listing location: a study of MNCs and stock exchanges in eight countries', *Journal of International Business Studies*, 2nd Qtr: 319–41.

SEC (1997) *Report on Promoting Global Pre-eminence of American Securities Markets*, pursuant to Section 509(5) of the National Securities Markets Improvement Act of 1996, The United States Securities and Exchange Commission, October.

Siegel, S. and Castellan, N. J. (1988) *Non-Parametric Statistics for the Behavioural Sciences*. New York: McGraw-Hill.

Weetman, P. and Gray, S. J. (1991) 'A comparative international analysis of accounting principles on profits: the USA versus the UK, Sweden and the Netherlands', *Accounting and Business Research*, 21(84): 363–79.

Weetman, P., Adams, C. A. and Gray, S. J. (1993) *Issues in International Accounting Harmonisation: The Significance of UK/US Accounting Differences and Implications for the IASC's Comparability Project*. London: ACCA Research Report No. 33.

Wolk, H. I. and Tearney, M. G. (1997) *Accounting Theory: A Conceptual and Institutional Approach*. Cincinnati, OH: South-Western College Publishing.

22   *The European Accounting Review*

APPENDIX

Companies used in this study

Firm	Date of 1994/5 20-F
Attwoods plc	31.7.94
Automated Security (Holdings) plc	30.11.94
Barclays Bank plc	31.12.94
Bass plc	30.9.94
BET plc	1.4.95
BOC Group plc	30.9.94
British Airways plc	31.3.95
British Gas plc	31.12.94
British Petroleum plc	31.12.94
British Steel plc	1.4.95
British Telecommunications plc	31.3.95
Cable & Wireless plc	31.3.95
Cadbury Schweppes plc	31.12.94
Cantab Pharmaceuticals plc	31.12.94
Carlton Communications plc	30.9.94
Central Transport Rental Group plc	30.4.95
English China Clays plc	31.12.94
Enterprise Oil plc	31.12.94
Glaxo Holdings plc	31.12.95
Govett & Company Limited	29.6.95
Grand Metropolitan plc	30.9.94
Hanson plc	30.9.94
ICI Group plc	31.12.94
Lasmo plc	31.12.94
Medeva plc	31.12.94
Midland Bank plc	31.12.94
National Westminster Bank plc	31.12.94
NFC plc	1.10.94
Reuters Holdings plc	31.12.94
RTZ Corporation plc	31.12.94
Signet Group plc	28.1.95
Smith & Nephew plc	31.12.94
SmithKline Beecham plc	31.12.94
The Royal Bank of Scotland plc	30.9.94
Tomkins plc	29.4.95
United News and Media plc	31.12.94
Vodafone Group plc	31.3.95
Waste Management International plc	31.12.94
Waterford Wedgwood plc	31.12.94
Willis Corroon plc	31.12.94
WPP Group plc	31.12.94

[20]

The International
Journal of
Accounting

Assessing the Acceptability of International Accounting Standards in the US: An Empirical Study of the Materiality of US GAAP Reconciliations by Non-US Companies Complying with IASC Standards

Donna L. Street,* Nancy B. Nichols,* and Sidney J. Gray†

*James Madison University, Harrisonburg, VA, USA; and †University of New South Wales, Sydney, NSW, Australia

Key Words: IASC; US GAAP reconciliations; Net income; IOSCO; SEC

Abstract: With the International Accounting Standards Committee (IASC) reaching the completion of its core standards program, the International Organization of Securities Commissions (IOSCO) is considering its response to the IASC's application for endorsement of International Accounting Standards (IASs). A critical aspect of IOSCO's acceptance of IASs is likely to be the extent to which such standards are compatible with US Generally Accepted Accounting Principles (US GAAP). This issue is explored by an empirical study of US GAAP reconciliations by non-US companies complying with IASC standards. The results indicate that the impact of accounting differences between IASs and US GAAP is narrowing and suggest that the Securities Exchange Commission (SEC) should consider accepting IASC standards without condition. Alternatively, an SEC endorsement could include a short list of IASs where acceptance is subject to additional disclosures.

With the International Accounting Standards Committee (IASC) reaching completion of its core standards program, the International Organization of Securities Commissions (IOSCO) is considering its response to the IASC's application for endorsement of International Accounting Standards (IASs). Given the significance of the US capital market in the global context, a critical aspect of IOSCO's acceptance of IASs is likely to be the extent to which such standards are compatible with US Generally Accepted Accounting Principles (GAAP). It is unlikely that significant differences from US GAAP will be easily accepted by the Securities Exchange Commission (SEC) in the US, a key IOSCO member, without the requirement for non-US companies to continue to provide a reconciliation to US GAAP.

Direct all correspondence to: Donna L. Street, School of Accounting, James Madison University, Harrisonburg, VA 22807, USA; E-mail: streetdl@jmu.edu

The International Journal of Accounting, Vol. 35, No. 1, pp. 27–63   ISSN: 0020-7063.

The purpose of this project is to respond to the call for research to assist the SEC in assessing IASs for cross-border offerings of securities in the US (Turner, 1999a). Specifically, the research aims to identify the most important differences between IASC standards and US GAAP in practice and to assess the significance and materiality of these accounting differences with particular reference to the measurement of net income. To the extent that such accounting differences are not significant or material, the argument for accepting IASs without reconciliation to US GAAP will be supported. On the other hand, the contrary is likely to strengthen the argument for retaining the status quo.

THE IOSCO PERSPECTIVE

An important aspect of IOSCO's overall commitment to facilitating cross-border offerings and listings by multinational enterprises is the Technical Committee's participation in the IASC project to develop a core set of IASs (IASC, 1999). Following the March 1999 publication of the IASC interim standard on financial instruments, which resulted in the IASC substantially completing all key parts of the core standards, the IOSCO Technical Committee began its assessment of the core standards. The assessment will focus on whether the core standards are of sufficiently high quality to warrant permitting foreign issuers to utilize them to access a country's capital markets as an alternative to domestic standards.

In recent years, the IOSCO Technical Working Group on Multinational Disclosure and Accounting devoted substantial resources to participating in the development of the core standards. This process included providing commentary on key proposals in each standard. As part of the assessment, the Working Group is evaluating whether its concerns were addressed in the final core standards, whether the IASC's standards work together to form an operational whole, and the potential impact of the standards on investors, issuers, and the markets.

The Working Group has completed an analysis of its comment letters and has created a comprehensive inventory of outstanding issues on individual IASs. Currently, the Working Group is analyzing those comments to identify IASC standards that may be recommended for use on a cross-border basis without condition and those standards where acceptance may be subject to additional disclosures or other conditions.

After the Working Group has completed its analysis, the group will make a recommendation to the IOSCO Technical Committee. The Technical Committee will then decide whether to recommend that IOSCO members permit foreign issuers to use IASs in lieu of national standards for cross-border offering and listing purposes. The Technical Committee considers completion of the IOSCO assessment as a matter of great urgency.

THE SEC PERSPECTIVE

As a key member of IOSCO, the SEC has stated its commitment to support the IASC but, in line with the IOSCO agreement, has indicated (SEC, 1996) there are three key elements in the acceptance of IASC Standards. First, the standards must include a core set of standards that constitute a comprehensive generally accepted basis of accounting. Second, the standards must be of high quality and result in comparability, transparency, and full disclosure. Third, the standards must be rigorously interpreted and applied. As Zeff (1999) has pointed out, "The SEC is truly a control agency, and it has a low tolerance for ambiguity." The SEC requires non-US companies to report in the same way as US companies and thus, all foreign registrants must either use, or reconcile to, US GAAP. However, pressure on the SEC has been growing to adopt a more conciliatory approach to non-US companies. The New York Stock Exchange (NYSE) has been concerned for some time that many non-US companies have been deterred from seeking a listing in New York by the SEC's reconciliation requirement (Cochrane, 1992). In 1996, the US Congress (1996) charged the SEC to support the development of IASs and to report on "the outlook for successful completion of a set of IASs that would be acceptable to the Commission for offerings and listings by foreign corporations in United States markets." While the SEC is yet to decide on the acceptability of IASC standards, it seems clear that the key question will be whether these standards will be considered close enough to US GAAP to be acceptable.

THE IMPACT OF US GAAP RECONCILIATIONS

In order to investigate this issue further, the significance and materiality of recent US GAAP reconciliations by non-US companies claiming to comply with IASs are examined. These reconciliations, currently required by the SEC to be supplied on Form 20-F for non-domestic companies listing on a US stock exchange, provide a reliable source of information about the nature and impact of differences between IASC standards and US GAAP in practice. While recent research has endeavored to assess the nature of such accounting differences, this has been limited to an evaluation of their incidence in the case of US companies (Street and Gray, 1999).

At the same time, previous research analyzing the impact of accounting differences using US GAAP reconciliations has been limited to an assessment of country differences including the UK, the Netherlands, Sweden and Australia (e.g., Weetman and Gray, 1990, 1991; Weetman et al., 1998; Hellman, 1993; Norton, 1995). While the differences between UK and US GAAP have been reported as material and becoming larger in recent years, the significance of differences in the case of the Netherlands, Sweden and Australia is somewhat less clear. Further, the value relevance of US GAAP reconciliations (i.e., the impact on share prices and returns) is also not clear with mixed results from recent studies on this issue (see Amir et al., 1993; Bandyopadhajay et al., 1994; Rees, 1995, 1996; Barth and Clinch, 1996; Fulkerson and Meek, 1998).

The research reported in this article extends earlier research by incorporating an assessment of how IASC–US GAAP differences impact quantitatively on the measurement of net income and provides an analysis of whether or not these differences are significant or material in the case of non-US companies complying with IASC standards.

METHODOLOGY

Sample

Companies that comply with IASs and provide US GAAP reconciliations in Form 20-F were identified based on a list supplied by the SEC. The list included the names of 41 SEC registrants believed to follow IASs. Eleven companies were dropped from the SEC list based on the following criteria:

- Use US or UK as opposed to IASC GAAP (Adecco, Ashanti Goldfields, Huaneng Power International, Logitech International, Shangdon Huaneng Power Development);
- Acquired by another company (Basic Petroleum International);
- Italian companies that use IASs only in the absence of Italian guideline (Benetton, ENI);
- Auditors opinion and accounting policy footnote make no mention of IASs (Emco, CICB);
- Delisted (ISS International Service Systems).

The researchers also reviewed a list of companies appearing on both the IASC's "Companies Referring to Their Use of IAS" and "The Complete Depositary Receipt Directory" of the Bank of New York to identify any additional IAS companies that file Form 20-F. This step identified BHP as a 20-F company. A collection of over two hundred 1997 annual reports of IASC companies were also reviewed to identify companies that voluntarily provide reconciliations to US GAAP. This step added Atlas Copco and Scania to the sample. The sample of 33 companies consists of:

- Twenty-seven using IASs and filing form 20-F (the audit opinion states that the financial statements comply with IAS);
- Four stating their financials comply with IAS in all material aspects (in the accounting policy footnotes) and filing form 20-F; and
- Two stating their financials comply with IAS in all material aspects and voluntarily providing a reconciliation to US GAAP in their annual report.

The sample comprises seven companies from China; three each from Canada, the Netherlands, and Sweden; two each from Bermuda, France and Switzerland; and one each from Australia, the Cayman Islands, Finland, Germany, Hungary, Italy, Mexico, Papua New Guinea, Poland, Portugal, and Russia. A list of the sample companies is provided in Appendix A.

While the sample companies are not necessarily representative of all companies complying with IASs, they would appear to be a sample relevant to the SEC for the purposes of assessing US GAAP compatibility and the significance of the 20-F reconciliation requirement.

IAS/US Accounting Differences

Measurement practices of IASs that differ from US GAAP are described in several sources such as FASB's (1996) *The IASC–US Comparison Project* and Pricewaterhouse-Coopers' (1998) *International Accounting Standards: Similarities and Differences IAS, US GAAP, and UK GAAP*. The key differences that result in 20-F reconciliation adjustments for the sample companies are listed in Table 1. Panels A through M describe differences where compliance with IAS in 1997 will force or allow divergence from US GAAP. In some areas, such as measurement of deferred taxes (Panel B) and property, plant, and equipment (Panel C), IASs provide two options, one being compatible with US GAAP (i.e., comprehensive allocation/historical cost) and the other allowing for divergence (i.e., partial allocation/revaluation). As reflected in Table 1, disharmony may also arise in areas where US GAAP is more detailed or provides more guidance than IASs, for example, in selecting the method for foreign currency translation (Panel F) and accounting for associates (Panel L). Another area of concern lies in the absence of IASs addressing industry practices. While the US provides guidelines on general R&D and industry specific guidance for software development costs and oil and gas exploration, IASs cover only basic R&D (Panel M). Panels AA through DD illustrate another problematic area where, in the absence of an IAS, companies may adopt accounting practices that vary from US GAAP (i.e., restructuring provisions/Panel AA).

In recent years, the IASC has revised several standards and issued additional standards as part of its core standards project which was completed in December 1998 with the issuance of IAS 39 (*Financial Instruments*). Thus, the last column of Table 1 provides an update of the extent to which IASs have changed since the period covered by the study (1995–1997). In that many of the modifications to IASs have been in line with US GAAP, reconciling items arising from these areas will disappear or become less significant/material in forthcoming years. An SEC decision regarding IASs should consider the impact of these revised standards and new standards, which the IASC has just completed.

The Index of Comparability

In order to understand the significance of IASC–US GAAP differences in practice, it is necessary to have a methodology that will facilitate the assessment of how such differences impact on accounting results. Gray (1980) introduced an "index of conservatism" to compare profit measurement practices across countries. Weetman and Gray (1990, 1991), Weetman et al. (1993), Adams et al. (1993), Cooke (1993), Hellman (1993), and Norton (1995) utilized the index in a similar manner. Weetman et al. (1998) renamed the index to focus on "comparability" and to place more attention on relative accounting treatment without requiring a judgement regarding which accounting treatment is more or less conservative. The "index of comparability" indicates the measurement impact of accounting differences. The index may thus be differentiated from alternative harmonization measures such as the H, I, or C indices which quantify the *incidence* of accounting differences but not their bottom-line impact (van der Tas, 1988).

Formula of the Index of Comparability

Where IAS reported income is compared to US GAAP income, the index is expressed by the formula:

$$1 - \frac{(\text{Net income}_{USA} - \text{Net income}_{IAS})}{|\text{Net income}_{USA}|}$$

THE INTERNATIONAL JOURNAL OF ACCOUNTING   Vol. 35, No. 1, 2000

Table 1. Key Differences between US and IASC GAAP as Reflected in 1997 20-F Reconciliations

Item and companies	US GAAP	IASC GAAP	Comments
Panel A: Inventory			
Impairment: Hoechst	ARB 43: inventories carried at lower of cost or market	IAS 2: inventories carried at lower of cost and net realizable value	
Costing: Hoechst, Nova	Under certain circumstances idle capacity costs may be absorbed into inventory costs	IAS 2: allocation of fixed production overhead based on normal capacity levels, with unallocated overheads expensed as incurred	
Measurement: Hoechst	ARB 43: permits FIFO, weighted average, and LIFO	IAS 2: benchmarks FIFO and weighted average. Allowed alternative LIFO	Although US and IASC GAAP are comparable, LIFO is not acceptable in some countries
Panel B: Deferred tax			
Method: Astra (partial), Banco Comercial Portugês, Beijing Yanhau (deferred tax asset), BioChem Pharma, BHP (based on announced tax rate), Fiat (partial), Hoechst (1995 only), Ispat (partial), Mexican Maritime (partial), Netia (1995 and 1996 only), New Holland, Nokia (partial), Nova (deferral method), Scandia (partial), Usinor (deferred tax asset), Yanzhou Coal Mining (deferred tax asset)	FAS 109: liability method with comprehensive allocation. Tax benefit from operating loss carry forward recorded if "more likely than not" to be realized. Change in tax rate not recognized until enacted	Old version IAS 12: (effective 1995–1997) allows full or partial allocation of timing differences. Allows deferral or liability method. Deferred tax assets only carried forward when reasonable expectation of realization. Under liability method, change in tax rate may be recognized when announced	IAS 12 Revised (effective years beginning on or after 1 January 1998). Accrue deferred tax liability for nearly all taxable temporary differences. Accrue deferred tax asset for nearly all deductible temporary differences if probable a tax benefit will be realized. Accrue unused tax losses and tax credits if probable will be realized. Use tax rates expected at settlement

continued overleaf

	US GAAP	IAS	Commentary
Panel C: Property, plant, and equipment			
Measurement: Atlas, Beijing Yanhau Petrochemical, BHP, China Eastern, China Southern, Fiat, Guangshen Railway, Ispat, Jilin Chemical, New Holland, Shanghai Petrochemical, Yanzhou Coal Mining	Measurement after initial recognition must be at historical cost	IAS 16 benchmark: property, plant, and equipment at historical cost following initial recognition. Allowed alternative: revaluation of classes of assets	Most revaluations not voluntary (i.e., all Chinese companies related to restructuring during mid-1990s associated with privatization; Fiat compliance with specific laws; New Holland in accordance with laws of certain countries in which the Company operates). A future IAS may reduce options in this area
Investment Properties: Banco	Treated same as property, plant, and equipment	Treated as property per IAS 16 or as long-term investments per IAS 25	
Impairment: China Southern, Nova	FAS 121: impaired PPE written down to fair value	IAS 12: impaired PPE written down to recoverable amount	IAS 36: (effective for years beginning on or after 1 July 1999) addresses impairment of PPE. FAS 121 and IAS 36 differ in key respects and G4 + 1 is working to minimize such differences
Panel D: Leases			
Sale and leaseback accounting: China Southern, Mexican Maritime, Nokia	FAS 13: defer and amortize profits up to certain limits. Immediately recognize losses	IAS 17: defer and amortize profit arising on sale and finance lease-back. If operating lease arises, profit recognition depends on sale proceeds compared to fair value of asset	The G4 + 1 members are discussing proposed revisions to leasing standards based on the discussion paper, *Accounting for Leases: A New Approach.*

(continued)

Table 1. (Continued)

Item and companies	US GAAP	IASC GAAP	Comments
Panel E: Retirement benefits Pensions: Banco (gain amortization), Hoechst, Matav (OPEB), Mexican Maritime (pensions and compensated absences), New Holland	FAS 87: accrued benefit method Use of current market assumptions Actuarial gains/losses which exceed "corridor" amortized over expected remaining working lives of participating employees	IAS 19: permits accrued benefit valuation (benchmark) and projected-benefit (alternative) methods Use of long-term assumptions Actuarial gains/losses recognized systematically over remaining working life of employees	1998s IAS 19 Revised (effective for years beginning on or after 1 January 1999), compatible with FAS 87 Accrued benefit method Use of discount rate based on market yields on high quality corporate bonds Actuarial gains/losses exceeding "corridor" amortized over expected remaining working lives of employees Accrual basis for other employee benefits
	FAS 106: similar rules for other post employment benefits	Does not specifically address other post employment benefits (para 4) or employee benefits such as compensated absences	
Panel F: Foreign currency translation Method: Astra	FAS 52: current rate method when functional currency is foreign currency Temporal method when functional currency is reporting currency	IAS 21: similar to US GAAP but sparse guidance may create diversity in practice (i.e., only four brief paragraphs provide guidance for determining the functional currency for foreign operations)	
Hyperinflation: Ispat	FAS 52: reporting currency used as the functional currency and the temporal method used for translation	IAS 21: statements restated to current purchasing power (via IAS 29) prior to translation into the reporting currency of the reporting enterprise	SEC has endorsed IAS 29 for foreign issuers

continued overleaf

Translation of foreign goodwill and fair value adjustments: LVMH, Mexican Maritime	FAS 52: closing exchange rate used	IAS 21: either historical exchange rate or closing rate may be used	FASB comparison notes this aspect of IAS 21 as a significant difference with US GAAP likely to impair comparability
Panel G: Goodwill Goodwill amortization: Atlas, Scandia, Usinor	APB 17: maximum amortization period of 40 years	IAS 22: amortization period may not exceed 5 years unless a longer period not to exceed 20 years can be justified	IASC's 20-year ceiling becomes rebuttable presumption via 1998 revision of IAS 22 (effective for period beginning on or after 1 July 1999); does not permit assignment of an infinite useful life to goodwill
Negative goodwill: Ispat	APB 16: reduces proportionately values assigned to noncurrent assets (other than marketable securities) in determining their fair values, any excess recognized as a deferred credit Negative goodwill amortized to income on a systematic basis over a period not exceeding 40 years	IAS 22 benchmark: fair value non-monetary assets acquired reduced proportionately until excess eliminated, any excess negative goodwill and treated as deferred income Alternative: any excess of acquirer's interest in fair values of identifiable assets/liabilities over cost is negative goodwill and treated as deferred income Amortize negative goodwill over period not exceeding 5 years, unless period not exceeding 20 years can be justified	

(continued)

Table 1. (Continued)

Item and companies	US GAAP	IASC GAAP	Comments
Miscellaneous: Netia		IAS 22 may be ambiguous where items are covered in the form of background material and implementation guidance (para 23–26)	
Panel H: Old goodwill standard			
Capitalize or Charge to Reserves: Banco Comercial Portugues, Fiat, Hoechst, New Holland, Mexican Maritime	APB 16: goodwill must be capitalized	IAS 22: (as revised in 1993) goodwill must be capitalized. However, original version allowed goodwill to be charged to reserves	Goodwill on acquisitions prior to 1995 may give rise to reconciling adjustments in that companies were not required to reinstate goodwill previously charged to reserves
Panel I: Minority interests			
Minority interests: Credicorp (not specified), Hoechst, Mexican Maritime	APB 16: stated at acquirer's share of pre-acquisition carrying value of assets. APB 17: allocate value to all intangibles based on appraised values, including acquired in-process R&D. In-process R&D with no alternative future use is immediately expensed	IAS 22: stated at either the acquirer's share of the pre-acquisition carrying value of assets or fair value of the net assets. Following an acquisition, only record intangibles as an acquired asset if they meet the definition of and recognition criteria for an intangible asset, otherwise, intangibles subsumed within goodwill and amortized accordingly	Minority interests may differ for US and IAS GAAP due to differences in assignment of costs to intangible assets such as in-process R&D. FASB is considering a new standard that would wipe out instant write-offs for the value of as-yet-undeveloped products picked up in an acquisition

continued overleaf

Panel J: Borrowing costs Atlas, Hoechst, Ispat, Netia, Swisscom, and Unisor	FAS 34: under certain conditions *interest* capitalized as part of acquisition cost of an asset	IAS 23 benchmark: expense all borrowing costs in the period incurred
China Southern, Jilin, Shanghai Petrochemical		Alternative: capitalize borrowing costs if attributable to acquisition of qualifying asset	Under allowed alternative, borrowing costs are defined broader than FAS 34, i.e., foreign currency exchange gains/losses capitalized to extent regarded as adjustment to interest costs
Panel K: Accounting for investments Credicorp, LVMH, Rostelecom	FAS 115: investments in marketable debt/equity securities carried at market except for held to maturity debt securities that are carried at amortized cost Holding gains/losses on trading securities (current) charged to net income, while holding gains/losses on available for sale securities (non-current) charged to stockholder's equity (comprehensive income, effective for 1998 financial statements)	IAS 25: current investments at either: market or lower of cost or market Holding gains/losses on current investments carried at market recognized as income/expense or per paragraph 32 Long-term investments carried at either: cost, revalued amounts, or for marketable securities, lower of cost and market value Per paragraph 32, holding gains on revaluation of long term investments credited to equity Holding losses may be charged against existing revaluation surplus, if valuation of security falls below cost the charge must go to income	IAS 39 (effective for periods beginning on or after 1 January 2001): all financial assets recognized on the balance sheet Subsequent to initial recognition, all financial assets (with limited exceptions including held to maturity debt securities) remeasured to fair value

(continued)

38   THE INTERNATIONAL JOURNAL OF ACCOUNTING   Vol. 35, No. 1, 2000

Table 1.   (Continued)

Item and companies	US GAAP	IASC GAAP	Comments
Panel L: Accounting for associates Equity Method: Banco, Hoechst, Netia	APB 18: equity method (investor should present its share of the associate's profit/loss at a post-tax level)	IAS 28: equity method (not clear at what level investor should report its share of the associates' profit/ loss, pre-tax or post-tax)	Equity method as described in IAS 28 essentially the same as APB 18, but IAS 28 is not as detailed and may provide for variation in interpretation
Panel M: Research and development Development: Banco Comercial Portugues, Nokia, Nova	FAS 2: expense all research and development costs as incurred	IAS 9: expense research cost as incurred and must capitalize/ amortize development costs if stringent criteria (i.e., satisfy definition of asset) met	1998's IAS 38 (effective for years beginning on or after 1 July 1999) reaffirms IASC position on R&D
Industry Practice: BHP (area of inter- est method for oil exploration), Lihir Gold, Swisscom (software)	Some software development costs must be capitalized For oil and gas exploration may use successful efforts or full cost	No industry specific standards	1998's IAS 38 (effective for years beginning on or after 1 July 1999) does not apply to miner- al rights and expenditure on exploration for, or development and extraction of, minerals, oil, natural gas and similar non- regenerative resources

continued overleaf

Items appearing in 20-F reconciliations that are not covered by IAS

Item	US GAAP	Note on IAS coverage	Comments
Panel AA: Restructuring provisions The G4 + 1's *Provisions: Their Recognition Measurement, and Disclosure in Financial Statements* states there is little published guidance on recognition/measurement of provisions in general and outlines group's view on restructuring: BHP, Fiat, Hoechst, Ispat, LVMH, New Holland, Swisscom, Usinor	FAS 5: allowed if management is committed and process has effectively begun EITF 94-3 allows setting up of reserves only if certain conditions met For employee termination, employees must be informed regarding key provisions of plan prior to period end Certain costs may be accrued as a part of restructuring charge under IAS are not allowed Restructuring plan must be scheduled within a period of time which indicates significant changes to plan are not likely	IAS 10 addresses contingent liabilities (record if probable and a reasonable estimate of the amount can be made) but does not specifically address restructuring costs No limit on the period of time to complete are structuring plan	IAS 37 (effective for periods beginning on or after 1 July 1999): a provision for restructuring costs should be recognized only if a formal plan for the restructuring exists and management has raised a valid expectation in those affected that it will carry out the restructuring by starting to implement that plan or announcing its main features to those affected by it Based on G4 + 1 Discussion Paper
Panel BB: Employee stock compensation Employee stock compensation (including stock options): Cayman Water, Gucci, Matav, Netia, (Usinor also had a violation but there was no income effect)	Cost of share awards/options charged over period of employee's performance via one of two options: APB 25, cost measured based on intrinsic value or FAS 123, cost based on fair value using an option pricing model For companies electing APB 25, FAS 123 requires disclosure of amount of compensation expense that would be recorded if stock options were carried at fair market value	Disclosures are required, but there is no standard or proposals on measurement	IAS 30 (effective for years beginning on or after 1 January 2001): financial assets/liabilities recognized on balance sheet After initial recognition most financial liabilities measured at original recorded amount (less principle repayments and amortization)—only derivatives and liabilities held for trading remeasured to fair value

(continued)

Table 1. (Continued)

	Items appearing in 20-F reconciliations that are not covered by IAS		
Item	US GAAP	Note on IAS coverage	Comments
Panel CC: Accounting for forwards			
Accounting for forward exchange contracts and hedging: Astra, LVMH, Scandia	FAS 52: hedged foreign currency receivables/payables translated at exchange rate at balance sheet date, with unrealized exchange gains/losses recorded in income Difference between amount of forward exchange contract translated at forward rate and exchange rate at date of inception amortized over life of contract Forward contract translated at exchange rate at balance sheet date and any unrealized exchanges gains/losses recognized in income	Accounting for forward exchange contracts and hedging excluded from the scope of IAS 21 However, IAS 21 does not preclude hedge accounting	Per IAS 39 (effective for years beginning on or after 1 January 2000) hedging means designating a derivative or (for hedges of foreign currency risks) a non-derivative financial instrument as an offset in net profit/loss, in whole or in part, to the change in fair value or cash flows of a hedged item Hedge accounting is permitted in certain circumstances, provided hedging relationship is clearly defined, measurable, and effective
Panel DD: Accounting for intangibles/deferred costs			
See below	Strict criteria for asset recognition and amortization	No specific IAS addressing intangible assets	IAS 38 (effective periods beginning on or after 1 July 1999) prescribes accounting for intangible assets and establishes specific criteria for asset recognition

continued overleaf

LVMH capitalized brands with no amortization	APB 17: maximum life of intangibles 40 years	IAS 38 will require that depreciable amount of an intangible asset be allocated on a systematic basis over estimated useful life
Banco Comercial Portugues includes costs of publicity campaigns in sundry assets	Advertising and publicity costs expensed as incurred	IAS 38 will require that expenditure on advertising and promotional activities be expensed as incurred
Scandia capitalized preoperating expenses	Organizational costs expensed under US GAAP	IAS 38 will require that start-up costs be expensed as incurred
Banco Comercial Portugues capitalized issuance costs	Issuance costs expensed as incurred	No IAS on capital transactions
China Southern incremental costs directly attributable to equity securities offering deferred and later charged against proceeds from initial offering	The deferred amount would be expensed in an earlier accounting period (upon the postponement of the earlier proposed offering of equity securities)	No IAS on capital transactions
		In August 1998, the G4 + 1 agreed that the most appropriate treatment of share issuance costs is to account for them as a reduction in the proceeds of the capital raising

(continued)

Table 1. (Continued)

Policy followed/company	Companies that violate IAS	
	IAS requirement	Comments
Panel AAA: Retirement benefits		
Astra: do not take future salary increases into account	IAS 19 (like US GAAP): future salary increases taken into account in calculation of future pension commitments	Some sample companies might argue IAS 19 is not applicable for their pension plans; however, the IASC argues that several such companies are not complying with IAS 19
BHP: charges to income contributions to pension plans	IAS 19: use either accrued benefit valuation (benchmark) or projected-benefit (alternative) method	The IASC (1998) states that some argued that the old IAS 19 did not work well for plans in countries such as Germany, Japan, and the Netherlands
Nokia: various pension schemes in accordance with local conditions/practices and the schemes are funded through payments to insurance companies or to trustee-administered funds as determined by periodic actuarial calculations	Nokia and Scandia do not appear to adhere to the measurement criteria of IAS 19 (post Comparability Project), nor do they provide the significantly expanded disclosures which include:	IASC now holds that as these countries were represented on the Retirement Benefits Steering Committee, such arguments will have little force in the future
Scandia: provisions based on actuarial-projections, the Swedish plan administered by Pension Registration Institute	• Accounting policies including a description of the actuarial valuation methods used • Actuarial present value of promised retirement benefits at the date of the most recent actuarial valuation • Fair value of the plan assets • Principle actuarial assumptions used in determining the cost of retirement benefits	

continued overleaf

Panel BBB: All inclusive income
Banco Comercial Portugues charges "bonus to employees" against reserves
Fiat does not charge entire tax on equity and substitute equalization tax to income

IAS 8: all items of income/expense included in profit/loss unless prohibited by an IAS

Panel CCC: Foreign currency transactions
Biochem Pharma: part of foreign currency translation adjustment recognized in earnings on repatriation of capital from foreign operations

IAS 21: a pro rata portion of exchange gains/losses accumulated in equity recognized in income upon disposal of an investment in a self-sustaining operation
Only a dividend constituting a return of the investment is considered a disposal

Canadian Handbook acknowledges this as a difference between Canadian GAAP and IASs

BioChem Pharma, IPL, and Nova: deferral and amortization of exchange differences on long-term monetary items

IAS 21 benchmark: on settlement of monetary items or on reporting monetary items at rates different from those at which initially recorded, resulting gains/losses recognized in period they arise (allowed alternative not applicable)

Method followed by these companies eliminated as part of IASC Comparability Project
Canadian Handbook acknowledges as a difference between Canadian GAAP and IASs

Panel DDD: Accounting for associates
BHP only discloses effect of accounting for associates on an equity basis

IAS 28: equity method used for investments in associates when there is significant influence

Legal impediment has been removed in Australia and new standard will require that investments in associates be recognized on an equity accounting basis

Usinor states that some investments in non-consolidated subsidiaries are carried at lower cost or fair value as defined by the COB

Usinor states that under US GAAP the equity method would be used to account for these investments
Hence, it appears that Usinor exercises significant influence and should also use equity method under IASC GAAP

(continued)

Table 1. (Continued)

Policy followed/company	Companies that violate IAS	
	IAS requirement	Comments
Panel EEE: Treasury stock LVMH: carried as asset on balance sheet; recorded a loss associated with sale of treasury stock Usinor: treated as a cash equivalent and valued at 1 cm	Under IASC and US GAAP when a company's own shares are repurchased, the shares are shown as a deduction from shareholder's equity	Fiat carries treasury stock as a fixed asset, but there were no entries to income for the year related to treasury stock
Panel FFF: Capitalization of costs Usinor: charged change in accounting policy for furnace relining costs in 1994 to income to conform with French accounting principles	IAS GAAP requires capitalization of such costs	In 1996 financial statements Usinor acknowledges that the nonrecurring charge is in violation of IASs

The denominator is US net income because 20-F reconciliations are addressed to investors accustomed to US GAAP (Weetman et al., 1998). Consequently, these investors view differences as departures from US net income rather than as departures from IAS net income. Net income is chosen for the denominator rather than a scale factor, such as sales or market value, because the research seeks to evaluate the materiality of accounting differences.

ISA 320, *Audit Materiality*, provides general guidance regarding an assessment of materiality. However, like the publications of other professional bodies and standard setters, the International Federation of Accountants' (IFAC) ISA 320 does not provide specific materiality guidelines to practitioners. In practice, auditors assessing materiality in relation to the impact on users make reference to percentages. Audit practice indicates a useful guideline as being 5–10 percent of income before taxation (Grant Thorton, 1990). As firm policy, Ernst and Young (1998) states that audit differences require consultation whenever the gross or net unrecorded differences exceed 5 percent of pretax income. While the SEC asserts that both qualitative and quantitative factors must be considered in determining materiality, SEC Chief Accountant Turner has stated that traditionally, 5 percent of earnings is believed to be the cut-off point for determining if an item is material or not (Burns, 1999). The current research provides findings based on bands at 5 percent and 10 percent of net income.

The neutral value of 1.0 is utilized for consistency with previous literature. An index value exceeding 1 indicates the IAS net income is greater than that reported according to US GAAP (or an IAS loss is not as large as a US loss). An index value less than 1 indicates that the IAS reported net income is less than that reported under US GAAP (or an IAS loss is larger than a US loss).

Since the 20-F reconciliation contains considerable detail, partial index values may be determined based on the formula:

$$1 - \frac{(\text{partial adjustment})}{|\text{ Net income}_{\text{USA}}|}$$

The partial index values measure the contribution of each 20-F reconciling item. The neutral value of 1 is retained for consistency. The indexes of partial adjustments sum to the total index by the formula:

$$\text{Total comparability index} = \sum_{1}^{n} \text{adjustment}_n - (n - 1)$$

Evaluation of Index

The comparability index carries the disadvantage of reporting extreme index values if US net income/loss approaches zero. Fortunately, such occurrences are rare in the current data set and do not seriously affect interpretation. The presence of outliers must be weighed against the association of the "index of comparability" with the accounting concept of materiality that is usually judged in relation to profit. Such outliers result in comparable problems in practical interpretation of their impact on financial statement users. Further, it has been asserted that materiality cannot be judged on a relative value basis when net income is small or the item causes a change from a small net income to a small net loss.

Use of the index to evaluate annual data may carry the risk of including in any given year a short-term timing difference that reverses in the following year due to a difference in recognition criteria. Fortunately, in that the 20-F provides 3 years of data, it allows for consideration of this aspect. An examination of the 3-year comparisons within each 20-F revealed two reversals (both associated with restructuring) in reconciling items that are observable for each of the separate adjustments analyzed. The impact of the two reversals on the overall index and the appropriate partial index was considered. The impact on the overall index of comparability was less than 1 percent in all years, and the impact on the restructuring partial index was less than or equal to 1 percent in all years.

RESULTS

Data were pulled from the 1997 20-Fs (or annual reports) of the 33 sample companies. Hence, the data cover the years 1995–1997. This section presents the (1) frequency of, and (2) tests of materiality for the 20-F reconciling adjustments and discusses the main causes of adjustments. Table 2 reports the relevant index of comparability measured as a mean and a median over the group as a whole (after excluding outliers) and for each type of reoccurring adjustment. Table 2 also reports the number of reconciling adjustments overall and by category. Each category in Table 2 represents a grouping of more than one type of adjustment (as reflected in Table 1), so that the total number of adjustments presented by companies in their 20-F reconciliations are considerably greater than the number of line items indicated in Table 2.

Index of Comparability for IAS Income

The *overall* index of comparability reveals that in 1995, 1996, and 1997, the adjustment to profit under IASs represents 7 percent (increase in IAS income), 20 percent (increase in IAS income), and 8 percent (increase in IAS income) of profit under US GAAP, respectively. *T*-tests (Table 3a) indicate that the mean index of comparability for IAS Income is significantly greater than 1 only in 1996 ($p = 0.01$). The median values are 1.03, 1.01, and 1.00 for 1995, 1996, and 1997, respectively, and the non-parametric Wilcoxon tests (Table 3b) indicate no statistically significant differences (at $p < 0.05$). Throughout Table 3, outliers are eliminated from the calculation of the *t*-statistics but not the Wilcoxon test.

According to Table 2, in all 3 years, the most frequently occurring sources of adjustments representing differences in US GAAP and IASs were associated with property, plant, and equipment; deferred taxes; goodwill; and capitalization of borrowing costs. Less frequently occurring adjustments are due to restructuring; research and development; foreign currency translation; retirement benefits/pensions; employee stock compensation; intangibles; minority interests; investments; accounting for associates; sale leasebacks; and inventory. In each year, a few adjustments are associated with adoption of new IASs or FASs (i.e., accounting changes). Of particular concern in each year is that several adjustments are associated with what appears to be violations of IASs.

Table 2. Excluding Outliers. Number of Companies Making Each Category of Adjustment to Net Income Including Mean and Median Index of Comparability for 1997, 1996, and 1995

Description of adjustment	1997 Count	1997 Mean	1997 Median	1996 Count	1996 Mean	1996 Median	1995 Count	1995 Mean	1995 Median
Overall	31	1.08	1.00	33	1.20	1.01	28	1.07	1.00
Revised	31	1.06	1.00	33	1.18	1.01	28	1.11	1.00
Violations of IASs	11	1.07	1.02	10	1.06	1.01	10	0.90	0.99
PP&E Revaluations	14	0.91	0.94	11	0.95	0.98	8	0.97	0.99
Deferred Taxes	11	1.06	1.03	13	0.99	0.99	16	0.93	0.97
Goodwill	10	1.08	1.01	9	1.21	1.03	7	1.03	1.02
Capitalized Borrowing Costs	8	0.93	0.95	6	0.99	1.00	6	1.01	0.99
Restructuring	6	1.03	1.01	6	1.06	1.06	5	0.64	1.02
Research and Development	4	1.00	1.00	6	1.14	0.99	5	1.27	1.02
Foreign Currency Translation	5	1.03	1.03	5	1.13	1.01	5	1.32	1.04
Retirement Benefits/Pensions	4	1.02	1.02	4	1.12	1.01	4	1.29	1.29
Accounting Changes	4	0.97	0.96	3	1.10	1.07	3	0.50	1.01
Employee Stock Compensation	4	1.06	1.06	3	1.09	1.07	2	1.63	1.63
Intangibles	3	1.01	1.00	3	0.98	1.00	4	1.09	1.05
Minority Interest	3	1.23	1.01	3	1.03	0.99	2	0.96	0.96
Investments	3	1.02	1.03	3	1.01	1.02	3	1.01	0.99
Accounting for Associates	3	1.38	1.02	3	1.28	1.10	2	0.65	0.65
Sale leasebacks	3	1.11	1.00	3	0.98	0.97	3	0.93	0.97
Inventory	2	1.04	1.04	2	0.98	0.98	2	1.03	1.03
Other	11	1.04	1.02	12	1.07	1.01	13	1.11	1.01

Notes: The following outliers were excluded from calculations of the mean and median values with regard to:

Hoechst (1997 overall index of comparability and 1995 overall index of comparability and partial index of comparability for goodwill and minority interest);

Swisscom (1997 overall index of comparability and partial index of comparability for restructuring and research and development);

Ispat (1995 overall index of comparability and partial index of comparability for goodwill) (full sample only);

Magyar (1995 overall index of comparability and partial index, of comparability for other);

Lihir (1997 partial index of comparability for research and development).

Table 3. Index of Comparability for Net Income

3a. Mean value and t-statistic

	N	M	SD	SEM	t	p value
Net Income 1997	31	1.083	0.3509	0.0630	1.318	0.197
Net Income 1996	33	1.197	0.4381	0.0762	2.588	0.014
Net Income 1995	28	1.073	0.3317	0.0627	1.172	0.252
Revised net income 1997	31	1.057	0.3305	0.0594	0.964	0.343
Revised net income 1996	33	1.179	0.4278	0.0744	2.409	0.022
Revised net income 1995	28	1.109	0.02843	0.0809	2.036	0.052
Partial Adjustments						
IAS Violations 1997	11	1.072	0.1776	0.0535	1.361	0.203
IAS Violations 1996	10	1.059	0.1315	0.0416	1.434	0.185
IAS Violations 1995	10	0.899	0.3117	0.0985	-1.021	0.334
PP&E Revaluations 1997	14	0.905	0.1607	0.0429	-2.198	0.046
PP&E Revaluations 1996	11	0.955	0.1562	0.0471	-0.959	0.360
PP&E Revaluations 1995	8	0.970	0.0581	0.0205	-1.439	0.193
Deferred Taxes 1997	11	1.060	0.0991	0.0298	2.009	0.072
Deferred Taxes 1996	13	0.993	0.0948	0.0263	-0.275	0.787
Deferred Taxes 1995	16	0.934	0.4076	0.1019	-0.649	0.526
Goodwill 1997	10	1.076	0.2088	0.0660	1.149	0.279
Goodwill 1996	9	1.211	0.4207	0.1402	1.503	0.171
Goodwill 1995	7	1.025	0.0428	0.0162	1.573	0.166
Capitalized Borrowing Costs 1997	8	0.926	0.1029	0.0364	-2.025	0.082
Capitalized Borrowing Costs 1996	6	0.989	0.0334	0.0136	-0.747	0.488
Capitalized Borrowing Costs 1995	6	1.008	0.1468	0.0599	0.137	0.896

3b. Actual median and Wilcoxon statistic

	1995				1996				1997			
	N	Median	Wilcoxon statistic	p value	N	Median	Wilcoxon statistic	p value	N	Median	Wilcoxon statistic	p value
Net income	31	1.03	184	0.104	33	1.01	201	0.077	33	1.00	266	0.398
Revised net income	31	1.02	162	0.046	33	1.01	207	0.094	33	1.00	250	0.293
IAS Violations	10	0.99	15	0.101	10	1.01	30	0.399	11	1.02	31	0.430
PP&E Revaluations	8	0.99	9	0.104	11	0.98	8	0.013	14	0.94	30	0.079
Deferred taxes	16	0.93	41	0.081	13	0.99	31	0.155	11	1.06	29	0.361
Goodwill	9	1.04	31	0.157	9	1.03	35	0.069	10	1.01	46	0.030
Capitalized Borrowing costs	6	0.95	12	0.377	6	1.00	13	0.300	8	0.99	8	0.080

Overall Materiality of Adjustments

The mean and median data in Table 2 provide summary indicators for the group of companies as a whole, but, when making investment decisions, investors are concerned with individual companies. Thus, the findings are presented as distributions of adjustments in bands of materiality in Tables 4 and 6. Discussion is in terms of adjustment to net income but could also apply to adjustments to net loss. Tests of statistical significance are again reported in Table 3.

In regard to overall net income, Table 4 presents the distribution bands of net income that an accountant might view as "immaterial" (i.e., differences less than 5%) or "material at 10 percent or more" or "material at 5–10 percent." In 1995, 1996, and 1997, respectively, three (of 31 or 10%), two (of 33 or 6%) and two (of 33 or 6%) companies report IAS income less than US income where the adjustment represents 5–10 percent of US income. One (of 31 or 3%), two (of 33 or 6%) and four (of 33 or 12%) report IAS income exceeding US income by 5–10 percent of US income. In 1995 and 1996, four (of 31 or 13%) and five (of 33 or 15%) report IAS income lower than US GAAP where the adjustment is at least 10 percent of US income. In 1997, eight (of 33 or 24%) report IAS income lower than US GAAP where the adjustment is at least 10 percent of US income. In 1995 and 1996, 11 (of 31 or 35%) and 12 (of 33 or 36%) companies report IAS income exceeding US GAAP income by 10 percent or more. This drops to nine (of 33 or 27%) companies in 1997. These trends suggest recent revisions and additions to IASC standards may be limiting the ability of companies to report materially higher profits in relation to US GAAP.

Violations of IAS—IAS Income Revised

Panels AAA through FFF of Table 1 describe areas where some sample companies appear to be violating IASs. The panels describe the accounting policies followed by these companies and review the appropriate accounting treatment as prescribed by IASs. In considering the materiality of differences between IASs and US GAAP, an argument can be made that IAS income should be adjusted for these violations. Alternatively, statistical tests may indicate significant differences between IASC and US income, where in the absence of violations of IASC accounting guidelines, there are no material differences.

For most items listed in panels AAA through FFF, IASC standards are very similar to US GAAP. For the adjustments listed in Panels BBB through FFF, the companies' adjustments to arrive at US GAAP reported in Form 20-F would also be required to arrive at a more accurate measure of IASC GAAP. While the differences between US GAAP and IAS 19 are more pronounced, the companies' explanations of their 20-F adjustments (see Panel AAA) clearly reveal they are also violating IASC GAAP. Adjusting reported income for the 20-F adjustments associated with retirement benefits for these companies does not provide an exact measure of IASC income; however, it does provide a more accurate measure than that reported by the companies. Thus, "IASC Income Revised" is calculated by starting with IASC income as reported by the companies and adjusting for the items described in Panels AAA through FFF of Table 1.

Table 4. Frequency Table of Distribution of Values of Index and Revised Index of Comparability for Net Income

Level of materiality	Index values	Index of comparability			Revised index of comparability		
		1997	1996	1995	1997	1996	1995
Adjustment of IAS profit is −10% or more of the amount of US profit	≤ 0.90	8	5	4	7	5	2
Adjustment to IAS profit between −5% and −10% of the amount of US profit	0.91–0.94	2	2	3	3	2	3
Adjustment to IAS profit within ±5% of US profit	0.95–1.04	10	12	12	11	12	12
Adjustment to IAS profit is between +5% and +10% of the amount of US profit	1.05–1.09	4	2	1	4	2	3
Adjustment to IAS profit is +10% or more of the amount of the US profit	≥ 1.10	9	12	11	8	12	11
Total		33	33	31	33	33	31
Range:							
Lowest value		−16.60	0.76	0.21	−16.60	0.76	0.86
Highest value		3.56	2.89	31.98	3.56	2.89	31.98

52   THE INTERNATIONAL JOURNAL OF ACCOUNTING   Vol. 35, No. 1, 2000

Table 5. Summary of Violations of IASs

Company name	Violations as a percentage of IAS reported income		
	1995 (%)	1996 (%)	1997 (%)
Astra Group	0.1369	−0.5185	0.0588
Banco Comercial Portugues	−3.1196	−9.0912	2.1893
Biochem Pharma	−54.8419	0.9702	−4.5705
Broken Hill Proprietary	0.9868	3.2504	−0.7317
Fiat	−4.4247	−4.4285	−7.6127
IPL	5.9815	0.6655	−4.4178
LVMH			0.7287
Nokia	5.9589	−0.5822	2.3006
Nova	−4.2735	−2.0881	−35.3846
Scandia	0.7012	1.0600	0.6045
USINOR	2.0541	−27.2666	−1.8004

Table 2 reports the mean and median values of the index of comparability for IAS Income Revised. The difference between IAS Income Revised and US GAAP represented 11 percent, 18 percent, and 6 percent of net income under US GAAP in 1995, 1996, and 1997, respectively. T-tests (Table 3a) indicate the mean index of comparability for IAS Income Revised is significantly greater than 1 in 1995 ($p = .05$) and 1996 ($p = .02$) but not 1997. The median values are 1.02, 1.01, and 1.00, for 1995, 1996, and 1997, respectively. The Wilcoxon tests (Table 3a) indicate a statistically significant difference only in 1995 ($p = .05$).

According to Table 4, IAS Income Revised is less than US income for three (of 31 or 10%), two (of 33 or 6%), and three (of 33 or 9%) companies in 1995, 1996, and 1997, respectively, where the adjustment represents 5–10 percent of US income. IAS Income Revised exceeds US income by 5–10 percent for three (of 31 or 10%), two (of 33 or 6%), and four (of 33 or 12%) companies in 1995, 1996, and 1997, respectively. In 1995, 1996, and 1997, IAS Income Revised is less than US income for two (of 31 or 6%), five (of 33 or 15%), and seven (of 33 or 21%) companies, where the adjustment represents at least 10 percent of US income. IAS Income Revised exceeds US income by 10 percent or more for 11 (of 31 or 35%) and 12 (of 33 or 36%) companies in 1995 and 1996. This drops to eight (of 33 or 24%) companies for 1997. Again, the trend suggests revisions and additions to IASs in recent years are limiting companies' ability to report higher profits in relation to US GAAP.

Table 5 provides information regarding the materiality of the IAS violations for each of the relevant companies. While several of the violations may be viewed as immaterial, some of the violations fall in the 5–10 percent range and others exceed 10 percent of income for the company. Items representing 5–10 percent of the company's income include:

- Banco Comercial Portugues' charging of bonuses to employees against reserves as opposed to observing the IASC's all inclusive income philosophy (overstated IAS income by 9 % in 1996);
- Fiat's not charging the entire tax on equity and substitute equalization tax to income—the policy followed is allowed by Italian law (overstated IAS income by 8 % in 1997);

Table 6. Frequency Table of Distribution of Values of Index of Comparability for PP&E Revaluations, Deferred Taxes, Goodwill, and Capitalized Borrowing Costs

Level of materiality	Index values	PP&E revaluations			Deferred taxes			Goodwill			Capitalized borrowing costs		
		1997	1996	1995	1997	1996	1995	1997	1996	1995	1997	1996	1995
Adjustment of IAS profit is –10% or more of the amount of US profit	≤ 0.90	5	4	1	0	3	3	0	1	0	1	0	1
Adjustment to IAS profit between –5% and –10% of the amount of US profit	0.91–0.94	3	0	1	0	0	3	1	0	0	3	0	0
Adjustment to IAS profit within ±5% of US profit	0.95–1.04	5	6	6	8	7	7	6	3	5	4	6	4
Adjustment to IAS profit is between +5% and +10% of the amount of US profit	1.05–1.09	1	0	0	0	2	0	2	2	1	0	0	0
Adjustment to IAS profit is +10% or more of the amount of the US profit	≥ 1.10	0	1	0	3	1	3	1	3	3	0	0	1
Total		14	11	8	11	13	16	10	9	9	8	6	6
Range (excluding outliers):													
Lowest value		0.41	0.68	0.84	0.97	0.83	–0.40	0.93	0.88	0.97	0.68	0.95	0.83
Highest value		1.06	1.31	1.02	1.31	1.17	1.68	1.66	2.24	9.79	1.01	1.03	1.28

- IPL's use of Canadian guidelines for foreign currency translation (understated IAS income by 6% in 1995);
- Nokia's decision to follow local practices in accounting for pensions (understated IAS income by 6% in 1995).

Violations that exceed 10 percent of income include:

- Biochem Pharma's use of Canadian guidelines for foreign currency translation (overstated IAS income by 55% in 1995);
- Nova's use of Canadian guidelines for foreign currency translation (overstated IAS income by 35% in 1997);
- Usinor's (all violations combined overstated IAS income by 27% in 1996):

    1. utilization of lower of cost or market accounting for some investments as defined by the Commission des Operations de Bourse—per IAS GAAP investments in associates where the company exercises significant influence should be accounted for using the equity method—(overstated IAS income by 14%),
    2. decision to carry treasury stock as an asset (overstated IAS income by 5%),
    3. and expensing (as opposed to capitalizing) furnace relining costs in order to conform to French accounting principles as interpreted by the Commission des Operations de Bourse (overstated IAS income by 8%).

Most of the above "violations" yield an overstatement of IAS income.

The above descriptions reveal that one violation representing between 5 percent and 10 percent of income is associated with Fiat following national law as opposed to IASs. Further, Usinor's 1996 violations, which exceed 10 percent of income, are associated in part with following practices approved by the Commission des Operations de Bourse in France as opposed to IASs.

Following Canada's guidelines for foreign currency translation results in IPL deviating from Revised IAS Income by an amount falling in the 5–10 percent range and Biochem Pharma and Nova deviating from Revised IAS Income by an amount exceeding 10 percent of income. The Canadian Handbook acknowledges some deviations from IASC GAAP in regard to foreign currency translation (see Table 1, Panel CCC). In January 1998, the Canadian Accounting Standards Board (AcSB) discussed the status of a project aimed at eliminating such differences. The AcSB re-affirmed the position taken in an Exposure Draft to eliminate Canada's unique standard of deferral and amortization of exchange gains/losses relating to foreign currency items having a fixed or ascertainable life extending beyond the end of the following fiscal year. However, the AcSB decided that the status of this project should remain unchanged until completion of the IASC's Financial Instruments Project that is targeted for mid-year 2000.

These findings suggest that national regulators and standard setters need to work with the IASC with an aim toward convergence of national GAAP and IASs. Differences between IASC requirements and national guidelines will be even more troublesome under IAS 1 Revised (effective for periods beginning on or after 1 July 1998), which will prohibit companies from stating that they follow IAS unless they comply without exception. In 1999 financial statements, legislated conflicts with IASC GAAP will prohibit companies from noting compliance with IASs.

It is important to note that none of the violations exceeding 10 percent of income are associated with companies whose audit opinion asserts compliance with IASs (see Appendix A). However, two violations representing 5–10 percent of income are attributable to companies whose audit opinions claim that the financial statements are prepared according to IAS. While Nokia's audit opinion makes no note of the violation, Banco Comercial Portugues' auditor notes the exception to IAS in the audit opinion. This suggests auditors may not place as much significance on a claim in the accounting policy footnotes that the statements comply with IASs or comply with IASs in all material aspects as they do to stating compliance with IASs within the audit opinion. Indeed, this is in line with a recent comment by the SEC Chief Accountant.

SEC Chief Accountant Turner has noted that in some situations where a foreign registrant's *footnotes* assert that the financial statements "comply in all material aspects with IAS" or "are consistent with IAS" the company may have applied only certain IASs or omitted certain information without giving any explanation of why the information was excluded (Turner, 1999b). Chief Accountant Turner indicates that the SEC staff has challenged such assertions and will continue to do so. He warns that where such an assertion cannot be sustained, the SEC will require either changes to the financial statements to conform with IASs or removal of the assertion of compliance with IASs. Hence, when auditing SEC foreign registrants claiming to follow IASs, auditors must begin to place more emphasis on identifying and requiring corrections of violations such as those identified by the current research.

Measurement Practices where IAS GAAP is Not Compatible with US GAAP

Panels A through M of Table 1 list the measurement practices where IASs differ from US GAAP for the sample companies between 1995 and 1997. Panels AA through DD lists the areas where the absence of guidance from the IASC allows for material departures from US GAAP for the sample companies. Table 2 reveals the areas where differences as described in Table 1 occur frequently (property, plant, and equipment; deferred tax; goodwill; and capitalization of borrowing costs). The other types of adjustments appear in the 20-F reconciliations on an infrequent basis. Thus, only the former items are discussed in terms of materiality.

Property, Plant, and Equipment

Table 2 reports all the accounting consequences of IASC policy for accounting for property, plant, and equipment that differ from US GAAP as reflected in the 20-F reconciliations (eight in 1995, 11 in 1996, and 14 in 1997). As shown in Panel C, these differences are associated primarily (12 companies) with the existence of IASC options for the measurement of property, plant, and equipment following initial recognition. Other differences include: IASC options for accounting for investment properties (one company) and IASC rules for impairment (two companies).

While the IASC benchmark is consistent with US GAAP for measurement of property, plant, and equipment after initial recognition, the allowed alternative provides for revaluation of classes of assets. It is important to note that most revaluation adjustments are not a function of companies "electing" the IASC-allowed alternative. All of the Chinese companies in the sample revalued fixed assets as part of a restructuring/ reorganization associated with privatization during the mid-1990s. Furthermore, two companies' (Fiat and New Holland) revaluations were associated with compliance with company law or tax regulations. Only three companies (Atlas, as permitted by Swedish GAAP; BHP, as permitted by Australian GAAP; and Ispat as permitted by IASs) voluntarily chose the IASC allowed alternative.

Table 2 reports the mean and median partial indices for property, plant, and equipment and indicates they represent 3 percent (reduction in IAS income), 5 percent (reduction in IAS income), and 9 percent (reduction in IAS income) of US profit in 1995, 1996, and 1997, respectively. T-tests (Table 3a) indicate that overall mean adjustments are significantly less than 1 in 1997 ($p = .05$). The median values are 0.99, 0.98, and 0.94 in 1995, 1996, and 1997, respectively. The Wilcoxon tests (Table 3b) indicate the overall adjustments are significant only in 1996 ($p = .01$). The significance of these adjustments may be explained by the relatively large number of Chinese companies in the sample that were subject to large restructuring/reorganization revaluations associated with privatization and Hong Kong Stock Exchange listing requirements. Insignificant differences in 1995 may be linked to some of the companies with revaluations:

1. not providing data for 1995 (China Eastern Airlines), or
2. revaluing assets during the 3-year period (Beijing Yanhau Petrochemical, April 1997; China Southern 31 December 1996; Guangshen Railway March 1996; and Ispat 31 December 1996).

Table 6 reveals that the individual adjustments for property, plant, and equipment tend to either yield immaterial differences with US income or result in IAS income being less than US income. For one (of eight or 13%), none, and three (of 14 or 21%), in 1995, 1996, and 1997, respectively, IAS income is lower than US income, where the adjustment represents between 5 percent and 10 percent of US income. The adjustment exceeds 10 percent of US income and IAS income is lower for one (of eight or 13%), four (of 11 or 36%), and five (of 14 or 36%) companies in 1995, 1996, and 1997, respectively. These adjustments are the result of higher depreciation charges on the revalued assets. The one instance in 1996 where IAS income is more than 10 percent higher than US income is also associated with revaluations of property, plant, and equipment. Fiat's adjustment to reverse revaluations of property, plant, and equipment reduces the company's net assets (as reflected in the reconciliation of IAS to US stockholder's equity) and the depreciation adjustment increases net income. Neither the IASC or FASB are considering proposals to modify the measurement basis of property, plant, and equipment following initial recognition. Thus, adjustments of this nature will likely continue into the foreseeable future.

The sole 1997 adjustment associated with higher IAS profit, where the adjustment represents between 5 percent and 10 percent of US income, is due to differences in accounting for impaired assets under IASC and US GAAP. Nova states that US accounting principles require impaired assets to be written down to fair market value whereas Canadian (and IAS) principles require assets to be written down to recoverable value. The G4 + 1's *International Review of Accounting Standards Specifying a Recoverable Amount Test for Long-Lived Assets* (Paul, 1997) details the primary differences between IASC and US GAAP in this area. And, the G4 + 1 is working on converging existing standards of the member bodies. Hence, it is possible that differences between IASC and US GAAP may be minimized in the not so distant future.

Accounting for Deferred Taxes

Table 2 reveals the occurrence of adjustments associated with accounting for deferred taxes (16 in 1995, 13 in 1996, and 11 in 1997). Table 1 (Panel B) shows that the differences are associated with the flexibility in IAS 12 (prior to its recent revision) which allows use of partial or comprehensive allocation (US GAAP requires comprehensive allocation) and the deferral or liability method (US GAAP requires the liability method). Under the deferral method, the tax rate in effect when the timing difference originates is utilized to measure the amount of deferred tax liability. Under the liability method as reflected in FAS 109, the enacted rate for the periods in which the temporary differences are expected to reverse is utilized to measure the deferred tax liability. However, under the liability method as defined by the IASC, a change in tax rate may be recognized when announced, while US GAAP delays such recognition until the change in rate has been enacted into law. IASC standards also differ regarding when a tax benefit from an operating loss carry forward may be recorded.

Table 2 reports the mean and median partial indices for deferred taxes and indicates they represent 7 percent (reduction in IAS income), 1 percent (reduction in IAS income), and 6 percent (increase in IAS income) of profit under US GAAP in 1995, 1996, and 1997, respectively. The median values are respectively 0.93, 0.99, and 1.06 in 1995, 1996, and 1997. The *t*-tests and Wilcoxon tests (Table 3) indicate no significant differences (at $p < .05$).

Table 6 reveals that, while several of the individual deferred tax adjustments are immaterial, some are material. IAS profit is lower and the adjustment exceeds 10 percent of US GAAP for three (of 16 or 19%) and three (of 13 or 23%) in 1995 and 1996. In 1995, an additional three (of 16 or 19%) report IAS income less than US income where the adjustment represents 5–10 percent of US income. And, in 1995, 1996, and 1997, three (of 16 or 19%), one (of 13 or 8%), and three (of 11 or 27%) report IAS income exceeding US income by 10 percent or more. In 1996, two (of 13 or 15%) additional companies report IAS income that exceeds US income by an amount in the 5–10 percent range.

Reconciliation items associated with deferred taxes will be minimized, and perhaps almost eliminated, beginning with the filing of 1998 20-Fs. In 1996, IAS 12 was revised along the lines of FAS 109 and effective for years being on or after 1 January 1998 requires the use of the liability method and comprehensive allocation. The decline in the occurrence of reconciling differences over the 3-year period studied may be associated with the early adoption of the new requirements of IAS 12 Revised by some sample

58   THE INTERNATIONAL JOURNAL OF ACCOUNTING   Vol. 35, No. 1, 2000

companies. Upon adopting IAS 12 Revised, Hoechst and New Holland reported no adjustments for deferred taxes.

Accounting for Goodwill

Table 2 reports the overall occurrence of adjustments associated with goodwill (seven in 1995, nine in 1996, and 10 in 1997). Panels G and H of Table 1 reveal that the adjustments are primarily associated with:

1. charging goodwill to reserves prior to 1995 which yields no goodwill amortization charge to IAS net income (five companies), and
2. differences in the maximum amortization period which yield higher goodwill amortization charges to IAS income (three companies).

Given that the index of comparability exceeds 1 in each year, the former appears to be the driving factor. As revised during the Comparability Project, IAS 22 now prohibits the write-off of goodwill to reserves and, like US GAAP, requires capitalization and amortization. However, in that companies were not required to reinstate goodwill charged to reserves prior to 1995 when the revision became effective, these adjustments may continue for years. Adjustments arising from the varying amortization periods for goodwill may also continue. While the IASC has dropped the 20-year maximum amortization period with the 1998 revision of IAS 22, the US is considering moving from a 40-year to a 20-year ceiling. However, it is possible that the G4 + 1 convergence project on accounting for business combinations (see *Recommendations for Achieving Convergence on the Methods of Accounting for Business Combinations*) may result in the US and IASC attempting to minimize differences in regard to the goodwill amortization period. However, the G4 + 1 members view the convergence of guidelines concerning the goodwill amortization period to be secondary to the convergence of methods of accounting for business combinations.[1]

Table 2 reports the mean partial indices for goodwill that represent 3 percent (increase in IAS income), 21 percent (increase in IAS income), and 8 percent (increase in IAS income) of profit under US GAAP in 1995, 1996, and 1997, respectively. The t-tests (Table 3a) indicate that the overall differences between IAS and US income associated with goodwill are not significant ($p < .05$). The medians are 1.04, 1.03, and 1.01 in 1995, 1996, and 1997. The Wilcoxon tests (Table 3b) indicate the goodwill adjustments are significant for 1997 ($p = .03$).

Table 6 indicates that several of the adjustments for goodwill over the 3-year period are immaterial. However, in 1996, one (of nine or 11%) adjustment reflects IAS income being less than US income, where the adjustment represents at least 10 percent of US income. This is related to Usinor amortizing goodwill over 5–20 years under IAS GAAP and over 40 years for US GAAP. In 1997, one (of 10 or 10%) adjustment reflects IAS income being less than US income where the adjustment represents 5–10 percent of US income. In 1995, 1996, and 1997, one (of nine or 11%), two (of nine or 22%), and two (of 10 or 20%) adjustments are associated with IAS income exceeding US income by an amount that represents 5–10 percent of US income. IAS income exceeds US income and the adjustments exceed 10 percent of US income for three (of nine or 33%), three (of nine or 33%), and one (of 10 or 10%) companies in 1995, 1996, and 1997, respectively. Differences where IAS income exceeds US GAAP by more than 10 percent are associated with:

- Hoechst (1995, 1996, and 1997) and Banco charging goodwill to reserves prior to 1995 (1995 and 1996),
- Ispat's treatment of negative goodwill (1995 and 1996).

Capitalized Borrowing Costs

Table 2 shows the occurrence of adjustments associated with capitalized borrowing costs (six in 1995, six in 1996, and eight in 1997). According to Table 1 (Panel J), the differences are a function of six companies following the IAS 23 benchmark whereby all borrowing costs are expensed in the period incurred. Differences for the three Chinese companies are associated with the broad definition of borrowing costs provided by the IAS allowed alternative that provides for the capitalization of more costs than does US GAAP.[2] In respect to the IASC benchmark, Atlas (Sweden) and Usinor (France) state that national GAAP excludes the capitalization of interest. Shanghai Petrochemical, which uses the allowed alternative, states that in years prior to those presented, adjustments arose with regard to capitalization of interest; however, no material adjustments are related to the capitalization of construction interest for the years presented. Accordingly, the adjustments for 1995, 1996, and 1997 represent the amortization effect of differences originating prior to 1995.

Table 2 indicates that the mean partial indices represent 1 percent (increase in IAS income), 1 percent (reduction in IAS income), and 7 percent (reduction in IAS income) of US income in 1995, 1996, and 1997. The *t*-tests (Table 3a) reveal no significant differences. The medians are 0.95, 1.00, and 0.99. Wilcoxon tests (Table 3b) also indicate no significant differences.

Table 6 reveals that in 1995 one (of 6 or 17%) company reports IAS income lower than US income where the adjustment is at least 10 percent of US income, and one (of 6 or 17%) reports IAS income at least 10 percent higher than US income. All 1996 adjustments were immaterial. In 1997, one (of eight or 13%) company reports IAS income lower than US income where the adjustment is at least 10 percent of US income and three (38%) others report lower IAS income where the adjustment represents between 5 percent and 10 percent of US income. The difference that exceeds 10 percent in 1997 arises from Swisscom's use of the IASC benchmark.

SUMMARY AND CONCLUSIONS

The purpose of this research was to identify important differences between IASC standards and US GAAP and to assess the significance and materiality of these differences by means of an empirical analysis of data from the US GAAP reconciliations provided by non-US companies complying with IASs. This is a critical issue as the SEC and IOSCO consider eliminating the requirement that companies using IASs provide a 20-F US GAAP reconciliation to achieve access to US capital markets.

60   THE INTERNATIONAL JOURNAL OF ACCOUNTING   Vol. 35, No. 1, 2000

The results show *overall* that the adjustments to net income from IASC Standards to US GAAP in 1995–1997 were significant, without adjusting for IAS violations, *only* in 1996 with adjustments of 7 percent, 20 percent and 8 percent, respectively. However, when violations of IASs were taken into account, the differences were significant in 1995 and 1996, but *not* in 1997. The mean adjustments were 11 percent, 18 percent, and 6 percent of profit under US GAAP, respectively. Instances of IAS violations highlight the need to work toward the convergence of certain national regulations that currently impede the implementation of IASs, which is the case with respect to certain items in some countries (e.g., Canada, Finland, France, and Sweden).

The findings associated with violations of IASs also raise very important issues for the international auditing profession. Our analysis reveals that for a few sample companies, the 20-F reconciliations (prepared by US audit partners of then Big-6 firms) required adjustments (and disclosures) that would also be necessary for compliance with IAS. Yet, audit partners based in the country of domicile (representing the same auditing firm) had signed opinions where the audit opinion and/or accounting policy footnotes indicated the financial statements complied in all material aspects with IASs. This finding supports the IFAC's concern that auditors are asserting that financial statements comply with IASs when the accounting policies and other notes show otherwise (Cairns, 1997). The SEC and World Bank have expressed similar concerns about the quality of corporate audits performed by Big Five subsidiaries in Asia (Schroeder, 1998). Turner, Chief Accountant of the SEC, has noted that accounting firms are lending their credibility to foreign financial statements that do not measure up to US standards. Turner (1999b) has also stated that if SEC staff identify violations of IASs in financial statements claiming to comply with IASs, then the SEC will require either changes to the financial statements to conform with IASs or removal of the assertion of compliance with IASs. Hence, it logically follows that if the SEC drops the reconciliation requirement for companies using IASs, the audit profession must be prepared to provide assurance that the statements indeed comply with IASs regardless of domicile of the office signing the opinion.

The most important research finding of this study is that the differences between IASs and US GAAP are narrowing. Indeed, in 1997 such differences were not statistically significant. Given the changes implemented following the recent completion of the IASC core standards work program, differences are also likely to be reduced even further by 2000 and beyond. Thus, it could be argued that IASC standards, in terms of their overall impact on net income, are sufficiently close to US GAAP to be acceptable to the SEC and IOSCO.

Alternatively, the SEC may consider it necessary that disclosures be provided where companies utilize certain IASC alternatives that have historically yielded significant/ material deviations from US GAAP. The IOSCO's Technical Working Group is now in the process of identifying IASs that may be acceptable for cross-border offerings without condition as well as IASs where acceptance may be subject to additional disclosures or other conditions. The current research findings are likely to assist in identifying candidates for the latter group. For example, the findings reveal that use of the IASC allowed alternative for property, plant, and equipment, tends to yield a significant deviation from US income. Yet, in some countries such as China, it may not be feasible to utilize the IASC benchmark. Hence, the SEC could require that companies utilizing the IASC allowed alternative for property, plant, and equipment measurement disclose the impact on US net income and net assets of using the alternative as opposed to the IASC benchmark.[3] Based on the current research and recent international developments, it appears that, if deemed necessary by the IOSCO Working Group, the list of IASs recommended for cross-border listings subject to additional disclosures could feasibly comprise quite a short list.

APPENDIX A

Company Names, Country, and Indication of IAS Compliance

Company Name	Country	Indication of IAS Compliance*
Aramex International	Bermuda	AR, Footnote
AB Astra	Sweden	Footnote
Atlas Copco	Sweden	Footnote
Banco Comercial Portugues	Portugal	AR, Footnote
Beijing Yanhau	China	AR, Footnote
Biochem Pharma	Canada	Footnote
Broken Hill Proprietary	Australia	Footnote
Cayman Water	Cayman Islands	AR, Footnote
China Eastern Airlines	China	AR, Footnote
China Southern Airlines	China	AR, Footnote
Credicorp	Bermuda	AR, Footnote
Fiat	Italy	Footnote
Guangshen Railway	China	AR, Footnote
Gucci Group	Netherlands	AR, Footnote
Hoechst	Germany	AR, Footnote
IPL Energy	Canada	Footnote
ISPAT International	Netherlands	AR, Footnote
Jilin Chemical Industrial	China	AR, Footnote
Lihir Gold	Papua New Guinea	Footnote
LVMH	France	Footnote
Magyar Távközlési Rt. (MATAV)	Hungary	AR, Footnote
Mexican Maritime Transportation	Mexico	AR, Footnote
Netia Holdings	Poland	AR, Footnote
New Holland	Netherlands	AR, Footnote
Nokia	Finland	AR, Footnote
NOVA	Canada	Footnote
OAO Rostelecom	Russia	AR, Footnote
Scania	Sweden	Footnote
Shanghai Petrochemical	China	AR, Footnote
Sulzer Medica	Switzerland	AR, Footnote
SwissCom	Switzerland	AR, Footnote
USINOR	France	Footnote
Yanzhou Coal Mining	China	AR, Footnote

AR: Compliance with IAS indicated in audit opinion.
Footnote: Compliance with IAS indicated in accounting policy footnote.

NOTES

1. Only one company reported an adjustment associated with different accounting methods utilized to account for a business combination.

2. Ispat did not have an adjustment in 1997.
3. IAS 16 requires that companies carrying items of property, plant, and equipment at revalued amounts disclose the carrying amount of each class of property, plant, and equipment that would have been included in the financial statements had the assets been carried under the benchmark treatment.

REFERENCES

Adams, C. A., P. Weetman, and S. J. Gray. 1993. "Reconciling National with International Accounting Standards: Lessons from a Study of Finnish Corporate Reports." *European Accounting Review, 2*(3): 471– 494.

Amir, E., T. S. Harris, and E. K. Venuti. 1993. "A Comparison of the Value-relevance of U.S. versus Non-U.S. GAAP Accounting Measures Using Form 20-F Reconciliations." *Journal of Accounting Research, 31(Supplement)*: 230 –275.

Bandyopadhyay, S. P., J. D. Hanna, and G. Richardson. 1994. "Capital Market Effects of U.S.–Canada GAAP Differences." *Journal of Accounting Research, 32*(Autumn): 262–277.

Barth, M. and G. Clinch. 1996. "International Accounting Differences and Their Relation to Share Prices: Evidence from U.K., Australian and Canadian Firms." *Contemporary Accounting Research, 13*(Spring): 134 –170.

Burns, J. 1999. "SEC's View on Materiality Goes Beyond Size, Official Says." *Dow Jones Newswires,* February 28.

Cairns, David. 1997. "IFAC—20 Years On." *World Accounting Report,* (October): 2.

Cochrane, J. L. 1992. "Helping to Keep U.S. Capital Markets Competitive: Listing World-class Non-U.S. Firms on U.S. Exchanges." *Journal of International Financial Management and Accounting, 2*: 165–170.

Cooke, T. E. 1993. "The Impact of Accounting Principles on Profits: The US versus Japan." *Accounting and Business Research, 23*(Autumn): 460 – 476.

Ernst and Young. 1998. Revisions to Requirements to Consult on Audit Differences. June 12.

Financial Accounting Standards Board. 1996. *The IASC–U.S. Comparison Project: A Report on the Similarities and Differences between IASC Standards and U.S. GAAP.* Financial Accounting Standards Board.

Fulkerson, C. L. and G. K. Meek. 1998. "Analysts' Earnings Forecasts and the Value Relevance of 20-F Reconciliations from Non-U.S. to U.S. GAAP." *Journal of International Financial Management and Accounting, 9*: 1–15.

Grant, Thornton. 1990. *Audit Manual.* London: Longman.

Gray, S. J. 1980. "The Impact of International Accounting Differences from a Security-Analysis Perspective: Some European Evidence." *Journal of Accounting Research, 18*(Spring): 64–76.

Hellman, N. 1993. "A Comparative Analysis of the Impact of Accounting Differences and Return on Equity." *European Accounting Review, 3*: 495–530.

IASC. 1998. "IASC Board Approves Revised IAS 19." *IASC Insight,* (March): 4–5.

IASC. 1999. "IOSCO Aims for a Timely Review of Core Standards." *IASC Insight,* (June): 1–2.

Norton, J. 1995. "The Impact of Accounting Practices on the Measurement of Profit and Equity: Australia versus the United States." *Abacus, 3*(3): 178–200.

Paul, Jim 1997. *International Review of Accounting Standards Specifying a Recoverable Amount Test for Long-lived Assets.* Norwalk, CT: Financial Accounting Standards Board.

PricewaterhouseCoopers. 1998. *International Accounting Standards—Similarities and Differences— IAS, US GAAP and UK GAAP.* UK: Pricewaterhouse Coopers.

Rees, L. L. 1995. "The Information Contained in Reconciliations to Earnings Based on U.S. Accounting Principles by Non-U.S. Companies." *Accounting and Business Research, 25*: 301–310.

Rees, L. L. 1996. "A Comparison of Investors' Abilities to Assimilate US GAAP Disclosures." *Journal of Accounting and Public Policy, 15*: 271–287.

Schroeder, M. 1998. "SEC Increases Accounting-fraud Probes." *The Wall Street Journal,* December 9: B8.

SEC. 1996. Press Release April 11.

Street, D. L. and S. J. Gray. 1999. "How Wide is the Gap between IASC and US GAAP? Impact of the IASC Comparability Project and Recent International Developments." *Journal of International Accounting, Auditing and Taxation, 8*(1): 133–164.

Turner, L. E. 1999a. *A Message from the Chief Accountant of the US Securities Exchange Commission, COSMOS Accountancy Chronicle,* January 5.

Turner, L. E. 1999b. Financial Reporting Issues Critical to European SEC Registrants/Users of US GAAP, Speech at the European FASB—SEC Financial Reporting Conference, April 8.

US Congress. 1996. National Securities Market Improvement Act.

van der Tas, L. G. 1988. "Measuring Harmonization of Financial Reporting Practice." *Accounting and Business Research, 18*(70): 157–169.

Weetman, P., C.A., Adams, and S.J., Gray. 1993. *Issues in International Accounting Harmonisation,* Research Report No 33. Chartered Association of Certified Accountants.

Weetman, P., E. A. E. Jones, C. A. Adams, and S. J. Gray. 1998. "Profit Measurement and UK Accounting Standards: A Case of Increasing Disharmony in Relation to US GAAP and IASs." *Accounting and Business Research, 28*(3): 189–208.

Weetman, P. and S. J. Gray. 1990. "International Financial Analysis and Comparative Accounting Performance: The Impact of UK versus US Accounting Principles on Earnings." *Journal of International Financial Management and Accounting, 2*(2/3): 111–130.

Weetman, P. and S. J. Gray. 1991. "A Comparative International Analysis of the Impact of Accounting Principles of Profits: The USA versus the UK, Sweden and The Netherlands." *Accounting and Business Research, 21*(84): 363–379.

Zeff, S. 1999. "The SEC: Rampant Speculation but what Happens Next?" *Accounting and Business, 2*(February): 16–21.

[21]

Journal of Business Finance & Accounting, 25(3) & (4), April/May 1998, 0306-686X

THE USE OF FOREIGN ACCOUNTING DATA IN UK FINANCIAL INSTITUTIONS

SAMANTHA MILES AND CHRISTOPHER NOBES*

INTRODUCTION

The globalisation of securities markets (Smith, 1991; and Scott-Quinn, 1991) has led to an increased use of foreign financial information and to a need for international comparability of financial information. The need for comparability has been recognised by securities regulators (IOSCO, 1995) but the fulfilment of it is some years away. In the meantime, one way of dealing with the problem is for regulators to demand expensive dual reporting or reconciliations.[1] Another way is to pretend that there is no problem, i.e. to negotiate mutual recognition of accounting regulations.

In most markets, the participants use various mechanisms to cope with international accounting differences, such as adjustments of accounting numbers to a benchmark or reliance instead on economic data or comparisons of financial information within a regulatory environment but not from one environment to another. This paper examines the reactions to foreign accounting data of participants in the global equity[2] market who are based in London, which has the world's most international major equity market.[3] The argument proceeds by looking first at previous findings relating to the use of accounting data in a domestic context, then at the few studies in an international context, then at our own survey. In order to interpret the results, it is important to discuss briefly the opposing theories of market efficiency and hence any implications for accounting policy choice which result from international accounting diversity.

USE OF ACCOUNTING DATA IN A DOMESTIC CONTEXT

Some research into UK equity valuation suggests that the annual report is the most important source of information for analysts, although they also use

* The authors are, respectively, Lecturer in Accounting at the University of Bristol and Coopers & Lybrand Professor of Accounting at the University of Reading. They are grateful for the many hours provided by the analysts and fund managers who were interviewed for this research, and to David Ashton, Judy Day, Don Egginton, Alan Roberts and the anonymous referees for comments on earlier drafts of this paper. (Paper received October 1996, revised and accepted August 1997)

Address for correspondence: C.W. Nobes, Coopers and Lybrand Professor of Accounting, Department of Economics, Faculty of Letters & Social Sciences, The University of Reading, P.O. Box 218, Whiteknights, Reading RG6 6AA, UK.

310   MILES AND NOBES

several other sources to build up their picture of a company (Lee and Tweedie, 1981; Arnold and Moizer, 1984; and Day, 1986). Nevertheless, Lee and Tweedie found that analysts had a limited understanding of accounting data; and Day found that few analysts had accounting qualifications, and noted that annual reports are not seen as containing price sensitive information. Arnold and Moizer suggested that analysts may have exaggerated their use of annual reports in order to avoid suspicions of insider dealing. More recent papers (Pike et al., 1993; and Breton and Taffler, 1995) do indeed show an increased reliance on company contacts.

Day reports that analysts make extensive use of ratios (e.g. gearing), and Arnold and Moizer show the use of price/earnings ratios. Pike et al. confirm the importance of price/earnings or price/cash flow ratios, followed by the ratio of net assets per share. They also found only a small usage of technical analysis or of betas. This contrasted with a greater use of technical analysis for domestic purposes in Germany (Darrat, 1987).

Given (i) the heavy reliance on ratios in the UK, and (ii) the lack of accounting sophistication, there would appear to be a temptation for management to engage in various forms of 'creative accounting'. It is widely believed that UK management succumb to the temptation (Griffiths, 1986; Jamieson, 1988; and Smith, 1992 and 1996). This is despite good evidence that major stock markets are efficient, at least in semi-strong form (e.g. Firth, 1976; and Cooper, 1982). Anecdotal evidence (e.g. as discussed by Watts and Zimmerman, 1986, p. 75) concerning the behaviour of managers and the investment community appears to suggest that they may not believe the general empirical evidence supporting market efficiency. It also seems that analysts may be 'functionally fixated' on the 'bottom line' without attending to the details of its calculation (Ashton, 1976; and Abdel-Khalik and Keller, 1979), so that an earnings decreasing accounting change is accompanied by a negative abnormal stock return regardless of the effect of a change in the present value of cash flows.

Running counter to these arguments: (i) it is possible to explain management behaviour in other ways, (ii) anecdotal evidence should be treated carefully, and (iii) belief in inefficiency by market participants does not imply inefficiency. First, some actions of management might be explained via the contracting hypothesis without contravening a belief in market efficiency. Many contracts, such as debt covenants and compensation plans within the firm, rely on accounting numbers. Management may be motivated to select certain accounting procedures because of the implications that they have for such contracts. This has some empirical support, e.g. Zmijewski and Hagerman (1981) and Healy (1985).

Secondly, the anecdotal evidence should be interpreted carefully. It is often considered less informative than more carefully constructed research, although this does not mean that it should be dismissed (Beaver, 1989, p. 142).

Thirdly, belief of inefficiency within the market by individuals does not imply that there actually is market inefficiency. For example, prices may

FOREIGN DATA AND UK FINANCIAL INSTITUTIONS 311

reflect a richer information set than the one accessed by one individual. Certainly, Beaver regards the statement that 'market efficiency implies that fundamental research is useless' as fallacious. This is because analysts competing for information play an important role in the process of generating and disseminating information (including much that is not accounting based) to the investment community. Thus the net effect of their activities need not be valueless but can contribute to market efficiency by producing a richer information system.

Grossman and Stiglitz (1976) suggest that the market can never be fully efficient because there are constantly new shocks to the economy, so that the market can never fully adjust to, and therefore prices can never fully reflect, all the information possessed by informed individuals. The inefficiency may be just enough to provide the revenue required to compensate the informed investors for their analytical activities.

It has also been suggested that the market contains both functionally fixated investors and those who are more sophisticated (Hand, 1990), although this is unproven (Tiniç, 1990). Foster (1988, p. 444) also suggests a myopic hypothesis which states that the capital market has a short term focus on the current year's reported earnings, rather than a focus on a multi-year horizon. This theory helps to explain Hand's hybrid hypothesis. As Tiniç (1990) argues, if both sophisticated and unsophisticated market participants determine stock prices, there must be restrictions on the behaviour of the sophisticated investors which prevent them from exploiting the profit opportunities offered by mispriced securities. De Long et al. (1990) suggest that such restrictions may be a limited time horizon (as proposed by Foster), risk aversion or lack of wealth. For this theory to stand, unsophisticated investors must also be unable to learn that there are profit opportunities from mispriced securities.

In terms of particular accounting choices used to test market efficiency, the cases of LIFO in the US and of goodwill in the UK are instructive. The former is a real accounting choice with economic consequences via the tax advantage of adopting LIFO, and the latter is a cosmetic accounting example. Despite a large amount of empirical work on LIFO adoption (e.g. Biddle, 1980; Ricks, 1982; Abdel-Khalik and McKeown, 1978; Biddle and Ricks, 1988; and Jennings, Mest and Thompson, 1992), it is still not clear whether the market can see through a change in accounting policy, although a large number of factors (rather than just the reaction of the market to the 'bottom line') has been suggested to explain why management might forgo the tax advantages of LIFO. Examples include Fellingham's (1988) signalling theory, Beaver's (1989, p. 41) contracting perspective and Morse and Richardson (1983) who suggested firm size.

The fear of an unsophisticated market reaction to the effects of goodwill rules on profit seems to have been an important driving force in standard setting discussions in the UK (Holland, 1990; Waller, 1990; and Nobes,

1992). Empirical research does suggest that UK companies pay more for subsidiaries than US companies do because of the different goodwill rules (Choi and Lee, 1992). This may be partly due to lack of information (Duvall et al., 1992), or to the existence of different corporate governance systems resulting in different constraints being placed on management.

Breton and Taffler (1995) show that, in practice, UK analysts are not good at correcting for creative accounting when calculating ratios. The UK's Accounting Standards Board has attempted to reduce the scope for creative accounting in certain areas (e.g. by including all exceptional and extraordinary items within earnings).[4] Ironically, this has led analysts to create the concept of 'headline earnings' (IIMR, 1993) which excludes extraordinary and certain exceptional items, thereby preserving and expanding the scope for creative interpretation of these words. In Germany, the analysts' association (DVFA) has a definition of earnings which is designed to exclude several discretionary and tax-based items (Busse von Colbe et al., 1991). Some research (e.g. Rees et al., 1992; and Harris et al., 1994) suggests that DVFA adjusted information is more value-relevant than the original German annual reports.

In a domestic context, it is therefore at best unproven that the market is efficient in deciphering accounting numbers, given the empirical evidence supporting efficient markets, functional fixation and Hand's hybrid system, and anecdotal evidence of the proliferation of creative accounting. When adding an international dimension, further issues arise, as examined below.

CROSS-BORDER ANALYSIS

Choi and Levich (1991) interviewed users of cross-border data in 52 organisations in five major financial centres. They found that over half the users reported an effect on their market decisions due to accounting diversity. The others adopted local perspectives or relied on economic data. Those reporting an effect mostly tried to re-state foreign financial statements to a more familiar accounting basis. Some, however, avoided certain countries because of accounting differences.

Choi et al. (1983) looked at the interpretation of financial ratios from overseas. They suggested that there needs to be adjustment for institutional and other issues, as well as for accounting differences, before there can be successful international comparisons. Aron (1991) showed the difference in average price/earnings ratios between certain stock markets. There are also several studies concerned with differential degrees of conservatism across countries in the measurement of earnings (e.g. Weetman and Gray, 1991; Emenyonu and Gray, 1992; and Norton, 1995). These studies use reports published by foreign companies listed on the New York Stock Exchange which reconcile domestic accounting to US rules.

FOREIGN DATA AND UK FINANCIAL INSTITUTIONS   313

We have drawn on this cross-border research in order to establish areas of investigation about the behaviour of analysts with respect to foreign accounting data. It also seems reasonable to extrapolate from the research summarised above relating to domestic analysis. For example, it seems likely that analysts are at least as unsure about comparative international accounting practices as they are about domestic ones. The following propositions are suggested in the context of the assessment of foreign companies by London-based analysts and fund managers:

1. Analysts and fund managers are not qualified accountants.
2. Accounting differences affect[5] the work of users.
3. Users rely more heavily on non-accounting data than on accounting data.
4. Users restate accounts before analysis.
5. Users restrict investment to countries or sectors with more familiar accounting.
6. Users are not knowledgeable about the major international accounting differences.

INTERVIEWS

Some of the above propositions might be susceptible to market-based research. For example, Choi and Lee's (1992) work might be extended to examine aspects of restatement of accounting data. However, the above propositions examine behavioural issues and would generally seem to require questionnaire or interview methodology which does not allow elaborate statistical analysis.

A questionnaire approach has been used elsewhere (Weaver, 1996). This paper, which can be seen as a series of case studies, reports on interviews with 17 London-based international analysts and fund managers. Interviews have the advantage over questionnaires of the ability to collect a richer series of answers by reducing ambiguity and investigating interesting lines of enquiry. There are disadvantages, such as a limited sample size and the likelihood of interviewer bias. Attempts can be made to reduce the bias (e.g. Clarkson, 1967; and Day, 1986), and in the case of this research, there were always two interviewers present, who made simultaneous notes and compared them soon after each interview. The interviews were semi-structured, using a template of questions in the same order, but allowing extra questions where they seemed relevant, for example following up interesting lines of enquiry.

The 17 interviewees worked for six large institutions (one ultimately controlled in the UK, one from the US, and four from continental Europe). The institutions were self-selecting in the sense that they agreed to take part in the interview process. This may introduce a bias if this means that certain

314   MILES AND NOBES

types of institution were excluded, e.g. those which were uncomfortable with their lack of international accounting expertise or those opposed to assisting outside research. The number of interviewees compares with those used in previous research: 18 individuals by Day (1986); 12 London-based firms by Choi and Levich (1991) and participants from five firms by Breton and Taffler (1995). Nevertheless, our findings can only be regarded as indicative, and may not accurately represent the whole population of UK analysts who use foreign accounting data in their work.

A pilot interview was conducted in March 1994 with four fund managers from a continental European based institution. The pilot was instructive, particularly in identifying the need to establish the organisational structure of the firm, e.g. whether analysts/fund managers concentrated on certain geographical areas or on sectors, international accounting diversity being potentially more important to the latter because inter-country comparisons must be made. It also became clear that some interviewees would be nervous about their lack of accounting knowledge, and would be more forthcoming if the interviews were not tape-recorded. It was therefore decided to use two interviewers for each interview, without tape-recording.

The 17 interviewees (nine analysts, five fund managers, and three analyst managers) were seen individually between April 1994 and March 1995, the interviews lasting about 45 minutes. The data which follows is based on the survey excluding the pilot. The Appendix summarises some biographical data relating to the interviewees, which has been used to cross reference the results.

In general, the analysts provided reports for external fund managers. As will be seen, the fund managers assume that the analysts make accounting adjustments for international diversity. The former are, therefore, less likely to see accounting diversity as a problem. Where useful, the findings below distinguish between analysts and fund managers. Another possibly relevant distinction for the *analysts*, which is brought out below, is between those specialising in particular sectors and those specialising in particular countries. By contrast, all the fund managers were basically geographically specialised.

FINDINGS

Our findings are explained here in the order of the six propositions outlined above.

Accounting Expertise

As may be seen from the Appendix, only two of the 17 interviewees had accounting qualifications (and none of the four pilot interviewees had). This is consistent with a similar finding by Day (1986) relating to domestic analysts.

Are Users Affected by International Differences?

Table 1 shows findings relating to whether the interviewees perceived inter-national accounting differences to affect investment decisions. This was explained as whether there were difficulties in understanding foreign financial statements or problems with the comparability of accounts which caused the users to alter their investment criteria. The interviewees were nearly equally split on this subject, with no evidence that greater experience leads to more effect. However, if the subjects are grouped into 'sector' and 'country' experts, a strong association can be seen between sector expertise and a tendency to perceive an effect on investment decisions: seven out of eight sector experts reported an effect, whereas only two out of nine country experts did. This is not driven by the analyst/manager classification because the fund managers were equally split between 'yes' and 'no'; nor is it due to any greater experience of sector specialists (they had average experience of 5.2 years, against country specialists' 8.6 years).

Those nine interviewees who reported an effect were asked follow-up questions on the nature of the effect on their behaviour. Assessment of foreign companies was said to be affected in the following ways:

(i)   reluctance to rely on accounting information (1 out of 9);
(ii) necessity to restate to some degree which was considered time-consuming (3 out of 9);
(iii) avoidance/reduction of investment due to a lack of understanding foreign accounting (3 out of 9); and
(iv) problems experienced in understanding accounting but not insurmountable ones (2 out of 9), e.g. requiring a more detailed analysis of the notes to the accounts than usual.

Those eight interviewees who saw no problem with accounting diversity fell into the following categories:

(i)   reliance on reports of brokers (3 out of 8);
(ii) lack of use of accounting information (1 out of 8);
(iii) lack of perception of accounting diversity (1 out of 8);
(iv) markets viewed from domestic perspective because price setters are domestic (1 out of 8); and
(v)   international comparisons not undertaken due to being a country specialist (2 out of 8).

Thus, these case studies suggest that investment decisions are generally affected by accounting diversity for sector experts but not for country experts.

Coping Techniques

Macro-economic data was used by 14 out of 17 interviewees, for purposes including:

Table 1

Do Accounting Differences Affect Capital Market Decisions? (No. of Interviewees)

Profession	Yes	No	Total
Analyst-sector	6	1	7
Analyst/manager-sector	1	–	1
Analyst-country	–	2	2
Fund manager (– basically country specialists)	2	2	4
Analyst/manager-country	–	3	3
Total	9	8	17

- to identify growth areas in an economy,
- to check that a company's forecasts were plausible,
- to identify cyclical factors, such as inflation and interest rates.

Two interviewees did not use macroeconomic data because they were fund managers who relied on analysts, and one analyst adopted a 'bottom-up' approach which focused on individual companies without looking at the macro-economy.

All interviewees (including the fund managers) reported the use of trend analysis and ratio analysis. About half the interviewees looked at companies over five to ten years in order to cover at least one business cycle. The others used two to four years, partly because the lack of availability of data was a problem (e.g. in emerging countries) and partly because comparability was made difficult after accounting changes (e.g. as a result of the implementation of EU Directives).

Ratio analysis ranged from the comprehensive by some analysts to a check for anomalies by three fund managers. Standard spreadsheets were in common use, with between six and nine ratios being normal. Six out of 17 interviewees preferred cash flow ratios (i.e. ratios based on an adjusted profit figure) but price/earnings ratios were seen as the most important by the other 11.

In conclusion, although non-accounting data is generally used, it does not supplant the use of accounting data.

Restatement

Restatement of foreign accounting data to a benchmark before analysis is not common. Only one interviewee (an analyst) undertook substantial, but not full, restatement (to a UK basis). Two more analysts made a few adjustments, particularly by adding back goodwill amortisation. Two analysts and one fund manager said that, where available, they used a company's reconciliation data to US or International Accounting Standards (IASs), and another used DVFA[6] figures.

On further investigation, it was clear that these analysts were unaware that, at least up until 1995, IASs were sufficiently flexible that almost any US or UK practice was acceptable. This flexibility meant that it was also quite possible for most continental European companies to choose national options in order to comply with IASs while retaining practices very different from either UK or US accounting.

The remaining eleven interviewees (i.e. 7 out of 8 fund managers and all the manager/analysts) did not adjust or use available reconciliation data. Further questioning revealed that the reasons for this included:

(i)   7 out of 8 fund managers assumed that analysts had already made the necessary adjustments (7 out of the 11 interviewees who did not adjust/reconcile);

(ii) accounting data is not sufficiently important to use resources to adjust it (2 out of 11);

(iii) cultural differences are more important than accounting differences and cannot be adjusted for by restatement (1 out of 11); and

(iv) domestic figures should be used for single-country portfolios, and even for international portfolios because price-setting is done by investors using domestic data (1 out of 11).

Some comment seems appropriate on the implications of these responses. Reason (i) above is especially interesting, as the fund managers' assumption is wrong (based on our study). Reasons (ii) and (iii) are unimpressive, given that all interviewees used accounting data for ratio analysis, at least to some extent. Although ratio analysis may overcome some of the problems for country analysts, extensive use of provisions for income smoothing in some countries[7] may make apparent trends misleading. For cross-country sectoral analysis, the use of ratios will not solve problems in cases where numerator and denominator are affected in opposite directions.[8] Reason (iv) may not be true for the large listed companies which our interviewees were generally concerned with. Even for single-country portfolios, accounting differences are important for analysis: otherwise how would one know, for example, that it is important to adjust for the highly varied goodwill treatments in France (see below)?

It is now possible to summarise our findings with respect to restatement. Full restatement was not undertaken by any interviewee. Six interviewees (five of them analysts, i.e. a slight majority of the nine analysts) made some adjustments or used available reconciliations. One fund manager did this, but most of them incorrectly assumed that analysts made full-scale restatement.

Avoidance of Countries/Sectors

On the matter of avoiding particular countries, most interviewees (9 out of 17) were not in a position to do this because they had been allocated one country or a small range of countries. However, three interviewees (all of them fund managers or manager analysts) did avoid certain countries, particularly those with low regulation and lack of disclosure rather than those with incomprehensible accounting. China, Turkey and Vietnam were mentioned in this context, but there was also concern over Austria, Greece, India and Portugal. The treatment of provisions in Germany and Switzerland was seen as suspect. One fund manager who had a free rein for continental Europe avoided Austria, Italy and Germany because of a perception of poor accounting despite the strength and importance of the economies.

Three of the country specialists (3 out of 9) who did have a choice of sectors avoided certain of them because of accounting difficulties. In particular, this applied to financial services, including insurance companies.

In summary, there is some evidence to show that users avoid countries (3 out of 8) and sectors (3 out of 9) but most interviewees had little choice for at least one of the two dimensions.

Awareness of International Differences

Interviewees were asked whether they could rank countries in terms of conservatism of the measurement of earnings (for example, as in Radebaugh and Gray, 1993). Most interviewees (12 out of 17) made suggestions which were consistent with that literature. For example, UK accounting was universally thought to be less conservative than US accounting, which in turn was seen as less conservative than Japanese. Several interviewees were alert to the relevance, for these comparisons, of inflation, exchange rate movements and stage of the business cycle.

Interviewees were asked about awareness of international differences in certain major areas of accounting: goodwill, inventory costing and deferred tax. Although the range of countries covered was large, the interviews focused on differences between France, Germany, Japan, the UK and the USA.

In the case of goodwill, all sector analysts correctly identified UK practice, but most other interviewees did not, as Table 2 shows. This finding is consistent with those above concerning the greater use of adjustments by sector analysts. Table 3 shows that a similar overall picture emerges for recognition of US practices, but that there is decreasing knowledge for Germany, then France and Japan. Again, for these four countries, the greatest proportion of correct answers was given by the sector analysts, but this detail is not shown in order to avoid a proliferation of similar tables. As usual, the fund managers relied on analysts' reports to have corrected for the goodwill differences, but some analysts did not know the goodwill treatments (as noted

FOREIGN DATA AND UK FINANCIAL INSTITUTIONS   319

Table 2

Recognition of UK Goodwill Practices (interviewees by category)

	Correct Treatment Identified	Incorrect Treatment Identified	Not Important/ Don't Know	Country Not Relevant[1]	Total
Analyst-sector	6	–	–	1	7
Analyst-country	–	–	2	–	2
Fund manager	2	–	2	–	4
Analyst/manager-sector	–	–	1	–	1
Analyst/manager-country	1	–	2	–	3
Total	9 (53%)	– (–%)	7 (41%)	1 (6%)	17 (100%)

Note:
[1] Accounting knowledge relating to a country is not relevant because that country is not focused upon for investment.

Table 3

Recognition of Goodwill Practices (no. of interviewees)

	Correct Treatment	Incorrect Treatment	Not Important/ Don't Know	Country Not Relevant	Total
UK	9 (53%)	–	7 (41%)	1 (6%)	17 (100%)
US	8 (47%)	–	6 (35%)	3 (18%)	17 (100%)
Germany	2 (12%)	1 (6%)	4 (23%)	10 (59%)	17 (100%)
France	1 (6%)	–	7 (41%)	9 (53%)	17 (100%)
Japan	–	–	6 (35%)	11 (65%)	17 (100%)

above) and only one analyst adjusted for goodwill differences. However, some analysts stripped goodwill and its amortisation out of the accounts for analysis for any country.

Several country analysts tended to think that goodwill was either unimportant or uniformly treated within a country, but neither of these ideas is likely to be the case for the group reports of listed companies.[9] As examples of the importance of goodwill:

- Daimler-Benz' Form 20-F reconciliation for 1993 showed adjustments of DM287m (47% of earnings) and DM2284m (13% of net assets) from German to US rules.

- The French group, Total, would show earnings 20% higher for 1995 if they had adopted the UK practice of writing goodwill off against reserves.

- On average,[10] for the 42 UK companies listed on the New York Stock Exchange in 1993/4, the US reconciliation adjustment for goodwill

320   MILES AND NOBES

Table 4

Recognition of Inventory Flow Assumptions (no. of interviewees)

	FIFO*	LIFO Also Allowed and Common*	Not Important/ Don't Know	Country Not Relevant	Total
UK	3 (18%)	–	13 (76%)	1 (6%)	17 (100%)
US	–	3 (18%)	11 (65%)	3 (18%)	17 (100%)
Germany	–	–	7 (41%)	10 (59%)	17 (100%)
France	–	–	8 (47%)	9 (53%)	17 (100%)
Japan	–	–	6 (35%)	11 (65%)	17 (100%)

Note:
* Shaded areas represent correct recognition.

amounted to a decrease in earnings of 33% and an increase in net assets of 76%.

Turning to inventory valuation, the interviews covered the flow assumptions for the determination of cost (e.g. FIFO/LIFO). As Table 4 shows, there was very little knowledge on this subject, although a few recognised that LIFO is not acceptable in the UK but is in the US and in some other countries. All interviewees thought that inventory valuation was an unimportant area, and none adjusted for it. The fund managers relied on analysts. Upon further investigation as to why the analysts thought the issue unimportant, the following reasons were raised:

(i)   low inflation, therefore little difference between FIFO, LIFO, etc. (5 out of 17),
(ii) the effects of different methods cancel out over time (4 out of 17),
(iii) stock levels are low in the sector dealt with (e.g. capital goods) (4 out of 17),
(iv) high stock turnover (1 out of 17).

These are unconvincing reasons because:

(i)   The use of LIFO accumulates an 'error' in the balance sheet valuation, so that inflation of 20 years ago may be relevant. It is true that lack of price movements reduce the current earnings effect, except that, when stocks are physically reduced, earnings *rise* because old stocks are deemed to be used up.
(ii) Most accounting differences cancel out over time, but analysis concentrates on yearly earnings figures and values shown at a particular date. As noted in (i), a LIFO error will accumulate in the balance sheet.
(iii) Stock levels are unlikely to be so low as to make this factor irrelevant in most sectors.

(iv) High stock turnover has no effect on LIFO valuation,[11] and would actually *increase* the difference between LIFO and FIFO.

As examples of the effects of LIFO even in a period of low inflation, the US companies, General Motors (1992) and Caterpillar (1994), respectively report LIFO undervaluation 'errors' in the balance sheet amounting to 43% and 70% of net assets. General Motors also report an 11% 'error' in the calculation of earnings for 1992.[12]

The third area investigated was deferred tax. As an example of how important this topic can be, research elsewhere (Weetman and Gray, 1991) has shown that it contributes a major difference for UK companies reconciling to US rules; on average an increase of 4.9% to earnings in 1988. For Germany, France and Japan, the timing/temporary differences which cause deferred tax are often unimportant at the level of individual companies, but can become substantial in group financial statements, especially for France (Scheid and Walton, 1992, ch. 13).

As Table 5 shows, the lack of knowledge in this area was almost total, with only one interviewee correctly identifying partial allocation as the UK practice, but four of them incorrectly suggesting that deferred tax is generally larger in UK than in US financial statements. Two interviewees recognised that the causes of deferred tax were unlikely to be significant in Germany. Three interviewees thought that deferred tax was the amount provided (and soon to be paid) relating to the year's profit. A few analysts ($^3/_{17}$), suggested that they sometimes removed deferred tax balances from liabilities before analysis. Even Scandinavian analysts were not alert to the large deferred tax balances now being generated, for example, by application in Sweden of US-style principles to the treatment of untaxed reserves in consolidated balance sheets.[13]

In some cases, interviews extended to discussion of such issues as pension costs and the capitalisation of leases. Most interviewees were unaware of

Table 5

Recognition of Deferred Tax Practices (no. of interviewees)

	Full Allocation*	Partial Allocation*	Generally Does Not Arise*	Not Important/ Don't Know	Country Not Relevant	Total
UK	4 (23%)	1 (6%)	–	11 (64%)	1 (6%)	17 (100%)
US	–	3 (18%)	–	11 (64%)	3 (18%)	17 (100%)
Germany	–	–	2 (12%)	5 (29%)	10 (59%)	17 (100%)
France	–	–	–	8 (47%)	9 (53%)	17 (100%)
Japan	–	–	–	6 (35%)	11 (65%)	17 (100%)

Note:
* Shaded areas represent correct recognition.

international differences and there was a consensus that these issues were not adjusted for by analysts in their reports.

Summarising the discussion above concerning Tables 3 to 5, it is clear that there was a lack of knowledge of international differences. Of the three major areas investigated, even knowledge of UK practices was largely restricted to the area of goodwill and particularly to sector analysts.

The somewhat greater expertise and concern of sector analysts with international differences is presumably, in some measure, due to their being forced to address financial statements from several countries. The existence of accounting differences then becomes unavoidably plain, whereas a country analyst may be misled by a mask of national uniformity of presentation which may cover important sectoral accounting differences and may also encourage the analyst to ignore differences between the base country and the target country.

IMPLICATIONS FOR MARKET EFFICIENCY

Evidence has been presented here indicating a strong reliance on accounting numbers, principally through ratio analysis, when undertaking international investment appraisal. Restatement of these accounting numbers back to a common benchmark was not undertaken nor was published reconciliation data generally utilised. An interesting finding was the assumption made by fund managers that analysts undertake full restatement when compiling reports, thus fund managers believed that these reports contained comparable ratios. If an analyst/manager is not aware of accounting differences which influence accounting numbers, as evidenced in this study, the resulting analysis is likely to be misleading and may result in inefficient distributions of resources.

Even if an analyst/manager invests in only one foreign country, then ignorance of the foreign accounting practices may lead to incorrect decisions even if there is no bias in the expectation of values or returns. This is because variations in practices between companies within a country (e.g. with respect to goodwill amortisation lives or to income smoothing using provision movements) may distort the interpretation of the comparative prospects of those companies.

Where there is a choice of countries, the ratios of foreign companies may differ from an analyst's domestic norms without reflecting an increase or decrease in financial risk or rewards. As noted earlier, German and Japanese companies traditionally (and on average) measure profit more conservatively than US or UK companies; and Japanese companies have had lower liquidity ratios for a long period. When inserted into ratio analysis without adjustment, such figures may lead to long-run under-investment into such countries because their companies look noticeably worse than UK or US companies for most ratios. Even *after* restatement, international ratio analysis can be misleading due to underlying cultural, economic and legal differences (e.g. McLeay, 1995).

An extreme form of this problem is country-avoidance due to (i) lack of familiarity with accounting, (ii) accounting which discloses too little information, (iii) foreign exchange risk, or (iv) repatriation or expropriation risks. These are, of course, different issues. The first is related to potential inefficiency. Country-avoidance due to this first issue is clearly significant when it relates to economically important countries such as Germany and, to a lesser extent, Austria and Italy. It suggests that their corporate cost of capital will be higher than it needs to be, and it may explain the increasing use of US rules or international standards in Germany and Switzerland.[14]

The evidence presented here which provides *prima facie* support for the functional fixation hypothesis does not in itself dispute market efficiency within national stock exchanges, as domestic share prices tend to be determined principally by domestic investors. Furthermore, it is still unclear exactly how international stock markets assimilate information because research in this area is inconclusive.

Our findings are behavioural and anecdotal, and should therefore be treated with care, as noted earlier. Nevertheless, there is no reason to believe that our sample was atypical, except to the extent that the interviewees may have been *better* informed than the world's average analyst/fund manager because they were volunteers and because they worked for offices of very large international institutions in the world's most 'international' market.

SUMMARY AND CONCLUSIONS

Previous research on the UK investment community has related to domestic analysis. Much of it was carried out before the extensive globalisation of markets from the middle of the 1980s. The only earlier analogous paper dealing with cross-border issues (Choi and Levich, 1991) did not concentrate on one financial centre nor on financial institutions. It covered only some of the issues examined here, and in less detail. The present research reports on the behaviour of members of the London investment community with respect to foreign accounting data. Interviews were conducted with 17 users of such data in six institutions. The results may not be representative of the whole population of users of foreign accounting data, but there is no reason to believe that the population is more sophisticated on average than our sample.

The findings can be summarised under six propositions:

1. Most interviewees had no accounting qualification.
2. Most sector experts saw accounting differences as having an effect on investment decisions but most country experts did not.

324   MILES AND NOBES

3. Most interviewees used macro-economic data but not instead of trend and ratio analysis using accounting data.
4. A large majority of the analyst interviewees (and all the fund managers) did not restate accounting data to a benchmark, and most did not use available reconciliation data. However, the fund managers assumed that analysts do restate.
5. There is some evidence that, where there is scope to do so, users avoid some countries or sectors because of accounting problems.
6. A large majority of interviewees were not aware of accounting differences in major topic areas, and only the sector analysts were, in some cases, aware of UK or US practices.

Previous research (either domestic or cross-border) did not deal with the differences between analysts and fund managers, which are seen as major here. Nor had the difference between sector analysts and country analysts been pointed out. Also, although not surprising in the light of domestic research, the degree of ignorance on international differences has not been documented before.

Previous research is not conclusive as to how stock markets assimilate information and set prices, some of the evidence suggesting that there is scope for successful window dressing in the domestic UK market. In an international context, it would appear that there may be even greater scope if all participants use accounting data (point 3 above), but they do not restate it (point 4), perhaps partly because they are inexpert (point 1) and unaware of the international differences (point 6). Country experts are probably wrong to be blasé about the differences (point 2) because in many countries (with the clear exception of the US) disclosure is worse than in the UK and the rules allow even more flexibility for the manipulation of earnings figures. This all suggests that incorrect investment advice and decisions are likely. To the extent that companies in certain countries or sectors are avoided (point 5), their cost of capital will rise due to the perception of poor accounting.

There would seem to be scope for better accounting training for users of international information and advantages from continuing harmonisation of accounting rules and practices.

APPENDIX

The Interviewees

Countries/Sectors Covered	Length of Experience in International Investment (Years)	Fund Manager or Analyst	Accounting Qualification
Japan	10	Fund Manager	No
Continental Europe	3.5	Fund Manager	No
Asia	25	Fund Manager	Partial
South East Asia	6.5	Fund Manager	No
UK (US in the past) Consumer goods, Beverages, Media, Pharmaceutical	12	Fund Manager	Yes
Far East: Mining, Tobacco, Food & Beverages	4	Analyst	No
USA and Canada	12	Both	No
Europe: Chemicals, Oil, Pharmaceuticals, Paper	4	Both	No
Capital Goods: UK, US, France, Germany, Sweden, Switzerland, Italy, Luxembourg	5	Both	No
European Chemicals	6	Analyst	No
Transport & Aviation: Europe, US, Japan	14	Analyst	No
France	4	Analyst	No
Switzerland & Belgium: Food, Oil & Gas in UK	2	Analyst	No
Sweden, Germany, France: Capital goods	0.5	Analyst	Yes
Turkey	4	Analyst	No
Scandinavian Banks	3	Analyst	No
Central Europe and Mediterranean	7	Analyst	No

NOTES

1 As, for example, demanded by the SEC for foreign registrants who wish to be listed on the New York Stock Exchange.
2 The analysts and fund managers in this survey dealt only with equities. Foreign bond markets are covered by other personnel. This suggests that the information costs of dealing in foreign markets are, to some extent, duplicated. This is a research issue to be pursued elsewhere.
3 For example, Cochrane (1994) shows that foreign equity turnover in 1992 was 43.2% for London, 6.8% for New York, 1.5% for Germany, 8.5% for Zurich and 0.3% for Tokyo.

4   Previously, large numbers of debit items were shown as extraordinary in order to escape from *SSAP 3*'s original definition of earnings. However, *FRS 3* defines 'ordinary' so widely that there will seldom be any items that are extraordinary. Furthermore, *FRS 3* amends the definition of earnings to include extraordinary items.

5   That is, affect decision-making due to difficulties of understanding, comparability, etc.

6   *Deutsche Vereinigung für Finanzanalyse und Anglageberatung*, the German analysts association (see Busse von Colbe et al., 1991).

7   See, for example, the corrections for German provisioning in the US GAAP reconciliations in the Annual Reports of Daimler-Benz AG for 1993 or 1994.

8   For example, UK goodwill practice makes income higher and net assets lower, compared to US, French or Japanese practice.

9   Goodwill is often important in such reports, particularly in its effects on earnings. Even listed Japanese companies may have bought many overseas subsidiaries. Practices vary dramatically within France, Germany and Japan (e.g. Nobes and Parker, 1995, chs. 11 to 13).

10 This is a simple average. The figures collate the data shown in Ernst & Young (1994).

11 High stock turnover would bring more up-to-date costs into a LIFO calculation of cost of sales but would still deem the oldest stock ever bought to be left in the balance sheet.

12 The 1992 Annual Report (p.24) shows a $294.7m increase in earnings due to the effect of LIFO in the context of falling inventory quantities. The post-tax loss (before effects of accounting changes) was $2,620.6m.

13 Arguably these would be treated as reserves under UK practices. The effect can be very important. For example, the shareholders' funds of Telia AB for 1994 are shown as SEK 19,842m, but would be 9.4% higher if deferred tax had been treated as reserves.

14 For example, from 1994, Bayer and Schering have used international standards for their group accounts. The same applies to Adidas, Deutsche Bank and Hoechst from 1995. Nestlé and many other Swiss companies do the same.

15 So far, two of the five institutions that we used for the research have asked for training courses on these issues, partly as a result of this research. See a similar point in Breton and Taffler (1995).

REFERENCES

Abdel-Khalik, A.R. and T.F. Keller (1979), *Earnings or Cash Flows: An Experiment on Functional Fixation and Valuation of the Firm* (American Accounting Association).

———— and J.C. McKeown (1978), 'Understanding Accounting Changes in an Efficient Market: Evidence of Differential Reaction', *Accounting Review* (October).

Arnold, J. and P. Moizer (1984), 'A Survey of the Methods Used by UK Investment Analysts to Appraise Investments in Ordinary Shares', *Accounting and Business Research* (Summer).

Aron, P. (1991), 'Japanese P/E Ratios in an Environment of Increasing Uncertainty', ch. 8 in Choi (1991).

Ashton, R.H. (1976), 'Cognitive Changes Induced by Accounting Changes: Experimental Evidence on the FFH', *Journal of Accounting Research*, Vol. 14, Supplement.

Beaver, W.H. (1989), *Financial Reporting: An Accounting Revolution* (2nd ed., Prentice Hall, Englewood Cliffs, New Jersey).

Biddle, G.C. (1980), 'Accounting Methods and Management Decisions: The Case of Inventory Costing and Inventory Policy', supplement to *Journal of Accounting Research*, Vol. 18.

———— and W.E. Ricks (1988), 'Analyst Forecast Errors and Stock Price Behaviour near the Earning Announcement Dates of LIFO Adopters', *Journal of Accounting Research*, Vol. 26 (Autumn).

Breton, G. and R. Taffler (1995), 'Creative Accounting and Investment Analyst Response', *Accounting and Business Research* (Spring).

Busse von Colbe, W., K. Geiger, H. Haase, H. Reinhard and G. Schmitt (1991), *Ergebnis nach DVFA/SG* (Schäffer Verlag, Stuttgart).

Choi, F.D.S. (1991), *Handbook of International Accounting* (Wiley, New York).

———— and C. Lee (1992), 'Effects of Alternative Goodwill Treatments on Merger Premia:

Further Empirical Evidence', *Journal of International Financial Management and Accounting*, Vol. 4.

Choi, F.D.S., H. Hino, S.K. Min, S.O. Nam, J. Ujiie and A. Stonehill (1983), 'Analyzing Foreign Financial Statements: The Use and Misuse of International Ratio Analysis', *Journal of International Business Studies* (Spring/Summer).

_____ and R.M. Levich (1991), 'Behavioral Effects of International Accounting Diversity', *Accounting Horizons* (June).

Clarkson, G.E.P. (1967), *Portfolio Selection: A Simulation of Trust Investment*, The Ford Foundation doctoral dissertation series (Prentice Hall, Englewood Cliffs, New Jersey).

Cochrane, J.L. (1994), *Are US Regulatory Requirements for Foreign Firms Appropriate?* (NYSE Inc. Publication).

Cooper, J.C.B. (1982), 'World Stock Markets: Some Random Walk Tests', *Applied Economics*, No. 5 (October).

Darrat, A.F. (1987), 'Money and Stock Prices in West Germany and the UK: Is the Stock Market Efficient?', *Quarterly Journal of Business Economics* (Winter).

Day, J. (1986), 'The Use of Annual Reports by UK Investment Analysts', *Accounting and Business Research* (Autumn).

De Long, J.B., A. Schleifer, L.H. Summers and R.J. Walderman (1990), 'Noise Trader Risk in Financial Markets', *Journal of Political Economy*, Vol. 98, No. 4.

Duvall, L., R. Jennings, J. Robinson and R.B. Thompson II (1992), 'Can Investors Unravel the Effects of Goodwill Accounting?', *Accounting Horizons* (June).

Emenyonu, E.N. and S.J. Gray (1992), 'European Community Accounting Harmonisation: An Empirical Study of Measurement Practices in France, Germany and the United Kingdom', *Accounting and Business Research* (Winter).

Ernst & Young (1994), *UK/US GAAP Comparison* (Kogan Page, ch. 6).

Fellingham, J. (1988), 'Discussion of the LIFO/FIFO Choice: An Asymmetric Information Approach', *Journal of Accounting Research*, Vol. 26, supplement.

Firth, M. (1976), 'The Impact of Earnings Announcements on the Share Price Behaviour of Similar Type Firms', *Economic Journal* (June) 1976.

Foster, G. (1988), *Financial Statement Analysis* (2nd ed., Prentice Hall, Englewood Cliffs, New Jersey).

Griffiths, I. (1986), *Creative Accounting: How to Make Profits What You Want Them to Be* (Sidgwick and Jackson, London).

Grossman, S.J. and J.E. Stiglitz (1976), 'Information Competitive Price Systems', *American Economic Review*, Vol.66, Papers and Proceedings.

Hand, J.R.M. (1990), 'A Test of the Extended Functional Fixation Hypothesis', *Accounting Review*, Vol. 65, No. 4 (October).

Harris, T.S., M. Lang and H.P. Möller (1994), 'The Value Relevance of German Accounting Measures: An Empirical Analysis', *Journal of Accounting Research* (Autumn).

Healy, P. (1985) 'The Impact of Bonus Schemes on the Selection of Accounting Principles', *Journal of Accounting and Economics*, 7 (April).

Holland, A. (1990), *Accounting for Goodwill: The UK Stock Market Implications of the Proposed New Rules* (Yamaichi International (Europe) Limited, January).

Institute of Investment Management and Research (IIMR) (1993), *The Definition of Earnings* (IIMR, Kent).

IOSCO (1995), 'IASC and IOSCO Reach Agreement', Press Release by IOSCO and IASC (11 July).

Jamieson, M. (1988), *A Practical Guide to Creative Accounting* (Kogan Page), London.

Jennings, R., D.P. Mest and R.B. Thompson II (1992), 'Investor Reaction to Disclosures of 1974–5 LIFO Adoption Decisions', *Accounting Review*, Vol. 67, No. 2 (April).

Lee, T.A. and D.P. Tweedie (1981), *The Institutional Investor and Financial Information* (ICAEW, London).

McLeay, S. (1995), 'International Financial Analysis', in C. Nobes and R. Parker (eds.), *Comparative International Accounting* (Prentice Hall, ch. 5).

Morse, D. and G. Richardson (1983), 'The LIFO/FIFO Decision', *Journal of Accounting Research*, Vol. 21, No. 1 (Spring).

Nobes, C.W. (1992), 'A Political History of Goodwill in Britain: An Illustration of Cyclical Standard Setting', *Abacus* (September).

328   MILES AND NOBES

Norton, J. (1995), 'The Impact of Financial Accounting Practices on the Measurement of Profit and Equity: Australia Versus the United States', *Abacus* (September).

Pike, R., J. Meerjanssen and L. Chadwick (1993), 'The Appraisal of Ordinary Shares by Investment Analysts in the UK and Germany', *Accounting and Business Research* (Autumn).

Radebaugh, L.H. and S.J. Gray (1993), *International Accounting and Multinational Enterprises* (Wiley, New York), p. 390.

Rees, W.P., P.F. Pope and C.M. Graham (1992), 'The Information Content of German Analysts' Adjustments to Published Earnings', Working paper 92/040 (University of Strathclyde).

Ricks, W.E. (1982), 'The Market's Response to the 1974 LIFO Adoptions', *Journal of Accounting Research*, Vol. 20, No. 1 (Autumn).

Scheid, J-C. and P. Walton (1992), *European Financial Reporting: France* (Routledge, London).

Scott-Quinn, B. (1991), *Investment Banking: Theory and Practice* (Euromoney, London).

Smith, R.C. (1991), 'Integration of the World's Financial Markets: Past, Present and Future', ch. 2 in Choi (1991).

Smith, T. (1992), *Accounting for Growth: Stripping the Camouflage from Company Accounts* (Century Business, London).

———— (1996), *Accounting for Growth* (2nd ed., Blackwell).

Tiniç, S.M. (1990), 'A Perspective on the Stock Market's Fixation on Accounting Numbers', *Accounting Review*, Vol. 65, No. 4 (October).

Waller, D. (1990), 'If Balance Sheets Don't Balance: On Blue Arrow's Widely Differing US and UK Figures', *Financial Times* (30 January).

Watts, R. and J.L. Zimmerman (1986), *Positive Accounting Theory* (Prentice Hall).

Weaver, S. (1996), 'International Financial Statement Analysis: The Reaction of the UK Investment Community to International Accounting Differences', Unpublished Ph.D. Thesis (University of Reading).

Weetman, P. and S.J. Gray (1991), 'A Comparative International Analysis of the Impact of Accounting Principles on Profits: The USA versus the UK, Sweden, and The Netherlands', *Accounting and Business Research* (Autumn).

Zmijewski, M. and R. Hagerman (1981), 'An Income Strategy Approach to the Positive Theory of Accounting Standard Setting/Choice', *Journal of Accounting and Economics*, Vol. 3 (August), pp. 129–49.

[22]

International Variations in the Accounting and Tax Treatments of Goodwill and the Implications for Research

Christopher Nobes and Julie Norton

This paper sets out the rules and practices in a number of countries with respect to different types of goodwill. the accounting and tax rules for goodwill are different in many cases. The need for the paper derives from the confusion in some previous research which has led to mis-specified hypotheses and incorrect conclusions.

INTRODUCTION

This paper is an attempt to clarify the international rules and practices relating to the accounting and tax treatments of goodwill. The paper deals with regulations and practices in 11 countries, also showing the rules of the International Accounting Standards Committee (IASC) and the European Union (EU) for comparison. The paper is necessary because there is confusion in the literature, particularly on tax treatments. Evidence of the confusion can be found in papers in several journals, including this one, as will be pointed out below. Failure to distinguish between different types of goodwill has led to errors of fact which invalidate some of the hypotheses of several frequently cited papers. In particular, it is intended here to add to (and, in some cases, subtract from) the debate about competitive advantage and economic consequences of goodwill rules (e.g., Choi and Lee 1991; Dunne and Rollins 1992; Lee and Choi 1992; Dunne and Ndubizu 1995).

Christopher Nobes and **Julie Norton** • Department of Economics, P.O. Box 218, Whiteknights, Reading, RG6 6AA, UK.

Journal of International Accounting, Auditing & Taxation, 5(2):179-196   ISSN: 1061-9518

180   INTERNATIONAL ACCOUNTING, AUDITING & TAXATION, 5(2)   1996

This paper is not designed to investigate the history of goodwill rules or practices (e.g., see instead Lee 1971, 1973, 1974; Andrews 1981; Hughes 1982; Carnegie and Gibson 1991; Nobes 1992) nor to examine the arguments in favour of particular procedures (e.g., see instead Nobes 1989; Stacy and Tweedie 1989; Grinyer et al. 1990; Archer et al. 1995; Miller 1995).

TYPES OF GOODWILL

One of the contributory factors to the confusion on goodwill is that many authors do not distinguish between the several different types of accounting goodwill. Of course, there are also uses of the word "goodwill" outside of accounting, for example, a businessman may refer to his customer list, or an analyst may refer to future streams of super-profits. This paper deals with goodwill as a technical accounting term.

For simplicity, all enterprises in the discussion here will be companies, although many of the points would still apply if they had not been. It is useful to distinguish three types of goodwill: (a) internally generated goodwill, (b) goodwill purchased when buying assets other than by buying the shares in a company (hereafter called nonconsolidation goodwill), and (c) goodwill purchased by a group when buying the shares in a company (hereafter called consolidation goodwill).

ACCOUNTING TREATMENTS

The Calculation of Goodwill

In many countries (including U.S. and UK) both nonconsolidation goodwill and consolidation goodwill are calculated as the difference between the cost and the fair value of what is purchased. Of course, the measurement of "fair value" can be complex. For example, the U.S. practice (APB opinion 16) is to take an acquiror's perspective, whereas the UK practice (FRS 7, para.1) is to take a neutral or market perspective. This can lead to great differences, as the UK rules do not allow the purchaser to take account of his intentions (e.g., they do not allow provisions for proposed redundancy costs or closures). Even establishing "cost" can be problematic when the purchase consideration is not entirely cash.

In some countries at certain times, goodwill has been measured as the difference between cost and the *book value* of the net assets purchased. This was generally the practice in continental Europe before the EU Seventh Directive (e.g., see Diggle and Nobes 1994). An echo of this is found in the Seventh Directive's option to use a method of calculation which starts with book values. German companies often use this *Buchwertmethode* (Ordelheide and Pfaff 1994, 185).

Appendix I to this paper provides numerical illustrations of these different ways of calculating goodwill. A further point to examine is the treatment of negative goodwill, but this will be done at the end of this section. Until then, it is assumed that the goodwill being discussed is always positive.

Another issue is that, when a company buys less than 100% of the shares in a subsidiary, the fair value exercise may involve all the subsidiary's net assets (as in the UK) or only the group's proportion of them (as in the U.S.). The International Accounting Standard (IAS 22, paras. 31 to 34) allows both.

Internally Generated Goodwill

It is universal practice not to recognize internally generated goodwill on balance sheets since there is no reliable measure of cost or value. The rules of some countries specifically cover this (e.g., Australia[1] and the UK[2]). Ma and Hopkins (1988) discuss the differences between internally generated and other goodwill.

Another concept of relevance here might be called "unrecognized" (or inherent) goodwill, which could be defined as the difference between a company's market value at a particular date and its accounting net asset value (usually measured at book carrying amounts rather than at fair values). Of course, this means that such "unrecognized goodwill" would also include any assets (net of liabilities) that should have been separately recognized, any under-valuation of recognized net assets, and any purchased goodwill which is not recorded on balance sheets in some countries (see below). Therefore, it would be misleading to use the terms "unpurchased" or "internally generated" goodwill here.

In some countries, it is within the rules for identifiable intangible assets to be capitalized when they have been internally generated (e.g., this seems to be allowed by APB Opinion 17 in the United States, and by Sch. 4 to the Companies Act 1985 in the UK). This creates an important blurred borderline between goodwill and other intangible assets.

In particular, in certain countries (e.g., the UK and the Netherlands) where many companies write off consolidation goodwill against retained earnings (see below), a way of helping to fill the resulting "hole in the balance sheet" is to capitalize such internally generated intangibles as brand names or newspaper mastheads (see Barwise et al. 1989). The advantage of having the brands rather than the goodwill in the balance sheet is that the amortization rules for the former are not so well specified in these countries. For example, it is common not to amortize brands names in the UK. A similar point arises for purchased intangibles, as discussed later.

Nonconsolidation Goodwill

As noted above, this second type of goodwill can arise when a company buys some of the net assets of another company (possibly the whole business) without

182   INTERNATIONAL ACCOUNTING, AUDITING & TAXATION, 5(2)   1996

buying the company itself, that is, without buying the shares in the company. No parent-subsidiary relationship is created, and no consolidation processes are triggered. However, since it is common to pay more than the fair value of the net assets acquired, goodwill often arises. It is also possible for nonconsolidation goodwill to arise in connection with certain types of business combinations, for example, in legal mergers in Japan.

In many countries (e.g., the U.S. and the UK), the accounting treatment of nonconsolidation goodwill is the same as that for consolidation goodwill. Indeed, in the United States, since there is almost exclusive concentration on consolidated financial statements, it would seldom be useful to distinguish this goodwill from consolidation goodwill for financial reporting purposes. However, in most countries other than the United States, individual company balance sheets (including those of the parent company) are prepared and published, so nonconsolidation goodwill is sometimes seen.

To show that the distinction between the two types of goodwill can be important, some countries have different terms for them. For example, in France, nonconsolidation goodwill is *fonds commercial*,[3] whereas consolidation goodwill is *écart d'acquisition*, which is what remains of the consolidation difference (*écart de première consolidation*) after a sort of fair value exercise. In Italy, nonconsoli-

TABLE 1
Accounting Regulations for
Nonconsolidation Goodwill

Country	Accounting Regulation
Australia, Canada, Netherlands, Spain, Sweden, UK, U.S. and IASC	Same as goodwill on consolidation—refer to table 2.
France	Capitalize, with no systematic amortization required, but provide for diminution in value. [a]
Germany	1. Amortize over 4 years, or
	2. amortize over period of usefulness, giving justification. [b]
Italy	1. Amortize over up to 5 years, or
	2. amortize over a limited period not exceeding the asset's life. [c]
Japan	Amortize systematically over a maximum of 5 years, with at least one fifth each year.[d]
EU Fourth Directive	1. Where classified as an asset, write off within a maximum period of 5 years, or
	2. write off systematically over a limited period exceeding 5 years provided that this does not exceed useful economic life. [e]

Notes: [a]Scheid and Walton (1992) p. 199.
[b]Macharzina and Langer (1995) p. 275;   Ordelheide and Pfaff (1994) p. 126.
[c]Zambon (1995) p. 479.
[d]Cooke and Kikuya (1992) p. 202;   Coopers & Lybrand (1993) p. 25.
[e]Article 34 (1a) and 37 (2).

TABLE 2
Accounting Regulations for Consolidation Goodwill

Country	Accounting Regulation
Australia	Amortize systematically over the period of benefit not exceeding 20 years. [a]
Canada	Amortize over a maximum of 40 years. [b]
France	1. Amortize systematically over useful life, or
	2. exceptionally, write off immediately to reserves. [c]
Germany	1. Write off immediately to reserves,
	2. amortize over up to 4 years, or
	3. amortize over useful economic life. [d]
Italy	1. Write off immediately to reserves, or
	2. amortize over up to 5 years, or
	3. amortize over a limited period not exceeding the asset's life. [e]
Japan	Amortize in an amount no less than that computed on a straight-line basis over appropriate periods. [f] Certain companies registered with the SEC of the USA are allowed to follow U.S. rules.
Netherlands	1. Immediate write-off to reserves,
	2. immediate write-off to income statement,
	3. amortize over not more than 5 years, or,
	4. if reasonable, amortize over a longer period to a maximum of 10 years. [g]
Spain	1. Amortize over 5 years, or
	2. with explanation, amortize over a maximum of 10 years. [h]
Sweden	Amortize over expected economic life:
	1. maximum 10 years, or,
	2. exceptionally, up to 20 years. [i]
UK	1. Normally, write off immediately to reserves, or
	2. amortize on a systematic basis over useful economic life. [j]
U.S.	Amortize over expected economic life. Maximum 40 years. [k] SEC often requires shorter lives.
IASC	Amortize over expected useful life:
	1. maximum 5 years, or,
	2. up to 20 years, with justification. [l]
EU Seventh Directive	1. Treat in accordance with the 4th Directive, or
	2. immediately deduct from reserves. [m]

Notes: [a] AAS 18.40-41 and AASB 1013.35-36; Price Waterhouse (1993a) p. 102.

[b] Coopers & Lybrand (1992a) p. 29.

[c] Coopers & Lybrand (1992b) p. 40; Scheid and Walton (1992) p. 23; Blake and Amat (1993) p. 124.

[d] Coopers & Lybrand (1992b) p. 40; Ordelheide and Pfaff (1994) p. 190; Macharzina and Langer (1995) p. 283; Seckler (1995) p. 248*l*

[e] Coopers & Lybrand (1992c) p. 36; Riccaboni and Ghirri (1994) p. 164; Blake and Amat (1993) p. 154; Zambon (1995) p. 487.

[f] Business Accounting Deliberation Council (1977), Section 4, para. 2(2).

[g] Dijksma and Hoogendoorn (1992) p. 135; Hoogendoorn (1995) p. 585; Parker and Nobes (1995) p. 344.

[h] Coopers & Lybrand (1992c) p. 36; Gonzalo and Gallizo (1992) p. 91, 114 and 169; Martinez (1995) pp. 839 and 847.

[i] Coopers & Lybrand (1994a) p. 34; Blake and Amat (1993) p. 196; Heurlin and Peterssohn (1995) p. 1196; Price Waterhouse (1995a) p. 77.

[j] SSAP 22.39-41; CA 1985 Sch. 4.21.

[k] APB Opinion 17.1 and 17.25-30.

[l] IAS 22.42 and 22.46; Coopers & Lybrand (1994b) p. 39.

[m] Article 30.

184   INTERNATIONAL ACCOUNTING, AUDITING & TAXATION, 5(2)   1996

dation goodwill is *avviamento*, whereas consolidation goodwill is *differenza da consolidamento*.

Table 1 examines the rules for nonconsolidation goodwill in eleven countries (plus EU and IAS rules). Table 2 shows the consolidation goodwill rules. As may be seen, in some countries, there are particular rules for nonconsolidation good-will which are different from those for consolidation goodwill. Generally, in these countries the accounting rules for nonconsolidation goodwill are tied in with the tax rules, as explained later.

Table 3 is concerned with *practices* rather than rules, and it particularly relates to consolidation goodwill.

Consolidation Goodwill

As noted earlier, consolidation goodwill is that arising in group financial statements when a group purchases the shares of another company. This is the type of goodwill most familiar to U.S. users of financial statements. Many writers on comparative accounting do not distinguish between nonconsolidation goodwill and consolidation goodwill (e.g., Brunovs and Kirsch 1991; Choi and Lee 1991; Lee and Choi 1992; Dunne and Rollins 1992; Miller 1995; Clinch 1995). In general, it is clear that the writers are addressing themselves to consolidation good-will. To the extent that the countries covered are English-speaking, problems seldom arise because the accounting rules are generally the same for the two types

TABLE 3
Practices of Large Companies with Respect to
the Treatment of Consolidation Goodwill

Australia	Capitalize. Amortize over useful life, frequently the maximum of 20 years.
Canada	Capitalize. Amortize over useful life, frequently the maximum of 40 years.
France	Capitalize. Amortize usually over a period in excess of 5 years, including 10, 20, 30 or 40 years.
Germany	A mixture of capitalization and equity write-off is found, even in the same company. Amortization lives vary greatly, with 5 and 15 years being common.
Italy	Capitalize usually. A variety of amortization lives is found, including 5 and 20 years.
Japan	Capitalize or, less commonly, expense immediately. Amortization usually over five years or less. Some companies listed on US exchanges can use US rules.
Netherlands	Equity write-offs are the most common but capitalization is also found, with amortization usually over a period longer than 5 years.
Spain	Capitalize. Amortization often over 5 years or the maximum of 10 years.
Sweden	Capitalize. Amortization usually over a period in excess of 5 years.
UK	Normally an equity write-off.
U.S.	Capitalize. Amortization over useful life, frequently the maximum of 40 years, unless the SEC has required a shorter period.

Notes: Sources=see Appendix II.

of goodwill (e.g., IAS 22 and the UK's SSAP 22 where no distinction is made). However, as discussed below, this lack of distinction can lead to difficulty when the discussion turns to other countries or to tax.

As Tables 2 and 3 show, the international differences in the rules and practices for consolidation goodwill are large. This has led to the "unlevel playing field" argument, whereby U.S. or Australian corporations, for example, complain that they are at a disadvantage when bidding for a company against a UK competitor because the latter will not suffer subsequent goodwill amortization changes. This issue is investigated in some detail by Miller (1995) and Clinch (1995). The latter also summarizes the equivocal findings of the capital markets research into the effects of goodwill capitalization and amortization on stock market value and share returns, as reported in such papers as Amir et al. (1993) and Chauvin and Herschey (1994). Included in this research is investigation of whether different goodwill rules lead to merger premia paid by UK corporations over and above prices paid by U.S. corporations (e.g., Choi and Lee 1991; Ivancevich 1993). The tax aspects of this are discussed later.

Another effect of the rules in some countries is the attempt to allocate purchase price to assets other than goodwill. It was noted earlier that internally generated intangibles are capitalized in some countries. In most countries, the rules also allow or encourage the recognition of identifiable intangibles when purchased (either separately or as part of a business combination). Where the rules on the amortization of intangibles are unclear (e.g., in Australia and the UK), this may encourage companies to allocate the purchase price of a business combination to intangibles rather than to goodwill. This is particularly likely in cases where goodwill has to be amortized because it cannot be written off against reserves. For instance, the rules in Australia (AASB 1013/AAS 18) require goodwill to be capitalized and amortized over up to 20 years, whereas there is no clear rule on the amortization of other intangibles. As an example of the results of this, The News Corporation (TNC), which is based in Australia, has a large figure for other intangibles in its balance sheet. When adjustments are made towards U.S. GAAP, this issue is very important, as shown in Table 4. The effect on TNC's income of the extra amortization charges caused by adjusting to U.S. GAAP is a reduction in earnings of 17%.

Some further points relating to purchased goodwill are that:

- No goodwill arises on a pooling of interests, because the method assumes that nothing has been purchased.
- Goodwill can arise on the purchase of shares in companies that are equity accounted (either subsidiaries, associates, or joint ventures).

Negative Goodwill

The treatment of negative goodwill varies internationally as shown in Table 5, which particularly refers to consolidation goodwill.

186   INTERNATIONAL ACCOUNTING, AUDITING & TAXATION, 5(2)   1996

TABLE 4
U.S. GAAP Reconciliation of The News Corporation, 1995

	U.S.$
Shareholders' equity (Australian rules)	16,582
Publishing rights, etc: revaluation and other	(4,203)
amortization	(1,491)
Goodwill: effect of SFAS 109 and other	988
amortization	140
Accounts payable	(1,464)
Associates	(967)
Minority interests	(502)
Other	(63)
Shareholders' equity (US GAAP)	9,020

TAX TREATMENTS

It is in the discussion of tax treatments that the confusion between the different types of goodwill becomes serious. The vital initial point is that, in all countries, consolidated financial statements as prepared for financial reporting purposes are irrelevant for tax purposes (except by coincidence; see below). In most countries, corporate income tax is calculated company by company, that is, tax-paying legal entity by tax-paying legal entity. For some aspects of tax calculations in some countries, some parts of the group may be aggregated (Lamb 1995) but even then the consolidated income statement is not directly used. For example, even in "consolidated returns," there are exclusions of one or more of (a) overseas subsidiaries,[4] etc., (b) joint ventures, (c) equity-accounted companies, or (d) subsidiaries in which the holding is less than 75% or 80%.[5]

Since the consolidated income statement is not directly relevant for tax purposes, and since amortization charges for consolidation goodwill only appear in such statements, then such charges are not tax deductible.

It would be possible to imagine a simple group in which all the subsidiaries were domestic and wholly-owned, there were no equity-accounted or proportionally consolidated companies, and there were no amortization charges for consolidation goodwill. In such a case, the group income statement might be equivalent to the aggregation of group income for tax purposes. However, this is clearly a special case, and it does not affect the argument about deductibility of consolidation goodwill.

In certain countries, amortization of nonconsolidation goodwill is wholly or partially tax deductible. As Table 6 shows, this is the case in Canada, Germany, Italy, Japan, Sweden and, since 1993, the United States.[6] In countries where charges must generally appear in the financial statements in order to be tax deductible (e.g., Japan and Germany),[7] this normally leads to the use in the financial statements of the shortest possible tax amortization periods.

TABLE 5
Accounting Regulations for Negative Consolidation Goodwill

Country	Accounting Regulation
Australia	Eliminate by proportionate reduction of the fair values of nonmonetary assets. Any remainder should be classified as a gain and taken to income. [a]
Canada	Eliminate by assigning to nonmonetary assets.[b]
France	1. Normally, carry as a deferred credit (provisions for risks and charges), or 2. exceptionally, credit to reserves. [c]
Germany	Carry as a reserve, liability or in between.[d]
Italy	Depending on its nature: 1. carry as a provision, or 2. credit to reserves. [e]
Japan	When consolidation differences appear on the debit and the credit side these amounts may be offset in the consolidated statement.[f]
Netherlands	Credit to revaluation reserve, unless it represents future losses, when a provision must be made.[g]
Spain	Carry as a provision or as deferred income depending on its nature. Take to income on realization.[h]
Sweden	1. Eliminate by reducing acquired assets, or 2. carry as long-term liability released to equity over a number of years. [i]
UK	Credit to reserves. May be written back to profit if it relates to anticipated losses or if subsidiary is sold.[j]
U.S.	Eliminate by proportionate allocation against the fair values of fixed assets other than investments. Carry any remainder as a liability (deferred credit) and amortize to income over the period of benefit, not to exceed 40 years.[k]
IASC	1. Eliminate by reducing the values of non-monetary assets, or 2. carry as a liability (deferred income), and then amortize over 5 years or, if justified, up to 20 years. [l]
EU Seventh Directive	Show as a separate item in the consolidated balance sheet. Positive and negative amounts may be offset. May be transferred to the income statement on realization or on the occurrence of anticipated losses of the subsidiary.[m]

Notes: [a] AAS 18.43 and AASB 1013.40; Price Waterhouse (1993a) p. 102; Parker (1995b) p. 195.

[b] Coopers & Lybrand (1992a) p. 29.

[c] Archer *et al.* (1995) p. 43.

[d] Blake and Amat (1993) p. 134; Ordelheide and Pfaff (1994) p. 187 and 191; Seckler (1995) p. 248.

[e] Coopers & Lybrand (1992c) p. 36; Riccaboni and Ghirri (1994) p. 163; Blake and Amat (1993) p. 154; Zambon (1995) p. 487-88.

[f] Business Accounting Deliberation Council (1977), Note 7.

[g] Dijksma and Hoogendoorn (1992) p. 135; Blake and Amat (1993) p. 154; Hoogendoorn (1995) p. 585; Parker (1995a) p. 214.

[h] Gonzalo and Gallizo (1992) p. 170; Martinez (1995) p. 839.

[i] Coopers & Lybrand (1994a) p. 33-34; Blake and Amat (1993) p. 197; Heurlin and Peterssohn (1995) p. 1196.

[j] SSAP 22.40.

[k] APB Opinion 16.91; Parker and Nobes (1995) p. 344.

[l] IAS 22.49 and .51.

[m] Article 19 (1c) and Article 31.

Previous Research

Several writers have speculated on the advantages of goodwill tax deductibility for acquirers based in certain countries (e.g., Pensler 1988; Dunne and Rollins 1992, 1994; Lee and Choi 1992; Touche Ross 1993; Dunne and Ndubizu 1995). However, in all cases, their context is consolidated financial statements and the purchase of shares. Therefore, when they refer to the tax deductibility of goodwill, they are mistaken because deductibility relates to goodwill arising on the acquisition of the assets of a business rather than the shares in it.

For example, Dunne and Rollins (1992, 193) state that goodwill is tax deductible in Canada, Germany, Japan, Italy, the Netherlands[8] and Spain. However, the context of their paper is the purchase of companies not of assets. It is Dunne and Rollins' detailed analysis of Japan which particularly suffers from this

TABLE 6
Tax Regulations for Nonconsolidation Goodwill

Country	Tax Regulation
Australia	Not a tax deductible item. [a]
Canada	75% of cost is eligible capital expenditure which may be amortized at a maximum annual rate of 7% on a declining balance basis.[b]
France	Not a tax deductible item.[c]
Germany	Amortize (straight-line) over exactly 15 years.[d]
Italy	Allowance of a maximum of 20% per annum.[e]
Japan	As set out in the Commercial Code (see Table 1), i.e. usually straight-line over 5 years.[f]
Netherlands	Not a tax deductible item.[g]
Spain	Not a tax deductible item.[h]
Sweden	Depreciate by a 30% declining balance method to allow 100% depreciation of cost over 5 financial years.[i]
UK	Not a tax deductible item (i.e., no capital allowances given).[j]
U.S.	Amortize (straight-line) over 15 years.[k]

Notes: [a] Price Waterhouse (1993a) p.137.

[b] Price Waterhouse (1994) p.146.

[c] Price Waterhouse (1995b) p.149; and implied by Scheid and Walton (1992) p.199; but the French case is complex.

[d] Ordelheide and Pfaff (1994) p.126; Macharzina and Langer (1995) p.275.

[e] Zambon (1995) p.480.

[f] Price Waterhouse (1993b) p.131.

[g] Dijksma and Hoogendoorn (1992) p.61.

[h] Gonzalo and Gallizo (1992) p.63.

[i] Price Waterhouse (1995a) p.102.

[j] CAA (1990) Ss 24, 25 and 159.

[k] s. 197 Internal Revenue Code (1986); Doering (1993).

problem. In Japan, the rules relating to nonconsolidation and consolidation goodwill are to be found in quite separate sources of authority. The nonconsolidation rules (which are relevant for tax deductibility purposes) come from the Commercial Code; the consolidation rules are the concern of the Securities and Exchange Law and the Business Accounting Deliberation Council (Cooke and Kikuya 1992, 209-210). In the same way as for the other countries, no nonconsolidation goodwill arises in a Japanese parent's financial statements when it pays cash to buy the shares in a company, so there is nothing to depreciate for tax purposes. Within Japan, legal mergers[9] are the more common method of business combination, and these can lead to nonconsolidation goodwill. However, in the context of the acquisition of overseas subsidiaries, the purchase method (which is Dunne and Rollins' context) is the relevant one.

This means that Dunne and Rollins (1992, 196) are in error when they state that the goodwill arising when Sony purchased CBS would be tax deductible. In the case of Sony's purchase, the $700m is consolidation goodwill[10] which is being amortized over 40 years both under Japanese group accounting and under U.S. GAAP for U.S. filing purposes. It is not tax deductible, and presumably Sony would have chosen the shorter amortization period appropriate to the tax rules if it had been.

This muddling of consolidation and nonconsolidation rules is carried through to the hypothetical cash flow calculations for Japan (Dunne and Rollins 1992, 198 and 200, Tables 3 and 4). Consequently, the main conclusion of the paper that "this increase in cash flow gives Japan Acquirer a competitive edge in the bidding process" (Dunne and Rollins 1992, 205) is wrong.

Tax Planning

At first sight it might appear that, in countries where goodwill is deductible, companies should arrange their purchases as acquisitions of assets not of shares. In this way, tax-deductible amortization of nonconsolidation goodwill can arise over a number of years for the purchaser. However, the acquisition is likely to give rise to immediate taxable income for the selling company, which would not have arisen if the company's shares had been bought.

For cross-border acquisitions, the purchaser and the seller are likely to have different tax rates, so the analysis of the tax effects will be complex. It seems unlikely that it will generally be advantageous for purchases to be arranged as acquisitions of assets, even in countries where goodwill is tax deductible.

A further point of relevance here is that the U.S. Tax Code allows certain domestic acquisitions to be deemed to be acquisitions of assets. Section 338 of the Internal Revenue Code allows a bidder company to elect to have a target company treated as though it had sold all its assets and bought them back again at the time

190   INTERNATIONAL ACCOUNTING, AUDITING & TAXATION, 5(2)   1996

of acquisition. Among other things, this gives rise to deductible goodwill. However, it also gives rise to taxable gains on the assets. Under most circumstances, it is therefore not advantageous to take the election.[11]

CONCLUSION

Many writings on the accounting or tax treatments of goodwill do not make clear whether they are examining nonconsolidation goodwill or consolidation goodwill. This is not surprising for writers in English, particularly North Americans, because the context of accounting is largely or exclusively seen as consolidated financial statements. However, individual company financial statements are given greater weight elsewhere in the world, particularly as a basis for the calculation of distributable or taxable income. Therefore, the lack of appreciation of the distinction between the types of goodwill can be a problem.

Confusion arises particularly when considering tax issues since it is only for nonconsolidation goodwill that amortization is tax deductible, and then only in some countries. It would seem to be important for researchers to specify the context of their examinations in this field as accurately as possible, and for readers to be alert to errors or confusion in past writings.

Acknowledgments: The authors are, respectively, Coopers & Lybrand, Professor of Accounting and Lecturer in Accounting at the University of Reading, England. They are grateful for advice from Paul Cherry (Coopers & Lybrand, Toronto), Pat McConnell (Bear Stearns, New York) and Etsuo Sawa (Japanese Institute of Certified Public Accountants); and for comments on an earlier draft to Margaret Lamb (University of Warwick), Malcolm Miller (University of New South Wales), R.H. Parker (University of Exeter), Alan Roberts (University of Reading), and Stefano Zambon (University of Padua).

NOTES

1. AAS 18.36 and AASB 1013.20.
2. Companies Act 1985, Sch. 4, note 3 to formats.
3. These are the elements of *fonds de commerce* which cannot be allocated to other captions on the balance sheet (commercial code, art.D.19).
4. This is the case in the United States (section 1504(b)(3) of the Internal Revenue Code), although Canadian and Mexican subsidiaries are, to some extent, an exception.
5. 75% applies in the UK; and 80% in the United States.
6. The U.S. treatment for goodwill changed in 1993, when Section 197 of the Internal Revenue Code was changed to allow the straightline amortization of certain intangibles over 15 years. See, for example, Doering 1993.

7. See, for example, Haller 1992.
8. It seems that they are wrong about the Netherlands, even for non-consolidation goodwill. See Table 6 and its references.
9. See, for example, IAS 22, para.6. Such legal mergers are also found in France as the *fusion* or in Italy as the *fusione*.
10. We are most grateful for interpretation of the Japanese language balance sheet to Etsuo Sawa of the Japanese Institute of Certified Public Accountants.
11. One case where the election might be advantageous is where the target has unused past tax losses which can be absorbed by the gain caused by the election.

REFERENCES

AICPA. 1995. *Accounting Trends and Techniques*. New York, NY: AICPA.

Amir, E., T. Harris, and E. Venuti. 1993. A comparison of the value-relevance of U.S. versus non-U.S. GAAP accounting measures using form 20-F reconciliations. *Journal of Accounting Research*, Supplement:230-64.

Andrews, W.T. 1981. The evolution of APB opinion no. 17: accounting for intangible assets; a study of the U.S. position on accounting for goodwill. *Accounting Historians Journal* 8(1):37-49.

Archer, S., D. Alexander, L. Collins, and D. Pham. 1995. *The Treatment of Goodwill and Other Intangibles: Theory, Standards and Practice in France and the UK*. London, UK: ICAEW.

Barwise, P., C. Higson, A. Likierman, and P. Marsh. 1989. *Accounting for Brands*. London, UK: LBS/ICAEW.

Blake, J., and O. Amat. 1993. *European Accounting*. London, UK: Pitman.

Brunovs, R., and R.J. Kirsch. 1991. Goodwill accounting in selected countries and the harmonisation of international accounting standards. *Abacus* September:135-161.

Business Accounting Deliberation Council. 1977. *Financial Accounting Standards on Consolidated Statements*. Tokyo, Japan: Ministry of Finance.

Carnegie, G., and R.W. Gibson. 1991. The evolution of accounting standards for goodwill in the English language countries following APB opinion no. 17 (1970). *Advances in International Accounting* 4:3-17.

Chauvin, K., and M. Hirschey. 1994. Goodwill, profitability, and the market value of the firm. *Journal of Accounting and Public Policy* 13:159-80.

Choi, F.D.S., and C. Lee. 1991. Merger premia and national differences in accounting for goodwill. *Journal of International Financial Management and Accounting* 3(3):219-240.

Clinch, G. 1995. Capital markets research and the goodwill debate. *Australian Accounting Review* June:22-30.

Cooke, T.E., and M. Kikuya. 1992. *Financial Reporting in Japan*. Oxford, UK: Blackwell.

Coopers & Lybrand. 1992a. *Accounting Comparisons: UK—Canada and USA*. London, UK: Gee.

Coopers & Lybrand. 1992b. *Accounting Comparisons: UK—Europe. Vol. I*. London, UK: Gee.

Coopers & Lybrand. 1992c. *Accounting Comparisons: UK—Europe. Vol. II*. London: Gee.

Coopers & Lybrand. 1993. *Accounting Comparisons: UK—Japan*. London, UK: Gee.

Coopers & Lybrand. 1994a. *Accounting Comparisons: UK—Europe. Vol. V*. London, UK: Gee.

Coopers & Lybrand. 1994b. *Accounting Comparisons: UK—International Standards*. London, UK: Gee.

Diggle, G., and C.W. Nobes. 1994. European rule making in accounting: the seventh directive as a case study. *Accounting and Business Research* Autumn:319-333.

Dijksma, J., and M. Hoogendoorn. 1992. *European Financial Reporting: The Netherlands*. London, UK: Routledge.

Doering, J.A. 1993. The amortization of intangibles: before and after section 197. *Taxes* October:621-635.

Dunne, K.M., and G.A. Ndubizu. 1995. International acquisition accounting method and corporate multinationalism: evidence from foreign acquisitions. *Journal of International Business Studies* 26(2):361-377.

Dunne, K.M., and T.P. Rollins. 1992. Accounting for goodwill: a case analysis of US, UK and Japan. *Journal of International Accounting, Auditing and Taxation* 2:91-207.

Dunne, K.M., and T.P. Rollins. 1994. Accounting for goodwill: a case analysis of US, UK and Japan. In *Readings and Notes on Financial Accounting: Issues and Controversies*, eds. S.A. Zeff and B.G. Dharan, 339-354. New York, NY: McGraw Hill.

FEE. 1994. *FEE 1994 Investigation of Emerging Accounting Areas*. London, UK: Routledge.

Gonzalo, J., and J. Gallizo. 1992. *European Financial Reporting: Spain*. London, UK: Routledge.

Grinyer, J., A. Russell, and M. Walker. 1990. The rationale for accounting for goodwill. *British Accounting Review* 22(3):223-235.

Haller, A. 1992. The relationship of financial and tax accounting in Germany: a major reason for accounting disharmony in Europe. *International Journal of Accounting* 27:310-323.

Heurlin, S., and E. Peterssohn. 1995. Sweden. In *European Accounting Guide*, eds. D. Alexander and S. Archer, 1185-1247. San Diego, CA: Harcourt Brace.

Hoogendoorn, M. 1995. The Netherlands. In *European Accounting Guide*, eds. D. Alexander and S. Archer, 555-659. San Diego, CA: Harcourt Brace.

Hughes, H.P. 1982. *Goodwill in Accounting: A History of the Issues and Problems*. Atlanta, GA: Georgia State University.

Ivancevich, D.M. 1993. Acquisitions and goodwill: the United Kingdom and the United States. *International Journal of Accounting* 28:156-169.

Lamb, M. 1995. When is a group a group? Convergence of concepts of "group" in European Union corporate tax. *European Accounting Review* 4(1):33-78.

Lee, C., and F.D.S. Choi. 1992. Effects of alternative goodwill treatments on merger premia: further empirical evidence. *Journal of International Financial Management and Accounting* 4(3):220-236.

Lee, T.A. 1971. Goodwill. An example of will-o'-the wisp accounting. *Accounting and Business Research* Autumn:318-328.

Lee, T.A. 1973. Accounting for goodwill. *Accounting and Business Research* 11 Summer:175-196.

Lee, T.A. 1974. Accounting for and disclosure of business combinations. *Journal of Business Finance and Accounting* Spring:1-33.

Ma, R., and R. Hopkins. 1988. Goodwill. An example of puzzle-solving in accounting. *Abacus* March:75-85.

Macharzina, K., and K. Langer. 1995. Financial reporting in Germany. In *Comparative International Accounting*, eds. C. Nobes and R. Parker, 265-287. Hemel Hempstead, UK: Prentice Hall.

Martinez, F.J. 1995. Spain. In *European Accounting Guide*, eds. D. Alexander and S. Archer, 821-911. San Diego, CA: Harcourt Brace.

Miller, M.C. 1995. Goodwill discontent: the meshing of Australian and international accounting policy. *Australian Accounting Review* June:3-16.

Nobes, C.W. 1989, 21 December. ASC puts goodwill on the balance sheet. *Financial Times*, p. 25.

Nobes, C.W. 1991. *Accounting and Financial Reporting in Japan*. Dublin, Ireland: Lafferty Publications.

Nobes, C.W. 1992. A political history of goodwill in Britain: an illustration of cyclical standard setting. *Abacus* September:142-167.

Nobes, C., and R. Parker. 1995. *Comparative International Accounting*. Hemel Hempstead, UK: Prentice Hall.

Ordelheide, D., and D. Pfaff. 1994. *European Financial Reporting: Germany*. London, UK: Rout-
      ledge.
Parker, R. 1995a. Financial reporting in the Netherlands. In *Comparative International Accounting*,
      eds. C. Nobes and R. Parker, 206-222. Hemel Hempstead, UK: Prentice Hall.
Parker, R. 1995b. Financial reporting in the United Kingdom and Australia. In *Comparative Interna-
      tional Accounting*, eds. C. Nobes and R. Parker, 171-205. Hemel Hempstead, UK: Prentice
      Hall.
Parker, R., and C. Nobes. 1995. Consolidation. In *Comparative International Accounting*, eds. C.
      Nobes and R. Parker, 325-347. Hemel Hempstead, UK: Prentice Hall.
Pensler, S. 1988, March 24. Accounting rules favor foreign bidders. *Wall Street Journal*, p. 26.
Price Waterhouse. 1993a. *Doing Business in Australia*. New York, NY: Price Waterhouse.
Price Waterhouse. 1993b. *Doing Business in Japan*. New York, NY: Price Waterhouse.
Price Waterhouse. 1994. *Doing Business in Canada*. New York, NY: Price Waterhouse.
Price Waterhouse. 1995a. *Doing Business in Sweden*. New York, NY: Price Waterhouse.
Price Waterhouse. 1995b. *Doing Business in France*. New York, NY: Price Waterhouse.
Riccaboni, A., and R. Ghirri. 1994. *European Financial Reporting: Italy*. London, UK: Routledge.
Ryan, J.B., and C.T. Heazlewood. 1995. *Australian Company Financial Reporting: 1995* (Account-
      ing Research Study No. 13). Melbourne, Australia: Australian Accounting Research Federa-
      tion.
Scheid, J.-C., and P. Walton. 1992. *European Financial Reporting: France*. London, UK: Rout-
      ledge.
Seckler, G. 1995. Germany. In *European Accounting Guide*, eds. D. Alexander and S. Archer, 223-
      322. San Diego, CA: Harcourt Brace.
Stacy, G., and D.P. Tweedie. 1989, 7 December. Setting a standard for the value of goodwill. *Finan-
      cial Times*, p. 15.
Touche Ross. 1993. *Goodwill and Intangible Assets*. London, UK: Touche Ross.
Zambon, S. 1995. Italy. *European Accounting Guide*, eds. D. Alexander and S. Archer, 379-533.
      San Diego, CA: Harcourt Brace.

APPENDIX I

The Calculation of Goodwill

This appendix sets out the various methods of calculation of the size of goodwill at acquisition. It is assumed throughout that there are no minority interests.
Otherwise, further complications arise.

Under the "classical method," goodwill is the difference between the cost of
the investment and the book value of the net assets at the date of acquisition. This
is shown as G_0^C in Table A1. This is the method used, for example, originally in
Britain and in much of continental Europe until the late 1980s.

The "modern" UK method calculates goodwill as the difference between the
cost of the investment and the fair values of net assets (G_0^u in Table A1). This
method was formally adopted in the UK in SSAP 14 in 1978 and was previously
in use in the United States (e.g., in APB Opinion 17). It is one of the two methods
allowed by the EU Seventh Directive (Article 19, 1, b) and is found in the laws of

194   INTERNATIONAL ACCOUNTING, AUDITING & TAXATION, 5(2)   1996

TABLE A1
Goodwill at Acquisition

Case I

Cost of investment = I = 8m

Book value of net assets = B_0 = 3m

Fair value of net assets = F = \$4.5m

Method 1: Classical (e.g., French early 1980s)

$G_0^C = I-B_0 = 8-3 = 5$

Method 2: Modern UK

$G_0^u = I-F = 8-4.5 = 3.5$

Method 3: Modern European

(i) $I-B_0 = x = 5$

(ii)   Allocate x to the net assets up to the extent (y) that fair values allow this.
        $y = F-B_0 = 1.5$

(iii) $G_0^E = I-(B_0 +y) = 8-(3+1.5) = 3.5$

Case II

However, take the case where the facts are the same, except that I = 3.5. Then:

1. $G_0^C = I-B_0 = 3.5-3 = 0.5$

2. $G_0^u = I-F = 3.5-4.5 = (1)$

3. $I-B_0 = x = 0.5$

        As before, $y = F-B_0 = 1.5$

        but allocation of x does not exhaust y, so:

        $G_0^E = I-(B_0 +x) = 3.5-(3+0.5) = 0$

Case III

Suppose that I = 2.5. Then:

1. $G_0^C = I-B_0 = 2.5-3 = (0.5)$

2. $G_0^u = I-F = 2.5-4.5 = (2)$

3. $I-B_0 = x = (0.5)$

This cannot be allocated, so $G_0^E = (0.5)$

---

some member states; examples in Table A2. Of course, as noted in the text, the calculation of fair values can differ internationally, and does so between the United States and the United Kingdom. A further variation is that negative goodwill is recognized in the UK but is eliminated in the U.S. (see Table 5).

The effects of this are, for example, that goodwill figures tend to be lower under Anglo-Saxon calculations than under traditional continental calculations. This is especially the case, given conservative continental book valuations. Also, negative goodwill is most likely to arise under the USA/UK method. Coupled with conservatism, this factor will lead even 'modern European' goodwill to be on average higher than /UK goodwill (see Table A1, Cases II and III).

The "modern European" method first calculates an amount, called "x" in Table A1, like classical goodwill. Then x, if positive, is allocated to the assets and

TABLE A2
Seventh Directive Goodwill Calculations

	Methods Allowed (see Table A1)
Belgium	2 and 3
Denmark	2 and 3
France	2 and 3
Germany	2 and 3
Italy	3
Netherlands	2
Portugal	2 and 3
Spain	2 and 3
UK	2
For comparison	
Australia	2
U.S.	2

Notes: In summary:

If $I > F > B_0$, then $G_0^C > G_0^E = G_0^U$.

If $F > I > B_0$, then $G_0^C > G_0^E = G_0^U$ and $G_0^C = 0, G_0^U$ is negative

If $F > B_0 > I$, then $G_0^C > G_0^E = G_0^U$, and all are negative.

liabilities of the subsidiary, but only to the extent that this would not exceed fair values. Any remaining difference is then called goodwill (G_0^E in Table A1). This method is allowed in the Seventh Directive (Article 19, 1, a); is taken up as optional or compulsory in some member state laws (see Table A2); and, where optional, is frequently practised, for example, in Germany.

As may be seen from Table A1, methods 2 and 3 lead to smaller goodwill figures than does method 1, assuming that the fair value exceeds the book value of the net assets. Also, assuming the normal case where the investment exceeds or equals the fair value of the assets, methods 2 and 3 lead to the same goodwill figures. However, where the investment is lower than the net asset values, methods 2 and 3 diverge, as shown in Table A1. However the German version of method 2 does not allow negative goodwill to be created or enlarged because of an excess of fair value over book value. So the result is the same as for method 3.

Appendix II
Survey of Practice for Consolidation Goodwill

	Australia	France	Germany	Italy	Japan	Netherlands	Spain	Sweden	United Kingdom	USA
Number of companies disclosing consolidation goodwill[a]	100	10	10	9	32	9	7	10	9	437
Accounting policy:										
Write-off to equity	—	—	2	1	—	7	—	—	9	—
Capitalize and amortize [b]	93	10	11	13	18	1	7	12	1	437
Expense immediately	1	—	—	—	9	1	—	1	—	—
No disclosure	6	—	—	—	5	—	1	—	—	—
Amortization period: [b]										
Equal to or less than 5 years	2	—	3	3	(c)	—	4	2	—	—
Greater than 5 years	86[d]	10	3	4	n/a	1	3	9	1	299[e]
Useful economic life	7	—	1	4	n/a	—	—	1	—	43
Other	—	—	3	2	n/a	—	—	—	—	95
No disclosure	—	—	1	—	n/a	—	—	—	—	—

Notes: [a] The total in the survey is shown in "sources" below.

[b] More than one response possible.

[c] Cooke and Kikuya (1992) suggest that goodwill is written off over a period exceeding one year, but with a maximum of 5 years.

[d] Includes life or 20 years, whichever is shorter.

[e] Including 171 companies stating 40 years; and 81 stating "not exceeding 40 years."

Sources:

1. For France, Germany, Italy, Netherlands, Spain, Sweden and UK: FEE (1994) survey based on the 1992 reports of ten quoted companies in each of the countries. Further evidence for France and the UK can be found in Archer *et al.* (1995).

2. For Japan: Nobes (1991) survey based on the reports of 50 companies.

3. For Australia: Ryan and Heazlewood (1995) survey based on the 1994 reports of the top 150 listed holding companies selected on the basis of market capitalization.

4. For U.S.: the AICPA (1995) survey of the 1994 reports of 600 corporations.

Name Index